PROGRAM EVALUATION
FOR SOCIAL WORKERS

PROGRAM EVALUATION
FOR SOCIAL WORKERS

FOUNDATIONS OF EVIDENCE-BASED PROGRAMS   7TH EDITION

Richard M. Grinnell, Jr.
Western Michigan University

Peter A. Gabor
University of Calgary

Yvonne A. Unrau
Western Michigan University

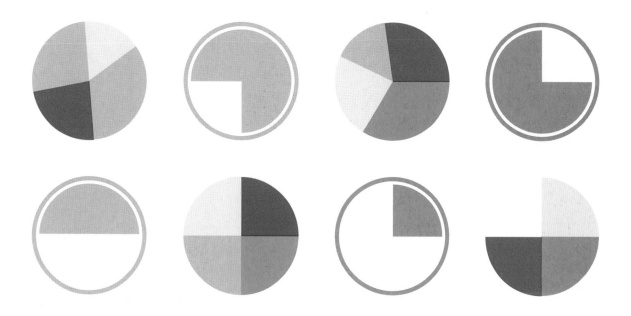

OXFORD
UNIVERSITY PRESS

OXFORD
UNIVERSITY PRESS

Oxford University Press is a department of the University of
Oxford. It furthers the University's objective of excellence in research,
scholarship, and education by publishing worldwide.

Oxford   New York
Auckland   Cape Town   Dar es Salaam   Hong Kong   Karachi
Kuala Lumpur   Madrid   Melbourne   Mexico City   Nairobi
New Delhi   Shanghai   Taipei   Toronto

With offices in
Argentina   Austria   Brazil   Chile   Czech Republic   France   Greece
Guatemala   Hungary   Italy   Japan   Poland   Portugal   Singapore
South Korea   Switzerland   Thailand   Turkey   Ukraine   Vietnam

Oxford is a registered trademark of Oxford University Press
in the UK and certain other countries.

Published in the United States of America by
Oxford University Press
198 Madison Avenue, New York, NY 10016

Library of Congress Cataloging-in-Publication Data
Program evaluation for social workers : foundations of evidence-based practice / Richard M. Grinnell, Peter A. Gabor,
Yvonne A. Unrau, editors. — Second Edition.
    pages cm
Revised editon of Program evaluation for social workers, 2012.
Includes bibliographical references and index.
ISBN 978–0–19–022730–2
1. Human services—Evaluation.   2. Human services—Evaluation—Case studies.   3. Social work administration.
I. Grinnell, Richard M., editor.   II. Gabor, Peter, (Sociologist) editor.   III. Unrau, Yvonne A., editor.   IV. Grinnell, Richard M.
Program evaluation for social workers.
HV40.P716 2015
361.3′2—dc23
2015008417

9 8 7 6 5 4 3 2 1
Printed in the United States of America
on acid-free paper

Contents in Brief

Contents in Detail

PART IV: MAKING DECISIONS WITH DATA

PART V: EVALUATION TOOLKIT

Preface

The first edition of this book appeared on the scene over two decades ago. As with the previous six editions, this one is also geared for graduate-level social work students—as their first introduction to evaluating social service programs. We have selected and arranged its content so it can be mainly used in a social work program evaluation course. Over the years, however, it has also been adopted in graduate-level management courses, leadership courses, program design courses, program planning courses, social policy courses, and as a supplementary text in research methods courses, in addition to field integration seminars. Ideally, students should have completed their required foundational research methods course prior to this one.

Before we began writing this edition we asked ourselves one simple question: "What can realistically be covered in a one-semester course?" You're holding the answer to our question in your hands; that is, students can easily get through the entire book in one semester.

GOAL

Our principal goal is to present only the core material that students realistically need to know in order for them to appreciate and understand the role that evaluation has within professional social work practice. Thus unnecessary material is avoided at all costs. To accomplish this goal, we strived to meet three highly overlapping objectives:

1. To prepare students to cheerfully participate in evaluative activities within the programs that hire them after they graduate.
2. To prepare students to become beginning critical producers and consumers of the professional evaluative literature.

3. Most important, to prepare students to fully appreciate and understand how case- and program-level evaluations will help them to increase their effectiveness as beginning social work practitioners.

CONCEPTUAL APPROACH

With our goal and three objectives in mind, our book presents a unique approach in describing the place of evaluation in the social services. Over the years, little has changed in the way in which most evaluation textbooks present their material. A majority of texts focus on program-level evaluation and describe project types of approaches; that is, one-shot approaches implemented by specialized evaluation departments or external consultants. On the other hand, a few recent books deal with case-level evaluation but place the most emphasis on inferentially powerful—but difficult to implement—experimental and multiple baseline designs.

> *This book provides students with a sound conceptual understanding of how the ideas of evaluation can be used in the delivery of social services.*

We collectively have over 100 years of experience of doing case- and program-level evaluations within the social services. Our experiences have convinced us that neither of these two distinct approaches adequately reflects the realities in our profession or the needs of beginning practitioners. Thus we describe how data obtained through case-level evaluations can be aggregated to provide timely and relevant data for program-level evaluations. Such information, in turn, is the basis for a quality improvement process within the entire organization. We're convinced that this integration will play an increasingly prominent role in the future.

We have omitted more advanced methodological and statistical material such as a discussion of celeration lines, autocorrelation, effect sizes, and two standard-deviation bands for case-level evaluations, as well as advanced methodological and statistical techniques for program-level evaluations.

The integration of case- and program-level evaluation approaches is one of the unique features of this book.

Some readers with a strict methodological orientation may find that our approach is simplistic, particularly the material on the aggregation of case-level data. We are aware of the limitations of the approach, but we firmly believe that this approach is more likely to be implemented by beginning practitioners than are other more complicated, technically demanding approaches. It's our view that it's preferable to have such data, even if they are not methodologically "airtight," than to have no aggregated data at all. In a nutshell, our approach is realistic, practical, applied, and, most important, student-friendly.

THEME

We maintain that professional social work practice rests upon the foundation that a worker's practice activities must be directly relevant to obtaining the client's practice objectives, which are linked to the program's objectives, which are linked to the program's goal, which represents the reason why the program exists in the first place. The evaluation process presented in our book heavily reflects these connections.

Pressures for accountability have never been greater. Organizations and practitioners of all types are increasingly required to document the impacts of their services not only at the program level but at the case level as well. Continually, they are challenged to improve the quality of their services, and they are required to do this with scarce resources. In addition, few social service organizations can adequately maintain an internal evaluation department or hire outside evaluators. Consequently, we place a considerable emphasis on monitoring, an approach that can be easily incorporated into the ongoing activities of the social work practitioners within their respective programs.

In short, we provide a straightforward view of evaluation while taking into account:

- The current pressures for accountability within the social services
- The current available evaluation technologies and approaches
- The present evaluation needs of students as well as their needs in the first few years of their careers

WHAT'S NEW IN THIS EDITION?

Publishing a seventh edition may indicate that we have attracted loyal followers over the years. Conversely, it also means that making major changes from one edition to the next can be hazardous to the book's long-standing appeal.

New content has been added to this edition in an effort to keep information current while retaining material that has stood the test of time. With the guidance of many program evaluation instructors and students alike, we have clarified material that needed further clarification, deleted material that needed deletion, and simplified material that needed simplification.

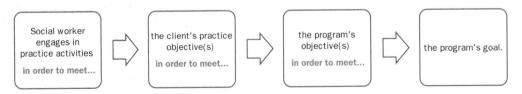

Like all introductory program evaluation books, ours too had to include relevant and basic evaluation content. Our problem here was not so much what content to include as what to leave out. We have done the customary updating and rearranging of material in an effort to make our book more practical and "student friendly" than ever before.

We have incorporated suggestions by numerous reviewers and students over the years while staying true to our main goal—providing students with a useful and practical evaluation book that they actually understand and appreciate.

Let's now turn to the specifics of "what's new."

- We have substantially increased our emphasis throughout our book on:

  - How to use stakeholders throughout the entire evaluation process.
  - How to utilize program logic models to describe programs, to select intervention strategies, to develop and measure program objectives, and to aid in the development of program evaluation questions.
  - How professional social work practice rests upon the foundation that a worker's practice activities must be directly relevant to obtaining the client's practice objectives, which are linked to the program's objectives, which are linked to the program's goal, which represents the reason why the program exists in the first place.

- We have included two new chapters:

  - Chapter 8: Theory of Change and Program Logic Models
  - Chapter 9: Preparing for an Evaluation

- We have included eight new tools for the Evaluation Toolkit:

  Tool A. Hiring an External Evaluator
  Tool B. Working with an External Evaluator
  Tool D. Meeting Evaluation Challenges
  Tool F. Budgeting for Evaluations

  Tool G. Using Evaluation Management Tools
  Tool I. Training and Supervising Data Collectors
  Tool J. Effective Communication and Reporting
  Tool K. Developing an Action Plan

- We have moved the Evaluation Toolkit to the end of the book (Part V).
- We have significantly increased the number of macro-practice examples throughout the chapters.
- We have expanded the book's Glossary to over 620 terms.
- Study questions are included at the end of each chapter. The questions are in the order the content is covered in the chapter. This makes it easy for the students to answer the questions.
- A student self-efficacy quiz is included at the end of each chapter. Instructors can use each student's score as one of the measurements for a behavioral practice objective that can be reported to the Council on Social Work Education (2015).

  Students are encouraged to take the chapter's self-efficacy quiz before reading the chapter and after they have read it. Taking the quiz before they read the chapter will prepare them for what to expect in the chapter, which in turn will enhance their learning experience—kind of like one of the threats to internal validly, *initial measurement effects*.

- We repeat important concepts throughout the book. Instructors who have taught program evaluation courses for several years are acutely aware of the need to keep reemphasizing basic concepts throughout the semester such as validity and reliability; constants and variables; randomization and random assignment; internal and external validly; conceptualization and operationalization; theory of change models and program logic models; case-level evaluations and program-level evaluations; accountability and quality improvement; standardized and nonstandardized measuring instruments; confidentiality and anonymity; data sources and data collection methods; internal and external evaluations; practice activities, practice objectives, program objectives, and program goals; in addition to standards, ethics, and cultural considerations.

Thus we have carefully tied together these major concepts not only within chapters but across chapters as well. There's deliberate repetition, as we strongly feel that the only way students can really understand fundamental evaluation concepts is for them to come across the concepts throughout the entire semester—via the chapters contained in this book. Readers will, therefore, observe our tendency to explain evaluation concepts in several different ways throughout the entire text.

Now that we know "what's new" in this edition, the next logical question is: "What's the same?" First, we didn't delete any chapters that were contained in the previous one. In addition, the following also remains the same:

- We discuss the application of evaluation methods in real-life social service programs rather than in artificial settings.
- We heavily include human diversity content throughout all chapters in the book. Many of our examples center on women and minorities, in recognition of the need for students to be knowledgeable of their special needs and problems.

    In addition, we have given special consideration to the application of evaluation methods to the study of questions concerning these groups by devoting a full chapter to the topic (i.e., Chapter 6).
- We have written our book in a crisp style using direct language; that is, students will understand all the words.
- Our book is easy to teach from and with.
- We have made an extraordinary effort to make this edition less expensive, more

esthetically pleasing, and much more useful to students than ever before.
- Abundant tables and figures provide visual representation of the concepts presented in our book.
- Numerous boxes are inserted throughout to complement and expand on the chapters; these boxes present interesting evaluation examples; provide additional aids to student learning; and offer historical, social, and political contexts of program evaluation.
- The book's website is second to none when it comes to instructor resources.

PARTS

Part I: Preparing for Evaluations

Before we even begin to discuss how to conduct evaluations in Part III, Part I includes a serious dose of how evaluations help make our profession to become more accountable (**Chapter 1**) and how all types of evaluations (**Chapter 2**) go through a common process that utilizes the program's stakeholders right from the get-go (**Chapter 3**). Part I then goes on to discuss how all types of evaluations are influenced by standards (**Chapter 4**), ethics (**Chapter 5**), and culture (**Chapter 6**).

So before students begin to get into the real nitty-gritty of actually designing social service programs (Part II) and implementing evaluations (Part III), they will fully understand the various contextual issues that all evaluative efforts must address. Part I continues to be the hallmark of this book as it sets the basic foundation that students need to appreciate before any kind of evaluation can take place.

Part II: Designing Programs

Students are aware of the various contextual issues that are involved in all evaluations after reading Part I. They then are ready to actually understand what social work programs are all about—the purpose of Part II.

This part contains two chapters that discuss how social work programs are organized (**Chapter 7**) and how theory of change and program logic models are used not only to create new programs, to refine the delivery services of existing ones, to guide practitioners in the development of practice and program objectives, but to help in the formulation of evaluation questions as well (**Chapter 8**).

> *The chapters and parts were written to be independent of one another. They can be assigned out of the order they are presented, or they can be selectively omitted.*

We strongly believe that students need to know what a social work program is all about (Part II) before they can evaluate it (Part III). How can they do a meaningful evaluation of a social work program if they don't know what it's supposed to accomplish in the first place? In particular, our emphasis on the use of logic models, not only to formulate social work programs but to evaluate them as well, is another highlight of the book.

Part III: Implementing Evaluations

After students know how social work programs are designed (Part II), in addition to being aware of the contextual issues they have to address (Part I) in designing them, they are in an excellent position to evaluate the programs.

The first chapter in Part III, **Chapter 9**, presents a comprehensive framework on preparing students to do an evaluation *before* they actually do one; that is, students will do more meaningful evaluations if they are prepared in advance to address the various issues that will arise when their evaluation actually gets underway—and trust us, issues will arise.

When it comes to preparing students to do an evaluation, we have appropriated the British Army's official military adage of "the 7 Ps," **P**roper **P**lanning and **P**reparation **P**revents **P**iss **P**oor **P**erformance. Not eloquently stated—but what the heck—it's *official* so it must be right. Once students are armed with all their "preparedness," the following four chapters illustrate the four types of program evaluations they can do with all of their "planning skills" enthusiastically in hand.

The remaining four chapters in Part III present how to do four basic types of evaluations in a step-by-step approach. **Chapter 10** describes how to do basic needs assessments and briefly presents how they are used in the development of new social service programs as well as refining the services within existing ones. It highlights the four types of social needs within the context of social problems.

Once a program is up and running, **Chapter 11** presents how we can do a process evaluation within the program in an effort to refine the services that clients receive and to maintain the program's fidelity. It highlights the purposes of process evaluations and places a great deal of emphasis on how to decide what questions the evaluation will answer.

Chapter 12 provides the rationale for doing outcome evaluations within social service programs. It highlights the need for developing a solid monitoring system for the evaluation process.

Once an outcome evaluation is done, programs can use efficiency evaluations to monitor their cost-effectiveness/benefits—the topic of **Chapter 13**. This chapter highlights the cost-benefit approach to efficiency evaluation and also describes the cost-effectiveness approach.

In sum, Part III clearly acknowledges that there are many forms that evaluations can take and presents four of the most common ones. Note that the four types of evaluation discussed in our book are linked in an ordered sequence as outlined in the following figure.

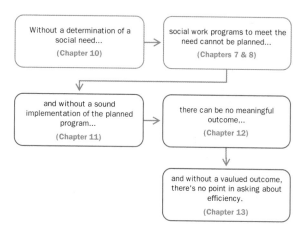

Part IV: Making Decisions with Data

After an evaluation is completed (Part III), decisions need to be made from the data collected—the purpose of Part IV. This part contains two chapters; the first describes how to develop a data information system (**Chapter 14**), and the second (**Chapter 15**) describes how to make decisions from the data that have been collected with the data information system discussed in the previous chapter.

Part V: Evaluation Toolkit

 Part V presents an Evaluation Toolkit that contains 13 basic "research methodology–type tools," if you will, that were probably covered in the students' foundational research methods courses. The tools are nothing more than very brief "cheat sheets" that create a bridge between Part III (four basic types of evaluations) and Part IV (how to make decisions with data). So in reality, the tools briefly present basic research methodology that students will need in order for them to appreciate the entire evaluation process.

For example, let's say an instructor requires students to write a term paper that discusses how to do a hypothetical outcome evaluation of their field placement (or work) setting. This of course, assumes they are actually placed in a social work program that has some resemblance to the content provided in Chapter 7. It would be difficult, if not impossible, to write a respectable program outcome evaluation proposal without using the following tools:

Tool E.   Using Common Evaluation Designs
Tool H.   Data Collection and Sampling Procedures
Tool L.   Measuring Variables
Tool M.   Measuring Instruments

Obviously, students can easily refer to their research methods books they purchased for their past foundational research methods courses to brush up on the concepts contained in the toolkit. In fact, we prefer they do just that, since these books cover the material in more depth and breadth than the content contained in the toolkit. However, what are the chances that these books are on their bookshelves? We bet slim to none. That's why we have included a toolkit.

We in no way suggest that all the research methodology students will need to know to do evaluations in the real world is contained within the toolkit. It is simply not a substitute for a basic research methods book (e.g., Grinnell & Unrau, 2014) and statistics book (e.g., Weinbach & Grinnell, 2015).

INSTRUCTOR RESOURCES

Instructors have a password-protected tab (Instructor Resources) on the book's website that contains links. Each link is broken down by chapter. They are invaluable, and you are encouraged to use them.

- Student Study Questions
- Power Point Slides
- Chapter Outlines
- Teaching Strategies
- Group Activities
- Computer Classroom Activities
- Writing Assignments
- True/False and Multiple-Choice Questions

The field of program evaluation in our profession is continuing to grow and develop. We believe this edition will contribute to that growth. An eighth edition is anticipated, and suggestions for it are more than welcome. Please e-mail your comments directly to rick.grinnell@wmich.edu.

If our book helps students acquire basic evaluation knowledge and skills and assists them in more advanced evaluation and practice courses, our efforts will have been more than justified. If it also assists them to incorporate evaluation techniques into their practice, our task will be fully rewarded.

Richard M. Grinnell, Jr.
Peter A. Gabor
Yvonne A. Unrau

Preparing for Evaluations

Part I contains six chapters that set the stage for all types of evaluations. They provide the foundational knowledge that students need to appreciate and understand before they should even consider undertaking any type of program evaluation; that is, the chapters provide important background material that prepares them for the evaluation enterprise.

Our students have told us that they refer to Part I as "fixin' to get ready."

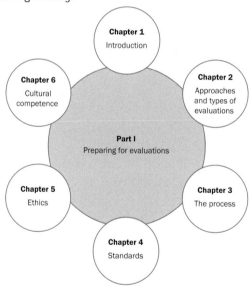

Chapter 1 discusses how social work practitioners are accountable to various stakeholder groups via program evaluations. It presents the quality improvement process as an integral part of any social service program and highlights the various stakeholder groups that must be consulted before doing any kind of evaluation. It also discusses the concept of evaluation within the person-in-environment perspective and program-in-environment perspective. The chapter ends with a brief distinction between "research" and

"evaluation" and ultimately provides a definition of program evaluation.

Chapter 2 presents the advantages and disadvantages of the two common approaches to evaluation: the project approach and the monitoring approach. It then goes on to discuss the four generic types of evaluations: need, process, outcome, and efficiency. The chapter ends with an introduction to what internal and external evaluations are all about.

Chapter 3 presents the generic six-step evaluation process (i.e., engage stakeholders, describe the program, focus the evaluation design, gather credible data, justify conclusions, ensure usage and share lessons learned).

Chapter 4 discusses the four evaluation standards (i.e., utility, feasibility, propriety, accuracy). The next part presents how professional evaluation standards sometimes collide with politics. The remainder of the chapter discusses what happens when standards are not followed.

Chapter 5 presents the various ethical issues that need to be taken into account when doing program evaluations. The chapter describes how informed consent and assent are obtained in addition to delineating the ethical issues that arise in all phases of the evaluation process.

Chapter 6 describes how we, as professional evaluators, must be culturally sensitive in our evaluation endeavors. It provides numerous guidelines to prepare the evaluator to be as culturally sensitive as possible while doing an evaluation.

In sum, the six chapters in Part I provide an "evaluation context springboard" by getting readers ready to actually evaluate programs via the four types of program evaluations that are found in Part III—needs assessments (Chapter 10), process evaluations (Chapter 11), outcome evaluations (Chapter 12), and efficiency evaluations (Chapter 13).

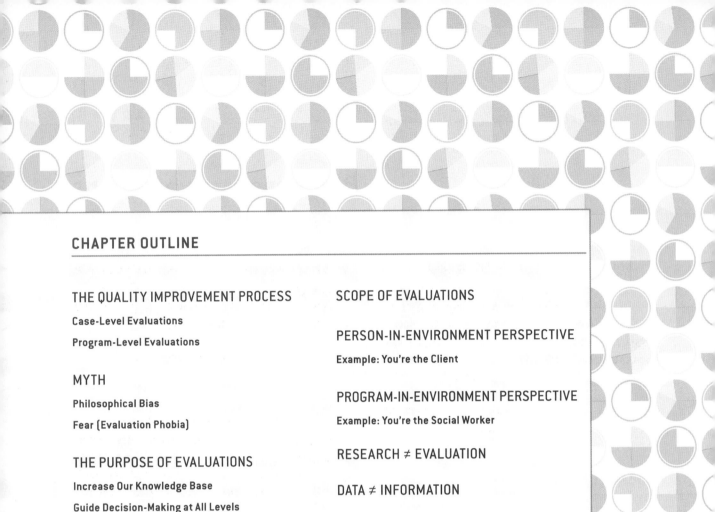

CHAPTER OUTLINE

One of the great mistakes we make is to judge policies and programs by their intentions rather than their results.

~ Milton Friedman

The profession you have chosen to pursue has never been under greater pressure. Our public confidence is eroding, our funding is diminishing at astonishing rates, and folks at all levels are demanding us to increase our accountability; the very rationale for our professional existence is being called into question. We've entered a brand new era in which only our best social work programs—those that can demonstrate they provide needed, useful, and competent client-centered services—will survive.

THE QUALITY IMPROVEMENT PROCESS

How do we go about providing these "client-centered accountable services" that will appease our skeptics? The answer is simple. We utilize the quality improvement process—not only within our individual day-to-day social work practice activities but also within the very programs in which we work. The evaluation of our services can be viewed at two basic levels:

- The case level
- The program level

In a nutshell, case-level evaluations assess the effectiveness and efficiency of our individual cases while program-level evaluations appraise the effectiveness and efficiency of the programs where we work.

The goal of the quality improvement process is to deliver excellent social work services, which in turn will lead to increased accountability.

We must make a commitment to continually look for new ways to make the services we offer our clients more responsive, effective, and efficient. Quality improvement means that we must continually monitor and adjust (when necessary) our practices, both at the practitioner level and at the program level.

Case-Level Evaluations

As you know from your previous social work practice courses, it's at the case level that practitioners provide direct services to client systems such as individuals, couples, families, groups, organizations, and communities. At the case level, you simply evaluate your effectiveness with a single client system, or case. It's at this level that you will customize your evaluation plans to learn about specific details and patterns of change that are unique to your specific client system. For example, suppose you're employed as a community outreach worker for the elderly and it's your job to help aging clients remain safely living in their homes as long as possible before assisted living arrangements are needed.

The support you would provide to an African American male who is 82 years of age with diabetes would likely be different from the support you would provide to an Asian female who is 63 years of age and is beginning to show signs of dementia. Furthermore, the nature of the services you would provide to each of these two very different clients would be adjusted depending on how much family support each has, their individual desires for independent living, their level of receptivity to your services, and other assessment information that you would gather about both of them. Consequently your plan to evaluate the individualized services you would provide to each client would, by necessity, involve different measures, different data collection plans, and different recording procedures.

Program-Level Evaluations

In most instances, social workers help individual clients through the auspices of some kind of a social service program. It's rarely the case that they would be self-employed and operating solely on their own to provide client services. In other words, social service programs generally employ multiple workers, all of whom are trained and supervised according to the policies and procedures set by the programs in which they work.

Typically, every worker employed by a program is assigned a caseload of clients. Simply put, we can think of the evaluation of any social service program as an aggregation of its individual client cases; that is, all clients assigned to every worker in the same program are included in the evaluation. When conducting program-level evaluations we are mostly interested in the overall characteristics of all the clients and the average pattern of change for all of them served by a program. We are interested in them as a group, not as individuals. Figure 1.1 illustrates how case- and program-level evaluations are the building blocks of our continued quest to provide better services for our clients.

> *The evaluation of a social service* program *is nothing more than the aggregation of its individual client cases.*

As shown in Figure 1.1, the quality improvement process is accomplished via two types of evaluations: case and program. This process then produces three desired benefits that are relevant to social workers at all levels of practice (discussed later in this chapter), which in turn leads to providing better services to clients and enhances our accountability.

MYTH

Few social work practitioners readily jump up and down with ecstasy and fully embrace the concepts of "case- and program-level evaluations," "the quality improvement process," and "accountability" as illustrated in Figure 1.1. However, in today's political environment, it's simply a matter of survival that we do. Moreover, it's the ethically and professionally right thing to do.

Nevertheless, some social work students, practitioners, and administrators alike resist performing or

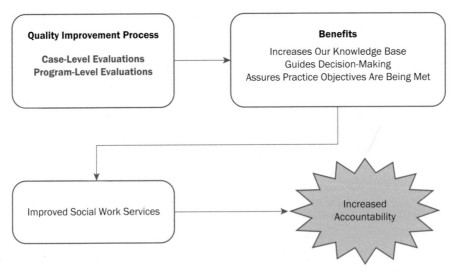

Figure 1.1: **The continuum of professionalization.**

participating in evaluations that can easily enhance the quality of the services they deliver, which in turn enhances our overall creditability, accountability, and usefulness to society. Why is there such resistance when, presumably, most of us would agree that the pursuit of improving the quality of our services is a highly desirable aspiration? This resistance is unfortunately founded on one single myth: *Evaluations that guide the quality improvement process within our profession cannot properly be applied to the art of social work practice.* And, since social work practice is mainly an art form, *accountability* is a non-issue.

> *On myths . . .*
>
> *Myths which are believed in tend to become true.*
>
> ~ *George Orwell*

This myth undercuts the concept of evaluation when in fact evaluations are used to develop evidence-based programs. The myth springs from two interrelated sources:

- Philosophy
- Fear

Philosophical Bias

A few diehard social workers continue to maintain that the evaluation of social work services—or the evaluation of anything for that matter—is impossible, never really objective, politically incorrect, meaningless, and culturally insensitive. This belief is based purely on a philosophical bias.

Our society tends to distinguish between "art" and "evaluation" where "evaluation" is incorrectly thought of as "science" or, heaven forbid, "research/evaluation." This is a socially constructed dichotomy that is peculiar to our modern industrial society. It leads to the unspoken assumption that a person may be an "artist" or an "evaluator" but not both, and certainly not both at the same time. It's important to remember that evaluation is not science by any stretch of the imagination. However, it does use conventional scientific techniques whenever possible, as you will see throughout this entire book.

Artists, as the myth has it, are sensitive and intuitive people who are hopeless at mathematics and largely incapable of logical thought. Evaluators, on the other hand, who use "scientific techniques," are supposed to be cold and insensitive creatures whose ultimate aim, some believe, is to reduce humanity to a scientific nonhuman equation.

Evaluation is not science.

Both of the preceding statements are absurd, but a few of us may, at some deep level, continue to subscribe to them. Some of us may believe that social workers are artists who are warm, empathic, intuitive, and caring. Indeed, from such a perspective, the very thought of evaluating a work of art is almost blasphemous.

Other social workers, more subtly influenced by the myth, argue that evaluations carried out using appropriate evaluation methods do not produce results that are useful and relevant in human terms. It's true that the results of some evaluations that are done to improve the quality of our social service delivery system are not directly relevant to individual line-level social workers and their respective clients. This usually happens when the evaluations were never intended to be relevant to those two groups of people in the first place. Perhaps the purpose of such an evaluation was to increase our knowledge base in a specific problem area—maybe it was simply more of a "pure" evaluation than an "applied" one.

Or perhaps the data were not interpreted and presented in a way that was helpful to the social workers who were working within the program. Nevertheless, the relevance argument goes beyond saying that an evaluation may produce irrelevant data that spawn inconsequential information to line-level workers. It makes a stronger claim: that evaluation methods cannot produce relevant information, because human problems have nothing to do with numbers and "objective" data. In other words, evaluation, as a concept, has nothing to do with social work practice.

As we have previously mentioned, the idea that evaluation has no place in social work springs from society's perceptions of the nature of evaluation and the nature of art. Since one of the underlying assumptions of this book is that evaluation does indeed belong in social work, it's necessary to explore these perceptions a bit more.

Perceptions of the Nature of Evaluation

It can be argued that the human soul is captured most accurately not in paintings or in literature but in advertisements. Marketers of cars are very conscious that they are selling not transportation but power, prestige, and social status; their ads reflect these concepts. In the same way, the role of evaluation is reflected in ads that begin, "Evaluators (or researchers) say. . . ."

Evaluation has the status of a minor deity. It does not just represent power and authority; it *is* power and authority. It's worshiped by many and slandered with equal fervor by those who see in it the source of every human ill.

> *On perceptions . . .*
>
> *All our knowledge has its origins in our perceptions.*
>
> *~ Leonardo da Vinci*

Faith in the evaluation process can of course have unfortunate effects on the quality improvement process within our profession. It may lead us to assume, for example, that evaluators reveal "truth" and that their "findings" (backed by "scientific and objective" research and evaluation methods) have an unchallengeable validity. Those of us who do social work evaluations sometimes do reveal "objective truth," but we also spew "objective gibberish" at alarming rates.

Conclusions arrived at by well-accepted evaluative methods are often valid and reliable, but if the initial clarification of the problem area to be evaluated is fuzzy, biased, or faulty, the conclusions (or findings) drawn from such an evaluation are unproductive and worthless. Our point is that the evaluation process is not infallible; it's only one way of attaining the "truth." It's a tool, or sometimes a weapon, that we can use to increase the effectiveness and efficiency of the services we offer to our clients.

The denigration of evaluation can have equally unfortunate results. If it's perceived as the incarnation of all that is materialistic, in possible opposition to common social work values, then either evaluative methods will not be applied or their results will not be believed—and hence, not incorporated into day-to-day practice activities.

> *The evaluation process is not infallible; it's only one way of attaining the "truth."*

In other words practitioners will have deprived themselves and their clients of an important source of knowledge. A great deal will be said in this book about what evaluation can do for our profession. We will also show what it cannot do, because evaluation, like everything else in life, has its drawbacks.

Evaluations are only as "objective" and "bias-free" as the evaluators who do them. For example, people employed by the tobacco industry who do "objective" evaluations to determine if smoking causes lung cancer, or whether the advertisement of tobacco products around school yards influences children's using tobacco products in the future, may come up with very different conclusions than those people employed by the American Medical Association to do the same studies. Get the point?

> *Evaluations are only as "objective" and "bias-free" as the evaluators who do them.*

Perceptions of the Nature of Art

Art, in our society, has a lesser status than evaluation, but it too has its shrines. Those who produce art are thought to dwell on an elevated spiritual plane that is inaccessible to lesser souls. The forces of artistic creation—intuition and inspiration—are held to be somehow "higher" than the mundane, plodding reasoning of evaluative methods. Such forces are also thought to be delicate, to be readily destroyed or polluted by the opposing forces of reason, and to yield conclusions that may not (or cannot) be challenged.

Art is worshiped by many who are not artists and defamed by others who consider it to be pretentious, frivolous, or divorced from the "real world." Again, both the worship and the denigration can lead to unfortunate results. Intuition, for example, is a valuable asset for social workers. It should neither be dismissed as unscientific or silly nor regarded as a superior form of "knowing" that can never lead us astray (Grinnell, Unrau, & Williams, 2014).

Evaluation and Art Unite!

The art of social work practice and the use of concrete and well-established evaluative methods to help us in the quality improvement process can easily coexist. Social workers can, in the best sense *and* at the same time, be both "caring and sensitive artists" and "hard-nosed evaluators." Evaluation and art are interdependent and interlocked. They are both essential to the survival of our profession.

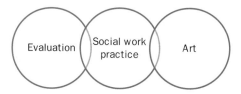

Fear (Evaluation Phobia)

The second myth that fuels resistance to the quality improvement process via evaluations is that an evaluation is a horrific event whose consequences should be feared. Social workers, for instance, can easily be afraid of an evaluation because it's they who are being evaluated; its their programs that are being judged. They may be afraid for their jobs, their reputations, and their clients, or they may be afraid that their programs will be curtailed, abandoned, or modified in some unacceptable way. They may also be afraid that the data an evaluation obtains about them and their clients will be misused. They may believe that they no longer control these data and that the client confidentiality they have so very carefully preserved may be breached.

 Learn how to reduce evaluation anxiety in Tool C in the Evaluation Toolkit.

In fact, these fears have some basis. Programs are sometimes axed as a result of an evaluation. In our

view, however, it's rare for a program to be abandoned because of a negative evaluation. They are usually shut down because they are not doing what the funder(s) originally intended, or they are not keeping up with the current needs of their local community and continue to deliver an antiquated service that the funding source(s) no longer wish to support. They can also be terminated because of the current political climate.

On the other side of the coin, a positive evaluation may mean that a social work program can be expanded or similar programs put into place. And those who do evaluations are seldom guilty of revealing data about a client or using data about a staff member to retard career advancement. Since the actual outcome of an evaluation is so far removed from the mythical one, it cannot be just the results and consequences of an evaluation that generate fear: It's the idea of being judged.

It's helpful to illustrate the nature of this anxiety using the analogy of the academic examination. Colleges and universities offering social work programs are obliged to evaluate their students so that they do not release unqualified practitioners upon an unsuspecting public. Sometimes, this is accomplished through a single examination set at the end of a course. More often, however, students are evaluated in an ongoing way, through regular assignments and frequent small quizzes. There may or may not be a final examination, but if there is one, it's worth less and feared less.

Most students prefer the second, ongoing course of evaluation. A single examination on which the final course grade depends is a traumatic event, whereas a midterm, worth 40%, is less dreadful, and a weekly, 10-minute quiz marked by a fellow student may hardly raise the pulse rate. It is the same way with the evaluation of anything, from social service programs to the practitioners employed by them.

An evaluation of a program conducted once every 5 years by an outside evaluator is a traumatic event, to say the least. On the other hand, ongoing evaluations conducted by the practitioners themselves as a normal part of their day-to-day activities becomes a routine part of service delivery and is no big shakes. The point is that "evaluation phobia" stems from a false view of what an evaluation necessarily involves.

Of course one of the disadvantages of doing an ongoing evaluation of a program is that the workers have to carry it out. Some may fear it because they do not know how to do it: they may never have been taught the quality improvement process during their university studies, and they may fear both the unknown and the specter of the "scientific."

One of the purposes of this book is to alleviate the fear and misunderstanding that presently shroud the quality improvement process and to show that some forms of evaluations can be conducted in ways that are beneficial and lead to the improvement of the services we offer clients.

THE PURPOSE OF EVALUATIONS

We have discussed two major reasons why social workers may resist the concept of evaluation—philosophical biases and fear. The next question is: Why should evaluations not be resisted? Why are they needed? What are they for? We have noted that the fundamental reason for conducting evaluations is to improve the quality of our services. As can easily be seen in Figure 1.1, evaluations also:

- Help increase our knowledge base.
- Help guide decision-making.
- Help assure that client objectives are met.

All three reasons to do evaluations within our profession are highly intertwined and are not mutually exclusive of one another. Although we discuss each one in isolation of the others, you need to be fully aware that they all overlap. We start off our discussion with how evaluations are used to increase our knowledge base.

Increase Our Knowledge Base

One of the basic prerequisites of helping people to help themselves is knowing what to do. Knowing how to help involves social workers possessing both practice skills and relevant knowledge. Child sexual abuse, for example, has come to prominence as a social problem only during the past few decades, and many questions still remain. Is the sexual abuse of children usually due to the individual pathology in the perpetrators, to dysfunctions in the family systems, or to a combination of the two?

> *Knowledge-based evaluations can be used in the quality improvement process in four ways:*
>
> 1 *To gather data from social work professionals in order to develop theories about social problems*
> 2 *To test developed theories in actual practice conditions*
> 3 *To develop treatment interventions on the basis of actual program operations*
> 4 *To test treatment interventions in actual practice settings*

If individual pathology is the underlying issue, can the perpetrator be treated in a community-based program, or would institutionalization be more effective? If familial dysfunction is the issue, should clients be immediately referred to family support/preservation services, or should some other intervention be offered such as parent training? In order to answer these and other questions, we need to acquire general knowledge from a variety of sources in an effort to increase our knowledge base in the area of sexual abuse.

One of the most fruitful sources of this knowledge is from the practitioners who are active in the field. What do they look for? What do they do? Which of their interventions are most effective? For example, it may have been found from experience that family therapy offered immediately is effective only when the abuse by the perpetrator was affection based, intended as a way of showing love.

On the other hand, when the abuse is aggression based, designed to fulfill the power needs of the perpetrator, individual therapy may be more beneficial. If similar data are gathered from a number of evaluation studies, theories may be formulated about the different kinds of treatment interventions most likely to be effective with different types of perpetrators who abuse their children. Once formulated, a theory must be tested. This too can be achieved by using complex evaluation designs and data analyses.

The data gathered to increase our general knowledge base are sometimes presented in the form of statistics. The conclusions drawn from the data apply to groups of clients (program-level evaluation) rather than to individual clients (case-level evaluation) and thus will probably not be helpful to a particular practitioner or client in the short term. However, many workers and their future clients will benefit in the long term, when evaluation findings have been synthesized into theories, those theories have been tested, and effective treatment interventions have been derived.

As it stands, the day-to-day interventions that we use in our profession could benefit from a bit of improvement. For instance, we lack the know-how to stop family violence, to eradicate discrimination, and to eliminate human suffering that comes with living in poverty, be it in our own country where poverty is found in isolated pockets or in developing countries where poverty is more pervasive.

Through social work education we learn theory/research/evaluation that, in turn, we are expected to translate into useful interventions to help our clients. You only need to come face-to-face with a few social work scenarios to realize the limits of our profession's knowledge base in helping you to know exactly *what* to do, *where* to do it, *when* to do it, and *who* to do it to.

> Evaluations will eventually help social workers to know exactly what to do, where to do it, when to do it, and who to do it to.

For example, imagine that you are the social worker expected to intervene in the following situations:

- An adolescent who is gay has been beaten by his peers because of his sexual preference
- A neighborhood, predominantly populated by families of color with low incomes, has unsafe rental housing, inadequate public

transportation, and under-resourced public schools
- A family is reported to child protection services because the parents refuse needed medical attention for their sick child based on their religious beliefs
- Officials in a rural town are concerned about the widespread use of methamphetamine addiction in their community

Despite the complexity of the preceding scenarios, there's considerable public pressure on social workers to "fix" such problems. As employees of social work programs, social workers are expected to stop parents from abusing their children, keep inner-city youth from dropping out of school, prevent discrimination in society, and eliminate other such social problems.

If that's not enough, we're expected to achieve positive outcomes in a timely manner with less than adequate financial resources. And all of this is occurring under a watchful public eye that is only enhanced by numerous 24-hour news reporting television broadcasts.

One Client and One Program at a Time

So how is it that we are to both provide effective client services *and* advance our profession's knowledge base—all at the same time? The answer is simple. We do this with one client and one program at a time by evaluating our individual practices with our clients and evaluating our programs as a whole.

We fully support the National Association of Social Workers' philosophy of quality improvement by continually and systematically looking for new ways to make the services we provide our clients more responsive, efficient, and effective. As we know by now, this is the ultimate goal of the quality improvement process in the social services.

Our profession—and all the social workers that comprise it—must be able to provide solid reasons for the policies and positions we take. As we know, evaluation procedures are an integral part of competent social work practice. Just as practitioners must be prepared to explain their reasons for pursuing a particular intervention with a particular client system, a social service program must also be prepared to provide a rationale for the implementation of its evidence-based treatment intervention that is utilized within the program.

Using a Knowledge Base

You are expected to have not only good intentions but the skills and knowledge to convert your good intentions into desired practical results that will actually help your clients. It all boils down to the fact that that we need to acquire the knowledge and skills to help our clients in an effective and efficient manner as possible.

Professional social workers have an influential role in helping to understand and ameliorate the numerous social and economic problems that exist in our society. The very nature of our profession puts us directly in the "trenches" of society; that is, we interface with people and the problems that prevent them from a quality of life enjoyed by the majority of our society. We practice in such places as inner-city neighborhoods and hospices and work with people such as those who are homeless and mentally challenged.

> On knowledge . . .
>
> In general, the public knowledge base and thus decision-making behaviors are far more influenced by advertisement than with current science.
>
> ~ David Perlmutter

Consequently, many social workers experience firsthand the presenting problems of clients, many of which result from societal injustices. Of course individual social workers, as part of our profession, are expected to help make things better, not only for our clients but also for the society in which we all live.

Guide Decision-Making at All Levels

A second reason for doing evaluations is to gather data in an effort to provide information that will help our stakeholder groups to make decisions. The people who make decisions from evaluation studies are called *stakeholders.* Many kinds of decisions have to be made about our programs, from administrative decisions about funding a particular social work program to a practitioner's decision about the best way to serve a particular client (e.g., individual, couple, family, group, community, organization).

Collaborating with Stakeholders

The process of evaluation can also help open up communication among our stakeholders at all levels of a program's operations. Each stakeholder group provides a unique perspective, as well as having a different interest or "stake" in the decisions made within our programs.

Evaluation by its very nature not only has us consider the perspectives of different stakeholder groups but it can also facilitate an understanding of the priority interests among the various parties and promote collaborative working relationships. Their main involvement is to help us achieve an evaluation that provides them with useful recommendations that they can use in their internal decision-making processes. There are basically six stakeholder groups that should be involved in all evaluations:

1   Policymakers
2   General Public
3   Program Funders
4   Program Administrators
5   Social Work Practitioners
6   Clients (i.e., potential, current, past)

Policymakers. To policymakers in governmental or other public entities, any individual program is only one among hundreds—if not thousands. On a general level, policymakers are concerned with broad issues of public safety, fiscal accountability, and human capital. For example, how effective and efficient are programs serving women who have been battered, youth who are unemployed, or children who have been sexually abused?

> A major interest of policymakers is to have comparative data about the effectiveness and efficiency of different social service programs serving similar types of client need.

If one type of program is as effective (produces beneficial client change) as another but also costs more, does the nature or type of service offered to clients justify the greater expense? Should certain types of programs be continued, expanded, modified, cut, or abandoned? How should money be allocated among competing similar programs? In sum, a major interest of policymakers is to obtain comparative data about the effectiveness and efficiency of different social service programs serving similar types of client need. See Chapter 12 for effectiveness evaluations and Chapter 13 for efficiency evaluations.

Policymakers play a key role in allocation of public monies—deciding how much money will be available for various programs such as education, health care, social services, mental health, criminal justice, and so on. Increasingly, policymakers are looking to accreditation bodies to "certify" that social service programs deliver services according to set standards.

General public. Increasingly, taxpayers are demanding that policymakers in state and federal government departments be accountable to the general public. Lay groups concerned with special interests such as the care of the elderly, support for struggling families, drug rehabilitation, or child abuse are lobbying to have their interests heard. Citizens want to know how much money is being spent and where it's being spent. Are taxpayers' dollars effectively serving current social needs?

The public demand for "evidence" that publicly funded programs are making wise use of the money entrusted to them is growing. The media, Internet, and television in particular play a central role in bringing issues of government spending to the public's attention. Unfortunately, the media tends to focus on worst-case scenarios intent on capturing public attention in a way that will increase network ratings and the number of consumers tuning in.

Evaluation is a way for social service programs to bring reliable and valid data to the public's attention. Evaluation data can be used to build public relations and provide a way for programs to demonstrate their "public worth." As such, evaluation is more often used as a tool for educating the public—sharing what

is known about a problem and how a particular program is working to address it—than a means to report definitive or conclusive answers to complex social problems.

> *The general public wants to know how much money is being spent and where it's being spent.*

When evaluation data reveal poor performance, then the program's administrators and practitioners can report changes made to program policy or practice in light of the negative results. On the other hand, positive evaluation results can help highlight a program's strengths in an effort to build its public image. A report of data showing that a program is helping to resolve a social problem such as homelessness may yield desirable outcomes such as allaying the concerns of opposing interest groups or encouraging funders to grant more money.

Program funders. And speaking of money . . . the public and private funding organizations that provide money to social service programs have a vested interest in seeing their money spent wisely. If funds have been allocated to combat family violence, for example, is family violence declining? And if so, by how much? Could the money be put to better use?

Often funders will insist that some kind of an evaluation of a specific program must take place before additional funds are provided. Program administrators are thus made accountable for the funds they receive. They must demonstrate to their funders that their programs are achieving the best results for the funder's dollars.

Program administrators. The priority of program administrators is concern for their own program's functioning and survival, but they also have interest in other similar programs, whether they are viewed as competitors or collaborators. Administrators want to know how well their programs operate as a whole, in addition to the functioning of their program's parts, which may include administrative components such as staff training, budget and finance, client services, quality assurance, and so on.

The questions of interest to an administrator are different but not separate from those of the other stakeholder groups already discussed. Is the assessment process at the client intake level successful in screening clients who are eligible for the program's services? Is treatment planning culturally sensitive to the demographic characteristics of clients served by the program? Does the discharge process provide adequate consultation with professionals external to the program?

Like the questions of policymakers, the general public, and funders, administrators also have a vested interest in knowing which interventions are effective and which are less so, which are economical, which intervention strategies should be retained, and which could be modified or dropped.

Social work practitioners. Line-level practitioners who deal directly with clients are most often interested in practical, day-to-day issues: Is it wise to include adolescent male sexual abuse survivors in the same group with adolescent female survivors, or should the males be referred to another service if separate groups cannot be run? What mix of role-play, educational films, discussion, and other treatment activities best facilitates client learning? Will a family preservation program keep families intact? Is nutrition counseling for parents an effective way to improve school performance of children from impoverished homes? The question that ought to be of greatest importance to a practitioner is whether the particular treatment intervention used with a particular client at a particular time is working.

> *A social work practitioner wants to know whether a particular treatment intervention used with a particular client is working.*

However, sometimes interests from stakeholders external to the program impose constraints that make practitioners more concerned with other issues. For example, when an outreach program serving homeless people with mental illness is unable to afford to send workers out in pairs or provide them with adequate communication systems (e.g., cell phones), workers may be more concerned about questions related to personal safety than questions of client progress. Or workers employed by a program with several funding streams may be required to keep multiple records of services to satisfy multiple funders, thus leaving workers to question the sensibility of duplicative paperwork instead of focusing on the impact of their services on clients.

Clients. The voice of clients is slowly gaining more attention in evaluation efforts, but our profession has a long way to go before clients are fully recognized as a legitimate stakeholder group. Of course clients are a unique stakeholder group since they depend on a program's services for help with problems that are adversely affecting their lives. In fact, without clients there would be no reason for a program to exist.

Clients who seek help do so with the expectation that the services they receive will benefit them in some meaningful way. Clients want to know whether our social service programs will help resolve their problems. If the program claims to be able to help, then are ethnic, religious, language, or other matters of diverse client needs evident in the program's service delivery structure?

> *Clients simply want to know whether our social service programs will help resolve their problems.*

In short, is the program in tune with what clients really need? Client voices are being heard more and more as time goes on. And rightfully so! A brief glimpse at the effectiveness and efficiency of the immediate relief services provided by FEMA to the survivors of Hurricane Katrina should ring a bell here. The total fiasco of the Veteran's Administration's not scheduling appointments for our vets in a timely manner is another example of a social service organization not meeting its clients' needs.

A Word About Collaboration Among Stakeholder Groups

Collaboration involves cooperative associations among the various players from the different stakeholder groups for the purposes of achieving a common goal—building knowledge to better help clients. A collaborative approach accepts that different stakeholders will have diverse perspectives.

Rather than assume one perspective is more valuable than another, each stakeholder group is regarded as having relative importance to achieving a better understanding of how to solve problems and help clients. For example, if a program's workers want to know how a new legislation will change service provision, then the perspective of policymakers and administrators will have great value. But if a program administrator wants to better understand why potential clients are not seeking available services, then the client perspective may be the most valuable of all the stakeholder groups.

> *On being equal . . .*
>
> *Find the appropriate balance of competing claims by various groups of stakeholders. All claims deserve consideration but some claims are more important than others.*
>
> ~ *Warren G. Bennis*

Unfortunately, and as it presently stands, a respectable collaborative working relationship among multiple social service agencies within any given community is neither the hallmark nor a natural phenomenon in today's social service arena—in fact it approaches disgraceful. It's been our experience that most social service programs do not play and work well with others (sound familiar from one of the checkmarks on your grade school report card?). The dominant structure is a hierarchy, which can be thought of as a chain of command with higher levels possessing greater power and authority over lower levels. Typically, policymakers and funders are at the top of the hierarchy, program administrators and workers in the middle, and clients at the bottom.

Critics of this top-down way of thinking might argue the need to turn the hierarchy upside down, placing clients at the top and all other stakeholder groups at varying levels of support beneath them. Whatever the power structure of stakeholders for a particular social work program, evaluation is a process that may do as little as have us consider the multiple perspectives of various stakeholder groups or as much as bringing different stakeholder groups together to plan and design evaluation efforts as a team.

Assure That Client Objectives Are Being Met

The third and final purpose of evaluations is to determine if clients are getting what they need. Contemporary social work practitioners are interested in knowing to what degree each of their individual client's practice objectives, and those of their caseloads are being achieved; that is, they are interested in evaluating their effectiveness with each and every client.

> *Our profession has the responsibility to continually improve our programs in order to provide better services to our clients.*

Clients want to know if the services they are receiving are worth their time, effort, and sometimes money. Usually these data are required while treatment is still in progress, as it's scarcely useful to conclude that services were ineffective after the client has left the program. A measure of effectiveness is needed while there may still be time to try a different intervention if the current one is not working. As we know from the beginning of this chapter, case-level evaluations are utilized to determine if client objectives are being achieved. More will be said about this in Chapter 15.

ACCOUNTABILITY CAN TAKE MANY FORMS

The three main purposes of conducting evaluations will improve our service delivery system, which in turn will increase our accountability. (See Figure 1.1.) As mentioned, administrators are accountable to their funders for the way in which money is spent, and the funders are similarly accountable to the public. Usually, accountability will involve deciding whether money should be devoted to this or that activity and then justifying the decision by producing data to support it.

Demonstrating accountability, or providing justification of a program, is a legitimate purpose of an evaluation insofar as it involves a genuine attempt to identify a program's strengths and weaknesses. Sometimes, however, an evaluation of a demonstration project may be undertaken solely because the terms of the grant demand it.

Accountability means that we are answerable for the actions and decisions we make.

For example, a majority of state and federally funded social work programs are required to have periodic evaluations or their funds will be taken away. In such cases, a program's staff, who are busy delivering services to clients, may inappropriately view the required evaluation as simply a "data-gathering ritual" that's necessary for continued funding.

Accountability in our profession can be viewed from many vantage points:

- **Coverage accountability:** Are the persons served those who have been designated as target clients? Are there any other beneficiaries who should not be served? (See Chapter 10.)
- **Cultural accountability:** Are program employees culturally competent? To what extent are the cultures of clients served represented in the program's administrative

and service delivery structures? We use the broad meaning of *culture* here to reflect diversity in areas of race, class, ethnicity, religion, sexual orientation, and other classifications identifying groups of people that are oppressed or discriminated against in our society. (See Chapter 6.)

- **Service delivery accountability:** Are a reasonable number of services being delivered? To what extent is service delivery supported by an evidence base? (See Chapters 7, 8, and 11.)
- **Fiscal accountability:** Are funds being used properly? Are expenditures properly documented? Are funds used within the limits set within the budget? (See Chapter 13.)
- **Legal accountability:** Are relevant laws, including those concerning affirmative action, occupational safety and health, and privacy of individual records, being observed? (See Chapter 4.)
- **Professional accountability:** Are our professional codes of ethics and accreditation standards being met? (See Chapters 4 and 5.)

SCOPE OF EVALUATIONS

The word *program* can refer to many different things. It may refer to something small, specific, and short term, such as a film developed for use during a training session on AIDS or PTSD. It may refer to a nationwide effort to combat family violence and include all the diverse endeavors in that field, with different program objectives and their corresponding intervention strategies. Or it may refer to a specific treatment intervention used with a specific social worker and undertaken with a specific client.

Obviously these different types of programs need to be evaluated using different evaluative methods. One size shoe doesn't fit all! Thus we need to know what the characteristics of the program are before it can be evaluated. The scope of any evaluation has to be sensitive to the following program characteristics:

- **Boundary:** The program may extend across a nation, region, state, province, city, parish, county, or community, or it may be extremely limited—for example, a course presented in an individual agency or school.
- **Size:** The program may serve individual clients, such as people seeking individual therapy, or many clients, such as people infected with the HIV virus.
- **Duration:** The program may be designed to last for half an hour—a training film, for example—or it may be an orientation course on child safety lasting for two days, a group therapy cycle lasting for 10 weeks, or a pilot project designed to help the homeless being evaluated after 2 years. Or, as in the case of a child protection agency, it may be intended to continue indefinitely.
- **Complexity:** Some programs offer integrated components, combining, for instance, child protection services, individual therapy, family therapy, and educational services under one common umbrella. Such a program is obviously more complex than one with a simpler, singular focus—for example, providing nutrition counseling to pregnant adolescents.
- **Clarity and time span of program objectives:** Some programs have objectives that can readily be evaluated: for example, to increase the number of unemployed adolescents who find full-time jobs 2 months after a 6-week training course (the intervention). Others have objectives that will not become evident for some time: for example, to increase the utilization by seniors of a meals-on-wheels program.
- **Innovativeness:** Some social service programs follow long-established treatment interventions, such as individual treatment; others are experimenting with new ones designed for use with current social problems, such as AIDS and PTSD.

PERSON-IN-ENVIRONMENT PERSPECTIVE

A hallmark of our profession is the person-in-environment concept. It's a perspective that affects how we view clients and the social problems they are experiencing. It's also a perspective that is useful for thinking about our programs and the role that evaluations play within them.

Viewing persons or entities in the context of their environments is a concept that comes from ecological theory, which is best known for its idea of nested environments, as shown in Figure 1.2. In ecological theory, the micro level represents the individual or family

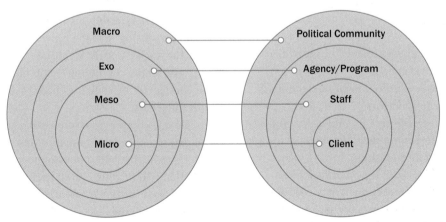

Figure 1.2: **Person-in-environment perspective.**

environment, the meso level accounts for interactions of micro-environments, the exo level represents entities that influence the micro-environment but do not always do so in a direct fashion, and, finally, the macro level is the outermost level represents distant connectivity such as our community or the broader society.

> *On environment . . .*
>
> *Our environment, the world in which we live and work, is a mirror of our attitudes and expectations.*
>
> ~ *Earl Nightingale*

Social work practitioners can use this thinking structure of ecological theory to assess interaction and interdependence among the four levels in order to better help clients as individual persons, groups, families, or communities.

The nested thinking structure within Figure 1.2 is a useful aid to better understand how clients interface with the human service programs, how programs interface with their societal environment, and how evaluations fit in this context. Figure 1.2 shows an example of how nested levels can help us understand individual persons (micro level) in the context of a social service program environment since they will have interactions with individual staff (meso level), receive services according to program policy and procedures (exo level), and deal with consequences of the community (macro level) such as having to cope with societal stigma that comes from using the program's services. In sum,

- The *micro level* represents the individual or family environment.
- The *meso level* accounts for interactions of micro-environments.
- The *exo level* represents entities that influence the micro-environment but does not always do so in a direct fashion.
- The *macro level* as the outermost level represents distant connectivity such as our community or the broader society.

Note that t
the "political c
ture of the env
and we discuss
we introduce
cal connected
ing critical in
program are
program itse

Viewin
through a pe
mon notion
perspective
client as a
connected w....
(e.g., friends, family), exo-level organizations (e.g., educational, occupational, religious) and macro-level communities or society (e.g., law enforcement, politics).

Example: You're the Client

Suppose, for a moment, you sought the help of a social worker at your university's counseling center because you have been feeling heightened sensations of anxiety such as shortness of breath and tightness in your lungs and chest when you think about upcoming final exams. Although your presenting problem (test anxiety) is very specific, you could expect the worker assigned to your case to ask you a broad set of questions to better evaluate the problem that brought you to the counseling center in the first place.

You could also expect to answer questions related to your ties with your university- and home-based friends, teachers, family, as well as your general sense of comfort fitting into the university scene. In addition, the social worker would also be mindful that your visit to the counseling center has itself added to the complexity of your life space or environment at your university.

By considering your presenting problem in the context of your environment, your social worker expects to be in a better position to suggest interventions that will fit your overall lifestyle and maximize your success at reducing test anxiety; the primary reason for you seeking help.

In addition, the worker would have a better idea about how to go about evaluating her work with you, the client. By considering a person-in-environment perspective a worker aims to develop ways to improve services to clients using micro-level interventions (e.g., counseling, problem-solving) and evaluation (e.g. case-level design, client satisfaction question-naire) methods.

PROGRAM-IN-ENVIRONMENT PERSPECTIVE

Viewing human service programs through an envi-ronment perspective is becoming more widespread among social workers, even among those who have no administrative aspirations. For example we can use a similar nested thinking structure previously described to conceptualize the human service pro-gram or agency (Level 1) within the context of both its local community environment (Level 2) and the broader societal and political environment (Level 3). Figure 1.3 has us consider all three levels against a backdrop of social justice (Mulroy, 2004).

Figure 1.3: **Program-in-environment perspective.**

Example: You're the Social Worker

Let's suppose, for a moment, that you have gradu-ated with your social work degree and you are now employed by the university counseling center to help students struggling with test anxiety. As a social work practitioner employed by the counseling center (Level 1), you have adopted a program-in-environment per-spective to help individual students.

In addition, you are bound by policy and proce-dures of your place of employment that calls for client services to benefit the client (i.e., effective) in a timely (i.e., efficient) and just (i.e., equity) manner. However, you are also aware of how your program (the counsel-ing center) is affected by the context of your univer-sity's environment (Level 2).

Various university-level factors could be at play, such as large class sizes, a majority of students being first in their families to attend college, astronomi-cal tuition costs, high textbook prices, peer pressure to "fit in," high dorm fees, or recent budget cuts for student support services on your campus. Thinking beyond your university's campus, you could gain fur-ther understanding of your capacity to help students at the counseling center by evaluating relevant soci-etal and political information (Level 3) such as the degree to which local, state, or federal government officials support higher education or the push in the global market economy to produce a more techno-logically skilled labor force.

The arrows flowing through the nested structure in Figure 1.3 communicate the idea that the bound-aries between the layers are porous. In other words, actions or events at one layer have an impact on all other layers. Thus the line-level social work prac-titioner, situated at in the center of Figure 1.3, as an employee of the program is concerned not just with the client but also with the many other people in the organizational environment.

By considering the program-in-environment per-spective, you as the social work practitioner assigned to help individual students with problem such as test anxiety may also be in a position to evaluate the prob-lem at a macro level—perhaps helping many students by your efforts.

Suppose you notice a trend whereby every month more and more students seek help for test anxiety. By considering the growing problem of student anxiety in the context of the program's environment, you would be in a better position to facilitate change that will fit the environmental context in which your counseling center is situated.

For example, you might enlist support of your supervisor to write a grant to fund student support groups, ask to chair or lead a committee to discuss instructional strategies to prevent student test anxiety, lobby your university's administration to raise awareness of student issues, or advocate for improvements to student support services on campus. In sum, by considering a program-in-environment perspective you could develop ways to improve services to your clients using macro-level interventions. In a sense, you're going from "case" to "cause."

RESEARCH ≠ EVALUATION

We have been using two words that somehow get interchanged in our day-to-day conversations: *research* and *evaluation*. They are not the same activities. Research is research, and evaluation is evaluation. According to the Centers for Disease and Prevention (2001), perhaps the greatest misunderstanding about the evaluation process is that it must follow the typical scientific method. Table 1.1 illustrates the basic principles that distinguish:

- **Research**, conducted, for example, to determine the *causes of domestic violence*.

  from

- **Evaluation,** conducted, for example, to find out whether a particular social work program (intervention) works with its intended audience—*victims of domestic violence*.

Social work professors love to debate the differences and similarities between research and evaluation. Their conversations can be mind-boggling, convoluted, longwinded, and more theoretical than practical. And speaking of practically, who cares?

In reality, evaluations are nothing more than applying basic "research" concepts to help us evaluate our effectiveness with individual cases and programs.

> *On research ...*
>
> *Research is what I'm doing when I don't know what I'm doing.*
>
> ~ *Wernher von Braun*

At this point we just want you to skim over Table 1.1 to see if you can remember what any of the words mean, since many of them should have been covered in your MSW foundational-level social work research methods course. After you finish this book, however, you'll not only know what the words mean but you will also know how they are used to evaluate your individual client cases in addition to the program where you work. And, more important, you'll be very comfortable in showing your peer group how to use the evaluation enterprise in professional social work practice.

As you will soon see, evaluation—at the case level and program level—does not occur in a vacuum and is influenced by real-world constraints: countless, practical, everyday constraints. All of our evaluations must be applied, practical, and feasible. In addition, they must be conducted within the confines of our available resources, time, and political contexts. An enormous—but extremely rewarding—undertaking.

DATA ≠ INFORMATION

Just as the words *research* and *evaluation* get discombobulated in most folks' brains, so do *data* and *information*. They too are often inappropriately used interchangeably. In this book, the term *data* signifies isolated facts, in numerical form (i.e., numbers) or in text form (i.e., words) that are gathered in the course of an evaluation. How we interpret the data when they have all been collected, collated, and analyzed is called *information*.

Table 1.1: **Differences Between "Research" and "Program Evaluation" Principles.**

Concept	Research Principles *(Topics covered in basic research methods books)*	Program Evaluation Principles *(Topics covered in this book)*
Planning	**Scientific method** • State hypothesis • Collect data • Analyze data • Draw conclusions from data	**Framework for program evaluation** • Engage stakeholders • Describe the program • Focus the evaluation design • Gather credible data • Justify conclusions • Ensure use and share lessons learned
Decision-making	**Investigator-controlled** • Authoritative	**Stakeholder-controlled** • Collaborative
Standards	**Validity** • Internal (accuracy, precision) • External (generalizability)	**Repeatability program evaluation standards** • Utility • Feasibility • Propriety • Accuracy
Questions	**Facts** • Descriptions • Associations • Effects	**Values** • Merit (i.e., quality) • Worth (i.e., value) • Significance (i.e., importance)
Design	**Isolate changes and control circumstances** • Narrow experimental influences • Ensure stability over time • Minimize context dependence • Treat contextual factors as confounding (e.g., randomization, adjustment, statistical control) • Understand that comparison groups are a necessity	**Incorporate changes and account for circumstances** • Expand to see all domains of influence • Encourage flexibility and improvement • Maximize context sensitivity • Treat contextual factors as essential information (e.g., system diagrams, logic models, hierarchical or ecological modeling) • Understand that comparison groups are optional (and sometimes harmful)
Data collection	**Sources** • Limited number (accuracy preferred) • Sampling strategies are critical • Concern for protecting human subjects **Indicators/Measures** • Mixed methods (qualitative, quantitative, & integrated)	**Sources** • Multiple (triangulation preferred) • Sampling strategies are critical • Concern for protecting human subjects, organizations, and communities **Indicators/Measures** • Mixed methods (qualitative, quantitative, & integrated)

(continued)

Table 1.1: (continued)

Concept	Research Principles *(Topics covered in basic research methods books)*	Program Evaluation Principles *(Topics covered in this book)*
Analysis and synthesis	**Timing** • One-time (at the end) **Scope** • Focus on specific variables	**Timing** • Ongoing (formative and summative) **Scope** • Integrate all data
Judgments	**Implicit** • Attempt to remain value-free	**Explicit** • Examine agreement on values • State precisely whose values are used
Conclusions	**Attribution** • Establish time sequence • Demonstrate plausible mechanisms • Control for confounding • Replicate findings	**Attribution and contribution** • Establish time sequence • Demonstrate plausible mechanisms • Account for alternative explanations • Show similar effects in similar contexts
Uses	**Disseminate to interested audiences** • Content and format varies to maximize comprehension	**Feedback to stakeholders** • Focus on intended uses by intended users • Build capacity **Disseminate to interested audiences** • Content and format varies to maximize comprehension • Emphasis on full disclosure • Requirement for balanced assessment

For example, data collected in reference to client referral sources gathered from a program's intake unit may indicate that the program accepts 90% of its referrals from other social service programs and only 10% of people who are self-referred. One of the many pieces of information (or conclusions or findings drawn from the data) generated by these data may be that the program is somehow more accessible to clients who were referred by other programs than to those who were self-referred. Thus case- and program-level evaluations yield data that are turned into information by practitioners and administrators, respectively, to improve client services.

Data Versus Information

The distinction between data and information is simple—data are the facts, while information is the interpretation that we give to these facts.

Together, data and information help guide various decision-making processes in an effort to produce more effective and efficient services to our clients. Producing meaningful and useful data and information for quality improvement in service delivery is a process that involves both the art and science of social work practice. While we might think of evaluation as a close cousin of science, it also has close relations with art.

Because evaluations occur in the real and "messy" world of social work practice—and not in an isolated, controlled laboratory—useful evaluation designs require creativity and ingenuity just as much as they need logic, procedural detail, and research principles. If evaluation is to help build the knowledge base of our profession, then we must—in the best sense and at the same time—be both "caring and sensitive artists" and "rigorous scientists."

DEFINITION

By now you're probably looking for the preverbal definition of *program evaluation*. Using all the previous content in this chapter, we define the term simply as the following:

> Program evaluations are systematic processes of collecting useful, ethical, culturally sensitive, valid, and reliable data about a program's current and future interventions, outcomes, and efficiency to aid in case- and program-level decision-making in an effort for our profession to become more accountable to our stakeholder groups.

Now let's see what chapters within this book directly address the contents of the preceding definition of program evaluation:

> Program evaluations are systematic processes (Chapter 3) of collecting useful (Chapter 4), ethical (Chapter 5), culturally-sensitive (Chapter 6), valid, and reliable data (Tools I and M) about a program's current (Chapter 10) and future interventions (Chapters 7 and 8), outcomes (Chapter 12), and efficiency (Chapter 13) to aid

in case- and program-level decision making (Chapter 14 and 15) in an effort for our profession to become more accountable to our stakeholder groups (Chapter 1).

SUMMARY

This chapter introduced the concept of quality improvement and explained how evaluation provides tools for us to use within the quality improvement process. We briefly discussed how evaluations can be done at the case and program levels and presented an introduction to why our profession needs evaluations: (1) to increase our knowledge base; (2) to guide decision-making for policymakers, administrators, practitioners, funders, the general public, and clients; and (3) to assure that clients' practice objectives are being met. We highlighted throughout the chapter that we need to work with all of our stakeholder groups when doing an evaluation so its findings will not only be useful to us—the evaluators—but to all of our stakeholder groups as well.

We also discussed the evaluation process within the person-in-environment perspective and the program-in-environment perspective. The chapter presented a brief discussion on the diversity of social work programs and thus how we need to take this diversity into account when doing evaluations. The chapter discussed how accountability can be viewed from different aspects: coverage, cultural, service delivery, fiscal, legal, and professional. The chapter ended with a definition of program evaluation.

The next chapter presents how we can utilize two different approaches to evaluation—the project approach and the monitoring approach—in addition to the four major types: need, process, outcome, and efficiency.

The goal of this chapter is to provide you with a beginning knowledge base for you to feel comfortable in answering the following questions. AFTER you have read the chapter indicate how comfortable you feel you are in answering each question on a 5-point scale where:

1	2	3	4	5
Very uncomfortable	Somewhat uncomfortable	Neutral	Somewhat comfortable	Very comfortable

If you rated any question between 1–3, reread the section of the chapter where the information for the question is found. If you still feel that you're uncomfortable in answering the question, then talk with your instructor and/or your classmates for more clarification.

	Questions	Degree of comfort? *(Circle one number)*
1	In your own words, define "the quality improvement process" and then discuss why it's important to our profession. Present your work to the rest of your class and utilize their feedback to refine your material even further.	1 2 3 4 5
2	In your own words, define "case-level evaluations" and then discuss why they are important for the social services. Describe how you would go about doing one with a theoretical student-client where you are helping her with her procrastination problem; that is, she procrastinates a whole bunch, like waiting until the last minute to read her program evaluation book. How would you go about evaluating your effectiveness with her—and only her? Present your work to the rest of your class and utilize their feedback to refine your material even further.	1 2 3 4 5
3	In your own words, define "program-level evaluations" and then discuss why they are important for the social services. Describe how you would go about doing one within your field placement (or work) setting. Present your work to the rest of your class and utilize their feedback to refine your material even further.	1 2 3 4 5
4	In your own words, discuss the relationship between case-level evaluations and program-level evaluations. Discuss how they complement one another and provide specific social work examples from your field placement (or work setting) to illustrate your main points.	1 2 3 4 5
5	List and discuss the two myths that surround the concept of "evaluation." Can you think of any more? If so, what are they?	1 2 3 4 5
6	Discuss how contemporary social work practice integrates "art" and "evaluation." Discuss how they complement one another and provide specific social work examples from your field placement (or work setting) to illustrate your main points.	1 2 3 4 5
7	List the three main roles that evaluation has within the social work profession, then discuss how each role enhances our profession's accountability by providing specific social work examples from your field placement (or work setting) to illustrate your main points.	1 2 3 4 5

8	List the various stakeholder groups that we have to be accountable to, then discuss how each one contributes to an evaluation by providing specific social work examples from your field placement (or work setting) to illustrate your main points.	1 2 3 4 5
9	List the various stakeholder groups for your social work program (i.e., BSW or MSW). Provide a rationale of why you listed each one. Who is the "client" stakeholder of your BSW or MSW program? Why? Could this be your parents who may be paying your tuition? If your parents aren't helping you out financially, are they still a stakeholder group? Why or why not? How about your instructor? Your future clients? Your children or significant others?	1 2 3 4 5
10	Are all stakeholder groups equal when it comes to contributing to an evaluation? Why or why not? Provide specific social work examples from your field placement (or work setting) to illustrate your main points.	1 2 3 4 5
11	List and discuss the six forms of accountability, then provide specific social work examples from your field placement (or work setting) to illustrate your main points.	1 2 3 4 5
12	There are many different types of social work programs, and they vary widely in their scope (characteristics). List and then discuss the various characteristics that a program can take. Provide an example of each one from your local social work community.	1 2 3 4 5
13	Define and discuss the evaluation process from a "person-in-environment perspective" (Figure 1.2) and provide specific examples from your field placement (or work setting) to illustrate your main points.	1 2 3 4 5
14	Define and discuss the evaluation process from a "program-in-environment perspective" (Figure 1.3) and provide specific social work examples from your field placement (or work setting) to illustrate your main points.	1 2 3 4 5
15	In your own words, and using Table 1.1 as a guide, discuss the differences between "research" and "evaluation." Provide as many social work examples as you can to illustrate your main points.	1 2 3 4 5
16	What's the difference between "data" and "information"? Provide as many social work examples as you can think of to illustrate your main points.	1 2 3 4 5
17	Review our definition of program evaluation. Then Google "definition: program evaluation" and locate at least five other definitions of program evaluation. Compare and contrast the ones you found with ours. What are their commonalities? What are their differences?	1 2 3 4 5
18	Now the hard part: Construct your own definition of "program evaluation" by integrating the contents of this chapter, our definition of program evaluation, and the five other ones you found on the Internet. Don't be shy; go for it! Present your definition to the rest of the class. What were their comments? Did they help you refine your definition even further?	1 2 3 4 5
19	At this point in the course, how comfortable are you in discussing the concept of evaluation with your field instructor (or your supervisor at work)? with your fellow classmates?	1 2 3 4 5

AFTER you have read this chapter AND have completed all of the study questions, indicate how knowledgeable you feel you are for each of the following concepts on a 5-point scale where

1	2	3	4	5
Not knowledgeable at all	Somewhat unknowledgeable	Neutral	Somewhat knowledgeable	Very knowledgeable

	Concepts	**Knowledge level?** *(Circle one number)*
1	The quality improvement process	1 2 3 4 5
2	Case- and program-level evaluations	1 2 3 4 5
3	The two myths surrounding the concept of evaluation	1 2 3 4 5
4	The three purposes of evaluations	1 2 3 4 5
5	The six forms of accountability	1 2 3 4 5
6	The six scopes of evaluations	1 2 3 4 5
7	The person-in environment perspective	1 2 3 4 5
8	The program-in-environment perspective	1 2 3 4 5
9	The differences between "research" and "evaluation"	1 2 3 4 5
10	The definition of "evaluation"	1 2 3 4 5
	Add up your scores (minimum = 10, maximum = 50)	Your total score =

A	48–50 = Professional evaluator in the making
A–	45–47 = Senior evaluator
B+	43–44 = Junior evaluator
B	40–42 = Assistant evaluator
B–	10–39 = Reread the chapter and redo the study questions

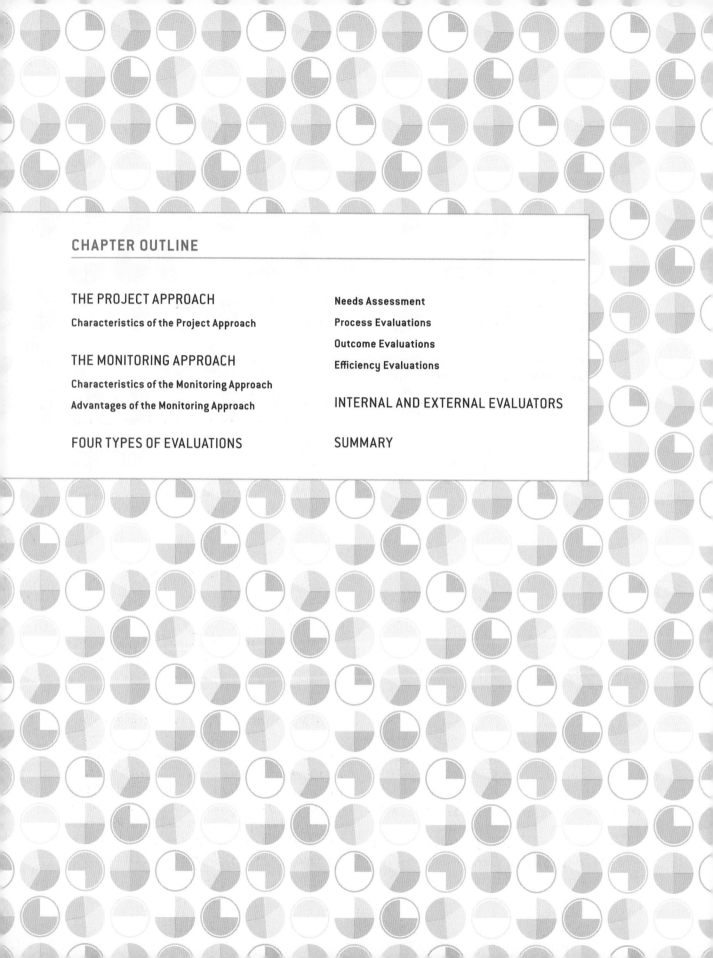

CHAPTER OUTLINE

*Everything should be made as simple
as possible, but not simpler.*

~ Albert Einstein

Chapter 2

APPROACHES AND TYPES
OF EVALUATIONS

A s we know from the last chapter, the quality improvement process provides us with an opportunity to continually monitor our individual practices (case level) and our programs (program level) in order to enhance our entire service delivery system. We found various ways to enhance our profession's accountability via the evaluation process that includes our stakeholder groups in our evaluative efforts.

This chapter continues our discussion on evaluation by describing two approaches that can be used within program-level evaluations in addition to discussing four types of program evaluations. Let's start by describing the two general approaches to program-level evaluations:

- The project approach
- The monitoring approach

Figure 2.1 is a refinement of Figure 1.1 contained in the previous chapter. Note that Figure 2.1 shows only program-level evaluations. It does not show case-level evaluations.

An evaluation whose purpose is to assess a completed social work program (or project) uses a project approach to program-level evaluations. Complementary to the project approach, an evaluation whose purpose is to provide feedback while a program is still underway has a monitoring approach to program-level evaluations; that is, it's designed to contribute to the ongoing development and improvement of the program as it goes along. We discuss the monitoring approach later in this chapter.

Sometimes the monitoring approach is called "formative evaluation," and the project approach is sometimes called "summative evaluation" as illustrated in Box 2.1.

THE PROJECT APPROACH

The first approach to a program-level evaluation is the project approach. It's usually initiated when the program has been in operation for a number of years.

Characteristics of the Project Approach

The project approach tends to give rise to evaluations with the following general overall characteristics they:

- Are externally driven
- Have to deal with resistant workers
- Are intrusive
- Provide only periodic (or no feedback) to social workers
- Recommend large program changes
- Are difficult to incorporate in practice settings

Externally Driven

A project evaluation will almost certainly be externally driven; that is, it will be initiated by someone who is not employed within the program who more often than not will decide on the evaluation questions to be answered and the data to be collected that will presumably answer the questions. Social workers who are employed within the program being evaluated by an "outsider" usually have very little input into the entire evaluative process within an externally driven project evaluation.

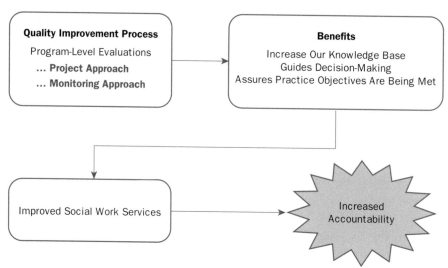

Figure 2.1: **The continuum of professionalization highlighting the two approaches to quality improvement.**

BOX 2.1   FORMATIVE AND SUMMATIVE EVALUATIONS

FORMATIVE EVALUATIONS (MONITORING APPROACH)

A formative evaluation typically involves gathering data during the early stages of your program. It focuses on finding out whether your efforts are unfolding as planned, uncovering any obstacles, barriers, or unexpected opportunities that may have emerged, and identifying mid-course adjustments and corrections that can help ensure the success of your program or intervention.

Essentially, a formative evaluation is a structured way of providing program staff with additional feedback about their activities. This feedback is primarily designed to fine-tune the implementation of the intervention, and it often includes information that is only for internal use by program managers, supervisors, and line-level social workers. Some formative data may also be reported in a summative evaluation of the program.

As we know, some social work programs evolve continuously, never reaching a stage of being finished or complete; formative evaluation activities may be extended throughout the life of a program to help guide this evolution.

SUMMATIVE EVALUATIONS (PROJECT APPROACH)

Summative evaluations typically involve the preparation of a formal report outlining the impact of a program's efforts.

For instance, an evaluation report will typically detail who participated in a program, what activities affected them, and what gains or improvements resulted from their participation.

Often this report will include details regarding what prerequisites or conditions are essential or helpful to the replication of the program, program costs and benefits, and disaggregated results showing findings for specific subgroups of participants.

There is no crisp dividing line between formative evaluation and summative evaluations. Much of the data gathered during formative evaluation activities may be reported in formal summative reports, particularly during the early development of new programs, in order to show how the program is responding to challenges and reaching benchmarks and milestones along the way toward intended outcomes.

Usually a compelling case that your program has had a positive impact requires the measurement of your program objectives before, during, and after implementation of the program. This requires careful program planning and early adoption of appropriate data collection methods and a management information database. In short, your summative evaluation report is a showcase for outcomes associated with your program.

The project approach to evaluation is usually initiated when the program has been in operation for a number of years.

Resistant Social Workers

Since social workers have very little involvement in a project evaluation—or in the evaluation process for that matter—they may react negatively to the evaluation, seeing it as unrelated, intrusive, irrelevant, and, more important, an extra burden. Additionally, they may fear the evaluation will be used in some way to judge them. When an evaluation is externally driven, social workers may resist implementation of an evaluator's recommendations, even if the program's administration insists that changes be made.

Intrusiveness

Evaluation procedures are very likely to be intrusive, no matter how hard the person doing the evaluation works to avoid this. Because the evaluation's procedures are not a part of a program's normal day-to-day routine but must be introduced as additional tasks to be performed, social workers have less time to spend on normal, client-related activities. This diversion of attention may be resented when workers feel obliged to spend less time with clients and more time participating in an evaluation process that was mandated "from above" or "from outside the program."

Periodic (or No Feedback) to Social Workers

The data obtained from a project-type evaluation, even if shared with the social work practitioners, is usually not directly or immediately relevant to them or their current clients. This is particularly the case if an evaluation is designed to answer questions posed by administrators or funders and workers' practice concerns cannot be addressed in the same evaluation project.

If, as sometimes happens, the project-type approach does yield useful information (via the data collected) for the social workers, and changes are made on the basis of these data, the next evaluation may not take place for a long time, perhaps not for years. If the evaluator is not on hand to analyze the benefits resulting from the changes, the social workers may not be sure that there were any benefits.

Large Recommended Changes

The changes recommended as a result of a project approach to evaluations can be major. Administrators and evaluators may feel that, with an evaluation occurring only once every few years, it's an event that ought to yield "significant" findings and recommendations to justify it. Large recommended changes can involve program renovations (e.g., overhauling the staff structure of a program) versus program refinements (e.g., adding or revising a component of staff training).

All evaluations must be based on well-established evaluation principles and methods. Project evaluations, however, are more likely to be based on the scientific rigor necessary to obtain cause-and-effect knowledge and use rigorous types of evaluation designs. Usually, rigorous experiments for the purpose of increasing knowledge are carried out in laboratory-type settings and not in practice settings. However, the same rigorous conditions may be suggested if the purpose is, for example, to evaluate the effectiveness and efficiency of a therapy group.

Learn more about different evaluation designs in Tool E in the Evaluation Toolkit.

The worker might argue that more time will be spent in the administration of the measuring instruments than conducting therapeutic work; the evaluator can easily reply that results will be valid only if scientific methods are strictly followed. The issue here is: Whose interests is the evaluation intended to serve? Who is it for—the social work practitioner or the external evaluator?

In a project approach, the answer is that sometimes it serves the evaluator or the administrative, academic, or funding body that has employed the evaluator. It should be stressed that this is not always the case. Many project approaches use unobtrusive evaluation methods geared to actual practice situations. If, however, the evaluation is undertaken only once in a number of years, intrusion can be considered warranted to obtain reliable and valid results.

Difficult to Incorporate in Practice Settings

A final characteristic of the project approach is that the evaluative methods used by the evaluator are difficult for social workers to learn and almost impossible for them to incorporate into their normal day-to-day practices. In fact, social workers are not expected to learn anything about evaluation procedures as a result of the program being evaluated. Nor is it expected that the evaluation methods employed will be used again before the next major periodic evaluation. The evaluator carries out the project approach, and, essentially until the next time, that's that.

THE MONITORING APPROACH

Most of the characteristics listed for the project approach are rather undesirable; without a doubt, the project approach is intrusive and traumatic, fails to meet the immediate needs of the workers, and may engender resentment and fear—especially if a program's workers have never been involved in a previous evaluation. We now turn to a second approach to program-level evaluations that complements the project approach and is the main focus of our book—the monitoring approach.

The monitoring approach is based on reliable and valid evaluation methods that can be integrated into a social work program as a part of—not an addition to—its normal operating routine. This approach measures the extent that a program is reaching its intended population and the extent to which its services match those that were intended to be delivered. In addition, this approach is designed to provide immediate and continuous feedback on the effectiveness of the client services being offered.

The monitoring approach is nothing more than the continual collection, analysis, reporting, and use of client-centered data. This ongoing and dynamic approach to evaluation is planned, systematic, and most important, timely. Ideally, such a system would be integrated with the program's records system so as to avoid duplication and enhance efficiency.

For example, data on the changes the program aims to effect (called *program objectives*—see Chapter 7) can be collected at intake, at specified times during the intervention (treatment), at termination, and at follow-up. In this way, a constant stream of systematic data are collected, analyzed, and reported in an effort to help the program focus on its clients as they come into (intake), go through (treatment), and leave (termination) the program, then go on with their lives (follow-up).

> *The monitoring approach to evaluation is based on reliable and valid evaluation methods that can be integrated into a social work program as a part of its normal operating routine*

As previously noted, the monitoring approach is done by folks who are employed within the program whereas the project approach is usually done by people who are hired outside the program. However, this is only a generality and does not hold for large social service organizations—especially those with research and evaluation departments actually housed within them. Nevertheless, it's absolutely important to think through the evaluators' role regardless of where the evaluator is housed—within the organization or outside the organization.

> *Learn more about an evaluator's role within different types of evaluations in Tools A and B in the Evaluation Toolkit.*

Characteristics of the Monitoring Approach

Evaluations resulting from a monitoring approach to program-level evaluations tend to have the following characteristics they:

- Are internally driven
- Have cooperative social workers

- Have ongoing continuous feedback procedures
- Recommend minor changes
- Are easily incorporated in practice settings

Internally Driven

Continuous routine use of evaluation methods may have been initially suggested by a program's administration, an outside consultant, or a funder. However, the evaluation methods are put into place and used by practitioners for their own and their clients' benefit without the request (or demand) from any outside source. The evaluative effort may thus be said to be internally driven.

Cooperative Social Workers

When evaluation is a process instead of an event, practitioners are more likely to collaborate in its efforts because it's an accepted part of the daily routine of delivering high-quality services to its clientele.

Integrated

By definition, an intrusion is something unrelated to the task at hand that interferes with that task. Evaluation methods that are routinely used to improve services to clients are part and parcel of the workers' daily tasks. Necessary client-centered changes for solving problems are usually agreed on by line-level practitioners and are usually accepted without difficulty because they result from informed decision-making; that is, decisions are made based on data that are available to all social workers.

Ongoing Continuous Feedback

Some activities in a social work program need to be monitored on a continuing basis. For example, client referrals are received daily and must be processed quickly. To estimate remaining program space, intake workers need a list of how many clients are presently being served, how many clients will be discharged shortly, and how many clients have recently been accepted into the program.

This continually changing list is an example of a simple evaluative tool that provides useful data.

The resulting information can be used to compare the actual number of clients in the program with the number the program was originally designed (and usually funded) to serve.

In other words, the list can be used to fulfill a basic evaluative purpose: comparison of what is with what should be, of the actual with the ideal. It might be found, in some programs, that the arithmetic of intake is not quite right. For example, suppose that a program has space for 100 clients. At the moment, 70 are being served on a regular basis. In theory, then, the program can accept 30 more clients. Suppose also that the program has five social workers; each will then theoretically carry a maximum caseload of 20.

In the caseloads of these five workers there should be just 30 spaces. But for some reason, there are more than 30. The supervisor, who is trying to assign new clients to workers, discovers that the workers can muster 40 spaces between them. In other words, there are 10 clients on the computer who are theoretically being served but who are not in any of the five workers' caseloads. What has happened to these 10 clients?

Investigation brings to light that the workers' records and the computer's records are kept in different ways. Computer records reflect the assumption that every client accepted will continue to be served until formally discharged. However, the practitioner who has not seen Ms. Smith for six months and has failed to locate her after repeated tries has placed Ms. Smith in the "inactive" file. The result of this disparity in record-keeping is that the program seems to have fewer available spaces, and clients who might be served are being turned away.

On Fear . . .

People always fear change. People feared electricity when it was invented, didn't they? People feared coal, they feared gas-powered engines . . . There will always be ignorance, and ignorance leads to fear. But with time, people will come to accept their silicon masters.

~ Bill Gates

Simply discussing inactive files at a staff meeting might solve the problem. What steps will be taken to locate a client who does not appear for appointments? How long should attempts at contact continue before the client is formally discharged? Which other involved professionals need to be informed about the client's nonappearance and the discharge? When and how should they be informed? Is it worth modifying the intake computer's terminal display to include inactive files, with the dates they became inactive and the dates they were reactivated or discharged? Once decisions have been made on these points, a straightforward procedure can be put in place to deal with the ongoing problem of inactive files.

Minor Recommended Change

When change is an expected and ongoing process that results from regular monitoring, program adjustments or modifications tend to be small. Of course continual monitoring can suggest that fundamental changes are needed in the way that the program is conceptualized or structured, but such large changes are rare. Most often, monitoring gives rise to continual minor refinements of programs over time.

Easy to Incorporate in Practice Settings

The monitoring approach, like the project approach, is based on well-established evaluation methods. The difference between them can lie in whom the evaluation is intended to serve: the line-level worker or the evaluator. When the workers themselves, for their own and their clients' benefit, undertake an evaluation, there is no doubt about whom the evaluation is intended to serve.

Advantages of the Monitoring Approach

Social workers who are interested in improving the quality of the services they offer via evaluations are well on their way to taking responsibility for providing the best possible service to clients through systematic examinations of their strengths and weaknesses via the quality improvement process.

Becoming a self-evaluating social work professional (or program) has definite advantages not only for clients but also for workers. For example, the monitoring approach to evaluation:

- Provides an increase understanding of programs
- Provides relevant feedback
- Provides timely feedback
- Provides self-protection
- Has a high level of practitioner and client satisfaction
- Strives for professionalism

Provides an Increased Understanding of Programs

As you know by now from your social work educational experience, social work programs are often complex entities with a large number of interlinked components. Practitioners' main concerns usually have to do with the effectiveness of their treatment interventions. How can the confused sexual identity of an adolescent who has been sexually abused best be addressed? What teaching technique is most effective with children who have learning disabilities? Is an open-door policy appropriate for group homes housing adolescents who are mentally challenged? Answers come slowly through study, intuition, hunches, and past experience, but often the issues are so complex that practitioners cannot be sure if the answers obtained are correct.

Many social workers stumble onward, hoping their interventions are right, using intuition to assess the effectiveness of their particular interventions (or package of interventions) with a particular client. We briefly discuss case-level evaluations in Chapters 14 and 15 to show how the use of simple evaluation designs can complement a worker's intuition so that an inspired guess more closely approaches knowledge.

However, no amount of knowledge about how well an intervention worked will tell the worker why it worked or failed to work. Why do apparently similar clients, treated similarly, achieve different results? Is it something about the client? about the worker? about the type of intervention?

Learn more about case-level evaluation designs in Chapters 14 and 15.

It's always difficult to pinpoint a reason for unsatisfactory achievement of a program's objectives because there are so many possible overlapping and intertwined causes. However, some reasons may be identified by a careful look at the program stages leading up to the interventions. For example, one reason for not attaining success with clients may be because they were inappropriate for a certain program and/or client group in the first place. Or perhaps the program's assessment procedures were inadequate; perhaps unsuitable clients were accepted because the referral came from a major funding body. In other words, perhaps the lack of client success at the intervention stage derives from simple screening problems at intake.

Social workers who have been involved with a do-it-yourself evaluation may become familiar with the program's intake procedures, both in theory and in reality. They may also become familiar with the planning procedures, discharge procedures, follow-up procedures, staff recruitment and training procedures, recording procedures, and so on.

The worker will begin to see a link between poor client outcomes at one program stage and inadequacies at another, between a success here and an innovation somewhere else. In sum, practitioners may be able to perform their own tasks more effectively if they understand how their program functions as a living organism. One way to gain this understanding is to participate in a hands-on, do-it-yourself evaluation.

Provides Relevant Feedback

A second advantage of the monitoring approach is that the workers within the program can formulate meaningful and relevant evaluation questions. They can use evaluation procedures to find out what they want to know not what the administrator, the funder, or a university professor want to know. If the data to be gathered are perceived as relevant, social workers are usually willing to cooperate in the evaluation. And if the information resulting from that data is relevant, it's likely to be used by the practitioners.

> *On Feedback . . .*
>
> *Question: What's the shortest word in the English language that contains the letters, abcdef?*
>
> *Answer: Feedback. Don't forget that feedback is one of the essential elements of good communication.*
>
> *~ Author unknown*

It's our belief that all evaluative efforts conducted in our profession provide feedback loops that improve the delivery of services. Feedback provides data about the extent to which a program's objective(s) is achieved or approximated. Based on these data, client services may be adjusted or changed to improve the achievement of the program's objective(s).

Provides Timely Feedback

A third advantage is that the workers can decide when the evaluation is to be carried out. Evaluation procedures can be undertaken daily, weekly, monthly, or only once in five years, as is discussed in the following chapters. The point here is that data are most useful when they help to solve a current problem, less useful when the problem has not yet occurred, and least useful after the event.

Provides Self-Protection

Some work programs are eventually evaluated by outside evaluators. If the social workers have already familiarized themselves with evaluation procedures and with their program's strengths and weaknesses, they are in a better position to defend the program when an externally driven evaluation occurs. In addition, because improvements have already been made as a result of self-evaluations, their program will be more defensible. Also, the social workers will indirectly learn about evaluation designs and methodology by monitoring their practices on a regular basis. Modifications recommended by an outside evaluator are hence likely to be less far-reaching and less traumatic.

Table 2.1: Approaches and Types of Evaluations

Approach	Type	Description	Purpose	Strength	Limitation	Sample Question
			Types of Program Evaluations			
Adversary-oriented evaluation	Process, outcome	Balances bias through a planned effort to generate opposing points of view within an evaluation	To assure fairness and illuminate program strengths and weaknesses by incorporating both positive and negative views into the evaluation design	Diverts a great deal of subsequent criticism by addressing anticipated	Time-consuming and expensive, requiring extensive preparation and investment of human and financial resources	How effective is the Healthy Start program in reducing child abuse rates?
Black-box evaluation	Outcome	Examines program output without consideration of program input	To determine program effects	Determines whether program is achieving its goals	Fails to consider why something is effective or ineffective	Do standardized test scores of high school students improve from the beginning of the term to the end?
Cluster evaluation	Process	Engages a group of projects with common funders, topics, or themes in common evaluation efforts to provide a composite overview of the success or failure of the cluster	To improve programs by identifying patterns of and lessons from the cluster	Allows multiple evaluation models, each designed for individual sites and programs based on local needs, to address collective themes or topics	Lack of standardization makes it difficult to describe how approach should be conducted	In what ways do prenatal programs for parents improve outcomes for infants?
Context evaluation	Need	Describes discrepancies between what is and what is desired	To develop a program rationale through the analysis of unrealized needs and unused opportunities	Potential for program effectiveness is enhanced when conceptual basis for program is perceived needs	Target audience may fail to recognize or articulate needs	What are the needs of low-income women in terms of prenatal health care?

Cost-effectiveness evaluation	Efficiency	Describes the relationship between program costs and outcomes for participants in substantive terms	To judge the efficiency of a program	Allows comparison and rank ordering of alternative interventions in addressing similar goals	Requires extensive technical and analytical procedures	How many dollars were expended to increase reading test scores of students?
Cost-benefit evaluation	Efficiency	Compares program costs and program outcomes in terms of dollars	To describe the economic efficiency of a program regarding actual or anticipated costs and known or expected benefits	Useful in convincing policymakers, funders, and decision-makers that dollar benefits justify the program	Difficult to quantify many outcomes in monetary terms and to express costs and benefits in terms of a common denominator	What was the total estimated savings to society as a result of decreases in teen pregnancy rates?
Evaluation research	Outcome	Generates knowledge of program effectiveness in general rather than judging the merit of individual programs	To generate knowledge for conceptual use	Introduces objectivity and scientific rigor	Nonsignificant statistical findings do not necessarily mean that group means are equal, nor that program is ineffective	Do employers who offer on-site child care have higher staff morale than those employers who do not offer on-site child care?
Goal-free evaluation	Outcome	Gathers data directly on program effect and effectiveness without knowledge of program goals	To gather data directly on program effect and effectiveness without knowledge of program goals	Attention to actual effects rather than alleged effects reduces tendency toward tunnel vision and increases likelihood that unanticipated side effects will be noted	Not goal-free at all but rather focuses on wider context goals instead of program-specific objectives	What are the actual effects of the mentoring program?

(continued)

Table 2.1: [Continued]

Types of Program Evaluations

Approach	Type	Description	Purpose	Strength	Limitation	Sample Question
Goals-based evaluation	Outcome	Emphasizes the clarification of goals and the program's effectiveness in achieving goals	To measure the degree to which goals are achieved	Evaluation is sensitive to a particular program and its circumscribed goals and objectives	Fails to consider additional effects of program and neglects why it succeeds or fails	Does a parent's knowledge of child development change as a result of the program?
Impact evaluation	Outcome	Addresses impact of program on program recipient	To describe direct and indirect program effects	Tests the usefulness of a program in ameliorating a particular problem	Difficult to establish causality in social sciences	Are participants able to secure meaningful employment as a result of the job-training program?
Implementation evaluation	Process	Examines if the program is functional and operating as it is supposed to be	To determine extent to which program is properly implemented (to seek out discrepancies between program plan and reality)	Examines program operations in context as implementation strategies are neither automatic nor certain	Provides no information regarding program efficiency or effectiveness	Is the program reaching the target population?
Input evaluation	Process	Describes strong and weak points of strategies toward achieving objectives	To identify and assess program capabilities	Provides useful information to guide program strategy and design	Approach can be complex and overwhelming if priorities are not set and followed	Are home visits or group sessions more appropriate for the target population?
Outcomes evaluation	Outcome	Comparison of actual program outcomes to desired program outcomes	To determine whether program objectives have been attained	Generally is easy to understand, develop, and implement	Lacks information regarding the actual nature of the program and what is producing observed outcomes	Do patients lose weight?

Evaluation type	Focus	Description	Purpose	Strengths	Weaknesses	Example question
Performance evaluation	Outcome	Assesses program results in terms of established performance indicators	To describe behavior changes as a result of the program	Establishes performance criteria for program recipients	Uncertainty regarding the extent to which program activities caused observed results	What study skills do youth display after participating in a tutoring program?
Process evaluation	Process	Focuses on internal dynamics and actual operations to understand strengths and weakness	To look at how an outcome is produced rather than the outcome itself	Provides feedback in development phase to improve program	Does not indicate if a program is successful or effective	How many hours of direct contact do program recipients receive?
Responsive evaluation	Process, outcome, need, efficiency	Responds to program activities and audience needs by allowing evaluation questions and methods to emerge from observation	To address the concerns and issues of the stakeholder audience	Directs the attention of the evaluator to the needs of those for whom the evaluation is being done	Reliance on individual stakeholder perspectives may lead to subjective designs and findings	What major questions would you like the evaluation to answer?
Theory-based evaluation	Process, outcome	Based on a model, theory, or philosophy about how a program works	To identify the causal relationships that affect, operate, and influence the program	Presents rationale for choice of variables, and results can contribute to growing body of scientific knowledge	Conclusions are based on whether theory is correct or accepted	Is there a fit between the outcomes predicted by the ecological theory and the observed outcomes for families?
Utilization-focused evaluation	Process, outcome, efficiency, need	Yields immediate, concrete, observable, and useful information on program decisions and activities as a result of evaluation findings	To increase the use of evaluation	Provides meaningful, relevant, and substantial information to empower users	Demands high expenditures of time, energy, and staff resources	What information is needed by stakeholders to improve future youth development programs?

Evaluations must never be new and frightening experiences but simply a part of the routine—a routine that tries to improve the quality of services for clients.

Another consideration is that the social workers themselves are likely to be less traumatized by the idea of being evaluated: Evaluation is no longer a new and frightening experience but simply a part of the routine—a routine that tries to improve the quality of services for clients.

Has a High Level of Practitioner and Client Satisfaction

A monitoring approach to a case-level evaluation can satisfy the worker that an intervention is appropriate and successful, and it can improve a client's morale by demonstrating the progress that has been made toward the client's practice objectives. Moreover, data gathered at the case level is always used at the program level. Thus, improvement of the program as a whole can follow from an improvement in one worker's practice—one client at a time.

Strives for Professionalism

A monitoring approach is consistent with the expectations of professional conduct in social work. Social workers who use systematic methods to evaluate their work can benefit from evaluation results through informed decision-making. Evaluation results can be used to support critical program changes or defend controversial program actions. They can also confirm or challenge workers' long-held beliefs about a mode of operation. Additionally, an evaluation can reveal a program's flaws and deficiencies that require corrective action.

FOUR TYPES OF EVALUATIONS

As can be expected by now, there are many types of evaluations that can be done to improve the delivery of the services we offer our clients. Table 2.1 presents various trendy approaches to evaluations with their fancy names in the left-hand column. The column to the immediate right is the generic type that it belongs to: need, process, outcome, or efficiency.

We briefly present the four types that are most relevant to our profession. Each is expanded on in detail in the chapters contained in Part III in this book:

1 Determining client needs, Chapter 10
2 Assessing how a program works, Chapter 11
3 Assessing client outcomes, Chapter 12
4 Determining a program's efficiency, Chapter 13

As we know from the preceding chapter, we need to understand that each evaluation is tied to a social service program that will be influenced to varying degrees by the environment in which the program operates. Figure 2.2 illustrates the four types of evaluations that we discuss in Part III of this book. They can be loosely classified under either the project approach or the monitoring approach to program-level evaluations.

Needs Assessment

As we will see in Chapter 10, the first type of evaluation is needs assessment. These are sometimes referred to as the *assessment of need*. These evaluations usually take place before a program is conceptualized, funded, staffed, and implemented (the topic of Chapters 7 and 8). In short, a needs assessment assesses the feasibility of (or need for) a given social service. A needs assessment is intended to verify that a social problem exists within a specific client population to an extent that warrants the implementation of a program.

On need ...

If I had asked people what they needed, they would have said faster horses.

~ Henry Ford

To do this, a needs assessment must produce fairly precise estimates of the demographic characteristics of individuals exhibiting the problem believed to exist. A needs assessment seeks to answer such questions as:

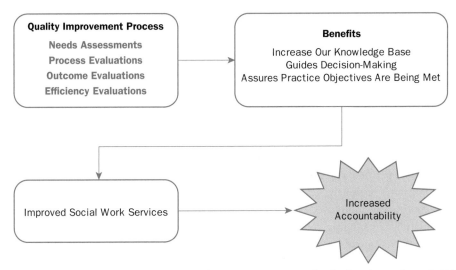

Figure 2.2: **The continuum of professionalization highlighting the four most common types of evaluations that can be used within the quality improvement process.**

- What is the socioeconomic profile of the community?
- What are the particular needs of this community with respect to the type of program being considered (e.g., physical health, mental health, employment, education, crime prevention)?
- What kinds of service are likely to be attractive to this particular community?
- Is the program meeting the needs of the people it believes it's serving?
- Is the program meeting the needs of people in the best possible way?
- Are there any other needs that the program could be meeting?

Social work programs should never gather data to justify their own maintenance needs. They must collect data to ascertain the real needs of the people they hope to serve and then tailor the structure of their service delivery to meet these needs.

As mentioned, an evaluation does not necessarily assess a whole program; particular parts of a program may be the focus, as in a needs assessment. For example, there may be some doubt that a program is currently addressing a specific community's needs. The composition of the local community may have changed since the program was first established, and there may now be a high proportion of Latino children being referred for service, whereas before the majority of referrals were African American and Caucasian.

The goal of a needs assessment may be to determine to what degree the program is responsive to the special needs of Latino children and to the present concerns of the Latino community. This may involve conducting a needs assessment within the community and comparing the community's current perceived needs with the program's original intent.

Experienced program executive directors and their funding sources know that the demographic characteristics of communities tend to change over time. Perhaps there's now a higher proportion of senior citizens than formerly, or perhaps the closure of a large manufacturing plant has meant high unemployment and an increase in all of the problems associated with job loss. Changes may also have occurred in the community's social service delivery network.

Perhaps a program for pregnant teens has had to close its doors or a meals-on-wheels service has recently been instituted for homebound seniors. Perceptive program directors try to keep abreast of changes like these by becoming members of interagency committees, consulting with local advisory boards and funding sources, establishing contact with community organizations, talking with social work professors, and taking other like action.

Despite all such preemptive measures, however, there is occasionally some doubt that a program is meeting the current needs of the people it was originally funded to serve. On these occasions, a needs assessment may be an appropriate type of evaluation, as it can ascertain what the community currently needs (if any) in the way of social services.

It's possible to avoid periodic and disruptive evaluative efforts if a program's responsiveness to its community needs is continually monitored. Indications that a target population is changing can be seen in changing referral patterns, novel problem situations presented by clients, and unusual requests from other programs.

We believe all programs should have monitoring systems through which such data are routinely collected and analyzed, and any lack of responsiveness to a community's needs can be easily picked up and dealt with immediately. We return to needs assessments in much more detail in Chapter 10.

Process Evaluations

A second type of evaluation is a process analysis, which is discussed in depth in Chapter 11. A process analysis is the monitoring and measurement of a treatment intervention—the assumed cause of client success or failure. As we will see shortly, an evaluation of efficiency determines the ratio of effectiveness or outcome to cost but says nothing about why the program is or is not efficient, either overall or in certain areas. To answer that question, we need to consider program process: the entire sequence of activities that a program undertakes to achieve its objectives, including all the decisions made, who made them, and on what criteria they were based.

> *On process...*
>
> *The beauty of empowering others is that your own power is not diminished in the process.*
>
> *~ Barbara Colorose*

An evaluation of process might include the sequence of events throughout the entire program, or it might focus on a particular program component: intervention, say, or follow-up. A careful examination of how something is done may indicate why it's more or less effective or efficient. To state the point another way: When a program is planned, correctly (Chapters 7 and 8), it should have included a definition of the population the program serves, a specification of the client needs it will meet, and a description of the specific social work interventions it will undertake to meet the client needs within the population. If client needs are not being met, or the population is not being adequately served, it may be that the practitioners' activities are not being carried out as originally planned. A process evaluation can ascertain whether this is so.

Sometimes a needs assessment will have determined that the program is serving a sufficient number of the people it's meant to serve. If not, a process evaluation will determine this and will also determine exactly what treatment interventions (activities) are being undertaken by its social workers with their clients. It addresses such questions as:

- What procedures are in place for assessment?
- Are staff members who do assessments thoroughly trained for the job?
- What modes of therapy are offered?
- What criteria are used to decide when a client should move from individual to family therapy, or into group therapy, or should be discharged or referred elsewhere?
- What follow-up procedures are in place?
- How much and what type of staff training is available?
- How are client records kept?
- What do staff do compared with what they are supposed to do?

In order for a process evaluation to occur, however, the program has to be specifically delineated in a written form that makes it extremely clear how a client goes through the entire program. In short, a client path flow must be established that depicts the key activities, decision points, and client flow through the program in a graphic format. We need to construct a logic model of our program and present a detailed diagram, sometimes called a *client path flow*, of the chronological order of how a client comes into and goes through our program. Logic models and client path flows are introduced in the following chapter and discussed in depth in Chapters 7 and 8.

The data necessary for a process evaluation will generally be available within the program itself but rarely in usable form. Client demographic and assessment data may be on file but will probably not be summarized. Services provided to clients are typically recorded by social workers in handwritten notes deposited in client files. Training courses taken by staff may be included in staff files, or general training files or may not be recorded at all.

Where no systematic management data system (sometimes referred to as management information system) is in place (see Chapter 14), gathering, summarizing, and analyzing data are extremely time-consuming endeavors. As a result, of course, it's rarely done until someone outside the program insists on it. Again, the use of routine monitoring procedures will avoid the need for intrusive evaluations initiated by outside sources.

> *The use of routine monitoring procedures will avoid the need for intrusive evaluations initiated by outside sources.*

We have assumed that both outcome and process evaluations are necessary components of any comprehensive program evaluation. If, however, we are concerned only with the client outcome of a specific program, it might be asked why we need to monitor the program's implementation. The answer is simple: An outcome analysis investigates any changes that are believed to be brought about by an orderly set of program activities. We cannot be certain, however, that any change was caused by the program's activities unless we know precisely what these activities were. Therefore, we need to study the program operations via process evaluations.

Outcome Evaluations

As we will see in Chapter 12, a third type of evaluation is an outcome evaluation. It's an evaluation that determines to what degree the program is meeting its overall program objectives. In a treatment program, this usually means the degree to which treatment interventions are effective. For example, a program in which a high proportion of clients achieve their individual practice objectives (sometimes referred to as treatment objectives or client objectives) can be considered a successful program. If the majority of clients terminate unilaterally without fully reaching their practice objectives, the program can be considered less than successful.

> *On outcomes . . .*
>
> *It's our attitude at the beginning of a difficult undertaking which, more than anything else, will determine its successful outcome.*
>
> *~ Barbara Colorose*

An outcome evaluation indicates whether the program is working, but it says nothing about why it's working (or failing to work). Nor is there any mention of efficiency; that is, the time and dollar cost of client success. After all, if a program achieves what it's supposed to achieve, via the attainment of its program objectives, what does it matter how it achieves it? If the program is to be replicated or even improved, it does matter; nevertheless, client outcome alone is the focus of many outcome assessments. Questions related to outcome generally fall into four categories:

- First, the evaluator wants to know to what degree the program is achieving its program objectives: For example, do people who participate in a vocational training program have improved job skills, and by how much have their job skills improved (a program objective)?
- Second, the evaluator wants to know whether people who have been through the program have better job skills than similar people who have been through similar programs.

- Third, and highly related to the previous point, is the question of causality. Is there any evidence that the program *caused* the improved job skills?
- Fourth, how long does the improvement last? Many clients who are discharged from social service programs return to the exact same environment that was more than likely responsible for their problem in the first place. Often client gains are not maintained, and equally often programs have no follow-up procedures to find out if they in fact have been maintained.

As we will see throughout this book, questions about how well the program achieves its objectives can be answered by aggregating, or bringing together, the data that individual social workers collect about their individual clients. Questions about how well client success is maintained can be answered in a similar way. However, comparisons between those who have and those who have not been through the program, as well as questions about causality, require a different sort of data, collected via explanatory evaluation designs involving two or more groups of clients.

Efficiency Evaluations

Chapter 13 describes efficiency evaluations—the fourth type of evaluation. These types of evaluations are always money-oriented and address such questions as

- How many hours of therapy are generally required before clients reach their practice objectives?
- What do these hours cost in clinical and administrative time, facilities, equipment, and other resources?
- Is there any way in which cost could be reduced without loss of effectiveness, perhaps by offering group therapy instead of individual therapy?

- Is a particular program process—intake, say—conducted in the shortest possible time, at minimum cost?

If an outcome evaluation has shown the program to be effective in achieving its program objectives, the efficiency questions become

- Does the program achieve its success at a reasonable cost?
- Can dollar values be assigned to the outcomes it achieves?
- Does the program cost less or more than other similar programs obtaining similar results?

Efficiency evaluations are particularly difficult to carry out in social work because so many of our client outcomes cannot be realistically (socially and professionally) measured in terms of dollars. In fact, it would be unthinkable to measure some client outcomes in terms of efficiency—such as counseling terminally ill cancer patients.

> *On efficiency …*
>
> *If all efficiency experts were laid end to end—I'd be in favor of it.*
>
> ~ Al Diamond

The benefits of a job-training program that removes its clients from welfare rolls can be more easily quantified in terms of efficiency (cost savings) than a program that is designed to reduce the feeling of hopelessness in terminal cancer patients. Nevertheless, there is only so much money available for social service programs, and decisions regarding which ones to fund, no matter how difficult, have to be made—especially if funding decisions are made on efficiency criteria. We do not need to put a price on program results in order to use costs in decision-making, but it's necessary to be able to describe in detail what results have been achieved via the expenditure of what resources.

Note that the four types of evaluation listed so far are linked in an ordered sequence as outlined in the following figure.

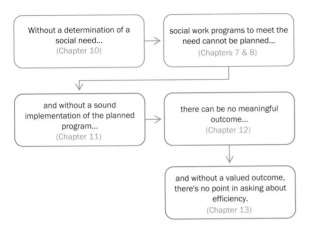

INTERNAL AND EXTERNAL EVALUATORS

Each of the four types of evaluations mentioned in the previous section can be done by an internal and/or external evaluator. In short, any evaluation may be internally driven; that is, they are initiated and conducted by staff members who work within a program. In other cases, the evaluation may be externally driven—initiated by someone outside the program to be evaluated, often a funding source.

On evaluators . . .

True genius resides in the capacity for evaluation of uncertain, hazardous, and conflicting information.

~ Winston Churchill

The main motive behind internal evaluations is usually to improve the quality of services to clients immediately. A distinct advantage of internal evaluations is that the evaluation questions framed are likely to be highly relevant to staff members'

interests. This is hardly surprising; staff members are responsible for conducting the evaluation, and, with their firsthand knowledge of the program, they are in a position to ensure that the evaluation addresses relevant issues. Thus feedback from an evaluation nurtures the quality improvement process. Moreover, practitioners (or organizations) who continually evaluate their practices are in a position to demonstrate accountability to their funders and other stakeholders.

A drawback to internal evaluators is that they may be viewed as lacking the credibility that comes with independent, outside evaluators. Sometimes, therefore, funding bodies are not content with data from internal evaluators and request external ones. Because they are carried out independently of the programs to be evaluated, external evaluators are often perceived to be more credible.

Because they are commissioned by people outside our programs, however, they tend to reflect those interests and may not address questions that are most relevant to program staff. As well, outside evaluators often impose an onerous data collection burden on staff and tend to be disruptive to normal program operations.

Learn more about hiring external evaluators in Tools A and B in the Evaluation Toolkit.

When externally driven evaluations are to occur, organizations that conduct internal evaluations are in an advantageous position. A priori, internal evaluations may identify some things that need to be improved before the outside evaluators appear. They may also identify programs' strengths, which can be displayed. As well, staff members are likely to be conversant with evaluation matters, allowing them to engage in knowledgeable discussions with outside evaluators and thus help ensure that the evaluation process will deal fairly with the programs' interests.

SUMMARY

This chapter started with a brief introduction to two common approaches to program-level evaluations: the project approach and the monitoring approach. We then summarized the four types of evaluations that will be presented in depth in the chapters contained in Part III: need, process, outcome, and efficiency. We ended the chapter by introducing the concept of internal and external evaluators.

With the contents of the previous chapter and this one under your belt, you are in an excellent position to appreciate the process that all evaluations go through—the content of the following chapter aptly titled, "The Process."

Study Questions   Chapter 2

The goal of this chapter is to provide you with a beginning knowledge base for you to feel comfortable in answering the following questions. AFTER you have read the chapter, indicate how comfortable you feel you are in answering each question on a 5-point scale where

1	2	3	4	5
Very uncomfortable	Somewhat uncomfortable	Neutral	Somewhat comfortable	Very comfortable

If you rated any question between 1–3, reread the section of the chapter where the information for the question is found. If you still feel that you're uncomfortable in answering the question, then talk with your instructor and/or your classmates for more clarification.

	Questions	Degree of comfort? (Circle one number)
1	In your own words, define "the project approach to program-level evaluations." Describe how you would go about doing one within your field placement (or work) setting.	1 2 3 4 5
2	In your own words, define "the monitoring approach to program-level evaluations." Describe how you would go about doing one within your field placement (or work) setting.	1 2 3 4 5
3	Discuss how the monitoring approach to program-level evaluations generates data for a project approach. Describe how this could be done within your field placement (or work) setting.	1 2 3 4 5
4	List and then discuss each of the characteristics of the project approach to evaluations. Then discuss how each is relevant by providing specific social work examples from your field placement (or work setting) to illustrate your main points.	1 2 3 4 5
5	List and then discuss each of the characteristics of the monitoring approach to evaluations. Then discuss how each is relevant by providing specific social work examples from your field placement (or work setting) to illustrate your main points.	1 2 3 4 5
6	List and then discuss each of the advantages of the monitoring approach to evaluations. Then discuss how each is relevant by providing specific social work examples from your field placement (or work setting) to illustrate your main points.	1 2 3 4 5

continued

	Study Questions for Chapter **2** Continued	
7	List the four main types of program evaluations. In your own words, briefly describe what each does. Then discuss how each could be done within your field placement (or work setting).	1 2 3 4 5
8	What questions do needs assessments address? Provide specific social work examples from your field placement (or work setting) to illustrate your main points.	1 2 3 4 5
9	What questions do process evaluations address? Provide specific social work examples from your field placement (or work setting) to illustrate your main points.	1 2 3 4 5
10	What questions do outcome evaluations address? Provide specific social work examples from your field placement (or work setting) to illustrate your main points.	1 2 3 4 5
11	What questions do efficiency evaluations address? Provide specific social work examples from your field placement (or work setting) to illustrate your main points.	1 2 3 4 5
12	In your own words, discuss the differences between internal and external evaluators. Then discuss how an internal one could be done within your field placement (or work setting). external?	1 2 3 4 5
13	Take a quick look at Table 2.1. Jot down a few questions that readily come to your mind when glancing at the table. What are your immediate impressions of the program evaluation enterprise by reviewing the contents of Table 2.1? Discuss these with your instructor and fellow classmates. Did they have the same impressions as you?	1 2 3 4 5

Chapter 2

Assessing Your Self-Efficacy

AFTER you have read this chapter AND have completed all of the study questions, indicate how knowledgeable you feel you are for each of the following concepts on a 5-point scale where

1	2	3	4	5
Not knowledgeable at all	Somewhat unknowledgeable	Neutral	Somewhat knowledgeable	Very knowledgeable

	Concepts	Knowledge Level? (Circle one number)
1	The project approach to program-level evaluations	1 2 3 4 5
2	The monitoring approach to program-level evaluations	1 2 3 4 5
3	Needs assessments	1 2 3 4 5
4	Process evaluations	1 2 3 4 5
5	Outcome evaluations	1 2 3 4 5
6	Efficiency evaluations	1 2 3 4 5
7	Internal evaluators	1 2 3 4 5
8	External evaluators	1 2 3 4 5
	Add up your scores (minimum = 8, Maximum = 40)	Your total score =

A 38–40 = Professional evaluator in the making
A– 36–37 = Senior evaluator
B+ 34–35 = Junior evaluator
B 32–33 = Assistant evaluator
B– 8–31 = Reread the chapter and redo the study questions

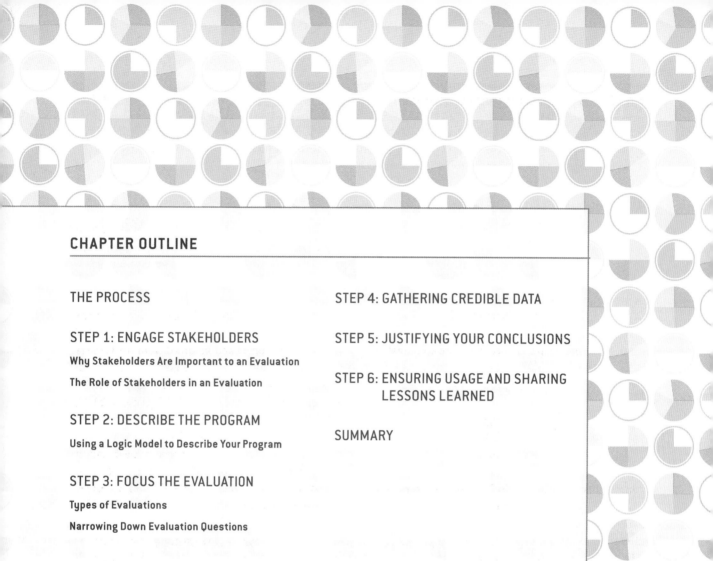

CHAPTER OUTLINE

Excellence is a continuous process and not an accident.

~ A. P. J. Abdul Kalam

Chapter 3

THE PROCESS

CENTERS FOR DISEASE CONTROL AND PREVENTION

The previous two chapters presented the rational of how case- and program-level evaluations (internal and external) help us to become more accountable to society. As you know, our programs are extremely complex and dynamic organizations that have numerous outside pressures to attend to, as well as concentrating on their own internal struggles—all at the same time providing efficient and effective services to clients.

Not only do program evaluations (i.e., need, process, outcome, efficiency) bring us a step closer to accountability; they also help line-level workers and evaluators alike learn about our clients' life experiences, witness client suffering, observe client progress and regress, and feel the public's pressure to produce totally unrealistic "magnificent and instant positive change" with extremely limited resources.

Integrating evaluation activities into our program's service delivery system, therefore, presents an immense opportunity for us to learn more about social problems, the people they affect, and how our interventions actually work. For organizational learning to occur, however, there must be an opportunity for continuous, meaningful, and useful evaluative feedback. And this feedback must make sense to all of our stakeholder groups. All levels of staff within a program have an influence on the program's growth and development, so they all must be involved in the "evaluative processes" as well. Thus we now turn our attention to the evaluative process.

THE PROCESS

What's this "evaluative process," you ask? The answer is simple. It's a tried-and-true method that contains six general steps as presented in Figure 3.1. As with the previous editions of this book, the steps and all related text have been adopted and modified from the Centers for Disease Control and Prevention (CDC; 1999a, 1999b, 1999c, 2005, 2006, 2010, 2011, 2013); Milstein, Wetterhall, and CDC Evaluation Working Group (2000), and Yarbrough, Shulha, Hopson, and Caruthers (2011).

It's our opinion that the CDC's evaluative framework that we use to describe the program evaluation process is the "gold standard" of all the evaluation frameworks that exist today. Hopefully you will agree after reading this chapter.

The steps are all interdependent on one another and, more often than not, are executed in a nonlinear sequence. An order exists, however, for fulfilling each step—earlier steps provide the foundation for subsequent steps. Now that we know there are six steps when evaluating social work programs we immediately turn our attention to the first step: engaging stakeholders in the evaluative process.

STEP 1: ENGAGE STAKEHOLDERS

For all four types of evaluations mentioned in the previous chapter and presented in depth in Part III of this book, the evaluation cycle begins by engaging all of our stakeholder groups. As we know by now, almost all social work evaluations involve partnerships with and among its stakeholders; therefore, any evaluation of a program requires considering the value systems of the various stakeholder groups. As you know from the previous two chapters, they must be totally engaged in

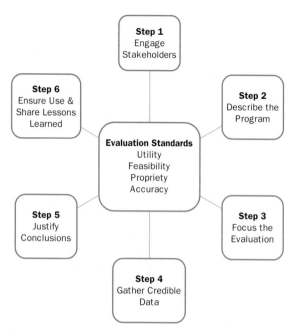

Figure 3.1: **The program evaluation process.**

the evaluation of your program in order to ensure that their perspectives are understood, appreciated, and, more important, heard. We simply cannot overemphasize this point enough—if you don't include your stakeholders in an evaluation it will fail. Guaranteed.

Stakeholders are people or organizations invested in your program, interested in the results of your evaluation, and/or with a stake in what will be done with the results of your evaluation. Representing their needs and interests throughout the process is fundamental to doing a good program evaluation.

When stakeholders are not engaged, your evaluation findings can easily be ignored, criticized, or resisted because your evaluation doesn't address your stakeholders' individual evaluation questions or values. After becoming involved, stakeholders can easily help to execute the other five steps. Identifying and engaging three stakeholder groups are critical to your evaluation:

> **Group 1: *Those involved in your program's operations,*** such as sponsors, collaborators, coalition partners, funding officials, administrators, executive

directors, supervisors, managers, line-level social workers, and support staff.

> **Group 2: *Those served or affected by your program,*** such as clients, family members, neighborhood organizations, academic institutions, elected officials, advocacy groups, professional associations, skeptics, opponents, and personnel at related or competing social service programs.

> **Group 3: *Primary users of your evaluation's results,*** such as the specific persons in a position to do and/or decide something regarding the findings that were derived from your evaluation.

Clearly, the three categories are not mutually exclusive; in particular, the primary users of evaluation findings are often members of the other two groups. For example, your program's executive director (Group 1) could also be involved in an advocacy organization or coalition (Group 2) in addition to being the main person who would utilize your evaluation's recommendations (Group 3).

Why Stakeholders Are Important to an Evaluation

Stakeholders can help (or hinder) an evaluation before it's even conducted, while it's being conducted, and after the results are collected and ready for use. Because so many of our social service efforts are complex and because our programs may be several layers removed from frontline implementation, stakeholders take on a particular importance in ensuring meaningful evaluation questions are identified and your evaluation results will be used to make a difference.

Stakeholders are much more likely to support your evaluation and act on the results and recommendations if they are involved in the evaluation process. Conversely, without stakeholder support, your evaluation may be ignored, criticized, resisted, or even sabotaged.

You need to identify those stakeholders who matter the most by giving priority to those stakeholders who:

IN A NUTSHELL	**3.1**	**Description of the Program Evaluation Process** *(Narrative for Figure 3.1)*
Steps (Figure 3.1)		**Description of Steps**
Step 1 Engage stakeholders		Evaluation stakeholders are people or organizations that are invested in your program, are interested in the results of the evaluation, and/or have a stake in what will be done with evaluation results. Representing their needs and interests throughout the process is fundamental to a good program evaluation.
Step 2 Describe the program		A comprehensive program description clarifies the need for your program, the activities you are undertaking to address this need, and the program's intended outcomes. This can help you when it is time to focus your evaluation on a limited set of questions of central importance. Note that in this step you are describing the program and not the evaluation. Various tools (e.g., logic and impact models) will be introduced to help you depict your program and the anticipated outcomes. Such models can help stakeholders reach a shared understanding of the program.
Step 3 Focus the evaluation design		Focusing the evaluation involves determining the most important evaluation questions and the most appropriate design for an evaluation, given time and resource constraints. An entire program does not need to be evaluated all at once. Rather, the "right" focus for an evaluation will depend on what questions are being asked, who is asking them, and what will be done with the resulting information.
Step 4 Gather credible data		Once you have described the program and focused the evaluation, the next task is to gather data to answer the evaluation questions. Data gathering should include consideration of the following: indicators, sources of methods of data collection, quality, quantity, and logistics.
Step 5 Justify conclusions		When agencies, communities, and other stakeholders agree that evaluation findings are justified, they will be more inclined to take action on the evaluation results. Conclusions become justified when analyzed and synthesized data is interpreted through the 'prism' of values that stakeholders bring, and then judged accordingly. This step encompasses analyzing the data you have collected, making observations and/or recommendations about the program based on the analysis, and justifying the evaluation findings by comparing the data against stakeholder values that have been identified in advance.
Step 6 Ensure use and share lessons learned		The purpose(s) you identified early in the evaluation process should guide the use of evaluation results (e.g., demonstrating effectiveness of the program, modifying program planning, accountability). To help ensure that your evaluation results are used by key stakeholders, it's important to consider the timing, format, and key audiences for sharing information about the evaluation process and your findings.

- Can increase the credibility of your efforts or the evaluation process itself
- Are responsible for day-to-day implementation of the activities that are part of your social work program
- Will advocate for (or authorize changes to) your program that the evaluation may recommend
- Will fund or authorize the continuation or expansion of your program

In addition you must include those who participate in your program and are affected by your program and/or its evaluation, such as:

- Program line-level staff, supervisors, managers, and administrative support
- Local, state, and regional coalitions interested in the social problem you are trying to solve
- Local grantees of your funds
- Local and national advocacy partners
- Other funding agencies, such as national and state governments
- State education agencies, schools, and other educational groups
- Universities, colleges, community colleges, and other educational institutions
- Local government, state legislators, and state governors
- Privately owned businesses and business associations
- Health-care systems and the medical community
- Religious organizations
- Community organizations
- Private citizens
- Program critics
- Representatives of populations disproportionately affected by the social problem you are trying to solve. This should include current clients and perhaps clients who have "graduated" from your program.
- Law enforcement representatives

The Role of Stakeholders in an Evaluation

Stakeholder perspectives should influence every step of your evaluation. Stakeholder input in Step 2:

Describe the Program, ensures a clear and consensual understanding of your program's activities and outcomes. This is an important backdrop for even more valuable stakeholder input in Step 3: Focus the Evaluation to ensure that the key questions of most importance are included.

Stakeholders may also have insights or preferences on the most effective and appropriate ways to collect data from target respondents. In Step 5: Justify Conclusions, the perspectives and values that stakeholders bring to your project are explicitly acknowledged and honored in making judgments about the data gathered.

> *The product of this step is a list of stakeholders to engage and a rationale for their involvement.*

Finally, the considerable time and effort you spent in engaging and building consensus among stakeholders pays off in the last step, Step 6: Ensure Use and Lessons Learned, because stakeholder engagement has created a market for the evaluation's results, or findings.

Stakeholders can be involved in your evaluation at various levels. For example, you may want to include coalition members on an evaluation team and engage them in developing relevant evaluation questions, data collection procedures, and data analyses. Or consider ways to assess your partners' needs and interests in the evaluation, and develop means of keeping them informed of its progress and integrating their ideas into evaluation activities. Again, stakeholders are more likely to support your evaluation and act on its results and recommendations if they are involved in the evaluation process from the get-go.

Involve Critics as Well

Have you ever heard the phrase, "keep your friends close and your enemies closer?" Well, this slogan aptly applies to the evaluation process as well. It's very important for you to engage your program's critics in your evaluation. Critics will help you to identify issues around your program's strategies and evaluation data that could be attacked or discredited, thus helping you strengthen the evaluation process. This information might also help you and others understand the opposition's rationale and will help you engage potential agents of change within the opposition. However, use caution: it's important to understand the motives of the opposition before engaging them in any meaningful way.

The emphasis on engaging stakeholders mirrors the increasing prominence of participatory models or "action" research in the research/evaluation community. A participatory approach combines systematic inquiry with the collaboration of diverse stakeholders to meet specific needs and to contend with broad issues of equity and justice.

STEP 2: DESCRIBE THE PROGRAM

Writing a good description of your program sets the frame of reference for all subsequent decisions in the evaluation process. Your description enables comparisons with similar programs and facilitates attempts to connect your program's components to its intended outcomes. Moreover, your stakeholders might have differing ideas regarding your program's overall goal and objectives. Evaluations done without agreement on your program's description will be of limited use.

Using a Logic Model to Describe Your Program

Your evaluation plan must include a logic model for your program as a whole. When developing your evaluation plan it's important to develop a logic model that specifically describes what your propose to evaluate. Simply put, the product of this step is a logic model of what is being evaluated, which must be accompanied by a text-based description.

Let's use a quick example of what we mean by a text-based description. Figure 3.1 presents the six steps of doing a program evaluation and the following illustration, "In a Nutshell 3.1," provides a text-based description of each step. One shows (i.e., Figure 3.1) and the other describes (In a Nutshell 3.1).

We strongly encourage you to develop a text-based description to accompany your logic model. This description must explain what you are proposing to evaluate and how this contributes to accomplishing your program's intended outcomes. This section should also describe important program features of what is being evaluated, such as the context in which your program operates, the characteristics of the population your program is intended to reach, and its stage of development (e.g., a pilot activity versus an activity that has been in place for a number of years).

> The product of this step is creation of a logic model accompanied by a text-based description.

Such descriptions are invaluable, not only for your own records but also for others who might be interested in implementing activities similar to those contained in your program. With a clear description of the activity and context in which your program resides, other social service programs will be better able to determine how likely it is that the evaluation results you obtained relate to what they would see if they chose to implement these same activities in their programs. Chapter 8 describes how to construct logic models in depth. Without a doubt, constructing logic models causes social work students a great deal of anxiety. It's hard to do, as it makes one think in a logical and consistent manner.

Logic models are nothing more than simple tools that help people physically see the interrelations among the various components of your program. They are concept maps with narrative depictions of programs in that they visually describe the logic of how your program is supposed to work.

Figure 3.2 presents the basic five elements of the standard run-of-the-mill logic model broken down into the work you plan to do (i.e., numbers 1 and 2) and the intended results that you expect to see from your work (i.e., numbers 3–5). Using Figure 3.2 as a guide, Figure 3.3 describes how to read a logic model (W. K. Kellogg Foundation, 2004).

In sum, a logic model is a pictorial diagram that shows the relationship among your program's components. It provides your program staff, collaborators, stakeholders, and evaluators with a picture of your

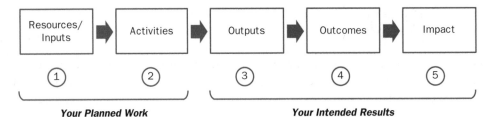

Figure 3.2: **The basic logic model.**

program, how it operates, and how it's intended to accomplish your program's objectives.

By discussing the logic model with different stakeholder groups, you can share your understanding of the relationships among the resources you have to operate your program, the activities you plan do, and the changes or results you wish to achieve from your activities. The CDC (2006) provides nine steps that you can follow when developing your logic model:

Step 1: *Establish a logic model work group.*
Your evaluation work group can be composed of program staff, collaborators, evaluators, and other stakeholders. Identify areas where each stakeholder is needed and contact them to discuss their potential interest in participating in the

discussion and any questions or concerns they have about your program.

Step 2: *Convene the work group to discuss the purpose and steps for constructing your logic model.* Review and summarize relevant literature, planning documents, reports, and data sources that will help explain your program's purposes, activities, and intended outcomes.

Step 3: *Provide an overview of the general logic modeling process.* Review the definitions of terms, outline the overall steps to construct or revise a logic model, choose the type of logic model that best fits your program needs, review your goals and objectives (if they already exist), or reach consensus on program goals and

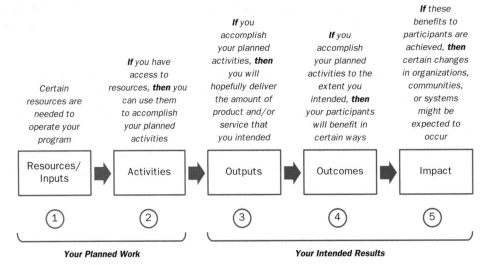

Figure 3.3: **How to read a logic model.**

IN A NUTSHELL	**3.2**	Step 1 *Engaging Stakeholders*

When a variety of stakeholders are involved in evaluation planning from the outset you can (a) plan and conduct evaluations that more closely fit your collective needs, (b) have greater buy-in for the use of your evaluation's results, and (c) avoid later critiques of your evaluation or the program by showing a transparent and open evaluation process.

Purpose	Fostering input, participation, and power-sharing among those persons who have an investment in the conduct of your evaluation and its findings; it's especially important to engage primary users of your evaluation's findings.
Role	Helps increase chances that your evaluation will be useful; can improve your evaluation's credibility, clarify roles and responsibilities, enhance cultural competence, help protect evaluation participants, and avoid real or perceived conflicts of interests.
Activities	Consulting insiders (e.g., leaders, staff, clients, and program funding sources) and outsiders (e.g., skeptics); taking special effort to promote the inclusion of less powerful groups or individuals; coordinating stakeholder input throughout the process of your evaluation's design, operation, and use; avoiding excessive stakeholder identification, which might prevent the progress of your evaluation.

It's time to engage a group of stakeholders to help you create your evaluation plan. The planning team for your evaluation should include individuals who are interested in—and perhaps affected by—the specific evaluation to be carried out.

There are three major categories of evaluation stakeholders to consider (Russ-Eft & Preskill, 2009, pp. 141–143):

- *Primary stakeholders.* Individuals who are involved in program operations and who have the ability to use evaluation findings to alter the course of a program. Examples of primary stakeholders include program staff and managers, as well as funders.
- *Secondary stakeholders.* Individuals who are served by the program and therefore are likely to be affected by any changes made as a result of the evaluation findings. Examples include program participants (e.g., workshop or training attendees) or others who are directly reached by your program.
- *Tertiary stakeholders.* Individuals who are not directly affected by programmatic changes that might result from the evaluation but who are generally interested in the results. Examples include legislators and other state social service programs.

A final set of stakeholders—often overlooked but important to engage—are *program critics*. These are individuals or groups that may oppose your program based on differing values about how to create change, what changes are necessary, or how best to utilize limited resources. Engaging opponents of the program in your evaluation can strengthen the credibility of your results and potentially reduce or mitigate some of the opposition.

Multiple stakeholder perspectives can contribute to rich and comprehensive descriptions of what's being evaluated while also facilitating a well-balanced and useful evaluation. Your stakeholders may also be engaged in carrying out your evaluation or in implementing its recommendations.

subsequently outline the objectives in support of each goal.

Step 4: *Decide whether you will use the "if-then" method, reverse logic method, or both to construct the logic model.* If you have a clear picture of what your inputs and activities will be, you will want to use the "if-then" approach, in which you construct your logic model from left to right, starting with the process components and working toward the outcomes.

The "reverse logic" approach can be used to work from the right to the left of the logic model, starting with the goal and working backward through the process components. If outputs are predetermined, you can start from the middle and branch out in both directions (an approach that combines the previous two methods).

Step 5: *Brainstorm ideas for each logic model column.* After brainstorming is complete, arrange these items into groups such as professional development, collaborations, and so on. Check that each activity logically links to one or more outputs and each output links to one or more outcomes.

Step 6: *Determine how to show your program's accomplishments and select indicators to measure your outputs and short-term outcomes.* The question number for each associated indicator should be placed under the output or short-term outcome that it measures.

Step 7: *Perform checks to assure links across logic model columns.* You should be able to read the logic model from both left to right and right to left, ensuring that a logical sequence exists between all of the items in each column. It's often helpful to color-code specific sections of your logic model to illustrate which sections logically follow one another.

Step 8: *Ensure that your logic model represents your program but does not provide unnecessary detail*. Review the items placed under the headings and subheadings of the logic model, and then decide whether the level of detail is appropriate. The work group should reach consensus in fine-tuning the logic model by asking: What items in the logic model can be combined, grouped together, or eliminated?

Step 9: *Revise and update your logic model periodically to reflect program changes.* Changes in your logic model may be needed to reflect new or revised programmatic activities or interventions or to account for a change in a new intervention or new evaluation findings.

Concept Maps

Logic models are nothing more than concept maps. Concept mapping is a tool that can be used to visually illustrate key elements of either the program's design or aspects of the evaluation plan. Concept mapping is a technique that is used to display information visually. Surely you have heard the expression "a picture is worth a thousand words." Concept mapping makes a complicated thing simple. As Albert Einstein said, "If you can't explain it simply, you don't understand it well enough," and "If I can't see it, I can't understand it." And this is the guy who came up with $E = mc^2$

Concept mapping facilitates communication through pictures; as such, it reduces the amount of text reading that would otherwise be needed in a planning process. Specifically, it's used to diagram concepts and the relationships between them. Concept maps can illustrate simple or complex ideas. For example, Figure 7.6 in Chapter 7 shows a simple concept map illustrating the relationship of the goal of an agency to the goals of three programs housed within the agency.

A more complex concept map is shown in Figure 3.4, which offers a visual illustration of a client-centered program design for a family and community support program. The illustration shows the relationship between the family and community support components of the program, which share both

Family and Community Support Program

Program Goal: To enhance quality of life for families that are living in the Edison neighborhood where such problems as poverty, substance abuse, mental illness, and domestic violence put children at risk for abuse and neglect. By improving the capacity of families and the community they live in, the program aims to build a safe neighborhood that values child well-being.

High Risk DCFS Neighborhood

Family Support

Activities

- Peer support hotline to families with children under 18 years old
- Short-term support counseling
- Peer support and support groups
- Emergency goods and services
- Liaising with courts, schools, and other service providers
- Employment training for community members in volunteer roles

Program Center

Friendly office space in highly visible part of neighborhood

*drop-in support
* meeting space
*volunteer hub
*emergency provisions
*telephone, fax, Internet
*referral information
*program office

Community Support

Activities

- Community outreach and awareness on child safety and well-being
- Time-limited improvement projects within community
- Recruit and sustain community board members and volunteers
- Resource and fund-raising efforts

Program Objectives

- Reduce child abuse reports
- Increase support to parents
- Increase community efficacy

Figure 3.4: **Concept map of a client-centered program design.**

office space and program objectives. Figure 3.4 also features the program's goal and details various activities that workers engage in. Indeed, Figure 3.4 highlights many key program design concepts that are discuss thoroughly in Chapter 7.

Another example of a concept map is shown in Figure 3.5. Rather than diagramming the relationship between program design concepts (as shown in Figure 3.4), the concept map featured in Figure 3.5 shows the fit of evaluation as a key phase of program operations in both components of the program. Furthermore, the picture reveals that the two program components (family support and community support) will have separate evaluations but the results of both will be considered together when shared with the community.

Communication tools. Concept maps are communication tools. Thus they can have the effect of answering evaluation questions about a group's thinking or generating new questions that aim for fuller understanding. It's important to understand that the concept

maps featured in Figures 3.4 and 3.5 present only two of many possible representations. In viewing the two illustrations, perhaps you had ideas about how the program design or the evaluation plan could be illustrated differently.

It may be that your idea is to add concepts not featured, such as identifying priority evaluation questions or specific measurement instruments. On the other hand, it may be your opinion that Figure 3.4 could be simplified by deleting parts of the illustration such as the program goal statement. Perhaps you see the relationships between concepts differently and would prefer to see the concept shapes in another arrangement.

Evaluation planning tools. Concepts maps are also planning tools. To be useful as a planning tool, the exercise of building concept maps should involve representatives of key stakeholder groups. Bringing different stakeholders—especially those with divergent views—together to build one concept map can generate rich discussion. Because communication

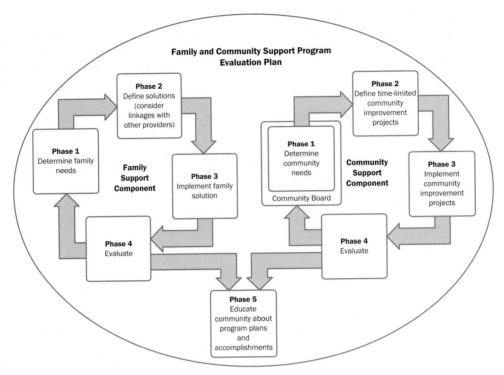

Figure 3.5: **Concept map of an evaluation plan.**

can result in intense and impassioned discussions as stakeholders promote different points of view, it's wise to have a skilled facilitator to accomplish the task.

Once concept maps are created they can be used as visual reminders throughout the planning and evaluation processes. The visual illustrations can function as literal maps that chart future discussion and planning decisions. As such, they should be easily accessible or displayed in clear sight of those working on the program and evaluation plans.

For example, suppose that stakeholders of the family and community support programs wind up spending 40 minutes of a 60-minute meeting in a heated debate about the type of activities that workers are expected to perform in the family support component of the program. It would be possible, and perhaps strategic, for a workgroup member to mention this fact, point to Figure 3.5, and add the suggestion that the group needs to wrap up discussion about family support to ensure that discussion about the community support component of the program does not get ignored.

STEP 3: FOCUS THE EVALUATION

After completing Steps 1 and 2, you and your stakeholders should have a clear understanding of your program and have reached a consensus on its description. Now your evaluation team needs to focus the evaluative efforts. This includes determining the most meaningful evaluation questions to ask and the most appropriate evaluation design to implement that would produce the most valid and reliable data that will be used to answer the questions.

Focusing your evaluation assumes that your entire program does not need to be evaluated at any specific point in time. Rather, the precise evaluation design to use entirely depends on what questions are being asked, who is asking the questions, and what will be done with the results.

Since resources for evaluation are always limited, we provide a series of decision criteria to help you determine the best evaluation focus at any point in time. These criteria are inspired by two of the four CDC's evaluation standards that are discussed in the following chapter:

- **Utility** (who will use the results and what information will be most useful to them)
- **Feasibility** (how much time and resources are available for the evaluation)

The logic model developed in the previous step, Step 2: Describing Your Program, sets the stage for determining the best evaluation focus. The approach to focusing an evaluation in the CDC Evaluation Framework differs slightly from traditional evaluation approaches. Rather than a summative evaluation conducted when your program had run its course and asking "Did your program work?", the CDC framework views evaluation as an ongoing activity over the life of a program that asks," Is your program working?"

A description of formative and summative evaluations is presented in Box 2.1. This may be an excellent time to revisit it before reading further.

In short, your social service program will always be ready for some kind of an evaluation. Because your logic model displays your program from inputs through activities/outputs through to the sequence of outcomes from short term to most distal, it can guide a discussion of what you can expect to achieve at a given point in the life of your program.

Should you focus your evaluative efforts on distal outcomes or only on short- or midterm ones? Conversely, does a process evaluation make the most sense right now?

Types of Evaluations

Many different questions can be part of a program evaluation, depending on how long your program has been in existence, who is asking the question, and why the evaluation information is needed. As we know from the previous chapter, there are four types of evaluations: need, process, outcome, and efficiency. This section ignores needs assessments for the moment and concentrates on questions that the remaining three types of evaluations can answer for a program that is already in existence:

- Process evaluations
- Outcome/efficiency evaluations

Process Evaluations

As we know, process evaluations—sometimes referred to as implementation evaluations—document whether a program has been implemented as intended and the reasons why or why not. In process evaluations you might examine what activities are taking place, who is conducting the activities, who is reached through the activities, and whether sufficient inputs have been allocated or mobilized. How to do process evaluations is discussed in depth in Chapter 11.

> *The products of this step include a final set of evaluation questions and the evaluation design that will be used to answer the questions.*

Process evaluations are important to help distinguish the causes of poor program performance—was your program a bad idea in the first place, or was it a good idea that could not reach the standard for implementation that you previously set? In all cases, process evaluations measure whether your actual program's performance was faithful to your initial plan. Such measurements might include contrasting actual and planned performance along all or some of the following:

- The locale where your services or program are provided (e.g., rural, urban);
- The number of people receiving your services;
- The economic status and racial/ethnic background of people receiving your services;
- The quality of your services;
- The actual activities that occur while the your services are being delivered;
- The amount of money the evaluation going to cost;
- The direct and in-kind funding for your services;
- The staffing for your services or programs;
- The number of your activities and meetings; and
- The number of training sessions conducted.

When evaluation resources are limited—as they usually are—only the most important issues of implementation can be included. The following are some

IN A NUTSHELL	**3.3**		Step 2: *Describing Your Program*

Program descriptions set the frame of reference for all subsequent decisions in an evaluation. The description enables comparisons with similar programs and facilitates attempts to connect program components to their effects. Moreover, stakeholders might have differing ideas regarding your program's goal and objectives.

Evaluations done without agreement on the program definition are likely to be of limited use. Sometimes, negotiating with stakeholders to formulate a clear and logical description will bring benefits before data are available to evaluate your program's effectiveness.

Content areas to include in a program description are presented below.

Purpose	Scrutinizing the features of the program being evaluated, including its purpose and place in the larger social service delivery context. Description includes information regarding the way your program was intended to function and the way that it actually was implemented. Also includes features of your program's context that are likely to influence conclusions regarding your program.
Role	Improves evaluation's fairness and accuracy; permits a balanced assessment of strengths and weaknesses; and helps stakeholders understand how program features fit together and relate to a larger context.
Activities	Characterizing the need (or set of needs) addressed by your program; listing specific expectations as goals, objectives, and criteria for success; clarifying why program activities are believed to lead to expected changes; drawing an explicit logic model to illustrate relationships between program elements and expected changes; assessing your program's maturity or stage of development; analyzing the context within which your program operates; considering how your program is linked to other ongoing efforts; avoiding creation of an overly precise description for a program that is under development.
Suggested content areas to address when describing your program	Questions to ask and answer about each content area when describing your program are listed below. Your main goal is to end up with a logic model that clearly paints an accurate picture of what your program is all about.
Need	What problem or opportunity does your program address? Who experiences it?
Context	What is the operating environment around your program? How might environmental influences such as history, geography, politics, social and economic conditions, secular trends, or efforts of related or competing organizations affect your program and its eventual evaluation?
Stage of development	How mature is your program? Is your program mainly engaged in planning, implementation, or effects? Is your program the only game in town, or are there similar programs in your immediate area?

continued

Resources (will go in logic model)	What assets are available to conduct your program's activities, such as time, talent, technology, information, and money?
Activities (will go in logic model)	What steps, strategies, or actions does your program take to effect change?
Expected effects (will go in logic model)	What changes resulting from your program are anticipated? What must your program accomplish to be considered successful?
Logic model	What is the hypothesized sequence of events for bringing about change? How do your program's elements (i.e., resources, activities, expected effects) connect with one another to form a plausible picture of how your program is supposed to work? Logic models are discussed in Chapter 8.

"usual suspects" that compromise a program's implementation and might be considered for inclusion in a process evaluation:

- **Transfers of accountability:** When a program's activities cannot produce the intended outcomes unless some other person or organization takes appropriate action, there is a transfer of accountability.
- **Dosage:** The intended outcomes of a program's activities (e.g., training, case management, counseling) may presume a threshold level of participation or exposure to the intervention.
- **Access:** When intended outcomes require not only an increase in consumer demand but also an increase in supply of services to meet it, then the process evaluation might include measures of access.
- **Staff competency:** The intended outcomes may presume well-designed program activities delivered by staff that are not only technically competent but also matched appropriately to the target audience. Measures of the match of staff and target audience might be included in the process evaluation

Outcome/Effectiveness Evaluations

Outcome evaluations assess progress on the sequence of outcomes your program is to address.

Programs often describe this sequence using terms like "short-term," "intermediate," and "long-term outcomes," or "proximal" (close to the intervention) or "distal" (distant from the intervention). How to do outcome evaluations is discussed in depth in Chapter 12.

Depending on the stage of development of your program and the purpose of the evaluation, outcome evaluations may include any or all of the outcomes in the sequence, including:

- Changes in client's attitudes, behaviors, feelings, cognitions, and beliefs;
- Changes in risk or protective behaviors;
- Changes in the environment, including public and private policies, formal and informal enforcement of regulations, and influence of social norms and other societal forces; and
- Changes in trends in morbidity and mortality.

While process and outcome evaluations are the most common of all four types of evaluations, there are several other types of evaluation questions that can be central to a specific program evaluation. These include the following:

- **Efficiency:** Are your program's activities being produced with minimal use of resources such as budget and staff time? What is the volume of outputs produced by

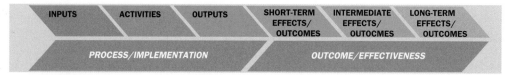

Figure 3.6a: Using logic models to determine types of possible evaluations.

the resources devoted to your program? (This topic is covered in Chapter 13.)

- **Cost-effectiveness:** Does the value or benefit of your program's outcomes exceed the cost of producing them? (This topic is covered in Chapter 13.)
- **Cause-effect:** Can the your program's outcomes be related to your program, as opposed to other things that are going on at the same time? (This topic is covered in Tool E.)

All of these types of evaluation questions relate to a part, but not all, of your logic model. Figures 3.6a and 3.6b show where in the logic model each type of evaluation focuses. As can be seen in Figure 3.6a, process evaluations would focus on the inputs, activities, and outputs and would not be concerned with outcomes/effectiveness. Effectiveness evaluations would do the opposite—focusing on some or all outcome boxes but not necessarily on the activities that produced them.

As can be seen in Figure 3.6b, efficiency evaluations care about the arrows linking inputs to activities/outputs—how much output is produced for a given level of inputs/resources. Cause-effect focuses on the arrows between specific activities/outputs and specific outcomes—whether progress on the outcome is related to the specific activity/output.

Determining the Focus of an Evaluation

Determining the "correct" evaluation focus is solely determined on a case-by-case basis. Several

guidelines inspired by the *utility* and *feasibility* evaluation standards (discussed in the following chapter) can help you determine the best focus.

Utility Considerations

1. *What is the purpose of your evaluation?* "Purpose" refers to the general intent of your evaluation. A clear purpose serves as the basis for your evaluation questions, evaluation design, and data collection methods. Some common purposes are:

   - Gain new knowledge about your program's activities;
   - Improve or fine-tune an existing program's operations (e.g., program processes or strategies);
   - Determine the effects of your program by providing data concerning your program's contributions to its long-term goal; and
   - Affect your program's participants by acting as a catalyst for self-directed change (e.g., teaching).

2. *Who will use the results from your evaluation?* Users are the individuals or organizations that will utilize your evaluation findings. The users will likely have been identified during Step 1 in the process of engaging stakeholders. In this step you needed to secure their input in the selection of evaluation questions

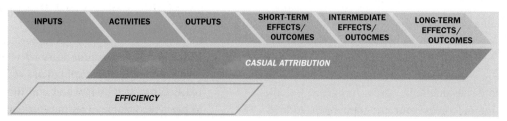

Figure 3.6b: Using logic models to determine types of possible evaluations.

and the evaluation design that would gather data to answer the questions. As you know by now, support from the intended users will increase the likelihood that your evaluation results will be used for program improvement.

3. ***How will the users actually use the evaluation results?*** Many insights on use will have been identified in Step 1. Data collected may have varying uses, which should be described in detail when designing your evaluation. Some examples of uses of evaluation findings are as follows:

- To document the level of success in achieving your program's objectives;
- To identify areas of your program that need improvement;
- To decide on how to allocate resources;
- To mobilize community support;
- To redistribute or expand the locations where your program or intervention, is being carried out;
- To improve the content of your program's materials;
- To focus your program's resources on a specific client population; and
- To solicit more funds or additional partners.

4. ***What do other key stakeholders need from your evaluation?*** Of course the most important stakeholders are those who request or who will use the results from your evaluation. Nevertheless, in Step 1, you may also have identified stakeholders who, while not using the findings of the current evaluation, have key questions that may need to be addressed in your evaluation to keep them engaged. For example, a particular stakeholder may always be concerned about costs, disparities, or cause-effect issues. If so, you may need to add those questions when deciding on an evaluation design.

Feasibility Considerations

The first four questions will help you to identify the most useful focus of your evaluation, but you must also determine whether it's a realistic and feasible one. Questions 5 through 7 provide a reality check on your desired focus:

5. ***What is the stage of development of your program?*** During Step 2 you identified your program's stage of development. There are roughly three stages in program development—planning, implementation, and maintenance—that suggest different focuses. In the planning stage, a truly formative evaluation—who is your target clientele, how do you reach them, how much will it cost—may be the most appropriate focus.

An evaluation that included program outcomes would make little sense at this stage. Conversely, an evaluation of a program in a maintenance stage would need to include some measurement of progress on developing program outcomes, even if it also included questions about its implementation.

6. ***How intensive is your program?*** As you know, some social work programs are wide-ranging and multifaceted. Others may use only one approach to address a large problem. Some programs provide extensive exposure ("dose") of a program, while others involve participants quickly and superficially. Simple or superficial programs, while potentially useful, cannot realistically be expected to make significant contributions to distal outcomes of a larger program, even when they are fully operational.

7. ***What are relevant resource and logistical considerations?*** Resources and logistics may influence decisions about your evaluation's focus. Some outcomes are quicker, easier, and cheaper to measure, while others may not be measurable at all. These facts may tilt the decision about the focus of your evaluation toward some outcomes as opposed to others. Early identification of inconsistencies between utility and feasibility is an important part of the evaluation focus step. But

we must also ensure a "meeting of the minds" on what is a realistic focus for a specific program evaluation at a specific point in time.

Narrowing Down Evaluation Questions

As should be evident by now, social work programs are complex entities. In turn, any evaluation within them can also be multifaceted and can easily go in many different directions. For example, a program evaluation can produce data to answer many different questions, such as, "Is a program needed in the first place?" (Chapter 10); "What exactly is my program?" (Chapter 11); "Is my program effective?" (Chapter 12); and "Is my program efficient?" (Chapter 13)?

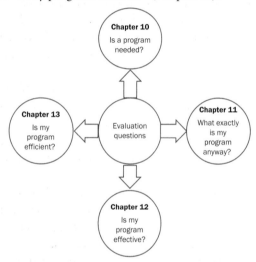

The list of possible evaluation questions is limitless, but program resources—human and fiscal—are not. As such, an essential planning task of any evaluation is to decide on a reasonable number of questions that will be the main focus of your evaluation. The W. K. Kellogg Foundation (1998) provides four tips for developing evaluation questions:

Tip 1: Ask yourself and evaluation team members why you are asking the questions you are asking and what you might be missing.

Tip 2: Different stakeholders will have different questions. Don't rely on one or two people (external evaluator or funder) to determine questions. Seek input from as many perspectives as possible to get a full picture before deciding on what questions to answer.

Tip 3: There are many important questions to address. Stay focused on the primary purpose for your evaluation activities at a certain point in time and then work to prioritize which are the critical questions to address. Because your evaluation will become an ongoing part of project management and delivery, you can and should revisit your evaluation questions and revise them to meet your current needs.

Tip 4: Examine the values embedded in the questions you are asking. Whose values are they? How do other stakeholders, particularly evaluation participants, think and feel about this set of values? Are there different or better questions the evaluation team members and other stakeholders could build consensus around?

Sources for Questions

By focusing a program evaluation around clearly defined questions, evaluation activities can be kept manageable, economical, and efficient. All too often stakeholders identify more interests than any single evaluation can reasonably manage.

A multitude of stakeholder-related sources can be utilized to generate a list of potential evaluation questions. The W. K. Kellogg Foundation (1998) lists nine stakeholder-related sources for our consideration:

Source 1: *Program Director:* Directors are usually invaluable sources of information because they are likely to have the "big picture" of the project.

Source 2: *Program Staff/Volunteers:* Staff members and volunteers may suggest unique evaluation questions because they are involved in the day-to-day operations of the program and have an inside perspective of the organization.

Source 3: *Program Clientele:* Participants/ consumers offer crucial perspectives for the evaluation team because they are directly affected by the program's services. They have insights into the program that no other stakeholder is likely to have.

Source 4: *Board of Directors/Advisory Boards/Other Project Leadership:* These groups often have a stake in the program and may identify issues they want addressed in the evaluation process. They may request that certain questions be answered to help them make decisions.

Source 5: *Community Leaders:* Community leaders in business, social services, and government can speak to issues underlying the conditions of the target population. Because of their extensive involvement in the community, they often are invaluable sources of information.

Source 6: *Collaborating Organizations:* Organizations and agencies that are collaborating with the program should always be involved in formulating evaluation questions.

Source 7: *Program Proposal and Other Documents:* The program proposal, funder correspondence, program objectives and activities, minutes of board and advisory group meetings, and other documents may be used to formulate relevant evaluation questions.

Source 8: *Content-Relevant Literature and Expert Consultants:* Relevant literature and discussion with other professionals in the field can be potential sources of information, and of possible questions, for evaluation teams.

Source 9: *Similar Programs/Projects:* Evaluation questions can also be obtained from executive directors and staff of other programs, especially when their programs are similar to yours.

Techniques to Focus Questions

Figure 3.7 shows a simple survey that we used to aid us in an evaluation planning session within a rural literacy program. The 24 questions shown in Figure 3.7 are only a sample of those generated by the program's stakeholders, which included representation from the program's steering committee, administration, and workers, as well as other professionals and local citizens; a total of 20 stakeholders participated in the planning process. The complete brainstorm list (not shown) included more than 80 questions—far too many to focus the program's evaluation, which had a modest budget.

The simple survey shown in Figure 3.7 was created to gather stakeholder input that would help identify priority questions of interest. The questions listed were created by the program's stakeholders. Thus the survey itself also had the added benefit of showing stakeholders that their ideas were both valued and were being put to good use in planning the program's evaluation strategy.

Evaluations that are not sufficiently focused generally result in large and unwieldy data collection efforts. Unfortunately, when mass quantities of data are collected without a forward thinking plan—linking the data collected to the evaluation questions to be answered—the data may be compromised by poor reliability and validity. On the other hand, evaluation data derived from carefully focused questions make it much easier to maintain the integrity of the data collection process and produce credible results.

Focusing an evaluation does not imply that only one part or aspect of a program or service will be of interest. In fact, there are usually a number of different interests that can be accommodated within a single evaluation. Figure 3.7, for example, suggests that, depending on the stakeholders' ratings, the literacy program's evaluation could end up focusing on questions related to client characteristics (Questions 1–10), program services (Questions 11–18), or client outcomes (Questions 19–24), or a combination of all three.

Focusing evaluation questions means that program interests are first identified and the evaluation's activities are then organized around those interests. Thus there can be multiple points of focus within a

Figure 3.7: **Example of a simple survey determining the priority of the evaluation questions that were selected for the final evaluation.**

Evaluation Question Priority Survey			
Instructions: (1) Rate each question by *circling one number* using the scale to the right of each question. (2) Feel free to add questions that you consider to be a priority for evaluation.			
Client Characteristic Questions:	Definitely Keep	Deserves Consideration	Throw Out
1. Who referred family to the program?	1	2	3
2. How many children in the family?	1	2	3
3. How old is each family member?	1	2	3
4. How long has the family lived in the community?	1	2	3
5. What is the family structure?	1	2	3
6. Does the family live in town or rural?	1	2	3
7. Does the family access other community services?	1	2	3
8. What languages are spoken in the home?	1	2	3
9. What are the education levels of parents?	1	2	3
10. Does family have (or want) a library card?	1	2	3
Program Service Questions:			
11. How many visits were made to the family?	1	2	3
12. How long was each visit?	1	2	3
13. How many scheduled visits were missed? Why?	1	2	3
14. How many times was family *not* ready for the visit?	1	2	3
15. Did family readiness improve over time?	1	2	3
16. How satisfied were parents with program?	1	2	3
17. How satisfied was family with the worker?	1	2	3
18. What was easiest/most difficult for you in the program?	1	2	3

continued

Figure 3.7: (continued)

Client Outcome Questions:			
19. Do clients show change after the program?	1	2	3
20. Do children's literacy skills improve?	1	2	3
21. Do reading behaviors change?	1	2	3
22. Were the parents' expectations of program met?	1	2	3
23. What is the support worker's evaluation of services?	1	2	3
24. Has enjoyment for reading increased?	1	2	3

single evaluation, but it's important that these be clearly identified and planned from the beginning.

The focal questions selected for a program's evaluation need not remain static. Questions may be added or deleted as circumstances and experiences dictate. In other words, a specific set of questions may guide the focus of an evaluation for a limited period of time.

STEP 4: GATHERING CREDIBLE DATA

In this step you will work with your stakeholders to identify the data collection methods and sources you will use to answer your evaluation questions. You will need to review your data collection plan in light of the work you did in your evaluation planning process:

- Are there new data sources you may want to incorporate?
- Do your methods meet your stakeholders' needs for information?
- Do you need to adjust your data collection timeline?
- Are there measures you might standardize across evaluations?

For new evaluative efforts, you may want to build in a pilot test or more small-scale data collection efforts before conducting a more intensive effort. As you develop your data collection approach, it's critical

to keep in mind why you are collecting the data and how you will use them. Being explicit about the use of data before they are collected helps you to conserve resources and reduces respondent burden.

The products of this step include data collection methods and indicators that will be used to answer your evaluation questions.

Your stakeholders may also help identify indicators that could be used to judge your program's success. Let's say you have chosen to evaluate a relatively new educationally oriented type of intervention designed to educate line-level social workers within your community about how the Affordable Care Act (aka, Obamacare) will affect their clientele. You want to know, for example, to what extent your intended target audience is attending (item 1 below) and completing the training, or your intervention (item 2 below) broken down by the type of practitioner they are (item 3 below). Your stakeholders decide that training attendance logs will be maintained and recommend including the following three specific indicators:

1. Attendance
2. Proportion of attendees who complete the training
3. Type of social work practitioner (community organizers, group workers, school social workers, medical social workers,

IN A NUTSHELL	**3.4**	Step 3: *Focusing Your Evaluation Design*

The direction and process of your evaluation must be focused to assess issues of greatest concern to stakeholders while using time and resources as efficiently as possible. Not all design options are equally well suited to meeting the information needs of your stakeholders.

After data collection begins, changing procedures might be difficult or impossible, even if better methods become obvious. A thorough plan anticipates intended uses and creates an evaluation strategy with the greatest chance of being useful, feasible, ethical, and accurate.

Content areas to include when focusing your evaluation design are presented below.

Purpose	Planning in advance where your evaluation is headed and what steps will be taken; process is iterative (i.e., it continues until a focused approach is found to answer evaluation questions with methods that stakeholders agree will be useful, feasible, ethical, and accurate); evaluation questions and methods might be adjusted to achieve an optimal match that facilitates use by primary users.
Role	Provides investment in quality; increases the chances that your evaluation will succeed by identifying procedures that are practical, politically viable, and cost-effective; failure to plan thoroughly can be self-defeating, leading to an evaluation that might become impractical or useless; when stakeholders agree on a design focus, it's used throughout the evaluation process to keep your project on track.
Activities	Meeting with stakeholders to clarify the real intent or purpose of your evaluation; learning which persons are in a position to actually use the findings, then orienting the plan to meet their needs; understanding how your evaluation results are to be used; writing explicit evaluation questions to be answered; describing practical methods for sampling, data collection, data analysis, interpretation, and judgment; preparing a written protocol or agreement that summarizes your evaluation procedures, with clear roles and responsibilities for all stakeholders; revising parts or all of your evaluation plan when critical circumstances change.
Suggested content areas to address when focusing your evaluation design	Questions to ask and answer about each content area when focusing your evaluation design are listed below. Your main goal is to end up with an evaluation design that is useful, feasible, ethical, and accurate.
Purpose	What is the intent or motive for conducting your evaluation (i.e., to gain insight, change practice, assess effects, or affect participants)?
Users	Who are the specific persons that will receive your evaluation findings or benefit from being part of your evaluation? How will each user apply the information or experiences generated from your evaluation?
Uses	How will each user apply the information or experiences generated from your evaluation?

continued

Questions	What questions should your evaluation answer? What boundaries will be established to create a viable focus for your evaluation? What unit of analysis is appropriate (e.g., a system of related programs, a single program, a project within a program, a subcomponent or process within a project)?
Methods	What procedures will provide the appropriate information to address stakeholders' questions (i.e., what research designs and data collection procedures best match the primary users, uses, and questions)? Is it possible to mix methods to overcome the limitations of any single approach?
Agreements	How will your evaluation plan be implemented within available resources? What roles and responsibilities have the stakeholders accepted? What safeguards are in place to ensure that standards are met, especially those for protecting human subjects?

DHS workers, child protection workers, and so on)

Learn more about how to collect credible data to answer your evaluation questions in Tool H in the Evaluation Toolkit.

You can see from this list of indicators that it will be important to have a question on the attendance sheet that asks attendees what type of social work practitioner they are (item 3). Had you not discussed the indicators that will be used to determine the "success" of your intervention, it's possible this important question would have been left off the attendance log.

STEP 5: JUSTIFYING YOUR CONCLUSIONS

Planning for data analyses and interpretation of the data prior to conducting your evaluation is important to ensure that you collect the "right" data to fully answer your evaluation questions. Think ahead to how you will analyze the data you collect, what methods you will use, and who will be involved in interpreting the results.

Part of this process is to establish standards of performance against which you can compare the indicators you identified earlier. You may be familiar

with "performance benchmarks," which are one type of standard. In this example, a benchmark for the indicator "proportion of attendees who complete training" may be "more than 60% of attendees completed the training." Standards often include comparisons over time or with an alternative approach (e.g., no action or a different intervention). It's important to note that the standards established by you and your stakeholders do not have to be quantitative in nature.

The products of this step include a set of performance standards and a plan for synthesizing and interpreting evaluation findings.

Regardless of whether your "indicators" are qualitative or quantitative in nature, it's important to discuss with evaluation stakeholders what will be viewed as a positive finding. The standards you select should be clearly documented in the individual evaluation plan.

Make sure to allow time for synthesis and interpretation in your individual evaluation plan. At the completion of your evaluation, you will want to be able to answer such questions as:

- Overall, how well does what is being evaluated perform with respect to the standards established in the evaluation plan?
- Are there changes that may need to be made as a result of your evaluation's findings?

Persons involved in an evaluation should strive to collect data that will convey a well-rounded picture of your program and be seen as credible by your evaluation's primary users. Data should be perceived by your stakeholders as believable and relevant for answering their questions. Such decisions depend on the evaluation questions being posed and the motives for asking them. Having credible data strengthens evaluation judgments and the recommendations that follow from them.

Although all types of data have limitations, an evaluation's overall credibility can be improved by using multiple procedures for gathering, analyzing, and interpreting data. When stakeholders are involved in defining and gathering data that they find credible, they will be more likely to accept your evaluation's conclusions and to act on its recommendations.

The following aspects of data gathering typically affect perceptions of credibility.

Purpose	Compiling data that stakeholders perceive as trustworthy and relevant for answering their questions. Such data can be experimental or observational, qualitative or quantitative, or it can include a mixture of methods. Adequate data might be available and easily accessed, or it might need to be defined and new data collected. Whether a body of data are credible to stakeholders might depend on such factors as how the questions were posed, data sources, conditions of data collection, reliability of the measurement procedures, validity of interpretations, and quality control procedures.
Role	Enhances the evaluation's utility and accuracy; guides the scope and selection of data and gives priority to the most defensible data sources; promotes the collection of valid, reliable, and systematic data that are the foundation of any effective evaluation.
Activities	Choosing indicators that meaningfully address evaluation questions; describing fully the attributes of data sources and the rationale for their selection; establishing clear procedures and training staff to collect high-quality data; monitoring periodically the quality of data obtained and taking practical steps to improve their quality; estimating in advance the amount of data required or establishing criteria for deciding when to stop collecting data in situations where an iterative or evolving process is used; safeguarding the confidentiality of data and data sources.
Suggested content areas to address when collecting credible data	Questions to ask and answer about each content area in relation to collecting credible data are listed below. You main goal is to collect valid and reliable relevant data.
Indicators	How will general concepts regarding the program, its context, and its expected effects be translated into specific measures that can be interpreted? Will the chosen indicators provide systematic data that are valid and reliable for the intended uses?
Sources	What sources (i.e., persons, documents, observations) will be accessed to gather data? What will be done to integrate multiple sources, especially those that provide data in narrative form and those that are numeric?
Quality	Are the data trustworthy (i.e., reliable, valid, and informative for the intended uses)?
Quantity	What amount of data are sufficient? What level of confidence or precision is possible? Is there adequate power to detect effects? Is the respondent burden reasonable?
Logistics	What techniques, timing, and physical infrastructure will be used for gathering and handling data?

STEP 6: ENSURING USAGE AND SHARING LESSONS LEARNED

As we have seen, you can promote the use of your evaluation findings by the actions you take throughout your evaluation's planning process. Building a commitment to using evaluation results both internally and with your stakeholders is extremely important. Sharing what you have learned will also add to our knowledge base about what interventions work with specific clientele.

> *The product of this step includes a communication and reporting plan for your evaluation.*

Thinking about the use of your evaluation findings does not need to wait until your evaluation is completed and results are ready to be disseminated. Think early and often about how and at what points you can (and need to) make use of your evaluation's results. Pilot-test results can be used to improve program processes. Baseline results can help to better target your intervention. Preliminary findings can help you to refine your data collection strategies in future rounds. Build in time to your schedule to ensure your evaluation's findings are actually used. For example, will you have enough time after your results are finalized to develop an action plan for program improvement?

Dissemination of results and communication about lessons learned should not be an afterthought. To increase the likelihood that intended audiences will use your evaluation findings for program improvement, it's important to think through how and with whom you will communicate as you plan and implement each evaluation, as well as after the evaluation has been completed. Your strategy should consider the purpose, audience, format, frequency, and timing of each communication (Russ-Eft & Preskill, 2009).

As you develop your dissemination plan, keep in mind the following:

- Consider what information you want to communicate. What action do you hope each of your audiences will take based on the information you provide? Are you just keeping them informed, or do you want them to act in some way? Tailor your communication plan accordingly.
- Your audience will likely vary greatly across evaluations and also may change as an evaluation progresses. Think broadly about who to include in communication. For instance, at various points in time you may want to include executive directors, program managers, supervisors, individuals participating in planning the evaluation, legislators or funders, or individuals affected by your program.
- Formats can be formal or informal and may include a mix of e-mail correspondence, newsletters, written reports, working sessions, briefings, and presentations. Formats may differ by audience and may also differ over time for the same audience as information needs change.
- Consider your communication strategies when estimating the resources that will be required to carry out your evaluation. If your evaluation resources are limited, we recommend giving the greatest consideration to the information needs of the primary evaluation stakeholders (those who have the ability to use your evaluation's findings).

SUMMARY

This chapter presented a discussion on how the CDC's six-step evaluation process unfolds and stressed how our stakeholders need to be involved in every aspect of our evaluation. The next chapter discusses how we, as professional social workers, must follow strict professional standards when evaluating our programs, taking into account the contents of the first three chapters of this book.

IN A NUTSHELL	**3.6**	Step 5: *Justifying Your Conclusions*

The conclusions that you draw from your evaluation conclusions are only justified when they are directly linked to the data you gathered. They will be judged against agreed-on values or standards set by your stakeholders. Stakeholders must agree that your conclusions are justified before they will use the results from your evaluation with any confidence.

Purpose	Making claims regarding your program that are warranted on the basis of data that have been compared against pertinent and defensible ideas of merit, value, or significance (i.e., against standards of values); conclusions are justified when they are linked to the data gathered and consistent with the agreed-on values or standards of stakeholders.
Role	Reinforces conclusions central to the evaluation's utility and accuracy; involves values clarification, qualitative and quantitative data analysis and synthesis, systematic interpretation, and appropriate comparison against relevant standards for judgment.
Activities	Using appropriate methods of analysis and synthesis to summarize findings; interpreting the significance of results for deciding what the findings mean; making judgments according to clearly stated values that classify a result (e.g., as positive or negative and high or low); considering alternative ways to compare results (e.g., compared with program objectives, a comparison group, national norms, past performance, or needs); generating alternative explanations for findings and indicating why these explanations should be discounted; recommending actions or decisions that are consistent with the conclusions; and limiting conclusions to situations, time periods, persons, contexts, and purposes for which the findings are applicable.
Suggested content areas to address when justifying your conclusions	Questions to ask and answer about each content area when in comes to justifying your conclusions are listed below. Your main goal is to end up with conclusions that are based on solid reliable and valid data that your stakeholders will appreciate.
Standards	Which stakeholder values provide the basis for forming the judgments? What type or level of performance must be reached for your program to be considered successful? to be unsuccessful?
Analysis and synthesis	What procedures will you use to examine and summarize your evaluation's findings?
Interpretation	What do your findings mean (i.e., what is their practical significance)?
Judgment	What claims concerning your program's merit, worth, or significance are justified based on the available data (evidence) and the selected standards?
Recommendations	What actions should be considered resulting from your evaluation? (Note: Making recommendations is distinct from forming judgments and presumes a thorough understanding of the context in which programmatic decisions will be made.)

IN A NUTSHELL	3.7	Step 6: *Ensuring Usage and Sharing Lessons Learned*
Assuming that the lessons you learned in the course of your evaluation will automatically translate into informed decision-making and appropriate action would be naive. Deliberate effort is needed on your part to ensure that your evaluation processes and findings are used and disseminated appropriately. Preparing for use involves strategic thinking and continued vigilance, both of which begin in the earliest stages of stakeholder engagement and continue throughout the entire evaluation process.		
Purpose	Ensuring that stakeholders are aware of the evaluation procedures and findings; the findings are considered in decisions or actions that affect your program (i.e., findings use); those who participated in the evaluation process have had a beneficial experience (i.e., process use).	
Role	Ensures that evaluation achieves its primary purpose—being useful; however, several factors might influence the degree of use, including evaluator credibility, report clarity, report timeliness and dissemination, disclosure of findings, impartial reporting, and changes in your program or organizational context.	
Activities	Designing the evaluation to achieve intended use by intended users; preparing stakeholders for eventual use by rehearsing throughout the project how different kinds of conclusions would affect program operations; providing continuous feedback to stakeholders regarding interim findings, provisional interpretations, and decisions to be made that might affect likelihood of use; scheduling follow-up meetings with intended users to facilitate the transfer of evaluation conclusions into appropriate actions or decisions; disseminating both the procedures used and the lessons learned from the evaluation to stakeholders using tailored communications strategies that meet their particular needs.	
Suggested content areas to address when ensuring usage and sharing lessons learned	Questions to ask and answer about each content area when it comes to ensuring usage of your findings and sharing the lessons you learned. Your main goal is to be sure your findings are utilized in addition to sharing with others what lessons you learned from your evaluation.	
Design	Is your evaluation organized from the start to achieve the intended uses by your primary stakeholder groups?	
Preparation	Have you taken steps to rehearse the eventual use of your evaluation findings? How have your stakeholder groups been prepared to translate new knowledge into appropriate action?	
Feedback	What communication will occur among parties to the evaluation? Is there an atmosphere of trust among stakeholders?	
Follow-up	How will the technical and emotional needs of users be supported? What will prevent lessons learned from becoming lost or ignored in the process of making complex or politically sensitive decisions? What safeguards are in place for preventing misuse of the evaluation?	
Dissemination	How will the procedures or the lessons learned from your evaluation be communicated to your relevant stakeholders in a timely, unbiased, and consistent fashion? How will your reports be tailored to your various stakeholder groups?	

Study Questions   Chapter **3**

The goal of this chapter is to provide you with a beginning knowledge base for you to feel comfortable in answering the following questions. AFTER you have read the chapter, indicate how comfortable you feel you are in answering each question on a 5-point scale where

1	2	3	4	5
Very uncomfortable	Somewhat uncomfortable	Neutral	Somewhat comfortable	Very comfortable

If you rated any question between 1–3, reread the section of the chapter where the information for the question is found. If you still feel that you're uncomfortable in answering the question then talk with your instructor and/or your classmates for more clarification.

	Questions	Degree of comfort? *(Circle one number)*
1	Without peeking at Figure 3.1, list the six steps that you would have to go through in doing an evaluation. Then describe each step in relation to your field placement (or work setting) to illustrate your main points.	1 2 3 4 5
2	List the main stakeholder groups that you would need to formulate for your evaluation. Then describe the role that each stakeholder group would have in relation to your field placement (or work setting) to illustrate your main points.	1 2 3 4 5
3	In your own words, describe the purpose of a logic model when describing your program (Step 2). Then describe how it would be used in relation to your field placement (or work setting) to illustrate your main points.	1 2 3 4 5
4	List the five elements of a logic model and describe each element in detail. Then construct a logic model in relation to your field placement (or work setting) to illustrate your main points.	1 2 3 4 5
5	In reference to logic models, what are "if-then" statements? Make an "if-then" statement in relation to your field placement (or work setting) to illustrate your main points.	1 2 3 4 5
6	What are concept maps? How are they used when doing an evaluation? Provide specific social work examples from your field placement (or work setting) to illustrate your main points.	1 2 3 4 5
7	What are the differences between a formative and a summative evaluation? Describe how your field placement (or work setting) could use both of them.	1 2 3 4 5
8	When focusing an evaluation you must be concerned with two of CDC's standards: utility and feasibility. List the four questions that you will need to ask and answer under the utility standard and the three questions under the feasibility standard. Then describe the two evaluation standards in relation to your field placement (or work setting) to illustrate your main points.	1 2 3 4 5

continued

9	List and describe the four main types of evaluation questions that an evaluation can answer. Then describe each question in relation to your field placement (or work setting) to illustrate your main points.	1 2 3 4 5
10	What four chapters in this book describe how to do needs assessments, process evaluations, outcome evaluations, and efficiency evaluations?	1 2 3 4 5
11	In reference to formulating evaluation questions, list four tips that you can use to make the task easier. Then describe each tip in relation to your field placement (or work setting) to illustrate your main points.	1 2 3 4 5
12	In reference to formulating evaluation questions, list the nine stakeholder groups (sources) that you can use to make the task easier. Then describe how you can use each source in relation to your field placement (or work setting) to illustrate your main points.	1 2 3 4 5
13	Describe how you will work with stakeholders to describe your program (Step 2). Use your field placement (or work setting) to illustrate your main points.	1 2 3 4 5
14	Describe how you will work with stakeholders to focus your evaluation (Step 3). Use your field placement (or work setting) to illustrate your main points.	1 2 3 4 5
15	Describe how you will work with stakeholders to gather credible data (Step 4). Use your field placement (or work setting) to illustrate your main points.	1 2 3 4 5
16	Describe how you will work with stakeholders to justify your conclusions from an evaluation (Step 5). Use your field placement (or work setting) to illustrate your main points.	1 2 3 4 5
17	Describe how you will work with stakeholders to ensure that your evaluation's findings are used (Step 6). Use your field placement (or work setting) to illustrate your main points.	1 2 3 4 5
18	Discuss how you would engage "stakeholders" for a program evaluation. Then discuss how you would engage client systems within your field placement setting. Notice any differences between the two? If so, what are they? Provide specific social work examples throughout your discussion.	1 2 3 4 5
19	Discuss in detail how you would describe a program before it's evaluated. Then discuss in detail how you assess your client systems psychosocial environments before you intervene. Notice any differences between the two? If so, what are they? Provide specific social work examples throughout your discussion.	1 2 3 4 5
20	Discuss in detail how you would focus an evaluation. Then discuss how you would narrow down a client's presenting problem area so it can become more specific and manageable. Notice any differences between the two? If so, what are they? Provide specific social work examples throughout your discussion.	1 2 3 4 5

Chapter 3 — Assessing Your Self-Efficacy

AFTER you have read this chapter AND have completed all of the study questions, indicate how knowledgeable you feel you are for each of the following concepts on a 5-point scale where

1	2	3	4	5
Not knowledgeable at all	Somewhat unknowledgeable	Neutral	Somewhat knowledgeable	Very knowledgeable

	Concepts	Knowledge Level? (Circle one number)
1	Listing the six steps (in the order they are presented in this book) of doing an evaluation	1 2 3 4 5
2	Describing in detail each one of the six step of the evaluation process	1 2 3 4 5
3	Utilizing stakeholders to help you describe your program (Step 2)	1 2 3 4 5
4	Utilizing stakeholders to help you focus your evaluation (Step 3)	1 2 3 4 5
5	Utilizing stakeholders to help you gather credible data for your evaluation (Step 4)	1 2 3 4 5
6	Utilizing stakeholders to help you to justify your conclusions from your evaluation (Step 5)	1 2 3 4 5
7	Utilizing stakeholders to help you to ensure that the findings from your evaluation will be used (Step 6)	1 2 3 4 5
8	Constructing logic models	1 2 3 4 5
9	Constructing "if-then" statements for logic models	1 2 3 4 5
10	Developing concept maps	1 2 3 4 5
	Add up your scores (minimum = 10, maximum = 50)	Your total score =

A   48–50 = Professional evaluator in the making
A–   45–47 = Senior evaluator
B+   43–44 = Junior evaluator
B   40–42 = Assistant evaluator
B–   10–39 = Reread the chapter and redo the study questions

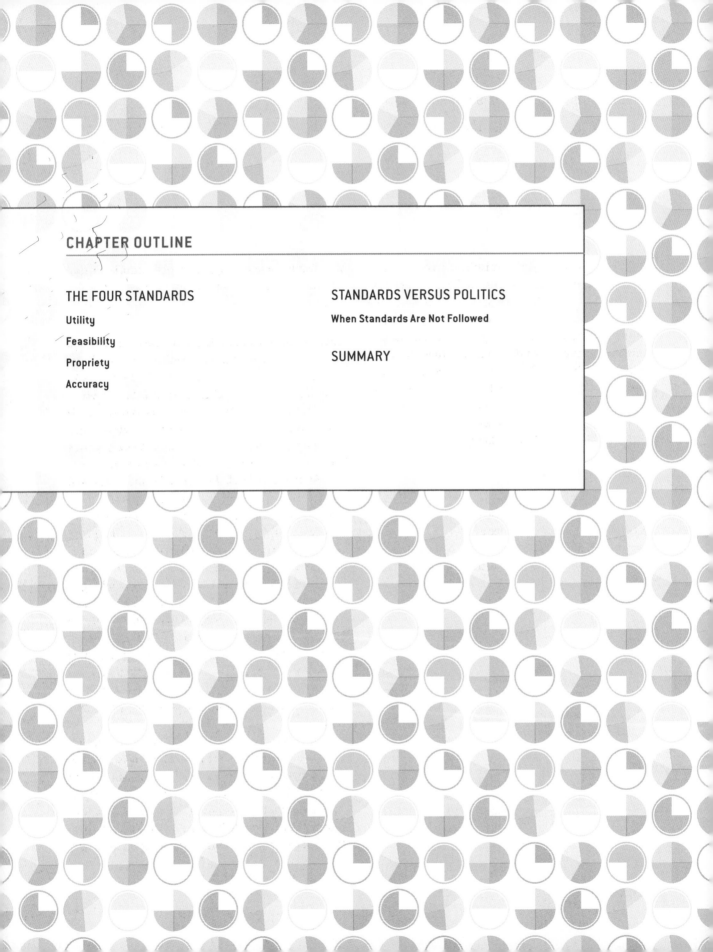

CHAPTER OUTLINE

The quality of leaders is reflected in the standards they set for themselves.

~ Ray Kroc

STANDARDS

To safeguard against the misdirection of the evaluation process or the misuse of the results, evaluators turn to professional standards for guidelines regarding the conceptualization and implementation of their work. There are four generic standards, and this chapter provides a description of those from the Joint Committee on Standards of Educational Evaluation (Yarbrough et al., 2011). The Committee was formed in 1975 and currently includes a large number of organizations concerned with maintaining high professional standards in evaluation practice.

THE FOUR STANDARDS

Notice the heavy overlap of the professional standards set out by the Joint Committee and the six steps of the evaluation process as described in the last chapter. Also note that they are in the center of the program evaluation process as illustrated in Figure 3.1. The Joint Committee

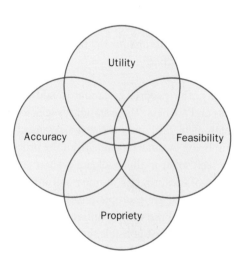

has identified four overlapping criteria against which all program evaluations should be judged.

Utility

The first standard is utility. The utility criteria are intended to ensure that your evaluations will provide useful data to one or more of your program's stakeholder groups. In other words, you are required to establish links between your evaluation's findings and the decisions you made that were derived from them. As we know, data obtained from an evaluation must be relevant to decision-makers and reported in a manner they can understand.

At the case level, for example, the client and the front-line social worker are, in most cases, joint decision-makers. Because workers usually carry out case-level evaluations, they will be able to decide on the type of data to be gathered, the method of analyses, and the way in which evaluation findings will impact their individual case-level decision-making.

At the program level, evaluation findings are usually documented in a written report. In a formative situation, the report may be one of a regular series, without formal recommendations; in a summative evaluation, there is likely to be a formal report, often ending with a series of recommendations. See Box 2.1 for a brief description of formative and summative evaluations.

In either case, to ensure that an evaluation has utility, you are responsible for determining in advance, with as much clarity as possible, the decisions that are to be based on the evaluation's findings. You are then responsible for reporting results in a manner that can inform the decisions to be taken. It's obviously important that your report be tailored to the decision-makers, who usually do not have an extensive background in evaluation, research methods, or statistics.

> *Utility Questions*
>
> - *Does the evaluation have a meaningful purpose?*
> - *Will the evaluation meet the information needs of the various stakeholders?*
> - *Will the evaluation provide relevant information in a timely manner?*

Thus statistical results, for example, should be provided so they are comprehensible to the users. When drafting recommendations, it's important that you keep in mind the social, political, economic, and professional contexts within which your recommendations will be implemented. The challenge is to provide recommendations that can result in meaningful and feasible improvement within the existing constraints of your program.

In sum, utility standards are intended to ensure that your evaluation will serve the information needs of its intended users.

Feasibility

Feasibility standards attempt to ensure that evaluations are conducted only when feasible, practical, and economically viable. These standards speak to minimizing disruption within the program where your evaluation is conducted; evaluators need to consider the impact of evaluation activities such as data collection and ensure that they do not impose an unreasonable burden on staff and on the organization itself.

> *Feasibility Questions*
>
> - *Are the planned evaluation activities realistic?*
> - *Are resources used prudently?*
> - *Is the evaluation minimally disruptive to your program?*

In addition, these standards address the issue of "political viability," suggesting that evaluators should anticipate political influence and possible attempts to misdirect the process or to misapply the results. These matters have already been discussed in detail in the previous three chapters. The feasibility standards require that you must be aware of these possibilities and ensure that the integrity of the evaluation process is maintained throughout.

In sum, feasibility standards are intended to ensure that your evaluation will be realistic, prudent, diplomatic, and frugal.

Propriety

Propriety standards provide a framework for the legal and ethical conduct of your evaluation. They also describe your responsibilities to ensure due regard for the welfare of those involved in your evaluation, as well as of those affected by its results.

These standards emphasize the obligation of those undertaking evaluations to act within the law, to respect those involved in the evaluation process, and to protect the rights and well-being of all evaluation participants. Colleges and universities generally maintain institutional review boards, which are concerned with ensuring that your evaluation methods are implemented in an ethical manner and the human participants who partake in your study are protected from harm or undue risk.

> *Propriety Questions*
>
> - *Is the evaluation ethical?*
> - *Does the evaluation protect the rights of individuals and protect the welfare of those involved?*

Finally, the propriety standards address completeness and fairness. These standards seek to ensure that a complete, fair, and balanced assessment of the program being evaluated results from the process. As we have seen so far in this book, an evaluation is only a snapshot of one program at one point in time. This means that there are multiple possible pictures of a program, each representing a different perspective.

Evaluators are responsible for creating a fair and balanced representation that can take into account

The second element of the Centers for Disease Control and Prevention framework is a set of 30 standards for assessing the quality of evaluation activities; these standards are organized into the four groups: Utility, Feasibility, Propriety, and Accuracy.

The standards answer the question, "Will this evaluation be effective?" They are an approved standard by the American National Standards Institute and have been endorsed by the American Evaluation Association and 14 other professional organizations.

Program professionals will recognize that the steps in evaluation practice are already a part of their routine work. Although informal evaluation occurs through routine practice, the standards help to assess whether a set of evaluative activities are well designed and working to their potential. The program evaluation standards make conducting sound and fair evaluations practical by providing guidelines to follow when having to decide among evaluation options. The standards help avoid creating an imbalanced evaluation (e.g., one that is accurate and feasible but not useful, or one that would be useful and accurate but is infeasible). Furthermore, the standards can be applied while planning an evaluation and throughout its implementation.

Utility Standard	Who needs the evaluation results? For what purpose do they need the evaluation results and/or why are they interested in the evaluation? Will the evaluation provide stakeholders with relevant information in a timely manner for them to actually use? The following utility standards ensure that your evaluation will serve the information needs of your stakeholders.
Stakeholder Identification	Persons involved in—or affected by—the evaluation should be identified, so that their needs can be addressed.
Evaluator Credibility	The persons conducting the evaluation should be both trustworthy and competent to perform the evaluation, so that the evaluation findings achieve maximum credibility and acceptance.
Information Scope and Selection	Information collected should be broadly selected to address pertinent questions about the program and be responsive to the needs and interests of clients and other specified stakeholders.
Values Identification	The perspectives, procedures, and rationale used to interpret the findings should be carefully described, so that the bases for value judgments are clear.
Report Clarity	Evaluation reports should clearly describe the program being evaluated, including its context and the purposes, procedures, and findings of the evaluation, so that essential information is provided and easily understood.
Final Report Timeliness and Dissemination	Significant interim findings and evaluation reports should be disseminated to intended users so that they can be used in a timely fashion.
Evaluation Impact	Evaluations should be planned, conducted, and reported in ways that encourage follow-through by stakeholders, so that the likelihood of the evaluation's results are increased.

Feasibility Standard	Are the planned evaluation activities realistic given the time, resources, and expertise at hand? How can planned evaluation activities be implemented with minimal program disruption? The following feasibility standards ensure that your evaluation will be realistic, prudent, diplomatic, and frugal.
Practical Procedures	Your evaluation procedures should be practical and keep disruption to a minimum while needed data are obtained.
Political Viability	Your evaluation should be planned and conducted with anticipation of the different positions of various interest groups, so that their cooperation may be obtained and so that possible attempts by any of these groups to curtail evaluation operations or to bias or misapply the results can be averted or counteracted.
Cost Effectiveness	Your evaluation should be efficient and produce information of sufficient value, so that the resources expended can be justified.
Propriety Standard	Does the evaluation protect the rights of individuals and protect the welfare of those involved? Does it engage those most directly affected by the program and changes in the program, such as participants or the surrounding community? The following propriety standards ensure that your evaluation will be conducted legally, ethically, and with regard for the welfare of those involved in the evaluation as well as those affected by its results.
Service Orientation	Your evaluation should be designed to assist organizations to address and effectively serve the needs of the full range of targeted participants.
Formal Agreements	Obligations of the formal parties to an evaluation (what is to be done, how, by whom, when) should be agreed to in writing, so that these parties are obligated to adhere to all conditions of the agreement or formally to renegotiate it.
Rights of Evaluation Participants	Your evaluation should be designed and conducted to respect and protect the rights and welfare of human subjects.
Human Interactions	Your evaluation should respect human dignity and worth in its interactions with other persons associated with it, so that participants are not threatened or harmed.
Complete and Fair Assessment	Your evaluation should be complete and fair in its examination and recording of the strengths and weaknesses of the program being evaluated, so that its strengths can be built upon and problem areas addressed.
Disclosure of Findings	The formal parties to your evaluation should ensure that the full set of evaluation findings along with pertinent limitations are made accessible to the persons affected by the evaluation and any others with expressed legal rights to receive the results.
Conflict of Interest	Conflict of interest should be dealt with openly and honestly, so that it does not compromise the evaluation's processes and results.

Fiscal Responsibility	Your allocations and expenditures of resources should reflect sound accountability procedures and otherwise be prudent and ethically responsible, so that expenditures are accounted for and appropriate.
Accuracy Standard	Will the evaluation produce findings that are valid and reliable, given the needs of those who will use the results? The following propriety standards ensure that your evaluation will convey technically adequate information regarding the determining features of merit of the program.
Program Documentation	Your program should be described and documented clearly and accurately, so that it is clearly identified.
Context Analysis	The context in which your program exists should be examined in enough detail that its likely influences on the program can be identified.
Described Purposes and Procedures	The purposes and procedures of your evaluation should be monitored and described in enough detail that they can be identified and assessed.
Defensible Data Sources	The data sources used in your program evaluation should be described in enough detail that the adequacy of the information can be assessed.
Valid Data	The data-gathering procedures should be chosen or developed and then implemented so that they will assure that the interpretation arrived at is valid for the intended use.
Reliable Data	The data-gathering procedures should be chosen or developed and then implemented so that they will assure that the data obtained are sufficiently reliable for the intended use.
Systematic Information	The information collected, processed, and reported in an evaluation should be systematically reviewed, and any errors found should be corrected.
Analysis of Quantitative Data	Quantitative data in an evaluation should be appropriately and systematically analyzed so that evaluation questions are effectively answered.
Analysis of Qualitative Data	Qualitative data in an evaluation should be appropriately and systematically analyzed so that evaluation questions are effectively answered.
Justified Conclusions	Your conclusions should be explicitly justified, so that stakeholders can assess them.
Impartial Reporting	Reporting procedures should guard against distortion caused by personal feelings and biases of any party to the evaluation, so that the final report fairly reflects the evaluation's findings.
Meta Evaluation	The evaluation itself should be formatively and summatively evaluated against these and other pertinent standards, so that its conduct is appropriately guided and, on completion, stakeholders can closely examine its strengths and weaknesses.

all reasonable perspectives. Often this means that no single picture will emerge as the result of an evaluation and you will need to explain how the several perspectives fit together and how they relate to the overall social, economic, political, and professional context in which your program operates.

In sum, propriety standards are intended to ensure that your evaluation will be conducted legally, ethically, and with due regard for the welfare of those involved in the evaluation, as well as those affected by its results.

Accuracy

The final set of standards address accuracy. This has to do with the technical adequacy of the evaluation process and involves such matters as validity and reliability, measurement instruments, samples, comparisons, and evaluation designs. These standards make clear your responsibility for maintaining high technical standards in all aspects of the evaluation process. You are also responsible for describing any methodological shortcomings and the limits within which findings can be considered to be accurate.

Accuracy Question

Will the evaluation produce valid and reliable findings?

In sum, accuracy standards are intended to ensure that your evaluation will reveal and convey technically adequate information about the features that determine worth or merit of the program being evaluated.

STANDARDS VERSUS POLITICS

The real-world pressures that affect—and sometimes buffer—the evaluation process exist because evaluations are often perceived to have serious consequences affecting people's interests. Consequently, people, factions, or groups sometimes seek to advance their personal interests and agendas by inappropriately influencing the evaluation process.

Politics may be at work within a program or outside of it; these can result in a very strong pressure on the evaluation process. Further, because politics often lead to personal contention, the actual implementation of an evaluation's findings and recommendations may become difficult.

On politics . . .

One of the penalties for refusing to participate in politics is that you end up being governed by your inferiors.

~ Plato

Politically charged situations may emerge within a program, in which case individuals internal to it are primarily involved. Administrators and staff are key players when it comes to internal politics. Program politics become apparent in situations in which staff interests are involved and where the evaluation's results may lead to changes in philosophy, organization, or approach to service provision. An evaluation must be prudent in dealing with internal politics because the cooperation of administrators and staff needs to be maintained in order to facilitate the evaluation process.

At other times, individuals who are outside of your program may wish to influence decisions about the future development or the allocation of its resources. External politics are at work when individuals outside your program attempt to influence your "evaluative efforts" in a negative way.

Further contention may develop when a program's staff members and external stakeholder groups hold different views about what events should take place and what decisions ought to be made. The nature of the decisions to be made, the invested interests of the respective parties, and the magnitude of potential change can all serve to raise the perceived consequences of the evaluation and the intensity of the political climate.

When Standards Are Not Followed

The six steps of the evaluation process discussed in the previous chapter and the four standards delineated in this chapter must be followed if our evaluations are to have any creditability.

However, any human endeavor, including evaluation, can be inappropriately or appropriately used; when stakes are high, the probability of misuse increases. As we know from the preceding three chapters and this one so far, a creditable program evaluation results in the production of a fair, balanced, and accurate report that contains meaningful recommendations.

At its best, the evaluation process should be open and transparent with sound recommendations evolving from its results. However, in a highly politicized situation, there may be little—if any—motivation of some folks to use the results in such a manner; their intent may be to use the evaluation process and/or its findings to further some other cynical purpose. Inevitably, a misuse of an evaluation's findings will occur.

Using Evaluations Inappropriately

When an evaluation's steps and standards are not followed, they can easily get side-tracked and misused in a variety of ways. Some of the more common misuses include the following.

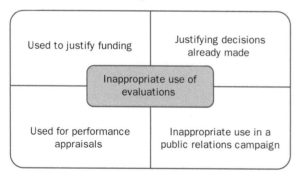

Justifying decisions already made. Perhaps the most frequent misuse of an evaluation's results is to justify decisions that were made in advance of the study. At the case level, for example, a worker may have decided, if only at the subconscious level, that a youngster in individualized treatment foster care should be referred to a group-care program. The worker may then select a standardized measuring instrument (see Tool M) that is likely to show that the youngster's functioning is highly problematic and then use these data to justify the previously taken decision.

> *Making decisions . . .*
>
> Too often we think we can act without explaining and take decisions without justifying them.
>
> *~ Peter Mandelson*

At the program level, an administrator may already have decided that a certain program within the agency should be reduced in size. The administrator may then commission an evaluation in the hope that the results will show the program to be ineffective. Inevitably, any evaluation will uncover some shortcomings and limitations; the administrator can then use these to justify the decision to reduce the size of the program. Similarly, outside funders who have already decided to curtail or cancel funding for a program may first commission an evaluation in the hope that the results will justify the preexisting decision.

Public relations. A second misuse of an evaluation is to distract attention from negative events and use the evaluation process as a public relations tool. From time to time within the social services, problems and incidents occur that bring unwelcome publicity. A worker in a group home, for example, may be indicted for sexual abuse of its residents, or a preschooler may be returned from a treatment foster home to her birth home and be subsequently physically abused by her biological parents. These types of incidents inevitably attract intense media scrutiny and public interest.

> *On public relations . . .*
>
> Some are born great, some achieve greatness, and some hire public relations officers.
>
> *~ Daniel J. Boorstin*

Some administrators may immediately respond to such incidents by commissioning "an evaluation" and then declining to comment any further. An administrator might announce, "I have today engaged Professor Rodriguez from the university to undertake a comprehensive evaluation of this program; until the evaluation results are available, I do not want to say anything further that might prejudge the findings." Sound familiar?

An evaluation may be an appropriate response in such a situation. However, its findings must be used to help decide on changes that need to be made to increase the likelihood that a similar problem will never again occur. When an evaluation is commissioned merely to distract attention or to avoid having to comment, much of the time, effort, and resources invested in it will be wasted. An evaluation in such a situation is mere window dressing—a diversion.

Performance appraisals. The third serious misuse of an evaluation occurs when it's used for purposes of performance appraisals. For example, data can be aggregated inappropriately across a worker's caseload, and the resulting "cumulative data" are then used for a performance appraisal. At the program level, the contents of an evaluation report, which focuses on an operating unit, may be used to evaluate the performance of a supervisor or administrator.

Although administrators do have a major responsibility for the performance of their unit, program, or department, other factors—beyond the control of the administrator—may also be involved; the point is that a program evaluation is not meant to link program performance and outcomes to individual social workers and their performances.

When an evaluation is used for purposes of a performance appraisal, the findings are likely to be used for political goals—to promote or undermine an individual. Such misuse of an evaluation is destructive, as administrators and workers alike will undoubtedly become defensive and concentrate their efforts on ensuring that evaluation data show them in the best possible light.

These efforts detract from the delivery of effective services and will also likely result in less reliable and valid data. Performance appraisals and program evaluations are two distinct processes, with different

purposes. Both are compromised if they are not kept separate.

Fulfilling funding requirements. Nowadays funders commonly require an evaluation of some kind as a condition of a program's funding, particularly in the case of new projects. Staff members who are trying to set up a new program or maintain an old one, for example, may see the evaluation requirement as a ritual without any direct relevance to them. They may thus incorporate an evaluation component into the funding proposal or graft evaluation activities onto an existing program, obediently jumping through hoops to satisfy funders that they are in compliance with evaluation requirements.

Often, these evaluation plans are not even implemented because they were designed for "show" only. At other times, the evaluation activities are undertaken but without any intention of making use of the results. It is, of course, a serious misuse (not to mention a waste of time, effort, and resources) to undertake an evaluation only to obtain program funds without any thought of using the data that were derived from the evaluation in any meaningful way.

Using Evaluations Appropriately

Having described a variety of possible misuses, it's appropriate to conclude this section of the discussion by reviewing two appropriate uses of evaluations. As discussed previously, evaluations are most properly used to guide an open and transparent decision-making process, where evaluation findings will be weighed and considered.

> *On decision-making . . .*
>
> Sometimes it's the smallest decisions that can change your life forever.
>
> ~ *Keri Russell*

Internal decision-making. The primary internal use of evaluation data is feedback; evaluation findings provide data about the degree to which a program's objectives are being met. When these data are available in a timely fashion, administrators and workers alike can continually monitor the impacts of their decisions and, where required, make adjustments to activities and program operations.

At the case level, for example, evaluation data can provide an objective basis for making clinical decisions. As described in Chapter 7, selected practice objectives are measured repeatedly while the client is receiving services. These data are then used as feedback on client progress and become an important consideration in decisions to maintain, modify, or change treatment activities and/or interventions.

At the program level, staff members' interest is in a broader picture of how the program functions. A good data collection strategy allows for a program to gather data continuously about its various components, practices, and procedures. The principal internal use for such data is developmental. The process is essentially as follows: data are collected continuously and analyzed periodically to provide ongoing feedback about the functioning of various aspects of the program.

Where the program is not performing as desired, there is an opportunity to make changes in structures, procedures, and practices. Subsequent data will then provide information about the impact of these changes. Through this process, administrators and staff can continuously fine-tune and improve the program.

Because the purpose of the evaluation is development, not judgment, people are more likely to take risks, innovate, and experiment. In such an environment, growth and development are more likely to occur. When staff members and teams feel encouraged to grow and learn, the program itself grows and learns.

External decision-making. External uses of evaluation data usually involve all stakeholder groups. Appropriate uses include the demonstration of accountability, decision-making about program and policy, and knowledge building.

As is stressed throughout our book, social service programs are, in a general sense, accountable to their clients, to their communities, and to professional peers. In a more specific way, they are also accountable to their funders. Accountability generally requires evidence that goals are consistent with community needs, that contracted services are actually provided as planned, and that these services are being provided effectively and efficiently. These are among the most common uses of evaluation data: to account for program activities and program results.

At the policy level, it's sometimes necessary to make decisions among various ways of meeting particular social needs. Or policymakers may decide to encourage the development of programs that are organized along certain intervention models. For example, in many jurisdictions, the development of treatment foster homes has been encouraged in recent years, while group-care facilities for young people are supported much more reluctantly. At other times, funders must make decisions regarding future funding for a specific program. In all three situations, evaluations could provide data that can help guide decisions.

Knowledge building is another way in which an evaluation's results may be used. Each completed evaluation study has the potential of adding to our profession's knowledge base. Indeed, at times, evaluations are undertaken specifically for the purpose of acquiring knowledge. Because most evaluations are conducted in field settings, they are particularly useful for testing the effectiveness of interventions and treatment models that actually occur in these settings.

Evaluations for external purposes are usually initiated by people outside the program, typically funding bodies such as governments or foundations. They are often also externally conducted by evaluation specialists on a project by project basis. When evaluations are externally initiated and externally conducted, there is a higher potential for problems to develop in the evaluation process and for the misuse of the findings. This is because an external evaluator may impose an evaluation framework that does not fit well with a program's operations or is not consistent with staff members' or administrators' expectations.

Learn more about hiring external evaluators in Tools A and B in the Evaluation Toolkit.

An effective safeguard is provided when administrators and staff are involved in decisions relating to the planning and execution of the evaluation. An alternative to the externally conducted evaluation is available to programs that establish internal evaluation systems. When internal systems are developed with stakeholders participating, the data collected through them often satisfy many of the data needs of the external stakeholders.

SUMMARY

This chapter presented a brief discussion of the professional standards we must follow within the evaluative process that was presented in the previous chapter. We presented the various considerations that should be taken into account when evaluating any social service program. Because programs are situated in the real world, politics and political influence are often unavoidable. Also, because they are complex entities, technical decisions can often influence the course of our evaluation, as well as its results.

We have a responsibility to ensure that our "evaluative" work provides accurate, fair, and complete information to decision-makers and that it's used in an open and constructive decision-making process. Professional standards for conducting evaluations provide guidance to ensure that our evaluations are constructive, ethical, and of the highest quality.

The next chapter is a logical extension of this one in that it discusses how we, as professional social workers, must follow strict ethical guidelines when evaluating our programs, taking into account the contents of this chapter.

The goal of this chapter is to provide you with a beginning knowledge base for you to feel comfortable in answering the following questions. AFTER you have read the chapter, indicate how comfortable you feel you are in answering each question on a 5-point scale where

1 Very uncomfortable	2 Somewhat uncomfortable	3 Neutral	4 Somewhat comfortable	5 Very comfortable

If you rated any question between 1–3, reread the section of the chapter where the information for the question is found. If you still feel that you're uncomfortable in answering the question, then talk with your instructor and/or your classmates for more clarification.

	Questions	Degree of comfort? *(Circle one number)*
1	List the four professional evaluation standards.	1 2 3 4 5
2	In your own words, define each of the four evaluation standards.	1 2 3 4 5
3	Discuss how you would incorporate each of the four evaluation standards within an evaluation you are doing within your field placement (or work setting).	1 2 3 4 5
4	List the four ways you could inappropriately use evaluation results.	1 2 3 4 5
5	In your own words, describe each of the four ways evaluation results can be misused. Then describe them in relation to your field placement (or work setting) to illustrate your main points.	1 2 3 4 5
6	Discuss how you would insure that you would not use your evaluation's results inappropriately within an evaluation you are doing within your field placement (or work setting).	1 2 3 4 5
7	List the two ways you could appropriately use evaluation results.	1 2 3 4 5
8	In your own words, describe each of the two ways evaluation results can be appropriately used. Then describe them in relation to your field placement (or work setting) to illustrate your main points.	1 2 3 4 5
9	Discuss how you would insure that you would use your evaluation's results appropriately within an evaluation you are doing within your field placement (or work setting).	1 2 3 4 5
10	Discuss how you would use your stakeholder groups to guard against the *inappropriate use* of your evaluation's results. Use your field placement (or work setting) to illustrate your main points.	1 2 3 4 5
11	Discuss how you would use your stakeholder groups to enhance the *appropriate use* of your evaluation's results. Use your field placement (or work setting) to illustrate your main points.	1 2 3 4 5

Chapter 4

Assessing Your Self-Efficacy

AFTER you have read this chapter AND have completed all of the study questions, indicate how knowledgeable you feel you are for each of the following concepts on a 5-point scale where

1 Not knowledgeable at all	2 Somewhat unknowledgeable	3 Neutral	4 Somewhat knowledgeable	5 Very knowledgeable

	Concepts	Knowledge Level? (Circle one number)
1	The *utility* evaluation standard	1 2 3 4 5
2	The *feasibility* evaluation standard	1 2 3 4 5
3	The *propriety* evaluation standard	1 2 3 4 5
4	The *accuracy* evaluation standard	1 2 3 4 5
5	The four inappropriate uses of evaluation results	1 2 3 4 5
6	The two appropriate uses of evaluation results	1 2 3 4 5
	Add up your scores (minimum = 6, maximum = 30)	Your total score =

A   29–30 = Professional evaluator in the making
A–   27–28 = Senior evaluator
B+   25–26 = Junior evaluator
B   23–24 = Assistant evaluator
B–   6–22 = Reread the chapter and redo the study questions

CHAPTER OUTLINE

Live one day at a time emphasizing ethics rather than rules.

~ Wayne Dyer

ETHICS

ANDRE IVANOFF AND BETTY BLYTHE

As you know from the previous chapter, there are four professional evaluation standards that must be followed when doing an evaluation (i.e., utility, feasibility, propriety, accuracy). The main focus of this chapter is devoted to one of them—propriety. At this point, it's extremely important for you to remember that the entire evaluation process is not a 100% linear one as Figure 3.1 may suggest.

All steps overlap to some degree. For example, it's impossible to clearly separate the activities you would do in Step 4 from Step 5 and Step 5 from Step 6. This may be a good time for you to review Figure 3.1 for a graphic presentation of the process and the following "In a Nutshell 3.1" that describes each step within the process.

During every step in any program evaluation, you will be called upon to make numerous ethical decisions. Since each step overlaps with the other steps, it's impractical to discuss ethical issues that need to be addressed within each step in a complete vacuum, isolated from the other steps: all steps are influenced by the ethical decisions made in the others (see Figure 5.1). This chapter mainly covers three of the steps (i.e., 3, 4, and 6) and discusses the ethical issues we need to address for each one.

Let's start off the topic of ethics by reviewing what the National Association of Social Workers (NASW) says about evaluation ethics.

CODE OF ETHICS

The NASW is the "practice organization" that works to enhance the professional growth and development of practicing social workers. The NASW believes that social work practitioners should also know the basics of evaluation as described in their *Code of Ethics* (1996). As you can see, the *Code* pertains to all of the four professional evaluation standards described in the previous chapter, especially propriety:

- Social workers should monitor and evaluate policies, the implementation of programs, and practice interventions.
- Social workers should promote and facilitate evaluation and research to contribute to the development of knowledge.
- Social workers should critically examine and keep current with emerging knowledge relevant to social work and fully use evaluation and research evidence in their professional
- Social workers should report evaluation and research findings accurately. They should not fabricate or falsify results and should take steps to correct any errors later found in published data using standard publication methods.
- Social workers engaged in evaluation or research should be alert to and avoid conflicts of interest and dual relationships with participants, should inform participants when a real or potential conflict of interest arises, and should take steps to resolve the issue in a manner that makes participants' interests primary.

On ethics . . .

Relativity applies to physics, not ethics.

~ Albert Einstein

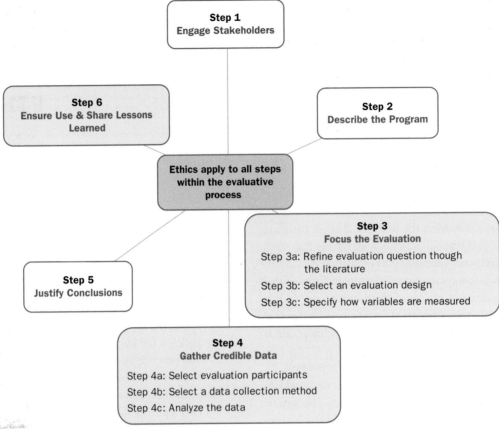

Figure 5.1: **Ethics apply to all steps of the evaluative process (from Figure 3.1).**

- Social workers should educate themselves, their students, and their colleagues about responsible research practices.
- Social workers engaged in evaluation or research should carefully consider possible consequences and should follow guidelines developed for the protection of evaluation and research participants. Appropriate institutional review boards should be consulted.
- Social workers engaged in evaluation or research should obtain voluntary and written informed consent from participants, when appropriate, without any implied or actual deprivation or penalty for refusal to participate; without undue inducement to participate; and with due regard for

participants' well-being, privacy, and dignity. Informed consent should include information about the nature, extent, and duration of the participation requested and disclosure of the risks and benefits of participation in the research.

- When evaluation or research participants are incapable of giving informed consent, social workers should provide an appropriate explanation to the participants, obtain the participants' assent to the extent they are able, and obtain written consent from an appropriate proxy.
- Social workers should never design or conduct evaluation or research that does not use consent procedures, such as certain forms of naturalistic observation and archival research,

unless rigorous and responsible review of the research has found it to be justified because of its prospective scientific, educational, or applied value and unless equally effective alternative procedures that do not involve waiver of consent are not feasible.

- Social workers should inform participants of their right to withdraw from evaluation and research at any time without penalty.
- Social workers should take appropriate steps to ensure that participants in evaluation and research have access to appropriate supportive services.
- Social workers engaged in evaluation or research should protect participants from unwarranted physical or mental distress, harm, danger, or deprivation.
- Social workers engaged in the evaluation of services should discuss collected information only for professional purposes and only with people professionally concerned with this information.
- Social workers engaged in evaluation or research should ensure the anonymity or confidentiality of participants and of the data obtained from them. Social workers should inform participants of any limits of confidentiality, the measures that will be taken to ensure confidentiality, and when any records containing research data will be destroyed.

On integrity . . .

Integrity is doing the right thing, even if nobody is watching.

~ Spencer Johnson

- Social workers who report evaluation and research results should protect participants' confidentiality by omitting identifying information unless proper consent has been obtained authorizing disclosure.

As you will see shortly, our entire book addresses the *Code of Ethics* in one way or another, especially this chapter. We now turn our attention to discussing how ethical issues are addressed within Steps 3, 4, and 6 of the evaluation process. Note that we do not discuss how ethical issues are involved in Steps 1, 2, and 5 as they are self-explanatory and have been discussed in depth in the previous chapters. Also, Step 6 is discussed in Tool J. Notice that Steps 3 and 4 in Figure 5.1 have three substeps each.

STEP 3: FOCUSING THE EVALUATION

As you know by now, you must answer a simple question: What is the purpose of my evaluation study? Sometimes your study can *directly benefit* those who participate in it, that is, the participants themselves. In addition, it may *indirectly benefit* others who share the same or a similar problem but are not actually participating in the study, that is, those who are not directly involved in your study as participants.

If your study does not directly or indirectly benefit its participants, then it must contribute to our professional social work knowledge base. If the question posed already has been answered, for example, what is the argument for answering it again? The program evaluator may believe it's important to replicate clinical findings and/or generalize the study's findings to other client populations, or to simply replicate the study using a more rigorous and creditable evaluation design, which in turn would produce more trustworthy findings (see Tool E).

Evaluation training is another acceptable reason for conducting an evaluation study that may not immediately benefit its participants. For example, the *Code of Ethics* contains an ethical standard that requires social work students to be educated in research and evaluation methodologies. In cases where there may be little direct or indirect benefit to the evaluation's participants, the level of risk posed by their participation must be minimal; that is, there should be little to no chance that clients' participation in the studies could harm them in any way.

At the end of the day, you have a responsibility to your evaluation participants—as well as to the larger professional community—to select an evaluation question that is actually worthy of investigation and will produce results that are meaningful, concrete, and useful, in addition to being reliable and valid. As Peter Drucker said, "The most serious mistakes are not being made as a result of wrong answers. The truly dangerous thing is asking the wrong question."

This section address the ethical issues that arise in relation to focusing your evaluation:

- Step 3a: Refining the evaluation question through the literature
- Step 3b: Selecting an evaluation design
- Step 3c: Specifying how variables are measured

Step 3a: Refine Evaluation Question Through the Literature

After identifying an evaluation question, the next goal is to refine it further by surveying the relevant literature. This involves a thorough review of the theory and other research studies related to the evaluation question. It's important to base any evaluation on a solid understanding of what came before: "What do we already know about the potential question under investigation?" Critical to refining the initial question is asking an answerable question. For example,

What social work intervention(s) will decrease gang-related "tagging" (marking) on public school grounds?

Once we have a question that can be answered, such as this one, we can then refine it a bit more. This part of the evaluation process is roughly analogous to the assessment phase in clinical social work practice. Once the client's presenting problem (the question) is posed, we then proceed to identify the parameters of the problem and explore its impact on the client's functioning.

As newer and more specific client information is drawn out during the assessment phase of social work practice, we then refine and increase the clarity and precision of the original problem statement. This process in clinical assessment is called *targeting*. Basing our choice of intervention on conclusions drawn quickly and imprecisely about the target problem compromises ethical practice.

Evaluate the Literature

What is acceptable knowledge? Is all information found on Google "good"? Is one search engine or bibliographic resource superior to another in the value of the information it generates? And what impact do the answers to these questions have on the services we provide to our clients? Even many elementary schools now inform their students that Wikipedia is not an acceptable reference source to be used in an academic paper.

Using search engines to find treatments for depression, for example, yields numerous links to psychotropic medication before psychosocial treatments are even cited. Indeed, information on how to commit suicide exists side by side with scholarly papers on factors related to preventing suicide!

Evaluating sources of knowledge was much easier (however inefficient) before the advent of the Internet. Professional journals and books, along with professional consensus, were considered the building blocks of our profession's knowledge base. These were available by subscription and in bookstores; most of us had to go to libraries or buy books to access this information. The Internet has broadened and extended our information sources beyond expectation and, at the same time, has made it much more difficult to critically assess the information found there.

Today, credible sources of practice information are available on the Internet, such as the Cochrane Collaboration (www.cochrane.org) and the Campbell Collaboration (www.campbellcollaboration.org). Both of these organizations' websites include systematic reviews and meta-analyses covering the assessment and treatment of health, mental health, and social welfare problems. Evidence-based practice guidelines represent the best of scholarly consensus and are available for mental health, substance abuse, and other areas of social work practice.

Step 3b: Selecting an Evaluation Design

The evaluation's research design (see Tool E) that is finally chosen to answer the evaluation question also warrants examination from an ethical perspective. In evaluation studies, in which participants are randomly assigned to either an experimental group or a control group, concerns often arise about withholding treatment or providing a less potent intervention for control group members. This is an evaluation design called the *classical experimental design* and illustrated in Figure 5.2.

The ability to randomly assign evaluation participants to groups significantly strengthens arguments about whether a particular intervention is responsible for the change (if any) that has occurred for the individuals in the intervention, or experimental, group. This decision, however, must be weighed against the reality of the participant's life or problem situation. Clients can be randomly assigned to two groups: one group receives the intervention (experimental group), and the other group does not receive it (control group) as illustrated in Figure 5.2.

If the experimental group does better than the control group after the study is completed, the control group would then be offered the same intervention that the experimental group received earlier. The control group just receives the intervention at a later date, so there are no ethical violations present in a true experimental design when implemented

correctly. However, a delay must always be weighed against the benefit as some delays may be detrimental or even fatal. This is discussed in much greater detail in Tool E.

Beneficence

Central to the consideration of the ethical issues in experimental designs is the question of *beneficence*. Researchers and the IRBs that guide them must consider how to maximize benefit and minimize harm to participants when considering how best to test the effectiveness of a social work intervention. The possibility of other viable treatment methods must be considered as well, as opposed to offering no treatment. Again, our *Code of Ethics* mandates that we must protect both clients and research participants from deprivation of access to evidence-based services.

Equipoise, or the Uncertainty Principle

This principle maintains that evaluation studies that randomize their participants to different treatment groups should be conducted only if there is a true uncertainty about which of the treatment alternatives is most likely to benefit them. Some questions are easy to answer, but some can pose dilemmas.

For instance, if an intervention being tested is known to be superior to an alternative inferior intervention, it's unethical to assign individuals to the inferior intervention. Similarly, an experimental study

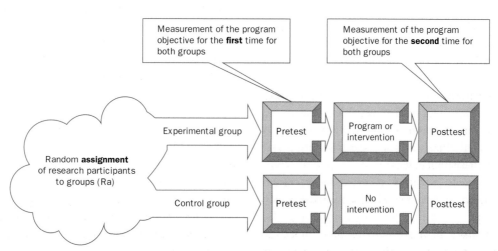

Figure 5.2: **Randomized pretest–posttest control group design (classical experimental design).**

that contains two interventions is unethical if a third intervention exists that is known to be more effective, unless the evaluators have questions about the efficacy of the effective intervention for a particular subgroup of clients.

All too often, however, a consideration of equipoise raises challenging questions for social workers, especially those working in fields where there are relatively little data to support the effectiveness of alternative interventions. Moreover, if the usual intervention has little or no evidence to support its effectiveness, can it be considered an appropriate comparison treatment?

Step 3c: Specifying How Variables Are Measured

After an evaluation design is chosen in Step 3b, the variables within our study need to be specified and eventually measured. Most of the time, however, our variables have already been selected for us such as a program's outcome variables called program objectives (see Chapter 7). See Box 7.1 in Chapter 7 for examples of a family support program that contains three program objectives and their measurements.

> *On variables . . .*
>
> *It's a little bit of a guessing game when you are using an unknown. I love his stuff. It's going to depend on the situation. So many variables.*
>
> ~ *Terry Francona*

If for some reason program objectives are not available, then you will have to formulate and measure them with the help of your stakeholders. All of the guidelines for measuring variables are covered in Tool H. This section presents a few tips on how to avoid potential ethical pitfalls in their selection and subsequent measurements.

For example, we need to avoid measurement methods and instruments with obvious biases, such as the biases related to gender, age, sexual orientation, and culture. If we are studying sexual habits of men and women, for example, the language of the

questions we formulate should not assume that all the participants are heterosexual.

As we will see in the following chapter, our *Code of Ethics* stresses the need for us to understand and respect the full extent of social diversity found within our client systems. This understanding and respect for individual differences must be reflected in the selection and measurement of the variables we wish to study and, hence, measure.

In selecting the variables for our study, we also need to base our selection from the literature, and not conduct a fishing expedition in which every variable imaginable is included in the study in an effort to search for "something of significance."

Having specific evaluation questions that guide each phase of your evaluation project is not just good evaluation practice—it's also good ethical practice. In a nutshell, your evaluation participants should not be asked to provide a wealth of information that may or may not answer the central question(s) of your study.

Be Aware of Cultural Issues

As we will see in detail in the following chapter, a study that fails to take into account cultural issues is likely to produce invalid and unreliable findings. Cultural issues must be considered at every step of the evaluation process, from developing the initial question to disseminating the study's findings.

As we know from our social work practice classes, perceptions and definitions of child sexual abuse are socially constructed and are shaped by specific cultural, social, and historical perspectives. Thus, we must take into account how our potential participants perceive and understand child sexual abuse, in addition to the cultural customs about discussing such a sensitive topic. These cultural contexts influence how your questions are asked, how your evaluation participants are recruited, and how your data are collected and finally analyzed.

We may find that little or no information is available on the social problem being addressed in the culture of the population in which we are interested. In this case, we need to consult representatives from the group we are studying for advice and guidance. *Focus groups* with these individuals will help to clarify many potential issues.

Pilot testing the measuring procedures using people from the group of interest is absolutely essential in an effort to avoid any misunderstandings, the possibility of offending our evaluation participants, and, ultimately, the production of data that are not reliable and valid. And of course, always involve your stakeholders as much as possible.

Examples. A proposed evaluation study of the experiences of political refugees to the United States from former Soviet Bloc countries is a relatively novel area of inquiry, with limited advice available in the professional literature. Thus, in designing an interview questionnaire, for example, we would likely find that talking to the immigrants and social workers who work with refugees will be the most helpful in understanding the challenges faced by this particular population.

Another example of an extremely important topic under the general area of cultural issues is that of language. If the data collection method(s), such as those discussed in Tool H, involve gathering data directly from our study's participants, then we need to be sensitive to issues related to language. Even when collecting data from participants who speak the same language as the social worker, we have to be sensitive to regional dialects, the age of the respondents, and the like. When doing evaluations with adolescents (aka, Millennials, Selfies, the Trophy Generation, or the App Generation) for example, we have to consider the trade-off between using standard English, slang, Webspeak, or other types of communication they commonly use.

As we will see later on in this chapter, when obtaining informed consent from potential participants, we must strive to explain our evaluation procedures in terms that can be easily understood by prospective participants. Our *Code of Ethics* and the next chapter clearly address the importance of considering cultural issues when designing an evaluation study. We are reminded to respect the cultural and ethnic backgrounds of the people with whom we work.

This includes recognizing the strengths that exist in all cultures—which is critical when designing questions, selecting variables to be studied, and conducting all other steps of the evaluation process itself. Thus, the aforementioned study of political refugees needs to consider their strengths as well as their challenges and difficulties.

STEP 4: GATHERING DATA

This section address three ethical issues that arise when it comes to gathering credible data for your evaluation,

- Step 4a: Selecting evaluation participants
- Step 4b: Selecting a data-collection method
- Step 4c: Analyzing the data

Step 4a: Selecting Evaluation Participants

As you know, one of our stakeholder groups is our clients. All types of evaluations require the input from our clients—past and present; that is, we use them to provide data as "evaluation participants." Thus, when using clients we need to be extremely careful not to violate any of their ethical and legal rights, which is the purpose of this chapter.

Not harming our clients, by commission or omission, is a cardinal rule within the evaluation process, as described in Chapter 3. There are a number of bodies that are devoted to ensuring that harm does not occur to our participants. In the United States, for example, there is a committee known as the National Commission for the Protection of Human Subjects of Biomedical and Behavioral Research.

All colleges and universities have ethics committees, or institutional review boards (IRBs), and many large social service agencies do as well. There are also various professional associations and lay groups that focus on protecting your evaluation participants. However, it's likely that the participants in your study will never have heard of any of these bodies. They will do what you ask them to do, either because they trust you or because they think they have no other choice but to participate. The responsibility of not hurting any of the participants in your program evaluations rests squarely on your shoulders—yes, yours.

How we select participants for their potential participation in our evaluation is a very important ingredient of the evaluation process. Although sampling methods are primarily driven by your evaluation's purpose, they are also are influenced by your own personal values and sometimes just convenience.

Ethical concerns include whether your potential participants are representative of the target population you really want to study. In other words, is this the group most affected by the question you are trying to answer? As you will see in Toolkit H, it's important to ask whether your group is diverse enough to represent those who are affected by the social problem you are concerned with.

On samples . . .

The proof of the pudding is in the eating. By a small sample we may judge the whole piece.

~ *Miguel de Cervantes Saavedra*

Evaluation studies with samples lacking in cultural diversity may limit generalization to the broader population under study, and they also compromise social work ethical tenets that address social justice and increased inclusion. Intentionally or inadvertently excluding certain individuals or groups from participating can markedly affect the quality of the data gathered and the conclusions drawn about the phenomena under investigation.

For instance, an evaluation study of immigrants that excludes non–English-speaking individuals, non-readers, and agency clients who come in before or after regular hours for the convenience of the evaluators introduces several types of sampling biases that will directly affect the generalizability of the study's results. This example also ignores the mandate that all social workers must engage in culturally competent practice and research/evaluation that respects client diversity.

Do We All Abide by IRBs?

It's very difficult to know how many social workers who engage in research fail to complete human subjects review processes or informed consent processes with their potential evaluation participants. Also, it's difficult to know how many of our social service agencies, especially smaller ones, do not have committees to review potential evaluation studies conducted by their staff.

We do not know how many agencies ask clients to sign "blanket" consent forms that indicate that the clients' information can be used for evaluation purposes. More important, many of these clients do not ask questions about consent forms because they may believe they are just another form to be signed at intake so they can receive the services they are requesting.

Moreover, some agencies may undertake routine evaluation activities to inform the delivery of their services that could raise ethical issues. For example, a focus group conducted by agency staff with certain client groups, such as rape survivors, may uncover personal or confidential information about the participants in the focus group discussion. Or clients who complete "client satisfaction with service questionnaires" might inadvertently disclose personal information that could be damaging to the client or significant others, or even to agency staff.

Recruitment of Evaluation Participants

How potential evaluation participants are recruited also requires an ethical lens. Four areas of concern, when it comes to recruitment, include:

- The consent and assent processes (ongoing or continuing)
- The possibility of coercion or undue influence (of both medium and message)
- Confidentiality and privacy
- Completeness (accuracy as well as truthfulness)

Assessing all possible ways that a potential participant might feel undue influence to participate—such as a personal appeal, a financial incentive, the status of being part of a special group, other tangible or intangible benefits, or just plain old fear of repercussions—can be a daunting task, to say the least.

Who is actually recruiting the participants? Does the gatekeeper—or the process of the recruitment effort itself—exert pressure, subtle or direct, to participate or not to participate? Social workers hold an ethical obligation to examine the fairness or equity of recruitment strategies within target populations and the representativeness (or diversity) of the sample finally selected to be included in the study.

As we know from earlier portions of this chapter, our *Code of Ethics* includes standards that mandate that we obtain potential research participants without threatening to penalize anyone who refuses to participate—and without offering inappropriate rewards for their participation. Just as clients have the right to self-determination in social work practice, so too do participants who volunteer for research projects.

Take a look at Boxes 5.1 and 5.2, which provide examples of consent (Box 5.1) and assent (Box 5.2) forms. Do you see any possibility that the potential participants were unduly influenced to participate and/or would not receive services if they did not participate? Why or why not?

Obtaining Informed Consent

Before you involve any human being in any kind of program evaluation, you must obtain the person's informed consent. The key word here is *informed*. The word *informed* means that all of your potential participants fully understand what is going to happen in the course of your study, why it's going to happen, and what its effect will be on them.

> **On informed consent . . .**
>
> *The key issue is informed consent so people know what they're getting into. Desperate people will go wherever hope is to be had, so it's important researchers know the benefits (of trials) are worth the risks to keep them safe.*
>
> *~ Tim Murphy*

If the people are psychiatrically challenged, mentally delayed, or in any other way incapable of full understanding, for example, your study must be fully and adequately explained to someone else who is very close to them—perhaps a parent, legal guardian, social worker, spouse, or someone to whom the participant's welfare is important. All written communications must be couched in simple language that all potential participants will understand—at an eighth-grade level.

It's clear that no potential participant may be bribed, threatened, deceived, or in any way coerced into participating in your evaluation. Questions must be encouraged, both initially and throughout the course of the project. People who believe they understand may have misinterpreted your explanation or understood it only in part. They may say they understand, when they do not, in an effort to avoid appearing foolish. They may even sign documents they do not understand to confirm their supposed understanding, and it's your responsibility to ensure that their understanding is real and complete.

It's extremely important for potential evaluation participants to know that they are not signing away their rights when they sign a consent form. They may decide at any time to withdraw from the study *without penalty*—without so much as a reproachful glance. When completed, the evaluation's results must also be made available to them.

Contents of an informed consent form. A written consent form should be only a part of the process of informing potential participants of their roles in your evaluation project and their rights as volunteers. Your consent form must give potential participants a basic description of the purpose of the evaluation, the evaluation's procedures, and their rights as voluntary participants. Certain bits of information must be provided in plain and simple language, including:

(a) That participants are being asked to participate in an evaluation study
(b) That their participation is voluntary and that they may discontinue participation at any time without penalty or loss of benefits to which they are otherwise entitled (e.g., in their standing as a patient, client, student, or employee)

(c) The purposes of the evaluation, simply explained

(d) What the procedures will be

(e) The expected duration of their participation

(f) Any reasonably foreseeable risks or discomforts

(g) Any safeguards to minimize the risks

(h) Any benefits to the participant or to others that may reasonably be expected from the evaluation study. In most cases, the study is not being performed for the benefit of the participants but for the potential benefit of others. This broader social benefit to the public should be made explicit.

(i) In cases where an incentive is offered, a description of the incentive and of how and under what conditions it is to be obtained

(j) Appropriate alternative procedures or courses of treatment, if applicable

(k) The extent, if any, to which confidentiality of records identifying the participant will be maintained (not an issue unless participants can be identified)

(l) Any restrictions on confidentiality (e.g., if any of the information gained during the study might have to be disclosed as required by law, as in instances of child abuse. In such cases, absolute confidentiality cannot be assured.)

(m) What monetary compensation or medical or psychological treatment will be provided for any "evaluation-related injury" (if more than minimal risk)

(n) The names of the evaluators and their official affiliations

(o) Contact information for questions about the study (name, office address, and phone contacts for the researcher, faculty advisor, and IRB staff). Do not include home phone numbers.

(p) That the evaluators will keep one copy of the signed consent form and give another signed copy to the participant

Using the aforementioned points, Box 5.1 provides an example of a consent letter that was written to elderly adults, a very vulnerable population. Working with vulnerable populations, in this case elderly adults, requires that you pay particular attention to ethical concerns that can arise during the consent process.

You must insure that your potential participants have sufficient knowledge and time to make an informed decision to participate in your project and that they are mentally and legally capable of doing so. For these reasons the evaluation contained in Box 5.1 offers two options for obtaining informed consent:

- Adults who are considered *mentally and legally competent* sign a consent form (e.g., Box 5.1).
- Individuals who are nonadults or mentally and/or legally incompetent and are under the care of a legal guardian sign an assent form (e.g., Box 5.2 *only after* a consent form from the person's legal guardian is signed).

Note that the legal guardian must first give permission for the person to participate in your project via a consent form. After a consent form is signed, then your potential evaluation participants decide on whether to participate via signing assent forms. This does not mean the person will chose to participate. In sum, a person can choose not to participate regardless of whether the person's legal guardian gave consent.

Regardless of their competency status, all of our potential participants followed the informed consent process outlined as follows:

- Introductory packets containing a letter of introduction, consent and assent forms, and a stamped, addressed response postcard was mailed to all individuals who met the study's eligibility criteria.
- These individuals were asked to contact a member of the evaluation team within 2 weeks of receiving the introductory packet to indicate their willingness to participate in the study.

BOX 5.1   EXAMPLE OF A CONSENT FORM
(NOTE: LETTERS IN BRACKETS CORRESPOND WITH THE CRITERIA IN TEXT.)

Project Description:
Comparison of Home and Community-Based Eldercare Programs Consent Form

You are invited to participate in a year-long evaluation study that explores the relative effectiveness of two home-based eldercare programs:

1. The Program of All Inclusive Care for the Elderly (PACE)
2. The Home and Community Based Services program (HCBS). **[a]**

What's the purpose of the study?

Both PACE and HCBS are social service programs that are designed to keep older adults such as yourself in their homes and out of nursing facilities. A brochure explaining both of these programs is attached to this consent form.

The purpose of this study is to determine which of these two eldercare programs, PACE or HCBS, is more effective at keeping elderly individuals at home. **[c]**

This study will interview you three times and will ask you about your:

1. Satisfaction and quality of life
2. Activities of daily living (dressing, bathing, mobility)
3. Emotional well-being
4. Utilization of hospital care

Your involvement in this study will provide valuable information that may help to determine future and effective methods to keep elderly persons in their homes.

Who's conducting this study?

This study is being conducted by graduate students enrolled in Western Michigan University's School of Social Work. The names and contact information for all members of the evaluation team can be found at the end of this consent form. **[n]**

Why are you asking me to participate in this study?

We are asking you to take part in this study because you meet the following three eligibility criteria:

1 You are 55 years of age or older
2 You meet the Michigan Medicare/Medicaid criteria to qualify for nursing facility level of care
3 You live within a PACE service area

Your participation in this study is completely voluntary. If you decide to take part in this study, you may withdraw your consent and remove yourself from the study at any time and without any penalty whatsoever. If you decide not to participate in this study, you will continue to receive your current level of care. **[b]**

What will I be asked to do?

If you choose to participate, you will be randomly assigned to one of three groups:

1 Group 1: These individuals receive services from the PACE program

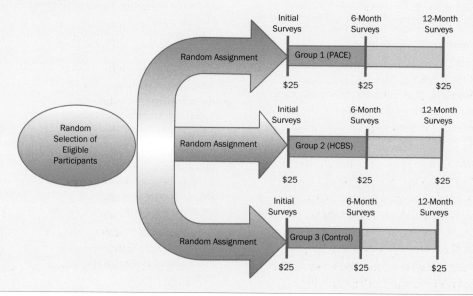

2 Group 2: These individuals receive services from the HCBS program

3 Group 3: These individuals do not receive any additional services

After you have been assigned to one of the three groups, you will be asked to take part in a series of three interviews. These interviews should take 1 hour or less to complete. You may choose not to answer any of the questions in any of the interviews without penalty.

Once you have completed the interviews, the individuals assigned to Groups 1 and 2 will begin receiving services through PACE and HCBS, respectively. These individuals will be interviewed again after receiving services for 6 months and after receiving services for 12 months.

The individuals assigned to Group 3 will be interviewed again 6 months and 12 months after the initial interview. **[d]** Your total time commitment for participating in all the interviews will be approximately 3 hours over the 12-month period. **[e]**

Will my privacy be protected?

Our evaluation team will take appropriate measures to insure that your privacy is protected. You will be assigned an identification number that will be used in place of your name. Names and identifying data will be kept in separate, secure files.

Data collected during the study will be kept in another secure file. These secure files will be stored in a locked room within the School of Social Work at Western Michigan University. Only members of the team will have access to these files.

All personal data will be destroyed at the end of the study. While the data you provide will be kept confidential, the results of this study may be published at a future date. **[k]**

Will my information be shared with others?

We will not share your information with anyone unless we believe that you are a danger to yourself or to another person. In that case, we are required by law to notify Adult Protective Services. **[l]**

What are the benefits to participating in this evaluation study?

If you are assigned to Group 1 or 2 you may receive care that improves your health and quality of life. Additionally, the data gathered during this study may prove beneficial to other elderly adults in Kalamazoo County. **[h]**

Compensation

You will receive $25 in cash before each interview. You may keep the cash and elect not to be interviewed. **[i]**

What are the risks associated with participating in this study?

It's important that you understand that you may be randomly assigned to Group 3, the group that does not receive any additional services. It's possible that you could experience a decline in either your physical or emotional health if you participate in this group. **[f]**

Continuing to see your doctor(s) on a regular basis may help to minimize these risks. If you do experience a decline in your health, you are free to end your participation in the study at any time without penalty. **[g]**

You may also contact, Elsie Evaluator (xxx-xxx-xxxx), a member of our evaluation team who will assist you in locating the resources needed to address your concerns. **[m]**

It's also important that you are aware that there are other eldercare programs available. A member of our team will discuss these alternatives with you prior to the beginning of the study. **[j]**

Considering Your Options

It's important that you take time to decide whether you are interested in participating in our study. You may want to discuss it with your family, friends, or one of your health care providers. You can also make a call collect phone call to any member of the team with questions or to indicate your willingness to take part in this study.

If you decide to take part in this study, a member of our team will meet with you to review this consent form and to obtain your signature. Our evaluation team will keep the original signed consent form, and you will be given a copy of the signed consent form for your records. **[p]**

By signing below you are indicating that you understand the contents of this consent form and agree to participate in our study.

Participant's signature
Participant's printed name
Name of person obtaining consent
Today's date

Contact Information [o]

Elsie Evaluator
Western Michigan University
Elsie.Evaluator@wmich.edu
Phone: xxx-xxx-xxxx

Edward Evaluator
Western Michigan University
Edward.Evaluator@wmich.edu
Phone: xxx-xxx-xxxx

BOX 5.2 EXAMPLE OF AN ASSENT FORM
(NOTE: LETTERS IN BRACKETS CORRESPOND WITH THE CRITERIA IN TEXT)

Project Description:
Comparison of Home and Community-Based Eldercare Programs Assent Form

- I have been invited to take part in a year-long evaluation study that will compare two home-based care programs for older adults:
  - The Program of All Inclusive Care for the Elderly (PACE)
  - The Home and Community Based Services program (HCBS). **[a]**
- The purpose of this study is to determine which of these two programs, PACE or HCBS, is better at keeping older adults in their own homes and out of nursing homes. **[c]**
- The data gathered during this study may help other elderly adults in Kalamazoo County. **[h]**
- This study is being conducted by graduate students from Western Michigan University's School of Social Work. Names and contact information for all members of the evaluation team are listed at the end of this form.
- I can contact any member of the team if I have any questions about this study. **[n]**
- Participating in this study is completely voluntary. If I take part in this study, I can change my mind at any time and stop participating without being penalized in any way. **[b]**
- During this study I will be randomly assigned to one of three groups:
  1 Group 1: People in this group will receive services from the PACE program.

- 2 Group 2: People in this group will receive services from the HCBS program.
- 3 Group 3: People in this group will not receive any additional services.
- After I have been assigned to a group I will be asked to complete interviews that will be offered three times:
  1 At the beginning of the study
  2 Six months after the study begins
  3 Twelve months after the study begins **[d]**
- I will spend approximately 3 hours of my time during the next year taking part in this study. **[e]**
- Each time I am interviewed my legal guardian will be paid $25 in cash. My legal guardian will still be paid $25 each time I am interviewed even if I choose not to answer some of the questions. **[i]**
- I do not have to answer any of the questions if I do not want to. I will not be penalized in any way if I decide not to answer any question.
- If I am assigned to Group 1 or Group 2, I can choose not to take part in any of the services offered by either PACE or HCBS. I will not be penalized in any way if I choose not to take part in the services offered.
- I understand that if I am assigned to Group 3, I will not receive any new eldercare services. My health may become worse because of this. **[f]**
- I understand that it's important that I continue to see my doctor(s) regularly in order to help reduce this risk. **[g]**

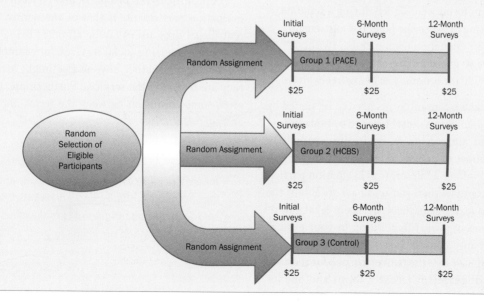

- If I decide to take part in this study and my health becomes worse, I can call a member of the evaluation team, Elsie Evaluator (xxx-xxx-xxxx), for help. **[m]**
- I understand that there are other eldercare programs available. A member of the evaluation team will talk with me about these other programs before this study begins. **[j]**
- My name will not be used during this study. I will be assigned a number to replace my name. **[k]**
- My privacy will be protected unless members of the evaluation team believe that I might hurt myself or someone else. If that happens, the evaluation team will have to tell my guardian and Adult Protective Services. **[l]**
- Results from this study may be shared with the general public at some time in the future.
- My signature on this assent form shows that I have read, or had someone read me, this form and that I agree to take part in this study.

- The evaluation team will keep the original, signed assent form, and I will be given a copy of this form to keep. **[p]**

Participant's signature
Participant's printed name
Name of person obtaining consent
Today's date

Contact Information [o]
Elsie Evaluator
Western Michigan University
Elsie.Evaluator@wmich.edu
Phone: xxx-xxx-xxxx

Edward Evaluator
Western Michigan University
Edward.Evaluator@wmich.edu
Phone: xxx-xxx-xxxx

- Within 2 weeks of receiving a positive response, a member of the evaluation team met with the interested individual (and his/her legal guardian if relevant) to review the consent/assent forms, answer any questions the individual had regarding the study, and obtained a signature on the consent form. Information on alternative eldercare programs was provided at that time.
- Assent forms were signed during a separate meeting between the potential participant and an evaluation team member (without the legal guardian present) to insure that the individual's consent was being freely given.

In a nutshell, consent forms need to be signed by adults and assent forms must be signed by nonadults—children and adolescents or, as in our example, a legally incompetent person. If your study is going to use children and/or adolescents as evaluation participants, for example, then you will have to obtain the consent of at least one of their parents or legal guardians (via consent forms) in addition to your evaluation participants' consent (via assent forms). In this case you will have to write two forms: one for the adolescents' legal guardians (consent form) and one for the adolescents (assent form).

Writing consent and assent forms takes time—lots of it. Never underestimate how much time it will take. Always pilot test your draft forms with a few potential evaluation participants to obtain their reactions and suggestions. These can then be used to refine your forms.

Anonymity Versus Confidentiality

A promise that is of a particular concern to many evaluation participants is that of anonymity. A current illegal drug user may be afraid of being identified. Folks receiving social services, for example, may be concerned whether anyone else might learn that they are receiving the services. Furthermore, there is often some confusion between the terms *anonymity* and *confidentiality*.

On confidentiality . . .

If I were to make public these tapes, containing blunt and candid remarks on many different subjects, the confidentiality of the office of the president would always be suspect.

~ Richard M. Nixon

Some evaluation studies are designed so that no one, not even the person doing the study, knows which evaluation participant gave what response. An example is a mailed survey form bearing no identifying marks and asking the respondent not to provide a name. In a study like this, the respondent is *anonymous.*

It's more often the case, however, that we do in fact know how a particular participant responded and have agreed not to divulge the information to anyone else. In such cases, the information is considered *confidential.* Part of our explanation to a potential evaluation participant must include a clear statement of what information will be shared and with whom (e.g., Boxes 5.1, 5.2).

Ensuring confidentiality. The first step in the process for ensuring confidentiality is often to assign a code number to each participant. The researcher and her assistants alone know that Ms. Smith, for example, is number 132. All data concerning Ms. Smith are then combined with data from all the other participants to produce summary aggregated results that do not identify Ms. Smith in any way. No one reading the final evaluation report or any publication stemming from it will know that Ms. Smith took part in the study at all.

Sometimes, however, complete confidentiality cannot be guaranteed. In a study undertaken in a small community, for example, direct quotes from an interview with "a" social worker may narrow the field to three because there are only three social workers there. The flavor of the quote may narrow it again to Mr. Jones, who said the same thing in church last Sunday. If there is any risk that Mr. Jones might be recognized as the author of the quote, then this possibility must be clearly acknowledged in the letter of consent that Mr. Jones is asked to sign.

Although the ideal is to obtain written consent from the potential participant before the study begins, it's not always possible to obtain the consent in writing. In a telephone interview, for example, the information that would have been contained in a consent letter is usually read to the participant, and oral consent is obtained over the phone. A mailed questionnaire that is sent out usually has an accompanying introductory letter that contains a statement that filling out the questionnaire and sending it back constitutes consent.

Bribery, deception, and other forms of coercion. It goes without saying that consent must never be obtained through bribery, threats, deception, or any form of coercion. You may feel insulted that such a possibility should even be mentioned in a text addressed to social workers, but consider what constitutes bribery. For example, if you offer $200, as an "honorarium," to the chief executive officer of an agency to persuade her to take part in your study, this is bribery.

> *On deception...*
>
> *It is double pleasure to deceive the deceiver.*
>
> ~ *Niccolo Machiavelli*

If you want to know how your evaluation participants *really* behave when no one else is looking, you will have to deceive them into believing that they are *not* being watched. You might think you can do this using an interviewing room with a one-way mirror, or you might pretend to be an ordinary member of a group when you are, in fact, a glint-eyed observer. Neither of these behaviors is ethically acceptable.

The only conditions under which deception might be tolerated—and it's a very large *might*—are when the data to be obtained are vitally important and there is no other way to get them. If you can persuade the various ethics committees that review your program evaluation proposal that both of these conditions exist, you *might* be given permission to carry out the study.

Even then, you would have to be sure that the deception was thoroughly explained to all the participants when the study was over (discussed later) and that arrangements had been made—free counseling, for example—to counter any harm they might have suffered.

Last but not least there are threats. No evaluator would ever persuade potential participants to

cooperate by threatening that, if they do not participate, worse things will befall them. But a *perceived*
threat, even if not intended, can have the same effect.
For example, a woman awaiting an abortion may
agree to provide private and very personal information about herself and her partner because she believes
that, if she does not, she will be denied the abortion.
It's of no use to tell her that this is not true; she may
simply feel she is not in a position to take any chances.
Her beliefs are her reality, not yours.

There are captive populations in prisons, schools,
and institutions who may agree out of sheer boredom
to take part in an evaluation study. Or they may participate in return for certain privileges or because they
fear some reprisal. There may be people who agree
because they are pressured into it by family members,
or they want to please their social workers, or they need
some service or payment that they believe depends on
their cooperation. Often, situations like this cannot be
changed, but at least you can be aware of them and do
your best to deal with them in an ethical manner.

Example 1. As we know from our earlier discussion,
deception can be tricky. Let's consider an example to
illustrate this point. José wanted to study racial/ethnic
bias in employment practices in family service agencies in Chicago. He mailed numerous fake application letters to all family service agencies in Chicago
that had current openings for full-time clinicians. He
sent the exact same qualifications, but he changed his
name to reflect four different groups of people: African
American, Latino, Asian, and Irish heritages. In short,
everything was exactly the same except his name.

José planned to simply count the number of
interview requests he received, broken down by each
group. Sounds harmless, you say? Read on.

In no way in his cover letter for employment did
José indicate he was conducting a research study. To
José's surprise, all of Chicago's executive directors of
family service agencies met at a local conference and
started talking about good job candidates they were
going to follow up on. José's name came up several
times in the conversation.

The executive directors soon became angry when
they found out they had been duped by José. Several
executive directors had not interviewed other qualified individuals because they were holding slots open
so that they could interview José when time permitted.

José, his school, his dean, and the federal government all became involved in addressing the consequences of his unethical use of deception. José's
actions ignored a key concept of our *Code of Ethics*:
whether acting as a practitioner, researcher, or evaluator, social workers are mandated to act with integrity
and in a trustworthy manner.

Generally it's good practice to avoid deception
whenever possible. Although it sounds reasonable to
say that good social work evaluators should *never* lie
to their potential participants or provide them with
less than a full disclosure about the methods of their
studies, in reality this is not always desirable.

Example 2. As an example, a social worker assessing bias toward developmentally delayed clients by
staff employed at correctional institutions initially
might not want to disclose the entire purpose of the
study because it might affect how the custodial staff
responds. We need to ask the ethical question: Is
deception absolutely necessary to carry out the study?
In other words, is deception necessary to prevent participants from trying to respond in a contrived and/or
socially desirable manner?

Next, we need to ask whether there is a possibility
that the deception will harm the participants, in either
the short or long term. If the deception causes or encourages participants to react in ways they might not otherwise, or allows them to make choices at odds with their
personal beliefs (e.g., a decision-making study that allows
a participant to lie, cheat, or steal), learning later about
their behavior might be psychologically distressing.

Our *Code of Ethics* mandates not only that we
protect our participants from mental distress but also
that we protect our clients from all harm to the fullest extent possible. The majority of deception that is
approved in evaluation studies is of minimal risk to
participants and is far less dramatic than José's study
of racial/ethnic bias in hiring practices.

For example, Jennifer would have been wiser if she
had used *more* deception in her study that monitored
children's seat-belt use on school buses. Climbing onto

a school bus after the young children had boarded, she cheerfully announced, "I am doing a study for your principal, and I'm counting the number of safe and smart children on this bus who buckle up!"

In this one simple, very honest sentence she immediately gave away the purpose of her study, which resulted in an immediate flurry of seat-belt–buckling behaviors—thus defeating her ability to get an accurate and realistic count of those children who would not have buckled up if it weren't for her disclosure of the study. On another topic: Do you think Jennifer needed permission from the children's parents to do her simple head count on the bus? Why or why not? After all, the children were minors.

Debriefing. One of the ways in which we can appropriately counteract the use of deception is by using debriefing procedures after our study is over. Debriefing involves explaining the true purpose of our study to the participants after our study is completed, along with why the deception was necessary. If there is a concern about psychological distress as a result of having been deceived by the study, then participants must be offered adequate means of addressing this distress.

In some cases of minimal-risk studies that involve deception, debriefing participants about the true nature of the study and their responses may cause greater distress than not fully understanding their actions in the study. In addition, experienced mental health professionals and IRBs might disagree on whether distressing self-knowledge can be mitigated effectively and how this should best be done, or they may even decide that the study should not be conducted given the psychological risks to potential participants. One possible way that our *Code of Ethics* offers to mitigate the situation is to offer participants "appropriate supportive services" after the study.

Step 4b: Selecting a Data Collection Method

Selecting a data collection method contains three ethical issues that surround the following:

- How data are collected
- Who collects the data
- The frequency and timing of data collection

How Data Are Collected

As we will see in Tool H, our choice of how to collect the data that best answer our evaluation question can introduce unintended bias, coercing some and potentially excluding other desired participants. Awareness is the key to understanding the ethical implications of data collection.

For example, Aisha wants to do a follow-up study with juveniles released from custody in her state's detention facilities. She goes about conducting a home phone survey during the hours she is at work (standard business hours) and calls the youths' "home" phone numbers. She is unaware that she is missing youths who have the following characteristics:

- Do not have land-line phones
- Have land-line phones but simply do not answer them
- Do not hang out at home during the day
- Operate primarily from cell phones

In addition, she might inadvertently inform housemates who answer that the person being called was formerly detained.

One of Aisha's colleagues, Barbara, is using an "anonymous" Internet-based survey to examine the educational aspirations of young adults. As part of her study, she asks participants about their recreational drug use and about any knowledge they might have about their parents' recreational use of illegal substances.

Although she does not ask for names or other identifying information, it's possible to trace respondents by their computers' Internet protocol (IP) addresses. Barbara forgot that all evaluators must protect their participants' identities, just as practitioners must protect clients' privacies, according to our *Code of Ethics.*

Further, although the youths have consented to participate via completion of the Internet survey itself, Barbara also was gathering data about the youths' parents. The parents have *not* consented to have their children give Barbara data about them.

Collecting data about parental substance abuse via their children without the parents' consent is not a good idea to say the least. A situation similar to this one resulted in the temporary shutdown of all federal research at one eastern university after an irate parent contacted the U.S. Department of Human Services' Office of Human Research Protection.

Who Collects the Data

Determining who is actually going to collect the data constitutes yet another ethical decision to be made. Anyone in a position of power or authority over the participant, such as teachers, social workers, health-care officials, administrators—anyone who can either supply or deny the resources that evaluation participants need—introduces the potential for undue influence. Coercion can easily result in less-than-willing participation.

It also may influence the quality of the data collected because the participants may respond differently than they normally would if they believe that individuals who have authority over them may see their responses. Paper-and-pencil surveys about anger and urges to act impulsively that are completed by clients arrested for interpersonal violence are an example. Our *Code of Ethics* also asserts that the presence of coercion violates the tenets of voluntary participation in both practice and research/evaluation activities.

Frequency and Timing of Data Collection

Finally, the choice we make about the frequency and timing of data collection activities also may raise privacy issues. Some evaluation designs require, by their very nature, to collect data from participants after the main part of the study has been completed. In situations such as these, the consent and/or assent letter(s) (e.g., Boxes 5.1, 5.2) must inform potential evaluation participants that they will be contacted in the future.

Step 4c: Analyzing the Data

Data analysis and, indeed, even drawing conclusions about data results is, unfortunately, one step in the evaluation process that many social workers most often wish to outsource or turn over to others. Those of us who are not "research oriented" are often unfamiliar with data analyses beyond basic statistics and may avoid reading the results section of journal articles. We simply skip ahead to the discussion section and assume that the author has reviewed what is most important.

We rely heavily on the peer review process in professional publications for assurance that appropriate methods of data analysis are used, but does this excuse us? Some have suggested that ethical data analyses begin with our moral responsibility to *understand* the analyses that data undergo before we make use of the evaluation's results.

Ethical problems in data analyses are rooted, broadly speaking, in the evaluation environment. Don't be more invested in supporting your theories than in testing them! The evaluator's personal attachment to specific theories, followed by the importance of obtaining statistical significance so that the study's results can be published or receive other indicators of peer approval, are real parts of the evaluation environment.

> *On quantitative data …*
>
> *You can use all the quantitative data you can get, but you still have to distrust it and use your own intelligence and judgment.*
>
> ~ *Alvin Toffler*

Our common understanding of an evaluation's "success" is based on the outcomes of the study; that is, whether the study's findings supported the study's hypotheses. Hearing an evaluator say the project did not "turn out" generally means that the results did not support the evaluator's expectations.

The following are guidelines related to data analysis. Social workers wishing to employ ethical analysis strategies should incorporate these principles into their own work:

- Research findings and results should be presented openly and honestly. This includes avoiding leaving out or omitting contradictory findings.

- Untrue or deceptive statements should be avoided in reports.
- The limits and boundaries of inference used should be delineated clearly. This may include considerations of the subjects sampled for participation or the levels of experimental variables.
- Complete and clear documentation should be provided, including how the data were edited, the statistical procedures used, and the assumptions made about the data.
- The role of the data analyst ideally is neutral so that statistical procedures may be applied without concern for a favorable outcome.

STEP 6: ENSURE USAGE AND SHARE LESSONS LEARNED

The final step, writing and disseminating the evaluation report, is fraught with potential ethical dilemmas. First, we often neglect to write a report and disseminate the findings of our evaluation studies. Somehow we get caught up in our busy schedules and the need to move on to the next project, and we fail to attend to this crucial last step. Not reporting our study's findings is a disservice to everyone who participated in and funded the study.

Moreover, our *Code of Ethics* calls for us to facilitate informed participation in the general community for shaping public social policy and human service institutions, as well as to engage in social and political action ourselves. Depending on the nature of the evaluation study, the findings might be important in advocating for social justice for our constituents, such as providing equal access to benefits and resources that will meet their basic needs and allow them to realize their full potential.

In addition to reporting to the community at large, we have a responsibility to report our findings to our participants and the community that is supposed to benefit from our study's findings. In particular, if our recruitment process involved promising to make a report available to potential evaluation participants, it's critical that we share our findings with them in clear and understandable language.

There are a host of methods for disseminating evaluation findings, including short summaries, journal articles, books, press releases, flyers, posters, brochures, letters of thanks to study participants, newsletters, local conferences, and seminars. Social workers need to consider the goal of the reporting and the needs of the target audience in selecting a distribution method.

For a broader audience, we need to find ways to make the content comprehensible and interesting. We need to be good storytellers when communicating our findings, while taking care not to distort them. As we will see in the following chapter, we must find culturally sensitive ways to report our evaluation's findings to both our participants and communities alike, when appropriate.

Our *Code of Ethics* also provides a thorough discussion of the importance of protecting clients' right to privacy. Providing feedback to our participants, while still maintaining their confidentiality, can be challenging in certain situations. To illustrate, our participants may have been in domestic violence shelters, mental health institutions, or juvenile justice placements and then returned home or released to more open settings. Simply obtaining a current address is often difficult, but even when the address is obtained, involuntary clients often do not want others to know that they have received social services. Hence they may not wish to receive an official report that, in some way, labels them as affiliated with a particular agency or service.

A cover letter thanking a woman for her involvement in an interpersonal violence study can "out" the participant and may even create a dangerous situation. Incarcerated youth, who were once eager to see the results of a study they participated in, may feel awkward and embarrassed 18 months later when the mailed report arrives at their homes.

Revealing Negative Findings

Another ethical dilemma that we sometimes face arises when there is conflict between the participants' program, policymakers, advocacy groups, and/or the group that funded the study. If stakeholders are displeased with certain findings, or with the way in which the evaluator has interpreted the findings, it can seriously complicate their dissemination. Our *Code of Ethics* highlights our responsibility to report our study's findings accurately—and, it should go without saying, not to fabricate the results.

> *On writing . . .*
>
> *I love being a writer. What I can't stand is the paperwork.*
>
> *~ Peter De Vries*

To the extent possible, we should come to some general agreement about how these issues will be resolved in the early stages of planning our study. In fact, our *Code of Ethics* cautions us to identify potential conflicts of interest, inform participants if a real or potential conflict of interest develops, and place primary importance on the participants' interests in resolving any conflicts of interest.

Often, the sharing of findings will be a delicate matter. Agency staff may be reluctant to hear, for example, that their program is less effective than they thought. If they were not engaged in the evaluation process in the first place and they know little about evaluation methodologies, they may be tempted to dismiss the findings and block any attempt on the part of the evaluator to discuss recommendations for improvement. Findings must be presented carefully, therefore, to the right people, in the right order, and at the right time.

Practitioners wrestle every day with a similar problem. Mr. Yen might not want to be told that his daughter is still threatening to run away despite all those parenting classes and family therapy sessions he attended. His daughter might not want him to know. His wife might not want him to know either in case this bit of data spurs him to inappropriate disciplinary steps. The social worker must decide whom to tell, as well as how, when, and how much. The same holds true when doing program evaluations.

SPECIAL CONSIDERATIONS

As communication becomes easier and the world a smaller place in many ways, more research needs and opportunities present themselves. For example, social workers may work with political and criminal prisoners, individuals with serious and persistent mental disorders or impaired cognitive functioning, refugees and internally displaced persons, and women and children who have been trafficked.

Social workers assessing needs and developing practice methods in global arenas require accurate information about the problems and the contexts in which these problems occur. This section addresses only a few of the ethical issues that surround three special considerations:

- International research
- Computer and Internet-based research guidance
- Students as subjects/students as researchers

International Research

Many social workers engage in international research. Our colleague Naselle, for example, is carrying out an HIV/AIDS risk reduction program in Kazakhstan with multiple-risk women. In order to do her research study, Naselle had to obtain permission from her own university, as well as from the minister of health in Kazakhstan and the national research ethics board there. In her home university's IRB application, Naselle was required to provide evidence that her research methods were culturally sensitive and appropriate and had been approved locally.

Depending on the level of risk associated with an international study, a researcher may need to demonstrate a sophisticated understanding of the country, culture, and customs before approval is granted to conduct the study. Our *Code of Ethics* reinforces this notion by mandating that social workers engage in culturally competent practice that respects diversity.

Computer and Internet-Based Research Guidance

Research with human subjects using Internet-based methods is a fast-developing data collection method used in social and behavioral sciences. The Internet provides efficient access and the ability to collect widely distributed information. Internet-based research must address the same risks—including violation of privacy, legal risks, and psychosocial stress—and must provide the same level of protection as other types of research involving human research participants. Recruitment procedures should follow institutional guidelines (usually found in IRB guidance) for recruiting research participants from traditional media such as newspapers and bulletin boards. Unsolicited e-mail messages to multiple users may be prohibited, and accurate disclosure of message origin and author is required in most cases.

Box 5.3 displays an excellent example of how a social work researcher obtained informed consent for his Internet-based research study. His request went out to over 1,500 social work educators who were signed up on the BSW List Serve at the time.

Researchers are advised to authenticate respondents, taking steps to assign participants personal

---

BOX 5.3 EXAMPLE OF OBTAINING INFORMED CONSENT FOR AN INTERNET-BASED RESEARCH STUDY

From: Allan Barsky <abarsky@fau.edu>
To: BPD-L@list.iupui.edu
Re: The Place of Faith in Social Work Education
Date: January 12, 2013: 7:29 PM

_____
_____
_____
_____
_____

The Place of Faith in Social Work Education:
Request for Your Consent to Participate in This Survey

Primary Investigator: Dr. Allan Barsky, School of Social Work, Florida Atlantic University

I am emailing to request your voluntary participation in a 26-question, online survey that should take 15 to 30 minutes to complete.

The purpose of this survey is to explore social work educators' views about the place of faith in social work education. The findings from this survey will be used to facilitate discussion on the place of faith in social work education with participants of the upcoming Baccalaureate Program Directors conference in Myrtle Beach, SC (March 2013), and perhaps at future social work conferences. The feedback from the survey may also be used to develop an article to be published in a scholarly social work journal.

I have emailed this request to you as a social work educator, whether you are in a teaching or administrative position. If you would like another member of your school or department to complete this survey, feel free to forward this request to that person.

Most of the questions are 5-point Likert-Type Scale Questions in which you'll be asked the extent to which you agree or disagree with certain statements. You will also have an opportunity to provide additional comments to present your views.

Feel free to answer any or all of the questions in this survey. You are also free to withdraw from the study at any time without penalty. The risks involved with participating in this study are no more than one would experience in regular daily activities. Potential benefits that you may receive from participation include helping you articulate your beliefs about the place of faith in social work education. Also, you will be contributing to an ongoing dialogue among social work educators on this topic.

I am not collecting any identifying information. I am using the encryption function on the online survey program (Google Docs) to prevent myself from having access to information about which computer or which IP address is submitting the survey. Although Google Docs has strict confidentiality and database security provisions in place, please note that there is always a possibility with Internet research that transmitted data can be intercepted by others.

If you experience problems or have questions regarding your rights as a research subject, you may contact the Florida Atlantic University

Division of Research at (561) 297-0777. For other questions about the study, please call me, the principal investigator, at (954) 558-5535 or email abarsky@fau.edu.

By completing clicking on the link below that says, "PLEASE CLICK HERE TO TAKE THE SURVEY" you will be giving consent to participate in this study. Thank you.

PLEASE CLICK HERE TO TAKE THE SURVEY

If this hyperlink does not work, you may cut and paste the following URL into your web browser:

https://docs.google.com/spreadsheet/view form?fromEmail=true&formkey=dCO3VFJ5cE hSYzIwZIZxekw1ZIVYdkE6MQ identification numbers to be used in any follow-up data collection endeavors. Data encryption is important for transmission, and acceptable software varies across countries. Whenever possible, using a professionally administered server is encouraged.

Finally, storing and destroying data also involve dual focus on privacy and technological methods. The goal is to provide the same level of protection to human subjects as with more traditional data collection methodologies.

Students as Subjects/Students as Researchers

The final special situations we briefly address are students as participants or subjects in research studies, and then students as researchers themselves.

Students who participate in agency or university research are a vulnerable group, subject to coercion and influence by faculty, their peers, their field instructors, and agency administrators alike. Students should be particularly well informed about the limits of privacy and confidentiality and should have a thorough understanding of the research goals and procedures prior to giving consent to participate. As with any research participant, students must be given the right to freely refuse participation without fear of adverse consequences in order for consent to be considered voluntary and informed.

Without such assurances, the research study does not meet the standards in our *Code of Ethics*. Research studies carried out by one's own classroom instructor or

---

BOX 5.4 HEART'S IN THE RIGHT PLACE BUT HEAD ISN'T

A beginning graduate social work student, Margaret, wants to recruit clients (evaluation participants) for an evaluation study. In her field practicum, Margaret is helping her professor recruit families for a study aimed at providing an intervention to improve the parenting skills of pregnant and parenting teenagers. She recruits potential participants at the local public social services office (her practicum setting), where the pregnant teenagers meet weekly with their child protection workers.

According to the study's recruitment protocol, recruitment takes place via colorful flyers handed out to clients by the receptionist as they enter the agency. The clients are asked by the receptionist to talk with Margaret to get further information on an "important study" in which they may wish to participate.

One day, Margaret notices a young pregnant teenager crying in the waiting room and asks her if she can do anything to help. Listening to her story, Margaret unwittingly finds herself strongly encouraging the teen to participate in the program (a new intervention, yet to be tested) by telling her how much the program would improve her parenting skills. She also suggests that her participation in the study would favorably impress the teen's social worker.

See Anything Wrong Here?

At this point, do you see anything wrong with Margaret's behaviors? Margaret responded to the teen's sad story based on what she believed to be in the teen's best interests, that is, participating in the study. Margaret tried to increase the teen's motivation to participate by telling her

it will improve her parenting skills.

In addition, Margaret asserts that the teen's participation would favorably impact the child protection worker's assessment of her. While Margaret's intentions may be understandable to the novice, she has in fact violated numerous ethical principles in one brief, 3-minute conversation. More specifically, and in no particular order, Margaret:

1. assumed she understood the teen's problem without conducting an adequate assessment
2. did not fully disclose to the teen the purpose of the study
3. exerted coercive influence over the teen to participate by telling her the program will work for her without actually knowing if it would; in fact, that's what the study was all about—finding out if the program worked in the first place
4. suggested that the teen's participation in the study would favorably affect the worker's perception of her
5. did not realize that the teen may have felt that she had to participate in the study to receive the services she was asking for in the first place
6. did not tell the teen that she may be randomly assigned to a control group (those who do not receive the treatment) and thus may receive no intervention whatsoever (at this time, that is)
7. did not obtain the consent of the teen's parents or legal guardian
8. did not obtain the teen's assent

field instructor may violate ethical research guidelines. According to our *Code of Ethics*, this situation may create a conflict of interest and fail to protect the best interests of the student/participant. Carrying out your own research project as a student, however, can be very exciting.

In that case as well, however, you are entitled to guidance and protection from your university and faculty in the ethical as well as methodological conduct of research. A faculty member should carefully review any student research proposal involving human subjects prior to its submission to the IRB. At many universities, students are considered "protected" within the university structure.

Therefore, the signing faculty sponsor ultimately is responsible for the ethical conduct of the student's research project. As a student, you have the right to receive education about how to ethically conduct an evaluation study.

By now you should be familiar with the ethical principles that need to be taken into account when doing an evaluation of some kind. This is an excellent time to see if you can point them out within the vignette contained in Box 5.4.

SUMMARY

This chapter briefly reviewed the ethical factors that affect Steps 3, 4, and 6 of the social work evaluation enterprise. By now you should know the place that program evaluations have in our profession (Chapter 1), what the quality improvement process is all about (Chapter 2), how the evaluation process unfolds (Chapter 3), the basics of the evaluation standards (Chapter 4), and how to behave in an ethical manner when doing an evaluation study (this chapter).

Since you are now a knowledgeable and ethical evaluator, you need to become a culturally sensitive one as well—the topic of the following chapter..

The goal of this chapter is to provide you with a beginning knowledge base for you to feel comfortable in answering the following questions. AFTER you have read the chapter, indicate how comfortable you feel you are in answering each of the following questions on a 5-point scale where

1	2	3	4	5
Very uncomfortable	Somewhat uncomfortable	Neutral	Somewhat comfortable	Very comfortable

If you rated any question between 1–3, reread the section of the chapter where the information for the question is found. If you still feel that you're uncomfortable in answering the question, then talk with your instructor and/or your classmates for more clarification.

	Questions	Degree of comfort? *(Circle one number)*
1	Discuss how you would *engage* your stakeholder groups to ensure your evaluation was ethical. Then describe how you would do this in relation to your field placement (or work setting).	1 2 3 4 5
2	Describe how you would *utilize* your stakeholder groups to help you cover all the ethical issues that may arise when you focus your evaluation (Step 3). Then describe how you would do this in relation to your field placement (or work setting).	1 2 3 4 5
3	Describe how you would *utilize* your stakeholder groups to help you cover all the ethical issues that may arise when you select an evaluation design (Step 3a). Then describe how you would do this in relation to your field placement (or work setting).	1 2 3 4 5
4	In your own words, describe *equipoise*, or the uncertainty principle.	1 2 3 4 5
5	Describe how you would *utilize* your stakeholder groups to help you cover all the ethical issues that may arise when it comes time to measuring your variables (Step 3b). Then describe how you would do this in relation to your field placement (or work setting).	1 2 3 4 5
6	Describe how you would *utilize* your stakeholder groups to help you cover all the cultural issues that may arise within your evaluation (Step 3b). Then describe how you would do this in relation to your field placement (or work setting).	1 2 3 4 5
7	Describe how you would *utilize* your stakeholder groups to help you cover all the ethical issues that may arise when you start to think about selecting evaluation participants (Step 4a). Then describe how you would do this in relation to your field placement (or work setting).	1 2 3 4 5

	Study Questions for Chapter **5** Continued	
8	Describe how you would *utilize* your stakeholder groups to help you cover all the ethical issues that may arise when you draft informed consent forms (Step 4a). Then describe how you would do this in relation to your field placement (or work setting).	1 2 3 4 5
9	List all the necessary statements that must go into an informed consent form (Step 4a).	1 2 3 4 5
10	Discuss the differences between anonymity and confidentiality. How would you go about ensuring your evaluation participants confidentiality? anonymity?	1 2 3 4 5
11	Describe *debriefing*. When would you use this technique within an evaluation?	1 2 3 4 5
12	Describe how you would *utilize* your stakeholder groups to help you cover all the ethical issues that may arise when you start to think about selecting a data collection method (Step 4b). Then describe how you would do this in relation to your field placement (or work setting).	1 2 3 4 5
13	List and discuss the three main ethical issues that must be taken into account when selecting a data collection strategy (Step 4b).	1 2 3 4 5
14	Describe how you would *utilize* your stakeholder groups to help you cover all the ethical issues that may arise when you start to think about the process of analyzing your data (Step 4c). Then describe how you would do this in relation to your field placement (or work setting).	1 2 3 4 5
15	Describe how you would *utilize* your stakeholder groups to help you cover all the ethical issues that may arise when you start to write your final evaluation report (Step 6). Then describe how you would do this in relation to your field placement (or work setting).	1 2 3 4 5

AFTER you have read this chapter AND have completed all of the study questions, indicate how knowledgeable you feel you are for each of the following concepts on a 5-point scale where

1	2	3	4	5
Not knowledgeable at all	Somewhat unknowledgeable	Neutral	Somewhat knowledgeable	Very knowledgeable

	Concepts	Knowledge Level? *(Circle one number)*
1	The NASW's *Code of Ethics*	1 2 3 4 5
2	The ethical issues that must be addressed when you focus your evaluation	1 2 3 4 5
3	The ethical issues that must be addressed when you select an evaluation design	1 2 3 4 5
4	The concept of *equipoise*	1 2 3 4 5
5	The ethical issues that must be addressed when you specify how your variables are to be measured	1 2 3 4 5
6	The ethical issues that must be addressed when you select evaluation participants	1 2 3 4 5
7	Informed consent procedures	1 2 3 4 5
8	Informed assent procedures	1 2 3 4 5
9	Ingredients of informed consent and assent forms	1 2 3 4 5
10	Anonymity and confidentiality	1 2 3 4 5
11	Bribery, deception, and other forms of coercion	1 2 3 4 5
12	Debriefing tactics	1 2 3 4 5
13	The ethical issues that must be addressed when you select a data collection method	1 2 3 4 5
14	The ethical issues that must be addressed when you analyze your data	1 2 3 4 5
15	The ethical issues that must be addressed when you ensure usage of your evaluation findings and share lessons learned	1 2 3 4 5
	Add up your scores (minimum = 15, maximum = 75)	Your total score =

A 71–75 = Professional evaluator in the making
A– 67–70 = Senior evaluator
B+ 63–66 = Junior evaluator
B 60–62 = Assistant evaluator
B– 15–59 = Reread the chapter and redo the study questions

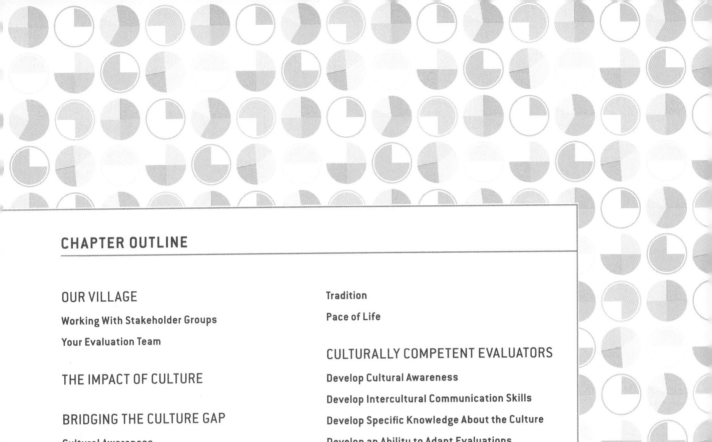

CHAPTER OUTLINE

*A nation's culture resides in the hearts
and in the soul of its people.*

~ Mahatma Gandhi

Chapter 6

CULTURAL COMPETENCE

CAROL ING

Using the five previous chapters as a background, this chapter explores a few of the cultural issues that also need to be taken into account when doing an evaluation. As you know from reading the previous chapter on ethics, many cultural and ethical issues are intertwined with one another.

This chapter is a logical extension of the previous one in that we provide a brief overview of culture and cultural competence, followed by a discussion of key issues in culturally competent evaluation practices. As the issues are discussed, we make use of examples of worldview perceptions, communications, and behaviors that may be characteristic of particular cultures. These are intended only as examples of cultural patterns and are not intended to suggest that any characteristics describe all members of the group.

We fully recognize that cultures are not monolithic and that a variety of cultural patterns may exist within broadly defined cultural groups. The descriptions provided within this chapter are for illustrative purposes only and are not meant to be stereotypical of the members of any culture.

We also know that each individual is unique, and we recognize that within any culture a wide range of individual perceptions, communications, and behaviors may exist. In social work evaluations, as in any other human interactive process, there is no substitute for meeting each person with openness and acceptance—regardless of cultural background.

OUR VILLAGE

Our village has grown to encompass the world. Faster means of transportation, the expansion of trade, and the human desire to seek a better life have created societies that no longer find their roots in one cultural tradition and their voice in one common language. Rather, migration trends and globalization activities have laid the foundations for complex, culturally diverse societies with representation from several racial, ethnic, and cultural groups.

Diversity is reflected throughout our society: in schools, in the workplace, and within all types of formal organizations. Social service organizations are no exception; there is increasing diversity both among staff and also among service recipients. Of course diversity also has an impact on the field of evaluation; the challenge for evaluators is to work effectively in culturally diverse settings.

Working With Stakeholder Groups

As is made clear throughout this book, evaluations are more than the technical practice of organizing and implementing data collection activities, analyzing data, and reporting findings. Although these are important activities, evaluations also involve working effectively with a variety of stakeholders in a wide range of organizations. The tasks include working with people to clarify expectations, identify interests, reconcile differences, and win cooperation.

Evaluators must therefore be adept in establishing interpersonal and working relationships in addition to bringing technical expertise to the evaluation process as illustrated in Chapter 3. When working with different cultural groups or in different cultural settings, for example, you must be culturally competent and also have the ability to adapt the technical processes of the evaluation enterprise so that they are appropriate for your evaluation setting.

Your Evaluation Team

To achieve community involvement with a lens toward cultural sensitivity, the following questions should be considered when forming an evaluation team from your various stakeholder groups that will guide you throughout your entire study:

- What history (e.g., prior practice and evaluation, knowledge of group and/or community) does the team have with the racial/ethnic group members included in your study?
- What efforts have been made to ensure the inclusion of the perspective of racial/ethnic group members in the design, conduct, and analysis of the study?
- What is the race/ethnicity of the team, including the principal investigator, consultants, data collectors, and coders?
- Have potential biases of the members been recognized?
- What efforts have been made to counter potential biases of the team in working with racial/ethnic minority groups?

It's not necessary for you to be a member of the racial/ethnic group you are studying; however, achieving culturally competent knowledge of the community is crucial. Cross-cultural evaluation is strengthened when evaluators study the beliefs, values, and social structures that form the context of the participants' worldview and incorporate that knowledge into the design and conduct of the study.

THE IMPACT OF CULTURE

Culture is many things: a set of customs, traditions, and beliefs and a worldview. These are socially defined and passed on from generation to generation (Porter & Samovar, 1997). Culture is manifested in the perceptions through which we view our surroundings and the patterns of language and behaviors through which we interact with others. Culture exists at the micro level and at the macro level:

- *Micro-level culture* is found within individuals. It's reflected in their personal values, beliefs, communication styles, and behaviors.
- *Macro-level culture* exists at the organizational level. It's found in institutions and communities and is manifested in their mandates, policies, and practices.

Culture acts as a filter through which people view, perceive, and evaluate the world around them.

Fundamentally, culture acts as a filter through which people view, perceive, and evaluate the world around them. At the same time, it also provides a framework within which people process information, think, communicate, and behave. Because different cultures establish different frameworks for perceiving and judging as well as for thinking and acting, misperceptions, miscommunications, and conflicts are not only possible but likely. Where people are unaware of how culture filters thinking, actions, perceptions, and judgments, the likelihood for misunderstanding is even greater.

The Japanese, for example, have traditionally used bowing as a form of greeting, but in North America handshakes are prevalent; in certain European countries, hugging and kissing are customary. It's easy to see that what is meant as a friendly gesture in one culture may be viewed as an intrusion in another. In a meeting, for example, a statement that is meant as a hypothetical example in one culture may be viewed as a firm commitment in another (see Box 6.1).

Moreover, what is valued in one culture may not be nearly as important in another. In North America,

BOX 6.1 THE "WHITE CULTURE" OF VIEWING THE WORLD

In most research studies conducted in the United States, the strategies, analytic techniques, and measurements used come from the "white culture." Evaluations that impose rules from the majority or dominant culture on people of different cultures may be restricted by a number of factors, such as conceptual mismatches, language barriers, different values, and differences in the meaning and manifestation of emotions. For example, the same behavior observed—or not observed—in people from different cultures can mean different things.

EXAMPLE

Anger is a trait that correlates highly with adolescent alcohol abuse in the Caucasian population, whereas in the American Indian population the expression of anger inversely correlates with alcohol abuse. Within this population, anger is a positive factor that can keep adolescents in school and help them stay motivated to improve the lives of their community members.

EXAMPLE

Research on marital communication involved a coding system that observers used to record conflicts in couples' interactions. Observers who were not of Asian heritage observed no conflicts among Asian couples. However, an observer who was brought in from the Asian community perceived numerous indications of conflicts those outside the culture were unable to detect.

---

for example, there is considerable emphasis on the "bottom line," which translates to program outcomes in evaluation. Thus evaluations are often concerned with assessing the outcomes of a social service program (see Chapter 12). In some cultures, however, the fact that a program has been created and now operates and provides employment for community members may be viewed as at least as important as the actual results of the services it provides.

What is valued in one culture may not be nearly as important in another.

BRIDGING THE CULTURE GAP

Under the principle "respect for people" as set out by the American Evaluation Association (2004), evaluators are expected to be aware of and respect differences among people and to be mindful of the implications of cultural differences on the evaluation process. Evaluators thus need:

- A clear understanding of the impact of culture on human and social processes generally and on evaluation processes specifically, and
- Skills in cross-cultural communications to ensure that they can effectively interact with people from diverse backgrounds.

Cultural Awareness

As the previous discussion suggests, culture provides a powerful organizing framework that filters perceptions and communications and also shapes behaviors and interactions. To practice effectively in different cultural settings, you will need a general awareness of the role that culture plays in shaping your perceptions, ideas, and behaviors.

Furthermore, evaluators need fundamental attitudes of respect for difference, a willingness to learn about other cultures, and a genuine belief that cultural differences are a source of strength and enrichment rather than an obstacle to be overcome. In particular, evaluators need cultural awareness: They need to be on guard that their perceptions, communications, and actions are not unduly influenced by ethnocentrism and enculturation—processes that act as barriers to effective communications and relationships.

Ethnocentrism

Because your own history is inevitably based in your own culture, and because you generally continue to be immersed in that culture, a natural human tendency is to judge others and other cultures by the standards of your own beliefs and values. This is known as ethnocentrism; it leads to defining the world in your own terms. This is natural.

Thus you might tend to view as normal that which is typical in your own culture; different practices, structures, or patterns that may be typical in other cultures are likely then viewed as "abnormal" or even problematic (Neuliep, 2000).

Among some social groups, for example, childrearing is viewed as a community responsibility, with extended family and other community members taking an active role when necessary. This is seldom typical in urban North American culture, where high mobility often places families in communities without extended family or other support networks.

Ethnocentrism is defining the world in your own terms.

Thus in a large urban setting an appropriate outcome for family support programs may be that the family remains intact. However, in communities located in rural or remote areas or on Native American reservations, a more appropriate outcome might be that suitable caregiving arrangements are identified within the family's kinship or community network. In short, an ethnocentric evaluator might, however unwittingly, apply mainstream North American values to a Native American family support program; this would clearly result in a distortion in the evaluation process.

Enculturation

Enculturation is a close cousin to ethnocentrism. It's a related process that refers to the fact that as children we learn to behave in ways that are appropriate to our culture. We also come to adopt a variety of core beliefs about human nature, human experience, and human behavior. This process teaches us how to behave, interact, and even think. Of course other cultural groups will have different ways of thinking, behaving, and interacting.

In some Asian cultures, for example, people value discussion, negotiation, and relationship, whereas in North America people tend to be more direct and task oriented (Hall, 1983). Similarly, some cultures such as the Swiss and Germans emphasize promptness, whereas in some Southern cultures, a meeting is seldom expected to start at the appointed time but only after everyone has arrived (Lewis, 1997).

The differences in behavior patterns and interactions are real; however, it's important for evaluators to recognize that others' patterns are as legitimate and appropriate as their own. When evaluators are unable to do this, stereotyping may occur, resulting in misunderstanding and misjudgment.

Enculturation is a process that refers to the fact that as children we learn to behave in ways that are appropriate to our culture.

For example, you may become frustrated because it's difficult to start meetings on time in a community or because it's not possible to keep to a tight schedule, and you may begin to stereotype the group you are working with as uninterested, noncooperative, and disorganized. Obviously such stereotypes will have the effect of creating additional barriers to communications and interactions and will hinder the evaluation process.

Intercultural Communication

Awareness of the impact of culture is important, but effective relationships depend on the actual communications. Because evaluation is as much a relationship process as a technical matter, effective communication is always important, particularly so in communication across cultures.

There are many models of intercultural communication. One of the more useful ones is offered by Porter and Samovar (1997). In this model, perceptions are regarded as the gateway to communications; they are the means by which people select, evaluate, and organize information about the world around them.

Perceptions, of course, depend in large part on individuals' worldviews, which are, in part, formed as a result of their cultural experiences. Thus perceptions help us select, organize, and interpret a variety of external stimuli, including the communications that others direct toward us.

After we process the communications that are directed toward us, we usually respond. Different cultures support different communication patterns and styles, and thus our response is also shaped and formed, at least in part, by our cultural background. Communications, then, are inextricably bound with culture. The opportunity for misunderstanding, ever present in any communication, is even greater when individuals from different cultural backgrounds interact.

Intercultural communication takes place at both the nonverbal and verbal levels. Anyone who interacts with members of another culture needs an understanding of both nonverbal and verbal communications patterns typical in that culture. We briefly look at communications at each of these two levels:

- Nonverbal
- Verbal

Nonverbal

An important part of human communications takes place nonverbally. Facial expressions, time, use of space, and gestures convey much information and are deeply based in culture. Without an understanding of the meaning of nonverbal communication symbols used by a culture, it's all too easy to misinterpret signs.

For example, a hand gesture that has virtually no meaning in one culture may be a vulgar symbol in another culture. For example, the OK sign, widely used in North America, is a circle formed by the thumb and the first finger; this sign is considered to be offensive and unacceptable in Brazil, and it means money in Japan (Morrison, Conway, & Borden, 1994).

> *On nonverbal language . . .*
>
> *The most important thing in communication is hearing what isn't said.*
>
> ~ *Peter F. Drucker*

Positioning oneself in relation to another may result in an inadvertent message of disinterest or aggression. North Americans usually feel comfortable standing at a distance of about two and a half to four feet from others. However, members of some cultures, among them Arabic, prefer to stand much closer when engaged in a conversation (Hall, 1983). An evaluator who positions himself at a North American distance may be perceived as cold, aloof, and disinterested by members of such cultures.

Similarly, the use of eye contact carries culturally specific meaning. In European-based cultures, eye contact is used extensively to demonstrate interest and to confirm that one is listening. Many other cultures, however, do not use eye contact extensively and may perceive it as disrespectful and even threatening. For example, prolonged eye contact in cultures such as that of the Japanese is considered to be rude (Samovar, Porter, & Stefani, 1998).

Verbal

On the verbal level, words also derive much of their meaning through culture. As language is the primary means through which a culture communicates its values and beliefs, the same words may have different meanings within different cultures. For example, the Japanese use the word *hai*, meaning "yes," to indicate that they have heard what was said and are thinking about a response. Because in many circumstances it's considered impolite to openly express disagreement, *hai* is used even when the listener is actually in disagreement with what is being said. Thus the meaning assigned to "yes" is quite different than that commonly understood by North Americans, who consider "yes" to mean that the listener is in agreement.

As the evaluation process involves extensive transmission of information through communications, it's obviously vital that verbal communications be accurate and effective. Without an understanding of intercultural communication generally and an ability to understand the specific patterns used by the group with whom the evaluator is dealing, communications problems may arise and derail the evaluation process.

CULTURAL FRAMEWORKS

As we have seen, culture often defines a group's values and beliefs and creates its communications patterns. In addition, culture also provides frameworks for other complex structures and processes. Different cultural groups, for example, have different methods of gathering information and of making decisions.

An understanding of these patterns is essential to ensure that data collection and analytical processes are appropriate and reports are practical and relevant. This section briefly looks at five aspects of cultural frameworks:

- Orientation to data
- Decision-making
- Individualism
- Tradition
- Pace of life

Orientation to Data

Some cultures thrive on "hard" data and greatly value processes, such as findings from evaluation studies, which produce data that can then be considered and acted upon (Lewis, 1997). These cultures, which include the North American mainstream culture, are considered data oriented.

On the other hand, some cultures such as Middle Eastern and Latin American cultures are viewed as "dialogue oriented," in that they pay more attention to relationships and process than to data. These groups tend to view statistics and data with some suspicion and regard it as only part of a picture. Such cultures consider relationships and context as more important than numbers.

Decision-Making

In many Western cultures, logic and rationality are highly valued and used extensively in making decisions about important matters (Hoefstede, 1997; Lewis, 1997). The evaluation designs (Tool E) upon which evaluation processes are based are examples of this style of "scientific" thinking. However, some cultures are less impressed by science and prefer intuition or more subjective, personal approaches to thinking and decision-making.

When evaluators prepare a report for people whose culture supports a scientific orientation to thinking, quantitative data with statistical analyses is quite appropriate; however, if the users are people who come from a culture that prefers more subjective and intuitive approaches to decision-making, a report

organized around the presentation of quantitative results will be less useful and comprehensible.

Individualism

Although most cultures support both individualistic and collectivistic tendencies, there is in every culture a bias toward one or the other (Hoefstede, 1997). In individualistic cultures, such as the mainstream North American culture, people work toward individual goals, and initiative, competition, and achievement are highly valued.

In collectivistic cultures, people are group oriented; loyalty, relationships, and overall community development are valued while individual goals are downplayed. In such cultures, the family, organizations with which people are affiliated (including the workplace), and the community are particularly important.

Keeping in perspective an organization's cultural view on individualism versus collectivism is important in understanding the behaviors, interactions, work processes, and structures that may be found in the course of an evaluation. What may appear from an individualistic perspective to be an unwieldy work process involving too many people may, in fact, be explained by a culture-based desire not to leave anyone out and to create as wide a network of involvement as is possible.

Tradition

Some cultures are more traditional and value the status quo and conformity, whereas others encourage innovation and view change as necessary if progress is to be made (Dodd, 1998). Change-oriented cultures such as mainstream North American society encourage experimentation, risk-taking, and innovation. They consider change to be an opportunity to improve.

In other cultures, such as with some traditional Asian cultures, values are centered on tradition and continuity. The young are expected to give way to the wishes of the older generation, and new ideas are not encouraged because they might disrupt the structure of society.

The reader will readily recognize that evaluation, as a change- and improvement-oriented activity, is grounded in Western cultural values. As such, the concept of evaluation itself may seem alien to those steeped in more traditional cultures. After all, evaluation is concerned with identifying areas for improvement, which therefore implies change, but traditional cultures value stability and continuity.

Inevitably, evaluators will sometimes work with organizations that are based in a tradition-oriented culture. In such circumstances, evaluators need to be sensitive to the fact that there may not exist a common understanding even about the basic premises of the evaluation process.

Pace of Life

In North America, especially in larger cities, we live our lives at an accelerated pace. Our schedules are jammed with many activities; agendas are overloaded, and there is an expectation that everything is a priority and must be done immediately. Time is viewed as linear and rigid; we live with the sense that if we miss an event it is forever gone. In such cultures, which are called monochromic, people tend to organize their lives by the clock (Hall, 1983).

Clearly, in such cultures it's important to be on time for meetings, to meet deadlines, and to stay on schedule (Samovar et al., 1998). In a sense, time is so central that members of the culture are hardly aware of its importance, but all things, including personal relationships, take second place to successful time management.

On the other hand, in polychromic cultures life is lived at a slower pace; activities grind to a halt on weekends, during rest times, and during festivals and important celebrations. Slower-paced cultures—for example, those in Latin America, the Middle East, and Indonesia—tend to be less aware of time and hold less of a concept of it as a commodity that must be managed.

On pace of life . . .

Adopt the pace of nature: her secret is patience.

~ Ralph Waldo Emerson

Time is seen as circular and flexible; the Indonesians even refer to it as "rubber time" (Harris & Moran, 1996). Time is not nearly as important an organizing force in people's lives as it is in monochromic cultures; if the scheduled start time passes without the event taking place, people are not unduly disturbed as another appropriate start time can be set. "Time is money" could not have arisen as a central idea in these cultures, which focus on relationships and interactions. Time management and business come second (Hall, 1983). In such cultures, it's vital to establish a personal relationship before conducting business.

Obviously evaluators need to have a good understanding of the concept of time held within the setting where they conduct their work. Tight schedules that provide few opportunities for cementing working relationships and disregard widely observed rest periods, holidays, and celebrations are obviously unrealistic and will be unsuitable in polychromic cultures. Attempting to impose such a schedule will be regarded as thoughtless and will impede rather than facilitate the evaluation process.

Furthermore, in assessing the achievement of milestones and other accomplishments, evaluations need to take into account the concept of time and the pace of life prevalent in the particular culture. In setting up a new social service program, for example, planning, procedure, policy development, initial staffing, and other preparatory activities may be accomplished in a much briefer period of time in one setting than in another. Both the concept of time and the pace of life might be, in fact, equally appropriate when cultural orientation toward time is taken into account.

CULTURALLY COMPETENT EVALUATORS

Although some evaluators come from minority backgrounds, many do bring a mainstream North American cultural orientation to their work. This orientation will result in part from their own cultural background and in part from their formation and education as evaluators. The methods of evaluation are, to a large degree, based in a Western or North American cultural tradition. Inevitably, evaluators will bring their own culturally based beliefs, values, and perspectives as well as their culturally based tool-kit, to the work.

More and more evaluations are conducted in settings that are culturally different from mainstream North American culture. Evaluations are conducted on reservations, at women's shelters, in organizations serving immigrants, and at agencies that grew from the needs and aspirations of minority communities and reflect the cultures of those communities.

> *The methods of evaluation are, to a large degree, based in a Western or North American cultural tradition.*

Evaluators who undertake work in culturally different settings or among people from different cultural backgrounds require the skills to effectively conduct their work and to make the evaluation process meaningful within those settings. These skills are:

- Develop cultural awareness
- Develop intercultural communication skills
- Develop specific knowledge about the culture being evaluated
- Develop an ability to appropriately adapt evaluation methods and processes

Develop Cultural Awareness

To be effective in intercultural work, evaluators need a degree of cultural awareness that will provide them with an understanding of the impact of culture on all human values, attitudes, and behaviors as well as interactions and processes. They need to understand how culture filters communications and how evaluation itself is a culture-based activity. Furthermore, evaluators should have an understanding of concepts such as ethnocentrism, enculturation, and stereotyping—all of which may subtly, or not so subtly, raise barriers to effective communications and relationships.

In addition, you need to bring attitudes of openness and acceptance to your work as well as a genuine belief that cultural differences need not pose barriers but can strengthen and enrich the evaluation process. Evaluators who wish to practice in diverse settings also need a high degree of self-awareness as well as understanding of their own cultural values and experiences and the impact of these values and experiences on their communications patterns, relationships, and professional work.

Cultural awareness increases through contact with other cultures and through experiencing differences. Travel, work in culturally different settings, and living in diverse communities are ways in which evaluators can develop their awareness and attitudes.

Develop Intercultural Communication Skills

The ability to approach others with openness and acceptance is foundational to effective communication, regardless of setting; in intercultural communication it's particularly important. However, effective intercultural communication also requires specific knowledge of the other culture and its communication symbols. As we now know, the meaning of nonverbal or verbal symbols is culturally defined. It's therefore important to know the meaning of common nonverbal and verbal communications symbols to ensure accuracy in both the transmission as well as the reception of messages.

Evaluators can prepare for their work by reading novels set in the culture, watching high-quality movies, and perusing books and guides that describe prevailing communications patterns. The use of cultural guides, to be discussed in the following section, is also helpful in learning to understand the meaning of common communication symbols.

Develop Specific Knowledge About the Culture

In the previous section, the importance of developing specific understandings about prevailing communication patterns in a specific culture was discussed. However, more than communication patterns must be understood by an evaluator who wishes to be effective in a culturally different setting. Specific knowledge about various details of the culture are important to ensure that effective relationships can be established, the work is planned in a realistic manner, and the resulting products will have utility.

> *On culture . . .*
>
> *No culture can live if it attempts to be exclusive.*
>
> ~ *Mahatma Gandhi*

Among other things, it's important to have some sense of the history of the group who comprise the culture in which the evaluation will be conducted. On Native American reservations, for example, the history of oppression and dislocation is vitally important and helps to frame values, attitudes, and beliefs. Among certain immigrant groups, escape from oppression is a dominant theme, and newly found freedoms and opportunities help to frame a highly individualistic and achievement-oriented culture.

Beyond history, it's vital to understand specific values, beliefs, and perspectives that shape individuals' and groups' perceptions and communications, in addition to the cultural structures, processes, and frameworks that are characteristic of the group. For example, in working with Native American groups on reservations, it's customary to include elders on advisory committees and listen with respect to the ideas and opinions that they express.

Furthermore, meetings begin with a prayer to the Creator and not with a review of the agenda, as is the case in most Western-oriented institutions. Concepts of time have been discussed previously; it's sufficient to say that the scheduled starting time for meetings may or may not be firmly fixed, depending on the setting.

There are a myriad of other details about culture, some of which may be important to understand to work successfully in the setting. For example, one of the authors of this book once conducted an evaluation on a reservation; the work included observing a restorative justice circle in action. The program had been conceived carefully with extensive use of traditional symbols.

One of these symbols was the circle itself, which symbolized a teepee; a convention had developed over time that participants entered and left the circle in one particular place that symbolized the entry to the teepee. Entering or leaving in any other place was regarded as the equivalent of walking through the walls of the teepee.

Of course an evaluator coming from the outside would not have been aware of this and would inevitably have committed a cultural faux pas at some point during the process. Happily, this was averted in this case because a member of the evaluation project, who was from the community itself, served as a cultural guide and had briefed the evaluator on the meaning of the cultural symbols involved as well as appropriate behaviors.

In general, specific cultural knowledge can be obtained through the same methods as suggested for understanding the specifics of communications patterns: travel, reading guidebooks and histories by writers from the culture, and watching movies. Engaging collaborators from within the cultural group, although not necessarily from within the organization itself, is perhaps the most effective way of learning about values, beliefs, traditions, behavior patterns, and the detailed texture of another culture.

Develop an Ability to Adapt Evaluations

Developing cultural awareness, intercultural communications skills, and specific knowledge of the culture of the group with which an evaluator is involved are foundational to conducting effective evaluations. The final set of skills involves adapting the evaluation processes and methods so that they will be appropriate and meaningful within the culture of the organization where the evaluation is being conducted. Adapting evaluations involves:

- Working with stakeholders
- Ensuring that the work processes are appropriate
- Ensuring that the products are meaningful and useful

Working with Stakeholders

As is discussed throughout this book, a variety of groups, including funders, staff members, program participants, and community members, may have an interest in how a program performs and, consequently, in the evaluation results. Different groups of stakeholders are likely to have different interests, and this will particularly be true in the case of evaluations conducted in settings with culturally different stakeholders.

Generally, funders represent powerful institutions such as governments and foundations within mainstream society. They will therefore articulate their interests from a North American or Western cultural perspective. In practice, funders will likely be interested in data that shed light on the extent to which the program is delivering the services that had been contracted and with what effect.

Furthermore, they will prefer to have the data packaged as a formal report, replete with quantitative data and statistics as well as specific recommendations for change and improvement. On the other hand, if the setting is based in a different culture, staff members, service recipients, and community members may be more interested in understanding the overall role that the program is playing within the community.

If they come from a dialogue-oriented culture, they may be interested in descriptions of the service process and service recipients' stories about their experiences with the service and its impact on their families. They will be looking not so much to receive data for the purpose of making changes but rather to develop broader and deeper understanding of the program and its place in the community.

Evaluators need to work at understanding each stakeholder group's perspectives, expectations, and interests and realize that these may be fundamentally different from one another. Therefore, a culturally competent evaluator must be committed to accommodating within the evaluation process the different perspectives and interests of diverse stakeholders.

Adapting Work Processes

Evaluation work always involves obtaining the cooperation of staff members and other stakeholder groups in carrying out the required evaluation procedures—particularly data collection. This is especially true when a monitoring system of quality improvement is put into place; the effectiveness of such a system depends on staff members carrying out their assigned roles in the evaluation process in a knowledgeable and consistent manner. It's therefore very important that the work processes be designed so that they are congruent with the culture within the organization.

For example, evaluators need to take into account the cultural meaning of time in the organization. If the organization is polychromic and operates at a relatively relaxed pace, the scheduling of evaluation events and activities must take this into account. A schedule that may be appropriate in an organization that operates from a monochromic cultural perspective may be totally unfeasible within a polychromic culture. Attempting to impose such a schedule will create tensions and stresses and is likely to result, at best, in very inconsistent implementation of evaluation activities. At worst, the entire evaluation enterprise may be discredited and collapse.

It's thus important that evaluators design work processes in a manner that is congruent with the cultural meaning of time. Scheduling should take into account the concept of time and orientation to time, not impose a burden that would be regarded by the culture as unduly stressful or inappropriate; it should ensure that holidays, community celebrations, and festivals are taken into account in the setting of schedules.

Similarly, data collection activities need to take into account the cultural orientation of the staff members who are likely to collect the data and the service recipients who are likely to provide them. In dialogue-oriented cultures, the collection of highly quantitative data involving the use of standardized measures, rating scales, and structured surveys may be inappropriate and result in inconsistent data collection at best.

At worst, service recipients and staff members will go through the motions of providing and collecting data without really understanding why the data are needed or how they are to be used. The reliability and validity of such data, of course, are likely to be low, compromising the entire evaluation effort.

Data collection protocols and procedures need to take into account whether evaluation participants are oriented to "data" or "dialogue" and should be designed to be as meaningful and culturally appropriate as possible. In dialogue-oriented cultures it may not be entirely possible, or advisable, to avoid the collection of quantitative data, but such data collection methods should be used sparingly. Ample explanations and support should also be provided to evaluation participants so that they can find meaning in these tasks and carry them out effectively.

Providing Meaningful Products

Ultimately, evaluations are undertaken to generate information products that stakeholders will find useful. It's particularly important that evaluation products be appropriate to the culture of stakeholders (McKinney, 2014). As discussed earlier, funders are likely to find reports useful when they address the extent to which the program meets its contractual obligations for providing services and describe the outcomes of those services. Furthermore, funders will look for quantitative data and statistical analyses that support the findings of the report. Managers who regularly deal with funders may also favor reports of this type.

However, other stakeholder groups may not find such products useful or understandable. This will be especially the case if stakeholders come from cultural backgrounds that are dialogue oriented. Reports with descriptions, stories, illustrations, and even pictures are likely to prove more meaningful to such stakeholders.

Culturally competent evaluators should accommodate all stakeholder groups who have a legitimate interest in an evaluation's results. Tailoring reports to funders' needs alone represents poor evaluation practice and is unlikely to result in meaningful program change. Program development necessarily comes from the inside and is based, primarily, on the initiative of the managers and staff. Evaluation products should support the efforts of managers and staff to develop the program by providing data that are meaningful, practical, and useful.

It's usually the case that quantitative and qualitative approaches can be combined within an evaluation. Although matters that interest funders are likely to be more suited to quantitative data collection and analyses, increased understanding can result from including descriptively oriented material that focuses on contextual matters.

Statistics describing the demographic makeup of service recipients, for example, can be supplemented by providing more detailed descriptions of a few selected service recipients. Often this can be accomplished by providing people the opportunity to tell their stories in their words.

As described throughout this book, all evaluations must abide by basic utility standards. These standards are intended to ensure that an evaluation will serve the information needs of intended users. Clearly this underscores the responsibility of evaluators to understand the intended audience for evaluations and to ensure that evaluation products are culturally appropriate and therefore comprehensible, meaningful, and useful.

Kiki Sayre (2002) presents a few guidelines for evaluators to consider in order to becoming more culturally competent:

- Develop specific cultural knowledge. Know the relationship between variables and behaviors in the group being evaluated. Only when the norms and values are clearly delineated can they be given proper consideration.
- Explicitly examine the theoretical framework that is the foundation of your evaluation study. Communicate clearly your own values, beliefs, approach, and worldview as the evaluator. Acknowledge and address how these may differ from the perspectives of the group to be studied. Whenever possible, have someone on the evaluation team who has knowledge and understanding of the group being studied.
- Define and measure ethnicity in a meaningful manner. To the degree possible, also define and measure key constructs, such as socioeconomic status, that are known to covary with ethnicity. If you suspect there is variability within a group, find out if other characteristics have an impact on the data.

- Measure the elements and factors that may covary to determine whether it's ethnicity or some other factor. If other factors are involved, the socioeconomic status or additional factors need to be measured along with race and ethnicity.
- Use measuring instruments that are appropriate for all the ethnic groups in your study and/or check those measures you use for their equivalence across groups. Make sure the measuring instruments you are using have cross-cultural equivalence.
- Make sure your analyses reflect your study's evaluation questions and that you have sufficient data to get accurate answers. The goal is to accurately interpret the experiences of particular groups of people in order to minimize errors throughout the study. For this reason, the evaluation team needs to be involved from the beginning of the study.
- Interpret results to reflect the lives of the people studied. Have someone with knowledge of the particular group analyze the data alongside the evaluators in order to point out variables that should be considered.
- Define the population precisely. Understand a group's country of origin, immigration history, sociopolitical status, level of education, and rules and norms. Without a clear understanding of the group's background, it's best to develop an evaluation team that has this background.
- Develop collaborations with the people you are studying. Community members need to be involved in the planning and implementation of the study. Define the pertinent evaluation questions at the outset of the study.
- Encourage buy-in. Know the community well and understand the pressures and external constraints operating among the population. State the goals of the evaluation team and determine the goals of the people being studied. Describe how the data will be used. Conduct interviews in a location that is comfortable to the group and without bias.

- Provide timely feedback and results in clear, useful formats conveyed through culturally appropriate methods. Ask those involved how best to disseminate the study's results. For example, you could share the results of your study with a Native American population in New Mexico in a "give-back" ceremony that uses storytelling and visuals, with no written material.
- Consider acculturation and biculturalism in the interpretation and utilization of data. Acculturation measures are often linear and one dimensional. Bicultural adaptation—or the adoption of some majority culture attitudes and practices coupled with the retention of ethnic group cultural practices and identity—is now considered a more useful measurement. Cultural identity can be bicultural or even tricultural. People generally do not lose one culture to gain another.
- Know when to aggregate the within-group data from a heterogeneous sample and still maximize external validity. Conduct within-group analyses that consider groups independently of each other to ensure that important data are not overlooked. Only aggregate the data if convincing similarities can be found.
- Avoid deficit model interpretations. Abandon stereotypes and models that measure diverse groups against a monocultural standard.

Box 6.2 sums up the various principles that we must follow when doing multicultural evaluations.

SUMMARY

This chapter presented the challenges of applying evaluation methods in culturally diverse settings. By reading the first six chapters of this book you should appreciate that conducting an evaluation is a complex endeavor, and undertaking evaluations that involve stakeholders from different cultural backgrounds adds considerable complexity.

BOX 6.2 GUIDING PRINCIPLES FOR MULTICULTURAL EVALUATION

INCLUSION IN DESIGN AND IMPLEMENTATION

- Multicultural evaluation is not imposed on diverse communities; communities understand and support the rationale for the evaluation project and agree with the methods used to answer key evaluation questions.
- Diverse beneficiary stakeholders are actively involved in all phases of the evaluation, including problem definition, development of research questions, methods chosen, data collection, analysis, and reporting.
- To the extent possible, multicultural evaluation empowers diverse communities to do self-evaluation through intentional capacity building in evaluation.

ACKNOWLEDGMENT/INFUSION OF MULTIPLE WORLDVIEWS

- Evaluators in multicultural evaluations have a genuine respect for communities being studied and seek deep understanding of different cultural contexts, practices, and paradigms of thinking.
- "Expert" knowledge does not exclusively reside with the evaluator; the grantee and/or community being studied is assumed to know best their issues, strengths, and challenges.
- The diversity of communities studied is represented in multicultural evaluation staffing and expertise whenever possible.

APPROPRIATE MEASURES OF SUCCESS

- Measures of success in multicultural evaluations are discussed and/or collaboratively developed with those being evaluated.

- Data collection instruments and outcome measures are tested for multicultural validity across populations that may be non-English speaking, less literate, or from a different culture.
- Multicultural evaluation data collection methods and instruments accommodate different cultural contexts and consider alternative or nontraditional ways of collecting data.

CULTURAL AND SYSTEMS ANALYSIS

- Multicultural evaluations take into account how historical and current social systems, institutions, and societal norms contribute to power and outcome disparities across different racial and ethnic communities.
- Multicultural evaluations incorporate and trace impacts of factors related to racial, cultural, gender, religious, economic, and other differences.
- Multicultural evaluation questions take a multilevel approach to understanding root causes and impact at the individual, interpersonal, institutional, cultural, system, and policy level, rather than focusing the analysis solely on individual behavior.

RELEVANCE TO DIVERSE COMMUNITIES

- Multicultural evaluations inform community decision-making and program design.
- Findings from multicultural evaluations are co-owned with diverse communities and shared in culturally appropriate ways.

This chapter concludes Part I of this book that deals with the contexts of your evaluation efforts. You are now well armed with all of the "behind-the-scenes" wisdom you must have to actually start to think about doing some kind of an evaluation. Now that you know how to prepare for an evaluation (Part I), you can proceed to actually doing one in Part III, appropriately titled "Doing Evaluations." However, before you can actually evaluate a social work program, for example, you need to know how they are designed and what they are trying to accomplish—the topic of the two chapters in the following part of this book: Part II: Designing Programs.

Study Questions   Chapter 6

The goal of this chapter is to provide you with a beginning knowledge base for you to feel comfortable in answering the following questions. AFTER you have read the chapter, indicate how comfortable you feel you are in answering each of the following questions on a 5-point scale where:

1 Very uncomfortable	2 Somewhat uncomfortable	3 Neutral	4 Somewhat comfortable	5 Very comfortable

If you rated any question between 1–3, reread the section of the chapter where the information for the question is found. If you still feel that you're uncomfortable in answering the question, then talk with your instructor and/or your classmates for more clarification.

	Questions	Degree of comfort? (Circle one number)
1	Discuss how you would form an evaluation team from your stakeholder groups to ensure your evaluation was culturally sensitive. Then describe how you would do this in relation to your field placement (or work setting).	1 2 3 4 5
2	In your own words, describe *ethnocentrism*. How is it relevant to program evaluations?	1 2 3 4 5
3	In your own words, describe *enculturation*. How is it relevant to program evaluations?	1 2 3 4 5
4	In your own words, describe the concept of intercultural communication. How is it relevant to program evaluations?	1 2 3 4 5
5	List the five aspects of cultural frameworks. Then describe how each pertains to doing a program evaluation.	1 2 3 4 5
6	List the four skill sets that you must possess to be a culturally competent evaluator. Then discuss how you will be sure you have each of these before you embark on an evaluation. Provide specific steps you will take to make sure you have them.	1 2 3 4 5

Chapter 6

Assessing Your Self-Efficacy

AFTER you have read this chapter AND have completed all of the study questions, indicate how knowledgeable you feel you are for each of the following concepts on a 5-point scale where

1 Not knowledgeable at all	2 Somewhat unknowledgeable	3 Neutral	4 Somewhat knowledgeable	5 Very knowledgeable

	Concepts	Knowledge Level? (Circle one number)
1	Working with stakeholder groups to form an evaluation team	1 2 3 4 5
2	The impact of culture on program evaluations	1 2 3 4 5
3	Ethnocentrism	1 2 3 4 5
4	Enculturation	1 2 3 4 5
5	Intercultural communication	1 2 3 4 5
6	Verbal and nonverbal forms of intercultural communication	1 2 3 4 5
7	The five aspects of cultural frameworks	1 2 3 4 5
8	Four skills needed to become a culturally competent evaluator	1 2 3 4 5
	Add up your scores (minimum = 8, maximum = 40)	Your total score =

A   38–40 = Professional evaluator in the making
A–   36–37 = Senior evaluator
B+   34–35 = Junior evaluator
B   32–33 = Assistant evaluator
B–   8–31 = Reread the chapter and redo the study questions

Designing Programs

Part II contains two very important chapters that explain how to construct social work programs with the aid of logic models. They provide the foundational knowledge that students need to appreciate and understand when it comes to knowing what their programs are actually trying to accomplish (program objectives) before the programs can be "evaluated" in any meaningful way (Part III).

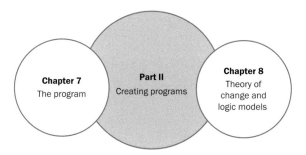

Chapter 7 discusses the "meat and potatoes" of a social work program. That is, we discuss agency mission statements and goals and how the programs within them are organized to meet the agency's overall goal. The chapter presents the requirements that are needed for a program to be labeled "evidence-based" and presents a few factors to consider when selecting one for any given community. The chapter then explains how to write goals and program objectives. In addition, it focuses on selecting indicators to measure program objectives and touches upon the relationship between practice objectives and practice activities. It ends with a brief discussion on why it's important for programs to have logic models.

Chapter 8 begins where Chapter 7 left off and is a logical extension of Chapter 7; that is, it describes in detail how to construct program logic models from theory of change models. More important, it describes how program logic models can aid us in designing program evaluations.

CHAPTER OUTLINE

A nation that continues year after year to spend more money on military defense than on programs of social uplift is approaching spiritual doom.

~ Martin Luther King, Jr.

With the background of the previous six chapters in mind, you're now in an excellent position to see how social work programs are actually designed. Remember, your evaluation will be done within a program so you have no other alternative but to understand how your evaluation will be influenced by its design.

We begin this chapter with the immediate environment of your program—the larger organization that it's housed within, commonly referred to as a social service agency.

THE AGENCY

A social service agency is an organization that exists to fill a legitimate social purpose such as:

- To protect children from physical, sexual, and emotional harm
- To enhance quality of life for developmentally delayed adolescents
- To improve nutritional health for housebound senior citizens

Agencies can be public and funded entirely by the state and/or federal government or private and funded by private funds, deriving some monies from governmental sources and some from client fees, charitable bodies, private donations, fund-raising activities, and so forth. It's common for agencies to be funded by many different types of funding sources. When several sources of funding are provided to an agency, the agency's funds (in their totality) are called "blended funds." Regardless of the funding source(s), agencies obtain their unique identities by their:

- Mission statements
- Goals

Mission Statements

All agencies have mission statements that provide the unique written philosophical perspective of what they are all about and make explicit the reasons for their existence. Mission statements sometimes are called philosophical statements or simply an agency's philosophy. Whatever it's called, a mission statement articulates a common vision for the agency in that it provides a point of reference for all major planning decisions.

> *You cannot do a meaningful evaluation of a social work program without first knowing how the program has been designed around its mission statement.*

A mission statement is like a lighthouse in that it exists to provide a general direction. It not only provides clarity of purpose to persons within the agency but also helps them to gain an understanding and support from the stakeholders outside the agency who are unquestionably influential to the agency's overall success (see Chapter 1).

Mission statements are usually given formal approval and sanction by legislators for public agencies or by executive boards for private ones. They can range from one sentence to 10 pages or more and are as varied as the agencies they represent such as,

- This agency strives to provide a variety of support services to families and children in need, while in the process maintaining their rights, their safety, and their human dignity.
- The mission of this agency is to promote and protect the mental health of the elderly people residing in this state by offering quality and timely programs that will deliver these services.
- The mission of this agency is to treat clients as partners in their therapy, and all services should be short-term, intensive, and focus on problems in day-to-day life and work.
- The mission of this agency is to protect and promote the physical and social well-being of this city by ensuring the development and delivery of culturally competent services that encourage and support individual, family, and community independence, self-reliance, and civic responsibility to the greatest degree possible.

In short, an agency's mission statement lays the overall conceptual foundation for all of the programs housed within it because each program (soon to be discussed) must be logically connected to the overarching intent of the agency as declared by its mission statement. Note that mission statements capture the general type of clients to be served as well as communicate the essence of the services they offer their clients. Creating mission statements is a process of bringing interested stakeholders together to agree on the overall direction and tone of the agency.

> *A mission statement articulates a common vision for the agency in that it provides a point of reference for all major planning decisions.*

The process of creating mission statements is affected by available words in a language as well as the meaning given to those words by individual stakeholders. Because mission statements express the broad intention of an agency, they set the stage for all program planning within the agency and are essential to the development of the agency's goal.

Goals

As should be evident by now, social service agencies are established in an effort to reduce gaps between the current and the desired state of a social problem for a specific client population. Mission statements can be lofty and include several philosophical declarations, but the agency goal is more concise; there is only one goal per agency. An agency's goal is always defined at a conceptual level, and it's never measured directly. Its main ambition is to guide us toward effective and accountable service delivery.

Requirements for Goals

It's essential that an agency's goal reflects the agency's mandate and is guided by its mission statement. This is achieved by forming a goal with the following four components:

1. The nature of the current social problem to be tackled
2. The client population to be served
3. The general direction of anticipated client change (desired state)
4. The means by which the change is supposed to be brought about

Agency goals can be broad or narrow. Let's look at two generic examples:

- **Agency Goal—National:** The goal of this agency is to enhance the quality of life of this nation's families (*client population to be served*) who depend on public funds for day-to-day living (*social problem to be tackled*). The agency supports reducing long-term dependence on public funds (*general direction of anticipated client change*) by offering innovative programs that increase the self-sufficiency and employability of welfare-dependent citizens (*means by which the change is supposed to be brought about*).
- **Agency Goal—Local:** The goal of this agency is to help youth from low socioeconomic households in this city (*client population to be served*) who are dropping out of school (*current social problem to be tackled*) to stay

in school (*general direction of anticipated client change*) by providing mentorship and tutoring programs in local neighborhoods (*means by which the change is supposed to be brought about*).

As discussed in Chapter 1, national agencies, for example, are clearly broader in boundary and size than local ones. Additionally, more complex agencies such as those serving multiple client populations or addressing multiple social problems will capture a more expansive population or problem area in their goal statements.

> *An agency's goal statement must be broad enough to encompass all of its programs; that is, each program within an agency must have a direct and logical connection to the agency that governs it.*

However small or large, an agency functions as a single entity and the agency's goal statement serves to unify all of its programs.

THE PROGRAM

Whatever the current social problem, the desired future state of the problem, or the population that the agency wishes to serve, an agency sets up programs to help work toward its intended result—the agency's goal. There are as many ways to organize social service programs as there are people willing to be involved in the task. And just about everyone has an opinion on how agencies should structure the programs housed within them.

Mapping out the relationship among programs is a process that is often obscured by the fact that the term *program* can be used to refer the different levels of service delivery within an agency (e.g., Figures 7.1, 7.2, and 7.3,). In other words, some programs can be seen as subcomponents of larger ones; for example, in Figure 7.3, "Public Awareness Services" falls under the "Nonresidential Program" for the Women's Emergency Shelter.

Figure 7.1: **Simple organizational chart of a family service agency.**

Figure 7.1 presents a simple structure of a family service agency serving families and children. Each program included in the Family Service Agency is expected to have some connection to serving families. The Family Support Program and the Family Counseling Program have an obvious connection, given their titles. The Group Home Program, however, has no obvious connection; its title reveals nothing about who resides in the group home or for what purpose.

Because the Group Home Program operates under the auspices of "family services," it's likely that it temporarily houses children and youth who eventually will return to their families. Most important, the agency does not offer programs that are geared toward other target groups such as the elderly, veterans, refugees, or the homeless.

By glancing at Figure 7.1, it can be easily seen that this particular family service agency has five programs within it that deal with families and children, the agency's target population: a group home program for children, a family counseling program, a child adoption program, a treatment foster care program, and a family support program.

Figure 7.2 provides another example of an agency that also deals with families and children. This agency (Richmond Family Services) has only two programs, a Behavioral Adaptation Treatment Program and a Receiving and Assessment Family Home Program. The latter is further broken down into two components—a Family Support Component and a Receiving and Assessment Component. In addition, the Receiving and Assessment Component is further broken down into Crisis Support Services, Child Care Services, and Family Home Provider Services.

How many programs are there in Figure 7.2? The answer is two—however, we need to note that this agency conceptualized its service delivery much more thoroughly than did the agency outlined in Figure 7.1. Richmond Family Services has conceptualized the Receiving and Assessment Component of its Receiving and Assessment Family Home Program into three separate subcomponents: Crisis Support

Services, Child Care Services, and Family Home Provider Services. In short, Figure 7.2 is more detailed in how it delivers its services than is the agency represented in Figure 7.1. Programs that are more clearly defined are generally easier to implement, operate, and evaluate.

Another example of how programs can be organized under an agency is presented in Figure 7.3. This agency, the Women's Emergency Shelter, has a Residential Program and a Nonresidential Program. Its Residential Program has Crisis Counseling Services and Children's Support Services, and the Nonresidential Program has Crisis Counseling Services and Public Awareness Services. This agency distinguishes the services it provides between the women who stay within the shelter (its Residential Program) and those who come and go (its Nonresidential Program). The agency could have conceptualized the services it offers in a number of different ways.

A final example of how an agency can map out its services is presented in Figure 7.4. As can be seen, the agency's Child Welfare Program is broken down

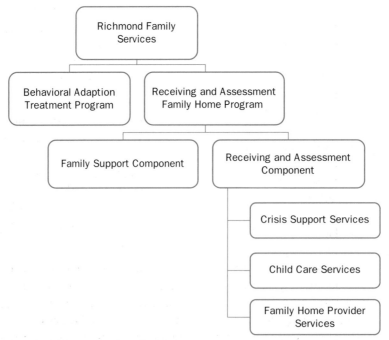

Figure 7.2: **Organizational chart of a family service agency (highlighting the Receiving and Assessment Family Home Program).**

Figure 7.3: **Organizational chart of a women's emergency shelter.**

into three services, and the Native Child Protection Services is further subdivided into four components: an Investigation Component, a Family Service Child in Parental Care Component, a Family Services Child in Temporary Alternate Care Component, and a Permanent Guardianship Component.

The general rule of ensuring that programs within an agency are logically linked together may seem simple enough that you might be wondering why we are emphasizing this point. The reality is that way too many programs are added to agencies on a haphazard, chaotic, and disorganized basis. This is because new programs spring out of last-minute funding opportunities that come available for new, but totally dissimilar, programs (to the agency's goal, that is). While a social service administrator must constantly seek new resources to provide better and/or additional services within the agency's programs, it's important that new and additional programs do not compromise existing ones.

By simply glancing at Figures 7.1–7.4 it can be seen that how an agency labels its programs and subprograms is arbitrary. For example, the agency that represents Figure 7.2 labels its subprograms as components and its sub-subprograms as services. The agency that represents Figure 7.3 simply labels its subprograms as services. The main point is that an agency must design its programs, components, and services in a logical way that makes the most sense in view of the agency's overall goal, which is guided by its mission statement and mandate.

Naming Programs

There is no standard approach to naming programs in the social services, but there are themes that may assist with organizing an agency's programs. We present four themes and suggest, as a general rule, that you pick only one (or one combination) to systematically name all of its programs:

- *Function,* such as Adoption Program or Family Support Program
- *Setting,* such as Group Home Program or Residential Program
- *Target population,* such as Services for the Handicapped Program
- *Social problem,* such as Child Sexual Abuse Program or Behavioral Adaptation Treatment Program

Program names can include acronyms such as P.E.T. (Parent Effectiveness Training), IY (Incredible Years: A Parent Training Program), or catchy titles such as Incredible Edibles (a nutritional program for children). The appeal of such program names is that

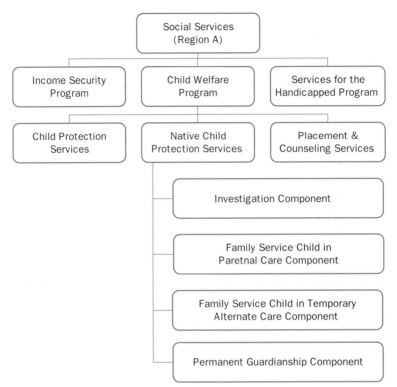

Figure 7.4: **Organizational chart of a state's social service delivery system (highlighting the Native Child Protection Services).**

they are endearing to the program's staff and clients alike who only are familiar with the program's services in the first place. Other's will not have clue to what the program is all about. However, unless the chic acronym (the program's name) is accompanied by a substantial marketing strategy, the program will go unnoticed by the general public, other social service providers, potential funders, and potential clients alike.

Therefore, the primary purpose of a program should be reflected in the program's name. Including the target social problem (or the main client need) in the program's name simplifies communication of a program's purpose. In this way, a program's name is linked to its goal, and there is less confusion about what services it offers.

Nondescript program names can lead to confusion in understanding a program's purpose. The Group Home Program in Figure 7.1, for example, suggests that this program aims to provide a residence for clients. In fact, all clients residing in the group home

are there to fulfill a specific purpose. Depending on the goal of the program, the primary purpose could be to offer shelter and safety for teenage runaways. Or the program's aim might be the enhanced functioning of adolescents with developmental disabilities, for example.

An Agency Versus a Program

What's the difference between an agency and a program? Like an agency, a program is an organization that also exists to fulfill a social purpose. There is one main difference, however: a program has a narrower, better defined purpose and is always nested within an agency. Nevertheless, sometimes an agency may itself have a narrow, well-defined purpose. The sole purpose of a counseling agency, for example, may be to serve couples who struggle with a sexual dysfunction.

In this case, the agency comprises only one program, and the terms *agency* and *program* refer to the same thing. If the clientele happens to include a high proportion of couples who are infertile, for example, it may later be decided that some staff members should specialize in infertility counseling (with a physician as a co-counselor) while other workers continue to deal with all other aspects of sexual dysfunction.

In this case, there would then be two distinct sets of social work staff (or the same staff who provide two distinct independent interventions), each focusing on a different goal, and two separate types of clients; that is, there would be two programs (one geared toward infertility counseling and the other toward sexual dysfunction). Creating programs that target specific problems and populations facilitates the development of evidence-based knowledge because workers can hone the focus of their professional development on specialized knowledge and skills. However, the agency, with its board, its senior administrator (executive director), and its administrative policies and procedures, would remain as a single entity.

DESIGNING PROGRAMS

Building or creating a social work program involves general and specific thinking about a program. The process begins by articulating a program's general intentions for solving identified social problems—the conceptualization or idea of the program's purpose. It also involves setting specific plans for how the program is to accomplish what it sets out to do.

A program for children who are sexually aggressive, for example, may aim to reduce the deviant sexual behavior of its young clients (i.e., the intention) by providing individual counseling (i.e., the plan for achieving the intention). A major purpose of a program's design is to easily communicate a model of service delivery to interested stakeholders. A program's design, via the use of a logic model, provides a blueprint for implementing its services, monitoring its activities, and evaluating both its operations and achievements.

Program designs present plausible and logical plans for how programs aim to produce change for their clients. Therefore, implicit in every program logic model

is the idea of theory—an explanation for how client change is suppose to be brought about (to be discussed in depth in the following chapter). The program for children who are sexually aggressive, for example, suggests that such children will reduce their sexual perpetration by gaining understanding or insight through sessions with an individual counselor. Programs that articulate a specific theoretical approach, such as psychoanalytic or behavior counseling, make their program theory more explicit. And, the more explicit, the better.

Figure 7.5 displays the four major components that are used to describe how programs deliver their services.

Box 7.1 displays a concise example of how the logic of Figure 7.5 is actually carried out within an evidence-based family support program. Included are:

- Program's goal
- Mission statement
- Three of the program's objectives (with literary support)
- Workers' sample activities to meet program objectives

Evidence-Based Programs

The knowledge we need to evaluate our programs is generally derived from your social work courses. There are many evidence-based interventions, or programs, in use today. All of them have been evaluated, to various degrees. Some have been evaluated in a rigorous manner—some less so. Some are very effective (e.g., Incredible Years) and some are downright dreadful (e.g., Scared Straight). The point is, however, that they all have been evaluated and have provided evidence of their degree of effectiveness. Go to the following websites to get a flavor of what social work programs are about and how they have been evaluated to be labeled "evidence based:"

- The Office of Juvenile Justice and Delinquency Prevention's Model Programs Guide
  http://www.ojjdp.gov/mpg
- National Registry of Evidence-Based Programs and Practices
  http://www.nrepp.samhsa.gov

Figure 7.5: **How a program's services are conceptualized from the case level to the program level.**

- Center for the Study and Prevention of Violence
  http://www.colorado.edu/cspv/blueprints
- Center for the Study of Social Policy
  http://www.cssp.org
- Promising Practices Network on Children, Families, and Communities
  http://www.promisingpractices.net/programs.asp
- Social Programs That Work
  http://evidencebasedprograms.org
- Social Development Research Group
  http://www.sdrg.org/rhcsummary.asp#6
- The Campbell Collaboration: C2-Ripe Library
  http://www.campbellcollaboration.org/selected_presentations/index.php
- The Cochrane Library
  http://www.thecochranelibrary.com/view/0/index.html
- National Prevention Dropout Center
  http://www.dropoutprevention.org
- What Works Clearinghouse
  http://ies.ed.gov/ncee/wwc
- Performance Well
  http://www.performwell.org
- Center for AIDS Prevention Studies (CAPS)
  http://caps.ucsf.edu

- Positive Behavior Supports and Interventions
  http://www.pbisworld.com
- Expectant and Parenting Youth in Foster Care: A Resource Guide 2014
  http://www.cssp.org/reform/child-welfare/pregnant-and-parenting-youth/Expectant-and-Parenting-Youth-in-Foster-Care_A-Resource-Guide.pdf

Selecting an Evidence-Based Program

As you can see from that preceding websites, there are hundreds of evidenced-based social work programs that you can implement within your agency. We suggest that all agencies should consider implementing evidence-based programs whenever possible. The following are 23 criteria that you need to consider when selecting one to implement within your local community's social service delivery system:

Program match
1. How well do the program's goals and objectives reflect what your agency hopes to achieve?
2. How well do the program's goals match those of your intended participants?
3. Is the program of sufficient length and intensity (i.e., "strong enough") to be effective with your particular group of participants?

BOX 7.1 EXAMPLE OF AN EVIDENCE-BASED FAMILY SUPPORT INTERVENTION (FROM FIGURE 7.5)

Program Goal

The goal of the Family Support Program is to help children who are at risk for out-of-home placement due to physical abuse (*current social problem to be tackled*) by providing intensive home-based services (*means by which the change is supposed to be brought about*) that will strengthen the interpersonal functioning (*desired state*) of all family members (*client population to be served*)

Mission Statement

This program strives to provide a variety of support services to families and children in need while also maintaining their rights, their safety, and their human dignity.

Program Objectives

1. Increase positive social support for parents by the end of the fourth week after the start of the intervention.

   - Literary Support: A lack of positive social support has been repeatedly linked to higher risk for child abuse. Studies show that parents with greater social support and less stress report more pleasure in their parenting roles.
     - Sample of Activities: Refer to support groups; evaluate criteria for positive support; introduce to community services; reconnect clients with friends and family.
       - Measuring Instrument: *Social Support Scale.*
2. Increase problem-solving skills for family members by the end of the eighth week after the start of the intervention.

   - Literary Support: Problem-solving is a tool for breaking difficult dilemmas into manageable pieces. Enhancing individuals' skills in systematically addressing problems increases the likelihood that they will successfully tackle new problems as they arise. Increasing problem-solving skills for parents and children equips family members to handle current problems, anticipate and prevent future ones, and advance their social functioning.
     - Sample of Activities: Teach steps to problem-solving; role play problem-solving scenarios; use supportive counseling.
       - Measuring Instrument: *The Problem-Solving Inventory.*
3. Increase parents' use of noncorporal child management strategies by the end of the intervention.

   - Literary Support: Research studies suggest that deficiency in parenting skills is associated with higher recurrence of abuse. Many parents who abuse their children have a limited repertoire of ways to discipline their children.
     - Sample of Activities: Teach noncorporal discipline strategies; inform parents about the criminal implications of child abuse; assess parenting strengths; and provide reading material about behavior management.
     - Measuring Instrument: *Checklist of Discipline Strategies.*

4. Are your potential participants willing and able to make the time commitment required by the program?
5. Has the program demonstrated effectiveness with a target population similar to yours?
6. To what extent might you need to adapt this program to fit the needs of your local community? How might such adaptations affect the effectiveness of the program?
7. Does the program allow for adaptation?
8. How well does the program complement current programming both in your organization and in your local community?

Program quality

9. Has this program been shown to be effective? What is the quality of this evidence?
10. Is the level of evidence sufficient for your organization?
11. Is the program listed on any respected evidence-based program registries? What rating has it received on those registries?
12. For what audiences has the program been found to work?
13. Is there information available about what adaptations are acceptable if you

do not implement this program exactly as designed? Is adaptation assistance available from the program's developer?

14. What is the extent and quality of training offered by the program's developers?

15. Do the program's designers offer technical assistance? Is there a charge for this assistance?

16. What is the opinion and experience of others who have used the program?

Organizational resources

17. What are the training, curriculum, and implementation costs of the program?

18. Can your organization afford to implement this program now and in the long term?

19. Do you have staff capable of implementing this program? Do they have the qualifications recommended (or required) to facilitate the program?

20. Would your staff be enthusiastic about a program of this kind, and are they willing to make the necessary time commitment?

21. Can this program be implemented in the time available?

22. What's the likelihood that this program will be sustained in the future?

23. Are your stakeholders supportive of your implementation of this program?

WRITING PROGRAM GOALS

A program goal has much in common with an agency goal, which was discussed previously:

- Like an agency goal, a program goal must also be compatible with the agency's mission statement as well as the agency goal and at least one agency objective. Program goals must logically flow from the agency as they are announcements of expected outcomes dealing with the social problem that the program is attempting to prevent, eradicate, or ameliorate.

- Like an agency goal, a program goal is not intended to be measurable; it simply provides a programmatic direction for the program to follow.

- A program goal must also possess four major characteristics:
  1. It must identify a current social problem area.
  2. It must include a specific target population within which the problem resides.
  3. It must include the desired future state for this population.
  4. It must state how it plans to achieve the desired state.

- In addition to the aforementioned four major criteria for writing program goals, there are seven additional minor criteria:
  5. *Easily* understood—write it so the rationale for the goal is apparent.
  6. Declarative statement—provide a complete sentence that describes a goal's intended outcome.
  7. Positive terms—frame the goal's outcomes in positive terms.
  8. Concise—get the complete idea of your goal across as simply and briefly as possible while leaving out unnecessary detail.
  9. Jargon-free—use language that most "non–social work people" are likely to understand.
  10. Short—use as few words as possible.
  11. Avoid the *use of double negatives*.

In sum, a program goal reflects the intention of social workers within the program. For example, workers in a program may expect that they will "enable adolescents with developmental disabilities to lead full and productive lives." The program goal phrase of "full and productive lives," however, can mean different things to different people.

Some may believe that a full and productive life cannot be lived without integration into the community; they may, therefore, want to work toward placing these youth in the mainstream school system, enrolling them in community activities, and finally returning them to their parental homes, with a view to making them self-sufficient in adult life. Others may believe that a full and productive life for these adolescents means the security of institutional teaching and care and the companionship of children with similar needs. Still others may believe that institutional care combined with community contact is the best compromise.

Program goal statements are meant to be sufficiently elusive to allow for changes in service delivery approach or clientele over time. Another reason that goals have intangible qualities is because we want enough flexibility in our programs to adjust program conceptualization and operation as needed. Indeed, by establishing a program design, we begin the process of crafting a theory of client change. By evaluating the program, we test the program's theory—its plan for creating client change. Much more will be said about this in the next chapter.

Preparing for Unintended Consequences

Working toward a program's goal may result in a number of unintended results that emerge in the immediate environment that surrounds the program. For example, a group home for adolescents with developmental disabilities may strive to enable residents to achieve self-sufficiency in a safe and supportive environment. This is the intended result, or goal. Incidentally, however, the very presence of the group home may produce organized resistance from local neighbors—a negative unintended result.

The resistance may draw the attention of the media, which in turn draws a sympathetic response from the general public about the difficulties associated with finding a suitable location for homes caring for youth with special needs—a positive unintended result.

On occasion, the unintended result can thwart progress toward the program's goal; that is, youth with developmental disabilities would not feel safe or supported if neighbors act in unkind or unsupportive ways. This condition would almost certainly hamper the youths' ability to achieve self-sufficiency in the community.

PROGRAM GOALS VERSUS AGENCY GOALS

Perhaps the group home mentioned earlier is run by an agency that has a number of other homes for adolescents with developmental disabilities (see Figure 7.6). It's unlikely that all of the children in these homes will be capable of self-sufficiency as adults; some may have reached their full potential when they have learned to feed or bathe themselves.

The goal of self-sufficiency will, therefore, not be appropriate for the agency as a whole, although it might do very well for Group Home X, which serves children who function at higher levels. The agency's goal must be broader to encompass a wider range of situations—and because it's broader, it will probably be more vague.

To begin, the agency may decide that its goal is "to enable adolescents with developmental disabilities to reach their full potential" as outlined in Figure 7.6:

- Group Home X, one of the programs within the agency, can then interpret "full potential" to mean self-sufficiency and can formulate a program goal based on this interpretation.
- Group Home Y, another program within the agency serving children who function at lower levels, may decide that it can realistically do no more than provide a caring environment for the children and emotional support for their families. It may translate this decision into another program goal: "To enable adolescents with developmental disabilities to experience security and happiness."
- Group Home Z, a third program within the agency, may set as its program goal "To enable adolescents with developmental disabilities to acquire the social and vocational skills necessary for satisfying and productive lives."

In short, Figure 7.6 illustrates the relationship among the individual goal of each of the three homes to the single goal of the agency. Note how logical and consistent the goals of the three programs are

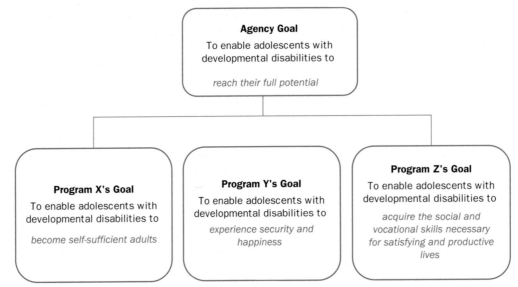

Figure 7.6: **Organizational chart of an agency with three highly related programs.**

with the agency's single overall goal. This example illustrates three key points about the character of a program goal:

- A program goal simplifies the reason for the program to exist and provides direction for its workers.
- Program goals of different but related programs within the same agency may differ, but they must all be linked to the agency's overall goal. They must all reflect both their individual purpose and the purpose of the agency of which they are a part.
- Program goals are not measurable. Consider the individual goals of the three group homes in Figure 7.6; none of them are measurable in their present form.

Concepts such as happiness, security, self-sufficiency, and full potential mean different things to different people and cannot be measured until they have been clearly defined. Many social work goals are phrased in this way, putting forth more of an elusive intent than a definite, definable, measurable purpose. Nor is this a flaw; it's simply what a goal is, a statement of an intended result that must be clarified before it can be measured. As we will see

next, program goals are clarified by the objectives they formulate.

PROGRAM OBJECTIVES

A program's objectives are derived from its goal. As you will see shortly, program objectives are measurable indicators of the program's goal; they articulate the specific client outcomes that the program wishes to achieve; stated clearly and precisely, they make it possible to tell to what degree the program's results have been achieved.

All program objectives must be client-centered; they must be formulated to help a client in relation to the social problem articulated by the program's goal. Programs often are designed to change client systems in three nonmutually exclusive areas:

- Knowledge
- Affects
- Behaviors

Knowledge-Based Objectives

Knowledge-based program objectives are commonly found within educational programs, where the aim is to increase the client's knowledge in some specific area. The words "to increase knowledge" are critical here: They imply that the recipient of the education will have learned something, for example, "to increase teenage mother's knowledge about the stages of child development between birth and 2 years." The hoped-for increase in knowledge can then be measured by assessing the mother's knowledge levels before and after the program. The program objective is achieved when it can be demonstrated (via measurement) that learning has occurred.

Affect-Based Objectives

Affect-based program objectives focus on changing either feelings about oneself or awareness about another person or thing. For example, a common affect-based program objective in social work is to raise a client's self-esteem, or interventions are designed to decrease feelings of isolation, increase marital satisfaction, and decrease feelings of depression. In addition, feelings or attitudes toward other people or things are the focus of many social work programs.

All program objectives are derived from its single goal.

To give just a few examples, programs may try to change negative views toward people of color, homosexuality, or gender roles. "Affects" here includes attitudes because attitudes are a way of looking at the world. It's important to realize that, although particular attitudes may be connected to certain behaviors, they are two separate constructs.

Behaviorally Based Objectives

Very often, a program objective is established to change the behavior of a person or group: for example, to reduce drug abuse among adolescents, to increase the use of community resources by seniors, or to reduce the number of hate crimes in a community. Sometimes knowledge or affect objectives are used as a means to this end. In other words, the expectation

is that a change in attitude or knowledge will lead to a change in behavior.

The social worker might assume that adolescents who know more about the effects of drugs will use or abuse them less, that seniors who know more about available community resources will use them more often, or that citizens that have more positive feelings toward each other will be less tolerant of prejudice and discrimination. Sometimes these assumptions are valid; sometimes they are not. In any case, when behaviorally based objectives are used, the program must verify that the desired behavior change has actually occurred.

WRITING PROGRAM OBJECTIVES

Whether program objectives are directed at knowledge levels, affects, or behaviors, they have to be SMART ones too; that is, they have to be **S**pecific, **M**easurable, **A**chievable, **R**ealistic, and **T**ime phased. All evidence-based social work programs cannot exist without SMART program objectives.

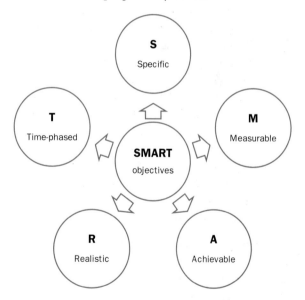

Specific (S)

In addition to being meaningful and logically linked to the program's goal (to be discussed shortly), program objectives must be specific. They must be complete and clear in their wording. Following are two columns. The left column contains active verbs that your program objective can start out with. The column on the right contains examples of possible types of program objectives you could be trying to achieve.

Examples of Active Verbs	Examples of Measureable Program Objectives
• Increase	• Social skills
• Decrease	• Feeling of depression
• Maintain	• Feelings of loneliness
• Obtain	• Attitudes toward authority
• Improve	• Aggressiveness
• Access	• Self-esteem levels

You need to mix and match to form appropriate objectives. For example, you could write the following:

- Increase self-esteem levels
- Decrease feelings of loneliness

Now that we know how to make a program objective specific, we turn to its measurability, the second quality required of a SMART program objective. Simply put, just ask the question, "Is the objective measurable?" If it can't be measured then it cannot be a program objective. As we know by now, the purpose of measurement is to gather data. A measure is usually thought of as a number: an amount of money in dollars, a numerical rating representing a level of intensity, or scores on simple self-administered standardized measuring instruments.

Measurable (M)

The purpose of setting a program objective is to bring focus to the desired change, which, if obtained, will contribute to the obtainment of the program's goal. One of the main purposes of making a measurement is to define a perceived change, in terms of either numbers or clear words.

A measurement might show, for example, that the assertiveness of a woman who has been previously abused has increased by 5 points on a standardized measuring instrument (a program objective), or that a woman's feelings of safety in her neighborhood have increased by 45 points (another program objective).

Learn more about how to measure program objectives in Tools L and M in the Evaluation Toolkit.

If the hoped-for change cannot be measured, then it's not a SMART program objective—it's missing the "M." Tools L and M present ways of measuring program objectives, but, for the time being, we turn to the third quality of a SMART program objective: achievability.

Achievable (A)

Not only must a program objective be specific and measureable, it must be achievable as well. Objectives should be achievable within a given time frame and with available current program resources and constraints. There is nothing worse than creating an unrealistic program objective that cannot be realistically reached by the client group it was written for. This unfortunately happens way more times than we wish to acknowledge. Just ask and answer the question, "Can the program's objective be reached given: (1) the clients' presenting problems, (2) the program's current overall resources, (3) the skill level of the workers, and (4) the amount of time the intervention is suppose to take?"

Realistic (R)

In addition to being specific, measurable, and achievable, program objectives must also be realistic. Having realistic program objectives ties in heavily with having achievable ones (mentioned earlier). A program objective is realistic when it bears a sensible relationship to the longer term result to be achieved—the program goal.

If a program's goal is to promote self-sufficiency of teenagers living on the street, for example, improving their ability to balance a monthly budget may be a realistic program objective; however, increasing their ability to recite the dates of the reigns of English monarchs is not, because it bears no relation to the program's goal of self-sufficiency.

The point here—and a point that will be stressed over and over in this text—is that an effective evidence-based program must demonstrate realistic and meaningful linkages among its overall goal (its reason for being) and its programs' objectives.

Time Phased (T)

Program objectives need to provide a time frame indicating when the objective will be measured or a time by which the objective will be met. Box 7.2 presents how the three program objectives in our Family Support Program illustrated in Box 7.1 were measured with SMART objectives. Notice that the three program objectives indirectly measure the program's goal; that is, the goal is achieved by the success of the three program's objectives.

INDICATORS

An indicator is a measurable gauge that shows (or indicates) the progress made toward achieving a SMART program objective. Some indicators include participation rates, income levels, poverty rates, attitudes, beliefs, behaviors, community norms, policies, health status, and incidence and prevalence rates. In the simplest of terms, indicators ultimately are used to measure your program objectives.

Sometimes these program objectives are called dependent variables, outcome variables, or criterion variables. The most important thing to remember is that your indicators must be based off your program's logic model (to be discussed shortly). A program objective can be measured with only one indicator, such as the following:

Program Objective	Single Indicator
Client obtains more stable housing	A. Percentage of clients who move to a transitional shelter, long-term housing, rehabilitative setting, or the home of a friend or family member.
Increase self-esteem	A. Hudson's Index of Self-Esteem (see Figure L.1 in Tool L)

And at other times, a program objective can be measured with more than one indicator, such as the following:

Program Objective	Multiple Indicators
Clients accesses needed services	A. Percentage of clients who agree to a recovery/treatment service plan by the end of their 30th day of shelter at that site. B. Percentage of clients who, as a result of their service plan, connected with supportive services within 30 days of the start of case management.

PRACTICE OBJECTIVES

Program objectives can be thought of as formal statements of a declaration of desired change for all clients served by a program. In contrast, practice objectives refer to the personal objectives of an individual client, whether that client is a community, couple, group, individual, or institution. Practice objectives are also commonly referred to as treatment objectives,

BOX 7.2 GRID FOR SMART PROGRAM OBJECTIVES (FROM BOX 7.1)

Program objectives	SPECIFIC	MEASURABLE	ACHIEVABLE	REALISTIC	TIME PHASED
Program objectives	It says exactly what you are going to do. It can't be too broad or vague.	There is a way of measuring the objective. It must be able to produce indicators.	The program objective can be actually achieved with your given resources and constraints.	The program objective is directly related to your program's goal.	The objective must have a date for its achievement.
To increase positive social support for parents by the end of the fourth week after the start of the intervention	This program objective is very specific. It is not vague.	This objective can produce a number of indicators. We have chosen two: (1) client logs, and (2) The Provision of Social Relations Scale.	This program objective can be easily achieved by the end of the first four weeks after the intervention starts given our resources and the skill levels of the social workers.	This program objective is directly related to the program's goal, which is to support family units where children are at risk for out-of-home placement due to problems with physical abuse.	"By the end of the fourth week after the intervention starts" is very specific in reference to time frames.
To increase problem-solving skills for family members by the end of the eighth week after the start of the intervention	This program objective is very specific. It is not vague.	This objective can produce a number of indicators. We have chosen one: The Problem Solving Inventory.	This program objective can be easily achieved by the end of the eighth week after the intervention starts given our resources and the skill levels of the social workers. We also believe that the clients have the motivation and capacity for the desired change to occur.	This program objective is directly related to the program's goal, which is to support family units where children are at risk for out-of-home placement due to problems with physical abuse.	"By the end of the eighth week after the intervention starts" is very specific in reference to time frames.

BOX 7.2 CONTINUED

| To increase parent's use of noncorporal child management strategies by the end of the intervention | This program objective is very specific. It is not vague. | This objective can produce a number of indicators. We have chosen two: [1] Goal Attainment Scaling and [2] Checklist of Discipline Strategies. | This program objective can be easily achieved by the end of the intervention given our resources and the skill levels of the social workers. We also believe that the clients have the motivation and capacity for the desired change to occur. | This program objective is directly related to the program's goal, which is to support family units where children are at risk for out-of-home placement due to problems with physical abuse. | "By the end of the intervention" is very specific in reference to time frames. |

individual objectives, therapeutic objectives, client objectives, client goals, and client target problems.

All practice objectives formulated by the social worker and the client must be logically related to the program's objectives, which are linked to the program's goal. In other words, all practice objectives for all clients must be delineated in such a way that they are logically linked to one or more of the program's objectives. If not, then it's unlikely that the clients' needs will be met by the program.

If a social worker formulates a practice objective with a client that does not logically link to one or more of the program's objectives, the social worker may be doing some good for the client but without program sanction or support. In fact, why would a program hire a social worker to do something the worker was not employed to do?

At the risk of sounding redundant, a program is always evaluated on its program objectives. Thus we must fully understand that it's these objectives that we must strive to attain—all of our "practice" efforts must be directly linked to them.

Example: Bob's Self-Sufficiency

Let's put the concept of a practice objective into concrete terms. Following is a simple diagram of how three practice objectives, if met, lead to increased life skills, which in turn leads to self-sufficiency. Is the diagram logical to you? If so, why? If not, why not?

These three interrelated practice objectives for Bob demonstrate a definite link with the program's objective, which in turn is linked to the program's goal. It should be evident by now that defining a practice objective is a matter of stating what is to be changed. This provides an indication of the client's current state, or where the client is. Unfortunately, knowing this is not the same thing as knowing where one wants to go. Sometimes the destination is apparent, but in other cases it may be much less clear.

PRACTICE ACTIVITIES

So far we have focused on the kinds of goals and objectives that social workers hope to achieve as a result of their work. The question now arises: What is that work? What do social workers do in order to help clients achieve the program's objectives such as obtaining knowledge (e.g., knowing how to make nutritional meals), feelings (feeling less anxious), or behaviors (reduce the number of truancies per school year)?

The question remains: What practice activities do social workers engage in to meet a program's objectives? The answer, of course, is that they do many different things. They show films, facilitate group discussions, hold therapy sessions, teach classes, and conduct individual interviews. They attend staff meetings, do paperwork, consult with colleagues, and advocate for clients.

The important point about all such activities is that they are undertaken to move clients forward on one or more of the program's objectives. All of evidence-based programs have SMART program objectives where each objective has practice activities associated with it.

A social worker who teaches a class on nutrition, for example, hopes that class participants will learn certain specific facts about nutrition. If this learning is to take place, the facts to be learned must be included in the material presented. In other words, our practice activities must be directly related to our client's practice objectives which are directly related to our program's objectives. It's critically important that social workers engage in practice activities that have the best chance to create positive client change.

Defining practice activities is an essential ingredient to understanding what interventions work. The list of practice activities is endless and dynamic in that workers can add, drop, and modify them to suit the needs of individual clients. Reviewing a list of practice activities with stakeholder groups gives them

Three Pracitice Objectives for Bob
1. Increase personal self-management skills
2. Increase general social skills
3. Increase drug resistance skills

Program Objective
Increase life skills

Program Goal
Become self-sufficient adults

Social worker engages in practice activities *in order to meet...*	the client's practice objective(s) *in order to meet...*	the program's objective(s) *in order to meet...*	the program's goal.

an idea of the nature of client service delivery offered by the program. Above is a diagram that presents the preceding discussion in graphic form.

LOGIC MODELS

Your program must have a logic model if it's to have any creditability. As you briefly saw in Chapter 3 and will see in depth in the following chapter, logic models are tools that help people physically see the interrelations among the various components of your program. A logic model is nothing more than a concept map that visually describes the logic of how your program is supposed to work.

Positions Your Program for Success

The W. K. Kellogg Foundation (2004) suggests that use of the logic model is an effective way to ensure a program's success. This would be a good time to review Figures 3.2 and 3.3 in Chapter 3. Using a logic model throughout the design and implementation of your program helps organize and systematize your program planning, management, and evaluation functions:

- In *Program Design and Planning,* a logic model serves as a planning tool to develop program strategy and enhance your ability to clearly explain and illustrate program concepts and approach for key stakeholders, including funders. Logic models can help craft structure and organization for program design and build in self-evaluation based on shared understanding of what is to take place. During the planning phase, developing a logic model requires stakeholders to examine

best-practice research and practitioner experience in light of the strategies and activities selected to achieve results.
- In *Program Implementation,* a logic model forms the core for a focused management plan that helps you identify and collect the data needed to monitor and improve programming. Using the logic model during program implementation and management requires you to focus energies on achieving and documenting results. Logic models help you to consider and prioritize the program aspects most critical for tracking and reporting and make adjustments as necessary.
- For *Program Evaluation and Strategic Reporting,* a logic model presents program information and progress toward goals in ways that inform, advocate for a particular program approach, and teach program stakeholders.

We all know the importance of reporting results to funders and to community stakeholders alike. Communication is a key component of a program's success and sustainability. Logic models can help strategic marketing efforts in three primary ways:

1. *Describing programs* in language clear and specific enough to be understood and evaluated.
2. *Focusing attention and resources* on priority program operations and key results for the purposes of learning and program improvement.
3. *Developing targeted communication* and marketing strategies.

Simple and Straightforward Pictures

A picture *is* worth a thousand words. The point of developing a logic model is to come up with a relatively simple image that reflects how and why your program will work. Doing this as a group brings the power of consensus and group examination of values and beliefs about change processes and program results.

Reflect Group Process and Shared Understanding

A logic model developed by all of a program's stakeholders produces a useful tool and refines the program's concepts and plans during the process. We recommend that a logic model be developed collaboratively in an inclusive, collegial process that engages as many key stakeholders as possible.

Change Over Time

Like programs, logic models change over time. Thus as a program grows and develops, so does its logic model. A program logic model is merely a snapshot of a program at one point in time. It's a work in progress—a working draft—that can be refined as your program develops.

SUMMARY

This chapter briefly discussed what a social work agency is all about and how programs fit within them. It touched on the fundamentals of evidence-based programs and presented a few criteria for selecting one out of the many that exist. We discussed how to construct program goals, objectives, indicators, practice objectives, and practice activities. The chapter ended with a brief rational of why evidence-based programs need to have logic models which is explored in-depth in the following chapter.

The goal of this chapter is to provide you with a beginning knowledge base for you to feel comfortable in answering the below questions. AFTER you have read the chapter, indicate how comfortable you feel you are in answering each of the following questions on a 5-point scale where

1 Very uncomfortable	2 Somewhat uncomfortable	3 Neutral	4 Somewhat comfortable	5 Very comfortable

If you rated any question between 1–3, reread the section of the chapter where the information for the question is found. If you still feel that you're uncomfortable in answering the question, then talk with your instructor and/or your classmates for more clarification.

	Questions	Degree of comfort? *(Circle one number)*
1	Discuss how mission statements are used within agencies.	1 2 3 4 5
2	Discuss how goals are used within agencies.	1 2 3 4 5
3	Discuss the differences between an agency's mission statement and its goal. Provide a social work example throughout your discussion.	1 2 3 4 5
4	List and then discuss the four requirements of an agency's goal. Provide an example of one using your field placement (or work) setting.	1 2 3 4 5
5	What's an agency? What's a program? Discuss the differences between the two?	1 2 3 4 5
6	List and then discuss the four themes that you can use in naming social work programs. Rename the program that you are housed within in reference to your field (or work) setting using the criteria presented in the book.	1 2 3 4 5
7	What are evidence-based programs? Select one from the websites presented in the book and discuss what the program is all about and how it was evaluated to become "evidence-based."	1 2 3 4 5
8	Discuss each one of the 23 criteria that need to be addressed when you select an evidence-based program to implement within your community.	1 2 3 4 5
9	List and then discuss the 11 criteria that need to be considered when writing a program goal.	1 2 3 4 5
10	Discuss the differences between an agency's goal and a program's goal.	1 2 3 4 5

continued

11	What are program objectives? Provide a social work example throughout your discussion.	1 2 3 4 5
12	What are knowledge-based objectives? Provide a social work example throughout your discussion.	1 2 3 4 5
13	What are affect-based objectives? Provide a social work example throughout your discussion.	1 2 3 4 5
14	What are behaviourally based objectives? Provide a social work example throughout your discussion.	1 2 3 4 5
15	What are SMART objectives? Provide a social work example throughout your discussion.	1 2 3 4 5
16	What are indicators of a program objective? Provide a social work example throughout your discussion.	1 2 3 4 5
17	What are practice objectives? Provide a social work example throughout your discussion.	1 2 3 4 5
18	What are practice activities? Provide a social work example throughout your discussion.	1 2 3 4 5
19	What are logic models? Why are they useful to social work programs.?	1 2 3 4 5

AFTER you have read this chapter AND have completed all of the study questions, indicate how knowledgeable you feel you are for each of the following concepts on a 5-point scale where

1 Not knowledgeable at all	2 Somewhat unknowledgeable	3 Neutral	4 Somewhat knowledgeable	5 Very knowledgeable

	Concepts	Knowledge Level? (Circle one number)
1	The differences between agencies and programs	1 2 3 4 5
2	Agency and program mission statements	1 2 3 4 5
3	Agency and program goals	1 2 3 4 5
4	Requirements for agency and program goals	1 2 3 4 5
5	Constructing program names	1 2 3 4 5
6	Designing social work programs	1 2 3 4 5
7	Evidence-based programs	1 2 3 4 5
8	Criteria for selecting evidence-based programs	1 2 3 4 5
9	Writing program goals	1 2 3 4 5
10	Writing program objectives	1 2 3 4 5
11	Selecting indicators for program objectives	1 2 3 4 5
12	Formulating practice objectives	1 2 3 4 5
13	Formulating practice activities	1 2 3 4 5
14	Logic models	1 2 3 4 5
	Add up your scores (minimum = 14, maximum = 70)	Your total score =

A   66–70 = Professional evaluator in the making
A–   63–65 = Senior evaluator
B+   59–62 = Junior evaluator
B   56–58 = Assistant evaluator
B–   14–55 = Reread the chapter and redo the study questions

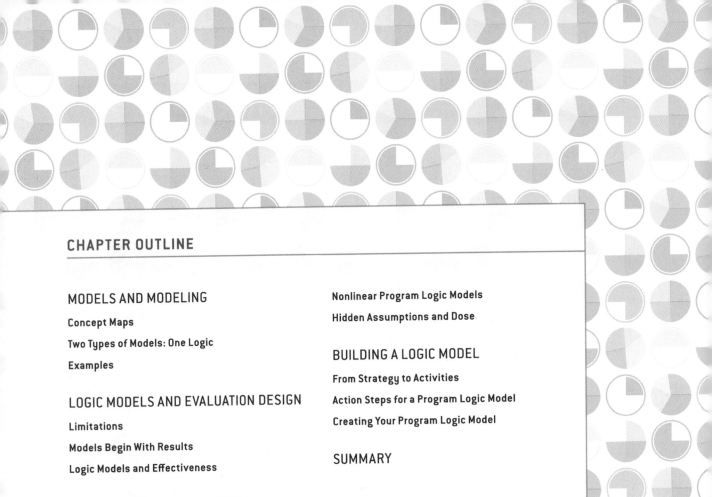

CHAPTER OUTLINE

If you don't know where you are going,
any road will get you there.

~ Lewis Carroll

THEORY OF CHANGE AND PROGRAM LOGIC MODELS

LISA WYATT KNOWLTON AND CYNTHIA C. PHILLIPS

Logic models were introduced in Chapter 3 when we discussed how they can be used to describe your social work program—Step 2 of the six-step process of doing an evaluation. They were then briefly discussed in the previous chapter in relation to how they can be used in actually designing a social service program.

Given what you already know about logic models from your previous readings, this chapter discusses them at a much more advanced level. In fact, this chapter presents two types of models that can be used in your modeling activities:

- **Theory of Change Models.** These are *conceptual*; that is, they are simply a general graphical representation of how you believe change will occur within your program. They are done *before* a program logic model is constructed.
- **Program Logic Models.** These are *operational*; that is, they are based off of your theory of change model. As depicted in Figures 3.2 and 3.3 in Chapter 3, they detail the resources, planned activities, outputs, and outcomes over time that reflect your program's intended goal. In an ideal world, they are constructed *after* a theory of change model is completed.

MODELS AND MODELING

Regardless of type—theory of change or program logic—good models are used to,

- explain an idea
- resolve a challenge
- assesses progress
- clarify complex relationships among a program's elements or parts
- organize information
- display thinking
- develop common language among stakeholders
- offer highly participatory learning opportunities
- document and emphasize explicit client and program outcomes
- clarify knowledge about what works and why
- identify important variables to measure and enable more effective use of evaluation resources
- provide a credible reporting framework
- lead to a program's improved design, planning, and management

Concept Maps

Models are concept maps that we all carry around in our minds about how the world does (or should) work. They are tools we can use to convey a scheme, program, or project in a brief, clear visual format. They describe our planned actions and the expected results from our actions. A model is a snapshot of an individual's or group's current thinking about how their social work program will work.

Modeling is also a technique that encourages the iterative development of a program. More specifically it creates a safe space for a program's stakeholders to start a debate, generate ideas, and support deliberations. More important, it allows us to think more clearly about specific relationships between and among variables. Models are a single, coherent logic that reflects a consistent thread that connects your program's overall design, implementation, and eventual evaluation. This thread of logic is critical to your program's effectiveness.

Modeling allows careful consideration of the relationship between what you actually do as a social worker (your day-to-day activities) and the results you obtain from your activities (outcomes). When tackled by a team—or a small group of stakeholders for that matter—models can be improved by engaging the knowledge and experience of others. The best models are socially constructed in a shared experience that is facilitated. The shared understanding and meaning they produce among social workers are valuable and enable success in subsequent steps of an evaluation's implementation.

Moreover, models are also used to calibrate alignment between the program's "big picture" and its various component parts. They can easily illustrate parts of a program or its whole system.

Two Types of Models: One Logic

As previously stated, there are two types of models: theory of change and program logic. They only differ by their level of detail and use. Nevertheless, they are both based on logic:

- **A theory of change model** is a very basic general representation of how you believe your planned change will occur that will lead to your intended results.

- **A program logic model** details the resources, planned activities, outputs, and their outcomes over time that reflect the program's intended results.

The level of detail and features distinguish theory of change models from program logic models. The two types of models and their relative features are highlighted in Table 8.1.

On one hand, the two models are different from one another in relation to time frame, level of detail, number of elements, display, and focus. On the other hand, they are alike because they share the same research, theory, practice, and/or literature. Essentially, the two types are simply different views of the same logic that have a shared origin. The two model also differ in purposes:

- **Theory of change models** display an idea or program in its simplest form using limited information. These models offer a chance to test plausibility. They are the "elevator speech" or "cocktail-napkin outline" of an idea or project.
- **Program logic models,** on the other hand, vary in detail but offer additional information that assists in a program's design, planning, strategy development, monitoring, and evaluation. Program logic models support a display that can be tested for feasibility. They are the proposal version of a social work program because they have fleshed out in detail—from a theory of change model—the resources, activities, outputs, outcomes, and other elements of interest to those creating and/or using the model.

Examples

The following two examples briefly explain the general concepts and terms related to theory of change models and program logic models. Although we show one of each type of model, it's important to keep in mind that these are only two examples from a much broader continuum of possibilities. There are many ways to express or display ideas and level of detail.

Table 8.1: **Features of Model Types.**

Features	Theory of Change	Program Logic
Time frame	No time	Time bound
Level of detail	Low	High
Elements	Few ("do + get")	Many
Primary display	Graphics	Graphics + text
Focus	Generic	Targets + specified results

Theory of Change Model Example

Theory of change models are the critical foundation for all social work programs. Often these models exist as part of an internal mental framework that is "dormant" or undisclosed. They can also imply considerable knowledge, experience, research, and practice. The evidence base for theory of change models typically is not made explicit.

Figure 8.1 shows a simple theory of change model for a community leadership program aptly titled "Community Leadership Program." Read from left to right, it illustrates that the program contains two strategies: an academy leadership curriculum (Strategy 1) and an academy leadership experience opportunity (Strategy 2).

These two strategies, when combined together and successfully implemented, will then lead to "more and better" community leaders, which in turn will lead to better community development. In short, the two strategies within the Community Leadership Program, when successfully implemented, leads to positive results.

Program Logic Model Example

Like theory of change models, program logic models are also visual methods of presenting an idea. And, like theory of change models, they are simply concept maps as mentioned in Chapter 3. They offer a way to describe and share an understanding of relationships (or connections) among elements necessary to operate your social work program. Logic models describe a bounded program: both what is planned (the doing) and what results are expected (the getting). They provide a clear road map to a specified end, with the end always being the outcomes and the ultimate impact of the program.

Common synonyms for logic models include concept maps, idea maps, frameworks, rich pictures, action, results or strategy maps, and mental models. Program logic models delineate—from start to finish—a specified program effort. For example, a program logic model for our Community Leadership Program (based on the theory of change model presented in Figure 8.1) would include the specified resources, activities, outputs, outcomes, and impact:

- Resources (or inputs) are what are needed to ensure the program can operate as planned. For example, money to pay your tuition is needed before you can enroll in your social work program, along with a host of other resources you will need.
- Activities are the tactical actions that occur within the program such as events, various types of services, workshops, lectures, publications, and the like. Together, activities make up your program's overall design—it's the intervention package. This is where the rubber hits the road. For example, one of the activities of your social work program is the courses you take. This is the "guts" of your social work program.

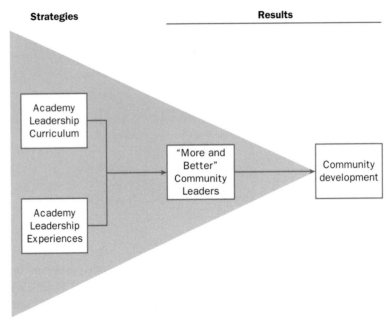

Figure 8.1: **Theory of change model for the Community Leadership Program.**

- Outputs are descriptive indicators of what the specific activities generate. For example, this could simply be the number of students who graduate each year after they complete the activities (i.e., courses).
- Outcomes are changes in our clients' awareness, knowledge levels, skills, and/or behaviors. The impact reflects changes over a longer period. For example, this could simply be the number of students who found social work jobs after graduating or the degree of your effectiveness as a social worker.

Figure 8.2 displays a simple program logic model for our Community Leadership Program shown as a theory of change model in Figure 8.1.

The program logic model illustrated in Figure 8.2 suggests that the program's desired results include more and better community leaders, which in turn will lead to better community development efforts. It implies the leadership development agenda is about resolution of community challenges and that, if resolved, will contribute to better community development.

To "read" this model, first note on the far right-hand column (column 6) the intended impact (ultimate aim) of the program: community development. Then move to the far left-hand column (column 1), where resources (or inputs) essential for the program to operate are listed. As you should know by now, program logic models employ an "if–then" sequences among their elements.

When applied to the elements in each column in Figure 8.2, it reads,

- IF we have these resources (column 1),
- THEN we can provide these activities (column 2).
- IF we accomplish these activities (column 2),
- THEN we can produce these outputs (column 3).
- IF we have these outputs (column 3),
- THEN we will secure these short-term outcomes (column 4).
- and so on.

Box 8.1 illustrates another version of how this "if–then" logic can be used.

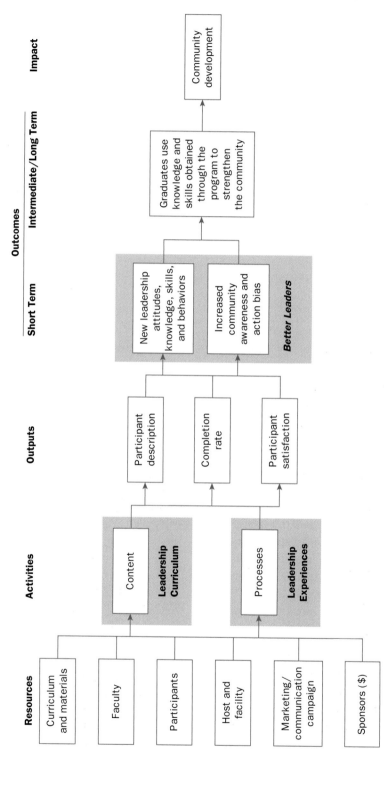

Figure 8.2: Program logic model for the Community Leadership Program (from Figure 8.1).

BOX 8.1 USING "IF-THEN" STATEMENTS IN DEVELOPING LOGIC MODELS

IF   a certain set of resources (such as staff, equipment, materials) are available,

THEN the program can provide a certain set of activities or services to participants.

IF   participants receive these services,

THEN they will experience specific changes in their knowledge, attitudes, or skills.

IF   individuals change their knowledge, attitudes, or skills,

THEN they will change their behavior and usual practice.

IF   enough participants change their behavior and practice,

THEN the program may have a broader impact on the families or friends of participants or on the community as a whole.

Thus a school-based alcohol prevention program could have the following theory:

Social worker provide alcohol prevention training to youth → Youth garin knowledge of alcohol avoidance strategies → Youth practice alcohol avoidance strategies → Youth reduce alcohol initiation and use

As a result of the reduced alcohol use of individual youth, alcohol problems in schools will decline.

LOGIC MODELS AND EVALUATION DESIGN

The program logic model depicted in Figure 8.2 is just one very simple representation of how a program might be designed. Many other variations of this example also exist that would still be logical and plausible.

A clear and coherent program logic model provides great assistance during an evaluation's design. It points out the key features and shows the relationships that may or may not need to be evaluated. At this level, evaluation questions are the foundation for an evaluation's design. If we apply this to our Community Leadership Program, for example, it's more than appropriate to focus on our program's intended results.

As illustrated in Box 2.1, a summative evaluation question could be: What difference did our program make in the community's development? Perhaps a place to begin is in determining the contribution the program made to the actual generation of more and better community leaders.

In this example, an evaluation could consider both changes in the awareness, knowledge, skills, and behavior of the program's participants as well as the impact they had on community development.

Stakeholders might also want to know about the content of the two activities (i.e., leadership curriculum, leadership experiences) and quality of training. They might be curious about implementation fidelity and adaptation too. Figure 8.3 demonstrates a program logic model with typical evaluation questions.

This program logic model represented by Figure 8.3 is serving as a concept map to guide the evaluation of the program. The five key evaluation questions are contained at the bottom of their respective columns in Figure 8.3. Key questions for our Community Leadership Program include:

1. Is the program doing the right things? (column 1)
2. Is the program doing things right? (column 3)
3. What difference has the program made among participants? (column 4)
4. What difference has the program made across the community? (columns 5 and 6)
5. What are the ways community needs can and should be addressed by the program? (columns 3–6)

Positioning questions on the logic model identifies where the data might be found to address any given inquiry:

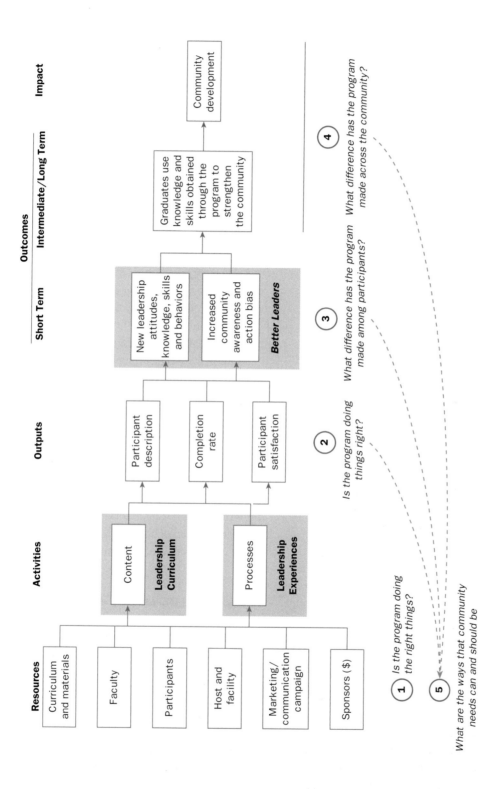

Figure 8.3: **Program evaluation model for the Community Leadership Program (from Figure 8.2).**

- Question 1 "tests" the logic constructed during the planning phase of the program. This question requires thoughtful connections to be drawn across activity accomplishment, implementation fidelity, and the attainment of desired outcomes/impact. It addresses the overall effectiveness of the selected activities and the related action in achieving the desired results.
- Question 2 examines implementation fidelity/variance as well as the scope, sequence, penetration, and quality of activities.
- Questions 3 and 4 focus on the extent to which outcomes and impact have been achieved.
- Question 5, like Question 1, should span the whole model to surface program improvement needs. Questions 1 and 5 are more reflective but are essential to a program's improved effectiveness.

These evaluation questions can be very helpful in the initial design and development of the program, as they help to aim the program's intervention(s). The next step is establishing indicators. Models also help us to guide the conversation and exploration needed to determine outcome indicators (see previous chapter), or the measures of progress, for any given social work program.

Limitations

It's important to note that the proper reference, "logic model," in no way guarantees that the model is, in fact, logical. While many models do demonstrate some modicum of logic, however, a logical representation does not always equal plausibility, feasibility, or success. There's some danger in seeing a graphic display on paper and considering it "true." This notion of omnipotence can stem from a worker's limited domain knowledge, vested interests, and lack of perspective. Typically, models do not take unintended consequences into account, although every social work program has negative side effects.

Realistically, even when program theory and logic models are constructed and build on the insights of a broad representative stakeholder group, can anyone be sure who's right? Every model must always be considered a draft. They are always incomplete and provide a simple illustration that makes evaluation and program improvement more accessible to individuals and groups. The mere existence of a model does not mean that the model—or the plans it represents—is ready for immediate implementation or that it will readily deliver its intended results.

It's essential to note that a logic model is a graphic display of the program captured at one point in time. It has to change in order to reflect best thinking and current evidence as these evolve over time. Creating and displaying variations of a model are experiences that can develop thinking about strategies/activities and their intended results. This development is a critical process in model quality and, ultimately, in the feasibility of the efforts described.

One of the greatest value of logic models is their use in an iterative, intentional process aimed at improving the thinking they illustrate. This is best done through a facilitated sequence with selected stakeholders. Obviously, logic models do not ensure perfect program implementation fidelity or even quality. Nor do they remedy any of the many concerns about organizational structure and culture that can deeply affect the program's effectiveness (see Chapters 5 and 6). Important action steps associated with quality include the identification of both the assumptions and the evidence used when developing models.

Models Begin With Results

Determining the results you desire is the first step in evaluating a program's overall effectiveness, because knowing where you are headed—or where you want to go—is critical to picking the best route to use (see quote at the beginning of this chapter). Logic models always begin with results. Results consist of outcomes and impact; each appears in a sequence over time. While impact is the ultimate end sought, sometimes synonymous with vision, outcomes are earlier indications of progress toward the results.

Results are the best place to begin when you are struggling with deciding which interventions (strategy) you should use to solve the social problem. It's important to avoid moving prematurely to specify what you want to do without knowing where you want to go. When it comes to program planning, specifying those outcomes most likely to occur soon and then those that will take more time to emerge helps determine what route (action path) might be best to use.

Social workers commonly complain their work is both activity focused and frantic. Considerable time and effort are spent on a flurry of tasks that frequently lack a clear relationship to the program's intended results. Logic models can assist in sorting priorities because they both rely on—and help build—a visual literacy that makes action and expected consequences clear. Through the models and modeling, stakeholders can identify strong evidence-based interventions likely to contribute to the results sought. And those interventions with less (relative) value can be sidelined or discarded.

Logic Models and Effectiveness

In the workplace (and in life), almost everyone is interested in effectiveness. To that end, you need to ask—and answer—three questions:

- Are you doing the right work?
- Can you make better decisions?
- Are you getting superior results?

All three of these questions apply in any context—whether it's in government or the private or nonprofit sector. They are among the most critical questions for social work administrators and line-level workers alike because they focus on key levers that influence performance. Doing the "right work" along with making "great decisions" secures "superior results."

Logic models can help to answer the three questions. Thus they are a useful tool for anyone interested in developing more effective social work programs.

Figure 8.4 demonstrates key points of the design, planning, implementation, and evaluation that the two types of models can support. Theory of change models are most helpful during the initial design of a program (left side of diagram). As plans or evaluation require greater detail, program logic models can make a substantial contribution to these later stages of work (right side of diagram). The types of models and their uses form a continuous loop that can provide feedback about a single program throughout its life cycle.

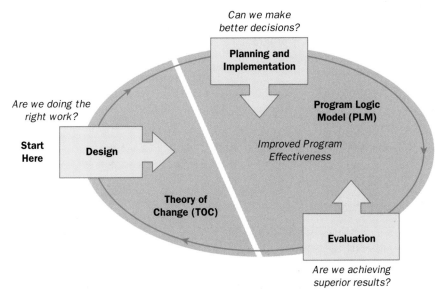

Figure 8.4: **The effectiveness continuum and models.**

Logic models as both a concept mapping tool and a strategic process offer considerable value to your program and, subsequently, its effectiveness. They can be used for different purposes at different times in the life cycle of a program. Theory of change models can dramatically influence program planning because they rely on knowledge to offer choices about doing the right work. In this stage, the selection of intervention strategies to produce the intended results occurs.

Program logic models help with more precise decisions about selecting the most promising evidence-based interventions that will be the most effective to achieve the intended results. They also aid in the design of an evaluation. They can assist in pointing to optimal areas of inquiry and help to determine whether progress is being made and what difference has occurred relative to results.

Some social service organizations use logic models routinely. They are a standard tool that promotes alignment and synergy. For example, a program evaluation can be designed and implemented more easily when a clear theory of change model and program logic model are already in existence.

BASIC PROGRAM LOGIC MODELS

The remainder of this chapter identifies the basic elements of program logic models. Generally, these models have enough detail to support a program's overall intervention strategy, design, implementation, and evaluation.

As we know, theory of change models are the foundation for program logic models. When well developed, theory of change models can ensure intellectual rigor for program logic models. Figure 8.5 illustrates the relationship of a theory of change model (composed of strategies and results) to the primary elements of a program logic model (composed of resources, activities, outputs, short-term outcomes, intermediate-term outcomes, long-term outcomes, and impact). The theory of change model is illustrated in the top horizontal row, and the program logic model is illustrated in the bottom horizontal row.

Notice that under the "Do" column in Figure 8.5, theory of change models use the term "strategies" and program logic models use the three terms "resources," "activities," and "outputs." Under the "Get" column, theory of change models use the term "results," and program logic models use the four terms, "short-term outcomes," "intermediate-term outcomes," "long-term outcomes," and "impact."

Assumptions Matter

It's important to be aware that specific assumptions are not illustrated in Figure 8.5. Recall that assumptions are informed by beliefs, past experiences, intuition, and knowledge. Too often, program logic models are built without the benefit of explicitly naming the assumptions and underlying the specific theory of change. This omission can help explain why tremendous conflict, even chaos, can erupt during program development, planning, implementation, and assessment.

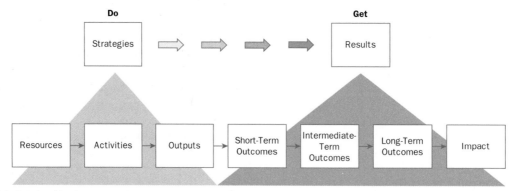

Figure 8.5: **Relationship of program and theory of change models.**

In the absence of explicitly named assumptions, either a clear theory of change does not exist and/or people hold multiple and conflicting variations that reflect their deeply held views about what should, or could, work and why. This can lead to diffused or diluted social work programs that lack the focus and intensity needed to produce their intended results. Because of these implications, omitting this "foundation" for your program undermines its potential for success.

As noted previously, conceptualization and learning styles differ from person to person. Organizational culture also affects how design, planning, monitoring, and measuring occur within any given program. Given these practical issues, we strongly suggest that both theory of change and program logic models eventually be created to form the foundation of shared meaning for all aspects of your program. The sequence in which they are developed certainly will reflect your stakeholders' preferences.

Key Elements of Program Logic Models

Program logic models display what a social work program might contain from start to finish. Its elements consist of the recipe for a bounded investment of financial and social capital for a specified result.

The level of detail within a logic model must show the relationships that illustrate the essential linkages that are needed in order to make a plan fully operational for each of the strategy strands identified in the theory of change model. The primary elements for each strand of a program logic model include resources, activities, outputs, outcomes, and impact.

Figures 3.2 and 3.3 in Chapter 3 are the basic templates of the elements for most program logic models. This is good time to review these two figures. The elements within these two figures are as follows:

- Resources are essential for activities to occur. They can include human, financial, organizational, community, or systems resources in any combination. They are used to accomplish specific activities. Sometimes resources are called inputs.

- Activities are the specific actions that make up the program. They reflect tools, processes, events, evidence-based interventions, technology, and other devices that are intentional in the program. Activities are synonymous with interventions deployed to secure the program's desired changes or results.

- Outputs are what specific activities will produce or create. They can include descriptions of types, levels, and audiences or targets delivered by the program. Outputs are often quantified and qualified in some way.

- Outcomes are about changes in our client system, often in program participants or organizations, as a result of the program's activities. They often include specific changes in awareness, knowledge levels, skills, and behaviors. Outcomes are dependent on the preceding resources, activities, and outputs. Sometimes outcomes are deconstructed by time increments into short, intermediate, and long term (e.g., Figure 8.3).

Time spans for outcomes are relative and should be specified for the program described. However, short term is often 1 to 3 years, intermediate term 4 to 6 years, and long term 7 to 10 years. The intervals specified for any given model would depend on the size and scope of the effort.

For example, a small-scale program such as an adult education typing class in one location might produce knowledge and skill outcomes in 6 weeks, where behavioral changes, such as changes in employment status, might take somewhat longer. Alternatively, a program targeting changes in global water quality might specify changes in the awareness and knowledge of international policymakers within 1 to 3 years; actual environmental improvements might not occur for several decades. Typically, dividing the project duration into thirds works pretty well as a starting point. Relying on additional evidence-based material also helps to inform us as to what's feasible and realistic.

Being exceedingly clear about timing and expected results is of paramount importance. The time span for outcomes is program specific. The logical sequencing of any given outcome chain also matters. Think about what will happen first, then what is likely to happen next.

Also keep in mind that the sequence may or may not be lockstep and barrel. Under some conditions, there may be different points of entry into a sequence. The important thing is to explore the interconnections and dependencies that do exist among the outcomes and impact you specify.

Impact is the ultimate intended change in an organization, community, or other client system. It carries an implication about time. It varies in its relative timing to the actual program or change effort. Sometimes impact occurs at the end of the program, but, more frequently, the impact sought is much more distant.

For some efforts, this may mean impact can be cited in 7 to 10 years or more. This can have important

implications, as it's well beyond the funding cycle for many typical grant-funded programs or the patience of many managers or politicians. A program logic model is one easy way to show how the work you do (your activities) within these constraints will hopefully contribute to a meaningful impact (your desired outcome that was obtained via your activities).

Nonlinear Program Logic Models

Just as in theory of change models, very few logic models of social work programs are developed in linear progressions. Purposely, to aid learning, we simplified the display of elements as a straight sequence. Reality suggests cycles, iterations (additional attempts), and interactions are very common. This more organic development is shown in Figure 8.6.

In this circular display, there is no specific starting point. Although the logic model elements are constant, the work of design, planning, managing, or evaluating might begin with any element.

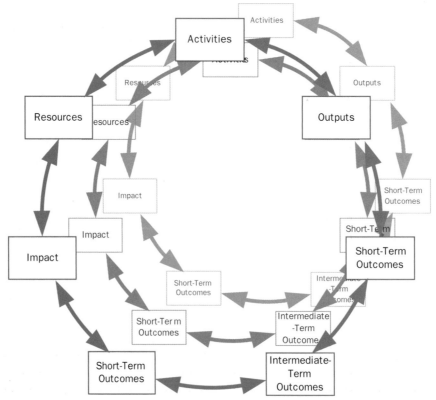

Figure 8.6: **Nonlinear logic model.**

In addition, this view shows how cycles of the same activity might occur over time. Keep in mind that Figure 8.6 groups activities together. A more detailed view could be staggering to portray. Sometimes capturing reality in a display impedes communication.

Hidden Assumptions and Dose

As we know by now, a program logic model displays the elements that are most critical to establishing and operating a social work program. It specifies the activities and their interdependent relationship as well as what they are expected to achieve. Program logic models do not necessarily include assumptions, but they rely on them.

They offer a view of the map that can inform a program's action plan and, later, its implementation. They can also quantify the "dosage" (e.g., number, type, and duration of activities) and describe the effects and benefits of the program for any given dosage, in addition to the ultimate change expected.

Getting the Dosage Right

Dosage is an important concept in effectiveness. A diluted dosage can have the same impact as no dosage at all. For example, if your mini-program's intended result is a large voter turnout in a local election (outcome), a classified ad may not be the best communication strategy (activity to achieve the outcome). A comprehensive media plan (Activity 1), for example, coupled with free transportation to the voting booths (Activity 2) has a greater chance of success (outcome). So it's tremendously important to design your program with enough of the right activities *and* dosage to secure your intended outcome.

BUILDING A LOGIC MODEL

An example of a program logic model for an improved-health program is displayed in Figure 8.7. As can be seen in the second column from the far left, the total intervention package, or overall interventive strategy, if you will, is actually composed of four activities. More often than not, a program's intervention package rarely relies on just one activity—they usually rely on multiple activities, as is evident in Figure 8.7.

The program logic model portrayed in Figure 8.7 suggests that IF we provide our participants with an exercise activity, a nutrition activity, a stress-reduction activity, and a retention activity, THEN their health will improve. Notice the word *activity* in the previous sentence and the "if-then" logic. Thus there are four activities (second column) that make up the complete intervention package for the improved-health (far right column) program. And we couldn't do the activities without the resources as outlined in the far left column.

Activities are sometimes called *components, services,* or *interventions.* The components of your social work program, for example, are all the courses you take in addition to other services your program makes available to you such as advising, providing/sponsoring a social work club, field trips, emergency loan funds, a social work library, study area, computer area, and so on.

Note the development of detail connecting the four activities (i.e., the total intervention package) to results in this program's logic model compared to a the theory of change model for the same program. The program logic model simply provides much more detail than the theory of change model for the same program by explicating the elements from a basic logic model for each activity strand. In a program logic model, for example, the details relative to the program's resources, activities, outcomes, impact, and other elements are labeled and placed in a sequential order.

Although still an overview and incomplete, the logic model illustration provides a detailed view of what this health-improvement program needs for resources, wants to do, plans to measure, and hopes to achieve. Beginning with the far left column with resources, this program's logic model includes funds, facility, faculty, and coaches, as well as eligible and willing participants, among its requisite inputs.

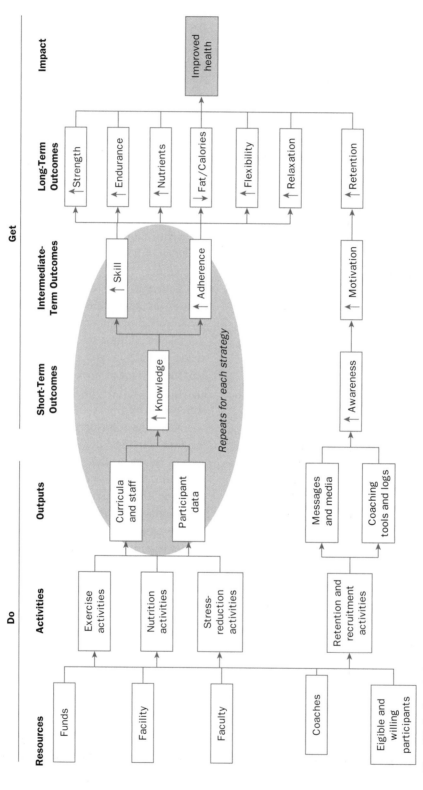

Figure 8.7: Logic model for an improved-health program.

Once again, the program's overall intervention contain four activities, or components. Outputs from the four activities could be numerous. For this illustration, we show only the overarching categories of information that could be considered.

Each activity would be repeated for each of the strands. These would include details about the scope, sequence, and quality of the curriculum; staffing qualifications; and information about participants and their participation. Activities "inside" these component strands contribute to changes in the participants' knowledge levels (short-term outcome), skills, and adherence (intermediate-term outcomes). Eventually, they can contribute to increases in the participants' strength, endurance, nutrients, flexibility, and relaxation (long-term outcomes).

Concurrently, over time, these same activities also yield reduced fat/calories (another long-term outcome). In fact, reducing fat/calories could indeed have a column of its own—to the immediate right of the long-term-outcomes. It would come just to the left of the program's impact, or improved health.

The retention and recruitment activity strand also generates some outputs and outcomes. Aggregated, activities within this component secure and keep participants in the program. Note that this model uses arrows to show relationships. Sometimes they reflect a cluster (indicating synergies) rather than just one-to-one relationships.

As is typical of many social work programs, several activities, or components, within an intervention package are shown as contributing collectively to outcomes rather than each component making its individual contribution to distinct outcomes in isolation. Collectively, the long-term outcomes generate improved health, which could be measured in a variety of ways (e.g., blood pressure, blood lipid, sugar profiles, weight, physical fitness).

In contrast to the big-picture view that theory of change models offer, program logic models provide a closer, more detailed picture of a program's operations. This view of the program provides adequate detail to create well-conceptualized and operationalized work plans. Program logic models provide a reliable outline for work plans that are then used to implement and manage a program. Just like theory of change models, program logic models are based on logic, but, here too, feasibility—given limited time and resources—is the appropriate standard for assessing their actual realistic value.

A common question about program logic models focuses on their level of detail. Essentially, their detail level is determined by their intended use and users. Although somewhat situational, they build out an overall intervention into activities. Sometimes they can even get into detailing the tasks that are contained within the activities, although more often that is described in the program's operations manual or action plan.

From Strategy to Activities

Some program logic models can be extremely complex, but the steps to create them are generally the same as for more simple efforts (see Figures 3.2 and 3.3 in Chapter 3). Large-scale programs or multiyear change efforts (sometimes called "initiatives") often are composed of many activities aimed at target audiences across many sites over a considerable time period. Often a single activity has numerous components—and sometimes even subcomponents.

As previously stated, program logic models usually do not display underlying beliefs or assumptions. They are nevertheless important elements in the conscious exploration of multiple target audiences. Sometimes social work programs are implemented in a cascade with some overlap in time, which requires a particular sequence of activities. When this is the circumstance, it can be helpful to focus on a function, a given intervention, or one partner's designated work.

The task is often simplified by thinking about a single aspect and then connecting it back to the whole with some of the inherent complexity reduced. Ultimately, program execution relies on integrated action—but the work that precedes it may require focused developmental attention on smaller parts.

Using our health-improvement program example, Figure 8.8 provides an orientation to how the exercise activity strand is reduced to subactivities. It breaks the activity into greater detail.

As can be seen in Figure 8.8, it becomes evident that exercise, as an activity, is made up of four key subactivities: physical exercise (strength), physical exercise (endurance), education, and assessment. Together, all four of the subactivities represent a comprehensive activity called *exercise*. And the exercise activity is just one of the four activities to improved health. Recall that the whole theory of change for this example includes three other activities to improved health: nutrition, stress reduction, and retention and recruitment.

It's the combination of the four activities reflected in the whole program that is most likely to secure the program's desired results. Each strand of a comprehensive program logic model needs to illustrate the contribution it makes to the overall desired result as well as its interdependence.

As you specify the subactivities content of your activity, you are naming more precisely what makes up the given activity. Later, the whole model is tested for feasibility—both practically before its implementation and literally when the program is evaluated. This may be a good time to reread Chapter 7 in reference to how a client system's practice objectives must be in congruent with the program's objectives.

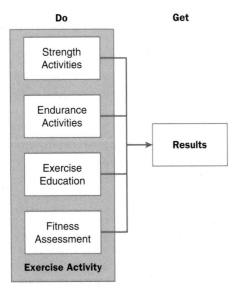

Figure 8.8: **The exercise activity with four subactivities.**

Action Steps for a Program Logic Model

The practical construction of a program logic model often begins with one or more information sources (e.g., research, interviews, past experiences, hunches, documents):

- First, we recommend that you begin with both a theory of change model and a program logic model with the named ends. You are most clear about your intended results (outcomes and impact). Our experience is that you must know what you want to accomplish before beginning a logic model. Put this on the far right in your model (impact).
- Second, name the changes or outcomes that will be part of your progress toward your program's intended impact. Unpacking this sequence is important because it makes it easier to see the strength of the connection between what you do (activities) and what you can get (outcomes).
- Third, we suggest tackling the specific activities, or interventions, that are required to achieve the outcomes you have specified in the second step. Interventions/activities are what causes the outcomes. Outcomes do not change by osmosis. They change because of interventions/activities.
- Fourth, list all the resources (inputs) that you need to implement your intervention package.
- Finally, outputs reflect the information needed to verify that activities named earlier in the process reach the right audiences and are of the quality and quantity needed to produce results.

So, according to Figure 8.9, the steps to draft a program logic model are ordered in this way:

Step 1: Identify the results that your total intervention package (various activities) will ultimately generate—the impact of your program.

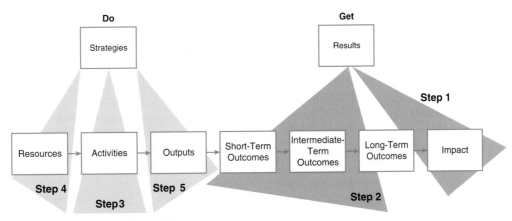

Figure 8.9: **Steps in creating a program logic model.**

Step 2: Describe the time-ordered series of outcomes (or changes) that will show progress toward your overall impact.

Step 3: Name all the activities needed to generate the outcomes.

Step 4: Define the resources (inputs) that are needed to produce the activities.

Step 5: Identify the outputs that reflect the accomplishment of activities.

Creating Your Program Logic Model

As should be evident by now, the format of your logic model helps you to organize your program's information in a useful way. Think of a program you are affiliated with now or want to create and its intended results. For each activity, brainstorm elements that might be cited in short-term outcomes first but are clearly linked to your intended results. Do the same for resources, activities, and outputs. It's important to make choices about the outcomes that are realistically and practically feasible with your limited financial resources.

With some experience you will begin to recognize commonly used activities that reflect knowledge from our profession. For example, marketing/communications, recruitment, retention, professional development or education, advocacy, and policy are activities often found in program logic models.

Examples of subactivities under a marketing/communications activity could include preparing a database of target markets, generating news releases, creating and sending a newsletter, establishing a website, and distributing public service announcements. We suggest you tackle one activity at a time. Aim to define the same level of detail for each activity. Box 8.2 presents some challenges when developing logic models and provides some possible solutions to each challenge.

Guiding Group Process

You can practice your group work skills when you develop logic models. The best method for generating a program logic model is to work with your stakeholders. Stakeholders are situational, but they generally are those who have an interest in—or are likely to—benefit from your program. As you know, stakeholders often include funders, program staff, and program participants. The facilitation of modeling requires some advance planning and a commitment to both discipline and quality during the process.

If you've already constructed a theory of change model, use it to catalyze the creation of a program logic model. If not, defining shared understanding for specified results gets your group process effort started. It's important to note that logic models need to be continually updated to respond to the dynamics of its external environment (context). They also reflect living systems that are not mechanistic but are constantly changing.

BOX 8.2   CHALLENGES AND POSSIBLE SOLUTIONS OF LOGIC MODEL DEVELOPMENT

Oftentimes stakeholders may have doubts or concerns about developing a logic model process. There may be concerns about the time and resources needed or the usefulness of the product. To help you alleviate these fears, we have listed some of the most common challenges to the logic model effort and suggested some possible solutions.

Challenge: "We've had trouble developing a logic model because our key stakeholders (e.g., staff, funders) cannot agree on the right services or outcomes to include."

- Although it might be difficult, keep key stakeholders involved, including staff, program participants, collaborators, or funders. Involving stakeholders does not mean they need to be involved with all tasks, and they do not need to have sign-off authority. Their role can be as simple as inviting them to review materials or help you think through some of your stickier questions or issues.
- Focus on the process, not the product. Take time to explore the reasons for disagreement about what should be captured in the logic model. Look for the assumptions, identify and resolve disagreements, and build consensus. Agencies that work through disagreements about the logic model typically end up with a stronger model with which everyone can be satisfied.

Challenge: "We're not really interested in developing a logic model, but our funder requires it."

- Look for examples of how other organizations have used logic models in meaningful and interesting ways. Many agencies have gone into the process with skepticism or lack of interest but ultimately found the process valuable.
- Try to focus on the fun and interesting aspects of the process. Building a logic model provides an opportunity—all too rare in the everyday provision of services—to discuss what it is about your work that is most meaningful and to renew your appreciation for the ways your program can change lives and communities. Focusing on the importance of this discussion—rather than seeing it as just a task to complete—can increase engagement in the process.

Challenge: "I just want to get my logic model finished. I don't want to spend much time on it."

- Logic models that are rushed often end up displaying faulty logic, insufficient evidence, or models copied from other programs that don't quite fit yours. Keep asking yourself "IF-THEN-WHY" questions to make sure that the model is sound. IF you provide a service, THEN what should be the impact for participants? WHY do you think this impact will result? What evidence do you have to support that connection?
- Make it more interesting by seeking a range of evidence. If you already know the published research by heart, look for additional types of evidence, such as theoretical frameworks, unpublished evaluation results, or experiences reported by program participants.
- If possible, recruit a facilitator from outside your agency who is trained and experienced in logic model development.

Challenge: "The goal of my program is to change an entire community, not just to influence the lives of a small group of participants."

- Think through each step that must occur. For instance, how does each activity impact individuals? In what ways does their behavior change? What has to occur in order for these individual changes to result in widespread community change?
- Consider issues or events outside the control of your agency that may promote or impede the change you are seeking. If needed, develop strategies for monitoring or documenting these issues.

Challenge: "My logic model is so complicated that nobody can understand it."

- Focus on the most important activities and outcomes. The model does not need to describe everything that you do; it should show the services and goals that are the most important to you.
- Avoid social work jargon at all costs. Describe your activities and outcomes in "real-life" language that is understood by a wide range of stakeholders. Try it out on someone unfamiliar with your work—a neighbor or a relative, for instance.
- Cut back on detail. Be specific enough to clearly explain what will happen as a result of your activities but without excessive detail.

Challenge: "I'm nervous about developing a logic model because it might make funders hold us more accountable for our results."

- Include (and subsequently measure) only outcomes that are realistic. If you do not want to be held accountable for something, it must not be an essential outcome goal. Outcomes are not hopes or wishes but reasonable expectations.
- Incorporate time frames into the logic model to show stakeholders the amount of time it will take to achieve long-term goals. Example: If you have only 1 or 2 years to show impact, you should not measure outcomes that may take longer to emerge. Instead, measure the intermediate steps toward those outcomes—the results that your program can reasonably expect to achieve.
- Remember that a logic model should be a dynamic tool that can and should be changed as needed; it is not a rigid framework that imposes restrictions on what you can do.

BOX 8.3 SELECTED ONLINE RESOURCES TO HELP CREATE LOGIC MODELS

- Everything You Want to Know About Logic Models
  http://www.insites.org/documents/logmod.htm
- Logic Models and How to Build Them
  http://www.uidaho.edu/extension/LogicModel.pdf
- Theory of Change Assistance and Materials
  http://www.theoryofchange.org
- Logic Model Development Guide
  http://www.wkkf.org/Pubs/Tools/Evaluation/Pub3669.
  pdf
- Community Tool Box
  http://ctb.ku.edu/tools/en/sub_section_main_1877.htm

- Logic Model Builder
  http://www.childwelfare.gov/preventing/developing/toolkit
- Using a Logic Model for Evaluation Planning
  http://captus.samhsa.gov/western/resources/bp/step7/
  eval2.cfm#b
- How to Build Your Program Logic Model
  http://captus.samhsa.gov/western/resources/bp/step7/
  eval3.cfm
- Developing a Logic Model: Teaching and Training Guide
  http://www.uwex.edu/ces/pdande/evaluation/pdf/
  lmguidecomplete.pdf

For these two reasons (and others), it's necessary to expect program logic models to be continuity revised. In association with some public specification of time, outcomes, and impact, can be explored and selected. This can be accomplished a number of ways.

We have had success in using the action steps noted, particularly when each participant contributed to brainstorming the model's elements by nominating contributions on sticky notes. This quickly generates a large number of possibilities for each element. Redundancies should be noted and celebrated as commonly held.

Then the group can sort them into those that must be kept, those that could be kept, and those that will not be kept (are not relevant). Once the results are named, then it's possible to compose content for the other elements. In this disciplined sequence, each stakeholder contributes to the whole, and each contribution has the benefit of an internal test relative to the program's design.

There are several variations on this approach. From a group, you could invite individuals or pairs to generate models in the sequence shown previously and then integrate and reconcile the variations. This approach helps avoid "groupthink" but requires strong process facilitation with content knowledge.

A generic model or template for a given program may be available. With some advance planning it's possible to identify one of these prototypes and introduce it to your group. Then the content adaptations can focus on improving it so that the content is relevant to your purposes, conditions, and planned results.

Regardless of the process, strategic decisions about your model's components and its relationships between elements should be made from among all the content generated. It's important to consider criteria for choices that reflect context, target audience(s), research, practice, literature, program benchmarking, as well as resource parameters. It can be very helpful to have draft models critically reviewed in a "mark-up."

Microsoft Visio is an excellent software program to construct logic models, but many other applications such as Word and PowerPoint are also useful. These as well as Inspiration software are all readily available. Take care in using technology for model creation because it can exclude valuable participation from your stakeholders. Box 8.3 lists a few online resources you can use to help you in developing logic models.

SUMMARY

Logic models are simply a visual display of the pathways from actions to results. They are a great way to review and improve thinking, find common understandings, document plans, and communicate and explicate what works under what conditions.

Now that you have mastered the contexts of evaluations (Part I) and know how to construct social work programs via logic models (Part II), you are now in an excellent position to evaluate the social work program you have constructed—Part III: Implementing Evaluations.

The goal of this chapter is to provide you with a beginning knowledge base for you to feel comfortable in answering the following questions. AFTER you have read the chapter, indicate how comfortable you feel you are in answering each question on a 5-point scale where

1 Very uncomfortable	2 Somewhat uncomfortable	3 Neutral	4 Somewhat comfortable	5 Very comfortable

If you rated any question between 1–3, please reread the section of the chapter where the information for the question is found. If you still feel that you're uncomfortable in answering the question, then talk with your instructor and/or your classmates for more clarification.

	Questions	Degree of comfort? *(Circle one number)*
1	In your own words, discuss what a theory of change model is all about and provide a social work example throughout your discussion.	1 2 3 4 5
2	In your own words, discuss what a program logic model is all about and provide a social work example throughout your discussion.	1 2 3 4 5
3	Compare and contrast a theory of change model and a program logic model. Demonstrate, via a social work example, how a theory of change model is needed before a program logic model can be produced.	1 2 3 4 5
4	List and then discuss each one of the advantages of using a program logic model. Provide a common social work example throughout your discussion.	1 2 3 4 5
5	Discuss how program logic models can be used in designing program-level evaluations. Use a social work example throughout your discussion.	1 2 3 4 5
6	Discuss the rationale of why a theory of change model and a program logic model always begin with "the results" in mind. Then construct a theory of change model and a logic model for your our social work program.	1 2 3 4 5
7	List and then describe in detail the six key elements of logic models. Use a social work example throughout your discussion.	1 2 3 4 5
8	Does a program logic model change over time? Why or why not?	1 2 3 4 5
9	List and then describe each one of the five action steps when developing a program logic model. What order do they occur in and why (see Figure 8.9)?	1 2 3 4 5

continued

10	Discuss how you would go about guiding the group process you would use when constructing a program logic model.	1 2 3 4 5
11	Ask your field instructor (or supervisor at work) for the program logic model that is currently being used in the program in which you are placed. Critique the model using this chapter as a guide.	1 2 3 4 5
12	What would you say to your field instructor if the answer is, "We don't have one because we don't need one"?	1 2 3 4 5
13	Pretend, for the moment, that your field instructor asks you to present a one-hour presentation to the line-level workers on the basics of program logic model development. What would you say to the group and why?	1 2 3 4 5
14	Using your field placement (or work setting) as a background, what would go under the "resource column" in its program logic model? Why did you list each one?	1 2 3 4 5
15	Using your field placement (or work setting) as a background, what would go under the "activities column" in its program logic model? Why did you list each one?	1 2 3 4 5
16	Using your field placement (or work setting) as a background, what would go under the "outputs column" in its program logic model? Why did you list each one?	1 2 3 4 5
17	Using your field placement (or work setting) as a background, what would go under the "outcomes column" in its program logic model? Why did you list each one?	1 2 3 4 5
18	Using your field placement (or work setting) as a background, what would go under the "impact column" in its program logic model? Why did you list each one?	1 2 3 4 5

AFTER you have read this chapter AND have completed all of the study questions, indicate how knowledgeable you feel you are for each of the following concepts on a 5-point scale where

1	2	3	4	5
Not knowledgeable at all	Somewhat unknowledgeable	Neutral	Somewhat knowledgeable	Very knowledgeable

	Concepts	Knowledge Level? (Circle one number)
1	Theory of change models (in general)	1 2 3 4 5
2	Program logic models (in general)	1 2 3 4 5
3	Why a program logic model is based off of a theory of change model	1 2 3 4 5
4	Modeling (no, not fashion)	1 2 3 4 5
5	Using logic models to aid in designing program-level evaluations	1 2 3 4 5
6	The key elements of program logic models	1 2 3 4 5
7	Nonlinear program logic models	1 2 3 4 5
8	Actually constructing a theory of change model	1 2 3 4 5
9	Actually constructing a program logic model	1 2 3 4 5
10	Guiding the group process that is needed to construct a program logic model	1 2 3 4 5
	Add up your scores (minimum = 10, maximum = 50)	Your total score =

A 47–50 = Professional evaluator in the making
A– 45–46 = Senior evaluator
B+ 43–44 = Junior evaluator
B 41–42 = Assistant evaluator
B– 10–40 = Reread the chapter and redo the study questions

Implementing Evaluations

Part III contains chapters that illustrate the four basic forms of program evaluations. All of the chapters present how to do their respective evaluations in a step-by-step approach.

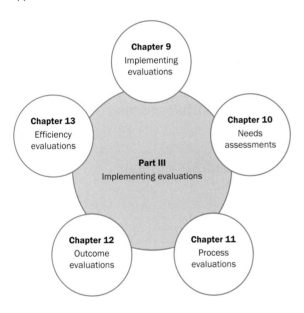

Chapter 9 sets the stage for the following four chapters in Part III. It contains nine evaluation implementation strategies that we believe support an evaluation's success. In short, it alerts the evaluator of what to expect in all types of evaluations.

Chapter 10 describes how to do basic needs assessments and briefly presents how they are used in the development of new social service programs as well as refining existing ones. It highlights the four types of social needs within the context of social problems.

Once a social service program is up and running, **Chapter 11** presents how we can do a process evaluation within the program in an effort to refine the services that clients receive and to maintain a program's fidelity. It highlights the purposes of process evaluations and places a great deal of emphasis on how to decide what questions the evaluation will answer.

Chapter 12 discusses the need for doing outcome evaluations within social programs. It highlights the need for developing a solid monitoring system for the evaluation process.

Once an outcome evaluation is done, social service programs can use efficiency evaluations to monitor their cost-effectiveness/benefits—the topic of **Chapter 13**. This chapter highlights the cost–benefit approach to efficiency evaluation and also describes in detail the cost-effectiveness approach.

In sum, Part III clearly acknowledges that there are many forms that evaluations can take within social service agencies and presents four of the most common ones. Each chapter builds on the previous one.

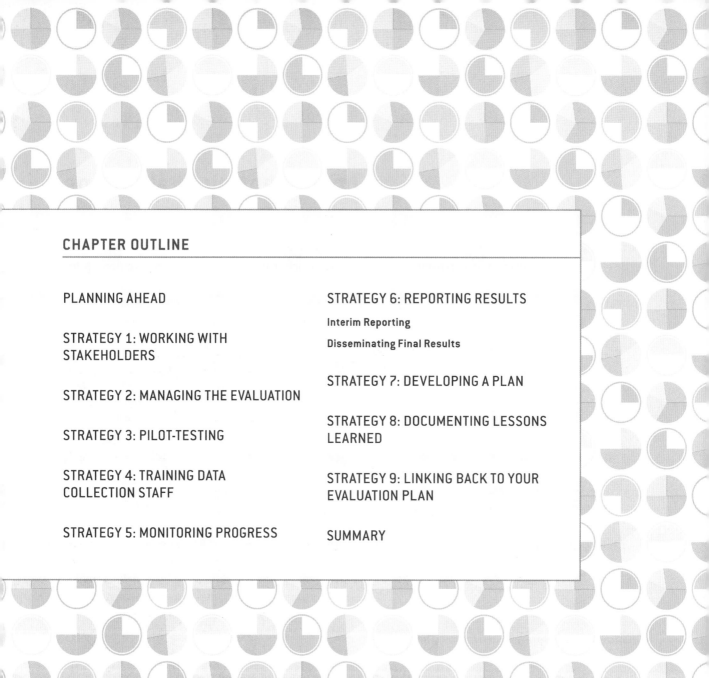

CHAPTER OUTLINE

Chapter 9

PREPARING FOR AN EVALUATION

CENTERS FOR DISEASE CONTROL AND PREVENTION

The six chapters in Part I provided you with the essential ingredients you need to digest before you can undertake any kind of evaluation: the evaluation process (Chapter 3) and standards (Chapter 4), in addition to ethical (Chapter 5) and cultural (Chapter 6) considerations. The two chapters in Part II provided information on how to design social work programs (Chapter 7) with the use of logic models (Chapter 8).

Simply put, you need to know what goes into a program before you can evaluate it. Otherwise, how would you know what you're evaluating? With Parts I and II under your belt you're now well on your way to getting your "feet wet" by actually doing one or more of the four different types of evaluations that are covered in the following four chapters: need (Chapter 10), process (Chapter 11), outcome (Chapter 12), and efficiency (Chapter 13).

No matter what type of evaluation your evaluation team decides to do, you have to know what to realistically expect before you start one—the topic of this chapter. Thus you need to begin thinking about how you are going to implement your evaluation *before* you actually carry it out. The expression "look before you leap" readily comes to mind here.

We have distilled the combined experience of a number of evaluation practitioners into nine evaluation implementation strategies contained in Box 9.1 that we believe will help support your evaluation's success.

PLANNING AHEAD

Although this chapter discusses evaluation *implementation* strategies, we still talk about *planning*. By doing so, we are asking that you "plan for the implementation of your evaluation" by incorporating the nine strategies in Box 9.1 to guide your evaluation team in conducting a particular evaluation. In a nutshell, they represent important steps you need to *plan* for that will help you to *implement* your evaluation more smoothly.

Reading through this chapter during the evaluation planning process will remind you of things you will want to incorporate into your actual evaluation plans as you think ahead toward implementing it. In addition to discussing these helpful implementation strategies, we also provide a checklist (see Table 9.3) that you can use to keep track of your own progress in preparing for the eventual implementation of your evaluation.

Each of the four types of evaluations can, at times, be a complex undertaking that requires the cooperation and coordination of multiple people and other resources. By managing your evaluation carefully, paying attention to the evaluation standards (i.e., utility, feasibility, propriety, accuracy), and closely following the steps in the evaluation process as presented in Chapter 3, you can facilitate a more smoothly run evaluation. Once again, key strategies developed by practitioners to minimize potential challenges and promote effective evaluation implementation are listed in Box 9.1.

BOX 9.1 IMPLEMENTATION STRATEGIES TO MAKE YOUR EVALUATION RUN SMOOTHLY

Strategy 1 Work with all stakeholder groups throughout the evaluation life cycle—from initial design through action planning and implementation—in order to help focus on questions of interest to them and to incorporate their perspectives

Strategy 2 Develop a concrete process for managing the tasks, resources, and activities necessary for your evaluation

Strategy 3 Pilot-test data collection instruments and procedures

Strategy 4 Train data collection staff

Strategy 5 Monitor the evaluation's progress, budget, timeline, and scope. Communicate frequently and

effectively with the evaluation implementation team and key stakeholders

Strategy 6 Disseminate results to all stakeholders in an accessible manner. Consider interim reporting where appropriate

Strategy 7 Develop an action plan to implement evaluation recommendations that includes clear roles, responsibilities, timeline, and budget

Strategy 8 Document lessons learned throughout the evaluation for use in future evaluations

Strategy 9 Link findings from the evaluation back to the strategic evaluation plan in case there are implications for the revision of the plan

---

On planning …

Planning is bringing the future into the present so that you can do something about it now.

~ Alan Lakein

In the pages that follow, we highlight what's involved in each of these general strategies, which aspects of your evaluation they can help you address, and what benefits you can expect from each strategy. Luckily, the majority of these strategies are simply a part of good project management, something most social workers do on a daily basis.

STRATEGY 1: WORKING WITH STAKEHOLDERS

Many of the causes of misunderstandings about evaluations—and of barriers to productive use of their findings—can be avoided or minimized when your stakeholders are included in key discussions at various points throughout your evaluation's life cycle. Including those who are important to your program in conversations about the program, the evaluation itself, and what you hope to learn from it can make them feel included and less anxious about the results (see Tool C on how to reduce evaluation anxiety). Their involvement can also offer you fresh perspectives on what your evaluation can potentially accomplish and

ways to make the entire evaluation process run more smoothly.

Some stakeholders you may want to consider involving in your evaluation (or with whom you will want to communicate about it in other ways) include all those folks we mentioned in Chapters 1 through 3. Table 9.1 presents a variety of ways to work with them throughout your evaluation. Note that to engage stakeholders effectively, you will first need to gauge their level of knowledge and experience regarding evaluation. It may also be necessary to provide them with an overview of program evaluation basics.

Perhaps you are wondering how you will manage the involvement of so many people in your evaluation, such as program directors, program staff, partners, evaluator(s), evaluation team members, and other program stakeholders. Questions you need to ask and answer are:

- Who will play what role(s)?
- Who is in charge of which aspects of the evaluation?
- Who has decision-making authority over which aspects of the evaluation?

As you explore working with your stakeholders, it's important to recognize that you have a range of options for how you can structure these relationships and that there's no "correct" or "incorrect" structure.

Table 9.1: **Ways to Work with Stakeholders.**

Category	Detail (if appropriate to your situation)
Upfront discussions with stakeholders about …	• Plans for the evaluation (yours and theirs) • Program priorities (yours and theirs) • Information needs and evaluation questions to explore (yours and theirs) • When information is needed • What evidence would be considered credible • How the data to be collected will answer the evaluation questions • How findings can be used • Community member perspectives to consider • Privacy, confidentiality, and cultural sensitivity • Limitations of evaluation • What to do if findings suggest immediate need for program modifications • A proactive approach to public relations, referred to as issues management, if the evaluation may reflect negatively on program or community
Frequent communication throughout the evaluation with stakeholders about …	• Results from pilot tests • Implementation progress • Early findings • Successes achieved • Challenges encountered • Other topics
Postevaluation discussions with stakeholders about …	• Turning findings into conclusions • Celebrating strengths • Developing recommendations grounded in findings • Developing strategies for disseminating results • Lessons learned • Limitations of the evaluation • Implications of the current evaluation for changes needed in the strategic evaluation plan • Designing an action plan with clear information on recommended strategies, roles and responsibilities, timeline, and budget

Benefits of working with stakeholders:

- *Encourages positive community response to your evaluation*
- *Builds "political will" to support your evaluation*
- *Develops support among program leadership for the program and/or for your evaluation in general*

- *Facilitates appropriate timing of your evaluation in relation to information needs*
- *Leads to development of relevant evaluation questions, which in turn supports use*
- *Promotes findings that are credible, used, understood, and accepted by all your stakeholder groups.*

The first step is to consider upfront what you want the roles, responsibilities, and lines of authority for those involved in your evaluation to look like. Here the evaluation literature can help you. For example, King and Stevahn (2002) have put considerable thought into the various roles an evaluator can play in relation to other evaluation stakeholders, within the organization sponsoring the evaluation, and in terms of managing interpersonal conflict. Tools A and B offer more information about these evaluator roles.

The second step is to clarify roles and responsibilities for everyone involved in order to avoid any misunderstandings. A "Roles and Responsibilities Table" lays out in detail who is responsible for what (shown as Table G.2 in Tool G),

As discussed further under Strategy 5, open and ongoing communication among evaluation stakeholders is paramount in conducting a successful evaluation. Tool G provides suggestions on ways to keep team members and other stakeholders informed as to the progress of your evaluation. Devising fair and minimally burdensome ways to obtain feedback is another important aspect of communication.

For example, depending on the size of your program's client catchment area and the dispersion of your stakeholders throughout your state, you may need to come up with creative ways for them to provide their input remotely, whether they are formally serving on your evaluation team or their expertise is being sought for other reasons.

Meeting by teleconference—rather than in person—or allowing stakeholders to provide input electronically are some ways to ease the burden of their potential participation. Webinar software, should you or one of your partners have access to it, allows remote stakeholders to view graphics and other documents online during tele-discussions. Some computer software packages of this type permit collaborative editing of documents, whereby all stakeholders can view edits on screen as they are being made.

Once you have drafted the final version of your evaluation plan, you will want to revisit the composition of your evaluation team to see if you wish to constitute it differently as you move toward the actual implementation of your evaluation. The design may have evolved in unexpected directions during planning, or new individuals or organizations may have joined your partnership with a stake in the proposed evaluation.

Should additional stakeholders review your draft plan? Should some of them join the evaluation team that will carry the evaluation forward—those able to facilitate as well as those able to obstruct its progress? Addressing concerns these individuals raise will help ensure your evaluation plan is feasible and that it receives the support it needs.

STRATEGY 2: MANAGING THE EVALUATION

Running a program evaluation is much like running any other project. The things you "worry about" may be a little different for an evaluation than for other kinds of projects, but the good management practices that help you elsewhere in your professional life will also work well for you with an evaluation. Good management includes thinking ahead about what is most important, which activities precede which other activities, who will do what, what agreements and clearances are needed, when important products are due, how far your budget will stretch, and how to make the budget stretch further.

You will also want to monitor progress and communicate frequently and efficiently with others on your evaluation team throughout the entire evaluation (see Strategy 5).

As part of your evaluation planning process, you must think ahead to the eventual implementation of your evaluation. We cannot stress this enough—think ahead. This is the purpose of this chapter: to encourage you to think ahead of what's to come. For example, if your own staff resources are lacking, either in terms of skill level or time available, you may want to reach out to partners and contractors to fill that gap. You may also need to develop memoranda of agreement or contracts to engage this external support in a timely fashion.

If required by your agency or one of the partners engaged in your program, you may need clearances for the protection of human subjects such as those that may be needed for an institutional review board (IRB) and Health Insurance Portability and Accountability Act (HIPPA). This can be requested as soon as your methodology has been finalized and your measuring instruments and consent (e.g., Box 5.2) and assent (Box 5.3) forms required by these entities have been developed.

Finally, you need to anticipate things that could cause problems down the road—such as the potential evaluation challenges presented in Tool D. Having identified potential challenges, you then need to put in place as many safeguards as possible to prevent them from happening, with contingency plans in

Table 9.2: **Management Evaluation Strategies.**

Category	What to Look For
Logistics	• Staff have skills required for evaluation tasks and are aware of their roles and responsibilities • Staff are available to work on evaluation activities or alternatives have been considered • Estimates of likely cost of evaluation in the individual evaluation plans are complete and feasible • Efficiencies possible across evaluations have been identified • Other sources of financial or staff support for evaluation (e.g., partner organizations, local universities, grant funding) have been identified • Actions to expand staff resources—such as contracting externally, training existing staff in needed skills, "borrowing" partner staff, interns from local colleges and universities—have been established • Agreements are developed and executed that may be needed to contract out a portion of the work (e.g., specific data collection activities, data analysis, development/distribution of reports), to access data sources, to facilitate meetings with partners (schools, workplaces, etc.) • Clearances/permissions that may be needed (such as IRB clearance, data-sharing agreements, permission to access schools or medical facilities) are in place
Data collection	• Appropriate data storage, data system capacity, data cleaning, and data preparation procedures are established and communicated • Procedures for protection of data are in place (considering such safeguards as frequent data backups, use of more than one audio recorder for interviews and focus groups) • Safeguards for respondent confidentiality and privacy have been developed • Those collecting or compiling data have been trained in the procedures • Monitoring systems are in place to assess progress and increase adherence to procedures for data protection, assurance of privacy and confidentiality • Cultural sensitivity of instruments has been tested • Respondent burden has been minimized (e.g., length of instrument considered, data collection strategies designed to be optimally appealing and minimally burdensome) • Ways to maximize respondent participation are in place • Existing data useful for the evaluation have been identified and permission to access those data has been obtained
Data analysis	• Procedures for how incoming data will be analyzed to answer the evaluation questions are in place • Table shells showing analyses to be conducted are developed

mind should things not go as planned. And yes, sometimes things do go south in an evaluation—way south.

> *Benefits of good evaluation management practice:*
>
> - *Maintains clarity among team members about everyone's roles and responsibilities*
> - *Identifies and secures resources to complete the evaluation*
> - *Keeps your evaluation on track in terms of timeline, budget, or scope*
> - *Provides a sound plan for managing incoming data*
> - *Enables all evaluation team members to follow clear procedures for working with contractors, consultants, and evaluation partners*

This type of planning should be undertaken with your evaluation team members, program stakeholders, and individuals experienced in evaluation in the areas outlined in Table 9.2. Depending on your own level of familiarity with evaluation logistics, you may or may not feel the need for outside help in working through this process.

In either case, it's important to consider how you will document the decisions made as part of this process so that you or others can refer back to them at a later date. How you do this is up to you and your evaluation team members.

You may find it helpful to integrate information on managing evaluation logistics into the individual evaluation plan, perhaps as an appendix. Or you may want to produce a separate document containing this information. The tips in Tool D will help you with this process, though you are not required to use them; they are there to use or not as you see fit.

STRATEGY 3: PILOT-TESTING

You should plan to pilot-test your data collection instruments and procedures. This is one good way to preempt some of the implementation challenges you might otherwise face. This is important whether you are conducting mail and/or telephone surveys; carrying out individual interviews, group interviews, or focus groups; or abstracting data from archival sources.

> *Benefits of pilot-testing measuring instruments and data collection procedures:*
>
> - *Generates effective data collection instruments that collect required data that work with the designed data analysis plan*
> - *Clarifies procedures for all data collection, whether carried out by your staff, contractors, consultants, or other data collection partners*
> - *Improves the validity and reliability of the data collected*

During the pilot test you will be looking at such issues as clarity of instructions, appropriateness and feasibility of the questions, sequence and flow of questions, and feasibility of the data collection procedures. Use lessons learned during the pilot test to modify your data collection instruments and/or your training materials for your data collectors. See Tool I for additional information on training data collectors.

STRATEGY 4: TRAINING DATA COLLECTION STAFF

Even if you are working with experienced individuals who are evaluation savvy, training those who will be involved in data collection on the specific measuring instruments and data collection procedures you will use in *this* evaluation is another good way to avoid difficulties during the data collection phase. Training helps to ensure that all staff with data collection responsibilities are familiar with the instruments and other forms that are part of your evaluation plan, as well as the procedures that will be followed and the safeguards that will be employed in implementing the plan. It will also promote consistency in data collection procedures across data collectors, thereby increasing the reliability of the data gathered.

Benefits of training data collection staff:

- *Promotes a consistent message about your evaluation to outside audiences*
- *Maintains consistency in data collection procedures*
- *Prevents loss of data and corruption of data integrity*
- *Guards against ethical breaches*
- *Improves the validity and reliability of the data collected*

Training should be required whether data collection is being done by your own staff, by partner staff, or by contractors/consultants. Training sessions should cover not only the logistics of the work but also the ethical aspects, such as issues in human subjects protection, maintenance of confidentiality (Chapter 5), and observance of cultural sensitivity (Chapter 6). Tool I presents guidelines to help you develop and deliver training to data collection staff.

STRATEGY 5: MONITORING PROGRESS

As mentioned earlier, an evaluation like any other project, needs to be carefully managed. This includes not only thinking ahead during planning about what needs to be accomplished, who will do what, and what time and budget constraints exist (per Strategy 2); it also includes monitoring progress and maintaining open lines of communication among members of your evaluation team as your evaluation proceeds.

Benefits of tracking and ongoing communication:

- *Maintains clarity among all your team members over their roles and responsibilities*
- *Keeps your evaluation on track in terms of timeline, budget, and scope*
- *Promotes effective communication with your stakeholders and maintains their engagement*

Strategies such as those found in the Evaluation Management Tool (Tool G) are useful for project tracking and ongoing communication. These tools are equally helpful in managing an evaluation with lots of "moving parts." You are not required to use these tools. However, you may find them helpful in identifying emerging issues that require your attention and in making sure you stay on track in terms of timeline and budget.

The tools are designed to help you track progress overall and against your established budget and timeline, identify performance issues by your staff or your contractor, identify implementation issues such as data access and data collection, and monitor the quality of your evaluation. Information to help you budget for your evaluation is included in Tool F.

STRATEGY 6: REPORTING RESULTS

Interim Reporting

Where appropriate, sharing interim findings derived from your evaluation not only helps maintain stakeholder interest in the evaluation process but also increases the likelihood that your stakeholders have the information they need in a timely manner. If you decide to share findings midway through the evaluation, be sure to couch the interim findings in terms of caveats that the data are only preliminary at this point. Furthermore:

- Share only what information you are comfortable sharing at any given point in time
- Focus on information you feel is important for stakeholders to begin thinking about
- Consider presenting the information as "food for thought" based on what you are seeing thus far

Disseminating Final Results

Dissemination of an evaluation's final results to stakeholders should be a process tailored to the information needs of your different stakeholder groups. While final reports are a common way to share findings, it's important to consider whether a large, formal final report is the most appropriate way to disseminate findings to the specific stakeholders with whom you are working.

By "appropriate way" we mean a tailoring of both message and format to the information needs of a given audience; that is, you need to consider the best way(s) to make the information you plan to share accessible to that particular audience. For example, some stakeholders may strongly desire a final report—they may even need it for documentation or accountability purposes. However, keep in mind that for other stakeholders a final report may include more information than they need or want.

> *Benefits of interim and final reporting:*
>
> - *Facilitates appropriate timing of your evaluation in relation to information needs*
> - *Facilitates the comprehension and use of the findings that were derived from your evaluation*
> - *Helps ensure, through interim reporting, that there are few or no "surprises" in the final evaluation report*

Figure 9.1 presents a list of some alternative means to disseminate evaluation findings. Depending on the composition of your stakeholder groups, you may want to experiment with one or more of these alternative approaches. Additional guidance for presenting the results of an evaluation is provided in Tool J.

Remember to set aside resources in your budget to support communication activities—something that is easy to forget to do. The communications portion of your budget can be based on the communication ideas put forward in your evaluation plans.

Depending on the communication venue(s) you choose, costs for communication activities might include such things as staff time for materials development and attendance at stakeholders' meetings, meeting space, refreshments, printing costs, or website maintenance.

Also remember to check with your funders about which of these costs are allowable under your grant(s). Communication may be something your partners can help with in various ways, but if tight resources limit you, then focus on your primary stakeholders.

STRATEGY 7: DEVELOPING A PLAN

Another important step in linking evaluation to action involves developing an action plan containing strategies for implementing evaluation recommendations. The action plan should, at a minimum, contain the following items:

- Rationale for recommended strategies
- Clear roles and responsibilities for implementing the elements of the action plan

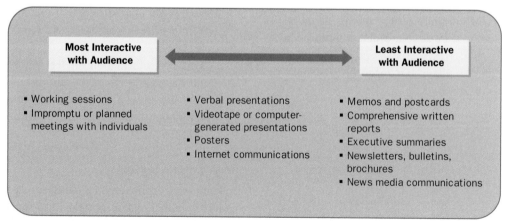

Figure 9.1: **Alternative communication formats.**

- Timeline
- Sources of funding for program or intervention modifications, if needed

Define roles for stakeholders and community members in the action planning and the action implementation processes. For example, you can convene a "working session" that combines a briefing on findings for stakeholders with joint planning on next steps and development of an action plan.

Benefits of action planning:

- *Facilitates the comprehension and use of the evaluation's findings*
- *Engages stakeholders in the improvement of your program*
- *Promotes accountability for use of your evaluation's findings*

Involving a variety of stakeholders in the action planning process will help facilitate stakeholder and decision-maker buy-in and thereby facilitate implementation of any recommendations that make sense for your program. Tool K contains an Action Plan template you can adapt to the needs of your own program.

STRATEGY 8: DOCUMENTING LESSONS LEARNED

History repeats itself—because we weren't listening the first time. That's as true for evaluation as it is anywhere else. Yet by documenting lessons learned from one evaluation for use in future evaluations you can begin building a historical record of knowledge about evaluation to pass on to future "generations" in your program. Consider adopting the habit of closing your evaluation team meetings by asking attendees:

- What have we learned?
- What can we do better next time?

Document these discussions in your meeting minutes for later reference. In this way you are encouraging your team members to reflect on their evaluation practice, and this will lead to evaluation capacity building.

Benefits of documenting lessons learned:

- *Avoids repeating past mistakes*
- *Builds evaluation capacity among you and your stakeholders*
- *Transfers knowledge to those who come after you*
- *Creates an archive of good evaluation practices over time*

As your various evaluations proceed and as you "learn by doing," make sure you and your team members pause occasionally to reflect upon what you have learned and document those things you want to remember to make your next evaluation go more smoothly. In some cases, you may learn things you would like to share more broadly, for example, through presentations at a grantee meeting, a professional conference, or even in a peer-reviewed journal article.

STRATEGY 9: LINKING BACK TO YOUR EVALUATION PLAN

Linking your evaluation findings back to your evaluation plan is a critical final strategy in ensuring an evaluation's use and promoting ongoing program improvement. It's not uncommon that an evaluation report raises more questions than it answers. This is actually a good thing. In a sense, each evaluation you conduct helps you set the agenda for future evaluations.

On planning . . .

Failing to plan is planning to fail.
                                 ~Alan Lakein

Findings from your evaluation may suggest, for example, that a particular component of the program was functioning well (e.g., a parent training component) but that another component you touched on only tangentially is functioning less well and should be looked into more closely (e.g., community awareness of available parent training classes). Or findings may demonstrate that another component of your program is not working well yet not really explain *why* that is so or *how* the problem could be remedied.

The *why* and *how* of what isn't working may then become grist for the mill of a future evaluation. Further, findings regarding issues encountered with the logistics of the evaluation itself may suggest that alternative approaches need to be tried in upcoming evaluations.

This is not to say that you need to completely revamp your evaluation plan every time you complete another individual evaluation. Rather, we propose that new information gleaned from each successive evaluation be viewed within the context of your long-range evaluation plans to see if any midcourse corrections are warranted.

While it's possible that recently compiled findings may occasionally imply that a planned evaluation should be scrapped and replaced with one of greater urgency, it's far more likely that your revised approach will involve only minor modifications to one or more proposed evaluations.

Findings may also help you generate ideas for an evaluation "wish list" pending the next evaluation cycle—or the sudden availability of additional evaluation funds. What you want is for your evaluation to continually inform not only your immediate program improvement efforts but also your longer range strategies for evaluations. That's why linking evaluation findings back to your strategic evaluation plan is so critical.

As a last check, before you call an evaluation plan "final" and begin to implement your evaluation, use the checklist in Table 9.3 to see if you have covered all the steps that will help lead to a successful implementation of your evaluation.

Table 9.3. **Preevaluation Checklist for the Successful Implementation of an Evaluation Plan.**

Category	Yes	No
Do we have an evaluation planning team composed of individuals with the knowledge, skills, and experience relevant to planning this evaluation?		
Do we have an evaluation implementation team of individuals who will take responsibility for implementing the evaluation, providing access to data, overseeing data collection, analyzing the data, and preparing the evaluation report?		
Have we identified our key stakeholders for this evaluation? See Chapters 1–3.		
Have we thought about how to work with our stakeholders? (Table 9.1) • Preevaluation? • During the evaluation? • Postevaluation? • To develop the Action Plan (Tool K)? • To manage public relations? • To minimize evaluation anxiety (Tool C)?		
Will the evaluation design (Tool E) and data collection methods (Tool H) result in ... • Methodology that is feasible given resource and practical constraints? • Data that are credible and useful to stakeholders? • Data that are accurate? • Data that will help answer the evaluation questions in a timely manner?		

continued

Table 9.3: **Continued**

Category	Yes	No

Are we prepared logistically? (Table 9.2)
 	
Do we have plans for …
 	
    • Staffing?
    • Budget (Tool F)?
    • Funding?
    • Data sharing and other types of contracts/agreements?
    • Human subjects (IRB), HIPAA, and organizational clearances/permissions?		

Are we prepared for data collection? (Table 9.2)
 	
Have we addressed …
 	
    • Finalization and approval of data collection instruments?
    • Propriety of the evaluation, including protection of human subjects?
    • Cultural sensitivity, clarity, and user-friendliness of instruments?
    • Respondent burden?
    • Methods to obtain high response rates or complete data?
    • Data handling, processing, storage?
    • Data confidentiality, security?		

Did we pilot-test our measuring instruments and data collection procedures?		
Did we train the data collection staff? (Tool I)		

Will the data analyses answer our evaluation questions?
 	
Have we specified the …
 	
    • Analyses to answer each evaluation question?
    • Table shells that show how the results will be presented?		

Do we have methods in place (Tool G) to track evaluation implementation and to promote communication within the evaluation implementation team?
 	
For example, do we have a …
 	
    • Timeline?
    • Budget?
    • Roles and responsibilities table?
    • Project description?
    • Project status form?		

Have we planned for sharing interim results (if appropriate) and for disseminating the final results? (See Tool J.)		

Spending some "quality time" over a glass of wine—or two—with your evaluation plan will pay off in the long run as you move forward to its implementation. With a solid individual evaluation plan in hand, you will be in the best possible position to implement an evaluation that meets the standards of utility, feasibility, propriety, and accuracy that were covered in Chapter 4.

Also, by following the strategies described here that relate to stakeholder engagement and sharing results—"Working with Stakeholders," "Monitoring Progress and Promoting Ongoing Communication," "Interim Reporting and Dissemination of Final Results," "Developing an Action Plan," "and "Linking Back to the Evaluation Plan"—you will be better able to translate your evaluation findings into shared action by you and your stakeholders alike.

SUMMARY

This chapter briefly provided the nine basic strategies that need to be followed when you are going to do any type of evaluation. Therefore, when reading the following four chapters, keep in mind that the strategies outlined in this chapter must be applied to each one. In a nutshell, they represent important steps you can take during the *planning* stages of your evaluation that will help you to *implement* your plans more smoothly.

The goal of this chapter is to provide you with a beginning knowledge base for you to feel comfortable in answering the following questions. AFTER you have read the chapter, indicate how comfortable you feel you are in answering each question on a 5-point scale where

1 Very uncomfortable	2 Somewhat uncomfortable	3 Neutral	4 Somewhat comfortable	5 Very comfortable

If you rated any question between 1–3, reread the section of the chapter where the information for the question is found. If you still feel that you're uncomfortable in answering the question, then talk with your instructor and/or your classmates for more clarification.

	Questions	Degree of comfort? *(Circle one number)*
1	List the nine strategies that you need to consider *before* doing any type of program evaluation.	1 2 3 4 5
2	Pretend, for the moment, that you have been hired to evaluate your social work program. However, you fully realize that you need to address several issues in reference to your program's stakeholders *before* you actually carry out your evaluation (Strategy 1). List, and then discuss, the issues you feel need to be addressed in relation to your stakeholder groups. Provide as many examples as you can throughout your discussion. And, more important, don't forget to utilize the tools contained in the Toolkit when appropriate.	1 2 3 4 5
3	Pretend, for the moment, that you have been hired to evaluate your social work program. However, you fully realize that you need to address several issues in reference to developing a good process for managing your evaluation *before* you actually carry out your evaluation (Strategy 2). List, and then discuss, the issues you feel need to be addressed in relation to developing a process to managing your evaluation. Provide as many examples as you can throughout your discussion. And, more important, don't forget to utilize the tools contained in the Toolkit when appropriate.	1 2 3 4 5
4	Pretend, for the moment, that you have been hired to evaluate your social work program. However, you fully realize that you need to address several issues in reference to pilot-testing your data collection instruments *before* they are used to collect data for your evaluation (Strategy 3). List, and then discuss, the issues you feel need to be addressed in relation to pilot-testing your measuring instruments and data collection procedures. Provide as many examples as you can throughout your discussion. And, more important, don't forget to utilize the tools contained in the Toolkit when appropriate.	1 2 3 4 5

continued

5	Pretend, for the moment, that you have been hired to evaluate your social work program. However, you fully realize that you need to address several issues in reference to training the folks who will be collecting data *before* they actually collect them (Strategy 4). List, and then discuss, the issues you feel need to be addressed in relation to training your data collectors when it comes to training data collection staff. Provide as many examples as you can throughout your discussion. And, more important, don't forget to utilize the tools contained in the Toolkit when appropriate.	1 2 3 4 5
6	Pretend, for the moment, that you have been hired to evaluate your social work program. However, you fully realize that you need to address several issues in reference to how you are going to monitor the progress of your evaluation in addition to how you are going to promote ongoing communication within your stakeholder groups *before* you actually carry out your evaluation (Strategy 5). List, and then discuss, the issues you feel need to be addressed in relation to monitoring your evaluation's progress in addition to promoting ongoing communication with your stakeholder groups. Provide as many examples as you can throughout your discussion. And, more important, don't forget to utilize the tools contained in the Toolkit when appropriate.	1 2 3 4 5
7	Pretend, for the moment, that you have been hired to evaluate your social work program. However, you fully realize that you need to address several issues in reference to how you are going to handle interim reporting procedures and the dissemination of your findings *before* you actually carry out your evaluation (Strategy 6). List, and then discuss, the issues you feel need to be addressed. Provide as many examples as you can throughout your discussion. And, more important, don't forget to utilize the tools contained in the Toolkit when appropriate.	1 2 3 4 5
8	Pretend, for the moment, that you have been hired to evaluate your social work program. However, you fully realize that you need to address several issues in reference to how you are going to develop an action plan *before* you even begin your evaluation (Strategy 7). List, and then discuss, the issues you feel need to be addressed in relation to developing an action plan for your evaluation. Provide as many examples as you can throughout your discussion. And, more important, don't forget to utilize the tools contained in the Toolkit when appropriate.	1 2 3 4 5

continued

9	Pretend, for the moment, that you have been hired to evaluate your social work program. However, you fully realize that you need to address several issues in reference to how you are going to document what you have learned from your evaluation (Strategy 8). List, and then discuss, the issues you feel need to be addressed in relation to documenting what you have learned from your evaluation. Provide as many examples as you can throughout your discussion. And, more important, don't forget to utilize the tools contained in the Toolkit when appropriate.	1 2 3 4 5
10	Pretend, for the moment, that you have been hired to evaluate your social work program. However, you fully realize that you need to address several issues in reference to how you are going to link your findings back to your original evaluation plan even *before* you begin the evaluation (Strategy 9). List, and then discuss, the issues you feel need to be addressed in relation to linking your evaluation findings back to your original evaluation plan. Provide as many examples as you can throughout your discussion. And, more important, don't forget to utilize the tools contained in the Toolkit when appropriate.	1 2 3 4 5

Chapter 9				Assessing Your Self-Efficacy

AFTER you have read this chapter AND have completed all of the study questions, indicate how knowledgeable you feel you are for each of the following concepts on a 5-point scale where

1 Not knowledgeable at all	2 Somewhat unknowledgeable	3 Neutral	4 Somewhat knowledgeable	5 Very knowledgeable

	Concepts	Knowledge Level? *(Circle one number)*
1	Overall, the nine strategies that can be implemented to increase the overall success of an evaluation	1 2 3 4 5
2	Working with stakeholders in an effort to increase the overall success of an evaluation	1 2 3 4 5
3	Developing a process for managing an evaluation in an effort to increase its overall success	1 2 3 4 5
4	Pilot-testing data collection instruments in an effort to increase the overall success of an evaluation	1 2 3 4 5
5	Training data collection staff in an effort to increase the overall success of an evaluation	1 2 3 4 5
6	Monitoring the progress of an evaluation in an effort to increase its overall success	1 2 3 4 5
7	Writing interim and final evaluation reports in an effort to increase the overall success of an evaluation	1 2 3 4 5
8	Developing an action plan in an effort to increase the overall success of an evaluation	1 2 3 4 5
9	Documenting the lessons learned from an evaluation in an effort to increase its overall success	1 2 3 4 5
10	Linking evaluation findings back to the evaluation's strategic plan	1 2 3 4 5
	Add up your scores (minimum = 10, maximum = 50)	Your total score =

A   47–50 = Professional evaluator in the making
A–   45–46 = Senior evaluator
B+   43–44 = Junior evaluator
B   41–42 = Assistant evaluator
B–   10–40 = Reread the chapter and redo the study questions

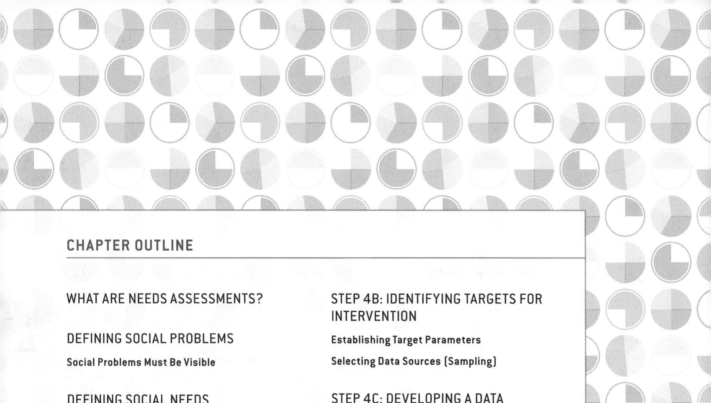

CHAPTER OUTLINE

Chapter 10

NEEDS ASSESSMENTS

Assessment is a key step in any change process where social workers are involved. A needs assessments is much more than simply establishing that a social problem exists (e.g., child prostitution, drug abuse, discrimination, violence, gang behavior, police violence); it also aims to identify a solution(s) to the problem.

WHAT ARE NEEDS ASSESSMENTS?

There are as many ways to define a needs assessment—or the assessment of need—as there are people willing to provide definitions of them:

- A tool used for identifying what a particular group of people is lacking that prevents them from achieving more satisfying lives (Reviere, Berkowitz, Carter, & Ferguson, 1996).
- A planning device that determines whether to embark upon or enhance specific programs and that determines how well recipients of services react to them (Ginsberg, 2001).
- A systematic approach to identifying social problems, determining their extent, and accurately defining the target population to be served and the nature of their service needs (Rossi, Lipsey, & Freeman, 2003).

As the preceding different definitions illustrate, needs assessments involve gathering data that ultimately will be used to match clients' needs (social problems) with potential programs (solutions to solve the social problem). In an ideal world, a needs assessment is conducted *before* establishing any new program. However, a needs assessment can generate data that are used to aid planning efforts at all stages of an existing program's development—start-up, expansion, renovation, or closure of particular "components" within a program.

A needs assessment for an existing program is particularly helpful when there's a poor fit between client needs and existing services. Signs of poor fit are indicated when:

- Services are made available to clients but not utilized by them
- A program fails to show it had a positive impact on its clientele
- Clients are dissatisfied about the nature or type of services they are receiving from a particular program

Thus not all needs assessments are done before a program is established. There are a few conditions that can trigger a needs assessment that can be conducted within an existing program, such as:

- Changes that occur in the community
- Changes in "the competition"
- Changes in understanding of the social problem
- The creation of more evidence-based interventions
- Changes in funding
- Changes in mandates

Regardless of when a needs assessment is carried out (before the program or during it), there are three interrelated concepts that are important to understanding the general framework of the needs assessment process:

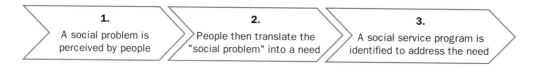

So to reiterate and as shown in the provided diagram above: a needs assessment determines what the social problem is (e.g., child prostitution, drug abuse, discrimination, violence, gang behavior, homelessness, bullying, child abuse) and turns the social problem into a need, then goes on to identify a tentative evidence-based social service program to address the need. We now turn our attention to a brief discussion of social problems.

DEFINING SOCIAL PROBLEMS

Defining a social problem is not a simple matter. Its definition depends on the definer's construction of reality. In other words, the definition of a social problem is connected to the unique perspective of the individual who creates the definition in the first place. Nevertheless, most people will accept that a social problem is an occurrence or event that is undesired by most or all of our society. They also must believe that the problem is changeable through social service interventions.

Some social problems present a visible and real threat to how our society is organized and to what people believe is necessary for a basic level of well-being. Citizens displaced by a natural disaster, parents abusing their children, high rates of unemployment, overt racism, police brutality, abject poverty, and people

committing suicide are examples of social problems that are presented in the media, have books written about them, and generally have been given a great deal of attention.

Social Problems Must Be Visible

Social problems have been the traditional focus of our profession since its beginning. As shown in Figure 10.1, our society has "drawn" a minimum line of acceptability for many of these visible social problems. Once the line is crossed—the physical abuse of a child is exposed, a teenager is caught selling drugs, a racist statement is made by a politician—there is some societal action that takes place.

The more visible the social problem, the more likely it is that action will follow. Table 10.1 provides a list of four crude indicators that can be used to assess whether an individual is willing to stand up and advocate for the elimination of a social problem. Generally speaking, the more indicators that are present (the more boxes checked as "yes"), the more concern an individual will have about a problem.

Other less explicit problems do not have a definite bottom line to indicate when and what action ought to take place. Children with behavior problems, individuals with low self-esteem, poverty, and unfair employment policies are examples of problems where the line of social acceptability falls within the gray area of society (see Figure 10.1).

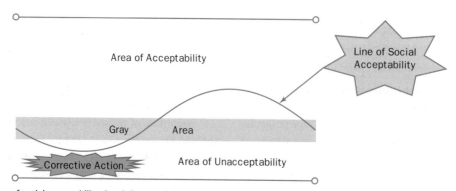

Figure 10.1: Line of social acceptability that defines social problems in society.

Table 10.1: **Four Indicators of a Social Problem's Visibility.**

Applies?		Indicator	Description
Yes	No		
☐	☐	*Proximity*	The physical distance between a person and the problem. For example, residents living in substandard rental accommodations are more likely to identify corrupt landlords as a problem than are residents living in adequate or superior housing conditions.
☐	☐	*Intimacy*	The level of personal familiarity with the problem, or the extent that you are personally affected by the problem. For example, someone close to you is hit by a drunk driver or afflicted by a fatal disease.
☐	☐	*Awareness*	The degree to which a problem has a presence in your daily thoughts. It is possible to have awareness of a problem without being intimately affected by it. For example, Hurricane Katrina hit Louisiana, Mississippi, and Alabama in 2005 and woke America up to the conditions of poverty in these areas as well as the limitations of the government to execute an immediate response to the large-scale crisis.
☐	☐	*Magnitude*	The scale or enormity of the condition. In other words, the more people affected by a condition, the more public attention the problem receives.

Consequently, these "problems" are less likely to see action—for example, to receive the assistance of public or grant monies—unless they are paired with more visible needs, as is the case when "prevention" measures are discussed; that is, the focus is to establish a connection between an identified social problem and preventing a subsequent undesired outcome.

Take children who have behavior problems, for example. These children, more than children without behavior problems, are likely to experience problems at home, at school, and in the community. Because child behavior problems can be disruptive to family relationships, classroom instruction, and community harmony, children experiencing such problems can be at risk for out-of-home placement, academic failure, truancy, and delinquency.

Thus, to highlight the issues of childhood behavior problems, we might discuss their importance in terms of preventing foster-care placement, school dropouts, and crime. These latter social issues are more likely to capture the public's attention than the general social problem of "children who behave badly."

DEFINING SOCIAL NEEDS

A social problem can be translated into various needs as illustrated in Table 10.2. At a minimum, a social need can be thought of as a basic requirement necessary to sustain the human condition, to which people have a right. For example, few in our society would dispute that people have the right to nutritional food, clean water, safe housing, and clean air.

However, there could easily be a debate about how the basic need for food should be defined. Some could argue that only direct food supplies should be given to families in need. Others may say that financial assistance should be provided to ensure that families can take care of their unique needs.

Table 10.2: **Example of Translating the Same Social Problem into Different Needs.**

Social Problem	⇒	Need
Family poverty	⇒	Food for basic nutrition
Family poverty	⇒	Money to purchase basic goods
Family poverty	⇒	Job to support family

Still others would argue that the need is to help parents of poor families find living-wage jobs to provide them with sustainable incomes. Like the definition of social problems, the translation of the problems into needs is subject to the individual views of how different people view "reality."

The Hierarchy of Social Needs

A popular framework for assessing human social needs is Abraham Maslow's (1999) hierarchy of human needs, shown in Figure 10.2. The physiological needs, shown at the base of the pyramid, represent the most basic conditions—food, water, shelter, and clothing—needed to sustain human life.

Maslow's model suggests that unless these foundational needs are met, a person will not grow or move to higher levels of well-being. In fact, the notion of hierarchy means that people must fulfill their needs at a lower level before they are able to move up the hierarchy, to higher levels of the pyramid.

Security needs in Maslow's hierarchy represent the human desire for safety—not only in the here and now but also in the future. When people fear for their safety, for example, it interferes with their social needs at the next level of the pyramid. In other words, without a sense of security, one's social needs such as love, friendship, and connection with others cannot be fully met.

Ego or esteem needs are at the next level and go beyond basic social relations to a sense of belonging in a social group in a way that adds to one's self-identify. Ego or esteem needs also reflect the desire to be recognized for one's accomplishments.

Finally, self-actualization, which is at the tip-top of the pyramid, is possible only when all other needs have been satisfied. People are said to be self-actualized when they reach their full potential as human beings. This full potential may be expressed through many arenas, such as in music, business, or humanitarian causes.

The framework for Maslow's hierarchy can be applied to human needs in many different contexts. An Internet search using "Maslow's hierarchy" combined with a second key search term such as "family," "community," "organization," or "education" will yield websites that apply the model to people living and working in these different environments.

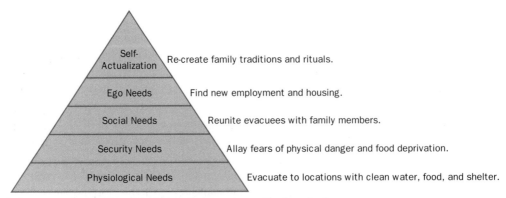

Figure 10.2: **Maslow's Hierarchy of Human Needs as applied to survivors of Hurricane Katrina.**

FOUR TYPES OF SOCIAL NEEDS

As seen earlier, Maslow's hierarchy of human needs is a helpful concept map to prioritize needs in relation to particular social problems. As we know, a "need" is a dynamic concept and can be conceived of from multiple perspectives. There are four types of needs that highly overlap with one another.

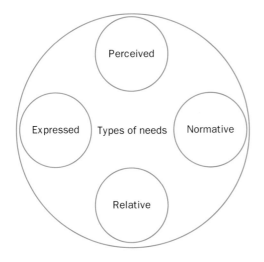

Perceived Needs

The first social need is a perceived need. It's also called a "felt" need. It's simply the perspective that individuals have about a social problem at a particular point in time. As individuals change over time, so do their perceived needs. Furthermore, perceived needs differ dramatically because "needs" are defined in the eyes of the beholders.

Everyone has an opinion on just about everything—especially social workers. Prison inmates, for example, will protest the removal of television sets from their cells, thereby demanding that television viewing is a necessary part of their recreational needs. The public, on the other hand, may not see a need for inmates to have access to television sets and may very well feel that the basic recreational outlets of inmates can be met through various educational magazines, exercise rooms, social clubs, and radio programming.

Normative Needs

The second type of need is a normative need. A normative need implies that there exists a standard with which a need can be compared. Need is then "calculated," usually from existing data, and the extent or magnitude of the need is numerically expressed as a ratio.

For example, accreditation standards may dictate the size of a social worker's caseload to be no greater than one worker to 15 clients—a ratio of 1:15. A program reporting a caseload ratio of 1:30 could use this normative need to illustrate a concern about its service quality and/or to argue for additional program resources.

Relative Needs

Like normative needs, relative needs also involve making comparisons. However, relative needs do not have normative standards like normative needs do. Instead, a relative need of one group is weighed against another comparable group. For example, Pecora and colleagues (2005) have shown the need for educational support after children in foster care leave the system.

They reported that only 1.8% of young adults (25–34 years of age) that formerly lived in foster care had completed a bachelor's degree. They also argued that this figure was significantly lower than 27.5%, which was the rate of completing a bachelor's degree among the general population of the same age.

This example shows the need of the general population *relative* to a subpopulation—foster care youth in Pecora et al.'s (2005) case. Many other relative comparisons are possible such as geography (e.g., one county versus another county), time (e.g., this year versus last year), or program (public programs versus private programs).

Expressed Needs

An expressed need is met or unmet by reporting the "demand statistics" related to a particular social service program or event. In other words, expressed needs tell us how many (or what percentage of) clients from a targeted group requested available services. A more difficult figure to report is the number (or percentage) of the targeted group that attempts but fails to access services.

For example, despite the fact that Latinos comprise the largest and most rapidly growing minority group

Table 10.3: **Four Types of Needs.**

Type of Need	Definition	Example
Normative	This need is defined by an existing normative standard to which a need can be compared	The number of people who live in substandard housing as defined by Federal housing standards
Perceived/ Demand	This need is defined in terms of what individuals, or groups, think their needs are	The number of people who believe they are living in substandard housing
Relative	This need is defined by the gap (if any) between the level of services existing in one community and those existing in similar communities	The percentage of people living in substandard housing in one community compared to those in another community
Expressed	This need is defined by the number of people who have requested a social service	The number of people who requested to receive low-income housing assistance

in the United States, there have been consistent reports of disproportionately low numbers of Latinos accessing essential services such as health care, social service, and education. Documentation of these attempts is often unreported.

Low expressed needs may be an indication that an existing social service is a poor fit with the identified client need. On the other hand, other mediating factors may be the problem. For instance, isolating language and cultural barriers or lack of awareness about social services are just two possible reasons that may help to explain the low levels of expressed needs by Latino groups. In this case, Latinos may want—or even demand—more services but are not accessing them because of language or other cultural barriers.

SOLUTIONS TO ALLEVIATE SOCIAL NEEDS

As an agency-based profession, social work solutions to alleviate social needs most typically come in the form of social work programs, or interventions. Sometimes the solution is accomplished through policies. On a simple level, these programs are aimed at improving the quality of life for people. This can be done either by proposing a new program in a location where it has not previously been provided or by suggesting new or alternative services within an existing program.

With a focus on social justice and a concern for vulnerable populations, most of us are employed by programs that target foundational human needs—physiological, security, and social, as shown in Figure 10.2. Every social work program is in fact a solution that is designed to resolve a social problem by addressing a specific need(s). In short, a social service program is established to eliminate a social need(s), which in turn will solve its related social problem. In Chapters 7 and 8 we covered the structure of programs in detail, and this may be a great time to review these two chapters to see how programs are conceptualized, implemented, and evaluated.

Table 10.4: **Relationship Among Problems, Needs, and Program Solutions.**

Problem	⇒	Need	⇒	Program Solution
Family poverty	⇒	Food for children's nutrition	⇒	Food bank
Family poverty	⇒	Money to purchase basic goods	⇒	Public assistance
Family poverty	⇒	Job to support family	⇒	Job training

Table 10.4 displays an example of the interrelatedness between social problems, needs, and program solutions; it illustrates how one problem can generate multiple needs as well as different program solutions. Indeed, a primary aim of a needs assessment is to find the best match.

STEPS IN DOING A NEEDS ASSESSMENT

As shown in Table 10.4, the main purpose of all needs assessments is to identify a social problem(s), translate that problem into a need(s), and propose a solution(s) to address the need(s).

Needs assessments achieve their purpose through well-established research/evaluation methods. Thus the steps used to carry them out must be clearly documented so other interested parties can evaluate the study's credibility. And because there's a great deal of flexibility in conducting any needs assessment, we must have a clear rationale for each step we take.

As with all types of evaluations, needs assessments do not develop out of thin air. They are born out of gaps in existing social services (or lack of them), public unrest, landmark cases, fluctuations in political and economic conditions, and changes in basic demographic trends. As such, the initial steps of conducting a needs assessment are in some ways predetermined.

A director of a family social service agency, for example, may notice that attendance at its parent support groups is low. The director then requests the line-level workers within the program to ask parents about the attendance problem and to see whether there are any concerns about access to the support group. Or a child may be abducted from a public school ground during the lunch hour and an inquiry may be called to look into the general safety of children and supervision practices at all public schools.

A third scenario could be that the number of street panhandlers may be perceived to be growing, so a municipal task force is formed to learn more about "the problem" and to decide what action, if any, the city should take. These examples illustrate that, once a needs assessment begins, a certain amount of momentum has already been established. Nevertheless, we must be able to take a step back and see if we have used a well-thought-out evaluation approach in examining the perceived need.

Although the entire process of conducting a needs assessment requires a certain amount of knowledge, skill, and diplomacy, the process can be easily incorporated into the general evaluation framework presented in Chapter 3 (also see Figure 10.3).

As can be seen from Figure 3.1 in Chapter 3, there are six nonmutually exclusive steps within the generic evaluation process. Figure 10.3 shows the steps of doing a needs assessment within the generic evaluation process. More specifically, this chapter discusses needs assessments within three of the six steps (i.e., 3, 4, 6).

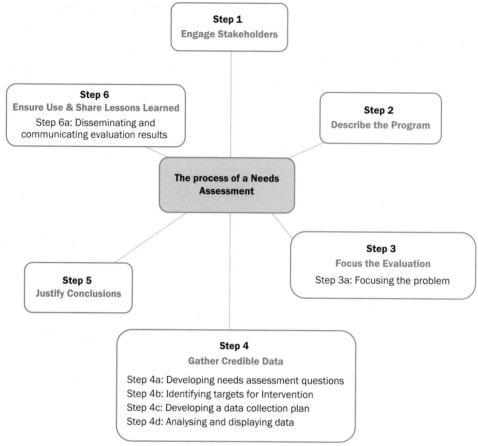

Figure 10.3: **The process of a needs assessment (from Figure 3.1).**

STEP 3A: FOCUSING THE PROBLEM

As we alluded to in our earlier discussion, needs and their tentative solutions are subject to politics, trends, biases, and opinions. The climate surrounding a particular social problem, therefore, can support or supplant our efforts to ascertain whether a social need really exists and which specific needs are given priority. Examples of events that can influence a needs assessment are political elections, heightened awareness of a social problem by the local media, lobbying from interest groups about a particular social problem, and economic change.

Before we start any needs assessment, however, we must give considerable thought to how a particular social problem is going to be defined. Once again, a needs assessment has three components: specific social problem(s), individual need(s), and possible solution(s) to address the need. How we define a specific social problem has a major impact on the types of data that we gather and how we proceed in collecting them.

Your definition of the social problem also has a great deal of influence on your proposed solution to resolve it. Thus it's imperative that you consider the social problem first and then, and only then, consider the scope of possible solutions to help solve the problem.

Example

Suppose, for example, a runaway shelter for teenagers reports that it's filled to capacity and is turning away runaways on a daily basis. It's tempting for a novice to declare that more shelter space is needed to accommodate the teens who are being turned away. In haste, the proposed solution to the problem is to expand the runaway shelter space. Has the problem been fixed? No! We must step back a bit more and ask more thoughtful questions such as the following:

- Who are the teens using the shelter?
- What are the teens running away from?
- When are teen runaways most likely to show up at the shelter?

The answers to these questions may suggest that providing more space is not the solution to the problem. A crisis counseling component could be added to the shelter, for example, to help teens negotiate with their parents to return home or arrange to stay with friends or relatives. There are many more possible solutions as well. Clearly, the definition of a need is crystallized by the assumptions and questions we ask about it.

STEP 4A: DEVELOPING NEEDS ASSESSMENT QUESTIONS

The type of questions asked in a needs assessment can easily shift the study's initial focus in different directions. Let's suppose Paula, a social worker, wants to examine the specific social problem of rising delinquency rates in the rural town where she lives and works (Hornick & Burrows, 1998).

- She could ask youth-focused questions:
  - Do youth perceive that they are a part of the community?
  - What do the youths perceive their role in the community to be?

- She could ask family-focused questions:
  - Are parents aware of their children's whereabouts and activities?
  - Do parents feel they are responsible for their children's behavior in the community?

- She could ask legal questions:
  - How are status offenses defined?
  - Are the penalties for juvenile crime adequate?

- She could ask intervention questions:
  - Is the probationary system able to accommodate the current number of juvenile delinquents?

Each of the aforementioned types of questions (i.e., youth, family, legal, intervention) frames the social problem from a different angle. They also imply different needs and that a different intervention approach is warranted:

- The youth-focused questions suggest solutions such as a campaign for recognizing the roles that youth play in the community.
- The family-focused questions hint that parent training and education might be in order.
- The legal questions target change for legislation, and the intervention questions shift focus to the operations of existing social services.

In short, it's always necessary to examine the problem from many different possible dimensions, or we run the risk of offering biased and premature solutions. Other considerations for developing needs assessment questions can be:

- Is the social problem acute or chronic?
- Is the problem long standing, or was it brought about by some recent event?

A list of possible questions to guide Paula's needs assessment for her rural town is presented in Box 10.1. Questions 1 and 2 were designed to find out more about the social problems, if any, within her

BOX 10.1 NEEDS ASSESSMENT QUESTIONS

1. With what social problems or issues are area residents confronted?
2. What perceptions do residents have regarding their community?
3. What types of services are viewed by residents as being important?

4. Which services are needed most?
5. To what extent are residents satisfied with the present level of social services in town?
6. Is there a transportation problem for residents who use services that are only available in Calgary?

community. Questions 3 to 6 were specifically geared toward possible solutions to the problems.

STEP 4B: IDENTIFYING TARGETS FOR INTERVENTION

As we have seen, how a social problem is defined is clearly influenced by a multitude of factors. The specific definition of need, however, is clarified by developing questions that guide the remaining steps of a needs assessment. The final questions developed are particularly useful in telling us who, or what, will be the target for the proposed solution(s) or proposed program(s).

Establishing Target Parameters

Targets for intervention can take many forms, such as individuals, groups, organizations, and communities. In reviewing the questions contained within Paula's needs assessment, for example, her target was the residents living in her rural town; that is, she was interested in what the townspeople thought about their community, the social problems they experienced (if any), and the social services that were available to them to solve the social problem.

Paula simply used a geographical boundary to define her target for intervention. It's necessary to develop explicit criteria so that there is no question as to who is and is not a target. Criteria that help define targets often include factors such as the following:

- Demographics, such as age, gender, race, and socioeconomic status

- Membership in predefined groups, such as families, professional work teams, and members in an organization
- Conditions, such as people receiving public assistance, residents of low-cost housing, and hospice clients

Direct and Indirect Interventions

Once a target for an intervention is defined, it can be tackled directly or indirectly. Proposed solutions can include direct services through programs established for the specified target. If we defined adolescents between 12 and 17 years of age who are at risk for alcohol and drug abuse (the target), for example, we might suggest that outreach services (the intervention) be established to reach them at their "hangouts," such as a nearby shopping mall or Dairy Queen.

Complementary to direct solutions are indirect solutions, which focus on changing policies and procedures that, in turn, affect the target. A possible indirect solution could be to institute a policy that increases the legal consequences (the intervention) for teens that are caught using drugs or alcohol (the target).

It should be clear by now that how we define a social need and pose needs assessment questions will influence the eventual targets for an intervention. In the case of Paula's needs assessment, for example, the residents in her town were targeted because they were all considered potential users of social services.

Another strategy might have been to target existing social service agencies (organizations) or specific neighborhoods (communities). She could have targeted the social services by asking questions such as:

- What's the profile of clients currently served?
- Do programs have waiting lists?
- How many clients are turned away because of inadequate resources?
- How many clients asked for services that were not available? What are these services?

Targeting neighborhoods may have led Paula to examine the number and type of social problems in each neighborhood. She could then have asked questions such as:

- What concerns do neighborhood residents have about the local area they live in?
- What were the existing social services in each neighborhood?
- What, if any, informal helping services existed in each neighborhood?

By selecting different targets and developing different needs assessment questions, Paula could have completely changed the direction of her study.

Selecting Data Sources (Sampling)

Defining a target logically leads you to identify your data source(s); that is, who (or what) you will collect data from. Therefore it's necessary for you to apply basic sampling principles if your study's findings are to have any generalizability. To have generalizability, however, you need to have a representative sample of your data sources. For now, let's take a closer look at how Paula arrived at a representative sample for the residents of her town (her target).

Paula defined the pool of residents who were eligible to participate in her needs assessment study. She defined the parameters of her sampling frame as all people over 18 years of age who resided within the town's borders. Although it may have been useful to collect data from youth as well (those under 18 years of age), it would also have added to the expense of actually carrying out the needs assessment.

Learn more about different sampling procedures in Tool H in the Evaluation Toolkit.

It may be that other local organizations such as a school or community center may recently have conducted a similar or related survey with this younger age group. If so, Paula might have used the existing survey information related to the younger group. Thus her needs assessment efforts would have been better spent targeting the older group.

Suppose that the population of Paula's town was a little over 2,000 people; it would be necessary for Paula to use random sampling procedures to select her sample of people. The size of Paula's sample would be influenced by time, money, resources, and the various possibilities on how to collect her data (Step 4c). To gather a random sample, Paula obtained a complete list of the town's residents from the electric company, as everyone in the town was billed for electricity use. She then took a random sample of 300 people from this list.

When deciding whom to include in the pool of data sources, you want to cast your net as far as possible. Ideally, you want to randomly choose from everyone who fits within the boundaries of those whom you have defined as a target.

STEP 4C: DEVELOPING A DATA COLLECTION PLAN

There is a critical distinction between a data collection method and a data source, which must be clearly understood before developing a viable data collection plan—the purpose of Step 4c. A data collection method consists of a detailed plan of procedures that aims to gather data for a specific purpose—that is, to answer our needs assessment question(s).

Learn more about developing a data collection plan in Tool H in the Evaluation Toolkit.

There are various data collection methods available: reviewing existing reports, secondary data analyses, individual interviews, group interviews, and telephone and mail surveys. Each data collection method can be used with a variety of data sources, which are defined by who (or what) supplies the data. Data can be provided by a multitude of sources, including people, existing records, and existing databases. (Table H.3 in Tool H presents a variety of data collection methods and Table H.4 provides an example of a data collection plan.)

Before we briefly discuss the various data collection methods, we must remember once again that a needs assessment has three main parts:

- The social problem(s)
- The need(s) derived from the social problem(s)
- The proposed solution(s) to the social problem

Given this, and as can easily be seen in Table 10.4, the social problem is family poverty where three needs of this population have been identified (i.e., food for children, money for basic goods, jobs). Each of the needs has a corresponding potential social service program associated with it (i.e., food bank, public assistance, job training).

Generally, when a needs assessment is sent out to the community it does not contain specific questions about "need." More often than not, it contains only questions about "perceived social problems" and "perceived potential solutions to them." Thus it's important to collect data for each part—the problem and solution.

If we collect data only about the potential social problem(s), for example, then we can only guess at the potential solution(s). If Paula asked only Questions 1 and 2 in her needs assessment (see Box 10.1), she would not have gathered any data to help decide what ought to be done (interventions in social work lingo) about the social problems that the townspeople identified.

Alternatively, if she only asked Questions 3 through 6 (see Box 10.1), she would have data to determine only what the residents think would solve the social problems in their community and would not have a clear indication about what social problems they perceive to exist, if any.

Paula could easily have developed her own set of "needs" from only the community's response to "social problems" (Question 1). She could then suggest corresponding social service programs to address these needs. So she could have asked only one open-ended question in her needs assessment: "What social problems or issues do area residents have?"

From the community's responses to this open-ended question she could then delineate (all by herself without any input from others) a set of "community's needs." She could even go on to suggest various evidence-based interventions to meet these needs. However, she wanted the community's input to possible solutions (Question 4). She simply wanted input from the community members in reference to what they felt was needed to address the social problems.

It should be clear by now that how a needs assessment question is defined guides the selection of the data collection method(s). This seemingly unimportant fact is actually quite critical in developing the best possible needs assessment. You must be careful not to subscribe to any one data collection plan in an effort to change your needs assessment questions to fit your preferred data collection method and/or data source.

Put simply, the combination of data collection method(s) and data source(s) that you choose influences the nature and type of data you finally collect and analyze. Therefore it's important that well-thought-out and meaningful questions are developed before plans to collect the data are set in stone.

How you go about collecting your data to answer your needs assessment questions depends on many practical considerations, such as how much time, money, and political support are available to you at the time of your study. Financial resources are usually limited, so it's worthwhile to begin a needs assessment study by using data that were previously collected by someone else.

If existing data are not adequate to answer your needs assessment questions, then you have no other alternative but to collect new data. To gain a broader understanding of the needs being examined, it's worthwhile to use numerous multiple data collection methods and data sources.

There are many ways to collect data, as presented in Table H.2 in Tool H. We present only the six that Paula actually used in her study:

- Existing reports
- Secondary data
- Individual interviews
- Group interviews
- Telephone and mail surveys

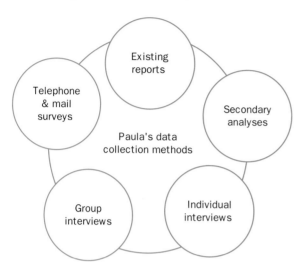

Existing Reports

Reviewing existing reports is a process whereby we closely examine data and information that are presented in existing materials, such as published research studies, government documents, news releases, social service agency directories, agency annual reports, minutes of important meetings, and related surveys, to name a few. The data provided from these many existing sources are generally descriptive and in the form of words.

Raw data may be presented in these existing sources, but most are presented in the form of information. That is, someone else has interpreted the data and drawn conclusions from them. Paula, for example, could have accessed information about her particular community through professional journals and government reports. She might also have had access to other needs assessments conducted in neighboring towns. At first glance, reviewing existing reports might seem like a time-consuming academic task, but it can be a real time-saver in the long run.

By looking over what others have already done, we can save valuable time by learning from their mistakes and avoiding reinventing the wheel. By taking the time to review existing documentation and reports at her town's planning office, for example, Paula was able to narrow the focus of her study by asking more specific questions, which she addressed in Step 3.

Data and information gleaned from existing published reports and articles provide us with a picture of how much attention the "social problem" has previously received. What other similar studies have been undertaken? In Paula's study, for example, she found that town residents had been polled about their opinions in the past.

The town had previously commissioned two other community assessment projects—the first assessed social needs and the second focused on housing and public transportation needs. In short, these types of reports provided her with a starting point to refine her needs assessment study in an effort to make it more useful to the townspeople.

Secondary Data

A secondary data analysis differs from the process of reviewing existing reports in that it involves working with raw data. The data, however, have typically been collected for some other purpose than answering our needs assessment question(s). Three common types of secondary data that are used in answering needs assessment questions are:

- Census data
- Client and program data

Using Census Data

Census data are periodic summaries of selected demographic characteristics, or variables, which describe a population. As you know, census takers obtain data (every 10 years) about variables such as age, gender, marital status, race, income level, education level, employment status, and presence of disabilities.

Census data are extremely useful for a needs assessment that compares its sample (target for intervention) with census data (general population). Census data for Paula's rural town, for example, showed that the city had doubled in size very quickly.

In addition to reporting how many residents lived in her town, the census data also provided a demographic profile of city residents, such as the number of people employed and unemployed, the number and ages of children living in single-parent and double-parent families, and the length of time people had lived in the city.

Thus Paula could compare the characteristics of her 300-person sample (randomly drawn from the town's electric company's files) with that of the city's total population (over 2,000). Census data also are useful for providing a general picture of a certain population at a specific point in time.

The more data obtained during a census, the more detailed the description of the population. The disadvantage of census data is that they can become outdated quickly. Census surveys take a considerable time to compile, analyze, and distribute. In addition, they give only a "general picture" of a population.

Census data, for example, provide data only on the average age of residents in a community or the percentage of childless couples living in a certain area. Although these data are useful for developing an "average community profile," they do not provide us with a clear idea of individual differences or how individual members of the community describe themselves.

Using Client Files and Program Records

Two other data sources that can be used for a secondary data analysis are existing client files and program records. More and more social work programs produce informal reports that describe the services they provide. They most likely use client data taken from intake forms and client files (e.g., Figure 14.3). Program data typically provide information about the demographic profile of clients served and the nature of the referral problems.

Simply counting the number of individuals served by a particular program provides us with data from which to calculate how big the problem is relative to a specified time period or for a particular client group. Remember our discussion of expressed needs presented earlier? Programs might keep data on the number of clients turned away because they were full

and/or the number of clients who were unwilling to be placed on a waiting list.

Client-related data are useful for needs assessments that focus on specific problem areas. If, for example, Paula's study focused specifically on the problems with teenage drug and alcohol abuse, she could have accessed programs serving this particular population and likely determined who the clients were based on these recorded data. If this was so, the following questions could have been asked:

- Were the teens mostly males or females?
- How old were the teens who were receiving social services?

The disadvantages of using data from programs are, first, they are not always complete or consistently recorded and, second, the data apply only to clients of a single program and for example do not tell us about teens who received services elsewhere or who were not receiving any help at all.

Individual Interviews

Face-to-face interviews with key informants produce new, or original, data. Interviewing key informants is a strategy that requires you to identify and approach specific people who are considered knowledgeable about the social problem you are interested in. Key informants are leaders in their community and include professionals, public officials, agency directors, social service clients, and select citizens, to name a few.

Your interviews can be formal and use a structured interview schedule, in which case you could ask all six questions in Box 10.1. If you would like to obtain more detailed data, you could develop questions that help you probe for more specific and detailed answers. In Question 4 in Box 10.1, for example, Paula could have also asked her key informants to consider services in the past and present or gaps in services.

On the other hand, when very little is known about your problem area, you can use informal unstructured interviews to permit more of a free-flowing discussion. Informal interviews involve more dialogue, in which questions you ask are generated by the key informants themselves. If, after interviewing a small number of key informants, for example, Paula consistently hears people express concerns about crime in the city, she may develop more specific questions to probe this social problem.

Using Key Informants

To help Paula define the parameters for her study, she used the key informant approach to interviewing at the beginning of her needs assessment study. This strategy was advantageous because it permitted her to gather data about the needs and services that were viewed as important by city officials and representatives of social service programs.

She was able to gather data about the nature of the social problems in her community and what specific groups of people faced these problems. Because Paula talked with public officials and people directly involved in the social services, she also was able to get some indication about what concerns might become future issues.

In addition, she got a glimpse of the issues that community leaders were more likely to support or oppose. Other advantages of interviewing key informants are that it's easy to do and relatively inexpensive. Moreover, because they involve interviewing community leaders, the interviews can be a valuable strategy for gaining support from these people.

One disadvantage of the key informant approach to data collection is that the views of the people you interview may not give an objective picture of the needs you're investigating. A key informant, for example, may be biased and provide a skewed picture of the nature of the social problem and its potential solution. Another drawback with key informant interviews occurs when you fail to select a good cross-section of people.

Paula, for example, was interested in learning about the range of social problems that her community was experiencing. If she had interviewed only professionals who worked with teenage or elderly populations, for example, then she would have run the risk of hearing more about the "social problems" that only these two groups face.

Group Interviews

A group interview is a data collection method that permits us to gather the perspectives of several individuals all at the same time. It's more complex than individual interviews because it involves interaction between and among the group members (data sources). There are strategies for structuring group interviews for needs assessments:

- Focus groups
- Nominal group techniques
- Public forms

Using Focus Groups

Like key informant interviews, focus groups collect new, or original, data on a specific topic from a selection of individuals who are reasonably familiar with the topic. The people within the groups are not necessarily familiar with each other. Focus groups are usually semistructured and often held in informal community settings where the group members are relaxed and comfortable in sharing their views and knowledge.

If you were to hold a focus group, for example, you would act as the group leader, provide some guidelines for the group process, and facilitate the dialogue for group members. You would prepare in advance a list of questions to ask your group members and to give some direction to the discussion. Again, Paula used the six questions in Box 6.1 in her needs assessment as a guide for her focus groups.

Your main task in conducting a focus group is to facilitate discussion and to keep your group members centered on the questions you're asking. Because you want to capture the divergent and similar views expressed in a focus group, you have several important tasks that must be considered.

First, you not only want to ensure that your group members are comfortable; you also want them to have clear expectations regarding why you are talking with them. Comfort can be increased by simple gestures of providing beverages and snacks, comfortable seating, and so on. Clarity of the task is ensured when meaningful and well-thought-out questions are prepared in advance and you offer a clear description of what you expect from the group.

Second, you need to record what group members say. The most accurate way of recording the discussion is to have it audiotaped and later transcribed. A second option is to bring a note-taker to the meeting who has the responsibility of writing down what people say.

Paula used focus groups that included community leaders, social service professionals, and selected groups of residents (e.g., elderly, parents, youth). The major advantages of focus groups are similar to those of using key informants. However, because a group process is used, focus group interviews are perhaps even more efficient than individual interviews. The disadvantages, of course, are that you will have less opportunity to explore the perspectives of individuals and your group members are always subject to the "groupthink" process.

Using Nominal Group Techniques

Nominal group techniques are useful data gathering tools for a needs assessment study because they can easily collect unbiased data from a group of people. The nominal group is composed of individuals who can answer a particular question of interest, and the process involves members working in the presence of others but with little structured interaction.

Paula, for example, wanted to select and recruit city officials, professionals, and city residents who had an opinion or knowledge about her six needs assessment questions. In doing so, she implemented the following steps:

1. Paula developed open-ended questions that were the focus for the group. The questions sought to generate problem dimensions such as Question 1: What social problems or issues are area residents confronted with? This question could also focus on generating solutions, in which case she would propose Question 4: What services are needed most? Ideally, a nominal group has six to nine members. If there

are considerably more, the technique can be used by forming smaller groups. Each group, or subgroup, should be seated comfortably and preferably in a circle.

2. Paula gathered the group together and gave an overview of the task. She gave each group member a sheet of paper with the questions written on it and explicit instructions that people were not to talk about their ideas with one another. She allowed about 15 minutes for the people to write down their responses privately.

3. Using a round-robin approach, she listed all answers generated in Step 2 on a flip chart. Because there was more than one group, each group listed their answers separately. The round robin continued until all responses were recorded. As in Step 2, this process was conducted without any discussion.

4. After all the responses were recorded on the flip charts, Paula engaged participants in some brief discussion about the responses listed. The discussion focused on clarifying what the responses meant so that everyone had a common understanding of each response.

5. Once all participants were familiar with the responses on the list, each person privately ranked the top five responses on an index card. These ranked lists were handed in and the popularity of responses was tallied on a flip chart. A second brief discussion was held to clarify any surprise rankings that occurred due to the misunderstanding of responses.

6. Paula ranked the responses so that the highest ranks reflected the social problems that were considered most important by the group members. If more specificity is desired, it's possible to rank the top responses, whereby another step of private rankings can occur.

The most obvious advantage of the nominal group technique for providing new data is that it promotes the sharing of ideas in an efficient manner. The nominal group process typically takes 2 to 4 hours depending on the size of the group and the number of questions asked (the entire cycle is applied for each question). Because of the game-like nature of the technique, participants can find the experience fun. When a cross-section of group participants is recruited, the process can yield a comprehensive response to needs assessment questions.

Using Public Forums

Public forums, as data collection methods, have far less structure than the other two methods of conducting group interviews. Holding a public forum involves inviting the general public to discuss matters that we wish to address in our needs assessment. A public forum can be a town hall meeting or even a phone-in radio talk show. It simply provides a place and an opportunity for people to assemble and air their thoughts and opinions about a specific social problem.

Paula invited the general citizens and leaders within her rural town to share their views on the social needs of the community. The discussion was guided by her six needs assessment questions but was less structured than other approaches she had used thus far.

The public forum approach was used at the beginning of Paula's study to kick-start the needs assessment process. The advantage of public forums is that they offer widespread advertising of the entire process. Their main disadvantage, however, is that they tend to draw a deliberate and select group of people who have strong opinions (in one way or another) that are not necessarily shared by the wider community.

Suppose, for example, that Paula held a public forum shortly after several layoffs had occurred within the local automotive industry. It's likely that her meeting would have been attended by many unemployed auto workers who, in addition to being concerned about community needs, had strong feelings about the loss of their jobs. When there is a strong unrest or there is an intense political agenda in a community, public forums may exacerbate the problem.

Telephone and Mail Surveys

The main goal of telephone and mail surveys is to gather opinions from numerous people in order to describe them as a group. A survey contains a list of questions compiled in an effort to examine a social problem in detail; it can be conducted by telephone or through the mail. The method chosen depends on how many questions are asked and how many people are sampled.

If we have only a few straightforward questions and a short time in which to collect data, it may be expedient to randomly select and interview people over the telephone. On the other hand, if our questions are more comprehensive, as was the case with Paula's study, and we have more time, it may be worthwhile to send out a mailed questionnaire.

The survey approach in collecting original data was a good one to use for Paula's study because it permitted her to systematically obtain the views of the townspeople in a very direct way; that is, she obtained opinions about the community from the residents themselves. In addition, Paula constructed her survey questionnaire from the data she obtained from interviews with her key informants. This meant that the data she collected from the survey meshed with the data she obtained from her key informants.

There are also several disadvantages to surveys. First, surveys are more resource intensive than many other data collection methods. The costs of constructing an appropriate survey, mailing, photocopying, and hiring someone to telephone or input the data from a mailed survey can add up quickly. Second, mailed surveys have low response rates, and people do not always complete all the questions. Third, constructing a mailed survey questionnaire is a complex task. Developing a useful survey questionnaire takes a great deal of knowledge and time.

For Paula, the advantages outweighed the disadvantages, and she opted to use a mailed survey. As a first step, Paula developed the mailed survey questionnaire. Because her task was to find out the community's needs, it was necessary for her to develop a survey that was directly relevant to the community. She tackled this task by examining other existing needs assessment mailed surveys, reviewing relevant literature, and, most important, talking to her key informants within the community.

Her mailed survey was carefully constructed so she could collect useful data about each of her questions. Her final survey was composed of seven sections: one for each of the six questions in Box 10.1 and an additional section to collect demographic data such as age, gender, marital status, employment status, income level, length of residence in the town, and the neighborhood in which people lived.

In sections addressing each of the six questions, respondents were asked to rate a number of statements using a predetermined measuring scale. Question 2, for example, aimed to find out how residents felt about living in the rural town. Respondents were also asked to rate statements such as "I enjoy living in this town" and "I feel that I am accepted by my community" on a 5-point scale where 1 meant "strongly disagree" and 5 meant "strongly agree."

To find out what services were needed most (Question 4), Paula listed a variety of social services (defined by her key informants) and asked respondents to rate the adequacy of the services. In this case, social services such as counseling for family problems, drop-in child care, and child protection services were listed. Respondents used a rating of 1 if they perceived the present level of the service to be "very inadequate" and 5 if they thought it was "very adequate." Because Paula anticipated that not all respondents would be familiar with all the social services in her town, she also included an "I don't know" response category.

The major part of her mailed survey required respondents to pick a number that best reflected their response to each question. Although Paula felt confident that she had covered all the critical areas necessary to fully answer her six questions, she also included an open-ended question at the end of the survey and instructed respondents to add any further comments or suggestions on the social services within the town. This allowed respondents an opportunity to provide commentary on some of the questions she asked and to voice any additional thoughts, ideas, beliefs, or opinions.

Because of her concern about the potentially low number of respondents to mailed surveys, Paula adopted several strategies to increase her response rate:

- A cover letter stating the purpose of her study was sent out with each mailed survey. The letter confirmed that all responses would be kept confidential and was signed by the town mayor and another city official.
- Extremely clear and simple instructions were provided
- A stamped, self-addressed return envelope was included with the survey
- Incentives to respondents were provided in the form of a family pass to a nearby public swimming pool or skating arena and access to the study's results
- A follow-up letter was sent out to all respondents as a prompt to complete the survey
- Information was provided to the respondents about when the study's results would be publicized in the media

STEP 4D: ANALYZING AND DISPLAYING DATA

Whether we use existing data or collect original data, there are several options on how to proceed when it comes to analyzing and displaying them. It's important to use a variety of strategies if we hope to develop an accurate and complete picture of the social need we are evaluating. As we have seen, no one method of data collection answers all that there is to know about a particular social need.

With a little effort, however, it's possible to design a data collection strategy that will provide useful quantitative and qualitative data. In a nutshell, qualitative data take the form of words, while quantitative data take the form of numbers. Paula was working with qualitative data when she examined archival reports from the town's Planning Commission and examined transcribed interviews. On the other hand, she was working with quantitative data when she analyzed respondents' numerical scores from her mailed survey.

Quantitative Data

Organizing and displaying data using quantitative approaches simply means that we are concerned with amounts. Quantitative data are organized so that occurrences can be counted. Basic statistics books describe counting in terms of frequencies: How frequently does an event occur? For instance,

- How many families live at or below the poverty line?
- What percentage of people over the age of 65 requires special medical services?
- How many families use the food bank in a given year?

If alcohol or drug use by teenagers was an important problem for Paula to consider, she would have counted the frequency of parents who perceive this as a problem in the community. Frequencies are usually reported as percentages, which is a rate per 100. If 45% of parents in Paula's sample perceived teen drug use as a problem, for example, then we would expect that 45 out of 100 parents in the total population would agree.

Because needs assessments often consider social problems on a larger societal level, we often find statistics reported using rates that are based on 1,000, 100,000, or more. Census data, for example, may report, that 8 per 1,000 babies are born with fetal alcohol syndrome (FES) in a certain community. These rates provide us with even more information when we have something to compare them with.

Suppose earlier census data, for example, reported that the rate of babies born with FES in the same community was 4 per 1,000. This means that the rate of FES has doubled between the two census reports. By making comparisons across time, we can look to the past, examine the present, and be in a better position to project into the future.

There are many other useful comparisons that can be made based on rates. Needs assessments can be used to compare a single specific situation with an established group norm. Remember normative needs, discussed earlier? We compare a norm with what we actually find. In other words, we might expect (norm) that unemployment in the rural town is at 10%, whereas when counted, it's actually at 20% (what we found).

What we expect is usually defined by existing standards or cutoff points. We can think of these as markers that set a minimum standard for most people. The poverty line, basic services provided by public welfare, and unemployment rate are a few examples where a known cutoff score is set.

Comparisons can also be made across geographic boundaries. Paula, for example, examined the ratio of employed social workers to the number of citizens living in the town. By reviewing existing published reports, Paula learned that there were two social workers practicing in her town to serve the needs of over 2,000 people. The specific ratio of the number of social workers to the number of people was 1 to 1,058. Paula compared these data with ratios in other cities.

She learned that a similar-sized city had four social workers serving a population of 2,557. The social-worker-to-population ratio in this other city was 1 to 639, which was about twice as high as that of her town. Paula was able to show a "relative need" for her community.

By comparing rates, we are in a better position to decide when a social problem is actually a problem. When counting problems in a needs assessment, we often report the incidence and/or the prevalence of a particular problem. Incidence is the number of instances of the problem that are counted within a specified time period. Prevalence is the number of cases of the problem in a given population.

The incidence of homelessness in the summer months, for example, may drop to 1 in 150 persons because of available seasonal employment. The prevalence of homelessness in a city, on the other hand, might be reported at a rate of 1 in 100 persons as an overall figure.

The purpose of this part of the survey is to learn more about your perceptions of these problems in the community. Listed below are a number of problems some residents of Northside have reported having.

Please circle a number from 1 to 3 on the line to the right of the question that represents how much of a problem they have been to you within the last year:

1. No problem (or not applicable to you)
2. Moderate problem
3. Severe problem

Questions	Responses		
1. Finding the product I need	1	2	3
2. Impolite salespeople	1	2	3
3. Finding clean stores	1	2	3
4. Prices that are too high	1	2	3
5. Not enough Spanish-speaking salespeople	1	2	3
6. Public transportation	1	2	3
7. Getting credit	1	2	3
8. Lack of certain types of stores	1	2	3
9. Lack of an employment assistance program	1	2	3
10. Finding a city park that is secure	1	2	3
11. Finding a good house	1	2	3

Figure 10.4: **Example of a nonstandardized needs assessment questionnaire that produces quantitative data.**

Reporting quantitative data provides a picture of the problem we are assessing, and the numbers and rates can be presented numerically or graphically. Using pie charts, bar graphs, and other visual representations helps to communicate data to all audiences. Many word processing programs and basic statistical packages have graphics components that can help us create impressive illustrations of our data. Figure 10.4 illustrates a nonstandardized needs assessment survey instrument that collected quantitative data.

Qualitative Data

Quantitative data analyses are useful in summarizing large amounts of numeric data that are expressed in numbers, but to capture the real "guts" of a problem we rely on qualitative data analyses. Rather than summarizing data with numbers, qualitative data analyses summarize data with words. Recall the final open-ended section in Paula's survey. By using a blank space at the end of her survey, respondents were able to add additional comments or thoughts in their own words.

Because not all respondents offered comments on the same topic, the data obtained in this section of her survey were not truly representative of the people who responded (sample). That is, the comments did not necessarily reflect the majority opinion of people who completed and mailed back the survey. Nevertheless, they did add important information to how Paula looked at and interpreted the data collected in other parts of her survey.

Many townspeople, for example, had views about the relationship between teen problems and the lack of supervision and recreational opportunities for the teens. Several respondents included comments that reflected this issue. The brief quotes that follow are examples of what some survey respondents said:

- "In regards to some younger people, some of the concerns I have heard of, and read about, would probably be decreased if there was something for them to do . . . The range of recreation activities in this town is poor."
- "Drug abuse is a very serious problem among 15- to 17-year-olds."
- "We need a recreation center for young teens 14 to 19 years old. Supervised dances, games, etc., as well as counselors."
- "The lack of entertainment facilities in this town encourages teens to congregate and use drugs and alcohol as substitutes for entertainment. These teens can get into trouble for the lack of things to do."
- "There's a definite need for activities and/or a drop-in center for teenagers. It would keep them off the streets and out of the mall."

As can be seen from these comments, these qualitative data (words) offer richer information than is available through numbers alone. The respondents were voicing their views about what was needed in their community, given that they believed a drug and alcohol abuse problem existed for teens in their community. These comments hint at possible solutions to solve the social problems.

On one hand, Paula could have taken the comments literally and proposed a youth center for the city. On the other hand, it may be that she needed to propose an educational or awareness program for parents so that they would gain a better understanding of the issues that youth face.

Qualitative data are typically collected through interviews, which are recorded and later transcribed and subsequently analyzed. Other forms of qualitative data collection occur through the reviewing of existing reports and client records in a program. A powerful form of qualitative data for a needs assessment is the case study approach. Usings an example of a single case can spark the attention of policymakers, funders, and the community when other attempts have failed.

STEP 6A: DISSEMINATING AND COMMUNICATING EVALUATION RESULTS

The final step in a needs assessment study is the dissemination and communication of findings. It goes without saying that a needs assessment is conducted because someone—usually the program stakeholder(s)—wants to have useful data about the extent of a social problem. It's important that the previous five steps of the needs assessment be followed logically and systematically so that the results to be communicated fit with the original intention of the evaluation.

Learn more about disseminating and communicating evaluating findings in Tool J in the Evaluation Toolkit.

The results of a needs assessment are more likely to be used if they are communicated in a straightforward and simple manner, and any written or verbal presentation of a study's findings must consider who the audience will be. In almost all cases, a report is disseminated only to the stakeholders.

In a nutshell, the final written report of a needs assessment address the proverbial three categories:

- The social problem(s)
- The need(s) derived from the social problem(s)
- The proposed solution(s) to the social problem

SUMMARY

This chapter presented the first kind of program evaluation we can do: needs assessments, or the assessment of need. We briefly discussed the process of doing a needs assessment within the steps of the generic evaluation process outlined in Chapter 3. A well-thought-out needs assessment has three components: (a) a social problem, (b) the specification of a social need, and (c) a potential solution to solve the social need. The next chapter presents the second type of program evaluation that you need to be aware of when you become a professional social worker: process evaluations.

The goal of this chapter is to provide you with a beginning knowledge base for you to feel comfortable in answering the following questions. AFTER you have read the chapter ,indicate how comfortable you feel you are in answering each question on a 5-point scale where

1	2	3	4	5
Very uncomfortable	Somewhat uncomfortable	Neutral	Somewhat comfortable	Very comfortable

If you rated any question between 1–3, please reread the section of the chapter where the information for the question is found. If you still feel that you're uncomfortable in answering the question, then talk with your instructor and/or your classmates for more clarification.

	Questions	Degree of comfort? *(Circle one number)*
1	In your own words, explain the concept of a needs assessment. Provide as many social work examples you can to illustrate the concepts.	1 2 3 4 5
2	Identify and define a social problem and proposed solution.	1 2 3 4 5
3	Let's say you have identified a social problem as "high tuition costs." Complete Table 10.1. What did you learn about yourself when it comes to "tuition costs" and the four indicators of a social problem's visibility?	1 2 3 4 5
4	Define and compare the four types of needs illustrated in Table 10.3 using "high tuition costs" as the social problem. Provide an example of each.	1 2 3 4 5
5	List and then discuss each step involved in doing a needs assessment. Provide one common social work example throughout your discussion.	1 2 3 4 5
6	Develop several types of needs assessment questions based on the social problem "high tuition costs."	1 2 3 4 5
7	Identify logical targets for intervention considering specific criteria factors in relation to Question 6.	1 2 3 4 5
8	Identify a sufficient sampling frame of data sources for Question 6.	1 2 3 4 5
9	Describe in detail the steps you would take to develop a data collection plan for Question 6.	1 2 3 4 5
10	Provide specific examples of data sources with respect to the various data collection methods in relation to Question 6.	1 2 3 4 5
11	What are qualitative data? Provide an example of qualitative data that you could generate from a needs assessment. What types of questions could you use in Question 6 that would produce qualitative data? Provide a couple of examples to illustrate your points.	1 2 3 4 5
12	What are quantitative data? Provide an example of quantitative data that you could generate from a needs assessment. What types of questions could you use in Question 6 that would produce quantitative data? Provide a couple of examples to illustrate your points.	1 2 3 4 5

AFTER you have read this chapter AND have completed all of the study questions, indicate how knowledgeable you feel you are for each of the following concepts on a 5-point scale where

1 Not knowledgeable at all	2 Somewhat unknowledgeable	3 Neutral	4 Somewhat knowledgeable	5 Very knowledgeable

	Concepts	Knowledge Level? *(Circle one number)*
1	Needs assessments in general	1 2 3 4 5
2	Social problems	1 2 3 4 5
3	Social needs	1 2 3 4 5
4	The hierarchy of social needs	1 2 3 4 5
5	Four types of social needs	1 2 3 4 5
6	Solutions to alleviate social needs	1 2 3 4 5
7	Steps in doing a needs assessment	1 2 3 4 5
8	Data sources	1 2 3 4 5
9	Qualitative data	1 2 3 4 5
10	Quantitative data	1 2 3 4 5
	Add up your scores (minimum = 10, maximum = 50)	Your total score =

A   47–50 = Professional evaluator in the making
A–   45–46 = Senior evaluator
B+   43–44 = Junior evaluator
B   41–42 = Assistant evaluator
B–   10–40 = Reread the chapter and redo the study questions

CHAPTER OUTLINE

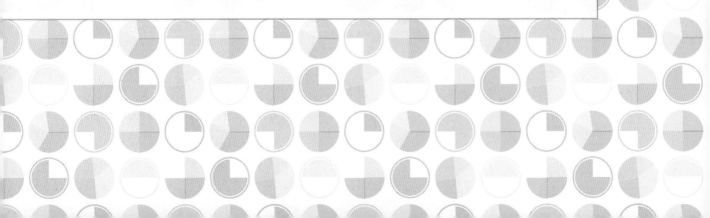

Excellence is a continuous process and not an accident.

~ A. P. J. Abdul Kalam

Chapter 11

PROCESS EVALUATIONS

As we found out in the last chapter, the main purpose of needs assessments is to determine the nature, scope, and locale of a social problem and to select an evidence-based social service program that will solve the problem. Once the program is up and running we can do a process evaluation that examines how its services are delivered to its clients and what administrative mechanisms exist within it to support the services it offers.

Unlike outcome evaluations discussed in the next chapter, process evaluations are not interested if the program achieved its objectives. There is, however, a direct connection between a process evaluation and an outcome evaluation. A process evaluation can be done if a program performs poorly on an outcome evaluation. In this case, we would be interested in finding out the reasons why the program had poor outcomes.

Ideally, a process evaluation occurs before or at the same time as an outcome evaluation. When new programs are being implemented, for example, it makes sense to check whether the programs were implemented in the way they were intended before evaluating their outcomes.

Therefore, by evaluating the program's processes (this chapter) and outcomes (next chapter), we are in a better position to suggest what specific processes lead to what specific successful client outcomes.

DEFINITION

Program processes refer specifically to the activities and characteristics that describe how a program operates. In general, there are two major categories of processes—the client service delivery system and the administrative support systems that sustain client service delivery.

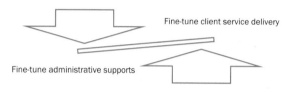

Client service delivery is composed of what workers do (e.g., interventions and associated activities) and what clients bring to the program (e.g., client profile, client problems). On the other hand, administrative support systems comprise the administrative activities that exist to support the program's client service delivery system.

In a nutshell, a process evaluation aims to monitor a program in an effort to assess the services it provides to its clients, including how satisfied key stakeholder groups are with the program's services. If we know exactly what type of services are being offered, how these services are being delivered, and how satisfied stakeholder groups are (especially clients) with the services, then we are in a better position to decide whether the program is, in fact, the best intervention to help clients with a specific problem configuration.

Example

Suppose, for example, we want to conduct a process evaluation of a family support program. Instead of focusing our evaluation efforts on the program's outcomes, as is done in an outcome evaluation (next chapter), we turn our attention to the program's day-to-day operations. Program Objective 2 in our family support program presented in Box 7.1 in Chapter 7, for example, aims "to increase problem-solving skills of family members."

In a process evaluation, we could ask the following questions:

- What treatment interventions do workers and clients engage in to increase family members' problem-solving skills?
- How much time do workers spend with family members on problem-solving interventions?

Like all four types of evaluations presented in Part III of this book, a process evaluation is simple to understand but challenging to carry out. Recall from Chapters 7 and 8 the issues involved in developing a program's goal and its related program objectives. There are similar problems in doing a process evaluation. To evaluate a program's approach to client service delivery, for example, social workers need to establish a common and useful "program language" that is meaningful and jargon free:

- Do workers and administrators alike, for example, mean the same thing when they refer to "counseling" versus "therapy?" Does referring a client to an additional service outside the agency, such as meals on wheels, constitute "counseling," or "therapy?" Or neither?
- How would we distinguish between "counseling" and "therapy?"
- Are these activities (remember, these are not program objectives) the same or different?

Using a consistent language to describe how a program delivers its services requires a level of precision that is difficult to achieve at the best of times. This is particularly true when workers come from different disciplines, different educational backgrounds, different skill levels, different motivational levels, and/or have different theoretical orientations and preconceived biases. Believe it or not, many of our programs do not have well-consolidated and well-thought-out treatment intervention approaches. They just plot along like they did in the 70s hoping for

the best and refusing to implement evidence-based interventions because "they know what works since they have been doing 'it' for years." Thus selecting a good evidence-based intervention, or program, for an agency to implement can easily become the first task of a process evaluation.

By defining, recording, monitoring, and analyzing a program's operations, we can easily gain a better understanding of what types of interventions (and associated activities) lead to what type of client outcomes (positive and negative). We can also gather data to assess whether the program's current administrative operations are adequately supporting the workers as they help their clients on a day-to-day basis. We can, for example, monitor the frequency of worker–client contact, the amount of supervision the workers receive, and the number of training sessions the workers attended over the past year or so.

PURPOSE

Clearly, there are many dimensions to conducting process evaluations. In general, however, they have three main purposes:

- Improving a program's operations
- Generating knowledge
- Estimating cost-efficiency

Improving a Program's Operations

A process evaluation can fine-tune the services that a program delivers to its clients. In this spirit, a process evaluation is a critical component of delivering good social work services. In the same way that we ask clients to monitor their progress using practice objectives (Chapter 7), workers must be willing to monitor their interventions and activities to assess whether they are helping their clients in the best way possible. It's also the responsibility of administrators to maintain a healthy work environment.

In general, data collected in a process evaluation are primarily used to inform decisions pertaining to the further development of the program's services. Even when a program is adequately conceptualized before it actually opens its doors for the first time, the day-to-day implementation of the program rarely—if ever—goes as smoothly as initially planned. There are many practical, legal, political, and ethical obstacles that prevent programs from being implemented as theoretically planned.

More often than not, these obstacles are not realized until the program gets underway. A family support program, for example, may unexpectedly find that the building in which it is located is locked on weekends, or that the program's funding source places last-minute demands on the workers' caseload size.

As seen in Box 2.1 in Chapter 2, a process evaluation is sometimes referred to as a formative evaluation: the gathering of relevant data for the continuous ongoing feedback and improvement of the client-related services a program offers. As will be seen shortly, a process evaluation provides us with important feedback about the two levels of program processes already discussed: its client service delivery system and its administrative supports.

We recommend that all process evaluations occur at the stage when new programs start to focus their efforts on developing well-thought-out client service delivery systems. After a well-conceptualized client service delivery approach is established via a logic model (a process that can take years), a process evaluation can shift its emphasis to the program's administrative operations.

The reason for beginning with direct client service delivery is that all worker supervision, training, and other administrative support should ultimately exist to support the workers' direct services to their clients. Unless we are clear about what the nature of the program's client service delivery approach is, our beginning attempts to design and implement supporting systems to help workers will be futile.

Generating Knowledge

The next chapter discusses how outcome evaluations help us to learn more about how clients demonstrate change (if any) when they go through a program. In comparison, process evaluations give us insight into what specific treatment interventions (and its associated activities) lead to these client changes (if any). Our profession has often referred to the client service delivery component of a program as a "black box."

This somewhat damaging label reflects the notion that clients enter and exit a program with no clear idea as to what actually took place while they were in it (thus a "black box"). As we know, process evaluations include the monitoring of our treatment interventions and activities, so they have much to offer us in relation to telling us what's really in the black box. Why do we want to go through all this trouble? The answer is simple,

- First, to monitor interventions and activities implies that we have labels and definitions for what we do with our clients. This, in turn, increases communication and reduces the need to reinvent labels for basic intervention approaches (e.g., educational, therapeutic, supportive) and activities (e.g., active listening, confrontation, clarification).
- Second, by monitoring what works (and what does not) with clients, we can avoid wasting time on treatment interventions and/or activities that do not work.
- Third, we can begin to respond to long-standing questions that are ingrained in our profession but have not been adequately answered, such as:
  - Are our interventions more effective in an office or community setting?
  - Is a 50-minute session the optimal duration for counseling?
  - What are the results of helping clients cope with poverty versus helping them challenge the system?

- Fourth, if process evaluations are conducted across several programs, for example, we can compare different client service delivery systems in terms of their differences and similarities. This information will help us to know what interventions work best and for whom.

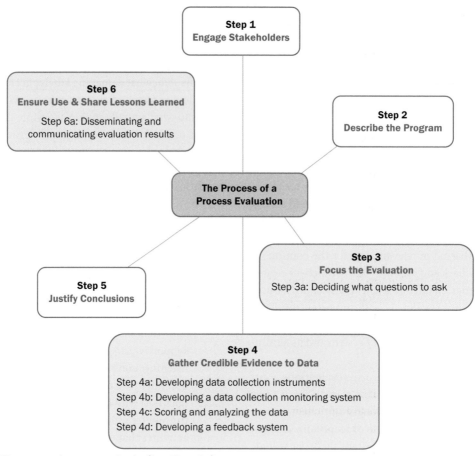

Figure 11.1: The process of a process evaluation (from Figure 3.1).

Estimating Cost Efficiency

The data collected for a process evaluation can be used to more precisely calculate the cost of delivering a specific program to a specific client population at a specific time. Chapter 13 discusses how to estimate the cost efficiency of programs: Does the program accomplish its objectives within a reasonable budget? On the other hand, a process evaluation permits us to ask more detailed questions that deal with a program's efficiency.

By monitoring the amount of time clients spend receiving individual and group interventions, and by keeping track of client outcomes, for example, we will be able to determine which interventions (e.g., group, individual) are more efficient—which ones cost less but produce similar client outcomes or results. Much more will be said about this in Chapter 13.

We always have to keep in mind that the major aim of a process evaluation is to determine whether a program is operating as it was intended. In this chapter, we discuss the steps, via Figure 11.1, of doing a process evaluation couched within the evaluation process model presented in Chapter 3.

STEP 3A: DECIDING WHAT QUESTIONS TO ASK

We have already discussed that a process evaluation can focus on two important dimensions of a program: its client service delivery system and its administrative operations. As such, it's important to develop clear questions for a process evaluation. There are eight questions that can be asked, such as:

1. What is the program's background?
2. What is the program's client profile?
3. What is the program's staff profile?
4. What is the amount of service provided to clients?
5. What are the program's interventions and activities?
6. What administrative supports are in place?
7. How satisfied are the program's stakeholders?
8. How efficient is the program?

Question 1: What Is the Program's Background?

Developing a program's goal and objectives, via the process delineated in Chapters 7 and 8, is part of the answer to this simple question. By defining a program's goal as illustrated in Chapter 7, we already know four important bits of information about a program:

1. Who it serves
2. What social problem it is tackling
3. What change it intends to accomplish
4. How it intends to create this change

The four bits of information in a program's goal clearly provides a description of the program in a straightforward way whereby we can easily grasp its scope and boundaries. We can now ask further background questions such as:

- What is the program's history?
- How did the program get started?
- What is the program's philosophy?

The answers to these types of questions provide you with the program's context—that is, the circumstances surrounding the program that will help you to interpret data derived from your process evaluation. A pro-life program, for example, will have a different philosophical approach to working with pregnant teens than a pro-choice program, yet both programs work with the same client population and tackle the same social problem. Furthermore, the two programs may have similar goals—to prevent teenage pregnancy.

We must always remember that programs often are initiated in response to political agendas or recommendations from needs assessments; other times they may begin simply on ad hoc bases when additional social service funds are available near the end of the fiscal year. Questions having to do with the program's history and philosophy provide us with information about the program's background in addition to the political and social environment in which it operates.

A program's history, for example, can be critical to fully understanding its day-to-day operations, and it helps us to work within its current political and social context. A program's philosophy can tell us how the major beliefs and values of the program's administrators (and workers) influence the program's operations.

Question 2: What Is the Program's Client Profile?

Knowing who is directly served by a program has implications for how the processes within it are operationalized and monitored. Clients are one of the stakeholder groups identified in Chapter 1. Remember that clients can be individuals, families, groups, communities, and organizations. If the clients are families, for example, we need to know their sociodemographic characteristics. Gathering relevant client data such as age, gender, income, education, race, socioeconomic status, and other relevant demographic characteristics gives us a general idea of whom we are trying to serve. We also want to know where our clients come from. In other words,

- How are clients referred to the program?
- Do they come primarily from one geographic area?
- How did they learn about the program?

Question 3: What Is the Program's Staff Profile?

Programs are staffed by individuals (e.g., workers, volunteers) with diverse backgrounds. Educational backgrounds and employment experiences can easily be used to describe the qualifications of workers. By monitoring worker qualifications, we can gain insight into establishing minimum-level qualifications for job advertisements. Are individuals with a master of social work degree substantially better than those with a bachelor of social work in providing family support services, for example?

Presumably, those with additional years of education have more to offer. If this is the case, what are the differentiating characteristics between the two levels of education? Sociodemographic data such as age, gender, and marital status are typical features used to describe workers and volunteers. Other meaningful descriptors for workers include salaries, benefits, and job descriptions.

There may be other staff characteristics that are important to a specific program. If we believe, for example, that being a parent is a necessary qualification for workers who help children in a foster-care program, we might collect data that reflect this interest. Developing profiles for workers and volunteers alike provides data by which to make decisions about further recruiting and hiring. By monitoring key characteristics of social workers, for example, we might gain some insights as to the type of individuals who are best matched for employment within the program.

Question 4: What Is the Amount of Service Provided to Clients?

Just because a program may be designed to serve clients for 1 hour per week for 6 weeks does not mean that it happens this way. Some clients may leave the program much earlier than expected, and some may stay much longer than anticipated. Thus we must record the clients' start and termination dates to determine how long they received services from the program.

When programs do not have clear-cut intake and termination dates (e.g., an outreach program for youth living on the street) or when these dates are not particularly meaningful (e.g., a long-term group home for adults with developmental disabilities), it may be necessary to collect data that are more useful. For instance, how long are street workers able to engage youth living on the street in a conversation about their safety? How many youth voluntarily seek outreach workers for advice? For adults with developmental disabilities who are living in a long-term group home, we might record the onset and completion of a particular treatment intervention.

Deciding when services begin and end is not as straightforward as it might seem. For instance, support services are sometimes provided to clients who are awaiting formal entry into a program, or follow-up services are offered to clients after a program's services have officially ended. Duration of service can be measured in minutes, hours, days, weeks, months, or years, and it provides us with data about how long a client is considered a client.

We might also want to know the intensity of the services we provide to clients. This can be monitored by recording the amount of time a worker spends with, or on behalf of, a client. Worker time, for example, can be divided into face-to-face contact, telephone contact, report writing, advocacy, supervision and consultation, and so on.

If we divide the amount of time spent in each one of these categories by the total time spent receiving services for one client, we can calculate the proportion of time spent in each category for that client. These simple calculations can produce the following data:

Overall worker time for Client A was as follows:

- 30% face-to-face contact
- 25% telephone contact
- 25% report writing
- 10% advocacy
- 10% supervision and consultation

These data can be used to formulate an estimate that can assist workers in gauging the timing of their interventions. We might determine, for example, that workers in a family support program spend an average of 55% of their time in client contact (30% face-to-face and 25% telephone contact). The other 45% is spent in meetings, writing up paperwork, participating in staff meetings, and so on.

If a few workers have particularly difficult families, it might be reflected in their reported hours. Perhaps their face-to-face hours are low for a family, say around 20%, because the families miss many appointments. It's also possible that their face-to-face hours are high, say 75%, because the families had a series of crises. These data alone can be useful when deciding whether to continue or change services being offered to any one family.

Question 5: What Are the Program's Interventions and Activities?

Looking into what the program's interventions and activities entail gets at the heart of the program's treatment strategy (and associated worker activities). It asks, "What approach do workers use (the intervention), and how do they do it (the activities within the intervention)?" Of all process evaluation questions, this one in particular can pose a threat to workers and administrators alike because it requires them to articulate the nature of the program's interventions and workers' activities related to these interventions in terms that others can understand. All of this was discussed in detail in Chapters 7 and 8.

This is simply not an easy task. Social workers who rely on professional jargon for efficient communication in the office should learn to explain what they do in lay terms so that nonprofessionals (especially clients) can understand what to expect from the program's services.

A process evaluation can also evaluate a program's fidelity; that is, it can be done to check the extent to which the delivery of an intervention adheres to the protocol or program logic model originally developed. Assessing a program's fidelity is extremely important.

Example: Checking on a Program's Fidelity

Gathering process evaluation data about the services provided to clients in a particular program is necessary to assess the fidelity or integrity of a program's services. Phrased as a question, we might ask, "Did the actual services delivered to clients match the original design of the program?" or, more realistically, "How close did the actual services delivered to the clients match the original program design and logic model?"

Box 11.1 displays a data collection form that was used by workers employed by a rural family literacy program as a part of their process evaluation.

Literacy workers in the program made brief home visits to families on a daily basis for 4 weeks (20 visits total) in an effort to accomplish two main program objectives, which are listed on the log:

- To increase literacy skills of children
- To increase parent(s) abilities to assist their children in developing literacy skills

In addition to specifying which program objective was targeted at each visit (Question 1), workers also identified the main activities used that day (Question 2) and rated family members in terms of the "readiness" to participate in services for each day's visit (Questions 3–6).

The form in Box 11.1 took only a few minutes to complete, and workers were trained to complete the form in their car immediately after a family visit ended in order to maximize accuracy of the data recorded. In turn, the aggregate log data from all the workers in the program provided useful program snapshots of several key aspects of program service delivery.

A list of several process evaluation questions were answered by the data collected from the workers across the program; the number of each process question corresponds with the particular item on the log (see Box 11.1) that generated the data to answer the questions:

① On average, how many minutes does a home visit by a literacy worker last?
② On average, how many miles do literacy workers travel to reach a family's home?
③ What proportion of family visits was devoted to increasing children's skills (program objective 1) versus increasing parents' skills (program objective 2)?
④ What program activity was used most often (least often) by program workers?
⑤ What percentage of visits were families "not at all ready" to participate?

As we saw in Chapter 5 on ethics, social workers should not be specifically evaluated on their own individual client "success" rates. In other words, it would be a misuse of a process evaluation to take data about one worker's client success rate and compare this rate with another worker's rate, or any other standard.

BOX 11.1 EXAMPLE OF A FORM THAT WAS USED TO MONITOR A PROGRAM'S FIDELITY

Rural Family Literacy Program Daily Family Visit Log

FAMILY: _____   WORKER: _____

Date: ____/____/_____   Visit Number (1 to 20, or follow-up): _____
    Day month year   Length of Visit (minutes): _____ ① _____
                  Distance traveled (km) (First Visit Only): _____ ② _____

1. What was the primary objective of today's visit? (Circle one.) ③

    1a. To increase literacy skills of children.
    1b. To increase parent(s)' abilities to assist their children in developing literacy skills.

2. What were the main activities of today's visit? (Circle all that apply.) ④

    2a. Pointing out parent's strengths in helping their children.
    2b. Teaching parents about child development.
    2c. Teaching parents about different learning/reading styles.
    2d. Teaching literacy games to family.
    2e. Teaching parents how to use resources (e.g., library).
    2f. Modeling reading with children.
    2g. Paired reading.
    2h. Listening to parent's concerns.
    2i. Identifying family priorities for children's activities.
    2j. Filling out Building Block Questionnaires.
    2k. Giving books/materials/written information.
    2l. Developing charts (sticker charts, reading checklists, etc.).
    2m. Providing referrals to other agencies.
        Other Describe: _____
        Other Describe: _____

3. How ready was the family for today's visit? (Circle one.) ⑤
    Not at all   1   2   3   4   5   Ready and Willing
4. Overall, how did the adult(s) participate in today's visit? (Circle one.)
    Not at all   1   2   3   4   5   Participated Fully
5. Overall, how did the child(ren) participate in today's visit? (Circle one.)
    Not at all   1   2   3   4   5   Participated Fully
6. Comments on today's visit (use other side if more space is needed):

Obviously, this type of analysis would influence the worker to record favorable data—whether accurate or not. Rather, monitoring of client success rates ought to be done in the spirit of program development and improvement, appealing to the curiosity of workers in learning about the effectiveness of their day-to-day activities.

Question 6: What Administrative Supports Are in Place?

Administrative supports include the "fixed" conditions of employment as well as the administrative operations that are designed to support workers in carrying out the program's client service delivery approach. Fixed conditions of employment describe things that remain relatively stable over time.

Examples include location of the intervention (e.g., in the office, client's home, community), staff–worker ratio, support staff, available petty cash, use of pagers and cell phones, hours of service delivery, and so on. Administrative operations, on the other hand, may change depending on current program stresses and include things such as worker training, supervision schedules, and program development meetings.

The most important thing to remember about a program's administrative supports is that they exist to support workers in carrying out their functions with clients. Workers who are paid poorly, carry pagers 24/7, have high caseloads, and consistently work overtime on weekends will likely respond to clients' needs and problems less effectively than will those who work under more favorable conditions.

Administrative supports should exist by design; that is, they ought to promote workers in offering sound client service delivery. What is most important to remember is that the approach to administrative support is not written in stone. As with all other aspects of a program, it remains flexible and open to review and revision.

Examples

A dramatic example of a how an administrative decision leads to change in client service delivery occurred when administrators of a group home program for delinquent youth questioned "group care" as the setting for client service delivery. The program's administrators questioned how living in a group home actually helped delinquent youth to improve on the program's objectives.

After collecting data about the effects of group living, the administrators determined that their program's objectives could best be achieved by using a less intrusive (and less expensive) setting for service delivery—providing interventions to youth while they continued living with their families.

In another example, an administrator of an outreach program for street youth noticed that the program's workers were consistently working overtime. By reviewing data collected on the amount of time workers spent "on the street" versus at the "store-front office" and by talking to the workers directly, the administrator learned that the social workers were feeling overwhelmed by the increasing number of youth moving to the streets.

The social workers were spending more time on the streets as the days went along in an attempt to help as many youth as possible; that is, they felt they were being reactive to the problems faced by youth on the street. They felt they did not have the time to reflect on their work in relation to the program's goal and objectives or have time to plan their activities. With these data, the program's administrator decided to conduct weekly meetings to help workers overcome their feelings of being overwhelmed and to develop plans to handle the increase in the number of clients.

Question 7: How Satisfied Are the Program's Stakeholders?

Stakeholder satisfaction is a key part of a process evaluation because satisfaction questions ask stakeholders to comment on the program's services. Using a client satisfaction survey when clients exit a program, for example, is a common method of collecting satisfaction data. In a family support program, for example, clients were asked for their opinions about the interactions they had with their family support workers, the interventions they received, and the program in general. Figure 11.2 presents a list of seven client satisfaction questions given to parents and children after they received services (at termination) from the program. Figures M.1, M.2, and M.3 contained in Tool M are three very useful standardized measuring instruments that you can use to measure client satisfaction with services. Remember, client satisfaction with services is relevant only to process evaluations—never to outcome evaluations.

The data collected from the questions in Figure 11.2 can be in the form of words or numbers. Clients' verbal responses could be recorded for each question using an open-ended interview format. On the other hand, clients could be asked to respond to each

How satisfied are you …
1. that the worker wanted what was best for you?
2. that the worker was pleasant to be around?
3. that you learned important skills to help your family get along better?
4. that the worker was fair and did not take sides?
5. with the amount of communication you had with the worker?
6. that you had a chance to ask questions and talk about your own ideas?
7. that the worker helped to improve your parent—child relationship?

Figure 11.2: **Family satisfaction questionnaire.**

question by giving a numerical rating on a 5-point category partition scale, for example. In this case, the rating scale would range from a response of 1, meaning "not at all satisfied," to 5, meaning "very satisfied."

Client responses to the seven questions in Figure 11.2 can easily provide a general impression about how clients viewed the program's services. Because questions were asked from parents and children alike, it was possible to compare parents' and children's views of the services provided. Suppose, for example, that the satisfaction data showed that parents reported higher satisfaction rates than their children. This finding alone could be used to reflect on how the program's treatment interventions were delivered to the parents versus their children.

Client satisfaction data can also be collected from other key stakeholder groups. Suppose the family support program operated under a child protection mandate. This would mean that each family coming into the program had an assigned child protection worker. Figure 11.3 shows the satisfaction questions asked of this group. Because client satisfaction involves the opinions of people "outside" the program, data collection has special considerations with respect to who collects them.

Question 8: How Efficient Is the Program?

Estimating a program's efficiency is an important purpose of a process evaluation. This question focuses on

> How satisfied are you …
> 1. with the amount of cooperation you received from the worker in his or her interactions with your department?
> 2. that the worker connected the family with appropriate resources?
> 3. that the worker was effective in helping the family get along better?
> 4. that the worker helped to improve communication between the parent(s) and your department?
> 5. that the worker helped to improve parent—child relationships?

Figure 11.3: **Child protection worker satisfaction questionnaire.**

the amount of resources expended in an effort to help clients achieve a desired program objective. Because a process evaluation looks at the specific components of a program, it's possible to estimate costs with more precision than is possible in a traditional outcome evaluation (next chapter). Data relating to the program's efficiency are available from the program's budget. Much more will be said about cost effectiveness in Chapter 13.

Given the eight questions that we can ask in a process evaluation, it's necessary to determine what questions have priority. Deciding which questions are the most important ones to be answered is influenced by the demands of different stakeholder groups, trends in programming, and plans for a program's future development and refinement.

STEP 4A: DEVELOPING DATA COLLECTION INSTRUMENTS

It's important to collect data for all question categories briefly discussed in Step 3a if we hope to carry out a comprehensive process evaluation. This might seem an unwieldy task, but data for several of the question categories usually already exist. Questions about program background, for example, can be answered by reviewing minutes of program meetings, memos, and documents that describe the phases of the program's development.

If written documentation does not exist, however, we can interview the people who created the program. Staff profiles can be gleaned from workers' resumes. A program's approach to providing administrative support can be documented in an afternoon by the program's senior administrator. Ongoing recording of training sessions, meeting times, worker hours, and so on can be used to assess whether administrative supports are being carried out as designed.

Data for the program's client service delivery approach should be routinely collected. To do so, it's necessary to develop useful data collection instruments that have three qualities:

- Easy to use
- Flow with a program's operations
- Designed with user input

Easy to Use

Data collection instruments that are used in a process evaluation should help workers to do their jobs better—not tie up their time with extra extensive paperwork. Instruments that are easy to use are created to minimize the amount of writing that workers are expected to do and the amount of time it takes to complete them. In some cases, data collection instruments have already been constructed (and tested) by other programs.

Learn more about different ways to measure variables in Tools L and M in the Evaluation Toolkit.

The National Center of Family Based Services, for example, has developed an intervention and activity checklist for generic family support programs. The checklist contains various interventions and activities in which workers are instructed to check appropriate columns that identify which family members (i.e., child or children at risk, primary caretaker, other adult) were involved in the intervention and related activities.

When standardized data collection instruments do not exist, however, workers may agree to use an open-ended format for a limited period of time. Workers' responses can then be reviewed and categorized to create a checklist that reflects the uniqueness of their program. The advantage of using an open-ended checklist versus a standardized, or uniform, one is that the listed interventions may be more meaningful to the workers.

Suppose, for example, we asked the workers within a drug and alcohol counseling program for youth to record the major interventions (and associated activities) they used with their clients. After reviewing their written notes, we list the following activities that were recorded by the workers themselves:

- Gave positive feedback
- Rewarded youth for reduced alcohol consumption
- Discussed positive aspects of the youth's life
- Cheered youth on
- Celebrated youth's new job

These descriptors all appear to be serving a common function—praise, or noting clients' strengths. Thus we could develop a checklist item called "praise." The checklist approach loses important detail such as the workers' styles or the clients' situations, but when data are summarized, a general picture of the workers' major activities soon emerges.

Another critical data collection instrument that exists in almost all programs is the client intake form (e.g., Figure 14.3 in Chapter 14), which typically asks questions in the areas of client characteristics, reasons for referral, and service history, to name a few. The data collected on the client intake form should be useful for case-level and program-level evaluations. Data that are not used (i.e., not summarized or reviewed) should never be collected.

Appropriate to the Flow of a Program's Operations

Data collection instruments that are used in process evaluations should be designed to fit within the context of the program, to facilitate the program's day-to-day operations, and to provide data that will ultimately be helpful in improving client service delivery. As mentioned previously, data that are routinely collected from clients, or at least relate to them, ought to have both case-level and program-level utility.

For instance, if the client intake form requires the worker to check the referral problem(s), these data can be used at the case level to discuss the checked items, or presenting problems, with the client and to plan a suitable intervention. These data can also be summarized across clients to determine the most common reason for referral to the program.

Client case records can be designed to incorporate strategies for recording the amount of time workers spend with their clients and the nature of the workers' intervention strategies. Space should also be made available for workers' comments and impressions. There is no one ideal design for any data collection instrument that can be used for process evaluations. Just as treatment interventions can be personalized by the workers within a program, so can data collection instruments.

When designed within the context of the program, data collection instruments used within process evaluations can serve several important functions:

- First, they offer a record of case-level interventions that can be used to review individual client progress.
- Second, components of the data collection instruments can be aggregated to produce a "program summary."
- Third, the instruments can be used as the basis for supervisory meetings. They can also facilitate case reviews as they convey the major client problems, treatment interventions, and worker activities in a concise manner.

Obtaining User Input

It should be clear by now that the major users of data collection instruments are the line-level workers who are employed within the program. Workers often are responsible for gathering the necessary data from clients and others. Therefore their involvement in the development and testing of the data collection instruments is critical. Workers who see the relevance of recording data will likely record more accurate data than workers who do not.

In some instances, the nature of the data collected requires some retraining of the social workers. Workers at a group home for children with behavior problems, for example, were asked to record the interventions and activities they used with children residing at the group home. The majority of the social workers, however, were initially trained to record observations about the children's behavior rather than their own. In other words, they were never trained to record the interventions and activities that they engaged in with their clients.

STEP 4B: DEVELOPING A DATA COLLECTION MONITORING SYSTEM

The monitoring system for a process evaluation relates closely to the program's supervision practices.

This is because program process data are integral to delivering client services. Data about a program's background, client profile, and staff characteristics can, more or less, be collected at one time period. These data can then be summarized and stored for easy access. Program changes, such as staff turnover, hours of operation, or caseload size, can be duly noted as they occur.

In contrast, process data that are routinely collected should be monitored and checked for reliability and validity. Time and resources are a consideration for developing a monitoring system. When paperwork becomes excessively backlogged, it may be that there is simply too much data to collect, data collection instruments are cumbersome to use, or the workers are not invested in the evaluation process. There are three considerations for developing a monitoring system for a process evaluation:

- Determining the number of cases to include
- Determining times to collect data
- Selecting a data collection method(s)

Determining Number of Cases to Include

As we will see in the next chapter, in an outcome evaluation we have to decide whether to include all clients served by the program or only a percentage of them. In a process evaluation, we need to make a similar decision. However, what constitutes a case can change depending on the questions we ask.

 Learn more about different sampling techniques in Tool H in the Evaluation Toolkit.

If we ask a question about the program's history, for example, the program is our unit of analysis and we have only to decide how many people will be interviewed and/or how many documents will be reviewed to get a sufficient answer to our history question.

When questions are aimed at individual clients, we can use the same sampling practices that are explained for outcome evaluations (next chapter). Data that are used for case-level activities should be collected from all clients within the program. Intake forms and assessment data are often used to plan client treatment interventions. Indeed, these data also serve important purposes, such as comparing groups of clients, which is often done in an outcome evaluation.

More often than not, client intake forms are far too lengthy and detailed. Thus a program may consider developing two intake forms, a short form and a long form. The short form could include only those data that workers deem relevant to their case-level work. In a sex offender program, for example, we might use the short form at client intake to gather data such as age of client, family composition, referral problem(s), service history, employment status, and so on.

In addition to these questions, a longer form could also collect data that enrich our understanding of the client population served by the program. For example, what services would the client have used if the sex offender program were not available? What is the length of employment at the client's current job? What community services is the client actively involved in?

If two forms are available (one short and one long), deciding which one to use is a matter for random sampling. Workers could use the long one with every second or third client. To maintain a true sense of "randomness," however, the assignment of a specific data collection instrument to a specific client should occur as close as possible to the actual intake meeting.

The use of short and long instruments can also apply to collecting data about a worker's activities. Data collection is always a balance between breadth (how many cases to include) and depth (what and how many questions to ask).

Whether the unit of analysis is the client, the worker, the administrator, or the program, our aim is to get a representative sample. For smaller programs, the number of administrators and workers may be low, in which case everyone can be included. In larger programs, such as public assistance programs, we might use random sampling procedures that will ensure that all constituents are represented in our evaluation. When outcome and process evaluations happen concurrently, we should consider developing sampling strategies that are compatible with both types of evaluations.

Data that are not used for the benefit of case-level evaluations may not need to be collected for all clients. Client satisfaction questionnaires, for example, are usually collected at the end of the program and are displayed only in an aggregate form (to ensure confidentiality). Because client satisfaction data aim to capture the clients' feelings about the services they received, the questionnaires should be administered by someone other than the worker who provided the services to the client. However, having a neutral individual (e.g., another worker, a program assistant, a supervisor) administer the client satisfaction questionnaire can be a costly endeavor.

Recall that, in our family support program example, client satisfaction questionnaires were given to the parents and their children. Although the questionnaires were not very long, they were completed in the clients' homes and thus involved travel costs. If a program's workers decide that client satisfaction data are a major priority, then creative strategies could be developed to collect relevant, valid, and reliable client satisfaction data. It may be possible, for example, to obtain these data over the telephone rather than in person.

A simple solution is to randomly select clients to participate in our client satisfaction survey. As long as an adequate number of clients are truly randomly selected, then we can generalize our results to all of the clients within the program who did not participate in our survey. Ideally, our client random selection process should occur at the time clients leave the program (i.e., terminate).

Determining Times to Collect Data

Earlier we discussed the uses of short and long data collection instruments to collect client-relevant data. If we decide that numerous data are to be collected from every client, we may choose to administer the short data collection instrument at one time period and administer the longer one at a different time period. Workers could decide what data will be collected at the intake interview (the shorter instrument) and what data can be collected later on (the longer instrument).

Learn more about collecting data in Tool H in the Evaluation Toolkit.

It may be that the intake procedures ask harmless questions such as age, gender, or employment status. After the worker has developed a rapport with the client, it may be more appropriate to ask questions of a more sensitive nature (e.g., service history, family income, family problems, family history). We should not make the mistake of collecting all data on all client characteristics at the initial intake interview. Many client characteristics are fixed or constant (e.g., race, gender, service history, problem history). Thus we can ask these questions at any time while clients are receiving services.

In a process evaluation, we can collect data that focus on the workers' treatment interventions and activities and the time they spend with their clients. We must decide whether they need to record all of their activities with all of their clients; because there are important case-level (and sometimes legal) implications for recording worker–client activity for each case, we recommend that they do.

In addition, we have already recommended that data on a worker's activity form be used for supervisory meetings. Ideally, case records should capture the nature of the worker's intervention; the rationale for the worker's actions; and changes in the client's knowledge, behavior, feelings, or circumstances that result from the worker's efforts (i.e., progress on client practice objectives).

Program administrators have the responsibility to review client records to determine what data are missing from them. The feedback from this review can, once again, be included in supervisory meetings. These reviews can be made easy by including a "program audit sheet" on the cover of each client file. This sheet lists all of the data that need to be recorded and the dates by which they are due. Workers can easily check each item when the data are collected.

If program administrators find there is a heavy backlog of paperwork, it may be that workers are being expected to do too much or the data collection instruments need to be shortened and/or simplified. Furthermore, we want to leave room for workers to record creative treatment interventions and/or ideas that can be later considered for the further refinement of the program.

Selecting a Data Collection Method(s)

Recording workers' activities is primarily a paperwork exercise. It's time consuming, for example, to videotape and systematically rate worker–client interactions. Because data on line-level workers' activities are often collected by the workers themselves, the reliability of the data they collect can easily come into question. Where supervision practices include the observation of the workers' interventions and activities with clients, it's possible to assess the reliability of workers' self-reports.

For example, if supervisors were to observe family support workers interacting with their families, they could also complete the therapeutic intervention checklist (discussed earlier) and compare the results with the ratings that workers give themselves. Through this simple procedure, interrater reliability scores can be calculated, which tells us the extent of agreement between the workers' perceptions and the supervisors' perceptions.

For client satisfaction data, social desirability can easily become an issue. If a worker who is assigned to a client administers a client satisfaction questionnaire (e.g., Figures 11.2, 14.8; M.1, M.2, and M.3 in Toolkit M) at the end of the program, the resulting data, generated by the client, will be suspect, even if the questionnaire is carried out in the most objective fashion.

Clients are less likely to rate workers honestly if the workers are present when clients complete the instrument. This problem is exacerbated when workers actually read out the questions for clients to answer. In this instance, it's useful to have a neutral person (someone not personally known to the client) read the questions to the clients.

Before clients answer satisfaction questions, however, it should be explained to them that their responses are confidential and that their assigned worker will not be privy to their responses. They should be told that their responses will be added to a pool of other clients' responses and reported in aggregate form. A sample of a previous report that illustrates an example of aggregated data could be shown to clients.

Learn more about training data collectors in Tool I in the Evaluation Toolkit.

How data are collected directly influences the value of information that results from the data. Data that are collected in a haphazard and inconsistent way will be difficult to summarize. In addition, they will produce inaccurate information. For example, during the pilot study, when the data collection instruments were tested for the amount of time workers spent with their clients, workers were diligent about recording their time in the first 2 weeks of a 6-week intervention program. After the initial 2-week period, however, workers recorded data more and more sporadically.

The resulting picture produced by the "incomplete" data was that the program appeared to offer the bulk of its intervention in the first 2 weeks of the program. A graph of these data would visually display this trend. Suppose such a graph was shown to the program's workers. With little discussion, the workers would likely comment on the inaccuracy of the data.

Moreover, the workers may share their beliefs about what the pattern of the remaining 4 weeks of the intervention looks like (in the absence of any recorded data). Rather than speculate on the "possible" patterns, the "hard" data could be used to encourage workers to be more diligent in their data-recording practices. Discussion could also center on what additional supports workers may need (if any) to complete their paperwork.

The bottom line is simple: doing paperwork is not a favorite activity of line-level social workers. When the paperwork that workers complete is not used for feedback purposes, they can become even more resistant to doing it. Thus it's important that we acknowledge data-recording efforts by providing regular summaries of the data they collected. For programs that are equipped with computer equipment and a management database system, it's possible for workers to enter their data directly into the computer. This luxury saves precious time.

STEP 4C: SCORING AND ANALYZING DATA

The procedures for collecting and summarizing process data should be easy to perform, and once the data are analyzed, they should be easy to interpret. As mentioned earlier, if a backlog occurs in the summarization of data, it's likely that the program is collecting too much data and will need to cut back on the amount collected and/or reexamine its data collection needs.

Thinking through the steps of scoring and analyzing data can help us decide whether we have collected too much or too little data. Consider a family support worker who sees a family four times per week for 10 weeks. If the worker completes a therapeutic activities checklist for each family visit, the worker will have a total of 40 data collection sheets for the total intervention period for this one family alone.

Given this large volume of data, it's likely that scoring will simply involve a count of the number of therapeutic activities used. Summary data can show which strategies the worker relied on the most. Because the dates of when data were recorded are on the data collection instrument, we could compare the worker's activities that were used at the beginning, in the middle, and at end of treatment. Other analyses are also possible if the data are grouped by client characteristics. For example,

- Do single-parent families receive more or less of a particular activity when compared with two-parent families?
- Do families where children have behavior problems take more or less worker time?
- What is the pattern of time spent with families over the 10-week intervention period?

Questions can also be asked in relation to any outcome data collected, such as the following:

- Is the amount of time spent with a family related to success?
- What therapeutic activities, if any, are associated with successful client outcomes?

Once data are collected and entered into a computer database system, summaries and analyses are simple matters.

STEP 4D: DEVELOPING A FEEDBACK SYSTEM

Because a process evaluation focuses on the inner workings of a program, the data collected should be shared with the workers within the program. The data collected on worker activities will not likely reveal any unknowns about how workers function on a day-to-day basis. Rather the data are more likely to confirm workers' and administrators' previously formed hunches. Seeing visual data in graphs and charts provides a forum for discussion and presents an aggregate picture of the program's structure—which may or may not be different from individual perspectives.

We have already discussed the utility of how process evaluations can help supervisors and their workers in supervisory meetings. Process data provide an opportunity to give feedback to individual workers and can form the basis of useful discussions. Program-level feedback can be provided to workers in program meetings.

Ideally, programs should set aside one half-day every 1 or 2 months for program development. During the program development meetings, program administrators could present data summaries for relevant or pressing questions. In addition, these meetings can be used to problem-solve difficulties in creating an efficient monitoring system.

Figure 11.4 presents the general stages of client service delivery for a program. Figure 11.5 and Table 11.1 show a detailed example of how clients can go through

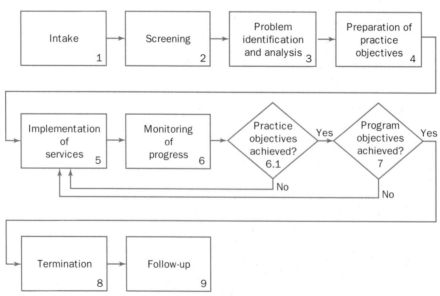

Figure 11.4: **Stages of a program that need to be considered in a process evaluation.**

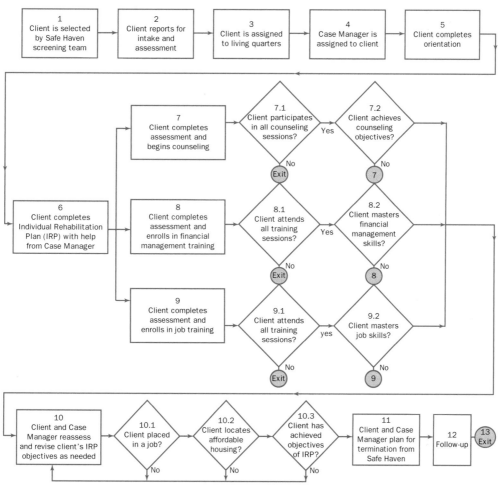

Figure 11.5: **Example of a client path flow (see Table 11.1 for narrative).**

the same program (Kettner, Moroney, & Martin, 2012). They are useful guides when considering the components of a program that need to be addressed when doing a process evaluation—they both show the key events in the program's client service delivery approach. In short, they reveal what's in the black box.

STEP 6A: DISSEMINATING AND COMMUNICATING EVALUATION RESULTS

Data collected through process evaluations can provide important clues as to which interventions work with what particular client problems. These data are a first step to uncovering the mystery of the black box. The results of a process evaluation, therefore, should be made available to programs that offer similar services.

Learn more about disseminating and communicating evaluating findings in Tool J in the Evaluation Toolkit.

By disseminating the results of a process evaluation in social work professional journals, at professional conferences, or through workshops, a program

Table 11.1: **Narrative Chart for Figure 11.5.**

Process Number	Title	Procedures	Documents
1	Client is selected by Safe Haven Shelter screening team	Appointment is made for client to meet with team. Team determines eligibility and makes selection	• Screening Form
2	Client reports for intake and assessment	Client meets with intake worker to complete all intake forms and to complete an assessment	• Intake Form • Social History • Data Entry Forms • Strengths and Needs Profile
3	Client is assigned to living quarters	Client is assigned to a room and given a tour of the facility	• Residential Assignment Form • Resident Responsibilities Form
4	Case manager is assigned to client	Case manager meets with client	• Data Entry Form • Case Notes
5	Client completes orientation	Client attends the next scheduled orientation session	• Orientation Log • Pretest and Posttest
6	Client completes Individual Rehabilitation Plan IRP with help from case manager	Case manager meets with client to assist in developing a plan to meet individual and program objectives	• IRP Form
7	Client completes assessment and begins counseling	Client meets with counselor to set up a schedule for individual and group counseling sessions. Initial assessment is completed and counseling objectives are established	• Data Entry Form • Counseling Plan • Case Notes
7.1	Client participates in all counseling sessions?	Counselor tracks attendance and evaluates quality of participation. Failure to participate can lead to exit from the program	• Attendance Form • Case Notes

continued

Process Number	Title	Procedures	Documents
7.2	Client achieves counseling objectives?	As client continues, progress is evaluated against objectives in the counseling plan. Work continues until objectives are achieved. Reassessments completed as needed	• Attendance Form • Data Entry Form • Case Notes
8	Client completes assessment and enrolls in financial management training	Client completes assessment of financial management skills and enrolls in the next available class	• Financial Management Skill Assessment Form • Training Enrollment Form
8.1	Client attends all training sessions?	Trainer tracks attendance and evaluates quality of participation. Failure to attend or participate can lead to exit from the program	• Attendance Form • Trainer Evaluation Form
8.2	Client masters financial management skills?	Mastery of skills is measured by testing. When client receives a passing grade on all units of the course she receives a certificate of completion. Reassessment is completed as needed	• Record of Progress and Completion Form
9	Client completes assessment and enrolls in job training	Client meets with job counselor to assess job skills. Training referral is made. Client meets with trainer	• Job Skills Assessment Form • Training Enrollment Form
9.1	Client attends all training sessions?	Trainer tracks attendance and evaluates quality of participation. Failure to attend or participate can lead to exit from the program	• Attendance Form • Trainer Evaluation Form
9.2	Client masters job skills?	Mastery of skills is measured by testing. When client receives a passing grade on all units of the course she receives a certificate of completion. Reassessment is completed as needed	• Record of Progress and Completion Form

continued

Process Number	Title	Procedures	Documents
10	Client and case manager reassess and revise client's IRP objectives as needed	When all activities of the IRP have been completed, client and case manager assess achievement and begin to prepare for termination if client is determined to be ready	• IRP • Case Notes • Data Entry Form
10.1	Client is placed in a job?	Client meets with job placement counselor to identify available job slots that fit with training. Job opportunities are continually explored until a job is secured	• Job Placement Referral Form
10.2	Client locates affordable housing?	Client meets with housing placement counselor to identify available housing and continues until housing is secured	• Housing Placement Referral Form
10.3	Client has achieved objective of IRP	Client and case manager review objective of IRP and assess level of success	• IRP Assessment Form • Strength and Needs Profile • Data Entry Form
11	Client and case manager plan for termination from Safe Haven	Client and case manager assess client's readiness to function independently in the community and make plans for follow-up contacts as needed	• Victims to Victors Termination Form • Safe Haven Termination Form • Data Entry Form
12	Follow-up	Case manager makes telephone contacts at the agreed-on times and otherwise follows up according to plan	• Case Notes • Data Entry Form
13	Exit	Follow-up contacts end by mutual agreement	• Case Closure Form • Case Notes • Data Entry Form

Note: IRP = Individual Rehabilitation Plan.

can take a leadership role in increasing our understanding of how to help specific groups of clients with specific problems.

SUMMARY

Process evaluations are aimed at improving services to clients. Data can be collected on many program dimensions in an effort to make informed decisions about a program's operations. Designing a process evaluation involves the participation of the program's administrators and workers. Program staff must decide what questions they want to ask, how data will be collected, who will be responsible for monitoring data collection activities, how the data will be analyzed, and how the results will be disseminated.

The following chapter presents another kind of evaluation: an outcome evaluation.

The goal of this chapter is to provide you with a beginning knowledge base for you to feel comfortable in answering the following questions. AFTER you have read the chapter, indicate how comfortable you feel you are in answering each question on a 5-point scale where

1 Very uncomfortable	2 Somewhat uncomfortable	3 Neutral	4 Somewhat comfortable	5 Very comfortable

If you rated any question between 1–3, reread the section of the chapter where the information for the question is found. If you still feel that you're uncomfortable in answering the question, then talk with your instructor and/or your classmates for more clarification.

	Questions	Degree of comfort? (Circle one number)
1	In your own words, define a process evaluation. Provide a social work example throughout your discussion.	1 2 3 4 5
2	List and then discuss the three purposes of doing a process evaluation. Provide a social work example throughout your discussion. Then discuss how each purpose would benefit your field placement (or work) setting.	1 2 3 4 5
3	List, and then describe all of the steps of doing a process evaluation. Then discuss how you would do one within your field placement (or work) setting.	1 2 3 4 5
4	List and then describe the eight questions that can be asked and answered in doing a process evaluation. Describe how you would go about asking and answering each of the questions in relation to your field placement (or work) setting.	1 2 3 4 5
5	List the three qualities of useful data collection instruments. Then discuss how you will be sure that they are met when you do a process evaluation.	1 2 3 4 5
6	List and then discuss the three considerations that must be taken into account when you develop a monitoring system for a process evaluation.	1 2 3 4 5
7	What are client path flows? Why are they important when it comes to a process evaluation?	1 2 3 4 5
8	Obtain a client path flow from your field placement (or work) setting. Is it up to date? Is it relevant? Do the other workers in your unit think it's useful to them? Why or why not?	1 2 3 4 5

AFTER you have read this chapter AND have completed all of the study questions, indicate how knowledgeable you feel you are for each of the following concepts on a 5-point scale where

1 Not knowledgeable at all	2 Somewhat unknowledgeable	3 Neutral	4 Somewhat knowledgeable	5 Very knowledgeable

	Concepts	Knowledge Level? (Circle one number)
1	Process evaluations, in general	1 2 3 4 5
2	Definition of process evaluations	1 2 3 4 5
3	Three purposes of process evaluations	1 2 3 4 5
4	Steps in doing process evaluations	1 2 3 4 5
5	The eight questions process evaluations can answer	1 2 3 4 5
6	Three characteristics of a good data collection instrument that can be used in process evaluations	1 2 3 4 5
7	Three considerations that must be taken into account when developing a monitoring system for process evaluations	1 2 3 4 5
8	Client path flows	1 2 3 4 5
9	Program fidelity	1 2 3 4 5
10	Differences between process evaluations and needs assessments (Chapter 10)	1 2 3 4 5
	Add up your scores (minimum = 10, maximum = 50)	Your total score =

A   47–50 = Professional evaluator in the making
A−   45–46 = Senior evaluator
B+   43–44 = Junior evaluator
B   41–42 = Assistant evaluator
B−   10–40 = Reread the chapter and redo the study questions

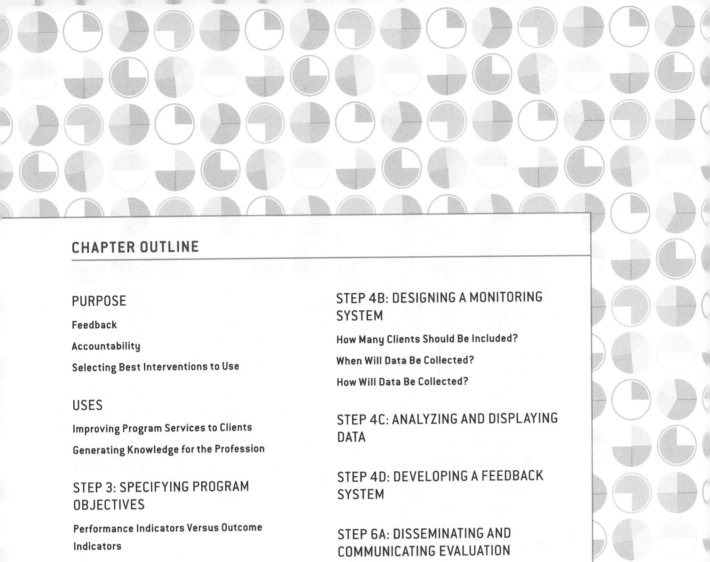

CHAPTER OUTLINE

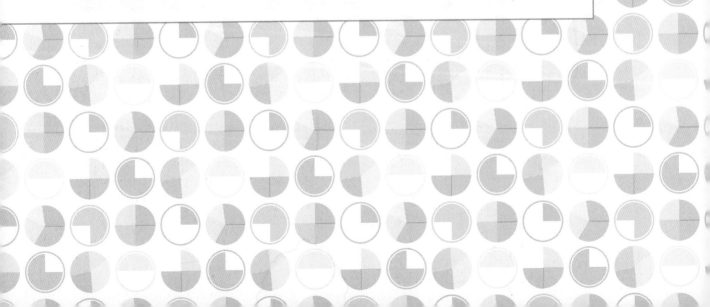

Chapter 12
OUTCOME EVALUATIONS

An outcome evaluation does nothing more than evaluate a program's objectives as presented in its logic model (see Chapters 7 and 8). As we know, program outcomes are what we expect clients to achieve by the time they leave our program. In most cases, we expect some positive change for the recipients of our services. When clients show improvement, we can feel optimistic that our program has had a positive impact on their lives.

A critical aspect of an outcome evaluation is that we must have a clear sense of what expected changes (the program's outcomes) we hope to see; as we know, these changes are not freely decided on. As we have seen throughout this book, program objectives are developed by giving consideration to the knowledge we have gained from the existing literature, available evidence-based interventions, past and present practice experiences, the current political climate, and, most important, our stakeholders.

Thus, by evaluating a program's objectives, we are, in effect, testing hypotheses about how we think clients will change after a period of time in our program. We would hope that clients participating in our family support program (see Box 7.1 in Chapter 7), for example, will show favorable improvement on its three program's objectives. This chapter uses the family support program as an example of how to develop a simple and straightforward program outcome evaluation.

In a nutshell, an outcome evaluation simply evaluates whether or not we achieved our program objectives. If we have not succinctly stated our program's objectives, however, any efforts at doing an outcome evaluation are futile at best. This fact places

some programs in a bind because of the difficulty they face in clearly defining concepts (or social problems) such as homelessness, self-esteem, child neglect, child abuse, and domestic violence. Most of these concepts are multifaceted and cannot be solved by focusing on any single program objective (e.g., behavior, knowledge, or affect).

Thus we must be modest about our abilities as helping professionals and feel comfortable with the fact that we can assess only one small component of a complex social problem through the efforts of a single social service program. Let's now turn our attention to the purpose of doing outcome evaluations.

PURPOSE

As we know by now, the main purpose of an outcome evaluation is to demonstrate the nature of change, if any, for our clients after they have received our services; that is, after they have left the program. Given the complexity of many social problems that our programs tackle, we must think about an outcome evaluation as an integral part of the program's planned activities and the intended results that were derived from these activities. This is accomplished by a program's logic model (see the left side of Figures 3.2 and 3.3 in Chapter 3 for its planned activities and the right side for intended results).

The far left-hand column in Box 7.2 lists the three program objectives for our Family Support Program that are described in Box 7.1. Suppose, for example, we want to evaluate only one of our three program objectives—to increase parents' knowledge about parenting skills—for parents who participate in our family support program.

If our program serves 10 parents and runs for 10 weeks, we gain a limited amount of knowledge by evaluating one round of the program's objective (to increase parents' knowledge about parenting skills). If we evaluate this single program objective each time we run the program and monitor the programs' accumulative outcomes over a 2-year period, however, we will have much more confidence in our program's results.

Feedback

There are many reasons for wanting to monitor and evaluate our program's objectives over time. One reason is to give concrete feedback to the program's stakeholders. As we know, a program's goal and its related program objectives are dynamic and change over time. These changes are influenced by the political climate, organizational restructuring, economic conditions, availability of new evidence-based interventions, staff turnover, and administrative preferences. Rarely are a program's goal and objectives changed or modified because of the results from a single outcome evaluation. They are changed through process evaluations as discussed in the previous chapter.

Accountability

Another reason for doing an outcome evaluation is so that we can demonstrate accountability in terms of showing whether or not our program is achieving its promised objectives. In this spirit, a program's logic model, in addition to its outcome evaluation plan, serves as a great concept map—it's a useful tool for telling us where we are headed and the route we plan to take to arrive at our destination which is always client success. This focus helps to keep program administrators and workers in sync with the program's mandate (which is reflected in the program's goal). If an outcome evaluation of your program is positive, you then have more of a justification to support and continue your program.

Selecting Best Interventions to Use

On the other hand, if the evaluation of a program's objectives turns out to be poor, we can investigate the reasons why this is so though a process evaluation. In either case, we are working with data with which to make informed case- and program-level decisions. Because we want our clients to be successful in achieving our program's objective(s), we select evidence-based interventions (and their associated practice activities) that we believe have the greatest chance of creating positive client change. Selecting rock-solid interventions in this way increases the likelihood that a program's objectives, the practice objectives, and the practice activities have a strong and logical link (see Chapters 7 and 8).

Programs are designed to tackle many complex social problems, such as child abuse, poverty, depression, mental illness, and discrimination. As we saw in Chapter 7, programs must develop realistic program objectives given what is known about a social problem, the resources available, and the time available to clients. Unfortunately, we attempt to do more than is feasibility possible. Evaluating a program's objectives gives us data from which to decide what can be realistically accomplished.

By selecting a few key program objectives, for example, we can place limits on what workers can really accomplish. It also places limits on the nature of the practice activities that workers might engage in. Suppose, for example, our family support program begins to receive referrals of childless couples who are experiencing violence in their relationships. Rather than trying to alter our program to meet clients whose current problems are not congruent with our program's objectives, we can educate our referral sources about the type of services we offer and the nature of the clientele we actually serve.

A program outcome evaluation is always designed for a specific program. Thus the results tell us about specific program objectives and not general social indicators. A 10-week employment training program showing that 75% of its participants found employment after being taught how to search for jobs cannot make any claims about impacting our nation's general unemployment rate (see Box 13.1 in Chapter 13). The results are *specific* to one *specific* group of participants, experiencing the *specific* conditions of one *specific* intervention over a *specific* time period.

USES

Given that a program outcome evaluation focuses on the program's objectives when clients exit a program, its uses may seem, at first blush, to be quite limited. The outcomes of a program's objectives, however, are pivotal points at which clients leave a program and begin life anew—equipped with new knowledge, skills, affects, or behaviors related to a specific social problem. Therefore evaluating the outcomes of a program's objectives gives us important information that can be used two ways:

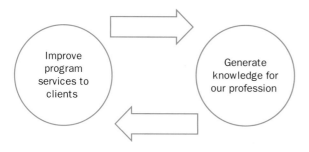

Improving Program Services to Clients

A primary use of any outcome evaluation is to improve a program's services (or interventions) that it delivers to clients. Thus data collected in an outcome evaluation tell us things such as how many clients achieved a program objective and how well the objective was achieved. Suppose, for example, a rural child abuse prevention program has as one of its program's objectives:

Program Objective:

To increase parents' awareness of crisis services available to them by the end of the program.

At the end of our program, however, we learn that, for 90% of our parents, their awareness level of the available crisis services remained the same—it did not change. Looking into the matter further, we find that there is only one crisis service available to parents living in the rural area and all of parents knew about this service *before* they became clients of the child abuse prevention program.

Influencing Decisions

Ideally, a program outcome evaluation should have a major impact on how concrete program decisions are made. Realistically, this is simply not the case. It's more likely that its results will assist us in resolving some of our doubts and confusion about a program or will support facts that we already know. The results contribute independent information to the decision-making process rather than carrying all the weight of a decision. The findings from an outcome evaluation usually assist us by reducing uncertainty, speeding things up, and getting things started.

When outcome data (program objectives) are routinely collected, results can be reviewed and compared at regular intervals. By reviewing outcome data, we improve on our ability to identify problem areas and any trends occurring over time. Such analyses assist us in pinpointing areas of our program that need further attention.

Generating Knowledge for the Profession

Evaluating a program's objectives can also lead us to gain new insight and knowledge about a social problem. As we saw in Chapter 7, program objectives are derived in part from what we know about a social problem (based on the literature and previous research studies). Thus when we evaluate a program's objectives, we are in effect testing hypotheses—one hypothesis for each program objective.

Learn more about different evaluation designs in Tool E in the Evaluation Toolkit.

We make an assumption that clients who receive a program's services will show more positive change on each program objective than if they did not receive the services. How well we are able to test each hypothesis (one for each program objective) depends on the evaluation design used.

If we simply compare pretest and posttest data, for example, we can say only that client change occurred over the time the program was offered, but we cannot be certain that the program actually *caused* the observed changes. On the other hand, if we use an experimental design and are able to randomly assign clients to a treatment group and to a control group, we will arrive at a more conclusive answer (see Figure E.10 in Tool E). The results obtained from a program evaluation provide supporting pieces of "effectiveness" rather than evidence of any "absolute truths."

In Chapters 7 and 8 we discussed how to conceptualize a program by defining its goal and stating its related objectives. A program outcome evaluation plan is unique to the context of the program for which it was designed and it's directly related to its logic model. Using our family support program as an example, there are six major steps in conducting an outcome evaluation as illustrated in Figure 12.1.

STEP 3: SPECIFYING PROGRAM OBJECTIVES

An outcome evaluation is a major collaborative effort. It's most successful when the social workers are included in its design and implementation. In programs where an "outcome evaluation mentality" does not exist, staff should be included in their designs. Eventually, as programs evolve to integrate evaluation activities with practice activities, planning for an outcome evaluation becomes an integral part of day-to-day program activities. If a program has clearly defined its goal and program-related objectives, the first step in an outcome evaluation is nearly

Figure 12.1: **The process of an outcome evaluation (from Figure 3.1).**

done. Theoretically, a program's objectives should be tied to theory which is then translated into its logic model. Thus an outcome evaluation, for all practical purposes, is theory driven (see theory of change model as discussed in Chapter 8).

By focusing on a program's objectives, we can be sure that we will not unnecessarily collect data on variables we do not want to know about. It's very tempting, for example, for program administrators—and workers alike—to make a last-minute decision to include an "interesting question" on an "evaluation form" or some other data recording instrument.

Learn more about the different ways to measure a programs' objectives in Tools L and M in the Evaluation Toolkit.

However, data are expensive to collect and analyze. Thus all data collected must be directly related to a program's objectives. Resources spent on collecting "extra" data detract from the quality of the data collected that are needed to monitor the attainment of a program's objectives. In other words, straying from a program's data collection plan seriously compromises the results of a carefully designed outcome evaluation plan.

Clearly specifying a program's objectives is a critical task because it defines how we understand our overall program in concrete terms. This is a very simple task when a program has a logic model as all of its objectives are clearly listed in the right hand columns (outcomes). As we saw in Chapter 7, the second program objective in our family support program outlined in Box 7.1 is "to increase problem-solving skills of family members." In short, this is only one of the three outcomes of the program.

Conceptually, we need to determine specifically how the social workers in the program define "problem-solving skills of family members."

- Is problem-solving the skill whereby family members apply prescribed steps in the problem-solving process?

- Is it the number of problems they successfully solve in a given day?
- Is it problem-solving in a general sense or problem-solving that is specific to family conflict?

Clearly there are many ways to define, and therefore measure, problem solving. To ensure that the program objective remains linked with the broader expectation of the program, we can look for direction from the program's goal. As a guide, the program goal is more helpful in telling us what problem solving is not, rather than what it is.

Although the idea of defining a program's objectives is relatively straightforward, we must be aware that there are many factors influencing the task. Evaluation of a program's objectives is more often than not an uphill battle. This is because major stakeholders want (and often demand) concrete objective results.

Performance Indicators Versus Outcome Indicators

Given the difficulties faced with measuring change in a client's self-esteem, for example, programs often opt to monitor variables such as the number of clients served in a given year and the number of hours of direct service contact between social workers and clients. These are performance (or output) indicators, not outcome indicators.

Nevertheless, these performance data are important to decision-making around client services and worker supervision, but they can seriously misguide the overall direction of an outcome evaluation if we're not careful. If, in fact, performance measures are used to define program outcomes, then social workers will focus on maximizing their direct service time without necessarily giving thought to how their time is spent or what it will accomplish.

Even more serious, by focusing on these types of performance outcomes, a program is at risk for developing an unhealthy culture among its workers. If workers in our family support program were to focus on increasing the number of direct service hours spent with clients, for example, then we might easily become misled into thinking that the social worker who spends the greatest number of hours in direct service hours with clients is in fact the "best" social worker. It may be, however, that this practitioner's work does not benefit clients at all. Focusing on these operational statistics has an important role for administrative decision-making and should be included in process evaluations (see Chapter 11).

STEP 4A: MEASURING PROGRAM OBJECTIVES

Now that we have specified our program objectives, we need to measure them. Selecting the best measurements for a program's objectives is a critical part of an outcome evaluation. To measure Program Objective 2 in our family support program introduced in Box 7.1, for example, we could use a standardized measuring instrument that has high validity and reliability.

If no such instrument is available or using a questionnaire is not feasible, we might ask clients a few direct questions about their problem-solving skills. We might ask them to talk about a problem-solving example they used in the past day or two and then ask them to tell us the number of steps they used to solve the problem.

Learn more about the different ways to measure variables in Tools L and M in the Evaluation Toolkit.

We could also rely on the individual client's own perspective and ask, "Since completing the program have your skills at problem-solving improved?" We could ask the client to respond "yes" or "no" or have the client rate the degree of improvement on a 5-point scale, where 1 means problem-solving skills are worse, 3 means they are about the same, and 5 means they have improved.

There are many different ways to measure program outcomes, ranging from simple to complex. Tools L and M present the importance of validity and reliability in choosing measuring instruments. At the very least, we can put our efforts into making sure

that the measurements of our program objectives have face validity. We want each question (in addition to the whole questionnaire) to accomplish the following:

- Directly relate to the program objective being measured
- Be part of a group of questions that together directly assess the program objective being measured
- Provide descriptive data that will be useful in the analysis of our findings

Pilot-Testing the Measuring Instrument

Once we have determined what measuring instrument(s) is going to be used to measure each program objective and who will provide the data (data source), we need to pretest or pilot-test the measuring instrument. A pilot test helps to ascertain whether in fact the instrument produces the desired data as well as whether any obstacles got in the way, such as when instructions are not clear or too many questions are asked at one time.

Therefore we want to pilot-test all instruments at all phases of an outcome evaluation, including pretest, in-program, posttest, and follow-up. Because we are interested in collecting data about (and not from) the data collection instrument (and not the content of our questions), we want to observe how clients react to completing it. To gain more information about the clients' understanding of questions, we might ask them to verbalize their thinking as they answer a question or ask them to comment on the process of providing the data.

When a self-report measuring instrument is used to measure a program's objective, we need to check the accuracy of the data it generates by using multiple data sources in the pilot study. In using self-report data, for example, we might ask clients for their permission to interview a family member or another person familiar with the problem.

Because we are only pilot-testing the self-report instrument, we might ask the opinion of the social worker currently working with the client. This pilot-testing activity gives us greater confidence as to whether we can rely on only client self-report data that will be collected later on in the outcome evaluation.

If we are having difficulty choosing between two closely related measuring instruments, or with the wording of a difficult question, we could ask clients to respond to two options and ask which one they prefer and why. We need to give extra attention to clients who do not complete measuring instruments or refuse to respond to certain questions. In these cases, we need to explore the reasons why a certain type of client did not answer, and we must do so in a manner that is sensitive to the client's needs.

After a measuring instrument that is used to measure a program objective has been selected and pretested, it's essential to establish clear procedures for scoring it. Scoring instructions accompany most standardized measuring instruments. Thus we need to decide only who will be responsible for carrying out the scoring task.

When a program develops its own nonstandardized measuring instrument, such as the one presented in Figure 10.4 in Chapter 10, it's necessary to agree on a systematic set of procedures for administering and scoring the instrument. Suppose, for example, that to measure Program Objective 2 in our family support program mentioned earlier we ask clients to talk out loud about a problem they encountered in the past week and tell us the steps they took in solving the problem.

Given that client responses will vary, we would need a consistent way to determine what steps were taken. First, we must agree, as a program, on what the steps of problem-solving are. Second, we need to examine the possible range of responses provided by clients. We might use several raters in the pilot test to establish a protocol for scoring and, later, use the established procedures to train the people who collect the data.

Determining how to best measure a program objective is a critical aspect of all types of evaluations and should not be taken lightly. Where possible, we need to look for means and methods to corroborate our data-generated results and strengthen the credibility of our results. Without at least the minimal pretesting of a measurement instrument, we cannot be confident about its ability to provide accurate data.

Tools L and M discuss in detail the importance of measuring outcome variables and selecting appropriate instruments to measure them. Box 12.1 presents numerous examples of how a few program objectives have been measured through various indicators.

BOX 12.1   EXAMPLES OF THREE LEVELS OF OUTCOMES AND INDICATORS FOR OUTPATIENT ADULT MENTAL HEALTH SERVICE PROVIDERS (THE THREE OUTCOMES ARE FROM A LOGIC MODEL. SEE CHAPTERS 7 & 8)

Initial Outcomes

Initial Outcome 1: Members of the community are aware of and are able to avail themselves to outpatient mental health services.
   Indicator 1: Number of consumers who received outpatient services during the quarter.
   • This is the total number of public mental health system consumers who received any type of service at your clinic at least once during the reporting period.
Initial Outcome 2: Consumers take responsibility for their mental health problems.
   Indicator 2: Number and percentage of consumers who had a treatment plan update this quarter.

Intermediate Outcomes

Intermediate Outcome 1: Consumers manage or reduce their presenting symptoms.
   Indicator 3: Number and percentage of consumers who managed symptoms or experienced a reduction in negative symptoms.
   • This is the total number of consumers who, with or without medication, reported an ability to manage their symptoms or had a reduction in negative symptoms as measured by a therapist using the General Assessment of Functioning score.
   • Number of consumers with improved General Assessment of Functioning score out of number of

continued

BOX 12.1 CONTINUED

consumers for whom follow-up assessment was completed during the reporting period.

- Each consumer should be assessed at intake and every 6 months and/or at discharge. There may be some consumers who happen to have two assessments in a quarter because case closure occurs a month or two after last assessment. In this case, report the case closure assessment.

Intermediate Outcome 2: Consumers experience an improved level of functioning.

Indicator 4: Number and percentage of consumers in an appropriate day program or other meaningful activity during all or part of the reporting period.

- This is the total number of active consumers from your clinic who were attending an appropriate day program, such as school, community centers, group meetings, or volunteer work, or engaging in other meaningful activity during all or part of the reporting period.

Long-Term Outcomes

Long-Term Outcome 1: Consumers do not require emergency hospital services.

Indicator 5: Number and percentage of consumers who had a psychiatric hospitalization.

- This is the total number of active consumers from your clinic who had to be admitted during this reporting period to a hospital for psychiatric reasons.

Indicator 6: Number and percentage of consumers who were treated in hospital emergency rooms.

- This is the total number of active consumers from your clinic who were treated at a hospital emergency room during this reporting period.

Long-Term Outcome 2: Consumers avoid first or new involvements with the criminal justice system.

Indicator 7: Number and percentage of consumers who were arrested, detained, diverted, or incarcerated.

- This is the total number of active consumers from your clinic who were arrested, detained, diverted,

or incarcerated at a correctional facility during this reporting period.

Long-Term Outcome 3: Consumers do not require homeless services.

Indicator 8: Number and percentage of consumers who were not housed in a homeless shelter during all or part of the reporting period.

- This is the total number of active consumers from your clinic who were housed in a shelter during all or part of this reporting period.

Long-Term Outcome 4: Consumers are employed.

Indicator 9: Number and percentage of consumers who were competitively employed during all or part of the reporting period.

- This is the total number of active consumers from your clinic who have been employed and earning wages during all or part of the reporting period.

Long-Term Outcome 5: Consumers feel more positive about their lives.

Indicator 10: Number and percentage of consumers who report an increase in well-being (life satisfaction).

- This is the total number of consumers who during the course of their treatment at your clinic reported an increase in well-being (life satisfaction) as measured by the attached eight questions of the Maryland version of the Mental Health Statistical Improvement Program. (Questions beginning "As a Direct Result of Services I Received . . ." as rated by consumers on a scale of 1 to 5.)
- The score is calculated by adding the eight scores and dividing by 8. So if a client checks "agree" for four questions ($4 \times 4 = 16$), "strongly agree" for three ($3 \times 5 = 15$), and "neutral" for one question ($1 \times 3 = 3$), the score would be 4.25. If a client scores 3.5 or higher, then the client is reporting an improvement in well-being/life satisfaction. Each consumer should be assessed every 6 months thereafter and/or at discharge. Some consumers may have two assessments in a quarter because case closure occurs a month or two after last assessment. In this case, report the case-closure assessment.

STEP 4B: DESIGNING A MONITORING SYSTEM

There are many procedural matters that must be thought through in carrying out an outcome evaluation. The evaluation is more likely to go smoothly when these matters are considered in advance. Practical steps are dictated by the need to minimize cost and maximize the number of clients included in the evaluative effort. Time and resources are important considerations for developing an outcome evaluation design.

Ideally, social workers should incorporate evaluation activities and tasks into their ongoing client service delivery. How we design our outcome evaluation can impact when the social workers meet with their clients. It may also change the nature of the worker–client interaction in their first meeting, as is the case when standardized measuring instruments are administered at intake.

Evaluation activity almost always affects the way social workers record client data. Because these evaluation activities directly impact a social worker's behavior, they have important implications for how clients are served and how evaluation data are collected. Much more will be said about designing monitoring data collection systems in Chapter 14.

- How many clients should be include?
- When will data be collected?
- How will data be collected?

How Many Clients Should Be Included?

In general, we want to collect data for as many clients as possible in an outcome evaluation. For programs with a few clients, such as a single group home program or a private social worker working independently, 100% coverage of clients served is more likely. For programs with many clients, however, such as child protection services or a large family and children service agency, we can use basic sampling techniques to develop a representative sample of all clients receiving services.

Sample Size

The major issue affecting sample size is whether program resources exist to collect data from all clients in the program. If it's not feasible to do so—an independent private social worker cannot afford to include 30 minutes of "testing" for each client, or a family service agency does not want to give up valuable "client time" for evaluation activities—then sampling is an option. The number of clients needed for an outcome evaluation is affected by the number of subgroups that may be included in the evaluation.

Suppose for example, our family support program wants to compare the levels of problem-solving skills (Program Objective 2) for single-parent and double-parent families. Ideally, we want to have roughly equivalent groups so that we do not end up comparing, say, 120 single parents with 240 double parents. Clearly, the double-parent families are better represented in this comparison. Ideally, we should aim to have a minimum of 30 clients for each subgroup included in our analyses. The more subgroups we include (say we are also interested in the age of parents, whether substance abuse is a factor, or what services our family has used previously), the more clients we need.

Sampling

When there are not enough resources to support data collection from all clients, the task can be lightened by randomly selecting clients for inclusion in the evaluation. As seen in Tool H, random selection can occur so long as the program aims to have a reasonable number of clients at critical points within the data analysis, such as when the program's semiannual and annual reports are due. The idea behind random sampling is that each client has an equal chance of being included in the study. In theory, this is a simple notion. In practice, however, there are many obstacles to consider.

The first matter to consider is deciding on what exactly constitutes the "total client population" served by the program. In our family support program, for example, it may be that parents periodically phone the program for crisis support and speak to a social worker on the telephone for a brief period, or, at times, an inappropriate referral is made and program time is used to reroute the client to a better matched service.

Learn more about the different sampling techniques and evaluation designs you can use in an evaluation in Tools H and E in the Evaluation Toolkit.

Although these clients may receive some assistance from our family support program, it would be unreasonable and even unimaginable to try and collect data related to the program's objectives. Rather, our family support program has as its primary client group families who are referred and accepted to the program to participate in the 12-week intervention.

Because clients of our family support program are referred on an ongoing basis, it's possible for random selection to occur by including every second or third client referred or by flipping a coin ("heads" our family is included, "tails" they are not) each time a client comes to the program, with a predetermined maximum number. If we are particularly interested in how outcomes relate to specific client groups (e.g., single-parent and double-parent families), we can use a stratified sampling strategy.

The critical aspect of random selection is that the decision to include clients is made without bias. That is, a program administrator does not select families because they appear to be cooperative, or social workers do not exclude families because they are concerned that the families might not respond positively toward the program.

Just as we allow clients the right to self-determinism—to say whether or not a particular intervention fits for them—we must also be willing to give clients the option to participate in any given evaluation activity. When clients decline to answer questions or fill out questionnaires, then we are faced with the problem of missing data. That is, we will have some unknowns in our final client sample. The less missing data we have, the more confident we will be that our evaluation results are reflective of all clients served within our program.

When Will Data Be Collected?

When the data are collected directly relates to the question asked in an outcome evaluation. An outcome evaluation indicates whether the program is meeting its program objectives, or working, but it says nothing about how it's working, or failing to work (see previous chapter). Nor is there any mention of efficiency; that is, the time and dollar cost of client success (see the next chapter).

After all, if a program achieves what it's supposed to achieve by the attainment of its program objectives, why does it matter how it achieves it? If the program is to be replicated or improved, it does matter, and efficiency assessments (Chapter 13) and process analyses (Chapter 11) can answer such questions. Questions related to outcome generally fall into four major categories, which have a direct link to the type of evaluation design used.

Outcomes Achieved?

First, the evaluator wants to know to what degree the program is achieving its objectives. Does participation in our family support program in relation to Objective 1, for example, increase positive social support for parents and by how much? This question requires that we collect data at (or near) the beginning of the program and at (or near) the end of the program to detect how much change has occurred.

As discussed earlier, we need to make a decision as to whether data will be collected for all incoming clients. Unless the data are in some way used to plan and implement a treatment intervention, data collection from all clients might be excessive, so a sampling strategy can be used.

Did One Group Do Better than Another?

Second, we want to know whether people who have been through our family support program have more positive social supports than similar people who have not been through the program. This question suggests that we collect data not only from clients in the program but also from clients who did not participate in the program. These could be clients who were turned away or perhaps are on a waiting list for program services. The aim of this question is to directly compare outcomes for clients receiving program services with those who do not.

Did the Intervention Cause the Change?

Third, there is the question of causality. Is there any evidence that services provided by our family support program caused the increase in positive social supports? This question requires the use of more complex evaluation designs such as those discussed in Tool E.

A related problem with collecting follow-up data is that clients may be receiving services from other programs during the follow-up period. How will we know if treatment effects are maintained as a result of our work with clients, or if the other current social service is somehow helping clients to do well? There are no perfect solutions to such a problem, but we can simply ask clients what additional social services they are involved with, if any. These data can be used to compare clients who are receiving additional social services with those who are not.

Did the Change Last?

Fourth, we might be interested in assessing the longevity of changes made by clients. In this case, we want to collect data from clients not only when they leave the program but also at some predetermined points afterward. Many clients who have exited from human service programs return to their previous social environments, which were at least partially responsible for their problems in the first place.

Often, clients' gains are not maintained; equally often, programs have no follow-up procedures to find out if they in fact have been maintained. Ideally, follow-up data are collected at intervals, such as 3, 6, or 12 months after clients exit a program. The time span should allow for enough time to pass in order to comfortably say that the program's effects were not simply temporary.

The challenge of collecting client follow-up data is that the task is not always easy. Sometimes it's very difficult to locate clients after they leave a program.

Programs working with underserved groups may have an especially difficult time because clients may not have telephones. Clients who are transient, have mental illness, have criminal backgrounds, and are homeless are hard to track down once they leave the program.

As we know, outcome data imply that we are interested in how clients change in terms of relevant program objectives at the end of our services. This assumption requires that a clear program end does in fact exist. In some cases, services to clients with ongoing difficulties may extend beyond those of the typical program. Suppose, for a moment, that a family within our family support program receives a 2-week extension of services because the family needs additional assistance for one reason or another.

When brief extensions are granted, the end of the program is also extended. If, however, longer term extensions are given such that the client essentially repeats the program, then the true program end technically is decided by the predefined program service time. The downside of looking at things this way is that the client may not show positive improvement at the predefined end of the program. This is unfortunate for our evaluation results, but it's a reality.

So far we have been discussing data collection from the vantage point of program-level evaluation. As we will see in Chapter 15, it's also possible to use aggregated case-level data to evaluate a program's outcomes. When case-level data are used, there are usually many more data collection points. Just how many there are will be determined by the worker and the client in designing an individual monitoring system for their unique practice objectives.

How Will Data Be Collected?

We can collect outcome data from clients by telephone, mail, or in person. Clearly, in-person costs are higher than if we collect data during our last contact with clients before they exit the program or if we contact clients by telephone (provided that the clients have phones). Ideally, we want to collect data from all clients who are represented in our program's objectives. In our example, Program Objective 2 within our family support program example focuses on problem-solving skills of all family members.

Data Sources

This raises the question of whether we should collect data from the children as well as the parents. We must decide how feasible it is to use more than one data source. If time and resources limit us to one data source, then we must pick the one we think is most representative or one that will provide the most meaningful data in relation to the program objective.

Who is going to be responsible for collecting data is a critical question. When data are collected at intake, workers usually will gather the facts from clients as part of the assessment process. When social workers collect data at program exit, there is great risk of biasing results, which can discredit the outcome evaluation. Because social workers and clients come to know each other well, the helping relationship can influence how clients respond to measuring instruments.

Furthermore, having social workers evaluate their own performance is not generally accepted as a way to provide accurate data. Another reason for not using social workers to collect outcome data is that the additional task is likely to overload them. As clients exit a program, new clients are admitted. It becomes unwieldy for social workers to juggle new admissions, terminations, clinical follow-ups, and evaluation follow-ups in addition to their ongoing caseloads.

Learn more about training and supervising data collectors in Tool I in the Evaluation Toolkit.

Quality data collection requires several explicit procedures that need to be laid out and strictly followed. Minimal training is needed for consistent data collection. It's rather inefficient to train all social workers within a single program to collect data (in addition to the disadvantages already stated). Thus it's advisable to assign data collection tasks to a small number of workers who are properly trained in the data collection effort. These individuals do not necessarily have to have any background in evaluation procedures; they simply need to have good interviewing skills and be able to follow basic standardized instructions.

STEP 4C: ANALYZING AND DISPLAYING DATA

It's possible that, by the time clients have answered questions on a program's intake form and completed any standardized measuring instruments used by a program, they may have produced 50 or more separate pieces of data. From marital status, to service history, to the level of a social problem, we must decide how each unit of data will be presented and what the possibilities for analyses are.

With outcome data, our data analyses tasks focus on the output of the program; that is, what is the condition (or situation) for clients at the time they exit the program and beyond? We may use demographic data on our intake form to present outcome data, according to subgroups, that reveal interesting results.

Suppose, for example, that overall family progress on problem-solving skills for our family support program was rather mediocre. But with further analyses, we are able to show that families with toddlers had great improvement compared with families with teens; in the latter, almost no improvement was observed. The additional information that can be gained from analyzing data in subgroups gives important detail for program decision-makers. It also helps to pinpoint a program's strengths and weaknesses, rather than simply looking at a program's results as a whole.

Aggregating Data

Although social workers may have some interest in analyzing client data on a question-by-question basis, outcome data are most useful when data can be aggregated and summarized to provide an overview on client outcomes. We must, therefore, decide how to aggregate responses to individual questions. When a standardized measuring instrument is used, the procedures for scoring and summarizing data derived from it are usually provided with the instrument.

Suppose we used a simple standardized measuring instrument to measure problem-solving skills, where a score of zero is considered "very low problem-solving skill" and a score of 100 is considered "very high problem-solving skill." If we measured clients at program intake (pretest data) and program exit (posttest data), we might report the average score for all clients at intake (e.g., 40) and the average score at program exit (e.g., 80), thereby reporting an "average" increase in problem-solving skills of 40 points.

Using Benchmarks

We can report additional information when normative data are available with standardized measuring instruments. For example, if our measuring instrument reported that when tested on a clinical population, the mean score was 50, and when tested on a nonclinical population, the mean score was 70, we could use these data to compare our client scores with these normative data. Normative data are particularly helpful for interpreting client data when measurement occurs only at program exit.

Because many stakeholders desire concrete and objective results, it's also worthwhile to consider reporting outcome data according to preset expectations, or benchmarks. We may have worded Program Objective 2, for example, as follows: "Seventy-five percent of families will show improvement in their problem-solving skills." We should measure outcomes in this way only if we have a sound rationale for estimating success.

Estimates may be derived from previous evaluation data, research studies, or general expectations of a given population. Estimates may focus on the amount of "average improvement" rather than the number of clients expected to show success. Including such estimates serves to educate stakeholders who might not be as well informed about a client population or a social problem.

It's important that stakeholders understand that 100% success in deterring runaways, family violence, drug addiction, child prostitution, crime, and welfare fraud is an unrealistic expectation for any program. In some cases, we may not expect a better than 50/50 chance of seeing improvement for clients. If this is the case, then outcome results should be interpreted in this context.

Analysis of outcome data is done by summarizing key outcome measures and reporting either the amount of change and/ or the number of clients achieving a certain predetermined level, or benchmark.

In addition to comparing outcome data with normative scores and preset expectations, we may also choose to present outcome data over time. It's possible, for example, to report client outcomes from one year to the next to show program trends. If outcome data from similar programs exist, it also is possible to compare the results of one program with another.

For the most part, analysis of outcome data is done by summarizing key outcome measures and reporting either the amount of change and/or the number of clients achieving a certain predetermined level, or benchmark. In either case, it's helpful to report these data using actual numbers and percentages. The numbers provide stakeholders with a realistic view of how many clients are included in each analysis, while percentages offer an easy way of comparing data across categories. We can also use basic graphing techniques and statistics to gain further insight into our data analysis.

STEP 4D: DEVELOPING A FEEDBACK SYSTEM

Outcome evaluation can produce useful and telling data about what is happening for clients after they receive program services. The results are most useful when they are routinely shared with key stakeholders. In most cases, the emphasis on outcome data is for the benefit of the stakeholders who are external to the program.

Funders and policymakers learn about program outcomes through annual reports or perhaps new proposals. Program outcomes may be disseminated more broadly as well. The local newspaper may be interested in doing a feature article on the services a program offers. In addition to providing anecdotes and general descriptions of a social problem, program administrators have the option of reporting outcome data, thereby increasing public awareness.

When it comes to program-level evaluations, developing a feedback system for internal stakeholders such as program administrators and social workers is absolutely essential. Making outcome data available to them on a regular basis helps to keep them focused on the program's goal and its related program objectives.

Discussing outcome data can also stimulate important questions such as the following:

- Why are our clients doing so well (or so poorly)?
- Are our program outcomes realistic?
- Are there any aspects of client outcomes that are being ignored?

When program personnel have an opportunity to respond to concrete data, discussions become more purposeful and focused. Much more will be said about developing a feedback system in Chapters 14 and 15.

STEP 6A: DISSEMINATING AND COMMUNICATING EVALUATION RESULTS

Disseminating and communicating outcome results need to be taken seriously if we want to see our evaluation used. As we have seen, the findings that emerge from an outcome evaluation give us objective data from which to make decisions about how clients make changes. Such results can affect program operations, funding, and even what we believe about our clients and the expectations we have of our programs. The likelihood of having evaluation results used is increased when results are presented in a straightforward manner.

It's useful to think about the obstacles that get in the way of putting evaluation results into practice. One obstacle occurs when we fail to remember the law of parsimony when presenting the final report. As mentioned in the last chapter, a report should be straightforward, clear, and concise. It should be designed for the intended audience (stakeholder group).

Note, however, that a program might have several versions of the same evaluation report—one version for each type of stakeholder. A report may be presented to the program's funders, while a pamphlet on the same information (presented differently) may be available for clients.

Another obstacle to using the findings of an outcome evaluation is created when the results contradict strong predetermined beliefs. It's fair to say, for example, that most social workers believe that their efforts are helpful to clients. We design programs with the hope and promise of improving human lives and social conditions. Thus when our outcomes show that no, or little, client change has occurred or that a client problem has worsened, it's easy to become defensive and to question the integrity of the evaluation methods.

Learn more about disseminating your evaluation results in Tool J in the Evaluation Toolkit.

Given that evaluation research methods are fraught with threats to internal and external validity, it's tempting to raise such concerns and then continue practicing as we always have. In other instances, the public may hold strong convictions about a particular social problem. An evaluation of a prison program, for example, may show that the program is unsuccessful in preventing prisoners from committing further crimes once they have been released. Yet the general public may have a strong opinion that people who commit crimes should be punished by being sent to prison. In such a case, the evaluation results will have little influence on program changes.

As we know from Chapters 4 and 5, whatever the form of reporting and disseminating our evaluation findings, confidentiality is of utmost importance. Confidentiality is most easily established when data are reported in aggregate forms. By summarizing data by groups, we avoid singling out any one client.

SUMMARY

Outcome evaluations are practical endeavors. We want to know whether client changes have occurred as a result of our intervention efforts. Thus our evaluation plan is designed to give us valid and reliable data that can be used for decision-making. To arrive at the best plan to answer our questions, we must consider how much time and money are available, what research design is feasible, and what biases exist.

Program outcome assessment is an evaluation that determines to what degree the program is meeting its overall program objectives. In our profession, this usually means the degree to which our interventions are effective. We have also provided a list of five myths regarding outcome evaluations that can be found at the end of this chapter.

We usually do outcome evaluations before or simultaneous to efficiency evaluations, the topic of the following chapter.

The goal of this chapter is to provide you with a beginning knowledge base for you to feel comfortable in answering the below questions. AFTER you have read the chapter, indicate how comfortable you feel you are in answering each of the following questions on a 5-point scale where

1 Very uncomfortable	2 Somewhat uncomfortable	3 Neutral	4 Somewhat comfortable	5 Very comfortable

If you rated any question between 1–3, reread the section of the chapter where the information for the question is found. If you still feel that you're uncomfortable in answering the question, then talk with your instructor and/or your classmates for more clarification.

	Questions	Degree of comfort? (Circle one number)
1	In your own words, define an outcome evaluation. Provide a social work example throughout your discussion.	1 2 3 4 5
2	List and then discuss the main purpose of doing an outcome evaluation. Provide a social work example throughout your discussion. Then discuss how the main purpose would benefit your field placement (or work) setting.	1 2 3 4 5
3	List and then discuss all of the steps of doing an outcome evaluation. Then discuss how you would do one within your field placement (or work) setting.	1 2 3 4 5
4	List and then discuss the two uses of outcome evaluations. Provide as many social work examples as you can to make your points.	1 2 3 4 5
5	Discuss the various ways that program objectives can be measured. Provide a social work example of each.	1 2 3 4 5
6	List and then discuss the three considerations that must be taken into account when you develop a monitoring system for an outcome evaluation.	1 2 3 4 5
7	Discuss why the contents of Chapters 7 and 8 have to be fully understood before embarking on an outcome evaluation. Provide as many social work examples as you can to make your points.	1 2 3 4 5
8	Discuss the relationship between outcome evaluations and process evaluations. How are they similar? How are they different? Is one better than the other? Why or why not? Provide as many social work examples as you can to make your points.	1 2 3 4 5

Chapter 12				Assessing Your Self-Efficacy

AFTER you have read this chapter AND have completed all of the study questions, indicate how knowledgeable you feel you are for each of the following concepts on a 5-point scale where

1 Not knowledgeable at all	2 Somewhat unknowledgeable	3 Neutral	4 Somewhat knowledgeable	5 Very knowledgeable

	Concepts	Knowledge Level? (Circle one number)
1	Outcome evaluations, in general	1 2 3 4 5
2	Purpose of outcome evaluations	1 2 3 4 5
3	Two uses of outcome evaluations	1 2 3 4 5
4	Steps of doing outcome evaluations	1 2 3 4 5
5	Three questions that need to be asked and answered when designing a monitoring system for outcome evaluations	1 2 3 4 5
6	Program objectives	1 2 3 4 5
7	Measurement of program objectives	1 2 3 4 5
8	Selecting indicators to measure program objectives	1 2 3 4 5
9	Disseminating and communicating results from outcome evaluations	1 2 3 4 5
10	Differences between outcome evaluations, process evaluations (Chapter 11) and needs assessments (Chapter 10)	1 2 3 4 5
	Add up your scores (minimum = 10, maximum = 50)	Your total score =

A   47–50 = Professional evaluator in the making
A–   45–46 = Senior evaluator
B+   43–44 = Junior evaluator
B   41–42 = Assistant evaluator
B–   10–40 = Reread the chapter and redo the study questions

12.1

Myth 1: *Evaluation is a complex science. I don't have time to learn it.*

No. It's a practical activity. If you can run an organization, you can surely implement an evaluation process.

Myth 2: *An outcome evaluation requires a whole new set of activities—we don't have the resources.*

No. Most of these activities in the outcome evaluation process are normal management functions that need to be carried out anyway in order to evolve your organization to the next level.

Myth 3: *An outcome evaluation is an event to get over with and then move on.*

No. Outcome evaluation is an ongoing process. It takes months to develop, test and polish—however, many of the activities required to carry out outcome evaluation are activities that you're either already doing or you should be doing.

Myth 4: *There's a "right" way to do outcome evaluation. What if I don't get it right?*

No. Each outcome evaluation process is somewhat different, depending on the needs and nature of the nonprofit agency and its programs. Consequently, each agency is the "expert" at its outcomes plan. Therefore start simple, but start and learn as you go along in your outcome planning and implementation.

Myth 5: *Funders will accept or reject my outcome plan.*

No. Enlightened funders will (or at least should) work with you, for example, to polish your outcomes, indicators, and outcomes targets. If your agency is a new nonprofit and/or a new program, then you very likely will need some help—and time—to develop and polish your outcomes plan.

CHAPTER OUTLINE

Efficiency is doing things right;
effectiveness is doing the right things.
~Peter Drucker

Chapter 13

EFFICIENCY EVALUATIONS

The previous three chapters examined three different types of evaluations (i.e., needs assessments, process evaluations, outcome evaluations). This chapter briefly describes the final type: evaluations to determine how efficient our programs are. The basic question addressed in an evaluation of efficiency is: "What did it cost to produce the program's outcomes?" A program that obtains its results (program objectives, or outcomes) at a lower cost than another similar program that achieves comparable results can be said to be more efficient.

Although the concept of "efficiency" is relatively straightforward, the techniques required to conduct an efficiency evaluation are quite complex, technical, and costly. For this reason, many evaluators often stop at the evaluation of a program's outcomes and ignore the question of its efficiency. Yet any program evaluation without consideration of the program's costs provides only an incomplete understanding of the program being evaluated.

The question of efficiency arises for a number of reasons. At a practical level, think of your own purchasing practices; if you're like most people, you want to obtain the goods and services you use at the lowest possible cost. By doing so, you can "stretch your dollar." It's no different in the social services field. By being efficient, we create savings, which in turn can then be used to meet other social needs (i.e., Chapter 10) via the establishment of other evidence-based social service programs (i.e., Chapters 7 and 8). In addition, because resources available to our profession are always scarce, it's a responsible practice to ensure that those resources are used wisely and in the most efficient manner as possible.

Finally, our profession has been under scrutiny for a number of years. There's a widely held perception among politicians and the general public alike that our social service programs are not good stewards of resources and that there is much waste in the delivery of the services we offer. Evidence of efficiency can serve to counteract such claims and shore up support for what we do.

COST EFFECTIVENESS VERSUS COST–BENEFIT

The evaluation of efficiency has two types of analyses: cost-effectiveness analyses and cost–benefit analyses. To illustrate the distinction between the two types, we use an example of our Aim High Program described in Box 13.1. This program seeks to prepare social assistance recipients for employment.

Generally speaking, a cost-effectiveness analysis seeks to examine the costs of a program in relation to its outcomes, expressed in terms of the program's objectives. A cost–benefit analysis also looks at the costs of a program. However, when looking at a program's outcomes, a cost–benefit analysis takes a further step by assigning a monetary value to the outcomes achieved, a process referred to as *monetizing outcomes*. In our example, a cost–benefit analysis would determine the exact dollar value it costs for one participant to find employment.

Both types of analyses provide information regarding efficiency. Cost-effectiveness analyses are somewhat easier to conduct than cost–benefit analyses because there is no requirement to place a

---

BOX 13.1 THE AIM HIGH PROGRAM

The Aim High Program is a state-funded program for the purpose of helping people who receive social assistance find competitive employment. One motivating factor in funding this program is to reduce the state's financial expenditures on social assistance. The program serves 130 unemployed social assistance recipients per year.

The program is designed as a 10-week on-site workshop followed by an 8-week follow-up session. The principal components of the program are delivered during the 10-week session. Some of these components are (a) short courses dealing with work-related issues, (b) job-finding skills, (b)

management of personal concerns, (d) adult academic upgrading, (e) a supported job search process, and (f) 3 weeks of work experience. During the 8-week follow-up, staff members contact participants several times per week and support them with the job-search process or in their employment (if they have found a position by that point).

Using the previous chapter as a guide, the program's outcomes were evaluated. These included changes in (a) reading and mathematics skills, (b) self-esteem, (c) employment status, (d) income earned, and (e) amount of social assistance received.

---

monetary value on the outcomes produced. This saves a difficult step in the evaluation process. Placing a dollar value on outcomes is often exceedingly difficult, particularly when we are dealing with intangible outcomes. For example, what dollar value should we assign to our clients' increased levels of self-esteem or their increased quality of life?

The decision about which type of analysis to conduct depends on the circumstances and on the type of data required. If our intent is to assess the efficiency of a single program or to compare two or more programs producing the same outcomes, for example, a cost-effectiveness analysis will provide the required information.

If, on the other hand, our desire is to compare two or more programs that produce different outcomes, a cost–benefit analysis will be appropriate because this procedure places a dollar value on outcomes, thereby making it possible to make the desired comparison. Box 13.2 presents an in-depth discussion on comparing cost-benefit analyses with cost–effectiveness analyses for a residential drug treatment program.

When to Evaluate for Efficiency

Ideally, efficiency-focused evaluations should be conducted in the planning phases of a social service program; that is, before the program is actually implemented. This is referred to as a *prospective approach* to efficiency-focused evaluations. The purpose of such an approach is to provide information about the advisability of launching the program as potential program

sponsors are provided information about the probable efficiency of the program.

Sponsors often have to choose among several proposed social service programs; prospective efficiency-focused evaluations can shed light on the costs of each program in relation to its outcomes. This allows potential sponsors to make more meaningful comparisons among the proposed alternatives and therefore make better informed decisions about which program(s) to fund.

A limitation of conducting a prospective efficiency-focused evaluation before a program gets up and running is that its costs and outcomes have to be estimated. Estimates, or best guesses, are seldom as accurate as actual records. Records can easily be obtained from a program that is already operating.

To compensate, evaluators often create a range of estimates, including low, medium, and high for both costs and outcomes. The estimates for costs may come from a number of sources, including the plans for the proposed program and the costs of similar programs. The estimates of outcomes can come from the literature and from previously evaluated comparable programs.

From these sources, information can be provided to decision-makers about the likely efficiency of the proposed program under a number of conditions ranging from "low efficiency" to "high efficiency." In a self-esteem program, for example, it might be possible to say that for each person who makes a 20-point improvement in his or her self-esteem (as measured

BOX 13.2   COST-BENEFIT VERSES COST-EFFECTIVENESS FOR A SUBSTANCE ABUSE TREATMENT PROGRAM

Cost-Effectiveness Analysis

A cost-effectiveness analysis is the relationship between program costs and program effectiveness, that is, patient outcome. Costs are measured as dollars spent, whereas effectiveness or outcome is measured as changes in patients' behaviors, thoughts, feelings, or biology. For example, the cost-effectiveness of an opiate treatment program might be measured as the cost of generating an opiate-free month for the average patient.

There is no single standard for "cost-effective." Generally, the term is used loosely as a way of saying that something probably costs less, or is more effective, than something else. Cost-effectiveness indices can be compared for different programs, different treatment modalities (such as residential versus outpatient clinics), and different treatment techniques (such as drug-free with or without acupuncture or drug-free versus methadone maintenance).

The overall cost-effectiveness of a program can be improved by first finding the parts of the program that contribute most to effectiveness and then discovering which of those program components have the lowest cost. Although substance abuse treatment programs are complex, it may be possible to improve cost-effectiveness by enhancing use of these more effective and less expensive components while decreasing use of less effective and more expensive components.

However, cost-effectiveness indicators vary somewhat over time and over patients because of many factors, not all of which are controlled by the program. It is easy to find an apparent difference in the cost-effectiveness of different program components or different programs. It is harder to show that the difference is real—for example, that it occurs reliably over months and for most patients and therefore should be used in program management decisions.

Cost–Benefit Analysis

A cost–benefit analysis is the measurement of both costs and outcomes in monetary terms. Costs and benefits can be compared between programs or contrasted within a single program. Cost–benefit analysis can also discover whether program expenditures are less than, similar to, or greater than program benefits.

The time it takes for program benefits to exceed program costs is also measured in some cost–benefit analyses. Cost–benefit findings can often stand alone. For example, consider the inherent value of finding that every $1 spent for a particular substance abuse treatment program results in average savings of $4.96 to the taxpayer.

Some drug treatment programs produce measurable monetary outcomes, like increased days of legitimate employment and decreased job absences. Increased employment can yield increased income, which yields increased tax revenues. In addition, drug treatment programs may reduce patients' use of food stamps, public health services, and other public assistance—a potentially huge cost savings.

These cost savings may not occur as soon as patients begin treatment. Social service costs may actually rise as patients are guided to social services they need for recovery. In a few months or years, however, social service costs may decrease, whereas patient income and taxes paid by patients may increase.

Other major benefits of substance abuse treatment programs are indirect or secondary, such as reduction in crime-related costs, including property losses; medical services required by victims; time taken off from work by victims; and costs of apprehending, trying, and incarcerating offenders. All of these income increments, tax payments, and cost savings can add up to a considerable total benefit that exceeds the cost of treatment several times over.

There are several ways to report the relationships between costs and benefits:

- The *net benefit* of a program can be shown by subtracting the costs of a program from its benefits. For example, if a substance abuse treatment program cost $100,000 per year but generated in the same year $500,000 in increased patient income, increased tax payments by patients, and reduced expenditures for social and criminal justice services, the net benefit of the program would be $500,000 minus $100,000, or $400,000, for that year.
- The *ratio* of benefits to costs is found by dividing total program benefits by total program costs. For example, dividing the $500,000 benefit of the program by its $100,000 costs yields a cost–benefit ratio of 5:1.
- Because neither net benefits nor cost–benefit ratios indicate the size of the cost (*initial investment*) required for treatment to yield the observed benefits, it is important to report this as well. We cannot assume that the same exact relationships between costs and benefits will exist at different levels of investment.

Sometimes an increase in cost allows new, more productive procedures to be used for treatment, increasing benefits dramatically. For example, increasing a program budget to allow hiring of a community liaison, vocational

continued

BOX 13.2 CONTINUED

counselor, or physician might dramatically increase patient outcome. Therefore it often is best to report the initial investment, the net benefit, and the cost–benefit ratio.

- The *time to return on investment* (the time it takes for program benefits to equal program costs) is yet another indicator used in cost–benefit analysis. For programs, benefits and costs occur at the same time, or at least in the same year. For individual patients, however, the investment in treatment may pay off substantially only after several months or years. Costs usually occur up front, but program benefits may take time to reach the point where they exceed costs.
- The decreasing value of benefits attained in the distant future can be calculated as the *present value* of benefits.

When most of the cost of treatment occurs in the first year of treatment but most benefits occur only several years after treatment, the value of those delayed benefits needs to be adjusted (decreased) to reflect the delay.

Analyses of cost, cost-effectiveness, and cost–benefit relationships can provide valuable insights into how a program operates and how its operations could be improved to serve more people better for less. Analyses of costs, cost-effectiveness, and cost–benefit also show funders that program managers are aware of the importance of accountability—accountability for how funds are used and what they are used to achieve.

---

by Hudson's *Index of Self-Esteem*—see Figure L.1 in Tool L) in the best-case scenario the cost will be $600/participant, in the most likely scenario the cost will be $700/participant, and in the worst-case scenario the cost will be $800/participant.

The limitations of using estimates cannot be ignored, but such analyses, known as *sensitivity analyses*, do provide decision-makers with useful information during the planning stages of a program. More commonly, efficiency-focused evaluations are undertaken as a final step of an outcome evaluation. When this is done, an efficiency evaluation is referred to as a *retrospective approach*.

For programs that are already operating, a completed outcome evaluation is required before an efficiency-focused evaluation can be undertaken. The basic logic of efficiency-focused evaluations requires that only incremental outcomes be considered—in other words, outcomes that would not have occurred without the program. Thus it's important that the outcomes considered in an efficiency-focused evaluation can be attributed to the program and only to the program.

As we know, evaluations that can attribute outcomes to an intervention require some form of an experimental design. Because such designs are, in practice, difficult to carry out, evaluators of efficiency often find themselves in a position where they must make the assumption that the outcomes they are using in their analyses can be directly attributed to the program.

The information provided by retrospective efficiency evaluations is useful in a number of ways. First, program administrators and sponsors can obtain a more complete understanding of the program. They can begin to weigh the outcomes against the costs and determine whether the costs are justifiable and whether it's worth it to continue with the program. Such considerations are often relevant within multiprogram agencies where administrators can use the information from efficiency assessments to manage their programs.

The efficiency of a program is also an important consideration when there are plans to expand or replicate the program. Finally, when scarcity of resources dictates reductions or cuts, an understanding of the efficiency of alternative program options can greatly assist in making those difficult decisions.

The following sections of this chapter describe the basic steps involved in conducting a cost–benefit evaluation and illustrate the procedures of conducting one by using an example of a social service program called the Aim High Program (Box 13.1). For purposes of this description, we assume that we are conducting a retrospective cost–benefit analysis: An analysis that was conducted after the program performed an outcome evaluation using the procedures presented in the previous chapter.

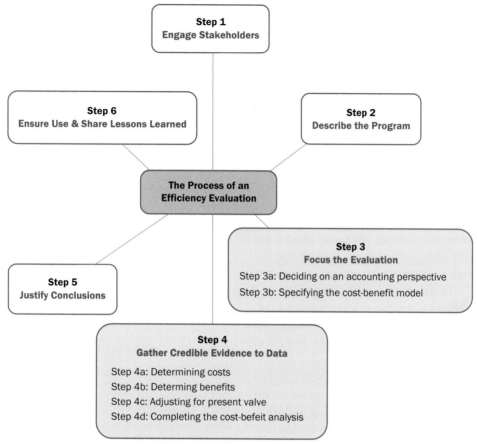

Figure 13.1: **The process of an efficiency evaluation (from Figure 3.1).**

For simplicity's sake, we discuss only the steps of doing an efficiency evaluation contained in Steps 3 and 4 of the generic evaluation model that was presented in Figure 3.1 in Chapter 3. However, in reality, you would have to go through all of the six steps contained in the evaluation process if you actually carried one out. Steps 3 and 4 are highlighted in Figure 13.1 to show you where the contents of this chapter fit into the generic evaluation process.

STEP 3A: DECIDING ON AN ACCOUNTING PERSPECTIVE

The first step in conducting a cost–benefit analysis is to decide on an accounting perspective to be used. A cost–benefit analysis can be conducted from a number of accounting perspectives. We discuss only two of the perspectives: the individual program's participants' perspective and the funding source's perspective. The perspective adopted determines what specific costs and benefits are to be considered in the analysis.

The Individual Program's Participants' Perspective

A program's participants' perspective is the narrowest perspective and is limited to considering the costs incurred and benefits obtained by the program's participants. For example, a cost–benefit analysis can be conducted using a participant's perspective to study the value, in monetary terms, of a college education.

Using hypothetical figures, suppose that the total cost to a student to obtain a college degree is $45,000 per year, or $180,000 over 4 years. These costs might include tuition and expenses for books, housing, and income not earned while attending college, to name a few.

Census data along with state and federal income statistics show that the average lifetime earnings of college graduates are $1,000,000 higher than those of non–college graduates. Having these data, we can now evaluate the cost–benefit of a college education; a graduate gains, on average, $820,000 over a lifetime as a result of graduating from college ($1,000,000 – $180,000 = $820,000).

The Funding Source's Perspective

Notice, however, that not all costs and benefits are included in the aforementioned calculations that use the individual program's participants' perspective. For example, the actual cost to the state-supported educational system of having students attend a college is typically much higher than the tuition paid by students—probably two-thirds higher (one-third state funds and one-third grant funds).

The state government usually provides annual funding to public universities to help make up the two-thirds difference, but this is not counted when a program's participants' perspective is adopted. This is because the state funding was not a cost to students—the program's participants. On the other hand, the state will gain in future years from the higher income earned by college graduates in the form of additional income taxes collected. These benefits are not considered, however, as they are not directly relevant from the participants' perspective.

When a funding source's perspective is adopted, the costs that are incurred by the funder in sponsoring a program and the benefits that accrue to the funder as a result of the program are the main focus. For example, a school district may wish to determine whether it's efficient to fund English as a second language instruction for students who have recently arrived in the country.

The costs of the program to the district budget would then be considered in relation to the benefits obtained. Such benefits might include a reduction in costs related to providing other resources and supports within schools, as students with increased English language skills can manage without special assistance.

Which perspective is adopted in a cost–benefit analysis depends on the sponsor of the evaluation and the questions to be answered.

Applying the Procedure

In the case of our Aim High Program, a funding source perspective was adopted, specifically that of the state government that funded the program. This perspective was taken because it was the state's senior managers who commissioned the evaluation as they sought to determine the impact of our Aim High Program on the state's budget. At the time of the evaluation, the state was extremely interested in employment training programs and was looking to identify the most efficient ones in order to establish similar programs throughout the state. This in turn would save the state money.

STEP 3B: SPECIFYING THE COST–BENEFIT MODEL

Once an accounting perspective is decided on, it's then possible to describe the general cost–benefit model to be used. This model specifies which specific costs and which specific benefits will be included in the model.

Looking at Costs

For program administrators, the cost of simply delivering the program is usually the largest cost to be considered. The most obvious cost for the individuals attending the program will be their enrollment fees (if any). These costs are considered direct costs. There are other "less visible" costs as well, known as hidden, indirect, and overhead costs.

To understand fully the costs from the individuals' perspectives, we need to look at these less obvious costs. For example, some participants may need to take time off from work and forego income, and they may need to acquire computer equipment and instructional texts. These are all hidden or indirect costs, and they need to be considered in a cost–benefit analysis from the individual's perspective.

Looking at Benefits

The same considerations apply to benefits as to costs. The students enrolled in our program may immediately benefit through an increase in salary from their current employers—that is, if they are currently employed. But they might also be able to obtain higher paying positions shortly after completing the program. Perhaps previous evaluations have shown that graduates typically benefit in this manner. This benefit has a monetary value and might be included in a cost–benefit analysis.

The participants may also gain in confidence and in their enjoyment of life. These are very important and real benefits but may be difficult, if not impossible, to convert into dollar terms. The evaluator would have to decide whether to monetize these benefits or to exclude them and note them as benefits to which a monetary value cannot be attached.

Having enumerated the exact costs and benefits from a selected accounting perspective, the cost–benefit model to be used can then be specified.

Applying the Procedure

The model used in conducting the cost–benefit analysis of our Aim High Program enumerates the main expenses incurred in funding and supporting the program from the state's perspective. The main cost factor of our Aim High Program is the funding provided by the state to run our program on a day-to-day basis. However, there are other costs of running our program as well. These include the costs incurred by the state in managing and administering the contract for our program. These are the professional, clerical, and other costs of contract management (at the state level), and these costs also need to be added to the model. In a nutshell, it costs the state money to administer the dollars it gives out for social service programs.

To make matters worse, our Aim High Program presently relies on state-funded social workers to refer clients to the program and to provide case management services. If we think about it, the time and state-funded resources expended in referring and providing case management services to the approximately 130 participants who attend the program yearly can be considerable.

In short, the social workers are also employees of the state and thus the value of their services must also be included in the costs of our Aim High Program. They do not work for our program for free just because they are "not officially" on the program's budget line. There is no such thing as a free lunch.

The benefits to be included in the model are, as is often the case, more difficult to specify than are the costs. In the case of our Aim High Program, there are a number of benefits to consider from the state's budget perspective. The most obvious is a reduction in social assistance payments for our program's participants as they are able to find competitive employment and therefore decrease their reliance on assistance from the state.

In addition, as income earners, the participants will now pay federal and state income taxes. As well, they will have more purchasing power and therefore engage in a variety of economic activities that benefit small businesses and corporations. This will result in more profitability for these businesses and hence more corporate taxes paid to the state.

It's important to keep in mind that our Aim High Program does produce other outcomes, but the ones included in the model are the ones that represent the main financial benefits accruing to the state's budget office as a result of the program. If we were using a program's participants' perspective, we might include benefits such as increased self-confidence due to finding employment, higher levels of self-esteem,

Table 13.1: **Costs and Benefits for the Aim High Program from a State Perspective.**

Costs	Benefits
1. Program payments	1. Reduction in social assistance payments
2. Contract administration costs	2. Increased state tax payments by participants
3. Costs of client referrals and case management services	3. Increased corporate taxes collected

and better qualities of lives. The items included in the cost–benefit model for our Aim High Program are presented in Table 13.1.

STEP 4A: DETERMINING COSTS

When considering costs, it's important to assign an accurate market value to each cost element. Occasionally, some goods and services are obtained through special arrangements and thus at a lower cost than would be normal. For example, a university professor may be interested in providing training, on a voluntary basis, to the participants in our program as part of a research project.

The professor, therefore, offers services without reimbursement. Because this service is unlikely to be obtained again without cost, it's common to use the normal market value (rather than the actual cost) of the service in the cost–benefit analysis. This process is known as shadow pricing.

Direct Costs

The first and usually most important cost factor to be accounted for is the direct cost of actually running the program. This information can usually be obtained from budgets, financial statements, or contracts between the funders and the program's administrators. When an agency delivers a single program, the total budget, or funding, can be considered to be the program cost.

However, in an agency that has several programs where it delivers its programs side by side, the accounting for direct costs becomes much more complicated. For example, some staff members may work in more than one program, and thus only a portion of their salary can be attributed to the program of interest. In some instances, separating out the costs to be attributed to a particular program can be a difficult and time-consuming task.

Indirect Costs

Next, indirect costs must be considered. By their very nature, indirect costs are difficult to pinpoint. Often only a portion of such costs can be directly attributed

to a particular program under review. For example, in a large agency operating several programs, part of the senior administration's time, some clerical time, as well as a portion of building costs and utilities would constitute overhead and would need to be attributed (via proportions) to the program being evaluated. The task of the evaluator in such circumstances is to identify the portion of indirect expenses that should be attributable to the cost of the program that is under review.

Applying the Procedure

Identifying direct costs for our Aim High Program was relatively simple because the agency and program were the same and thus had only our Aim High Program under its auspices. The total contract payment from the state to the program could be considered the direct cost for this program. Specifically, these costs were set by contract at $375,100 per year of program operations.

As described earlier, separating out the indirect costs that may be attributed to any single program can be a difficult exercise. Indeed, unless accurate accounting records are kept, it may be impossible to do so. Such was the case in examining the indirect costs of our Aim High Program. As indicated in the cost–benefit model, contract administration costs and the costs of case management services are the indirect costs to be considered. However, the departments within the state's government responsible for these functions did not keep records that would allow the costs associated with our Aim High Program to be separated from the costs of other activities within the various state departments.

The only way to identify these costs, under the circumstances, was to estimate them. After discussions with managers and accountants in the two state departments, it was estimated that indirect costs totaled 10% of direct costs. This formula was then used to complete the cost estimates for the program: $375,100 plus 10% equals $412,610, the total cost of the program per year—from the state's perspective.

Dividing the sum ($412,610) by the total number of clients served annually (130 participants) equaled

$3,174 per participant. In sum, and on a general level, our program spent, on average, $3,174 per participant per year.

Estimates are typically substituted when actual costs cannot be determined from the records, as is often the case for at least some of the cost factors. Although evaluators attempt to make well-founded estimates, this nevertheless becomes a limitation of the evaluation. In the following section, we will see how estimates are also used in determining benefits.

STEP 4B: DETERMINING BENEFITS

As we know, social service programs produce a variety of outcomes. These may include outcomes that are already expressed in dollar terms, such as an increase in annual income or a decrease in expenditures on medicines. However, more typically, programs produce outcomes that are not expressed in monetary terms. For example, a program might increase the self-esteem of its clients.

Another program might result in better communications between parents and their teenage children. Other outcomes might be expressed even more generally, such as increasing the overall happiness or improving the quality of life for individuals. It's a major challenge in cost–benefit analyses to monetize, or express in amounts of money, outcomes that are not inherently "financially oriented."

Suppose, for example, we are looking at the benefits of a smoking cessation program from the participants' point of view, or perspective. When participants stop smoking, the direct benefits can be easily quantified by calculating the amount of money saved on tobacco products. Indirect benefits would include savings to the individuals on future medical costs, among others. These indirect benefits can also be calculated with data obtained from findings derived from previous research studies and population statistics. The numbers from such analyses could be included in a cost–benefit evaluation.

However, other good outcomes will also be produced. For example, participants' children may be less likely to become smokers. A participant may also live

longer and enjoy a better quality of life. These gains may well be more important than the financial savings that can be identified. However, it would be very difficult to monetize these important benefits. What financial value can be attached to a child not starting to smoke, from not being physically abused, or from not taking drugs?

Some evaluators use complicated and, at times, imaginative methods in an attempt to place a value on happiness, enjoyment of life, and other warm and fuzzy benefits. However, the fact remains that there is no easy way to monetize such outcomes without making huge and sometimes contentious assumptions.

Under the circumstances, the most reasonable and prudent approach for evaluators to take is to monetize only those outcomes that can be reasonably converted into financial terms. Other outcomes, even if important, can be noted as unquantifiable benefits. The limitation of this approach is that other important benefits are not accounted for in the cost–benefit analysis.

Applying the Procedure

In the case of our Aim High Program, a variety of outcomes were produced and subsequently evaluated. These included changes in the basic educational levels of participants, changes in the self-esteem of participants, competitive employment for participants, wages earned by participants, and a reduction in social assistance payments to the participants. Although all of these outcomes could potentially be included in a cost–benefit analysis, not all were relevant to the accounting perspective selected, that of the state's budget office.

For example, although there is a meaningful value for increasing the participants' confidence levels via furthering their basic educational skills, this outcome (increasing confidence levels of participants) is not relevant to the state. Consequently, only outcomes relevant to the state were included in the analysis; these three outcomes are specified in the cost–benefit model included in the right-hand side of Table 13.1.

With reference to a reduction in social assistance payments (the first item in the list of benefits in the model), an outcome evaluation done prior to the cost–benefit analysis showed that social assistance payments to participants were reduced, on average, $230 per month.

The other financial benefits included in the model were increased state tax payments by participants resulting from their increased earnings as well as increased corporate taxes collected by the state government as a result of the increased economic activity generated by the program's participants. These benefits, although financial in nature, are very difficult to specify. To account for these benefits, a detailed examination of the income tax returns for each participant would be necessary. This was not possible because of the confidentiality provisions surrounding tax returns, and thus it was necessary to resort to estimates.

Tax accountants and economists were consulted, and, based on their assessments and recommendations, the assumption was made that the additional tax benefits to the state, resulting from the increased earnings of our program's participants, amounted to 3% of their earned income. As data relating to earned income was available from the outcome evaluation that was previously done, it was possible to calculate the tax benefits to the state at $5 per month per participant.

Adding the $5 per month tax increase to the $230 per month in reduced social assistance payments provides $235 per month per participant to the state's coffers. In the state's eyes, this works out to $2,820 of benefits per participant per year to be added to the state's bank account ($235 per month × 12 months = $2,820).

STEP 4C: ADJUSTING FOR PRESENT VALUE

In many instances, the benefits of a social service program may continue for a number of years. When that is the case, it's necessary to adjust the value of benefits in future years. This is a practice known as discounting and is based on the premise that the value of a sum of money at the present time (today) is higher than the value of the same amount in the future.

For example, if someone offered you a choice between receiving $1,000 today or receiving the same sum next year, you would be better off taking the money now. By having the money in your pocket now you could invest it and by next year have $1,000 plus the amount earned through your investment. This is known as an opportunity cost.

Suppose it costs a participant $500 to complete a smoking cessation program and this results in savings of $1,200 per year on tobacco products. This means that the person will only save $700 for the first year when the $500 enrollment fee is figured in ($1,200 – $500 = $700). The initial $500 cost of attending the program is incurred only once, but the benefit stream for the participants continues for years.

When we decide to compute the savings, we cannot simply add $700 for each future year to arrive at the total benefit because, as explained previously, the value of the $700 decreases as time marches on. In cost–benefit analyses, the following formula is used to discount the value of benefits in future years:

$$\text{Present Value} = \frac{\text{Amount}}{(1+r)^t}$$

where:
r = the discount rate
t = the number of years into the future

Tables providing discounted amounts at various rates are available from many financial institutions and on the Internet.

Before applying the discounting formula, the discount rate needs to be determined. There are a variety of ways for determining the discount rate, each requiring a number of economic assumptions that are far beyond the scope of our book. For purposes of the evaluation of social service programs, however, a reasonable way to set the discount rate is to set it at the opportunity cost of a safe investment (e.g., certified deposits). Thus if the money could be safely invested at 4%, the discount rate should be set at 0.04.

A second decision is to determine the number of years that the benefits will last. In some instances, the benefits may last for a set period of time. In other cases, such as those of smoking cessation or employment training programs, the benefits may continue without a fixed end. However, projecting benefits into the future is an imprecise proposition at best because it requires the assumption that the participants' statuses will not substantially change in the future.

In the absence of longer term follow-up data, such assumptions are necessarily speculative; the farther into the future projections are made, the more speculative they become. Nevertheless, evaluators must make some assumptions regarding the length of time that the benefit stream will continue. Usually, this determination is made after examining the literature regarding similar programs and having consultations with knowledgeable stakeholders and experts. An alternative approach is to conduct multiple analyses, each assuming a different duration for each level of benefit.

Applying the Procedure

In the case of our Aim High Program, our interest is on the benefits accrued to the state. As can be seen in Table 13.1, we have specified these to be reductions in social assistance payments and increased taxes (state and corporate). These benefits, as we have seen, result from the increased earning power of the program's participants, and we can expect that their increased earning power, and hence the benefits, will continue for a number of years.

For purposes of the cost–benefit analysis, it was decided to look at the efficiency of our program at three time periods after the participants exited our program (i.e., 12, 24, 36 months), rather than speculating about how long their benefit stream will

continue. The cost–benefit data at three future points in time should provide decisions-makers with a good understanding of the efficiency of the program—from the state's perspective, that is.

When examining the benefits in future years, it's therefore necessary to apply the discounting procedure to account for the reduced value of the benefits in future years. The discount rate was set at 0.045 to reflect the opportunity costs prevailing at the time.

As we know from Step 4, an outcome evaluation determined that the benefits on a per-participant basis were $2,820 per year. Using the formula to discount the value of benefits obtained in future years, it can be calculated that the present value of "per-participant benefits" after Year 1 is $2,699.

After Year 2 the value is $2,582, and after Year 3 it's $2,471. These values are then used to calculate the present value of the total benefits per participant. After 12 months, the total benefits are $2,699; after 24 months, the total benefits are $5,281; and after 36 months, the total benefits amount to $7,752. Table 13.2 shows these calculations in detail.

STEP 4D: COMPLETING THE COST–BENEFIT ANALYSIS

With the information obtained in the previous steps, a cost–benefit analysis can now be completed. This step involves a lot of numeric data, and tables are an effective way of presenting them. The program costs, benefits, and net benefit (or cost) are usually presented

Table 13.2: Calculating the Present Value of $2,820 for Three Future Time Periods.

Time Periods	Yearly Benefits[a]	Total Benefits over a Three-Year Period	Present Value of Total Benefits
12 months	$2,699	$2,699	$2,699
24 months	$2,582	$2,699 + $2,582	$5,281
36 months	$2,471	$2,699 + $2,582 + $2,471	$7,752

[a]After discounting, using a rate of 0.045.

at this step, both on a per-participant basis and on a program basis as a whole.

Sometimes a benefit–cost ratio is reported. This ratio can be readily computed by dividing the benefits by the costs (benefits/cost). A ratio of 1.0 indicates that the program's benefits equal its costs; this is sometimes known as the breakeven point. A ratio greater than 1.0 indicates that benefits outweigh the costs. A ratio below 1.0 indicates that costs are higher than benefits. Thus the higher the benefit–cost ratio, the greater the efficiency of the program.

Applying the Procedure

As was shown in Step 4a, the average annual cost for each participant in our Aim High Program was $3,174. As was shown in Step 4b, the annual benefit for each participant was $2,820 per year. As was shown in Step 4c, the adjusted benefit value was $2,669 for the first year. Table 13.3 reports the costs, benefits, net benefits, and benefit–cost ratios of our program at three time intervals after the participants completed our program. Note that the benefits have been adjusted, as described in Step 4c.

As can be seen in Table 13.3, after 12 months, on a per-participant basis, the costs exceed benefits by $475. At the program level, with 130 participants served per year, the costs exceed benefits by $61,750 ($475 × 130 participants = $61,750). The benefit to cost ratio for the first year was 0.85.

At 24 months, the benefits exceed costs by $2,107 on an individual client basis and by $273,910 at the program level; the benefit–cost ratio rose from 0.85 at 12 months to 1.66 after 2 years out of the program.

After 36 months, the benefits exceed costs by $4,578 on an individual client basis and by $595,140 when looking at the program level; the benefit–cost ratio was 2.44 after 3 years out of our program. As is the case with most social service programs, the efficiency of a program depends, in part, on the selection of time at which its results are viewed. The further into the future the benefits are projected, the higher the benefit–cost ratio and the more efficient the program appears.

Using cost–benefit data, we can calculate our program's breakeven point—when the cost of our program is balanced by its benefits. Dividing the present value of benefits (after 12 months, $2,699) by 12, it can be calculated that the monthly value of these benefits during the first year is $225. With benefits accruing at the rate of $225 per month, the program cost of $3,174 is recovered in just over 14 months.

COST-EFFECTIVENESS ANALYSES

As has been discussed, there are differences between a cost–benefit and a cost-effectiveness analysis. This section highlights those differences and describes how a cost-effectiveness evaluation is conducted.

Table 13.3: **Cost–Benefit Analysis of the Aim High Program.**

Months After Program Completion	Participant Level	Program Level (130 clients per year)	Benefit–Cost Ratio
12	Benefit $2,699 Cost $3,174 Net (cost) benefit $(475)	Benefit $350,870 Cost $412,620 Net (cost) benefit $(61,750)	0.85
24	Benefit $5,281 Cost $3,174 Net (cost) benefit $2,107	Benefit $686,530 Cost $412,620 Net (cost) benefit $273,910	1.66
36	Benefit $7,752 Cost $3,174 Net (cost) benefit $4,578	Benefit $1,007,760 Cost $412,620 Net (cost) benefit $595,140	2.44

As we now know, efficiency analyses require an "accounting-minded" approach and are focused on the financial and economic aspects of a social service program and its outcomes. As we also know, a program may produce other outcomes that cannot be readily or reasonably expressed in financial terms. An effectiveness analysis, which does not try to establish a monetary value for a program's outcomes, provides only one way of examining efficiency. Simply put, a cost-effectiveness evaluation establishes the cost of achieving each unit of a program's outcome.

On the cost side, a cost-effectiveness analysis proceeds in much the same way as a cost–benefit analysis. In identifying outcomes, cost-effectiveness analyses depend on prior outcome evaluations, which will have identified relevant program outcomes. The process then continues by selecting the outcomes to be analyzed and determining the number of units of each outcome that have been achieved. For each outcome, it's then possible to determine the cost of each unit achieved by dividing the total program cost by the total number of units of outcome achieved.

As has been seen, in cost–benefit analyses it's necessary to select an accounting perspective and to consider only those costs and benefits that are relevant to the chosen perspective. This results in some outcomes being excluded from the analyses. In cost-effectiveness analyses, it's possible to mix perspectives and to report the costs of outcomes that are relevant to individual participants as well as to the funding source or some other entity, such as the program's stakeholders.

Applying the Procedure

Like all social service programs, our Aim High Program produced a variety of outcomes. These included an increase in basic academic skills of participants, an increase in self-esteem of participants, and competitive employment for participants. With these results in hand, it's possible to calculate their cost per unit achieved.

For example, the outcome evaluation found that approximately 30% of our program participants found employment. Taking the program-level data reported in Table 13.3, we know the annual cost of the program is $412,620. At the program level, with 130 clients served per year, we can expect that 30% or 39 clients will find employment at a total program cost of $412,620.

We can now calculate the cost for each participant to find a job by dividing the total program costs by the number of participants who found jobs. In the case of our Aim High Program, it costs $10,580 per participant to find a job ($412,620/39 = $10,580).

If all of our participants found jobs, the cost per job found would be much lower, $3,174. Thus it should be noted that the very best our program could do, on the efficiency side of things, would be to have all of our 130 participants find jobs at $3,174 per participant.

A FEW WORDS ABOUT EFFICIENCY-FOCUSED EVALUATIONS

As shown, evaluations of efficiency put a clear focus on the financial and economic aspects of programs. This is particularly true in the case of cost–benefit analyses. Advocates of efficiency-focused evaluations argue that, unless there is a good understanding of the financial efficiency of a program, any evaluation will necessarily be incomplete. They contend that efficiency-focused evaluations will put decision-makers in a position where they can make better and more rational decisions.

As a result, the scarce resources available to support social service programs will be used most efficiently. Such thinking is consistent with the growing trend in our society to make decisions based on economic criteria.

Although there is a certain validity to these claims, critics point out that efficiency-focused evaluations are not without their limitations and shortcomings. First, from a practical point of view, as should be now evident by reading this chapter, the evaluation of efficiency, particularly cost–benefit analyses, requires a technical approach with a high level of skill on the part of the evaluator. Few social service organizations employ staff members with these skills; therefore, they face the additional expense of having to hire outside consultants to undertake such work.

Maintaining the kind of financial records and data that are required to analyze the costs and benefits of social service programs also adds to the costs of such evaluations. These costs will further increase when an agency operates several programs at the same time, shares social workers between and among programs, or uses common space such as a gym or playground—the list can be endless.

Also adding to the mix is that some clients are enrolled in more than one program within the same agency at the same time. Sometimes they are also being seen by another program in a different agency as well.

From a technical perspective, there may be a reliance on estimates and assumptions throughout the process. First, cost data are often not available to complete detailed cost analyses, and thus estimates must be used. Next, it's not easy to place a dollar value on many outcomes of interest, and assumptions must be made in assigning dollar values to such benefits.

Moreover, some benefits cannot be monetized at all and are therefore ignored in the calculations. Furthermore, projecting benefits into the future is difficult and again requires assumptions on the part of the evaluators. The more that estimates and assumptions are used in completing an evaluation, the more the results must be treated with caution.

From a more philosophical perspective, critics point to the fact that the evaluation of efficiency is based on a concept of utilitarianism. This is an economic-philosophical view that holds that social service organizations should weigh the costs and benefits of a proposed course of action and proceed to establish a program only if its "benefits" to the clients it will serve will exceed the program's "costs."

This perspective is clearly dominant within the for-profit sector where investments and products are judged by whether they will produce a profit. In the social services, however, it's not always desirable to make decisions based on utilitarian considerations. The ethics and values of our professions call for action based on what is right, is just, and enhances human dignity and well-being. Thus we strongly believe it may be desirable to proceed with a social service program even if its benefits cannot be shown to exceed its costs.

For example, many individual and group counseling programs are concerned with assisting people to live more effective and fulfilling lives. Although the costs of such programs can be established, it would be very difficult to place a dollar value on the program's outcomes. Should such programs therefore be abandoned?

Alternatively, consider the case of two assisted living programs for the elderly. Program A has been shown to be more cost efficient than Program B. However, the residents in Program B feel much happier and more comfortable than the residents in Program A. A decision based entirely on financial efficiency would dictate that the decision-maker chose Program A to fund as the desirable model. In cost–benefit calculations, little or no weight is given to outcomes such as the happiness or comfort of the residents.

SUMMARY

This chapter discussed two common types of efficiency-focused evaluations: cost–benefit evaluations and cost-effectiveness evaluations. There is little doubt that such evaluations have the potential to provide valuable information to decision-makers and stakeholders. At the same time, it's important to understand and recognize the limitations inherent in efficiency-focused evaluations.

The goal of this chapter is to provide you with a beginning knowledge base for you to feel comfortable in answering the following questions. AFTER you have read the chapter, indicate how comfortable you feel you are in answering each of the following questions on a 5-point scale where

1 Very uncomfortable	2 Somewhat uncomfortable	3 Neutral	4 Somewhat comfortable	5 Very comfortable

If you rated any question between 1–3, reread the section of the chapter where the information for the question is found. If you still feel that you're uncomfortable in answering the question, then talk with your instructor and/or your classmates for more clarification.

	Questions	**Degree of comfort?** *(Circle one number)*
1	In your own words, define an efficiency evaluation. Provide a social work example throughout your discussion.	1 2 3 4 5
2	Discuss the differences between a cost-effectiveness evaluation and cost-benefit evaluation. Provide a social work example of each one.	1 2 3 4 5
3	List and then discuss all of the steps of doing a cost-benefit evaluation. Then discuss how you would do one within your field placement (or work) setting.	1 2 3 4 5
4	Describe the similarities and differences between "an individual program's participants' perspective" and "the funding source's perspective" when it comes to cost–benefit analyses.	1 2 3 4 5
5	Discuss how you would go about determining your costs (e.g., Table 13.1) when doing a cost–benefit analysis of obtaining your social work degree. What are your costs?	1 2 3 4 5
6	Discuss how you would go about determining your benefits (e.g., Table 13.1) when doing a cost–benefit analysis of obtaining your social work degree. What are your benefits?	1 2 3 4 5
7	Using your responses to Questions 5 and 6, produce a table that is similar to Table 13.1 when it comes to your obtaining your social work degree.	1 2 3 4 5
8	In relation to Question 7, produce a table like Table 13.2. Simply make up reasonable data when it comes to determining the costs and benefits.	1 2 3 4 5
9	In relation to Question 8, produce a table like Table 13.3.	1 2 3 4 5

Chapter **13**				Assessing Your Self-Efficacy

AFTER you have read this chapter AND have completed all of the study questions, indicate how knowledgeable you feel you are for each of the following concepts on a 5-point scale where

1 Not knowledgeable at all	2 Somewhat unknowledgeable	3 Neutral	4 Somewhat knowledgeable	5 Very knowledgeable

	Concepts	Knowledge Level? *(Circle one number)*
1	Efficiency evaluations, in general	1 2 3 4 5
2	Cost–benefit analyses	1 2 3 4 5
3	Cost-effectiveness analyses	1 2 3 4 5
4	Calculating costs	1 2 3 4 5
5	Calculating benefits	1 2 3 4 5
6	The steps of doing a cost–benefit analyses	1 2 3 4 5
7	Calculating present value of total benefits	1 2 3 4 5
8	Calculating benefit–cost ratios	1 2 3 4 5
9	Advantages and disadvantages of efficiency-focused evaluations	1 2 3 4 5
10	Differences among efficiency evaluations, outcome evaluations (Chapter 12), process evaluations (Chapter 11), and needs assessments (Chapter 10)	1 2 3 4 5
	Add up your scores (minimum = 10, maximum = 50)	Your total score =

A	47–50 = Professional evaluator in the making
A–	45–46 = Senior evaluator
B+	43–44 = Junior evaluator
B	41–42 = Assistant evaluator
B–	10–40 = Reread the chapter and redo the study questions

PART IV

Making Decisions With Data

After your evaluation is completed (Part III), you need to make decisions from the data you collected—the purpose of Part IV.

This part contains two chapters. The first describes how to develop a data information system (**Chapter 14**), and the second describes how to make decisions from the data that have been collected in the data information system (**Chapter 15**).

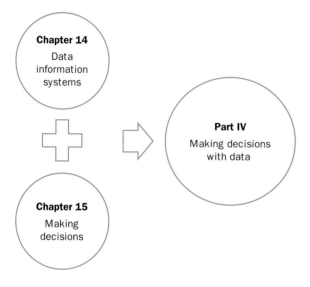

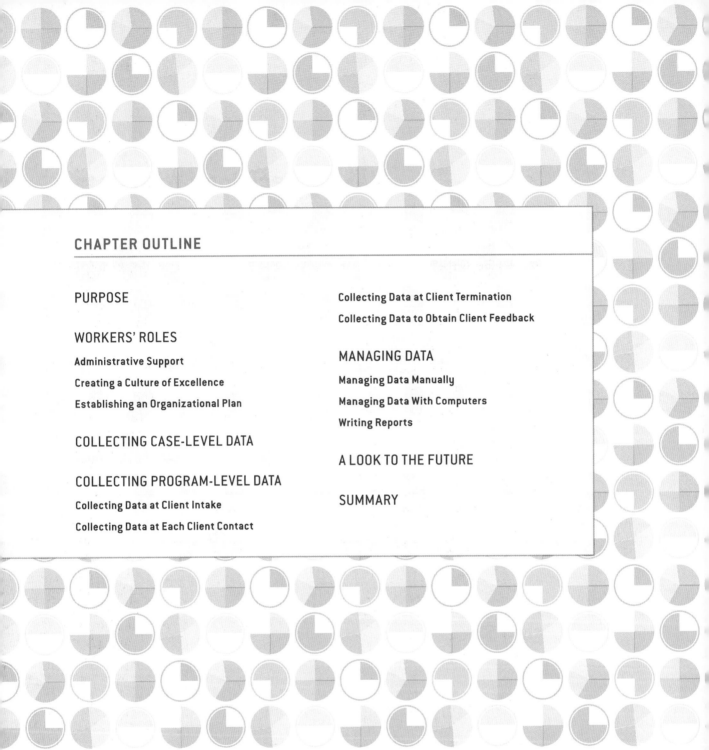

CHAPTER OUTLINE

Information is not knowledge.

~ Albert Einstein

Chapter 14

DATA INFORMATION SYSTEMS

As we know, data collection is not a haphazard activity. In short, it's not undertaken in the hope that the data we collect during an evaluation will somehow be useful to someone in some place at some time. Data collection procedures must reflect a careful analysis of information needs at all levels within the social service program and should provide for the collection of useful data in the least disruptive, most economical, and most efficient manner possible.

The data collected—and eventually stored—for evaluations of all kinds can be loosely characterized as a data information system. Within this system, specific data are collected, analyzed, and reported. Of course, systems of any kind may function well or not so well. Some evaluations are inadequately planned, resulting in a lack of coherence in data collection, analyses, and reporting. As we learned from Chapter 9, others can be nicely planned and function well in that they collect the right data, in the right form, and at the right time, so they can be readily analyzed and subsequently reported to the stakeholders.

PURPOSE

A data information system should be designed in a way that data collected at any stage of the program are demonstrably relevant to the future decisions to be made. Data collected by front-line workers, for example, should bear upon, in the first instance, the decisions they are required to make for their clients' practice and program objectives. Thus the data they collect must guide their clinical decision-making.

At the same time, these data must be capable of being aggregated in a timely manner that is relevant to administrators and other stakeholders interested in your program's outcomes. Essentially, an effective information system should:

- Recognize that different data needs exist among different stakeholder groups
- Be capable of delivering needed information to all levels of stakeholders in a timely manner and in a format usable at that level

WORKERS' ROLES

Designing, developing, and maintaining an effective information system is not only a technical matter; social service issues also need consideration. Staff members, as human beings, may have reactions that range from skepticism to resistance when faced with the introduction of a data information system. These reactions are related not only to the personality and experience of the individual but also to the collective experience of the evaluation workgroup and the organization. Where recent experience includes reorganization, restructuring, and questionable use of previous evaluation results, staff members will understandably react with suspicion, if not outright hostility (Gabor & Sieppert, 1999).

Establishing and maintaining a data information system requires the cooperation of all program staff, from line-level workers through senior administrators. Inevitably, much of the burden of data collection falls on the line-level workers. Involving them in the planning and design of the information system helps to ensure that information needs at the direct-service level will be met and that data can be collected without undue disruption to service provision. Moreover, the involvement of line-level workers helps to secure their cooperation and commitment to the entire evaluation process.

Administrative Support

Administrators must commit the necessary resources for the implementation of the system, including providing adequate training and continual support. The design and implementation of an information system is expensive—very expensive. Computer hardware and software may have to be purchased, and consultation fees and training costs probably will be incurred. Providing adequate training and support to professional workers and staff is not just a vital consideration—it's a must.

Training is particularly necessary if the new system introduces computerization. Often, administrators will not hesitate to spend tens of thousands of dollars on equipment but will skimp on training the personnel who are to use it. This is shortsighted; as a general rule, administrators should expect to spend at least one dollar for training for every dollar spent on equipment.

Creating a Culture of Excellence

It's very important that an evaluation be carried out within an organizational culture that acknowledges that social service programs inevitably fall short of perfection. As we know by now, the purpose of an evaluation is not to assign blame; it's to provide better client services by identifying a program's strengths and limitations so that the former can be reinforced and the latter corrected.

An attitude of continuous learning and developing is the essence of a progressive organization; the data information system generates feedback that facilitates good social work practice. When the overall goal is improvement and development, and workers can see how the contribution of an effective information system leads to that goal, they are more likely to cooperate and contribute to the effective functioning of the information system.

Establishing an Organizational Plan

As previously discussed, effective data information systems are the result of careful planning and design as well as negotiation and compromise. Early involvement in the planning of the system by front-line workers, administrators, and other relevant stakeholders is important. Any data collection plan must take into account at least three sets of needs:

- Data collection must meet **case-level decision-making needs**, serving decisions to be made immediately as well as those made throughout the client's progress within the program. Certain data, for example, are required at client intake to decide whether to accept a referral. Once accepted, the client may go through a formal assessment procedure, at which point further data will likely be collected. Other stages of service provision will require yet more data. The case-level information system should be designed to take advantage of—and build on—the existing data collection system.
- The system design must accommodate the program-level decision-making responsibilities of the **administrators and other stakeholders**. To avoid the creation of parallel evaluation systems at the case and program levels, the latter should be designed to make as much use of data collected for case-level evaluation as is possible. This often entails the aggregation of case-level data.
- Technical requirements of **the system** must also be considered. The system will require certain types of data, formats, data collection procedures, and analytic capabilities.

COLLECTING CASE-LEVEL DATA

Perhaps the best way to decide what data are needed at the case level is to follow a client through the program by way of a client path flow. Figure 14.1 presents an example of a client flowchart illustrating the sequence of events in a child protection program.

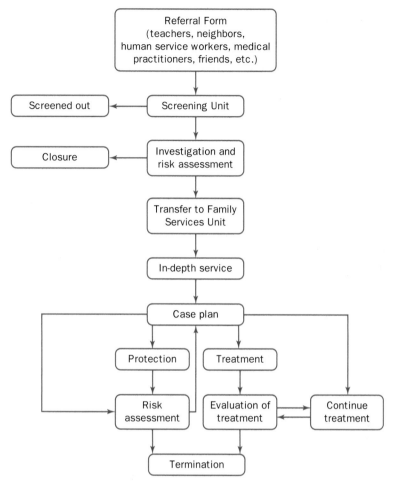

Figure 14.1: **Client flowchart for a child protection program.**

The beginning of the process is the referral. Suspected neglect or abuse may be reported by a variety of people, including relatives, teachers, neighbors, and health-care workers. All referrals are immediately directed to the screening unit. Because every allegation of child abuse must be looked into, at this point the two most relevant pieces of data are the age and place of residence of the alleged victim.

Within a short period, a screening worker normally contacts the referring source as well as the family to verify the complaint and to obtain further details. Based on this information, the worker decides whether a full investigation is warranted. If so, an investigating worker will likely interview the alleged victim and will probably interview relevant others as well.

As with every activity, each interview has a specific purpose. The purpose of interviewing the alleged victim is fourfold:

- To verify that the alleged abuse has in fact occurred
- To ensure the immediate safety of the child
- To determine whether treatment is needed
- To determine what treatment would be best in addition to informing the child and others connected to the case about what will happen next

The investigating worker will conduct this interview on the basis of data collected by the screening worker and will need data in the following general areas:

- Specific circumstances of the alleged abuse
- Specific circumstances in which it was disclosed
- Data about the child
- Data about the family

The screening form thus must be designed to incorporate these different data needs. From a case-level perspective, then, the data collected at screening serves two broad purposes:

- To make a decision about whether a further investigation is warranted
- To provide the investigating worker with initial information data

Because a monitoring system is intended to provide needed and timely data to staff members, and because front-line workers themselves will be in the best position to know what data they need to help them in their decision-making, front-line workers should be involved in designing forms.

When the investigation is complete, the data are used to assess the degree of continuing risk to the child. On this basis, the worker determines whether further services are required. Continuing cases are transferred from the screening unit to the family services unit, where a worker is assigned to the family to coordinate protection and treatment functions.

The family services unit worker then conducts a full assessment based on the data provided by the investigating worker in the screening unit as well as any additional data collected. The purpose of assessment is to develop an in-depth understanding of the situation and of child and family needs so that an appropriate intervention plan can be established. In other words, data collected during assessment are used in making decisions about the client's case plan.

As Figure 14.1 indicates, the case plan formulated may have both a protection component and a treatment component. Client practice objectives are established in relation to both of these components, and data collected during service provision are used to assess the degree to which activities are achieving the practice objectives. Case-level data will also be needed subsequently, in aggregated form, for program evaluation purposes. Thus, when determining what data are to be collected for case-level evaluations, it's also important to take into consideration the data that are needed for the program's evaluation needs.

Termination criteria for protection and treatment often differ. Protection workers are likely to focus on the continuing safety of the child, whereas treatment workers may focus on family functioning. The family may therefore still be undergoing treatment when protection services have been discontinued. Ultimately, when the decision to terminate all services is made, the case can be closed.

As is evident, data collection is not a matter of randomly assembling whatever data come to hand. The data collected in each phase should be fully and firmly linked to the objectives of the particular phase, the decisions to be made during the phase, and the data needs of subsequent phases. Insufficient data lead to poor decision-making; overly profuse and irrelevant data result in a lack of clarity and unnecessary costs.

To ensure that there is adequate congruence between the data collected and the decisions to be made, a data collection analysis can be undertaken. This analysis lists the following, in chronological order:

- The decisions to be made
- The data needed to make each decision
- The actual data collected

Data collection protocols need to be revised if there is a discrepancy between what data are needed and what data are actually being collected,

COLLECTING PROGRAM-LEVEL DATA

Data collection at any program stage must be designed to fulfill the data needs of both line-level workers and administrators alike. From the perspective of a multi-program agency, for example, it's often useful to identify the main data collection events for each program. Typically, a program collects data at intake, at every contact with a client, and at termination. Other data collection events may be planned, depending on circumstances and needs.

Forms	Programs				
	Information	Education	Parent Support	Counseling	Mediation
• Intake	X	X	X	X	X
• Assessment				X	X
• Contact Notes (Intervention period)			X	X	X
• Termination			X	X	X
Self-Report Satisfaction					
• Nonstandardized		X		X	X
• Standardized	X	X	X	X	X

Figure 14.2: **Example of a data collection plan.**

A specific plan for identifying the key data collection events for a family service agency, for example, across five of its programs is presented in Figure 14.2. As you can see, the agency has five programs: an Information Program, an Education Program, a Parent Support Program, a Counseling Program, and a Mediation Program.

Each cell marked with an "X" represents a major data collection event for which a corresponding data collection instrument (or form) can be designed. In the case of this agency, the four major data collection events are at client intake, assessment, client contacts (intervention period), and termination. In addition, two kinds of data relating to client satisfaction are also included in Figure 14.2:

- Nonstandardized self-report data
- Standardized self-report data

The nonstandardized data could be collected via Figure 14.8 for example, and the standardized data could be collected via Figures M.1, M.2, and M.3 in Tool M. Once the information needs are identified, data collection forms can be designed for each of these purposes.

To illustrate this point, consider the counseling program operated by the agency. The service is

funded by the Department of Social Services (DSS) to provide counseling services to DSS clients with psychosocial problems who need more help than the brief instrumentally oriented counseling of the DSS can provide. Figure 14.3 shows part of an intake form that new clients might complete in the center's office while they are waiting for a first interview.

Collecting Data at Client Intake

The intake form is usually the first document in the client's file. Of course, different programs need different or additional data. A job-training program, for example, will likely ask about jobs previously held, previous income, reason for present unemployment, and participation in other job-training programs.

An individual intake form provides data for a case record, but it's not very useful for program evaluation purposes unless the data are aggregated with other intake forms. Figure 14.4 provides four simple tabular reports on the counseling program compiled by aggregating the data from 200 individual client intake forms for the month of January. These reports are examples of information related to client characteristics.

Figure 14.4 shows at a glance that 200 new clients were accepted into the program during the month of

Name: _____

Current Address: _____

Telephone Number: _____

TYPES OF SERVICE SOUGHT (circle one number below):

    1. Individual counseling

    2. Couple counseling

    3. Family counseling

    4. Other (please specify _____)

SEX (circle one number below):

    1. Male

    2. Female

BIRTH DATE _____

REFERRAL SOURCE (circle one number below):

    1. Self

    2. Friends, family

    3. Physician

    4. Clergy

    5. Department of Social Services

    6. Other agency

    4. Other (please specify _____)

REASONS FOR SEEKING SERVICES (Program Objectives). Circle one number below:

    1. Marital problems

    2. Family problems

    3. Problems at school

    4. Problems at work

    5. Parent—child problems

    6. Health problems

    7. Substance abuse

    8. Personal adjustment problems

    9. Other (please specify _____)

Figure 14.3: **Example of a client intake form.**

January, 63% of whom were referred by DSS. The program is thus able to document the degree to which it's achieving one of its output objectives: providing services to clients referred by DSS.

Equally important, if referrals from DSS fall short of objectives, staff members will be able to spot this trend immediately and take steps to better meet the program's mandate, or perhaps to negotiate an adjustment of this mandate if new circumstances have arisen. The point of importance is that monitoring provides ongoing feedback that helps to ensure continuing achievement of a program's mandate: to see clients referred by DSS.

Contrast this with the situation of a program that undertakes occasional evaluations. By the time data indicating a problem with DSS referrals are analyzed and reported, the problem will have existed for a period of time and is likely to have serious consequences. In all likelihood, the program's reputation among the DSS workers will have suffered. The DSS may even have concluded that, because this program

Sex of Client		
Sex	Number	Percent
Male	90	45
Female	110	55
Total	200	100
Age of Clients		
Age Range	Number	Percent
10-19	30	15
20-29	78	39
30-39	42	21
40-49	28	14
50-59	12	6
60+	10	5
Total	200	100
Referral Sources of Clients		
Sources	Number	Percent
Self	8	4
Friends, family	12	6
Physicians	8	4
Clergy	10	5
DSS	126	63
Other agencies	28	14
Other	8	4
Total	200	100
Reasons Clients Requesting Services (Program Objectives)		
Presenting Problems	Number	Percent
Marital problems	18	9
Family problems	40	20
Problems at school	28	14
Problems at work	12	6
Parent—child problems	30	15
Health problems	20	10
Substance abuse	22	11

Figure 14.4: **Excerpts for a monthly intake report for January (from Figure 14.3).**

is not providing adequate service, alternative services should be contracted.

The report also provides other useful data. Tables reporting the frequency distribution of the sex and age of new clients provide the data required to ensure that the program is attracting the type of clients for whom it was established. Assume that another one of the program's output objectives is to attract 100 adolescents and young adults each month. Figure 14.4 indicates that 54% of new clients are 29 years of age or under. These kinds of data indicate that the program is on the right track.

On the other hand, if an objective had been to provide services to a large number of senior citizens, data revealing that only 5% of new clients are 60 years of age or over would be cause for concern (see Figure 14.4). A program is unlikely to undertake extensive changes on the basis of data for 1 month, but if several consecutive monthly reports were to indicate that older people constitute only a small percentage of new clients, staff may well conclude that a problem exists and needs to be addressed.

Collecting Data at Each Client Contact

The course of service provision can be followed by completing, after each session, a client contact form, such as the one illustrated in Figure 14.5. The form is designed to provide workers with the information they need to maintain a record of services provided and also to provide data to the information system for evaluation purposes.

The form is designed for easy completion, using primarily a check-box format for entering the data. At the end of the form, there is a space for the workers' anecdotal notes, which may be made in the manner preferred by each worker. All but the anecdotal information is designed to be ultimately transferred into the information system. After identifying data for the client and worker are entered, the type of service and service location are specified.

As discussed, these are the types of data that make it possible for service statistics to be compiled and reported on a regular basis. In this case, counseling is the service provided. Because the data are captured at this point, it will later be possible to track the number of counseling sessions provided to the client. The record also makes it possible to track the total number of counseling sessions provided within the program and the agency. Similarly, noting the service location or whether the service was provided by telephone will make it possible to generate a description of services provided by location.

Quality standards were also identified as one possible focus of an evaluation. The present client contact form records data about whether the service was provided to an individual or a larger unit within the family and also whether community resource suggestions were made. These data can later be compiled to provide a profile of the client system to which services are provided and the number of community resources suggested in this case. Because the agency had set objectives regarding these benchmarks, capturing the data on the client contact form tracks the extent to which these benchmarks have been met.

On this contact form, provision is also made for recording the length of the session and the length of preparation, including travel time and paperwork. These data reflect administrative needs. Management wanted to track the costs associated with moving services out of the center and decided that, for a period of time, data should be collected that would provide information about such costs. By tracking time spent in travel and preparation, the additional costs related to moving services out of the center can be easily determined.

Finally, the client contact form records the results of any measurements that were completed during service provision. In this case, a practice objective was self-esteem improvement, and Hudson's *Index of Self-Esteem* was used as the measure (see Figure L.1 in Tool L). The current week's score on the instrument, 39, is recorded for this practice objective. There is a provision for recording other scores as well.

These data can be used to follow changes in practice objectives during the course of the intervention, can be aggregated into monthly summaries (as shown at the bottom-half of Figure 14.7), and, ultimately, can be employed in a one-group pretest–posttest evaluation design (e.g., Figure E.6 in Tool E).

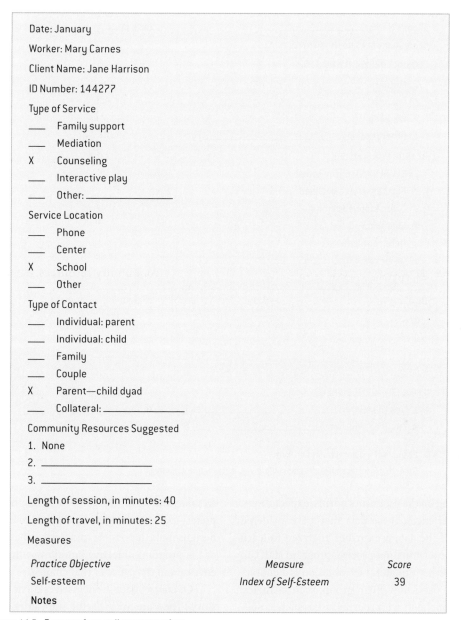

Date: January

Worker: Mary Carnes

Client Name: Jane Harrison

ID Number: 144277

Type of Service

____   Family support

____   Mediation

X   Counseling

____   Interactive play

____   Other: _____

Service Location

____   Phone

____   Center

X   School

____   Other

Type of Contact

____   Individual: parent

____   Individual: child

____   Family

____   Couple

X   Parent—child dyad

____   Collateral: _____

Community Resources Suggested

1. None

2. _____

3. _____

Length of session, in minutes: 40

Length of travel, in minutes: 25

Measures

Practice Objective	Measure	Score
Self-esteem	Index of Self-Esteem	39

Notes

Figure 14.5: **Excerpts from a client contact form.**

Note: This form measures practice objectives, not program objectives.

Collecting Data at Client Termination

When the case is closed, a termination form is completed. On this form, data regarding the nature of termination as well as the final level of outcomes can be recorded. Moreover, the need for any follow-up can also be noted. Data from client terminations can also be aggregated and summarized. An example of a client termination form is provided in Figure 14.6.

Figure 14.7 provides excerpts from a summary report of cases closed in the counseling unit during one recent month. These data are the result of aggregating data from clients' intake and termination forms. Aggregating data in this manner provides information that is very useful in understanding program functioning. We can readily see, for example, that over a third (36%) of the clients who terminated did so unilaterally.

Client's Name: _____   Date (M-D-Y) __ __ __

Client Identification Number: _____

CLOSURE DECISION WAS:

1. Mutual
2. Client's
3. Worker's
4. Other (specify _____)

REASON FOR CLOSURE:

1. Service no longer needed
2. Further service declined
3. Client stopped coming
4. Client moved
5. Referred elsewhere
6. Other (specify _____)

PROGRAM OBJECTIVES:

Objective	Score	Measuring Instrument
1.		
2.		
3.		
4.		

IS FOLLOW-UP REQUIRED?

1. Yes (if so, why _____)
2. No (if so, why not _____)

Figure 14.6: **Example of a client termination form.**
Note: This form measures program objectives, not practice objectives.

Depending on the program's norms, expectations, and past experiences, these data may be considered problematic. If the data are further analyzed to learn more about the termination process, program staff can determine whether unilateral termination is a characteristic of any particular client group, such as males, older clients, or clients with specific issues such as substance abuse. Such data are invaluable in diagnosing the problem and deciding on a program's adjustments and modifications. Data from subsequent reports will then shed light on the success of the measures adopted.

Data pertaining to the degree that our clients (as a group) achieved a program objective are also useful. Comparing the average objective score at the beginning with the average score at termination for a group of clients provides data about the group's net change achieved with respect to the program objective. Doing so takes the form, in research terms, of a one-group, pretest–posttest design (e.g., Figure E.6 in Tool E). Such designs make it possible to describe change in the level of the program objective but allow only limited inferences about the cause of that change.

Of course, data in themselves do not tell the whole story. They are very useful indicators, but their full interpretation requires careful attention to contextual variables and issues. For instance, it's possible that the relatively modest results achieved with clients experiencing marital and family problems is attributable to factors other than the way in which the program is designed and delivered. It may be that two of the more experienced workers have been on leave for the past several months.

Perhaps one of these positions was covered by temporarily reassigning a less experienced worker while the other position was left vacant. Thus, during

Cases Terminated		
Method of Termination	Number	Percent
Mutual consent	25	50
Client's decision	18	36
Worker's decision	7	14
Totals	50	100
Average of Clients' Program Objectives		
Objectives	Beginning	End	n
Self-esteem	61	42	12
Peer relations	57	37	4
Depression	42	27	4
Marital satisfaction	51	8	6
Clinical stress	47	41	9
Alcohol involvement	40	1	4
Partner abuse	52	42	1
Sexual satisfaction	66	60	5
Anxiety	52	41	5
Total			50

Note: All program objectives are measured with Hudson's Scales as reported in Nurius and Hudson, 1993. High scores = higher levels of problem.

Figure 14.7: **Excerpts from a monthly summary report of closed cases.**

the preceding several months, fewer marital counseling and family therapy hours may have been delivered, by less experienced staff. This could obviously have affected client outcomes. In general, interpreting the data resulting from evaluation requires consideration of contextual variables and cannot be done purely on the basis of quantitative results.

Collecting Data to Obtain Client Feedback

Satisfaction with a social service program often becomes a focus for a process evaluation. Thus staff members depicted in the earlier illustrations have determined that it would be useful to obtain feedback from program participants regarding various aspects of their satisfaction. Consequently, a satisfaction survey was developed, which clients are asked to complete at the time of service closure. An example

of a very simple nonstandardized client satisfaction survey instrument is provided in Figure 14.8. Also see Figures M.1, M.2, and M.3 in Tool M for standardized instruments that measure the clients' satisfaction with the services they have received.

Again, such data are most useful when aggregated across clients. An excerpt from such an analysis is provided in Figure 14.9. As may be seen, a large majority of clients consider the services helpful and the staff members supportive, and think themselves better off as a result of services. As well, two-thirds would recommend the services to others, and about 68% indicate a high or very high level of overall satisfaction with the program.

Staff members may react to summaries such as those shown in Figures 14.7 and 14.9 in a number of ways. They may resent that their work is being

Please provide us with feedback on our services by completing the following brief questionnaire. For each question, circle one response.

1. The services received were helpful:

   Strongly Disagree   Disagree   Agree   Strongly Agree

2. Staff members were supportive:

   Strongly Disagree   Disagree   Agree   Strongly Agree

3. I am better off as a result of these services:

   Strongly Disagree   Disagree   Agree   Strongly Agree

4. I would recommend these services to others:

   Strongly Disagree   Disagree   Agree   Strongly Agree

5. My overall satisfaction with these services is:

   Very Low   Low   Moderate   High   Very High

6. Comments or suggestions:

Figure 14.8: **Example of a nonstandardized client satisfaction survey.**

scrutinized, particularly if the monthly summary has been newly instituted. Where the results suggest that there is room for improvement (which is often the case), they may be uncertain of their own competence and, perhaps, feel that they are being judged. Alternatively, or perhaps in addition, they may be alerted to the fact that they may need to modify their interventional approaches to improve their clients' satisfaction.

Which of these feelings predominates depends to some extent on the way the information system was introduced to the practitioners. Workers who were consulted about the system's development, informed about its advantages, and involved in its design and implementation are more likely to regard the monthly summaries as useful feedback. Staff members that were neither consulted nor involved are likely to regard them with apprehension and resentment.

Equally important in shaping the attitudes of line-level workers to data collection is how the agency's administrators uses, or abuses, the data generated. If the data are used in a judgmental, critical manner, social workers are likely to remain skeptical and defensive about the monitoring process. Where the data are regarded as useful feedback and are used in a genuine, cooperative effort to upgrade and further develop services, workers will likely welcome such reports as tools that can help them—and the program—improve.

These considerations suggest that administrators should view evaluation data as a means of assisting them in identifying areas for improvement and in identifying factors in problems and difficulties. Obviously, this approach is far more likely to evoke a positive response than one in which undesirable results signal the beginning of a search to assign blame.

Administrators' responsibilities do not, however, end here. To foster a truly positive environment for evaluation, administrators should not only be concerned with pinpointing potential trouble spots but should also be committed to supporting their line-level workers' efforts to improve the program's overall effectiveness and efficiency. These are key roles for an administrator of any social service organization.

MANAGING DATA

Effective data information systems are powered by information gleaned from the data. As programs become more complex, and as evaluation becomes an increasingly important function, organizations require increasingly sophisticated data management capabilities. Data management includes collection and recording; aggregation, integration, and analyses; and reporting. These functions may be carried out manually, through the use of computers, or through

The services I received were helpful.		
	Number	Percent
Strongly Disagree	22	11
Disagree	36	18
Agree	94	47
Strongly Agree	48	24
Totals	200	100

Staff members were supportive.		
	Number	Percent
Strongly Disagree	18	9
Disagree	38	19
Agree	88	44
Strongly Agree	56	28
Totals	200	100

I am better off as a result of these services.		
	Number	Percent
Strongly Disagree	30	15
Disagree	46	23
Agree	98	49
Strongly Agree	26	13
Totals	200	100

I would recommend these services to others.		
	Number	Percent
Strongly Disagree	40	20
Disagree	30	15
Agree	74	37
Strongly Agree	56	28
Totals	200	100

My overall satisfaction with these services is...		
	Number	Percent
Low	24	12
Moderate	40	20
High	90	45
Very High	46	23
Totals	200	100

Figure 14.9: **Program-level report of results from a client satisfaction survey (from data collected via the form in Figure 14.8).**

a combination of manual and computer-based methods.

Managing Data Manually

Not long ago, most data management functions were undertaken manually. Data collection forms were designed, completed in longhand or by word processors, and usually placed in case files. The need to produce specific data—for example, looking at the referral sources of all new cases in the last 6 months—usually entailed a manual search of all new case files as well as manual aggregation and analyses of the data. Although such a system could unearth the required data, the process was cumbersome and labor intensive.

As organizations found that they were called upon to generate certain types of data on a regular basis, they developed methods for manually copying specific data (e.g., referral sources, age, sex of client, presenting problem) from client records onto composite forms or spreadsheets. In this way, manually searching files for the required data is easily avoided. However, the composite forms or spreadsheets were still analyzed manually.

Although these procedures were an improvement, such a system was limited not only because manual analyses were time consuming but also because they could provide only the data that had been identified for aggregation. A need for data other than that which had been included on the spreadsheet still entailed a manual search of all relevant files.

Obviously, manual methods are labor intensive and costly. They are also limited in their flexibility and in their capacity to quickly deliver needed data. It's not surprising that, with the ready availability of powerful desktop computers, social service organizations have increasingly turned to computer-based data management systems.

Managing Data With Computers

Computers can be used in both case- and program-level evaluations. Because computers increase the capacity for data management and make the process more efficient, their use in recent years has dramatically increased.

Even so, at this time, few social service organizations rely entirely on computers for data management. Usually, data management systems are a combination of manual and computer-based methods. Manual functions, however, are decreasing, and, correspondingly, computer-based functions are increasing. The trend is clear: computers are becoming increasingly important in evaluation. Typically, data are collected manually through the completion of forms and measuring instruments. At this point, the data are often entered into the computer, which maintains and manages the data and carries out the required aggregation and analyses.

The computer can easily assist, for example, with the aggregation and analysis of case-level monitoring data. Figure 14.7 illustrated this process, using the example of an agency where workers routinely use standardized measuring instruments to track changes in their clients' program objective(s). As may be seen, the computer has selected all clients who had program objectives related to self-esteem during a specified period of time and calculated the average initial (Beginning) and final (End) self-esteem scores for those clients.

There were 12 clients in the group, and the average score for the group dropped from 61 at the beginning of service to 42 at termination, a considerable decline in problems with self-esteem. In this instance, the data management capabilities of the computer readily allowed a one-group pretest–posttest evaluation design to be carried out.

Further analyses can be conducted on these results to determine whether the decline is statistically significant. A variety of computer programs can rapidly carry out such data analyses. This represents a major advantage over manual data analyses, as most statistical computations tend to be complex, cumbersome, and time consuming. With today's statistical software packages, the required computations can be easily and accurately accomplished; indeed, more sophisticated procedures, prohibitively time consuming when done by hand, also become possible.

Similarly, the computer analysis can readily provide data on other points of focus: service data, client characteristics, quality indicators, and client satisfaction. As in the case of the outcome data discussed previously, computers can refine analyses not only to provide data about the entire group but to answer more specific questions.

A computer can easily select clients who received services in conjunction with other family members (a quality indicator) and compare their outcomes with those who received individual services. Similarly, data pertaining to two or more operating periods can be compared. These are just two examples of powerful analyses that become possible through computers; the result is information, derived from data, that allows a deeper understanding of program and the services it provides.

There is a potential danger in the ready availability of such analytical power; people who have little knowledge or understanding of data analyses or statistics can easily carry out inappropriate procedures that may serve to mislead rather than inform. Nevertheless, when used knowledgeably, such statistical power makes more incisive analyses possible.

Using Relational Databases

Another group of software programs known as relational databases are also increasingly being used in data management. As the name suggests, these programs enable the linking of disparate data in a manner that makes it possible to look at and understand data in different ways.

Through linking the data contained on client contact forms with information on intake and termination forms, for example, it may be possible to analyze the relationship between initial presenting problems, the course of service provision, and client outcomes. Virtually unlimited flexibility in analyzing data is provided by such programs, which leads to an increasingly more sophisticated understanding of programs, services, and their specific elements. Peter Gabor and Jackie Sieppert (1999) provide a detailed example of one such system.

Writing Reports

Regular evaluation reports provide continuous feedback for line-level workers and administrators alike.

Essentially, they provide the same data, updated for new cases, on a regular basis. Examples of such reports are provided in Figures 14.4, 14.7, and 14.9.

As with other data management, computers are particularly useful in generating such reports. Software packages used to conduct statistical analyses or to maintain relational databases usually have provisions for repeating the same analyses. Basically, once a data analysis is specified, it can be run over and over again using updated data and producing updated reports.

Moreover, formats for reports containing tables, graphs, and charts as well as headings and labels can also be specified in advance. Using computers, there is an unlimited number of reports that can be generated, making it possible to provide timely information, tailored to the needs of staff members and other stakeholder groups. This, in turn, makes possible an ongoing, organization-wide quality improvement process.

A LOOK TO THE FUTURE

It's probably safe to predict that over the next few years computers, tablets, and other devices will play an increasingly important role in data management. With the ready availability of more powerful computer hardware and software programs, it's likely that many organizations will attempt to automate as much of their data management processes as is possible.

One prominent area for automation is the data entry process. Laptop computers make direct data entry feasible. Workers and clients will increasingly use electronic versions of forms, instruments, and questionnaires, entering data directly into laptop computers. Although it may be hard to picture workers and clients in the social services engaging in such activities, they are common practice in the business world.

It's only a matter of time until most people will have sufficient familiarity with computers to feel comfortable in interacting with and entering data into them. Already, many people are doing so through automatic tellers, voice mail, and electronic travel reservations.

Data entered directly into laptop computers will be electronically transferred into the organization's data management system, eliminating the need for completing paper copies and manually entering data into the system. This development will not only make data management more accurate and efficient but will also make possible the creation of larger, more powerful systems.

Such developments are probably inevitable. Though some might regard them with suspicion, computer-based information systems can be powerful tools in the service of quality improvement efforts. Ultimately, the technology represented by computerization is, in itself, neither good nor bad. Like any technology, it can be used well but it can also be misused. Clearly, evaluators and social service professionals alike will need to keep a close eye on such developments and ensure that computer use is congruent with professional values and ethics.

SUMMARY

This chapter stressed that the development of an information system in an existing social service program requires the full cooperation of both line-level workers and administrators. Front-line workers have an important role to play in the design and development of the system. Administrators must be prepared to provide training, support, and resources in addition to demonstrating that the monitoring system is intended to improve the program, not to assign blame.

The following chapter builds upon this one in that it presents how to make case- and program-level decisions using data.

The goal of this chapter is to provide you with a beginning knowledge base for you to feel comfortable in answering the following questions. AFTER you have read the chapter, indicate how comfortable you feel you are in answering each question on a 5-point scale where

1 Very uncomfortable	2 Somewhat uncomfortable	3 Neutral	4 Somewhat comfortable	5 Very comfortable

If you rated any question between 1–3, reread the section of the chapter where the information for the question is found. If you still feel that you're uncomfortable in answering the question, then talk with your instructor and/or your classmates for more clarification.

	Questions	Degree of comfort? *(Circle one number)*
1	In your own words, describe what data information systems are all about. Provide as many social work examples as you can to illustrate your points.	1 2 3 4 5
2	Describe the workers' roles when developing a data information system. Provide as many social work examples as you can to illustrate your points.	1 2 3 4 5
3	List and describe the three sets of needs when developing a data collection plan within a program. Provide as many social work examples as you can to illustrate your points.	1 2 3 4 5
4	Describe how you would go about collecting case-level data within your field practicum (or work) setting. Provide as many social work examples as you can to illustrate your points.	1 2 3 4 5
5	Describe how you would go about collecting program-level data within your field practicum (or work) setting. Provide as many social work examples as you can to illustrate your points.	1 2 3 4 5
6	Describe how you would go about collecting client intake data within your field practicum (or work) setting. Provide as many social work examples as you can to illustrate your points.	1 2 3 4 5
7	Describe how you would go about collecting client data for each contact you have with a client within your field practicum (or work) setting. Provide as many social work examples as you can to illustrate your points.	1 2 3 4 5
8	Describe how you would go about collecting client termination data within your field practicum (or work) setting. Provide as many social work examples as you can to illustrate your points.	1 2 3 4 5

continued

9	Describe how you would go about collecting client feedback data within your field practicum (or work) setting. Provide as many social work examples as you can to illustrate your points.	1 2 3 4 5
10	Describe how you would go about manually collecting data within your field practicum (or work) setting. Provide as many social work examples as you can to illustrate your points.	1 2 3 4 5
11	Describe how you would go about collecting data with computers within your field practicum (or work) setting. Provide as many social work examples as you can to illustrate your points.	1 2 3 4 5

AFTER you have read this chapter AND have completed all of the study questions, indicate how knowledgeable you feel you are for each of the following concepts on a 5-point scale where

1 Not knowledgeable at all	2 Somewhat unknowledgeable	3 Neutral	4 Somewhat knowledgeable	5 Very knowledgeable

	Concepts	Knowledge Level? *(Circle one number)*
1	Data information systems, in general	1 2 3 4 5
2	Designing an organizational plan to collect data within a program	1 2 3 4 5
3	Collecting case-level data	1 2 3 4 5
4	Collecting program-level data	1 2 3 4 5
5	Collecting data at client intake	1 2 3 4 5
6	Collecting data at each client contact	1 2 3 4 5
7	Collecting data at client termination	1 2 3 4 5
8	Collecting data to obtain client feedback	1 2 3 4 5
9	Managing data manually	1 2 3 4 5
10	Managing data with computers	1 2 3 4 5
	Add up your scores (minimum = 10, maximum = 50)	Your total score =

A   47–50 = Professional evaluator in the making
A−   45–46 = Senior evaluator
B+   43–44 = Junior evaluator
B   41–42 = Assistant evaluator
B−   10–40 = Reread the chapter and redo the study questions

A good decision is based on knowledge and not on numbers.

~ *Plato*

Ideally, all of our professional decisions should be arrived at via a rational process based on the collection, synthesis, and analysis of relevant, objective, and subjective data. As seen in Tools L and M, objective data are obtained by an explicit measurement process that, when carefully followed, reduces bias and increases the data's objectivity.

Subjective data, on the other hand, are obtained from our professional impressions and judgments that, by their very nature, incorporate the values, preferences, and experiences of the individuals who make them. It's our position that objective data—when combined with subjective data—offer the best basis for decision-making.

Thus the best practice- and program-relevant decisions are made when we understand the advantages and limitations of both objective and subjective data and are able to combine the two as appropriate to the circumstances—the purpose of this chapter.

USING OBJECTIVE DATA

Using objective data in decision making has its advantages and disadvantages.

Advantages

The main advantage of using objective data when making decisions is in the data's precision and objectivity. At the program level, for example, an agency may receive funding to provide an employment skills training program for minority groups such as our Aim High Program described in Box 13.1 in Chapter 13. If appropriate data are kept, it's easy to ascertain to what degree the eligibility requirement is being met, and it may be possible to state, for example, that 86% of our client base are in fact from minority groups.

Without objective data, the subjective impressions of community members, staff members, funders, and program participants would be the sources of the data. Individuals may use descriptors such as "most," "many," or "a large number" to describe the proportion of minority people served by our employment skills training program. Obviously, such subjective judgments are far less precise than objective data and they are also subject to biases.

Disadvantages

Objective data, however, are not without their own limitations. These include the following:

- Some variables are difficult to measure objectively
- Data may be uncertain or ambiguous, allowing conflicting interpretations
- Objective data may not take all pertinent contextual factors into account

Although considerable progress has been made in recent years in the development of standardized measuring instruments, not all variables of conceivable interest to social workers are convenient and feasible to measure. Thus objective data may not be available to guide certain practice and program decisions.

In the same vein, even if a variable can be measured, data collection plans may not call for its measurement—or the measurement may have been omitted for any of a variety of reasons that arise in day-to-day professional activity. Consequently, objective data are not always available to guide practice and program decision-making.

Where objective data are available, their meaning and implications may not always be clear. At the case level, a series of standardized measures intended to assess a 10-year-old's self-esteem may yield no discernable pattern. It would thus be difficult, on the basis of such objective data alone, to make decisions about further interventions and services.

At the program level, objective data may indicate that, over a 3-month period, people participating in a weight-loss program lose an average of 5 pounds per person. Although the results seem favorable, the average weight loss is not very great, making it unclear whether the program should be continued as is or whether modifications should be considered.

Finally, objective data seldom provide useful contextual information, although the context relating to them is important in their interpretation. In the example of our weight-loss program, the average 5-pound loss would probably be considered inadequate if the clientele were known to be a group of people who, for medical reasons, needed to lose an average of 60 pounds each. On the other hand, if the clientele were known to be a group of downhill skiers preparing for the ski season, the program could be considered quite successful.

USING SUBJECTIVE DATA

Using subjective data in decision-making also has its advantages and disadvantages.

Advantages

Although it might seem desirable to base all decisions on logically analyzed objective data, such information on all factors affecting a given practice or program decision is seldom available. Consequently, objective data are often supplemented by more subjective types of data, such as the workers' impressions, judgments, experiences, and intuitions.

As human beings, we assimilate subjective data continuously as we move through our daily life; competent social work professionals do the same, noting the client's stance, gait, gestures, voice, eye movements, and set of mouth, for example. At the program level, an administrator may have a sense of awareness of staff morale, history and stage of development of the organization, external expectations, and the ability of the organization to absorb change.

Seldom are any of these subjective data actually measured, but all of them are assimilated. Some subjective data are consciously noted; some filter through subconsciously and emerge later as impressions, opinions, or intuitions. Clearly, such subjective data may considerably influence case and program decision-making.

At the case level, for example, perceptions, judgments, and intuition—often called clinical impressions—may become factors in decision-making. A worker may conclude, based on the client's body language, eye contact, and voice, that her self-esteem is improving. Further case-level decisions may then be based on these subjective impressions.

At the program level, objective data may suggest the need to modify the program in the face of inadequate results. The administrator, however, may put off making any modifications on the basis of a subjective judgment that, because several other program changes had recently been implemented, the team's ability to absorb any additional changes is limited. To the extent that subjective data are accurate, such a decision is entirely appropriate.

Disadvantages

The main limitation of subjective data, however, is that impressions and intuition often spring to the mind preformed, and the process by which they were formed cannot be objectively examined. By their nature, subjective data are susceptible to distortion through the personal experience, bias, and preferences of the individual. These may work deceptively, leaving workers unaware that the subjective data on which they are relying actually distort the picture.

In reality, case- and program-level decision-making uses a blend of objective and subjective data. Together, the two forms of data have the potential to provide the most complete information on which to base decisions. Ultimately, the practitioner will have to use judgment in reconciling all relevant sources of data to arrive at an understanding of the situation.

In building an accurate picture, it's important not only to consider all sources of data but also to be aware of the strengths and limitations of each of these sources. Quality case and program decisions are usually the result of explicitly sifting through the various sources of data and choosing those sources in which it's reasonable to have the most confidence under the circumstances.

Having considered decision making in general, we now turn to an examination of the specifics of the process at the case and program levels.

MAKING CASE-LEVEL DECISIONS

If high-quality case-level decisions are to be reached, the social worker should know what types of decisions are best supported by objective data and what types will likely require the use of subjective data. As you know from your social work practice classes, your professional relationship with your client is a process that passes through a number of phases and follows logically from one to the next. There are essentially four phases, as illustrated in the diagram below,

problems (program objective) and have been assigned to a worker named Maria. From Ms. Wright's initial statement, the problem is that her partner does not pay enough attention to her. In Maria's judgment, Ms. Wright's perception is a symptom of yet another problem that has not been defined.

The client's perception, however, is a good starting point, and Maria attempts to objectify Ms. Wright's statement: In what ways, precisely, does her partner not pay enough attention to her? Ms. Wright obligingly provides data: Her partner has not gone anywhere with her for the past 3 months, but he regularly spends three nights a week playing basketball, two nights with friends, and one night at his mother's.

Mr. Wright, brought into the session under protest, declares that he spends most nights at home and the real problem is that his partner constantly argues. Further inquiry leads Maria to believe that Mr. Wright spends more nights away from home than he reports but fewer than his partner says; Ms. Wright, feeling herself ignored, most likely is argumentative; and the underlying problems are actually poor communication and unrealistic expectations on the part of both.

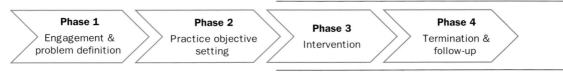

In practice, these phases are not likely to follow a clear sequence. Engagement, for example, occurs most prominently at the beginning of the professional relationship, but it continues in some form throughout the entire helping process. Problem definition is logically the first consideration after engagement, but if it becomes evident during intervention that the client's problem is not clearly understood, the problem-definition and objective-setting phases will have to be readdressed. Nevertheless, discernible phases do exist. The following describes how case-level decisions can be made in each phase.

Phase 1: Engagement and Problem Definition

Suppose a married couple, Mr. and Ms. Wright, come to a family service agency to work on their marital

Setting Practice Objectives

A host of other problems surfaced subtly during the interview and cannot be addressed until the communications problem is solved; communication, therefore, should be the initial target of the intervention—the first practice objective.

A second practice objective could be to reduce the Wrights' unrealistic expectations of each other. Let's consider that the Wrights have these two practice objectives that are specifically geared toward the program objective: "to increase marital satisfaction." Maria believes that the attainment of the two practice objectives will increase the Wrights' marital satisfaction—the main purpose for which they are seeking services.

Remember, the Wrights want a happier marriage (that's why they sought out services); they did not seek out help with their dysfunctional communication patterns and unrealistic expectations of one another. Thus to increase their marital satisfaction is the program objective, and communications and expectations are the two practice objectives.

> **Two practice objectives**
> 1. Increase communication skills
> 2. Increase realistic expectations
>
> **Program objective**
> Increase marital satisfaction

So far, Maria's conclusions have been based on her own impressions of the conflicting data presented by the Wrights. Unless the problem is straightforward and concrete, the engagement and problem-definition phase often depends more on the worker's subjective judgment, experience, and intuition than it does on objective data.

Using Standardized Measurements

Even when standardized measuring instruments are used to help clients identify and prioritize their problems, the choice of the problem to be first addressed will largely be guided by the worker's professional judgment. Once a worker's professional judgment has indicated what the problem might be, the magnitude of the problem can often be measured with more objectivity through the use of standardized measuring instruments.

In the Wrights' case, Maria has tentatively decided to formulate a practice objective of increasing the Wrights' communication skills. To confirm that communication skills are problematic, she asks Mr. and Ms. Wright to independently complete a 25-item standardized measuring instrument designed to measure marital communications skills.

The instrument contains such items as "How often do you and your spouse talk over pleasant things that happen during the day?" with possible responses of "very frequently," "frequently," "occasionally," "seldom," and "never." This instrument has a range of zero to 100, with higher scores showing better communication skills. It has a clinical cutting score of 60,

indicating effective communications above that level, and it has been tested on people of the same socioeconomic group as the Wrights and may be assumed to yield valid and reliable data.

The introduction of the measuring instrument at this stage serves two basic purposes. First, the scores will show whether communication is indeed a problem and to what degree it's a problem for each partner. Second, the scores will provide a baseline measurement that can be used as the first point on a graph in whatever case-level design Maria selects.

Phase 2: Practice Objective Setting

In the Wrights' case, the program objective is to increase their marital satisfaction. Thus, a related practice objective (one of many possible) is to increase the couple's communication skills to a minimum score of 60, the clinical cutting score on the standardized measuring instrument. The practice objective setting phase in this example thus relies heavily on objective data: It's framed in terms of a change from very ineffective communication (score of zero) to very effective communication (score of 100).

The same process applies in cases where the standardized measuring instrument selected is less formal and precise. Maria, for example, may ask each partner to complete a self-anchored rating scale indicating his and her level of satisfaction with the degree of communication achieved. The scoring range on this instrument could be from 1 to 6, with higher scores indicating greater levels of satisfaction and lower scores indicating lesser levels of satisfaction.

If Mr. Wright begins by rating his satisfaction level at 3 and Ms. Wright indicates hers at 2, the practice objective chosen may be to achieve a minimum rating of 4 for each partner. Here again, practice objective setting is based on objective data collected at the beginning of Maria's intervention.

Phase 3: Intervention

The selection of the intervention strategy itself will be based on objective and subjective data only to a limited degree. Perhaps Maria has seen previous clients with similar practice objectives and also has objective evidence, via the professional literature, that a specific treatment intervention is appropriate to use in this specific situation. But even though the intervention is chosen on the basis of data accumulated from previous research studies and past experience, each intervention is tailored to meet the needs of the particular client system, and decisions about strategy, timing, and its implementation are largely based on subjective data—the worker's professional judgment.

Objective data may play only one part in the selection of an intervention strategy, but once the strategy is selected, its success is best measured on the basis of consistently collected objective data. Ideally, objective data are collected using a number of different standardized measures. In the Wrights' case, for example, the scores from repeated administrations of the standardized instrument that measures the degree of communication will comprise one set of objective data for one particular practice objective.

Frequency counts of specifically selected behaviors may comprise another set: for example, a count of the number of conversations daily lasting at least 5 minutes, or the number of "I" statements made daily by each partner. The self-anchored rating scale, described in the previous section, could be a third source of data. These sets of data together provide considerable information about whether, and to what degree, progress is being made.

Maria is also likely to come to a more global opinion about how the couple is doing in regard to their communication patterns. This opinion will be based on a variety of observations and impressions formed as she works with the couple. The process by which such an opinion is formed is intuitive and—depending on the worker's skill, experiences, and the circumstances—may be quite accurate. The method by which it's arrived at, however, is idiosyncratic and is therefore of unknown validity and reliability. For this reason, relying on clinical impressions exclusively is inadvisable.

On the other hand, objective measures may have their own problems of validity and reliability. The best course is a middle one: determination of a client's progress should be based on a combination of objective data *and* subjective data. Where objective and subjective data point in the same direction, Maria can proceed with considerable confidence that she has a clear and accurate picture of her clients' progress.

Where objective and subjective data diverge, Maria should first attempt to determine the reasons for the difference and ensure that she has a good understanding of her clients' problems and needs. When Maria is satisfied that she has an accurate grasp of her client system's progress, she is ready to proceed to decisions about the most appropriate treatment intervention to use.

These decisions are guided by changes in the practice objective. Three patterns of change are possible:

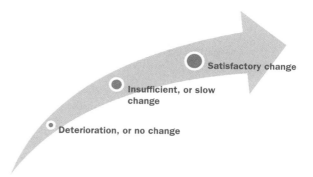

Deterioration or No Change

Suppose that Ms. Wright scored a 40 on the first administration of the standardized measuring instrument that measures the degree, or level, of communication patterns. Then she scores a 41 on the second, a 43 on the third, and a 42 on the fourth (Figure 15.1). Mr. Wright scores 50, 51, 53, and 52, respectively. How would Maria analyze and interpret such data?

First, Maria will want to consider what the other available sources of data indicate. Let's assume that, on the self-anchored communication satisfaction scale, Ms. Wright still rates her satisfaction at 2 and that, during the sessions, she avoids eye contact with Mr. Wright and tries to monopolize the worker's attention with references to "he" and "him." In this situation, the data all seem to point to the same conclusion: There has been virtually no change or progress. Under such circumstances, it's reasonable to place considerable reliance on the data contained in Figure 15.1.

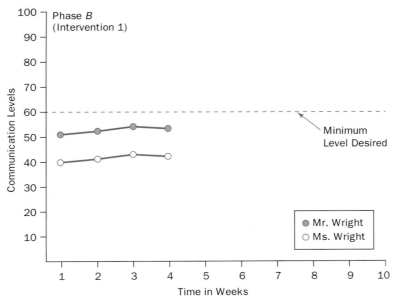

Figure 15.1: *B* design: The Wrights' communication levels over time, indicating no change.

As Figure 15.1 also indicates, the slope of the line connecting the measurement points is virtually flat—that is, it's stable, indicating neither improvement nor deterioration. Moreover, the level of the problem is well below the desired minimum score of 60 (dashed line in Figure 15.1). Such data would normally lead Maria to conclude that a change in the intervention is warranted—resulting in a *BC* design.

Here qualitative considerations may also enter the case-level decision-making process. Maria, for example, may be aware of disruptions in the lives of Mr. and Ms. Wright. Perhaps Mr. Wright received a layoff notice from his job during the second week of the intervention. Maria may now need to consider whether the effects of the intervention might not have been counteracted by these adverse circumstances. Ultimately, she will need to decide whether to continue the intervention in the hope that, once the couple has dealt with the shock of the impending layoff, the intervention will begin to have the desired effect.

It's also possible that the intervention is known to have a delayed impact. This characteristic could have been determined from the professional literature or from Maria's previous experience with using the intervention. Under such circumstances it may, again,

be reasonable to maintain the intervention for some time longer and see whether movement toward the practice objective begins.

How long it's sensible to continue an intervention in the absence of documented progress is a matter best left to Maria's and the couple's judgment. As long as there is reason to believe that an intervention may yet have the desired impact, it's justified to pursue that intervention.

If there is no evidence of change for the better, however, the intervention will need to be changed. Note that data will provide objective evidence supporting the need for a change in the intervention, but they will not indicate what future intervention strategies might be used instead. Formulation of a new intervention strategy will again call upon Maria's and her clients' judgment.

Insufficient or Slow Change

Insufficient or slow change is a familiar scenario in the social services. A gradual but definite improvement in the communication scores may be noted, indicating that Mr. and Ms. Wright are slowly learning to communicate. Their relationship continues to deteriorate, however, because their communication scores are still below 60—the minimum level of good communication; progress needs to be more rapid if the marriage is to be saved.

In general, many clients improve only slowly, or they improve in spurts with regressions in between. The data will reflect what is occurring—what the problem level is, and at what rate and in what direction it is changing. No data, however, can tell a worker whether the measured rate of change is acceptable in the particular client's circumstances. This is an area in which subjective clinical judgment again comes into play.

The worker may decide that the rate of change is insufficient, but just marginally so; that is, the intervention is successful on the whole and ought to be continued but at a greater frequency or intensity. Perhaps the number of treatment sessions can be increased, or more time can be scheduled for each session, or more intensive work can be planned. In other words, a B design will now become a B_1B_2 design (Figure 15.2).

Or, if baseline data have been collected, an AB design will become an AB_1B_2 design. If, on the other hand, the worker thinks that intensifying the intervention is unlikely to yield significantly improved results, a different intervention entirely may be adopted. In this case, the B design will become a BC design (Figure 15.3), or the AB design will become an ABC design.

Sometimes improvement occurs at an acceptable rate for a period and then the client reaches a plateau, below the desired minimal level; no further change seems to be occurring. The data will show the initial improvement and the plateau (Figure 15.4), but they will not show whether the plateau is temporary, whether it's akin to a resting period, or whether the level already achieved is as far as the improvement will go.

Again, this is a matter for clinical judgment. The worker and client system may decide to continue with the intervention for a time to see whether improvement begins again. The exact length of time during which perseverance is justified is a judgment call. If the client system remains stuck at the level reached beyond that time, the worker and client system will have to decide whether to apply the intervention more intensively, try a new intervention, or be content with what has been achieved.

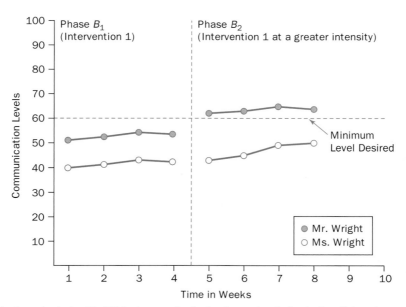

Figure 15.2: B_1B_2 changing intensity design: The Wrights' communication levels over time, indicating insufficient change at the B_1 followed by a more intensive B_2.

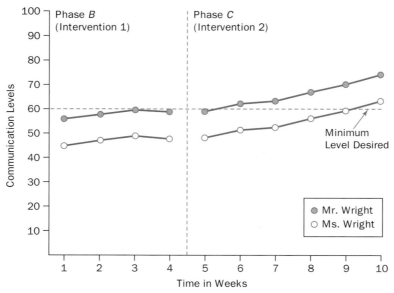

Figure 15.3: *BC* design: The Wrights' communication Levels over time, indicating insufficient change at the *B* intervention followed by a *C* intervention.

Satisfactory Change

Frequently objective data will show an improvement. At times the improvement will be steady and sustained, and at other times an overall trend of improvement will be punctuated with periods of plateau or even regression. This latter scenario is illustrated in Figure 15.5. Essentially, continuation of the treatment intervention is justified by

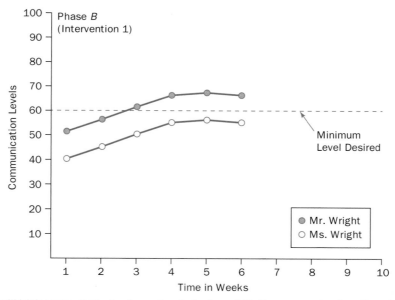

Figure 15.4: *B* design: The Wright's communication levels over time, indicating an initial improvement leveling off to a plateau.

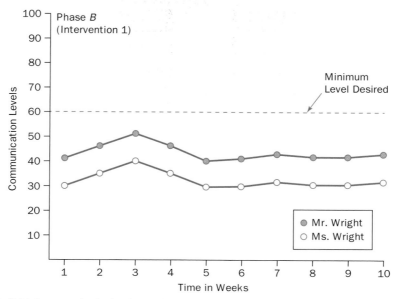

Figure 15.5: *B* design: The Wright's communication levels over time, indicating some improvement with periods of plateaus and regressions.

continuing client progress, although Maria may wish at times to make minor modifications in the intervention.

It's important to keep in mind that not all case-level designs permit the worker to conclude that the intervention has caused the change for the better. With many designs that are likely to be used in the monitoring of social work interventions, it's possible to conclude only that the client's practice objective has changed for the better. This is the situation in the B design shown in Figure 15.4 where Mr. Wright has obtained communication scores over 60 but Ms. Wright has yet to reach the minimum acceptable level of 60. From a service perspective, however, evidence that Mr. and Ms. Wright are improving is sufficient justification for continuing the intervention; it's not necessary to prove that the intervention is causing the change.

When the data show that a client has reached the practice objective, the worker will, if possible, initiate a maintenance phase, perhaps gradually reducing the frequency of contact with a view to service termination but also trying to ensure that the gains achieved are not lost. If other practice objectives need to be resolved, the maintenance phase for one objective may coincide with the baseline or intervention phase for another. It's quite

possible to engage in a number of case-level designs at the same time with the same client; because client practice objectives are usually interrelated, data obtained in one area will often be relevant to another.

The maintenance phase is important, ensuring that the practice objective really has been satisfactorily resolved. Assume that data show a steady improvement, culminating at a point above the target range (as in Figure 15.3). One measurement below the minimum desired level means only that the practice objective was not at a clinically significant level when that measurement was made. Subsequent measurements may show that a significant problem still exists.

A number of measurements are required before Maria can be confident that the practice objective has stabilized at the desired level. Similarly, where the trend to improvement included plateaus and regressions, measurements must continue beyond the achievement of the practice objective to ensure that the objective has indeed stabilized in the desired level and direction.

Phase 4: Termination and Follow-Up

Once it's decided that the program objective (not the practice objective) has been accomplished, the next step is termination and follow-up. The termination decision is straightforward, in theory: when the data show that the program objective has been achieved via the attainment of practice objectives, and the practice objective level is stable, services can be terminated.

In reality, however, other factors need to be taken into account, such as the number and type of support systems available in the client's social environment and the nature and magnitude of possible stressor events in the client's life. We must carefully weigh all these factors, including information yielded by objective *and* subjective data, in making a decision to end services.

Ideally, the follow-up phase will be a routine part of the program's operations. Many social work programs, however, do not engage in any kind of follow-up activities, and others conduct follow-ups in a sporadic or informal way. If the program does conduct routine follow-up, decisions will already have been made concerning how often and in what manner the client should be contacted after the termination of services. If no standardized follow-up procedures are in place, we will have to decide whether follow-up is necessary and, if so, what form it should take.

Data can help decide whether a follow-up is necessary. If data reveal that a client has not reached a program objective, or has reached it only marginally, a follow-up is essential. If data show a pattern of improvement followed by regression, a follow-up is also indicated to ensure that regression will not occur again.

The follow-up procedures that measure program objectives may be conducted in a number of ways. Frequently used approaches include contacting former clients by letter or telephone at increasingly longer intervals after the cessation of services. A less frequently used approach is to continue to measure the program objectives that were taken during the intervention period. As services to the Wrights are terminated, Maria could arrange to have them each complete, at monthly intervals, the Marital Satisfaction Scale (the measure of the program objective).

Maria could mail the scale to the Wrights, who, because they have already completed it during the course of the intervention, should have no problem doing so during follow-up. The inclusion of a stamped, self-addressed envelope can further encourage them to complete this task. In this manner, Maria can determine objectively whether marital satisfaction gains made during treatment are maintained over time.

At a minimum, collecting program-level data (not case-level data) during follow-up results in a *BF* design, as illustrated in Figures 15.6 and 15.7. If an initial baseline phase had been used, the result would be an *ABF* design. Where follow-up data indicate that client gains are being maintained, a situation illustrated in Figure 15.6 termination procedures can be completed.

Where follow-up data reveal deterioration after termination, as illustrated in Figure 15.7 Maria is at least in a position to know that her clients are not doing well. Under such circumstances, complete termination is not warranted. Instead, Maria should consider whether to resume active intervention, provide additional support in the clients' social environment, or offer some other service. The follow-up data will not help Maria to decide what she should do next, but they will alert her to the need to do something.

It should be noted that Figures 15.6 and 15.7 provide data for marital satisfaction scores and do not represent the couple's communication scores, as in Figures 15.1. This is because follow-up data are concerned only with program objectives (in this case, marital satisfaction), not practice objectives (in this case, communication and expectations of one another).

One other point needs to be clarified. All standardized measuring instruments do not measure their variables in the same way when it comes to what their high and low scores mean. For example, high scores on some instruments indicate there is more of a "problem" being measured than lower scores on the same instrument. For example, see Figures 15.6 and 15.7, where the higher the score, the worse their marital satisfaction; thus we try to get our clients' scores below the clinical cutting score of 30, where the lower the score, the better.

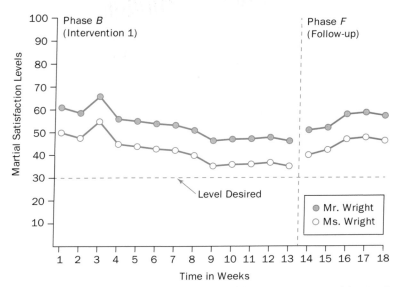

Figure 15.6: *BF* design: The Wrights' marital satisfaction levels during treatment (*B*) and after termination (*F*), indicating maintained improvement after termination.

Some instruments are scored exactly the opposite, where higher scores indicate the "problem" is less present than lower scores. For example, see Figures 15.1, where the higher the score, the better the communication. Here we try to get our clients' scores above the clinical cutting score of 60, where the higher the score, the better. All of this can be very confusing to novices and experts alike. It's always necessary to know exactly how each standardized measuring instrument is scored and what the scores mean.

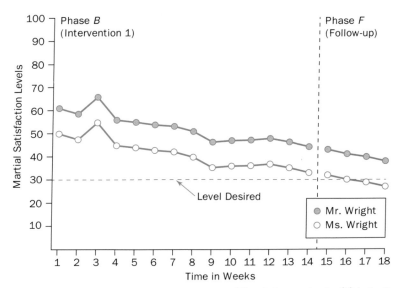

Figure 15.7: *BF* design: The Wrights' marital satisfaction levels during treatment (*B*) and after termination (*F*), indicating a deterioration after termination.

MAKING PROGRAM-LEVEL DECISIONS

The primary purpose of collecting data at the program level is to obtain feedback on the program in an ongoing manner so that the services provided can be continually developed and improved.

In the first instance, the program may be assessed with regard to the achievement of process objectives. Process objectives are analogous to facilitative practice objectives; their achievement makes it more likely that program objectives will also be achieved. In a sense, they speak to the effectiveness and efficiency of the service operation. Process objectives, for example, might address the type of clientele to be served, indicating that a minimum of 75% should come from minority backgrounds.

Or these objectives could speak to the length of waiting lists, specifying that no one should have to wait longer than 2 weeks before the commencement of services. Other process objectives could deal with the number of continuing education hours provided to staff members, premature termination of cases, service hours provided, and similar other matters.

The actual program objectives may be assessed in various ways. Success rates may vary with problem type. A particular social service program, for example, may achieve good success with children who have family-related problems but less success with children whose problems are primarily drug related. Or perhaps desirable results are achieved with one type of client but not another: a drug rehabilitation program may be more successful with adults than it's with adolescents, for example.

Or, again, a particular program within an agency may achieve its program objectives better than another program within the same agency. A child welfare agency, for example, may successfully operate an adolescent treatment foster-care program but have less success with its adolescent group-care program. If several residential programs are operated, an agency may achieve its program objectives to a higher degree than another.

Finally, the agency must be considered as a whole. How successful is it when all of its programs are assessed together? What might be done on a general organizational level to improve the agency's "overall" effectiveness and efficiency?

A picture of results can be readily achieved through the collection and analysis of objective and subjective data. The kinds of data collected and analyses performed will depend on the program being considered. This section begins with a few words about process evaluation and then deals in detail with outcome evaluation.

Process Evaluations

Usually, data can be readily gathered on matters of interest in a process evaluation as discussed in Chapter 11. Collecting data, for example, on the demographic characteristics of clients, the length of time spent on waiting lists, the types of services provided, and the total number of hours of each is a relatively straightforward matter.

These data are collected continuously and analyzed on a regular basis. Reports available to staff members make clear to what degree process objectives are being met. Process objectives usually pertain to good and desirable practices that are thought to lead to desired results.

Outcome Evaluations

Outcomes can be classified into three nonmutually exclusive areas as illustrated below:

| Problems and cases | Program | Agency |

Problems and Cases

As we know, many social service agencies offer services to people with a variety of needs: pregnant teens, disabled seniors, preadolescents with drug issues, couples seeking help with their marriages, and people who are trying to stop smoking. The agency will be interested in knowing, and is usually required by funders to document, to what degree its programs are helping people with particular types of social problems.

The results achieved by any one client, satisfactory or not, do not say much about the general effectiveness of the program as a whole. Program effectiveness is determined only by examining data from groups of clients, often using simple aggregation methods.

Assume, for example, that during a 6-month period of a smoking cessation program the program served 80 clients, 40 male and 40 female. Using the case-level monitoring techniques previously described, data will be available showing the number of cigarettes smoked by each client at the beginning and at the end of the intervention. Aggregating the individual client results indicates that the average number of cigarettes smoked daily at the beginning of the intervention was 34 and the average number smoked at the end of the program was 11.

Thus the clients smoked, on average, 23 fewer cigarettes per day after they completed the stop-smoking program. These aggregated data, after analysis, provide a method of assessing the outcome of the program. The aggregated data and the results of the analysis for all 80 clients are presented in Table 15.1.

The analysis presented in Table 15.1 is a simple one—the calculation of the difference between the beginning and ending average number of cigarettes smoked. The analysis could be extended to determine whether this difference might have come about by chance alone. This is what is meant by the term "statistical significance." Detailed treatment of statistical procedures is way beyond the scope of this text but is readily available in any introductory statistics book.

To return to our example, the decline in smoking can be documented as a net change of 23 cigarettes, on average, per client. Although the data available in this situation permit documentation of the program's objective, or outcome, it's not possible to attribute this change *solely* to the intervention.

The particular evaluation design used was the one-group pretest–posttest design (Figure E.6 in Tool E), and as we know, it does not support inferences about causality. Nevertheless, this type of design enables staff members to document the overall results of their services.

Further analyses of these data may provide additional and more specific information. Suppose, for example, that program staff had the impression that they were achieving better results with female smokers than with male smokers. Examining the results of males and females as separate groups would permit a comparison of the average number of cigarettes each group smoked at the end of the program. The data for this analysis are presented in Table 15.2.

Note that the average number of cigarettes smoked at the beginning of the program was exactly the same for the males and females, 34. Thus it could be concluded that there were no meaningful differences between the males and females in reference to the average number of cigarettes they smoked at the start of the intervention.

As Table 15.2 shows, at the end of the program males smoked an average of 18 cigarettes daily and females an average of 4 cigarettes. On average, then, females smoked 14 fewer cigarettes per day than did males. Essentially, this analysis confirms workers' suspicions that they were obtaining better results with female smokers than with male smokers.

The information obtained via the simple analysis presented earlier provides documentation of outcomes, a vitally important element in this age of accountability and increased competition for available funding. There is, however, a further advantage to compiling and analyzing evaluation data. By

Table 15.1: **Average Number of Cigarettes Smoked Per Day at the Beginning and End of the Smoking Cessation Program (N = 80).**

Beginning	–	After	=	Difference
34		11		23

Table 15.2: **Average Number of Cigarettes Smoked Per Day at the Beginning and End of the Smoking Cessation Program Broken Down by Sex (N = 80).**

Sex	Beginning	–	After	=	Difference	N
Male	34		18		16	40
Female	34		4		30	40
Totals	34		11		23	80

conducting regular analyses, social work administrators and workers can obtain important feedback about the program's strengths and weaknesses.

These data can be used to further develop services. The data discussed earlier, for example, may cause the services to be modified in ways that would improve effectiveness with male clients while maintaining effectiveness with female clients. This would not only improve services to the male client group but would also boost overall program outcomes.

Program

As we know from Chapters 7 and 8, a program is a distinct unit, large or small, that operates within an agency. An agency, for example, may comprise a number of treatment programs, or a child welfare agency may operate a treatment foster-care program and a residential child abuse treatment program as part of its operations. The residential program itself may comprise a number of separate homes for children of different ages or different problem types.

These programs should be evaluated if the agency as a whole is to demonstrate accountability and provide the best possible service to its clientele. A thorough evaluation will include attention to needs (Chapter 9), process (Chapter 10), and outcomes (Chapter 12), as well as efficiency (Chapter 13). Because the greatest interest is often in outcome, however, this section focuses on outcome evaluation, where the question is: "To what degree has a program succeeded in reaching its program objectives?"

If this question is to be answered satisfactorily, the program's objectives must be defined in a SMART way (Chapter 7) that allows them to be measured (see Tools L and M in the evaluation toolkit). Let's assume that one of the objectives of the residential child abuse treatment program is to enable its residents to return to their homes. The degree of achievement of this program objective can be determined through simple math: What percentage of the residents returned home within the last year?

If the agency includes several programs of the same type, in different locations, lessons learned from one can be applied to another. In addition, similar programs will likely have the same program objectives and the same ways of measuring them so that results can be aggregated to provide a measure of effectiveness for the entire agency. If the programs are dissimilar—for example, a treatment foster-care program and a victim-assistance program—aggregation will not be possible, but separate assessment of program outcomes will nevertheless contribute to the evaluation of the agency as a whole.

Agency

An outcome evaluation, whether in respect to an agency, a program, or a case, always focuses on the achievement of SMART objectives. How well has the agency fulfilled its mandate? To what degree has it succeeded in meeting its goal, as revealed by the measurement of its program objectives? Again, success in goal achievement cannot be determined unless the agency's programs have well-defined, measurable program objectives that reflect the agency's mandate.

As seen in Chapter 7, agencies operate on the basis of mission statements, which often consist of vaguely phrased, expansive statements of intent. The mission of a sexual abuse treatment agency, for example, may be to ameliorate the pain caused by sexually abusive situations and to prevent sexual abuse in the future. Although there is no doubt that this is a laudable mission, the concepts of pain amelioration and abuse prevention cannot be measured until they have been more precisely defined.

This agency's mandate may be to serve persons who have been sexually abused and their families living within a certain geographical area. If the agency has an overall goal, "to reduce the trauma resulting from sexual abuse in the community," for example, the mandate is reflected and measurement is implied in the word "reduce." The concept of trauma still needs to be operationalized, but this can be accomplished through the specific, individual practice objectives of the clients whose trauma is to be reduced: the primary trauma for a male survivor may be fear that he is homosexual, whereas the trauma for a nonoffending mother may be guilt that she failed to protect her child.

If logical links are established between the agency's goal, the goals of the programs within the agency, and the individual practice objectives of clients served by the program, it will be possible to use the results of one to evaluate the other. Practice objective achievement at the case level will contribute to the success of the program's objectives which will in turn contribute to the achievement of the agency's overall goal.

OUTCOME DATA AND PROGRAM-LEVEL DECISION-MAKING

Just as an outcome for any client may be acceptable, mixed, or inadequate, an outcome for a program can also be acceptable, mixed, or inadequate, reflecting the degree to which its program objectives have been achieved.

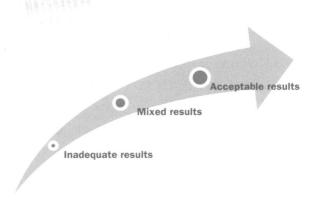

Acceptable results

Mixed results

Inadequate results

Acceptable Results

Before a result can be declared "acceptable," it's necessary to define clearly what counts as an acceptable result for a specific program objective. Let's return to the example of the residential program, where one of the program's objectives included enabling residents to return home: if 90% of residents succeed in making this move within 6 months of entry into the program, has the program's objective been achieved to an acceptable degree? What if 80% of residents return home within 6 months and a further 10% return home within a year? Or 100% return home within 6 months but half of the adolescents are eventually readmitted to the program?

Evidently, an acceptable result is largely a matter of definition. The program administrators and funders must decide what degree of objective achievement can reasonably be expected given the nature of the problems, the resources available, and the results of similar programs. Are the results for the smoking cessation program, for example, shown in Tables 15.1 and 15.2, indicative of success?

If the program comprises a number of subprograms, the same considerations apply with regard to each. Defining criteria for success should be done in advance of obtaining results, to avoid politicizing the results and to make it possible to set relevant program objectives.

Once the standards for an acceptable level of achievement have been set, evaluation becomes a matter of comparing actual outcomes against these standards. Where standards are met, program personnel can, with some degree of confidence, continue to employ existing procedures and practices.

If outcomes are analyzed on a regular basis, workers will be able to see not only whether program objectives are being achieved to an acceptable degree but also whether the level of achievement is rising or falling. Any persistent trend toward improvement or decline is worth investigating so that more effective interventions and processes can be reinforced and potential problems can be detected and resolved.

Mixed Results

Occasionally, the results of an outcome evaluation will show that the program is achieving its objectives only partially. A program may be successful in helping one group of clients, for example, but less successful with another. This was the situation in the smoking cessation program mentioned previously: female clients were being helped considerably, but male clients were obtaining much less impressive results (see Table 15.2). Similarly, an evaluation may reveal seasonal variations in outcomes: At certain times of the year a program may achieve its program objectives to an acceptable degree but not at other times.

Clients in farming communities, for instance, may be able to participate in the program in the winter more easily than during the growing season, when they are busy with the tasks of farming. This factor alone may result in reduced achievement at both the case and program levels. It's also possible that one program within an agency is achieving its objectives to a greater degree than another, similar program.

In such situations, staff members will undoubtedly wish to adjust practices and procedures so that the underperforming components can be upgraded. In making any adjustments, however, care must be taken not to jeopardize those parts of the operation that are obtaining good outcomes. In the case of the smoking cessation program, for example, the workers may be tempted to tailor several sessions more to the needs of male clients. Although this may indeed improve the program's performance with male clients, the improvement may come at the expense of effectiveness with females.

A preferable strategy might be to form separate groups for males and females during some parts of the program, leaving the program unchanged for female clients but developing new sessions for male clients to better meet their needs. Of course, it's impossible to predict in advance whether changes will yield the desired results, but ongoing monitoring will provide feedback about their efficacy.

Inadequate Results

One of the strengths of a program-level monitoring system is that it takes into account the entire program process, from intake to follow-up. A low level of program objective achievement is not necessarily attributable to the interventions used by the workers with their clients. It's possible that the problem lies in inappropriate eligibility criteria, unsatisfactory assessment techniques, inadequate staff training, or a host of other factors, including unforeseen systematic barriers to clients' involvement in the program.

If an outcome evaluation shows that results are unsatisfactory, further program development is called for. To diagnose the problem or problems, the program administrator and workers will want to examine data concerning all the stages that lead up to intervention as well as the intervention process itself. Once they have ideas about the reasons for suboptimal performance, usually obtained by process evaluations (see Chapter 10), they are in a position to begin instituting changes to the program's procedures and practices—and monitoring the results of those changes.

BENCHMARKS

This section discusses how a family service program uses benchmarks to guide decision-making in five areas.

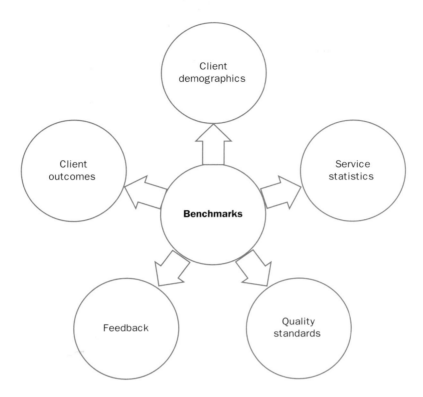

Client Demographics

It's always desirable to have reliable and valid data about the clientele actually being served by the program, not only to ensure compliance with funding contracts but also to identify any changes or trends in client profile. Client demographics data are useful in all types of evaluations. Table 15.3 provides a simple illustration of the types of variables that can be tracked in the client demographic area (left side) as well as methods of measuring these variables (right side).

As can be seen, the client demographics to be measured are stated in the form of simple straightforward benchmarks. The target values of each benchmark were derived from the program's funding contract as well as from the program's goal, which reflects what kind of clientele is targeted by the program. By specifying client demographics as benchmarks, the program has clear targets toward which to work. Criteria are also explicitly established against which evaluation results can be eventually assessed.

Alternatively, it's also possible to phrase benchmarks in the format of objectives. Recall the qualities of SMART objectives that were described in Chapter 7. These qualities apply to both client-centered objectives and to maintenance or instrumental objectives. Objectives differ from benchmarks in that they do not specify a target value, as is the case in Table 15.3.

Table 15.3: **Client Demographics.**

Benchmarks	Measures
Serve 200 individuals overall, per month	Count of Client Intake Forms
60% of clients will be single-parent families	Item on Client Intake Form

It may be, for example, that instead of setting a benchmark to serve 200 individuals per month, a program aims only to maintain the overall number of clients served from the previous year. Using objectives is preferable to using benchmarks when a specific target value is uncertain or cannot be reasonably estimated. Some people would also argue that using benchmarks alone tends to create a climate of "bean counting" more so than is the case with objectives.

In general, client demographics measure the number of clients served and their corresponding characteristics that are considered relevant to the program's services and outcomes. The two variables in Table 15.3 can be easily tracked by data gleaned from a client intake form. Data about whether a client is new to the program, for example, can be readily captured by including one extra item (perhaps a checklist) on the program's intake form such as the one displayed in Figure 14.3.

Of course it's important in the planning and focusing phase of an evaluation to determine that it's of interest to know whether a client is or is not new to the program. If the data collection system is designed to capture these data in advance, it will be a simple matter to track this issue. If not, it may be inconvenient, confusing, and costly to revise data collection or reconstruct the data at a later date, if it's possible. Using our example, the following simple item could be added to an intake form without much hassle:

Is this the first time you have received services from this program?

_____ Yes

_____ No

_____ Don't know

Client demographic data are important to funders, program administrators, and practitioners. By tracking these variables, program administrators can provide data to funders to verify that their programs' services are indeed being provided to the groups they intended. Funders, in turn, will welcome assurances that their funding is being used in the manner they have targeted.

Data about client demographic variables are useful for a number of reasons. If benchmarks are being met,

for example, program administrators will be reassured to continue the services that have been provided. On the other hand, unmet benchmarks will alert administrators and practitioners alike to explore the reasons behind the shortfall. Perhaps program practices can be adjusted to ensure that intended clients are informed of the services offered and are welcomed to the program.

Alternatively, it's possible that the social needs within the community have changed over time and earlier targets are no longer realistic, as would be the case in a transient community where population demographics change regularly. Immigrants, who had once lived downtown, for example, may now be moving into the suburbs and young professionals are perhaps moving in and replacing them. In such a case, the program will have an early indication that its services should be adjusted to meet current needs.

Service Statistics

Service statistics provide a second focal point for our evaluation example. Service statistics are similar to client demographic data. However, the focus is on the services provided by the program (i.e., program processes) rather than on the program's clientele. Service, or process, data are of interest for accountability purposes in addition to program feedback and development.

Again, program administrators and funders will take interest in these data to ensure that the quantity of the program services corresponds to initial funding expectations, as well as to expectations as set out in the program's logic model (see Chapter 8). In addition, service statistics can also add to a solid understanding of the program's service delivery structure.

By tracking changes in various components of service delivery, for example, program administrators are in a better position to make informed decisions about reallocating their scarce resources. In short, with relevant data they will be able to manage resources more effectively and efficiently. For example, data about the volume of services provided during evening hours may lead to the reduction (or increase) of those hours.

Table 15.4 provides a simple example of two benchmarks related to service statistics. The value set for the volume of services (in our case, 500

Table 15.4: **Service Statistics.**

Benchmarks	Measures
500 counseling sessions per month	From Contact Information Form
20% of counseling sessions will take place out of center	Item on Contact Information Form

Table 15.5: **Quality Standards.**

Benchmarks	Measures
Less than 25% of services will be provided only to single individuals	Item on Contact Information Form
A minimum of one community resource suggestion per family	Item on Contact Information Form

counseling sessions per month) corresponds to levels set in the funding agreement. The second service benchmark (in our case, 20% of services will be provided out of the center) reflects the program's intention to be more responsive to client needs by moving services out of the office and into the community. Tracking service statistics related to the location where the services were delivered provides feedback about whether the current practices are in line with this objective.

As indicated in Table 15.4, data about a program's services can generally be captured through data entered on a program's contact form or an equivalent document for recording case notes (see Figure 14.5). As long as the type of service is recorded along with the amount of services provided, the volume of each type of service can be easily tracked. To determine the location and the time of service, specific items may need to be added to the contact form or collected in a systematic way. To minimize paperwork, these items can be designed as check boxes.

Quality Standards

Quality standards are about practices that the program believes will lead to positive client outcomes. These practices may be described by relevant standard setting through the professional literature or by official accrediting agencies such as the Council on Accreditation. Quality standards are usually a focal point for process evaluations, as they relate to practices that are expected to lead to certain client outcomes. The assumption is that "good" social work practices lead to "good" client outcomes.

Most social service programs hold strong beliefs about practices thought to best serve clients, but very few actually monitor the implementation of them. Of course, many social work practices or interventions are relatively complex and difficult to capture within a single evaluation effort. Nevertheless, some quality standards, as the two shown in Table 15.5, can be addressed within an evaluative framework.

The benchmarks specified in Table 15.5 relate to program beliefs that the most effective services are those provided to larger client systems rather than an individual—for example, to a parent–child dyad or to an entire family. The benchmark speaks to this by specifying that over 75% of "client contacts" will involve more than one person. Similarly, the program believes in the impact and helpfulness of community resources in strengthening and supporting families. Thus another target is that at least one community resource suggestion per family will be made during the course of service provision.

The data needed to monitor these benchmarks can be collected through the creation of appropriate items on the "client contact form" or any other client log (see Figure 14.5). Again, through strategic design, a check-box format will easily allow the capture of the data needed to track these two simple objectives (or variables).

Data relating to the achievement of quality standard objectives are helpful in the program planning and development process of an evaluation. Through collecting such data over time, the program can ensure that its beliefs about effective practices are translated into actual practice. Results falling short of the benchmark could result in revising the set values included in the benchmark or revising the program operations in some way to increase the likelihood of achieving the original value.

Alternatively, it may be determined that the gap is the result of unmet training needs or attitudes held by staff members. In such a case, further staff development might be planned. On the other hand, if the benchmarks are met, as evidenced via credible data, existing practices and procedures could be examined in greater detail.

For example, program practices could be monitored to determine what approaches are most effective in getting individual clients to accept help as part of a larger group (e.g., a parent–child dyad, family). Additionally, benchmarks might be modified so that they align better with the professed quality standards.

In short, tracking quality standards provides data about the actual practices of a program and reveals when practices are not consistent with beliefs. Such data would lead to an examination of those practices with a view to further developing them.

Feedback

Feedback received from relevant stakeholders is another area to focus on in our evaluation example. Relevant groups may include clients, volunteers, referring agencies, or other stakeholder groups. More often than not, relevant feedback usually centers on client satisfaction of some kind. High client satisfaction, or an otherwise high opinion of a program, does not necessarily correspond with successful client outcomes.

In other words, clients may like a program but not experience any positive change as a result of it. Nevertheless, it's desirable that a program draws favorable opinions and comments from its stakeholders. If not, administrators and staff alike should be aware that satisfaction with the program is not high.

Table 15.6 provides a simple example of two benchmarks relating to feedback—in this case, client feedback. The data to track this objective are collected by asking clients to fill out a simple client satisfaction survey at the time of the completion of services (see

Table 15.6: **Feedback (Client).**

Benchmarks	Measures
70% of clients rate *helpfulness* item as "agree" or "strongly agree"	Satisfaction Survey Item 1
75% of clients rate *satisfaction* item as "high" or "very high"	Satisfaction Survey Item 5

Figure 14.8). In this case, there were five items on the survey, designed specifically for this program.

The items deal with such matters as the helpfulness of services, the supportiveness of staff, and overall satisfaction with the program's services. The first four items use a rating scale with four possible response categories. For example, helpfulness was measured by the item:

The services received were helpful (check one):

_____ Strongly Disagree

_____ Disagree

_____ Agree

_____ Strongly Agree

As Table 15.6 shows, the program set a benchmark that a minimum of 70% of service recipients will rate this item as "agree" or "strongly agree." To measure overall satisfaction, a fifth item was included that read:

My overall satisfaction with these services is (check one):

_____ Very Low

_____ Low

_____ Moderate

_____ High

_____ Very High

The benchmark meant that 75%, or more, of the clients should rate the satisfaction item as "high" or "very high." This would in turn indicate a minimum expected level of overall satisfaction with the services offered by the program.

Standardized client satisfaction scales can be found in Figures M.1, M.2, and M.3 in Tool M. We suggest using them whenever possible because they are much more valid and reliable than creating your own.

Client Outcomes

An evaluation system is seldom complete without some attention to client outcomes or client results, which is the reason that the social service organization exists in the first place. Thus client outcomes always lie outside of the program with the clients; they reflect changes in clients. Client outcomes are always directly tied to program objectives as stated in the program's logic model.

Table 15.7 provides three examples of benchmarks used to monitor program objectives or client outcomes. As can be seen, the first benchmark is expressed in terms of a minimum mean score of 3.4 on the first five items of a nonstandardized rating scale, designed specifically for the program. Of course, the value 3.4 has meaning only if we know the possible range of the rating scale.

If scores can range from 1 to 5 (and 5 is high), we would interpret the data more positively than if scores ranged from 1 to 10 (and 10 is high). Tools L and M discuss rating scales as methods of measurement; they can easily be constructed in such a way that they can directly and meaningfully monitor program objectives.

The next two benchmarks in Table 15.7 are expressed as an average minimum score and an average gain score on two separate standardized measuring instruments, Hudson's *Index of Self-Esteem* and Hudson's *Index of Peer Relations*. As seen in Tools L and M, standardized instruments are always preferable to use in outcome measurements because their reliability and validity have been previously determined and demonstrated. Thus such measures generally have more credibility than locally constructed instruments.

It should be noted that the last two outcome benchmarks imply different evaluation designs. Specifying a score of less than 30 on the exit from the program on the *Index of Self-Esteem* implies a one-group posttest-only design (Figure E.1 in Tool E). As we know, such a design allows a description of the level at which clients leave at the end of the service, but the design does not make it possible to determine the amount of change, if any, that has taken place. However, because the *Index of Self-Esteem* is known to have a clinical cutting score of 30 (i.e., scores higher than 30 indicate a clinical problem), the meaning of the objective can be interpreted more clearly.

The objective specifying an average improvement of 15 on the *Index of Peer Relations* (this would actually be a reduction of 15 points because this instrument uses higher numbers to indicate greater problems) implies a one-group pretest–posttest design (Figure E.6 in Tool E). That design not only provides a description of the group at the end of the service but also provides a description of the group at the time of entry and therefore allows a determination of what change has taken place.

Of course, because the design involves only clients who have received program services, it cannot be concluded that the program was the only cause of the change. A control group (a parallel group of clients who did not receive program services) is needed to conclude such causality.

Outcome measurement is an increasingly important topic among social service programs. Evaluation data relating to outcomes serve the needs

Table 15.7: **Client Outcomes.**

Benchmarks	Measures
Grand mean of 3.4 on first five items of Educational Outcomes Form	Educational Outcomes Feedback Form designed specifically for the program
Average self-esteem score less than 30 on exit from program	Hudson's *Index of Self-Esteem*
Average improvement of 15 points in peer relations on exit from program	Hudson's *Index of Peer Relations*

of multiple stakeholders. Funders and administrators can use it to assure themselves of the effectiveness of the program and thereby demonstrate accountability.

To ensure that the program is operating in the most effective manner possible, administrators and staff can examine outcome results and make program adjustments as necessary. For professionals providing direct services, outcome measures provide a framework for case-level evaluations and facilitate accurate and honest communications with clients.

SUMMARY

One of the most important reasons for incorporating evaluation techniques within programs is to obtain timely data on which further decisions about intervention plans or program development can be based. At the case level, the worker will continually monitor changes in the client problem; at the program level, data relating to needs, processes, and outcomes can help staff make informed decisions about program modifications and changes.

The goal of this chapter is to provide you with a beginning knowledge base for you to feel comfortable in answering the following questions. AFTER you have read the chapter, indicate how comfortable you feel you are in answering each question on a 5-point scale where

1 Very uncomfortable	2 Somewhat uncomfortable	3 Neutral	4 Somewhat comfortable	5 Very comfortable

If you rated any question between 1–3, reread the section of the chapter where the information for the question is found. If you still feel that you're uncomfortable in answering the question, then talk with your instructor and/or your classmates for more clarification.

	Questions	Degree of comfort? *(Circle one number)*
1	Discuss the similarities and differences between objective and subjective data. Provide a common social work example throughout your discussion.	1 2 3 4 5
2	List and then discuss the four essential phases in case-level decision-making. Provide a common social work example throughout your discussion.	1 2 3 4 5
3	List and then discuss the three possible patterns of change in relation to practice objectives. Provide a common social work example throughout your discussion.	1 2 3 4 5
4	Discuss the three areas of identification for decision-making within program-level outcomes. Provide a common social work example throughout your discussion.	1 2 3 4 5
5	Discuss how data results can be considered acceptable, mixed, or inadequate when considering whether a program's objectives have been achieved. Provide a common social work example throughout your discussion.	1 2 3 4 5
6	Discuss how each of the five benchmarks illustrated in this chapter can be applied to your field placement (or work) setting. Provide an example of each one in relation to your field placement (or work) setting.	1 2 3 4 5

AFTER you have read this chapter AND have completed all of the study questions, indicate how knowledgeable you feel you are for each of the following concepts on a 5-point scale where

1 Not knowledgeable at all	2 Somewhat unknowledgeable	3 Neutral	4 Somewhat knowledgeable	5 Very knowledgeable

	Concepts	Knowledge Level? [Circle one number]
1	Making decision with data, in general	1 2 3 4 5
2	Using objective data to make decisions	1 2 3 4 5
3	Using subjective data to make decisions	1 2 3 4 5
4	Making case-level decisions	1 2 3 4 5
5	Setting practice objectives	1 2 3 4 5
6	Using standardized measuring instruments	1 2 3 4 5
7	Making program-level decisions	1 2 3 4 5
8	Outcome data and program-level decision-making	1 2 3 4 5
9	Using data in process and outcome evaluations	1 2 3 4 5
10	Benchmarks	1 2 3 4 5
	Add up your scores (minimum = 10, maximum = 50)	Your total score =

A   47–50 = Professional evaluator in the making
A–   45–46 = Senior evaluator
B+   43–44 = Junior evaluator
B   41–42 = Assistant evaluator
B–   10–40 = Reread the chapter and redo the study questions

PART V

Evaluation Toolkit

This part contains 13 tools you can use within your evaluations. All of them are referred to within the previous 15 chapters.

Tool A. Hiring an External Evaluator

Tool B. Working With an External Evaluator

Tool C. Reducing Evaluation Anxiety

Tool D. Meeting Evaluation Challenges

Tool E. Using Common Evaluation Designs

Tool F. Budgeting for Evaluations

Tool G. Using Evaluation Management Strategies

Tool H. Data Collection and Sampling Procedures

Tool I. Training and Supervising Data Collectors

Tool J. Effective Communication and Reporting

Tool K. Developing an Action Plan

Tool L. Measuring Variables

Tool M. Measuring Instruments

Part V is your personal evaluation toolkit. Use it! These tools present basic "research methodology–type tools," so to speak, that were covered in your foundational research methods course. The tools contain a bridge between Part III (which presents the four basic types of evaluations) and Part IV (which discusses how to make decisions from the data you have collected from your evaluations). So in reality, Part V briefly presents basic research methodology that you will need to appreciate the complete evaluation process.

We in no way suggest that all the research methodology you need to know in order to do an evaluation is contained in this part. Part V is simply not a substitute for your research methods text! If you go on to do a real-life evaluation, however, you will have no other alternative but to obtain a social work research methods book in order to obtain an advanced understanding of what we cover briefly in Part V. Remember, we present only the very basics of the basics.

It's simple: just select the tools you need to do your evaluation. If you don't need any—that is, you aced your research methods course with flying colors and remembered everything that was covered—then just skip this part all together. If, for example, you're a measurement expert, then you don't need to use Tools L and M. However, if you haven't heard of the words *reliability* and *validity*, then start reading.

Your evaluation toolkit is filled with strategies to create, maintain, and repair your evaluation plans. As is the case in any line of work, those who master the proficient use of their tools produce better quality products than those who do not—and this includes you, as you prepare for your professional career as a social worker.

Using the image of a toolkit will help you to understand that there is little use in rummaging through your toolbox without having a meaningful evaluation project in mind. It's simply fruitless, for example, to debate strategies for measuring your clients' outcomes when your program objectives are not SMART ones.

It's also a waste of time to deliberate who ought to supply evaluation data in the absence of a clearly articulated evaluation question. When your program logic model is ambiguous and/or the reasons for conducting your evaluation are vague, there is not much in your toolkit that will help you produce a meaningful evaluation.

HIRING AN EXTERNAL EVALUATOR

This tool is to assist you with preparations in hiring an external evaluator—if you need one, that is. It should be particularly useful for social work agencies that do not have specific position descriptions tailored for evaluators. This tool is organized around the six steps of the evaluation process as outlined in Chapter 3. It lists some of the knowledge, skills, and abilities an evaluator needs to possess for each step of the process.

Please note we do not address formal educational requirements. Evaluation practitioners come from many academic disciplines, and many evaluators have learned the field by experience, rather than formal educational programs.

This list is not all-inclusive, nor are we "endorsing" this as the only list of appropriate attributes to look for in an external evaluator. In addition, it's likely you will be unable to hire an evaluator who possesses all the skills listed; however, we feel it's appropriate that you fill this position with someone with many of these skills and a willingness to learn those skills they do not currently possess. Our main goal is to provide you with useful guidance for your consideration.

PRINCIPLE DUTIES

- Work with stakeholders to develop a comprehensive program evaluation plan
- Ensure that evaluation activities are complementary to the program's operations and activities in addition to being consistent with its mission statement

KNOWLEDGE, SKILLS, AND ABILITIES

Overarching Items

- Knowledge of or familiarity with the evaluation framework as presented in this book
- Working knowledge of the Joint Committee on Standards for Educational Evaluation's program evaluation standards (i.e., utility, feasibility, propriety, accuracy)
- Knowledge of or familiarity with the American Evaluation Association's Guiding Principles for Evaluators (http://www.eval.org/p/cm/ld/fid=105)
- Ability to identify limitations of knowledge and methods for acquiring additional evaluation knowledge to supplement personal expertise when necessary
- Knowledge of how evaluation is different from research

Step 1: Engage Stakeholders

(See Figures 3.1, 5.1, 10.3, 11.1, 12.1, and 13.1.)

1a. Ability to educate program staff and partners about evaluation concepts and methods
1b. Ability to engage stakeholders based on shared priorities

- Meeting facilitation, presentation, conflict resolution, and negotiation skills
- Knowledge of strategies to engage stakeholders in the evaluation process

1c. Ability to work as part of an evaluation team to plan and execute evaluations of prioritized aspects of the program

Step 2: Describe the Program

(See Figures 3.1, 5.1, 10.3, 11.1, 12.1, and 13.1.)

2a. Ability to organize and summarize information in a clear and concise manner

2b. Ability to understand the context of a program and how it affects program planning, implementation, and outcomes

2c. Ability or experience in the development and use of logic models to describe programs

2d. Ability to provide leadership in a team setting, move members forward, and build consensus

2e. Skill in developing and articulating program goals and objectives in a structure supporting evaluation (i.e., SMART objectives)

Step 3: Focus the Evaluation Design

(See Figures 3.1, 5.1, 10.3, 11.1, 12.1, and 13.1.)

3a. Knowledge of various evaluation designs (e.g., experimental, quasi-experimental, nonexperimental, one-group, two-group)

3b. Experience with evaluations using mixed method approaches

3c. Knowledge or experience with approaches for generating, revising, and prioritizing evaluation questions

3d. Knowledge in the development of evaluation plans

3e. Knowledge of methods for designing evaluations so as to increase the likelihood that the findings will be used by primary evaluation stakeholders

Step 4: Gather Credible Data

(See Figures 3.1, 5.1, 10.3, 11.1, 12.1, and 13.1.)

4a. Ability to lead the program's staff in developing and testing data collection instruments

4b. Ability to identify and assess existing data sources for their potential use in a program evaluation

4c. Ability to gather data using qualitative and quantitative approaches such as interviews, group processes, participant observation, surveys, electronic data files, or other methods

4d. Ability to manage databases, construct data files, conduct and supervise data entry, and perform data edits/cleaning

4e. Knowledge of methods for protecting confidential data for those who participate in the evaluation

Step 5: Justify Conclusions

(See Figures 3.1, 5.1, 10.3, 11.1, 12.1, and 13.1.)

5a. Knowledge of appropriate quantitative and qualitative data analysis methods

5b. Ability to conduct analyses using appropriate analytic tools for quantitative data (e.g., SAS, SPSS, Minitab) and/or qualitative data (e.g., NVivo 8, Atlas.ti, MaxQDA)

5c. Ability to develop criteria and standards reflective of the values held by key evaluation stakeholders

5d. Experience with synthesizing information generated through an evaluation to produce findings that are clearly linked to the data collected

5e. Skill in working with stakeholders to develop feasible recommendations

Step 6: Ensure Use and Share Lessons Learned

(See Figures 3.1, 5.1, 10.3, 11.1, 12.1, and 13.1.)

6a. Ability to prepare and present evaluation results in a manner that increases the likelihood that they will be used and accepted by a diverse group of stakeholders

6b. Ability to develop action plans and systems to facilitate and track implementation of evaluation findings and recommendations

6c. Ability to work with stakeholders to present analyses, find common themes, and identify relevant and actionable findings from evaluations

6d. Skill in developing and implementing a communications and dissemination plan

WORKING WITH AN EXTERNAL EVALUATOR

You may want to consider hiring an experienced evaluator to support your evaluation efforts. We say *experienced* because there is no standard training or credential for professional evaluators. Instead, if you decide to seek outside help, you will be selecting evaluators based on their experiences rather than on their education. The following are a few tips for helping you decide whether to seek outside help, how to work with an evaluator to make sure your needs are met, and what to look for when selecting an evaluator.

NEED FOR AN EXTERNAL EVALUATOR

In certain situations, an external evaluator may be desired or needed. The following are some of the factors to consider when deciding whether to hire an external evaluation consultant.

Positives	Negatives
• Less work for you • Consultants bring an impartial point of view • Results might be seen as more objective to other members of the community	• You give up some control over the process • You may not build evaluation skills among program staff • It may be expensive—you need to find the funds • Consultants may not completely understand your program, and you are paying for their learning curve

WORKING WITH EXTERNAL EVALUATORS

Although hiring an external evaluator may lessen the work involved for you and your staff, managing an evaluation contract is demanding and time-consuming. You will not be able to turn over all responsibility for your evaluation to a third party. Consider what the evaluation consultant can do and what you will need to do.

Suggested roles for an external evaluator are listed in Table B.1. You might find that you prefer a different mix of "control" or "involvement" or that this evolves over time if you develop a good working relationship with an evaluator. Regardless, you will want to be clear about what tasks you are asking the evaluator to do and how you plan to interact with him or her throughout your evaluation.

SELECTING AN EVALUATOR

Your decision about the right evaluator for your program will depend on what you are looking for in terms of the mix of technical skills, familiarity with your program or context, and personal characteristics. In addition to the qualities you should look for in an evaluator that were presented in Tool A, there are a few more for you to consider:

- Experience with program evaluation
- Ability to communicate effectively
- Basic knowledge of your program's population
- Experience with the range of data collection strategies and evaluation designs that will

best serve your program or the particular evaluation activity or activities you are planning

- Good references (from sources you trust)

You should provide prospective evaluation consultants with a clear description of the project, including the goals, expectations, available data and resources, and a timeline, to enable the consultant to

Table B.1: **Suggested Role-Sharing Between Program Staff and an External Evaluator.**

Evaluation Steps	Program Staff	External Evaluator
1. Engage Stakeholders	**Lead Role** You know your stakeholders best and who should be engaged in the evaluation.	**Support Role** The evaluator should demonstrate an interest in engaging stakeholders and have sufficient skills and experience to engage stakeholders effectively (e.g., facilitation skills, conflict resolution skills, etc.).
2. Describe the Program	**Shared Role** You will need to share your knowledge of the program with the evaluator.	**Shared Role** The evaluator should engage program staff and possibly stakeholders in the process of describing the program. The evaluator should take the lead on developing a program description (logic model, program theory, etc.).
3. Focus the Evaluation	**Shared Role** Identifying the most important evaluation questions is not an activity you can delegate to an outsider, although the evaluator may well be able to help you refine the questions.	**Shared Role** A skilled evaluator will help you focus the evaluation, design good evaluation questions, and develop an evaluation design.
4. Gather Credible Data	**Support Role** Program staff may need to assist the evaluator in gaining access to existing data or in soliciting participation (e.g., invites or distribution lists for focus groups, interviews, surveys).	**Lead Role** An outside evaluator should be the lead on all data collection activities with oversight by program staff.
5. Justify Conclusions	**Shared Role** Program staff should help the evaluator interpret data and develop recommendations.	**Shared Role** An outside evaluator can be the lead on all data analysis activities with oversight by program staff.
6. Ensure Use and Share Lessons Learned	**Lead Role** Only you can ensure that the results are used to inform your program.	**Support Role** A skilled evaluator can present evaluation results (interim and final) in a way that promotes use.

prepare a formal proposal. Formal proposals from each consultant should be reviewed, and you should ask questions of the candidates.

If there are things you do not understand—ask! If you cannot clearly communicate with the prospective evaluator during this phase of the process, you might want to consider finding another evaluator. Ask the evaluator whether there are other things you should consider or ask about the planned evaluation; after all, he or she is the "expert" on the topic.

MANAGING AN EXTERNAL EVALUATOR

Once you have chosen your evaluator it's essential that you draw up a contract to cover the work. This will ensure there is clarity of expectations by both the evaluator and you. The contract will set out the main terms and conditions and may include the following:

- Who "owns" the data collected and the material that is produced
- How issues such as protection of confidentiality and conflicts of interest are to be addressed
- A detailed description of deliverables (e.g., presentations of work to stakeholders and others; frequency of communication; etc.)
- Timelines for all work and work products

- Budget and a payment schedule (periodic billing of actual hours, etc.)
- Discussion of sanctions and contract termination

Contract language should ensure that the deliverables and timeline are clearly described and that program staff has an opportunity to review major deliverables and request modifications if they do not meet expected quality. The terms of the agreement should be tight enough to ensure that you get what you want but flexible enough to ensure that mid-course changes are possible.

To ensure that you get what you want and need from the evaluation, it's important to designate a key member of your staff to manage the consultant and the evaluation process. This person will have responsibility for:

- Communicating with the evaluator
- Making sure the evaluator has access to the information required
- Troubleshooting problems that arise
- Ensuring that products are delivered and payments are made

As discussed in depth in Chapter 9, careful planning is the key to a successful evaluation experience. Once a plan is in place, all parties should attempt to adhere to it to the extent possible. While small changes are normal in the course of implementing a plan, substantial changes can affect both the cost and timing of an evaluation.

REDUCING EVALUATION ANXIETY

Evaluation anxiety—feeling anxious about an evaluation and its potential impacts—is quite common—especially for social work students. It can easily affect the staff and other stakeholders of a program being evaluated, *as well as* the evaluators themselves. Its effects can be detrimental to the quality of the evaluation. A few practical suggestions to minimize evaluation anxiety for the stakeholders and evaluators themselves are addressed in this tool.

STAKEHOLDERS' ANXIETY

Some sources of program staff and stakeholder anxiety include the following:

- Lack of experience
- Negative past experiences
- Fear of negative consequences

Most people experience anxiety when they believe their behaviors or achievements are being evaluated. Simply put, they're afraid that the evaluation's results will reflect poorly on them. If you are aware of—and take steps to—address this perception at the outset of your evaluation, you can minimize the chance that stakeholder anxiety will lead to the obstruction of your evaluative efforts or render your findings useless. Helping stakeholders understand the clear distinction between a personnel evaluation and a program evaluation is an important first step for you to take.

Several well-seasoned evaluators have analyzed the phenomenon of evaluation anxiety and offer a number of practical strategies—or tips—to recognize and deal with it (see Table C.1).

When present in excess, this type of anxiety may display itself in terms of conflict with evaluators; avoidance of or refusal to work with the evaluators; stalling, protesting, or failing to use evaluation results; hiding weaknesses; and displays of anger at negative findings.

At its worst, excessive evaluation anxiety can result in difficulty gaining access to required data, lack of cooperation by critical stakeholders, false reporting, challenges to the validity of evaluation results, lack of program improvement, decrease in performance and productivity, and a general dissatisfaction with program evaluations.

One particularly challenging area is the anxiety associated with communicating negative evaluation findings. The tips contained in Table C.2 address this type of challenge.

EVALUATORS' ANXIETY

Up to now, we have focused on anxiety among evaluation stakeholders. However, we recognize that the evaluator can also experience anxiety when planning for and conducting an evaluation.

This can arise from a number of sources, which may include the following:

- Relationship of evaluator to organization
- Competing priorities or roles
- Competing demands of different stakeholders
- Workload stress
- Personal conflicts
- Time/budget/logistical constraints

Table C.1: **Addressing Excessive Evaluation Anxiety.**

Tip #	Within your field practicum (or work) setting, pretend for a moment that you are asked to "evaluate" your practicum's social service program (or work) setting. Choose one of the three main types of evaluations that you could do: process (Chapter 11), outcome (Chapter 12), or efficiency (Chapter 13).
	Discuss how you would specifically address each of the following tips within your hypothetical evaluation in reference to "evaluation anxiety." Provide as many social work examples as you can to illustrate your points. What skill sets did you learn within your social work program that will help you deal with not only your evaluation anxiety as an evaluator but the anxieties of the other stakeholders as well?
1	*Expect and accept:* Be prepared for some evaluation anxiety and accept that you will have to account for and respond to it throughout the evaluation.
2	Work through "hangovers" from previous bad evaluation experiences.
3	Make sure that the anxiety experienced by the stakeholders isn't a legitimate opposition to you proposing a bad evaluation.
4	Determine the program "psychologic" (i.e., how the success or failure of the program being evaluated will affect stakeholders personally).
5	Thoroughly discuss the purposes of your evaluation in everyday language with all stakeholders.
6	Thoroughly discuss why honesty with the evaluator is not disloyalty to the group.
7	Thoroughly discuss the risk/benefit ratio of cooperation for individuals.
8	Provide balanced, continuous improvement feedback.
9	Allow stakeholders to discuss how the results of your evaluation will affect them.
10	Be prepared to wear your psychotherapy hat (i.e., in terms of trying to understand how stakeholders connected to the evaluation think and feel throughout the process).
11	Engage in role clarification on an ongoing basis (i.e., at a given moment are you functioning as a critic, a co-author, a trainer?).
12	Be a role model (i.e., allow stakeholders to evaluate the evaluation and accept criticism gracefully).
13	Distinguish the blame game from the program evaluation game.
14	Facilitate learning communities/organizations (i.e., stakeholder receptivity to evaluation as a means to enhance learning).
15	Push for culture change (i.e., toward a view of evaluation as routine and valuable).

Table C.2: **Communicating Negative Evaluation Findings.**

Within your field practicum (or work) setting, pretend for a moment that you are asked to "evaluate" your practicum's social service program (or work) setting. Choose one of the three main types of evaluations that you could do: process (Chapter 11), outcome (Chapter 12), or efficiency (Chapter 13).

Discuss how you would specifically address each of the following tips within your hypothetical evaluation in reference to "communicating negative evaluation findings." Provide as many social work examples as you can to illustrate your points. What skill sets did you learn within your social work program that will help you deal the task of communicating negative evaluation findings to your stakeholder group?

1	Hold regular debriefing sessions with program leadership throughout the evaluation to ensure that evaluation results are known early and are not "sprung on" participants at the end.
2	Conduct "mock sessions" early in the evaluation to discuss "what if" scenarios should negative results be obtained.
3	Ensure fair and balanced reporting of both positive and negative findings.
4	Promote the use of evaluation findings as "learning opportunities" for program improvement.
5	Engage stakeholders in evaluation decision-making process and communicate throughout the entire evaluation.
6	Keep stakeholder perspectives' in mind and directly address anxiety issues related to possible negative findings.

You can address or minimize many of these issues by applying some of the strategies previously listed in this tool. You may find that as the evaluation becomes routine and its value has been demonstrated, competing demands may lessen. In the following section we elaborate on some additional techniques that may be helpful in minimizing evaluator anxiety.

Evaluators who are aware of their role going into the evaluation and how it may change in relation to stakeholder needs may be better able to recognize potential sources of anxiety and address those stressors throughout the evaluation process. Three models presented by King and Stevahn (2002) describe the types of roles played by evaluators. They are summarized in the following.

Interactive Evaluation Practice Continuum

This model describes the role of the evaluator in relation to other evaluation participants by emphasizing the extent to which evaluation stakeholders are involved in the evaluation's decision-making and implementation processes. King and Stevahn (2002) lay out a continuum of stakeholder/evaluator involvement within an evaluation as illustrated in Table C.3.

Being clear about the relative involvement of the evaluator and other stakeholders in the evaluation decision-making and implementation processes can easily clarify expectations for all parties, although these roles will more than likely shift during the evaluation.

Evaluation Capacity Building Framework

This framework describes the relationship between the evaluator and the organization sponsoring the evaluation, specifically with respect to the evaluator's commitment to building within the organization the continuing capacity to conduct evaluation studies. This continuum places the evaluator in a range of roles from primarily providing evaluation findings,

Table C.3: **Degree of Stakeholder Involvement in the Evaluation Process.**

Traditional Evaluation	Participatory Evaluation	Action-Research
The evaluator takes primary responsibility for the evaluation design and conduct with input from stakeholders	There is joint responsibility for the evaluation between the evaluator and stakeholders	Stakeholders direct the evaluation, with the evaluator serving as a consultant or coach

to actively promoting evaluation participants' capacity to evaluate, or even to explicitly acting as an organizational change agent to promote organizational development.

Being explicit about the extent to which you will be engaged in building the evaluation capacity of your organization will help you to clarify relationships and expectations and reduce conflict related to your role as the evaluator.

Dual Concerns Model

This model provides a framework for examining interpersonal conflict. Two "concerns" are arrayed on a matrix that looks at the value placed on maintaining interpersonal relationships (from low to high) versus the value placed on achieving goals (from low to high). Each cell in the resulting schema suggests a "strategy" for minimizing or addressing conflict.

In this framework the strategies that emphasize equal attention to both relationships and goals are seen as most beneficial for evaluation. These strategies are labeled "compromising" (medium, medium) and "cooperative problem solving" (high, high). Other strategies known as "withdrawing" (low, low), "smoothing" (high, low), and "forcing" (low, high) are seen as unproductive strategies for dealing with conflict in an evaluation.

Conflict is an inevitable part of the evaluation enterprise. Recognizing and acknowledging the emphasis on relationships and goal attainment, as well as the strategies being used to resolve conflict by all participants, can move the group toward a more productive resolution of conflict. This resolution can sustain relationships while maintaining focus on evaluation goals.

MANAGING EVALUATION CHALLENGES

Good planning and strategies such as those discussed in Chapter 9 can help you anticipate and minimize potential evaluation challenges. Yet no matter how well you plan, challenges can—and will—occur. By promptly identifying and actively confronting evaluation challenges, you can help each of your evaluations meet the evaluation standards of utility, feasibility, propriety, and accuracy.

The five tables in this tool provide practical suggestions for meeting evaluation challenges you might encounter. The challenges are organized by type as follows:

- Evaluation Context—Table D.1
- Evaluation Logistics—Table D.2
- Data Collection—Table D.3
- Data Analysis—Table D.4
- Dissemination of Evaluation Findings—Table D.5

For each potential challenge, we suggest actions you can take upfront, during planning, to meet these challenges proactively. We also suggest actions you can take during implementation to minimize the effects of any challenges that arise despite your best planning efforts.

EVALUATION CONTEXT

No program—and no evaluation for that matter—occurs in a vacuum. Your program exists within an organizational hierarchy and is embedded within a community that can influence the ultimate success of your evaluation (see Chapter 1). Your interventions

may occur in multiple settings (e.g., homes, schools, workplaces, hospital emergency rooms, clinics), and therefore the evaluation of your interventions may require access to these places to collect critical data.

To gain this access, you will need to identify and cultivate "champions" for your evaluation in your organization and in the community at large. These champions can also encourage your key program stakeholders to consider—and eventually act on—your evaluation findings.

This type of "political will" in support of your evaluation is extremely valuable and should be thoughtfully and actively fostered. Think upfront about where reliance on your organization, its leadership, and your community will be most critical and incorporate ways to facilitate that interaction into your evaluation plan. Table D.1 offers steps you can take to address challenges relating to evaluation context.

EVALUATION LOGISTICS

An evaluation needs to be managed like any other project. Those working on it need to know who is doing what, when, how, and why. They also need clear guidelines about how many hours and other resources can and should be spent on individual work assignments.

Evaluation progress should be carefully monitored through a variety of means, and contingency plans should be developed if evaluation components, such as the timeline, budget, and/or scope, lose their trajectory. Good project management processes and

Table D.1: **Meeting Challenges in Evaluation Context.**

Within your field practicum (or work) setting, pretend for a moment that you are asked to "evaluate" your practicum's social service program (or work) setting. Choose one of the three main types of evaluations that you could do: process (Chapter 11), outcome (Chapter 12), or efficiency (Chapter 13).

Discuss how you would specifically address each one of the following tips within your hypothetical evaluation. Provide as many social work examples as you can to illustrate your points. What skill sets did you learn within your social work program that will help you deal with each tip?

Evaluation challenge	Tips for meeting challenges during *planning*	Tips for meeting challenges during *implementation*	Relevant standard(s)
Negative community response to evaluation	1. Discuss information needs and evaluation plans with your stakeholders 2. Include one or more stakeholders from the community (including program beneficiaries) on your evaluation team, if appropriate	3. Discuss your evaluation findings with stakeholders and explore implications for your program and community 4. Include stakeholders in developing your action plan to implement evaluation findings 5. Use an issues management approach to public relations if findings may reflect negatively on the community (see Table C.2 in Tool C)	• Utility • Feasibility
Lack of "political will" to support evaluation	6. Discuss information needs with stakeholders and incorporate their needs into evaluation design	7. Discuss evaluation successes, findings, and implications for program with stakeholders and organizational leadership postevaluation 8. Consistently send messages about the importance of your evaluation	• Utility • Feasibility
Changes in program priorities	9. Discuss program priorities with stakeholders and incorporate into design	10. When priorities shift, frankly discuss whether the evaluation should continue as planned or whether modifications need to be made 11. If evaluation continues to completion, discuss implications for program priorities with stakeholders after completion	• Utility • Feasibility

Table D.1: (Continued)

Evaluation challenge	Tips for meeting challenges during *planning*	Tips for meeting challenges during *Implementation*	Relevant standard(s)
Lack of support from program leadership	12. At the start of strategic evaluation planning, include frontline program leadership in stakeholder discussions about the evaluation	13. Keep leaders informed about your evaluation through progress reports and solicit their input 14. Consider alternate methods of dissemination that may be more useful to busy leaders 15. Should leadership change, inform new leaders about the evaluation and its progress and solicit their input 16. Include leaders in briefings on evaluation results and implications for program improvement	• Utility • Feasibility

tools, such as the ones presented in Table D.2, will support those managing the evaluation in reaching a successful conclusion. These good management practices and tools should be built into your evaluation plan.

DATA COLLECTION

There are many aspects of data collection activities to consider, both while planning and implementing an evaluation. This is true whether you are collecting new data through surveys, interviews, or focus groups; systematically reviewing archival data (such as medical records); or compiling and analyzing surveillance data and other types of data from existing sources. Any of these types of data collection activities requires that you have a clear plan (or protocol) for how the work will proceed and as many safeguards as necessary to ensure consistency, accuracy, and reliability of your findings.

Some important safeguards include documenting procedures to be used, pilot-testing data collection

procedures and measuring instruments, training individuals involved in data collection/compilation, and carefully cleaning the data in preparation for analysis. In addition, you will want to ensure procedures are in place to monitor the quality and consistency of incoming data. Protecting the rights of any program participants involved in your evaluation is another critical consideration that must be planned for upfront and managed carefully during its implementation. Table D.3 offers steps you can take to address data collection challenges.

DATA ANALYSIS

Nothing is more frustrating than approaching the conclusion of an evaluation only to discover that the data collected are not analyzable or do not meet the needs of program staff and stakeholders. With so many precious human and monetary resources invested in an evaluation, planning ahead for data analysis and use—and documenting those in the

Table D.2: **Meeting Challenges in Evaluation Logistics.**

Within your field practicum (or work) setting, pretend for a moment that you are asked to "evaluate" your practicum's social service program (or work) setting. Choose one of the three main types of evaluations that you could do: process (Chapter 11), outcome (Chapter 12), or efficiency (Chapter 13).

Discuss how you would specifically address each one of the following tips within your hypothetical evaluation. Provide as many social work examples as you can to illustrate your points. What skill sets did you learn within your social work program that will help you deal with each tip?

Evaluation challenge	Tips for meeting challenges during *planning*	Tips for meeting challenges during *implementation*	Relevant standard(s)
Difficulty communicating with evaluation staff, evaluation team members, and stakeholders	1. Develop a communication plan about whom you will need to communicate with at various stages of the evaluation and the best modes of communication for each audience type	2. Consult regularly with the communication plan to help make sure you are on track 3. Develop ways to obtain regular feedback from various audience types to help make sure they feel communication is adequate	• Utility • Feasibility • Propriety • Accuracy
Confusion among team members about roles and responsibilities	4. Plan around staff skills and availability, including looking across evaluations during strategic planning 5. Clearly document team members' roles and responsibilities in evaluation plan	6. Hold regular meetings with evaluation team during implementation to discuss progress and to address emerging issues	• Feasibility • Accuracy
Insufficient financial resources to complete evaluation	7. Have resource estimates developed by individuals experienced in evaluation 8. Consider efficiencies across evaluations during the strategic evaluation planning phase 9. Identify additional resources for evaluation 10. Consider delays in evaluation schedule to accommodate funding cycle 11. Allow for some "wiggle room" in your budget in case surprises occur	12. Regularly monitor evaluation budget during implementation 13. Consider reduction in scope and other cost- saving measures if budget monitoring indicates a need to economize. 14. Document effectiveness of cost-saving measures 15. Keep track of resources spent to help generate more realistic estimates in future evaluations	• Feasibility

Table D.2: (Continued)

Evaluation challenge	Tips for meeting challenges during *planning*	Tips for meeting challenges during *implementation*	Relevant standard(s)
Inadequate staff resources to complete evaluation	16. Plan around staff skills and availability, including looking across evaluations during strategic evaluation planning 17. Consider alternatives during strategic evaluation planning if staffing falls short of requirements, such as contracting externally, training existing staff in needed skills, "borrowing" partner staff, interns from local colleges and universities	18. Implement previously developed contingency plans to deal with staff shortages	• Feasibility
Evaluation off track in terms of timeline, budget, or scope	19. Plan at several levels: strategic planning for the big picture, individual planning for each specific evaluation	20. Monitor timeline, budget, and scope 21. Hold regular meetings with evaluation team to discuss progress and emerging issues 22. Respond quickly to emerging issues; include team members in devising solutions 23. Revise timeline, budget, and scope as feasible, considering any fixed deadlines 24. Document effectiveness of procedures used to address emerging issues	• Feasibility

individual evaluation plan—is critical. To the extent that such plans are developed in consultation with program leadership and stakeholders, the likelihood that evaluation findings will meet their information needs increases. Table D.4 offers steps you can take to address data analysis challenges.

DISSEMINATION OF EVALUATION FINDINGS

We conduct evaluations in order to put the data collected to good use. Findings from evaluations provide a means toward our accountability to our funders and

Table D.3: **Meeting Challenges in Data Collection.**

Within your field practicum (or work) setting, pretend for a moment that you are asked to "evaluate" your practicum's social service program (or work) setting. Choose one of the three main types of evaluations that you could do: process (Chapter 11), outcome (Chapter 12), or efficiency (Chapter 13).

Discuss how you would specifically address each one of the following tips within your hypothetical evaluation. Provide as many social work examples as you can to illustrate your points. What skill sets did you learn within your social work program that will help you deal with each tip?

Evaluation challenge	Meeting challenges during *planning*	Meeting challenges during *implementation*	Relevant standard(s)
Ineffective data collection instruments or data collection strategies	1. Consider utilizing or modifying existing measuring instruments that have already been tested 2. Where new instruments are needed, include stakeholders and individuals experienced in evaluation and in the design of effective, culturally sensitive instruments 3. Consider meeting with members of respondent population to inform instrument development 4. Pilot-test instruments before launching full data collection and revise instruments as needed 5. Use multiple methods, where possible, to triangulate findings and in case any one method or instrument does not work well	6. Train all data collection staff (even those with extensive experience) on written evaluation protocol containing the specifics of data collection for the evaluation 7. Regularly monitor data collection activities to ensure all is proceeding smoothly and to detect any emerging problems 8. If problems surface—particularly early in data collection—consider modifying that particular instrument or data collection strategy	• Feasibility • Accuracy
Lack of access to needed data	9. Identify potential data sources and determine the availability and accessibility of any existing data required for the evaluation 10. Develop memoranda of understanding and data sharing agreements for access to required data prior to launch	11. Discuss with evaluation team and stakeholders how to work around failures or divisions in data sharing agreements 12. If necessary, revise evaluation scope to accommodate lack of access and tap alternative data sources 13. Be alert for biases introduced from partners' points of view about data being collected or partners' relationships with respondents from whom data are being collected	• Feasibility • Accuracy

Evaluation challenge	Meeting challenges during *planning*	Meeting challenges during *implementation*	Relevant standard(s)
Difficulties recruiting participants	14. Include stakeholders and individuals experienced in evaluation in planning to maximize respondent participation in the evaluation 15. Solicit support from community members and explain to them the importance of the program and the importance of evaluation for improving the program 16. In designing instruments and recruitment materials, consider respondent burden and the costs and benefits to respondents in participating	17. Train data collectors in effective recruitment techniques 18. Solicit support from community members in identifying and gaining the cooperation from eligible respondents 19. Budget permitting, consider offering incentives (non-monetary only) to participants 20. Identify and minimize barriers to recruitment or participation in the evaluation (e.g., reduce length of instrument, change data collection strategies to be more appealing or less burdensome)	• Feasibility • Propriety • Accuracy
Difficulties working with contractors	21. Plan for which evaluation tasks will need to be contracted out and identify funds available for this work 22. Develop detailed agreements that clearly outline contractors' roles, responsibilities, products, timeline, and budget; include requirements and funds for regular meetings and progress reports	23. Train contractor staff to be involved in data collection on the written evaluation protocol containing the specifics of data collection for this evaluation 24. Monitor contractor timeline, budget, and performance through regular meetings and/or written progress reports 25. Have a back-up list of contractors to call in the event services cannot be rendered	• Feasibility • Accuracy

continued

Evaluation challenge	Meeting challenges during *planning*	Meeting challenges during *implementation*	Relevant standard(s)
Difficulties working with data collection partners (often volunteers)	26. Same as for "contractors" but with less formality as these are collaborative rather than business relationships	27. Pilot-test instruments and procedures and incorporate lessons learned from pilot test into data collectors' training manual 28. Train partner staff to be involved in data collection on the written evaluation protocol containing the specifics of data collection for this evaluation 29. Monitor data collection to ensure quality 30. Monitor partners' performance through regular meetings and/or written progress reports	• Feasibility • Accuracy
Difficulties managing volume of incoming data	31. Plan how incoming data will be managed, considering issues such as data storage, data system capacity, data cleaning, and preparation of data for analysis; also consider safeguards for respondent confidentiality and privacy 32. Document data management approach in individual evaluation plan	33. Develop data management systems 34. Test/review data collection systems 35. Clearly assign responsibilities for data cleaning and data entry	• Feasibility • Accuracy
Loss of data or corruption of data integrity	36. Plan how data will be collected and protected, considering issues such as frequent data backups, use of more than one audio recorder for interviews and focus groups, and safeguards for respondent confidentiality and privacy	38. Train all staff who will be involved in data collection (even those with extensive experience) on the specifics of data collection for this evaluation	• Accuracy

Table D.3: **(Continued)**

Evaluation challenge	Meeting challenges during *planning*	Meeting challenges during *implementation*	Relevant standard(s)
	37. Ensure up-to-date protection of computer systems to guard against corruption and loss of electronic files	39. Monitor data collection activities to ensure all is proceeding smoothly and to detect any emerging problems 40. Set up procedures and encourage data collection staff to use them to report issues	
Ethical breaches	41. Include stakeholders in planning for privacy, confidentiality, and cultural sensitivity 42. Document in individual evaluation plan and IRB package (if applicable) safeguards to protect privacy and confidentiality	43. Train staff who will be involved in data collection and analysis 44. Rigorously monitor data collection process 45. If severe breaches occur, notify IRB immediately	• Propriety

Table D.4: **Meeting Challenges in Data Analysis.**

Within your field practicum (or work) setting, pretend for a moment that you are asked to "evaluate" your practicum's social service program (or work) setting. Choose one of the three main types of evaluations that you could do: process (Chapter 11), outcome (Chapter 12), or efficiency (Chapter 13).

Discuss how you would specifically address each one of the following tips within your hypothetical evaluation. Provide as many social work examples as you can to illustrate your points. What skill sets did you learn within your social work program that will help you deal with each tip?

Evaluation challenge	Tips for meeting challenges during *planning*	Tips for meeting challenges during *implementation*	Relevant standard(s)
Data collected are not useful	1. Discuss with stakeholders their information needs and priorities 2. Incorporate stakeholder information needs and priorities into individual evaluation plan 3. Identify what type of data potential end users view as credible data (e.g., qualitative, quantitative, mixed)	8. If feasible, revise data collection strategies or instruments or clarify instructions to enhance data quality 9. Work with stakeholders to address evaluation findings in an action plan with clear roles, responsibilities, timeline, and budget	• Utility

continued

Table D.4: **(Continued)**

Evaluation challenge	Tips for meeting challenges during *planning*	Tips for meeting challenges during *implementation*	Relevant standard(s)
	4. Identify a study design (Tool E) that will provide credible data for end users (e.g., posttest only, pretest-posttest) 5. Specify how data analyses will help answer the evaluation questions 6. Draft table shells to show how data will be used to answer evaluation questions 7. Pilot-test instruments and revise as necessary to promote useful data collection	10. Discuss evaluation findings and implications for program with stakeholders post-evaluation 11. Conduct preliminary analysis of pilot data to check for usefulness of data and feasibility of analysis plan; revise data collection and analysis plans as necessary (including possible revisions to the sampling plan)	
Uncertainty about how to analyze the data	12. Include stakeholders and individuals experienced in evaluation and in data analysis in planning how incoming data will be analyzed 13. Cross-check analysis plans with evaluation data collection instruments to ensure data are collected in an appropriate manner for intended analyses 14. Document data analysis approach in individual evaluation plan (possibly including blank table shells) 15. Ensure availability of individuals (either staff or contractors) with the requisite skills and experience to implement the data analysis plan	16. Consult with analysts on staff or in partner organizations 17. If data cannot or will not be analyzed, consider dropping the data elements from data collection instruments 18. Do not report data with small cell sizes that might result in inadvertent disclosure of confidential information (e.g., when small numbers of cases further broken down by demographic factors could lead to identification of individuals). In these situations, it may be advisable to note the reason for not reporting on certain analyses.	• Feasibility • Accuracy • Propriety

Table D.4: (Continued)

Evaluation challenge	Tips for meeting challenges during *planning*	Tips for meeting challenges during *implementation*	Relevant standard(s)
Preliminary findings indicate need for program modifications	19. Discuss with stakeholders how to handle the situation if preliminary findings suggest a need for program modification 20. Consider preparing for a "mock" findings session in which possible results scenarios are presented	21. Discuss preliminary findings with stakeholders to decide whether program should be modified immediately or after evaluation concludes 22. If the program is modified, consider with evaluation team and stakeholders any implications for the evaluation	• Utility

other decision-makers. Yet evaluation findings that are not believable, or come too late to meet a particular information need, are unlikely to be able to inform programmatic decision-making.

Fortunately, there are things that can be done to help ensure use, during both the planning and implementation of an evaluation. Table D.5 offers steps you can take to address evaluation challenges relating to the dissemination of your evaluation's findings.

Table D.5: **Meeting Challenges in Dissemination of Findings.**

Within your field practicum (or work) setting, pretend for a moment that you are asked to "evaluate" your practicum's social service program (or work) setting. Choose one of the three main types of evaluations that you could do: process (Chapter 11), outcome (Chapter 12), or efficiency (Chapter 13).

Discuss how you would specifically address each one of the following tips within your hypothetical evaluation. Provide as many social work examples as you can to illustrate your points. What skill sets did you learn within your social work program that will help you deal with each tip?

Evaluation challenge	Tips for meeting challenges during *planning*	Tips for meeting challenges during *implementation*	Relevant standard(s)
Late timing of evaluation in relation to Information needs	1. Discuss with your stakeholder groups when they feel they will need the information	2. Monitor the evaluation's timelines to ensure you stay on track 3. If appropriate, disseminate interim findings prior to the completion of your evaluation, along with caveats that information provided at this stage is not final	• Utility

continued

Table D.5: (Continued)

Evaluation challenge	Tips for meeting challenges during *planning*	Tips for meeting challenges during *implementation*	Relevant standard(s)
Findings not used	4. Hold upfront discussions with program stakeholders about their information needs and how they can use your findings 5. Incorporate stakeholders' information needs into your evaluation design 6. Develop plans for the dissemination of your findings (including interim findings as they become available)	7. Ensure that your findings are communicated to decision-makers in useful formats at strategic times; share your interim findings if appropriate 8. Hold postevaluation discussions with program stakeholders about your evaluation findings and the implications for the entire program 9. Document proposed strategies to address your evaluation findings in an action plan with clear roles, responsibilities, timelines, and budget	• Utility
Findings not credible	10. Discuss with program stakeholders and decision-makers any design and data collection preferences they may have 11. Incorporate stakeholder, evaluator, and practitioner perspectives into evaluation design and development of data collection strategies 12. Document design and data collection strategies in your evaluation plan	13. Postevaluation, discuss findings and potential programmatic implications with stakeholders 14. Document proposed strategies to address your evaluation findings in an action plan with clear roles, responsibilities, timelines, and budget	• Utility • Accuracy

Table D.5: (Continued)

Evaluation challenge	Tips for meeting challenges during *planning*	Tips for meeting challenges during *implementation*	Relevant standard(s)
Findings from one evaluation have implications for later evaluations in the strategic evaluation plan	15. During strategic planning for evaluation, be aware of potential relationships and interdependencies between the various evaluations proposed	16. As part of postevaluation discussions, address whether any of the evaluation findings affect future planned evaluations (such as which evaluations to conduct or how to conduct them or how much of the resources have been expended) 17. If necessary, revise the strategic evaluation plan accordingly	• Utility • Feasibility
Findings not welcomed by some stakeholders	18. Discuss upfront with stakeholders their information needs and plans for evaluation 19. Discuss upfront with stakeholders how to handle a situation where findings do not show the program in a positive light or if findings suggest the need for program modification 20. Consider alternative modes of dissemination that may be more useful and accessible to stakeholders than the traditional final evaluation report	21. Communicate with stakeholders throughout the evaluation to avoid surprises at the end 22. At postevaluation, discuss evaluation findings with stakeholders and explore implications for program and community, emphasizing positive, constructive action that can be taken 23. Document proposed strategies to address evaluation findings in an action plan with clear roles, responsibilities, timeline, and budget; include roles for stakeholders in action planning	• Utility • Feasibility

USING COMMON EVALUATION DESIGNS

This tool covers the various research designs you can use in your evaluations. Does the term "research/evaluation designs" sound familiar? It should, because it was covered in your foundational research methods course. We present a brief discussion on how various designs can be used in your evaluations by categorizing them into two classifications:

- One-group designs
- Two-group designs

The main difference between the two classifications is that the one-group designs don't compare their evaluation participants with another group; they simply don't have another group of participants to compare to. On the other hand, the two-group designs do just that; they compare one group of research participants against another group—usually to ascertain if a particular group (experimental group) has more positive outcomes on a program objective than the other group (control or comparison group).

The designs presented in this tool cover the majority of the ones that are used in evaluating social service programs. There are obviously more designs than we present. However, they are very complicated to execute, and the chances of you needing one that is not included here are slim.

Let's begin our discussion with the simplest of all evaluation designs—those that use only one group of evaluation participants.

ONE-GROUP DESIGNS

These designs measure (a) the participants' success with an intervention (program objective) after they leave a program and (b) any nonprogram objective at any time. They are exceptionally useful for providing a framework for gathering data for needs assessments (Chapter 10) and process evaluations (Chapter 11). In fact, two-group designs are rarely used in needs assessments and process evaluations. There are numerous types of one-group evaluation designs; we present only five of them:

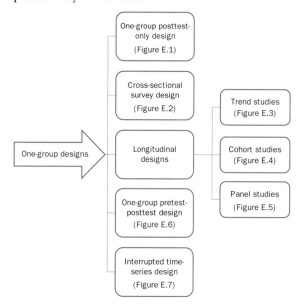

One-Group Posttest-Only Design

The one-group posttest-only design is sometimes called the one-shot case study or cross-sectional case study design. Suppose in a particular small community there are numerous parents who are physically abusive toward their children. The city decides to hire a school social worker, Antonia, to implement a social service program that is supposed to reduce the number of parents who physically abuse their children.

She creates a 12-week child abuse prevention program (the intervention) and offers it to parents who have children in her school who wish to participate on a voluntary basis. A simple evaluation study is then conducted to answer the rather simplistic question: "Did the parents who completed the program stop physically abusing their children?" The answer to this question will crudely determine the success of her program, or intervention.

There are many different ways in which her program can be evaluated. For now, and to make matters as simple as possible, we are going to evaluate it by simply calculating the percentage of parents that said they stopped physically abusing their children after they attended the 12-week program—the program's objective.

At the simplest level, the program could be evaluated with a one-group posttest-only design. The basic elements of this design can be written as shown in Figure E.1.

Where:

X = Child abuse prevention program, or the intervention
O = First and only measurement of the program objective

All that this design provides is a single measure (O) of what happens when one group of people is subjected to one intervention or experience (X). It's safe to assume that all the members within the program had physically abused their children before they enrolled, since people who do not have this problem would not have enrolled in such a program.

But even if the value of O indicates that some of the parents did stop being violent with their children after the program, it cannot be determined whether they quit because of the intervention or because of something else.

These "somethings" are called rival hypotheses, or alternative explanations. Perhaps a law was recently passed that made it mandatory for the police to arrest folks who behave violently toward their children, or perhaps the local television station started to report such incidents on the nightly news, complete with pictures of the abusive parents.

These or other extraneous variables might have been more important in persuading the parents to cease their abusive behavior toward their children than their voluntary participation in the program. All we will know from this design is the number and percentages of the people who self-reported that they stopped hurting their children after they successfully completed Antonia's 12-week program.

Figure E.1a presents the results from a simple survey question that Antonia included in a mailed survey that was completed by her past participants.

Survey Question:
Do you continue to physically abuse your children?

1. Yes
2. No

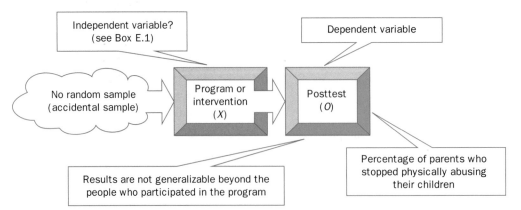

Figure E.1: **One-group posttest-only design.**

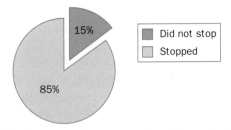

Figure E.1a: **Percentage of parents who stopped physically abusing their children after leaving Antonia's program (from Figure E.1).**

Notice that 85% of the parents reported they do not physically abuse their children after they completed Antonia's program. So Antonia could place the results of her survey question in a simple pie chart like Figure E.1a. And, yes, we are fully aware of the problems with parents self-reporting whether or not they continue to physically abuse their children, but for now, just go along with us.

The one-group posttest-only design is also used often in process evaluations when it comes to the collection of client satisfaction data.

Cross-Sectional Survey Design

Let's take another example of a design that does not have an intervention of some kind called a cross-sectional survey design. In doing a cross-sectional survey, we survey a cross-section of some particular population only once.

In addition to running her child abuse prevention program geared for abusive parents, Antonia may also want to start another program geared for all the children in her school (whether or not they come from abusive families)—a child abuse educational program.

Before Antonia starts her educational program geared for the children, however, she wants to know what parents think about the idea—kind of like a needs assessment discussed in Chapter 10. She may send out questionnaires to all the parents, or she may decide to personally telephone every second parent, or every fifth or tenth, depending on how much time and money she has. She asks one simple question in her mini–needs assessment survey:

Survey Question
Do you support our school offering a child abuse educational program that your child could enroll in on a voluntary basis and with your consent?

1. Yes
2. No

The results of her rather simplistic survey constitute a single measurement, or observation, of the parents' opinions of her proposed educational program (the one for the children) and may be written as shown in Figure E.2.

The symbol O represents the entire cross-sectional survey design, since such a design involves making only a single observation, or measurement, at one time period. Note that there is no X, since there is really no intervention. Antonia wants only to ascertain the parents' attitudes toward her proposed program—nothing more, nothing less.

This type of design is used often in needs assessment studies. Data that are derived from such a design can be displayed in a simple pie chart as in Figure E.2a Notice that 60% of the parents supported their children attending a voluntary child abuse educational program.

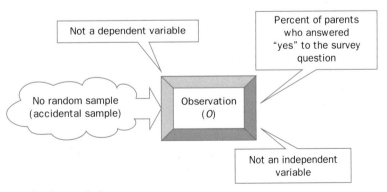

Figure E.2: **Antonia's cross-sectional survey design.**

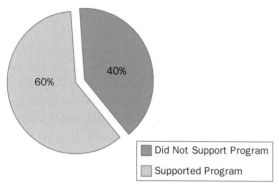

Figure E.2a: **Percentage of parents who supported a voluntary child abuse educational program in 2015 (from Figure E.2).**

Longitudinal Designs

The longitudinal design provides for multiple measurements (Os) of the program objective—or some other variable of interest over time, not just at one point in time. Notice that the two previous designs—the one-group posttest-only design and the cross-sectional survey design—measured a variable only once: not so with longitudinal designs; they measure variables more than once, thus the name "longitudinal." They can be broken down into three general types:

- Trend studies
- Cohort studies
- Panel studies

Trend Studies

A trend study takes different samples of people who share a similar characteristic at different points in time. Antonia may want to know whether parents of second-grade children enrolled in her school are becoming more receptive to the idea of the school offering their children a child abuse prevention education program. Her population of interest is simply the parents who have children in the second grade.

Remember, a trend study samples different groups of people at different points in time from the same population of interest. So, to answer her question, she may survey a sample of the parents of Grade 2 children this year (Sample 1), a sample of the parents of the new complement of Grade 2 children next year (Sample 2), and so on (Sample 3) until she thinks she has sufficient data to answer her question. Each year the parents surveyed will be different, but they will all be parents of Grade 2 children—her population of interest.

Antonia will be able to determine whether parents, as a group, are becoming more receptive to the idea of introducing child abuse prevention material to their children as early as Grade 2. In other words, she will be able to measure any attitudinal trend that is, or is not, occurring. The design can be written as shown in Figure E.3, and the data from Antonia's study could be displayed in a simple bar graph like Figure E.3a.

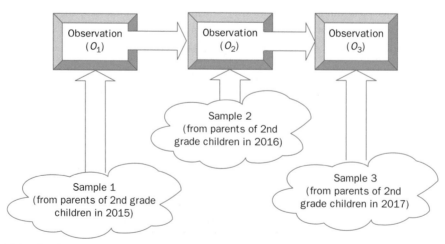

Figure E.3: **Antonia's trend study.**

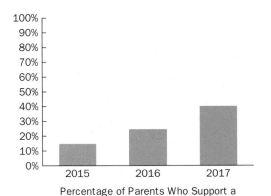

Figure E.3a: **Displaying data for a trend study (from Figure E.3).**

Notice that the percentage of parents desiring such a program is going up over time.

Where:

O_1 = First measurement of a variable in **Sample 1**

O_2 = Second measurement of the same variable in **Sample 2**

O_3 = Third measurement of the same variable in **Sample 3**

Cohort Studies

A cohort study takes place when evaluation participants who have a certain condition and/or receive a particular treatment are sampled over time. For example, AIDS survivors, sexual abuse survivors, or parents

of children can easily be followed over time. In a nutshell, and unlike a trend study that does not follow a particular cohort of individuals over time, a cohort study does just that—it follows a particular cohort of people who have shared a similar experience.

Antonia might select, for example, one particular group of parents who have adopted minority children and measure their attitudes toward child abuse prevention education in successive years. Again, the design can be written as shown in Figure E.4, and data could be presented in a format in a simple graph such as Figure E.4a.

Where:

O_1 = First measurement of a variable for a **sample** of individuals within a given cohort

O_2 = Second measurement of the variable for a **different sample** of individuals within the same cohort **1 year later**

O_3 = Third measurement of the variable for a **different sample** of individuals within the same cohort **2 years later**

Panel Studies

In a panel study, the same individuals are followed over a period of time. Antonia might select one random sample of parents, for example, and measure their attitudes toward child abuse prevention education in successive years. Unlike trend and cohort

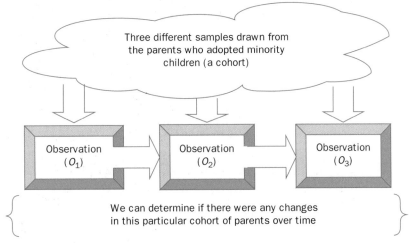

Figure E.4: **Antonia's cohort study.**

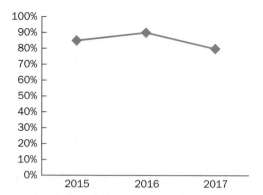

Percentage of Parents who Have Minority Children that Support a Prevention Educational Program by Year

Figure E.4a: Displaying data for a cohort study (from Figure E.4).

prevention education program in their children's school over a 3-year period (from 2015 to 2017).

Where:

O_1 = First measurement of attitudes toward child abuse prevention education for a **sample of individuals**

O_2 = Second measurement of attitudes toward child abuse prevention education for the **same individuals 1 year later**

O_3 = Third measurement of attitudes toward child abuse prevention education for the **same individuals 2 years later**

One-Group Pretest–Posttest Design

The one-group pretest–posttest design is also referred to as a before–after design because it includes a pretest of the program objective, which can be used as a basis of comparison with the posttest results. It should be obvious by now that this is the first design that uses a pretest of some kind. It's written as shown in Figure E.6, and hypothetical data could be displayed as in Table E.1.

Where:

O_1 = First measurement of the program objective
X = The program, or intervention (see Box E.1)
O_2 = Second measurement of the program objective

studies, panel studies can reveal both net change and gross change in the program objective for the same individuals. Additionally, panel studies can reveal shifting attitudes and patterns of behavior that might go unnoticed with other research approaches.

For example, if Bob was measured once at Time 1, he would then again be measured at Time 2 and so forth. We would do this for each individual in the study. Again, the design can be illustrated as in Figure E.5, and hypothetical data could be displayed in a simple graph as in Figure E.5a. For example, Figure E.5a presents the results of the percentages of the same parents who want to have a child abuse

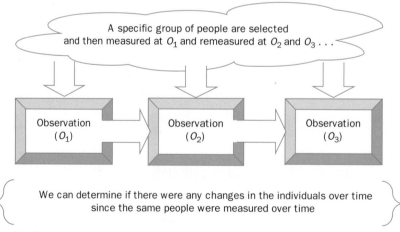

Figure E.5: Antonia's panel study.

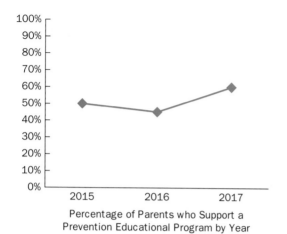

Figure E.5a: **Displaying data for a panel study (from Figure E.5).**

The pretest–posttest design, in which a pretest precedes the introduction of the intervention and a posttest follows it, can be used to determine, on a general level, how the intervention affects a particular group. The design is used often in social work decision-making. The differences between O_1 and O_2, on which these decisions are based, could be due to many other internal validity factors (to be discussed in the next section) rather than to the intervention.

Let's take another indicator of how Antonia's child abuse prevention program could be evaluated. Besides counting the number of parents who stopped physically abusing their children as the only indicator of her program's success, she could have a second outcome indicator such as a reduction in the parents' risk for abusive and neglecting parenting behaviors.

This program objective could be easily measured by an instrument that measures their attitudes toward physical punishment of children. Let's say that Antonia had the parents complete the instrument before participating in the child abuse prevention program (O_1) and after completing it (O_2).

In this example, all kinds of things could have happened between O_1 and O_2 to affect the participants' behaviors and feelings—such as the television station's deciding to publicize the names of parents who are abusive to their children. Just the experience of taking the pretest could motivate some participants to stop being abusive toward their children. Maturation—the children becoming more mature with age so that they became less difficult to discipline—could also affect the results between the pretest and posttest measurements.

Interrupted Time-Series Design

In the interrupted time-series design, a series of pretests and posttests are conducted on a group of evaluation participants over time, both before and after the independent variable, or intervention, is introduced. The basic elements of this design are shown in Figure E.7, where:

Os = Measurements of a program's objective
X = The program, or intervention (see Box E.1)

This design takes care of the major weakness in the descriptive one-group pretest–posttest design, which does not control for many rival hypotheses.

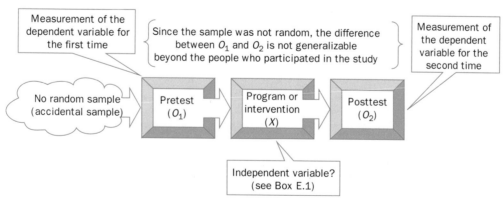

Figure E.6: **One-group pretest–posttest design.**

Table E.1: **Displaying Data: One-Group Pretest–Posttest Design (From Figure E.6).**

	Pretest Average (O_1)	Posttest Average (O_2)	Difference Average $(O_2 - O_1)$
Intervention Group $(N = 20)$	50	80	30

Suppose, for example, that a new policy is to be introduced into an agency whereby all promotions and raises are to be tied to the number of educational credits acquired by social workers.

Since there is a strong feeling among some workers that years of experience should count for more than educational credits, the agency's management decides to examine the effect of the new policy on morale.

Because agency morale is affected by many things and varies normally from month to month, it's necessary to ensure that these normal fluctuations are not confused with the results of the new policy.

Therefore, a baseline is first established for morale by conducting a number of pretests over, say, a 6-month period before the policy is introduced. Then a similar number of posttests is conducted over the 6 months following the introduction of the policy. The same type of time-series design can be used to evaluate the result of a treatment intervention with a client or client system, as in case-level designs described in Chapter 15. Again, without randomization, threats to external validity still could affect the study's generalizability, but most of the threats to internal validity are addressed.

These issues are referred to as "alternative explanations" and "rival hypotheses" and can make most of us question the results of just about any outcome evaluation. The only way you can control for all this messy stuff is by using two groups of people. So before going any further with a discussion of two-group designs, you should brush up on the concept of internal validity, the subject of the following section.

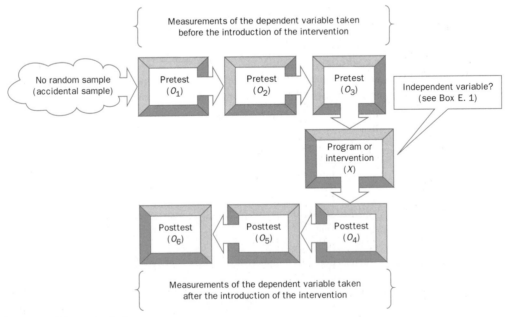

Figure E.7: **Interrupted time-series design.**

BOX E.1 TREATMENT: A VARIABLE OR A CONSTANT?

For instructional purposes, group designs are displayed using symbols where *X* is the independent variable (treatment) and *O* is the measure of the dependent variable. This presentation is accurate when studies are designed with two or more groups. When one-group designs are used, however, this interpretation does not hold.

In one-group designs, the treatment, or program, cannot truly vary because all research participants have experienced the same event; that is, they all have experienced the program. Without a comparison or control group, treatment is considered a constant because it is a quality shared by all members in the research study. In short, time is the independent variable.

There does not necessarily have to be an independent variable in a study, however; we may just want to measure some variable in a particular population such as the number of people who receive a certain type of social service intervention over a 10-year period. In this situation, there is no independent or dependent variable (see the section on cross-sectional surveys).

INTERNAL VALIDITY

Internal validity is a term we use to assess the "approximate certainty" about inferences regarding cause–effect or causal relationships. Thus internal validity is only relevant in studies that try to establish causal relationships. It's not relevant in all the one-group designs except the last one—the one-group pretest–posttest design—as this design *attempts* to establish a relationship between the intervention and program objective. In any causal study, we should be able to conclude from our findings that the intervention is, or is not, the only cause of change in the dependent variable, outcome variable, or program objective.

If our explanatory study does not have internal validity, such a conclusion is not possible, and the study's findings can be misleading. Internal validity is concerned with one of the requirements for an "ideal" evaluation—the control of rival hypotheses, or alternative explanations for what might bring about a change in the program objective.

The higher the internal validity, the greater the extent to which rival hypotheses (or alternative

explanations) can be controlled; the lower the internal validity, the less they can be controlled. There are numerous threats to internal validity. We discuss only the ones that are relevant to program evaluations:

- History
- Maturation
- Testing
- Instrumentation error
- Statistical regression
- Differential selection of evaluation participants
- Mortality
- Reactive effects of research participants
- Interaction effects
- Relations between experimental and control groups

Let's start by discussing the first threat in internal validity: history.

History

The first threat to internal validity, history, refers to any outside event, either public or private, that may affect the program objective and that was not taken into account in our design. Many times it refers to events that occur between the first and second measurement of the program objective (the pretest and the posttest). If events occur that have the potential to alter the second measurement, there is no way of knowing how much (if any) of the observed change in the program's objective is a function of the intervention and how much is attributable to these events.

Suppose, for example, we are investigating the effects of an educational program on racial tolerance. We may decide to measure the program objective (decreasing racial tolerance in the community) before introducing the intervention, the educational program. The educational program is then implemented and is represented by X. Finally, racial tolerance is measured again, after the program has run its course. This final measurement yields a posttest score, represented by O_2. As you know, the one-group pretest–posttest study design is presented in Figure E.6.

The difference between the values O_2 and O_1 represents the difference in the degree of racial tolerance in the community before and after the educational program. If the study is internally valid, $O_2 - O_1$ will yield a crude measure of the effect of the educational program on racial tolerance, and this is what we were trying to discover. Now suppose that before the posttest could be administered, a colossal terrorist attack occurs in the United States, such as the type that occurred in New York on September 11, 2001.

It may be fair to say that terrorism can be expected to have a negative effect on racial tolerance, and the posttest scores may, therefore, show a lower level of tolerance than if the terrorist act had not occurred. The effect, $O_2 - O_1$, will now be the combined effects of the educational program and the terrorist act, not the effect of the program alone, as we initially intended.

Terrorism is an extraneous variable that we could not have anticipated and did not control for when we designed the study. Other examples might include an earthquake, election, illness, divorce, or marriage—any event, public or private, that could affect the dependent variable, or program objective. Any such variable that is unanticipated and uncontrolled for is an example of history.

However, the effects of history are controlled for with the use of a control group; that is, the control group would theoretically have experienced the act of terrorism exactly like the experimental group. Thus both groups would have been exposed to the extraneous terrorism variable, and this would make it a constant in the evaluation design.

So whenever a control or comparison group is used in a study, it's usually safe to say that the effects of history have been controlled for. The most important thing to remember as a mortal is that you cannot control history—history marches on with or without us. You can, however, control for the effects of history by adding a control or comparison group to the evaluation design.

Maturation

Maturation, the second threat to internal validity, is a first cousin to history. It refers to changes, both physical and psychological, that take place in our evaluation participants over time and can affect the dependent variable, or program objective. Suppose that we are evaluating an interventive strategy designed to improve the behavior of adolescents who engage in delinquent behavior. Since the behavior of adolescents changes naturally as they mature, the observed change may have resulted as much from their natural development as from the intervention strategy.

Maturation refers not only to physical or mental growth, however. Over time, people grow older, more or less anxious, more or less bored, and more or less motivated to take part in a study. All these factors and many more can affect the way in which people respond when the program objective is measured a second or third time.

As previously discussed regarding the effects of history, the effects of maturation can indeed be controlled for with the use of a control or comparison group. Like history, you cannot control maturation; you can only control for the effects of maturation by using control or comparison groups in your designs.

Testing

Testing is sometimes referred to as *initial measurement effects*. Thus the pretests that are the starting point for many evaluation designs are another potential threat to internal validity. One of the most utilized designs involves three steps: (1) measuring some program objective, such as learning behavior in school or attitudes toward work; (2) initiating a program to change that variable; and (3) measuring the program objective again at the conclusion of the program. This design is known as the previously discussed one-group pretest–posttest design and is illustrated in Figure E.6.

The testing effect is the effect that taking a pretest might have on posttest scores. Suppose that Roberto, an evaluation participant, takes a pretest to measure his initial level of racial tolerance before being exposed to a racial tolerance educational program. He might remember some of the questions on the pretest, think about them later, and change his views on racial issues before taking part in the educational program. After the program, his posttest score will reveal his changed opinions, and we may incorrectly assume that the program was *solely* responsible, whereas the true cause was his experience with the pretest *and* the intervention.

Sometimes a pretest induces anxiety in a research participant, so Roberto may receive a worse score on the posttest than he should have. Or perhaps boredom caused by having to respond to the same questions a second time was a factor. To avoid the testing effect, we may wish to use a design that does not require a pretest.

If a pretest is essential, we then must consider the length of time that elapses between the pretest and posttest measurements. A pretest is far more likely to affect the posttest when the time between the two is short. The nature of the pretest is another factor. Measuring instruments that deal with factual matters, such as knowledge levels, may have large testing effects because the questions tend to be more easily recalled.

Instrumentation Error

The fourth threat to internal validity is instrumentation error. This is simply a list of all the troubles that can afflict the measurement process. The instrument may be unreliable or invalid, as discussed in Tools L and M. It may be a mechanical instrument, such as an electroencephalogram, which has malfunctioned. Occasionally, the term *instrumentation error* is used to refer to an observer whose observations are inconsistent or to measuring instruments that are reliable in themselves but that have not been administered properly.

Administration, with respect to a measuring instrument, refers to the circumstances under which the measurement is made: where, when, how, and by whom. A mother being asked about her attitudes toward her children, for example, may respond in one way in the social worker's office and in a different way at home, while her children are screaming around her feet.

Further, a mother's verbal response may differ from her written response, or she may respond differently in the morning than she would in the evening, or differently alone than she would in a group. These variations in situational responses do not indicate a true change in the feelings, attitudes, or behaviors being measured; they are only examples of instrumentation error.

Statistical Regression

The fifth threat to internal validity, statistical regression, refers to the tendency of extremely low and extremely high scores to regress, or move toward the average score for everyone in the study. Suppose an instructor makes her class take a multiple-choice exam and the average score is 50.

Now suppose that the instructor separates the low scorers from the high scorers and tries to even out the level of the class by giving the low scorers special instruction. To determine whether the special instruction has been effective, the entire class then takes another multiple-choice exam. The result of the exam is that the low scorers (as a group) do better than they did the first time, and the high scorers (as a group) do worse. The instructor believes that this has occurred because the low scorers received special instruction and the high scorers did not.

According to the logic of statistical regression, however, both the average score of the low scorers and the average score of the high scorers would move toward the total average score for both groups (i.e., 50). Even without any special instruction, and still in their state of ignorance, the low scorers (as a group) would be expected to have a higher average score than they did before. Likewise, the high scorers (as a group) would be expected to have a lower average score than they did before.

It would be easy for the instructor to assume that the low scores increased because of the special instruction and the high scores decreased because of the lack of it. But this is not necessarily so; the instruction may have had nothing to do with it. It may all be due to statistical regression, where the high group goes down and the low group goes up.

Differential Selection of Evaluation Participants

The sixth threat to internal validity is differential selection of evaluation participants. To some extent, the participants selected for a study are different from one another to begin with. "Ideal" evaluations, however, require random sampling from a population (if at all possible) and random assignment to groups. This assures that the results of a study will be generalizable to the larger population from which they were drawn (thus addressing threats to external validity to be discussed later).

This threat, however, is present when we are working with preformed groups or groups that already exist, such as classes of students, self-help groups, or community groups. It's probable those different preformed groups will not be equivalent with respect to relevant variables and that these initial differences will invalidate the results of the posttest.

A child abuse prevention educational program for children in schools might be evaluated by comparing the prevention skills of one group of children who have experienced the educational program with the skills of a second group who have not. To make a valid comparison, the two groups must be as similar as possible with respect to age, gender, intelligence, socioeconomic status, and anything else that might affect the acquisition of child abuse prevention skills.

We would have to make every effort to form or select equivalent groups, but the groups may not be as equivalent as we hoped—especially if we are obliged to work with preformed groups, such as classes of students or community groups. If the two groups were different before the intervention was introduced, there is not much point in comparing them at the end.

Accordingly, preformed groups should be avoided whenever possible. If it's not feasible to do this, rigorous pretesting must be done to determine in what ways the groups are (or are not) equivalent, and differences must be compensated for with the use of statistical methods.

Mortality

The seventh threat to internal validity is mortality, which simply means that evaluation participants may drop out before the end of the study. Their absence will probably have a significant effect on the study's findings because people who drop out are likely to be different in some ways from those participants who stay to the end. People who drop out may be less

motivated to participate in the intervention than are people who stay in, for example.

Since dropouts often have such characteristics in common, it cannot be assumed that the attrition occurred in a random manner. If considerably more people drop out of one group than out of the other, the result will be two groups that are no longer equivalent and cannot be usefully compared. We cannot know at the beginning of the study how many people will drop out, but we can watch to see how many do. Mortality is never problematic if dropout rates are 5% or less *and* if the dropout rates are similar for the both groups.

Reactive Effects of Research Participants

The eighth threat to internal validity is reactive effects. Changes in the behaviors or feelings of research participants may be caused by their reaction to the novelty of the situation or to the knowledge that they are participating in a study. The classic example of reactive effects was found in a series of studies carried out at the Hawthorne plant of the Western Electric Company, in Chicago, many years ago. Researchers were investigating the relationship between working conditions and productivity. When they increased the level of lighting in one section of the plant, productivity increased; a further increase in the lighting was followed by an additional increase in productivity.

When the lighting was then decreased, however, production levels did not fall accordingly but continued to rise. The conclusion was that the workers were increasing their productivity not because of the lighting level but because of the attention they were receiving as research participants in the study.

The term *Hawthorne effect* is still used to describe any situation in which the evaluation participants' behaviors are influenced not by the intervention but by the knowledge that they are taking part in an evaluation project. Another example of such a reactive effect is the placebo given to patients, which produces beneficial results because the patients believe it's medication.

Reactive effects can be controlled by ensuring that all participants in a study, in both the experimental and the control groups, appear to be treated equally. If one group is to be shown an educational film, for example, the other group should also be shown a film—some film carefully chosen to bear no relationship to the variable being investigated. If the study involves a change in the participants' routine, this in itself may be enough to change behavior, and care must be taken to continue the study until novelty has ceased to be a factor.

Interaction Effects

Interaction among the various threats to internal validity can have an effect of its own. Any of the factors already described as threats may interact with one another, but the most common interactive effect involves differential selection and maturation.

Let's say we are studying two preformed groups of clients who are being treated for depression. The intention was for these groups to be equivalent, in terms of both their motivation for treatment and their levels of depression. It turns out that Group A is more generally depressed than Group B, however. Whereas both groups may grow less motivated over time, it's likely that Group A, whose members were more depressed to begin with, will lose motivation more completely and more quickly than Group B. Inequivalent preformed groups thus grow less equivalent over time as a result of the interaction between differential selection and maturation.

Relations Between Experimental and Control Groups

The final group of threats to internal validity has to do with the effects of the use of experimental and control groups that receive different interventions. These effects include:

- Diffusion of treatments
- Compensatory equalization
- Compensatory rivalry
- Demoralization

Diffusion of Treatments

Diffusion, or imitation, of treatments may occur when members of the experimental and control groups talk to each other about the study. Suppose a study is designed to present a new relaxation exercise to the experimental group and nothing at all to the control group. There is always the possibility that one of the participants in the experimental group will explain the exercise to a friend who happens to be in the control group. The friend explains it to another friend and so on. This might be beneficial for the control group, but it invalidates the study's findings.

Compensatory Equalization

Compensatory equalization of treatment occurs when the person doing the study and/or the staff member administering the intervention to the experimental group feels sorry for people in the control group who are not receiving it and attempts to compensate them. A social worker might take a control group member aside and covertly demonstrate the relaxation exercise, for example.

On the other hand, if our study has been ethically designed, there should be no need for guilt on the part of the social worker because some people are not being taught to relax. They can be taught to relax when our study is over, as pointed out in Chapter 5 on ethics.

Compensatory Rivalry

Compensatory rivalry is an effect that occurs when the control group becomes motivated to compete with the experimental group. For example, a control group in a program to encourage parental involvement in school activities might get wind that something is up and make a determined effort to participate too, on the basis that "anything they can do, we can do better." There is no direct communication between groups, as in the diffusion of treatment effect—only rumors and suggestions of rumors. However, rumors are often enough to threaten the internal validity of a study.

Demoralization

In direct contrast with compensatory rivalry, demoralization refers to feelings of deprivation among the control group that may cause them to give up and drop out of the study, in which case this effect would be referred to as mortality. The people in the control group may also get angry.

Now that you have a sound understanding of internal validity, we turn our attention to two-group designs that have to minimize as many threats to internal validity as possible if they are to provide cause–effect statements such as "my intervention caused my clients to get better."

TWO-GROUP DESIGNS

Except for the one-group pretest–posttest design, one-group designs do not intend to determine cause–effect relationships. Thus they are not concerned with internal validity issues. Two-group designs, on the other hand, help us produce data for coming a bit closer to proving cause–effect relationships and so internal validity issues come readily into play. There are many two-group designs; we discuss only four of them.

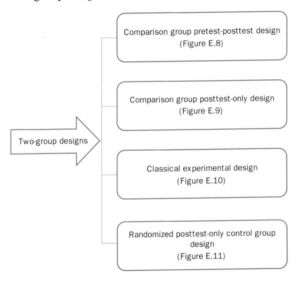

Comparison Group Pretest–Posttest Design

The comparison group pretest–posttest design simply elaborates on the one-group pretest–posttest design by adding a comparison group. This second group receives both the pretest (O_1) and the posttest (O_2) at the same time as the experimental group, but it does not receive the intervention. In addition, random assignment to groups is never done in this design. This design is written as shown in Figure E.8, and hypothetical data could look like those displayed in Table E.2.

Where:

O_1 = First measurement of the program objective
X = The program, or intervention
O_2 = Second measurement of the program objective

The experimental and comparison groups formed under this design will probably not be equivalent because members are not randomly assigned to the two groups (notice the 10-point difference at pretest). The pretest scores, however, will indicate the extent of their differences. If the differences are not statistically significant but are still large enough to affect the post-test, the statistical technique of analysis of covariance can be used to compensate.

As long as the groups are at least somewhat equivalent at pretest, then this design controls for nearly all of the threats to internal validity. But because random assignment to groups was not used, many of the external validity threats remain (to be discussed at the end of chapter).

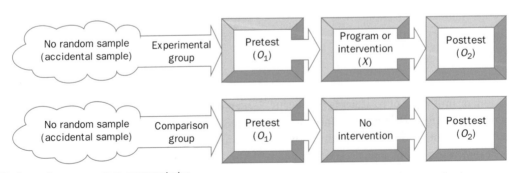

Figure E.8: **Comparison group pretest–posttest design.**

Table E.2: **Displaying Data for a Comparison Group Pretest–Posttest Design (From Figure E.8).**

Group	Pretest Average (O_1)	Posttest Average (O_2)	Difference Average ($O_2 - O_1$)
Intervention Group	50	80	30
Comparison	60	70	10
Difference			20

Comparison Group Posttest-Only Design

The comparison group posttest-only design improves on the one-group posttest-only design by introducing a comparison group that does not receive the intervention but is subject to the same posttest as those who do (the comparison group). The basic elements of the comparison group posttest-only design are as shown in Figure E.9, and hypothetical data could be displayed as in Table E.3.

Where:

X = The program, or intervention

O_1 = First and only measurement of the program objective

In Antonia's child abuse prevention program, if the January, April, and August sections are scheduled but the August sessions are canceled for some reason, those who would have been participants in that section could be used as a comparison group.

If the values of O_1 on the measuring instrument were similar for the experimental and comparison groups, it could be concluded that the program was of little use, since those who had experienced it (those who had received X) were not much better or worse off than those who had not.

A problem with drawing this conclusion, however, is that there is no evidence that the groups were equivalent to begin with. Selection, mortality, and the interaction of selection and other threats to internal validity are thus the major difficulties with this design. The use of a comparison group does, however, control for the effects of history, maturation, and testing.

Classical Experimental Design

The classical experimental design is the basis for all the experimental designs. It involves an experimental group and a control group, both created by a random assignment method (and, if possible, by random selection from a population).

Both groups take a pretest (O_1) at the same time, after which the intervention (X) is given only to the experimental group, and then both groups take the posttest (O_2) at the same time. This design is written as shown in Figure E.10, and the typical way to present data is displayed in Table E.4

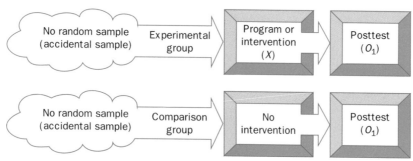

Figure E.9: **Comparison group posttest-only design.**

Table E.3: **Displaying Data for a Comparison Group Posttest-Only Design (From Figure E.9).**

Group	Posttest Average
Intervention	80
Comparison	70
Difference	10

Where:

R = Random selection (Rs) from a population and random assignment (Ra) to group

O_1 = First measurement of the program objective

X = The program, or intervention

O_2 = Second measurement of the program objective

Because the experimental and control groups are randomly assigned, they are equivalent with respect to all important variables. This group equivalence in the design helps control for many of the threats to internal validity, because both groups will be affected by them in the same way.

Randomized Posttest-Only Control Group Design

The randomized posttest-only control group design is identical to the comparison group posttest-only design, except that the participants are randomly assigned to two groups. This design, therefore, has a control group, rather than a comparison group.

This design usually involves only two groups: one experimental and one control. There are no pretests. The experimental group receives the intervention and takes the posttest; the control group only takes the posttest. This design can be written as shown in Figure E.11 and data generated from this design can be presented as in Table E.5.

Where:

R = Random selection (Rs) from a population and random assignment (Ra) to group

X = The program, or intervention

O_1 = First and only measurement of the program objective

In addition to measuring change in a group or groups, a pretest also helps to ensure equivalence between the control and the experimental groups. As you know, this design does not have a pretest. The groups have been randomly assigned, however, as indicated by R, and this, in itself, is theoretically

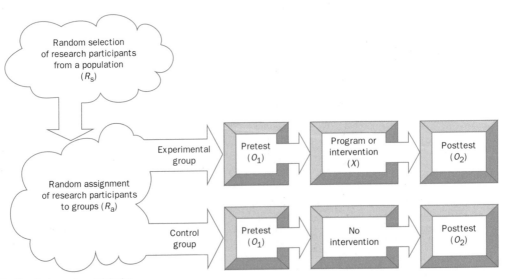

Figure E.10: **Classical experimental design.**

Table E.4: **Displaying Data for a Classical Experimental Design (From Figure E.10).**

Group	Pretest Average (O_1)	Posttest Average (O_2)	Difference Average $(O_2 - O_1)$
Intervention	50	80	30
Control	50	70	20
Difference			10

enough to ensure equivalence without the need for a confirmatory pretest.

This design is useful in situations where it's not possible to conduct a pretest or where a pretest would be expected to strongly influence the results of the posttest because of the effects of testing. This design also controls for many of the threats to internal validity (previously discussed) and external validity (discussed in the following section).

EXTERNAL VALIDITY

Generally speaking, *external validity* is the degree to which the results of a specific study are generalizable to another population, to another setting, or to another time. There are numerous threats to external validity; we discuss only the four that are most relevant to doing program evaluations:

- Selection–treatment interaction
- Specificity of variables
- Multiple-treatment interference
- Researcher bias

Selection–Treatment Interaction

The first threat to external validity is selection–treatment interaction. This threat commonly occurs when an evaluation design cannot provide for random selection of participants from a population. Suppose we wanted to study the effectiveness of a family service agency staff, for example. If our research proposal

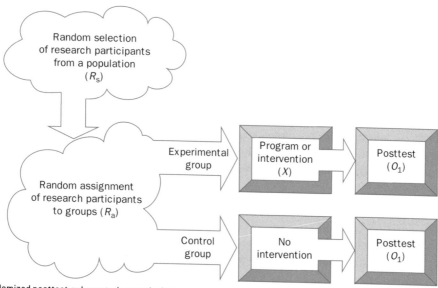

Figure E.11: **Randomized posttest-only control group design.**

Table E.5: **Displaying Data for a Randomized Posttest-Only Control Group Design (From Figure E.11).**

Group	Posttest Average
Intervention	80
Control	50
Difference	30

was turned down by 50 agencies before it was accepted by the 51st, it's very likely that the accepting agency differs in certain important aspects from the other 50. It may accept the proposal because its social workers are more highly motivated, more secure, more satisfied with their jobs, or more interested in the practical application of the study than the average agency staff member.

As a result, we would be assessing the research participants on the very factors for which they were unwittingly (and by default) selected—motivation, job satisfaction, and so on. The study may be internally valid, but, since it will not be possible to generalize the results to other family service agencies, it will have little external validity.

Specificity of Variables

Specificity of variables has to do with the fact that an evaluation project conducted with a specific group of people at a specific time and in a specific setting may not always be generalizable to other people at different times and in different settings.

For example, a measuring instrument used to measure the IQ levels of upper socioeconomic–level Caucasian suburban children does not provide an equally accurate measure of IQ when it's applied to lower socioeconomic–level children of racial minorities in the inner city.

Multiple-Treatment Interference

The third threat to external validity, multiple-treatment interference, occurs when an evaluation participant

is given two or more interventions in succession, so that the results of the first intervention may affect the results of the second. A client who attends treatment sessions, for example, may not seem to benefit from one therapeutic technique, so another is tried. In fact, however, the client may have benefited from the first technique, but the benefit may not become apparent until the second technique has been tried.

As a result, the effects of both techniques become commingled, or the results may be erroneously ascribed to the second technique alone. Because of this threat, interventions should be given separately if possible. If the research design does not allow this, sufficient time should be allowed to elapse between the two interventions in an effort to minimize the possibility of multiple-treatment interference.

In addition, your evaluation participants may be getting help in other places besides the program you are evaluating. They may, for example, be offered help by other caseworkers, probation officers, various self-help groups, hospitals, clinics, friends, clergy, and even their mothers and fathers in addition to the odd social work practicum student or two. All of these other helping sources will somehow affect the results of your study.

Researcher Bias

The final threat to external validity is researcher bias. Researchers, like people in general, tend to see what they want to see or expect to see. Unconsciously and without any thought of deceit, they may manipulate a study so that the actual results agree with the anticipated results. A practitioner may favor an intervention so strongly that the study is structured to support it, or the results may be interpreted favorably. The phrase "If I didn't believe it, I wouldn't have seen it" readily comes to mind.

If we know which individuals are in the experimental group and which are in the control group, this knowledge alone might affect the study's results. Students whom an instructor believes to be bright, for example, often are given higher grades than their performance warrants, whereas students believed to be dull are given lower grades. The way to control for researcher bias is to perform a double-blind experiment in which neither the evaluation participants nor the evaluator knows who is in the experimental or control group. Using standardized measuring instruments, thoroughly training data collectors, and having other people besides the evaluators collect the data are a few of the methods that you can use to control for the effects of research bias.

SUMMARY

Evaluation designs cover the entire range of evaluation questions and provide data that can be used to gain knowledge for our profession. No single design is inherently inferior or superior to the others. Each has advantages and disadvantages. Those of us who are familiar with them will be well equipped to select the one that is most appropriate to a particular evaluative effort.

BUDGETING FOR EVALUATIONS

Conducting an evaluation requires careful allocation of resources, including time and money. This tool provides basic information that will help you anticipate and plan for the resources you will need.

HOW TO BUDGET FOR AN EVALUATION

Developing accurate budgets for an evaluation takes both planning and expertise. How do you come up with an appropriate estimate, especially if you have little direct experience? Though other methods exist, two approaches to budget estimation you may want to consider are the historical and roundtable methods. For both approaches you will need to think through the justification for the estimate, the assumptions you make, and the known requirements of your current evaluation.

Historical Budgeting Method

If you have information on actual expenditures from prior evaluations, this is often the best place to start. Think carefully about the assumptions and requirements of these prior evaluations compared with your current requirements.

- Where do you need to make adjustments?
- Are you now conducting data collection over 4 months rather than 6 months?
- Do you have more or fewer staff than in the past?
- Do you have more or fewer respondents?

On a general level you may want to develop a "per unit" price from prior efforts (e.g., if you conducted five focus groups in a prior effort, how much did it cost to recruit, conduct, analyze, and report on each group?). However, keep in mind that you may experience increased efficiency per unit when you conduct the same activity more than once.

This means that you may tend to overestimate costs if you simply multiply by the number of additional units. The more evaluations you conduct over time, the more historical budget data you will have to work with and the more accurate your estimates will become.

Roundtable Budgeting Method

If you do not have historical data available as a guide for estimating the costs of your new evaluation or if prior evaluations were too different from current efforts, you can use "expert" opinions to help you develop your budget. Bring together three to four experienced staff or partners with knowledge of the level of effort required. For example, you may want to bring in a staff member who has experience working with your target population to help you estimate how much time will be needed for recruitment.

As you work with these experts, carefully document and describe the elements of your evaluation that will affect the costs:

- How many units, sessions, or modules will there be?
- How long will each of these last?
- Who will be involved?
- What experience level is needed?

- How many and what types of supplies, equipment, and materials will be required?
- Are there any fixed costs?
- What are the variable costs?

Work as a group to come up with your best estimates of staff time and additional resources needed for each component of your evaluation. As before, consider efficiencies in your evaluation processes as you add "units" to ensure you are not overestimating your resource needs.

It may be advantageous to combine the two approaches discussed here to come up with a more accurate estimate. A roundtable group can usually provide a better estimate when it is based on historical data. Historical estimates can benefit from the input of several experienced staff to assess where and how to make adjustments based on the requirements of the current evaluation.

Whichever approach you choose, the most important step in preparing an accurate estimate is to ensure that you are matching your estimated costs to current evaluation requirements or plans. If you find that your estimated costs are more than you have available to support the evaluation, you will need to scale back the evaluation plans to fit the available resources or identify additional resources to conduct the evaluation as planned. For multiyear evaluations, comparing your estimated costs against your actual expenditures each year can also help ensure that you are still on track to complete your evaluation.

TYPES OF COSTS TO CONSIDER IN BUDGETING FOR EVALUATION

The largest cost in conducting an evaluation is generally staff time. As you estimate the level of effort required to complete your evaluation, consider each of the steps of the general evaluation process outlined in Chapter 3.

When budgeting for an evaluation, think in terms of the tasks that need to be accomplished and the hours and costs these tasks will take. Often we tend to focus on the time it will take to collect data but underestimate the time it takes to plan the evaluation (especially when working with larger stakeholder groups), pilot-test data collection instruments, clean and prepare the data, analyze the data, and communicate the results.

By carefully thinking through each step, you are more likely to generate a realistic cost estimate. Initially, it may help to think in terms of the tasks that need to be accomplished and the hours they will take. Then translate the hours into dollars, also assessing the level of expertise required for each specific task.

Monitoring evaluation progress is another aspect of evaluation often missed during budget planning. Remember to allot staff and contractor time for regular team meetings and the preparation of progress reports. In addition to staff time, there are a number of additional costs you may incur. We list some categories of costs frequently encountered in the following. You can use Table F.1 to record these costs.

- **Consultants/contractors.** Consultants or contractors used to extend staff capacity or to provide special skills or experience
- **Communications.** Postage or telephone charges
- **Travel.** Long-distance or local travel for evaluation staff to conduct the evaluation or present the evaluation results
- **Printing and duplication.** Preparation of documents, data collection materials, reports, and other printed materials
- **Materials.** Purchased data collection instruments, library services, or datasets
- **Supplies.** Office supplies or software that must be purchased or leased for the evaluation
- **Specialized equipment.** Equipment needed to conduct the evaluation or data collection (e.g., laptop computers)
- **Purchased services.** Services purchased from outside vendors with a fixed per unit price (e.g., transcription or translation). These types of service relationships typically do not require a consultant type of arrangement
- **Incentives.** Small monetary or nonmonetary items provided to participants to encourage their participation in the evaluation

- **Institutional review board (IRB) review (if necessary).** If IRB review applies to your evaluation, check with your particular IRB to find out their fee structure
- **Training (if necessary).** Training associated with building staff capacity (e.g., analysis training, data collection training, software training) or to provide specific training instructions for your evaluation
- **Dissemination (e.g., conferences).** Costs associated with meeting or conference registration or for local facilities if you plan to convene a stakeholder session
- **Other.** Any other costs necessary for conducting your evaluation
- **Overhead costs and fees.** Any overhead fees or costs associated with staff time or other resource usage

Table F.1: **Evaluation Budget Template.**

Resource	Year 1 ($)	Year 2 ($)	Year 3 ($)	Year 4 ($)
Evaluation staff salary and benefits				
Consultants/contractors				
Communications (e.g., postage, telephone)				
Travel				
Printing and duplication				
Materials				
Supplies				
Purchased services (e.g., transcription)				
Specialized equipment				
Incentives				
IRB Review (if necessary)				
Training (if necessary)				
Dissemination (e.g., conferences)				
Other				
Overhead costs and fees				
Total				

Not all of these types of costs apply to every evaluation. You should tailor the template (Table F.1) to fit your evaluation. If you are using different sources of funds for your evaluation, you will also want to consult cost restrictions or budgeting requirements associated with each source.

If you hire an external evaluator for part or all of an evaluation, be sure to request an itemized work plan and budget that details labor hours/costs and other expenses using similar categories. Having these documents will avoid later misunderstandings about what was and was not included in the consultant/contractor's scope of work and budget.

Also, you may obtain in-kind contributions to help you with an evaluation, whether in the form of staff time (e.g., secretarial support) or material support (e.g., space, incentives, telephone, photocopying).

In-kind contributions should be carefully recorded at each stage in the evaluation. This will help you document the actual costs of your evaluation and will serve to illustrate the support and buy-in you have obtained for doing the evaluation. It will also ensure that you do not overlook people or organizations when acknowledging contributions.

Last, systematically keep track of your time and expenditures as you go along. By recording staff labor, expenditures, and in-kind contributions on every evaluation that you conduct, your ability to accurately estimate an evaluation budget will improve with time as you feed these data back into future estimation processes. The records you keep will also help you answer to your funders, managers, and other stakeholders about how program resources were used.

USING EVALUATION MANAGEMENT STRATEGIES

Basic project management strategies that you may have used on other projects are also useful in managing evaluations. Effective project management requires applying a set of techniques and principles in a disciplined way while simultaneously being ready to adapt your plans as unanticipated issues arise.

Good management practices will help you make sure your evaluation is on track and, if you encounter problems, will help your respond quickly. In this tool we provide a few simple management strategies to help you implement your evaluation successfully:

- Evaluation overview statement
- Evaluation roles and responsibilities
- Evaluation timeline
- Periodic evaluation reports

The management strategies we include in this tool are meant to be illustrative but are by no means the only ones that may be useful for managing your evaluation. You may have similar tools you typically use that will work well for your evaluations. Or you may choose to modify one or more of these tools to fit your needs.

Whatever management strategies you choose to use, we recommend that you include them as appendices or integrate them into the body of your evaluation plan so that you and your stakeholders have a common understanding of how you will manage the evaluation as you begin to implement it.

STRATEGY 1: EVALUATION OVERVIEW STATEMENT

An evaluation overview statement may be one of the most important pieces of text you write about your evaluation. It provides a concise but comprehensive summary of your evaluation and what you hope to gain by conducting it. In a few short sentences it should convey the main purpose of the evaluation, what is being evaluated, the major activities to be undertaken, and the proposed uses of the evaluation results.

The evaluation overview statement should be consistent with the evaluation purpose you described in your evaluation plan. However, we recommend that you provide additional detail in the statement that will make it suitable for broader communication with stakeholders who may never read your evaluation plan. Box G.1 provides an example of an overview statement.

Potential ways you could use your evaluation overview statement include:

- In materials used to recruit participants for the evaluation
- Communication with funders
- Communication with partners, such as in newsletters
- Communication with decision-makers (e.g., briefings or "elevator speeches")
- Communication with the general public (e.g., on websites or press releases)

BOX G.1 SAMPLE EVALUATION OVERVIEW STATEMENT

Evaluation of Asthma Self-Management Training Program

The purpose of this one-year evaluation is to determine whether participants' asthma self-management knowledge and skills increase as a result of asthma self-management training. Adults who obtain emergency department asthma care at a large urban hospital in [city] will be referred to the training program.

Trained asthma educators will deliver the training in a small-group classroom setting. Trainings will be periodically monitored to ensure a standard curriculum and consistency across asthma educators. We anticipate training 810 adults in this program over a 6-month period from March 20xx to August 20xx.

Data will be collected through self-administered questionnaires, which will be collected prior to and after the training. The questionnaire will ask about participant demographics, asthma self-management knowledge, asthma self-management skills, and intentions for changing behavior.

Questionnaires will only have an ID number to protect patient privacy, and the hospital will not have access to survey results of individual patients. The analysis will focus on changes in knowledge, skills, and behavioral intention from pre- to post-training.

We will also look at subgroups by race/ethnicity, age, and gender to understand whether the training was more beneficial for certain groups than others. The results will be used to determine whether to continue this training in the future and, if so, who should enroll.

- Title of the evaluation
- Name of the element or aspect of the program being evaluated
- Time period of the evaluation
- Overall goal of the evaluation
- Identified uses for the evaluation results
- Evaluation design and major data collection activities
- Intended audience(s) for project
- Any special considerations for how data will be collected or analyzed (e.g., issues related to evaluation standards)

STRATEGY 2: CREATING A ROLES AND RESPONSIBILITIES TABLE

A roles and responsibilities table is useful to help ensure that all aspects of your evaluation are assigned to a particular individual or individuals, to reduce confusion about roles, and to gain agreement from all those involved in the evaluation as to who will do what.

Remember to update your roles and responsibilities table as new staff, consultants, or partners join or leave the project. This helps ensure that no activity falls through the cracks if your personnel changes over time. You should also link roles and responsibilities to your evaluation timeline (see next section) to ensure that evaluation team members assigned to activities are available at the appropriate times.

As shown in Table G.1 each staff, consultant, or partner with responsibilities for carrying out some aspect of the evaluation should be listed. This list should include those involved at any stage of the evaluation, including those only involved in planning activities or in dissemination of findings.

The second column lists the individual's role in the evaluation—this may or may not be the same as his or her job title or other program roles. The "Responsibilities" column should be a brief but comprehensive bulleted list of what each team member will do throughout the evaluation period. Be sure to include responsibilities related to coordination or oversight as well as direct involvement in evaluation tasks.

Developing your evaluation overview statement is a valuable planning exercise to ensure that all stakeholders agree about your evaluation goals. The statement should be crafted with input from your evaluation team and should be widely used by team members and other partners when discussing the evaluation.

This ensures the messages that are disseminated to various audiences about your evaluation are accurate and consistent. Remember that it may be necessary to tailor your statement to a given audience in terms of reading level, level of detail, and/or level of technical content.

The format of the evaluation overview statement can vary, but basic elements include:

Table G.1: **Roles and Responsibilities Table.**

Names	Roles	Responsibilities	Tasks (from Table G.2)
Staff 1	Evaluation Leader	• Work with stakeholder groups to design evaluation, gain appropriate permissions, and develop measuring instruments • Obtain IRB clearance from hospital IRB • Train data collectors on evaluation protocol • Monitor trainings on quarterly basis throughout the implementation • Oversee analysis • Write up evaluation interim and final results • Conduct briefings on findings with stakeholders • Work with stakeholder groups on action plan for use of results	1–8
Staff 2	Data Analyst	• Compile statistics on attendance and response rates throughout data collection • Enter data from training forms • Check data quality • Conduct main analyses • Analyze subgroup data • Write up results	6, 7
Partner 1 Staff 1 and 2	Asthma Educator and Data Collector	• Attend data collector training • Conduct asthma self-management trainings • Conduct pre- and post-data collection	4, 5
Staff 3 Partner 1 Partner 2 Partner 3	Evaluation Team	• CParticipate in evaluation planning and design • CHelp develop data collection instrument • CReceive interim reports and provide feedback as necessary on evaluation progress • CProvide feedback on evaluation findings • CParticipate in action planning for program improvement	1, 2, 7, 8

The "Tasks" column allows you to explicitly list the major evaluation activities in which you believe the individual will be involved (see Table G.2 for an example of specific tasks). Some team members may be involved in all tasks, while others may be involved in only one or two. The more complicated the evaluation you are undertaking, the more useful you may find it to track responsibilities by tasks.

STRATEGY 3: TIMELINES

A timeline is a critical management tool that allows you to plan when evaluation activities should occur and to track whether activities are going as planned or if they are behind schedule. We recommend that you examine your timeline in relation to known resource constraints—whether financial or staffing—as well as

Table G.2: **Task Table.**

Task	Task Title
Task 1	Planning and evaluation design
Task 2	Data collection questionnaire development
Task 3	Obtaining necessary clearances
Task 4	Data collector training
Task 5	Data collection and monitoring
Task 6	Data management and analysis
Task 7	Communicating findings/reporting results
Task 8	Action plans for improvement of training

the timeline for other concurrent evaluations or program activities you may be conducting. Will you have the right staff available when you need them?

An evaluation timeline should be a living document. The sequence and timing of many activities are dependent on prior actions (e.g., you cannot analyze your results before your data are collected). This means you may need to make adjustments along the way to keep your evaluation moving forward.

Basic Yearly Progress Timeline

A sample of a basic yearly progress timeline can be seen in Table G.3. This template can be used to list major evaluation activities (column 2) and when they are expected to occur (column 1). Use the third column to note the data source or target audience for planned data collection or communication activities (this represents the "how" for each activity you have planned). The next column indicates which team members are involved in the activity. This column

Table G.3: **Timeline: Basic Yearly Progress.**

Timeline: Year 1 2015–2016				
Month (When)	**Evaluation Activity (What)**	**Data Source(s)/Audience (How)**	**Person(s) Responsible (Who)**	**Status Notes**
Ongoing	Monthly progress reporting	To program leadership	• Evaluation Leader	
January	Evaluation planning and instrument development	Self-administered questionnaire	• Evaluation Leader • Evaluation team	
February	Obtain clearance from hospital IRB	IRB forms	• Evaluation Leader	
	Train data collectors on protocol	Training materials	• Evaluation Leader	
March–August	Conduct asthma self-management training	With referred adult participants	• Asthma Educators	

Table G.3: (Continued)

Timeline: Year 1 2015–2016				
Month (When)	**Evaluation Activity (What)**	**Data Source(s)/Audience (How)**	**Person(s) Responsible (Who)**	**Status Notes**
	Conduct data collection/monitoring	Self-administered questionnaire—adults with asthma	• Asthma Educators • Evaluation Leader	
	Conduct data management	Self-administered questionnaire	• Data Analyst	
September	Data cleaning	Data quality assurance	• Data Analyst	
October	Analysis and interpretation		• Data Analyst • Evaluation Leader	
November	Develop evaluation reports and briefings		• Evaluation Leader • Data Analyst	
	Provide feedback on results		• Evaluation Team	
December	Develop action plan for use of results		• Evaluation Leader • Evaluation Team	

should match information included in the roles and responsibilities table. Use the last column to track progress toward accomplishing your planned activities (e.g., completed, delayed, etc.). You can also add notes about actions that may be needed to support moving the activity forward. Additional rows can be added if your evaluation spans multiple years.

Milestone Table

Another option to consider is a milestone table that simply lists key products or events and the dates by which they should be completed. In preparing this table, shown in Table G.4., think about the entire evaluation process from planning through data collection and analysis to the dissemination of findings and subsequent action planning. These may include fixed dates (such as a scheduled partnership meeting or training where you plan to collect data) or more dependent dates (e.g., 2 weeks after approval of new funding).

Include the dates when products are due or when key evaluation dissemination and communication activities are planned (such as a community meeting where you plan to discuss evaluation findings). Keeping the table up to date will allow you to track progress in meeting milestones as well as keep track of any schedule changes or deviations from the schedule.

Table G.4: **Timeline: Evaluation Milestone Table.**

Date	Description	Status
10th day of every month	Monthly progress report	
2/5/20xx	Submit completed hospital IRB material (including questionnaire)	
2/28/20xx	Obtain hospital IRB clearance	
2/15/20xx	Data collector training	
3/1/20xx—8/31/20xx	Conduct asthma self- management training	Once dates are scheduled add to table
Monthly from 3/1/20xx–8/31/20xx	Monitor one training session per month	Once dates are scheduled add to table
November 10, 20xx	Conduct briefing with Evaluation Team	
November 30, 20xx	Submit final evaluation report to stakeholders	
December 15, 20xx	Complete action plan for use of evaluation results	Add in dates for implementation of action plan

Gantt Chart

A Gantt chart is a valuable way to display the overall project timeline and activities. There are many ways to construct a Gantt chart, but the basic structure calls for lists of activities and the duration of each activity.

Start and stop dates and other milestones are indicated with larger dots or different colors. More complex Gantt charts can convey dependencies between activities (e.g., an activity that cannot start until after another is completed) or relative estimates of labor hours or other resources across activities.

A key consideration in constructing a Gantt chart is the level of resolution you need. During periods in which many activities will be ongoing simultaneously, it may be helpful to set up the chart by days or weeks. For a longer term view, months or quarters may be sufficient.

In Table G.5 the link between Task 3 and Task 5 indicates a dependency between those tasks in that data collection cannot occur without institutional review board (IRB) clearance. The dots in Task 5 indicate that monitoring of training will occur periodically on a monthly basis.

Shared Calendar

A final suggestion is to create a shared calendar for your evaluation project. This calendar can be used by all members of the evaluation team to focus on key dates for the evaluation. A calendar such as the one shown in Table G.6 can be kept on paper, but increasingly, electronic calendars are useful to keep all team members up to date. Online calendars can also be created and shared with team members and can be accessed from any location (e.g., Google calendars).

Table G.5: Timeline: Gantt Chart.

Activity	Start	Stop							YEAR 1 Timeline (20XX)					
			J	F	M	A	M	J	J	A	S	O	N	D
1. Planning and evaluation design	1/1/20xx	1/31/20xx	▨											
2. Data collection development	1/1/20xx	1/31/20xx	▨											
3. Obtaining clearances	2/5/20xx	2/28/20xx		▨										
4. Data collector training														
5. Data collection and monitoring	3/1/20xx	8/31/20xx			•	•	•	•	•	•				
6. Data management and analysis	9/1/20xx	10/31/20xx									▨	▨		
7. Communicate findings/report results	11/1/20xx	11/30/20xx											▨	
8. Action planning	12/1/2010	12/31/20xx												▨

Table G.6: **Timeline: Calendar.**

[APRIL]						
Sunday	**Monday**	**Tuesday**	**Wednesday**	**Thursday**	**Friday**	**Saturday**
					1	2
					Team Meeting 10 AM	
3	4	5	6	7	8	9
	Training 6 PM			Training 10 AM		
10	11	12	13	14	15	16
Training 12 noon			Training 7 PM [Monitoring]			
17	18	19	20	21	22	23
24	25	26	27	28	29	30
					Team Meeting 10 AM	

STRATEGY 4: PERIODIC EVALUATION PROGRESS REPORTS

Keeping a systematic record of your evaluation on a periodic basis can help ensure that key stakeholders have access to the information they need to play an active role in your evaluation. Periodic evaluation reports also help you maintain a history of your evaluation while it is in progress, rather than trying to reconstruct events once the evaluation is complete.

These reports can vary in format and audience, depending on project requirements and needs. Two types of reports that you may want to consider include:

- Evaluation progress reports
- Evaluation status reports

Evaluation Progress Report

An evaluation progress report is a record of progress and accomplishments during a specific time period. These reports can be prepared monthly or quarterly throughout the evaluation period and represent a valuable record for you in developing more detailed annual reports to funders (e.g., continuation applications) or other stakeholders.

They can also be a good way to get new staff or partners up to speed on progress. These reports can

BOX G.2 SAMPLE EVALUATION PROGRESS REPORT

Title: Evaluation Progress Report

Time Period: [month, year]

Evaluation Title: Evaluation of Asthma Self-Management

Prepared by: Evaluation Leader

Progress and Accomplishments for [Current Reporting Period]

- Program conducted eight trainings with 150 trainees
- Evaluation Leader monitored one training
- Data Analyst began entering data from completed questionnaire

Problems and Solutions

- Trainees for this month are 70% female. To have greater male participation, ensure that males are being appropriately referred to program; consider asking men who refuse the referral about their barriers to participation; strengthen recruitment materials for men; consider other times or dates for future trainings that may be more acceptable for men or male-only sessions.

Personnel Changes

- None; consider adding male trainer

Schedule Progress

- Trainings were well attended this month; evening trainings were most popular. Informal feedback suggests more weekend trainings are needed.

Planned Activities for [Next Reporting Period]

- Conduct additional trainings
- Monitor one (randomly selected) training
- Continue data entry of new questionnaires

Financial Report

- Hours incurred in month: XX
- Cumulative hours: XX
- Costs incurred in month: XX
- Cumulative costs: XX

either use a narrative format or rely on bullet points but are generally no more than one to three pages in length. Evaluation progress reports usually include the following types of information:

- Header information, including name of evaluation and person reporting
- Time period for report
- Accomplishments during time period
- Problems and proposed or enacted solutions during time period

- Personnel changes
- Progress in meeting planned schedule or deviations from schedule
- Planned activities for next reporting period
- Financial reporting for staff and other expenditures incurred during time period and percent of budget expended (you can include varying amounts of detail depending on audience needs and reporting requirements)

Title: Evaluation Status Report

Time Period: [month, year]

Evaluation Title: Evaluation of Asthma Self-Management

Prepared by: Evaluator Leader

Current vs. Expected Status for [Current Reporting Period]

- Program conducted eight trainings with 150 trainees
- Evaluation Leader monitored one training

Trainee Demographics	Expected Participants per Month (%)	Actual Participants for Reporting Month (%)
Gender		
• Male	67 (50)	45 (30)
• Female	68 (50)	105 (70)
Race/Ethnicity		
• White	86 (65)	95 (63)
• African American	21 (15)	23 (15)
• Latino	21 (15)	26 (17)
• Other	7 (5)	6 (4)
Age		
• 18–35	67 (50)	70 (47)
• 36–50	34 (25)	35 (23)
• 51+	34 (25)	45 (30)
Total	135	150

Deviations from Expected Progress

The number of trainees that were trained in the month exceeded expected targets. However, female trainees represented 70% rather than 50% of the expected number of trainees. Targets for trainees by race/ethnicity and age were met.

Proposed Solutions to Address Deviations

To increase male participation, ensure that males are being appropriately referred to the program; consider asking men who refuse the referral about their barriers to participation; strengthen recruitment materials for men; consider other times or dates for future trainings that may be more acceptable for men.

Expected Status for [Next Reporting Period]

Target recruitment for next month remains constant.

You may also want to include additional items during certain periods of the evaluation, such as:

- Lists of evaluation partners or your evaluation team members during planning
- Response rates for data collection activities during the data collection period
- Planned or actual requests for information received during the evaluation and any response
- Planned or actual communication activities related to evaluation findings
- Evaluation successes or lessons learned regarding evaluation
- Other items that you want to record in a systematic way

You should also require evaluation progress reports from your consultants and partners if they are engaged in autonomous activities. Be sure to build reporting requirements into any contracts or Memoranda of Understanding that you issue. If the progress of others is going to affect that of the evaluation as a whole, your evaluation manager needs to be aware of any problems or potential delays that others encounter.

Evaluation Status Report

An evaluation status report is similar to an evaluation progress report but has a primary focus on tracking where you are in relation to where you planned to be. Putting your evaluation progress in context allows you to record your accomplishments. It also allows you to focus on deviations from your plan so that you can proactively address them.

In our example, to determine your status during data collection, you would need to keep track of the number of people who were referred to the program, the number who were actually trained, and the number of participants who completed the questionnaire each month. This will tell you how well you are doing toward your goal of collecting information from 810 trainees. If you expect to conduct analyses by subgroup, you may also need to set subgroup participation expectations to ensure an adequate number to conduct the analysis. You can set these targets based on a number of sources depending on your needs, such as demographics of your area, population served by the institution where the intervention is being conducted, the literature, or prior experience.

This type of evaluation status reporting can also help you identify adjustments to strengthen your intervention and evaluation as it progresses. For example, you may find you need to enhance recruitment procedures, retrain data collectors, or change the logistics of training to help ensure that trainees do not leave before filling out the post-survey. You may want to combine elements of the two reports depending on your own needs.

DATA COLLECTION AND SAMPLING PROCEDURES

This tool provides you with three subtools, if you will, in your evaluation toolbox. It presents three basic procedures you will need to carry out your evaluation:

- Selecting a data source(s)
- Selecting a sample from your data source(s)
- Collecting data from your sample

Thus this tool will assist you in determining who will provide the data for your evaluation (data source), how your data sources will be selected (sampling), and how your data will be collected from your data source (data collection). See the diagram below:

for your evaluation. For example, federal and state personnel such as politicians, government officials, and staff from professional organizations can be data sources.

Among program workers there are therapists, caseworkers, and case aides as well as many collateral professionals such as teachers, psychologists, and workers from other programs to supply data. Clients, as a stakeholder group, are an extremely common data source. As you know, a client can refer to an individual, a family, a group, a community, or an organization, depending on how a program defines

Tool H₁

Selecting a data source(s)

Tool H₂

Selecting a sample from your data source(s)

Tool H₃

Collecting data from your sample

DATA SOURCE(S)

This section will guide you through the process of selecting exactly from whom you are going to get your data—known as data sources. Data sources can be:

- People
- Existing data

People

As we know, there could be any number of individuals in your stakeholder group who could provide the data

it. Table H.1 provides an example of six program outcomes (left column), the measurement, or indicator, that was used for each outcome (middle column), and the respective data source (right column).

Firsthand and Secondhand Data

The best data sources are those that provide firsthand or direct knowledge regarding the experience that is the subject of your evaluation. Adolescents, for example, have firsthand data relating to their perceptions about their futures. In contrast, data sources that have indirect knowledge about an experience

Table H.1: **Example: Program Outcomes, Indicators, and Data Sources.**

Mission/Objective: Ensure the physical and emotional well-being (safety) and normal development of children by placing them into stable, safe, high-quality foster homes.		
Outcome	*Outcome Indicator*	*Data Source*
Child safety		
1. Physical well-being	Number and percentage of children with serious health problems at follow-up	Agency records; trained observer ratings
2. Repeated abuse and neglect	Number and percentage of children identified as either abused or neglect by time of follow-up	Agency records; trained observer ratings; client survey
3. Safety concerns	Number and percentage of children removed from foster home by time of follow-up for other than permanent placement	Agency records; trained observer ratings
Child development		
4. Physical development	Number and percentage of children who met normal growth curves and height/weight expectations at time follow-up	Agency records; trained observer ratings
5. Social development	Number and percentage of children who displayed "age-appropriate" social skills at time of follow-up	Trained observer ratings; client survey
6. Educational development	Number and percentage of school-age children who were progressing satisfactorily in school at time of follow-up	Agency records; client survey

can provide only secondhand data. Adolescents, for example, can offer secondhand data about their parents' feelings either through speculation or by sharing observations about their parents' behaviors.

Given that firsthand data sources are not always available or easily accessible for evaluation purposes, we often look to secondhand data to inform us. Client records, for example, are filled with data that describe client problems and strengths as well as their patterns of change.

Practitioners and not the clients themselves, however, typically provide these data. As such, evaluation findings that are based solely on client records as a data source are weaker than those that use firsthand data sources and/or multiple data sources. Now for the questions:

- Who is in a better position to say which interventions most effectively help clients? Is it:

  - The clients themselves
  - The practitioners who work with clients, or
  - The funders who shell out the money to pay for services?

- Do practitioners' case notes truly reflect their perceptions about their cases, or is it necessary to interview them firsthand?

These types of questions have no easy answers. As a result, it's desirable for you to include a variety of data sources in your evaluation so that multiple perspectives are considered. Our bias is to give priority to data sources that have directly experienced the social need, the program process, or the program outcome that you are evaluating.

As mentioned earlier, firsthand data sources generally convey their experiences with more candor and accuracy than others who have had only indirect involvement. A pregnant teenager, for example, can more aptly speak to her fears of motherhood than anyone else, including her own mother.

Likewise, a social worker can more succinctly describe the details of an interaction with his client than can his supervisor or a professional colleague. Generally speaking, the farther removed a data source is from the experience or event in question, the greater the possibility for misrepresentation of the actual experience, or the vaguer the data will be.

Existing Data

Existing data sources are previously recorded documents or artifacts that contain data relevant to current evaluation questions. Paula also obtained existing data in her needs assessment study in Chapter 10. Generally speaking, existing data were originally collected for some purpose other than the current evaluation. Most likely, stakeholders supplied the data some time ago, and this data can be found in documents or databases in one of three areas:

- *Public data and information,* such as census data, government documents, or published literature

- *Client data and information,* such as client records, social histories, genograms, service plans, case notes, clinical assessments, or progress reports
- *Program data and information,* such as program logic models, previous evaluation reports, program contracts or funding applications, meeting minutes, employee time and activity logs, employee resumes, quality assurance records, or accounting records

People or Existing Data?

How do you decide whether to use people or existing data sources? The answer is simple: It depends on the specific focus of your evaluation. In particular, the final questions developed for your evaluation will guide you in deciding on the best data source for your inquiry.

For example, a needs assessment aimed at increasing understanding about the adolescents involved in crime in their community may phrase its evaluation questions to emphasize different data sources:

- Do adolescents who commit crimes see themselves as having a future in their community?
- To what degree do parents feel responsible for their children's criminal behavior in the community?
- What are the legal consequences for adolescents who commit crimes in the community?

Clearly, the first question targets adolescents as an essential data source, but the latter questions give priority to parents of adolescents and legal professionals or documents, respectively. Each question, of course, can be answered by any number of data sources. No doubt, parents have opinions about their children's futures, and, certainly, the legal community has a perspective on adolescent crime. Each data source, however, can speculate only about questions that ask what others are thinking or feeling.

SAMPLING METHODS

Knowing how to select a sample for your evaluation study is another tool in your toolkit. After selecting a data source, your next step is to develop a comprehensive list of every single person, document, or artifact that could possibly provide the data for your evaluation. This list is called a sampling frame, and it identifies all units (i.e., people, objects, events) of a population from which your sample is to be drawn. For example,

- A needs assessment (Chapter 10) may target people—every community member, regardless of what stakeholder group they represent.
- A process evaluation (Chapter 11), on the other hand, may target objects—all client records opened in the last fiscal year.
- Outcome and efficiency evaluations (Chapters 12 and 13) may target events—every client discharged after a minimum of 2 weeks of program services.

Of course any type of evaluation can sample people, objects, or events, depending on its focus. If our sampling frame includes only a small number of units, then it's feasible to include each one as a data source. A social service program employing 10 practitioners, for example, can easily collect data from all of its workers.

On the other hand, the 10 practitioners, each with caseloads of 40, together serve 400 clients at one time, which amounts to tons of data collection activities—perhaps more than the program can manage. Having more data source units than we can handle is a problem that our sampling tools can help fix.

After a sampling frame is defined, we then want to develop a plan that tells us how many units to pick and which specific units to choose. Do we want every member of a community to provide data, or only a select number? Do we review every client record opened in the last fiscal year, or just a portion of them? A sampling plan gives us explicit criteria so that there

is no question as to which units will provide data for our evaluation and which will not.

There are two sampling methods to consider for any evaluation:

- Probability sampling
- Nonprobability sampling

Probability Sampling

A probability sampling method is one that ensures that each unit in a sampling frame has an equal chance of being picked for your evaluation. Units are selected randomly and without bias. Those that are chosen will provide data for your evaluation, and units that are not picked will not.

The major benefit of probability sampling methods is that they produce samples that are considered to be representative of the larger sampling frame from which they were drawn. As such, data collected from the sample can be generalized or applied to the sampling frame as a whole.

Suppose that we randomly pick 100 out of a possible 1,000 members of the community that is the focus of a needs assessment evaluation. If the 100 people in our sample were picked using probability sampling approaches, then we can be confident that the data they provide will give the same information as if we had collected data from all 1,000 members.

Probability sampling, therefore, saves time and money by using a randomly selected subset to provide information about a larger group. Peter Gabor and Carol Ing (2001) summarize four types of probability sampling as follows:

- *Simple Random Sampling*

  Select each unit included in the sample using a chance procedure (e.g., rolling dice, picking random numbers, flipping a coin).

- *Systematic Random Sampling*

  1. Determine the total number of units in a population (e.g., $N = 400$ client sessions).
  2. Determine the desired sample size for the evaluation (e.g., $N = 100$ client sessions).

3. Calculate the interval to select units; that is, divide the total number of units by the desired sample size (e.g., 400/100 = 4, so every fourth session will be selected).

4. Randomly select the starting point using a chance procedure (e.g., rolling a die) to pick a number between 1 and 4 (e.g., 3).

5. Begin with session 3, and pick every fourth one thereafter (e.g., 003, 007, 011, up to session 399).

- *Stratified Random Sampling*

  1. Identify the variables or strata relevant to the evaluation (e.g., African American, Caucasian, Latino community members).

  2. Determine the percentage of each variable category in the population (e.g., African American, 28%; Caucasian, 60%; Latino, 12%).

  3. Determine the total sample size (e.g., N = 100).

  4. Calculate the strata totals (e.g., 28% of 100 = 28 African American, 60% of 100 = 60 Caucasian, 12% of 100 = 12 Latino).

  5. Use simple random sampling procedures to select units for each strata until all totals are filled.

- *Cluster Sampling*

  1. Determine the sample size (e.g., N = 250).

  2. Determine the percentage of each variable category in the population (e.g., African American, 28%; Caucasian, 60%; Latino, 12%).

  3. Use simple random sampling to select a portion of clusters (e.g., 40 residential blocks).

  4. Calculate the number of units within the selected clusters (e.g., 10 homes per block = 400 units).

  5. Use random sampling procedures to select 250 homes from 400.

Nonprobability Sampling

In contrast, nonprobability sampling methods do not give each unit in a sampling frame an equal chance of being picked for an evaluation study. In other words, individual people, objects, or events do not have an equal opportunity to supply data for your evaluation.

Thus individual people, objects, or events do not have an equal opportunity to supply data to your evaluation. Gabor and Ing (2001) summarize the four types of nonprobability sampling as follows:

- *Convenience or Availability Sampling*

  1. Include the nearest or most available units.

- *Purposive Sampling*

  1. Include units known or judged to be good data sources based on some theoretical criteria.

- *Quota Sampling*

  1. Identify variables relevant to the evaluation (e.g., gender, age).

  2. Combine the variables into discrete categories (e.g., younger female, younger male, older female, older male).

  3. Determine the percentage of each category in the population (e.g., 35% younger female, 25% younger male, 30% older female, 10% older male).

  4. Determine the total sample size (e.g., N = 200).

  5. Calculate quotas (e.g., 35% of 200 = 70 younger females, 25% of 200 = 50 younger males, 30% of 200 = 60 older females, 10% of 200 = 20 older males).

  6. Select the first available data sources possessing the required characteristics until each quota is filled.

- *Snowball Sampling*

  1. Locate a small number of data sources in the population of interest.

2. At the same time that data are collected from these sources, ask them to identify others in the population.

3. Contact the newly identified data sources, obtain their data, and request additional data sources from them.

4. Continue until the desired sample size is obtained.

Nonprobability sampling methods are used in situations where it's desirable to limit or pick your data sources based on some unique characteristic. It may be that you want to collect data only from clients who drop out of treatment before completion. Or you may want only data related to cross-cultural worker–client interactions.

When it's possible to decisively identify conditions or characteristics that define a subset of data sources, it's not necessary to sample beyond it. In other words, it's not necessary to sample from all units when the data of interest are possessed by only a select few.

Nonprobability sampling strategies aim to produce quality, firsthand data from sources that share something in common. They are often used when an evaluation question seeks a fuller understanding of the dynamics of a particular experience or condition rather than to generalize the characteristics of a sample to the larger sampling frame from which it was drawn. This latter aim is achieved by using probability sampling methods.

When is it necessary to use sampling strategies in an evaluation plan? Sampling strategies or tools can effectively address the following problems that are commonplace in all types of evaluations:

- The sampling frame is so large that data cannot realistically be collected from every unit (e.g., needs assessment of a community of 10,000 people, or a process evaluation of daily worker–client interactions in an institutional setting).
- Previous efforts to include all units in a sampling frame have failed (e.g., client response rate to satisfaction surveys is low, or client records are voluminous and not systematically organized).

- Only data sources with unique characteristics are desired (e.g., practitioners who balance their workload well, clients who successfully complete treatment, or client reports that influence courtroom decisions).
- Program resources are limited and can support data collection from only a portion of the sampling frame (e.g., program costs for evaluation are limited, or the program only employs one or two practitioners who are responsible for data collection).
- Multiple data sources are desired (e.g., data are collected from clients, workers, and/or records).

Thomas Black (1999), via Table H.2, provides us with a brief list of the advantages and disadvantages of the various sampling techniques that can be used in social work evaluation studies.

COLLECTING DATA

Now that you have your data source identified and have drawn a sample of your data sources, it's time to collect data from them. You're going to need some sort of data collection method that will consist of your detailed plans and procedures of exactly how you are going to obtain your data that will eventually answer your evaluation question.

No matter what data collection method you choose out of the many that exist, you want to develop protocols that will yield credible data. That is, you want your data to be judged as accurate and trustworthy by any reviewer. Debra Haffner and Eva Goldfarb (1997) provide an excellent summary, via Table H.3, of many ways to collect accurate and trustworthy data. Like all things in life, each data collection method has its advantages and disadvantages. You need to decide what the best one is given your specific situation.

It should be extremely clear by now that how you state your evaluation question guides the selection of your data collection method(s). As discussed earlier, you never want to subscribe to your favorite data collection method before you know your evaluation question. To do so risks collecting a flurry of data that in the end are 100% worthless.

Table H.2: **Advantages and Disadvantages of Various Sampling Methods.**

Type	Description	Advantages	Disadvantages
Simple Random	Random sample from whole population	Highly representative if all subjects participate; the ideal	Not possible without complete list of population members; potentially uneconomical to achieve; can be disruptive to isolate members from a group; time scale may be too long, data/sample could change
Stratified Random	Random sample from identifiable groups (strata), subgroups, etc.	Can ensure that specific groups are represented, even proportionally, in the sample(s) (e.g., by gender), by selecting individuals from strata list	More complex; requires greater effort than simple random; strata must be carefully defined
Cluster	Random samples of successive clusters of subjects (e.g., by institution) until small groups are chosen as units	Possible to select randomly when no single list of population members exists but local lists do; data collected on groups may avoid introduction of confounding by isolating members	Clusters in a level must be equivalent and some natural ones are not for essential characteristics (e.g., geographic: numbers equal but unemployment rates differ)
Stage	Combination of cluster (randomly selecting clusters) and random or stratified random sampling of individuals	Can make up probability sample by random at stages and within groups; possible to select random sample when population lists are very localized	Complex; combines limitations of cluster and stratified random sampling
Purposive	Hand-pick subjects on the basis of specific characteristics	Ensures balance of group sizes when multiple groups are to be selected	Samples are not easily defensible as being representative of populations due to potential subjectivity of researcher
Quota	Select individuals as they come to fill a quota by characteristics proportional to populations	Ensures selection of adequate numbers of subjects with appropriate characteristics	Not possible to prove that the sample is representative of designated population

continued

Table H.2: **(Continued)**

Type	Description	Advantages	Disadvantages
Snowball	Subjects with desired traits or characteristics give names of further appropriate subjects	Possible to include members of groups where no lists or identifiable clusters even exist (e.g., drug abusers, criminals)	No way of knowing whether the sample is representative of the population
Accidental	Either asking for volunteers, or the consequence of not all those selected finally participating, or a set of subjects who just happen to be available	Inexpensive way of ensuring sufficient numbers of a study	Can be highly unrepresentative

Put simply, the combination of data sources and data collection methods chosen can influence the nature and type of data collected. Having a well-thought-out and meaningful evaluation question before you reach for your data collection tools is absolutely essential. This will help you to stay clear of the impending disaster that will come when your evaluation data collection plan drifts away from your evaluation's initial purpose.

This happens all the time. Watch out for it so it doesn't happen to you. Remember the Cardinal Rule: Your evaluation question determines:

- Who you will collect data from (your data sources)
- How you are going to obtain a sample of your data sources
- How you plan on collecting data from your sample of data sources

How you exactly will go about collecting data to answer your evaluation question depends on many practical considerations—such as how much time, money, and political support is available to you at the time of your study. Political, ethical, and cultural factors that will affect your study were discussed in Chapters 4, 5, and 6.

For now, it's enough to say that, given the resource limitations affecting most programs, it's worthwhile for you to explore existing data options first. In the vast majority of evaluations, however, existing data may not be adequate to answer your evaluation question, and you will need to collect new data. For comprehensive coverage, an evaluation ought to use multiple data sources and data collection methods—as many as are feasible for a given evaluation.

There are various data collection methods available, and each one can be used with a variety of data sources, which are defined by who (or what) supplies the data. As discussed previously, data collection methods are concerned with existing data (i.e., data that have already been collected) or new data (i.e., data that will be collected).

Obtaining Existing Data

Given that existing data are previously recorded, they can be used to address questions that have an historical slant. Existing data can be used to profile recent and past characteristics or patterns that describe communities, clients, workers, or program services. For example, we may be interested in knowing the past demographic characteristics of a community, or a synopsis of worker qualifications for recent employees, or the general service trends of a program since its beginning.

When existing data are used, the method of data collection is primarily concerned with detailing the steps taken to assemble relevant materials. In other words, what are the rules for including or excluding existing data? The challenge of gathering existing data

Table H.3: Advantages and Disadvantages of Selected Data Collection Methods.

Data Collection Method	Description	Advantages	Disadvantages
Questionnaire (General)	A paper-and-pencil method for obtaining responses to statements or questions by using a form on which participants provide opinions or factual information	• Relatively inexpensive, quick way to collect large amounts of data from large samples in short amounts of time • Convenient for respondents to complete • Anonymity can result in more honest responses • Questionnaires are available • Well suited for answering questions related to what, where, and how many	• Limited ability to know whether one is actually measuring what one intends to measure • Limited ability to discover measurement errors • Question length and breadth are limited • No opportunity to probe or provide clarification • Relies on participants' ability to recall behavior, events • Limited capability to measure different kinds of outcomes • Must rely on self-report • Not well suited to answering questions related to how and why • Difficult with low-literacy groups
One-to-One Interview (General)	An interaction between two people in which information is gathered relative to respondent's knowledge, thoughts, and feelings about different topics	• Allows greater depth than a questionnaire • Data are deeper, richer, have more context • Interviewer can establish rapport with respondent • Interviewer can clarify questions • Good method for working with low literacy respondents • Higher response and completion rates • Allows for observation of nonverbal gestures	• Requires a lot of time and personnel • Requires highly trained, skilled interviewers • Limited number of people can be included • Is open to interviewer's bias • Prone to respondents giving answers they believe are "expected" (social desirability) • No anonymity • Potential invasiveness with personal questions

continued

Table H.3: [Continued]

Data Collection Method	Description	Advantages	Disadvantages
One-to-One Interview [Unstructured]	Totally free response pattern; allows respondent to express ideas in own way and time	• Can elicit personal information • Can gather relevant unanticipated data • Interviewer can probe for more information	• Requires great skill on part of interviewer • More prone to bias in response interpretation • Data are time consuming to analyze
One-to-One Interview [Semistructured]	Limited free response, built around a set of basic questions from which interviewer may branch off	• Combines efficiency of structured interview with ability to probe and investigate interesting responses	• Cannot do true exploratory research • Predetermined questions limit ability to probe further
One-to-One Interview [Structured]	Predetermined questions, often with structured responses	• Easy to administer • Does not require as much training of interviewer	• Less ability to probe for additional information • Unable to clarify ambiguous responses
Focus Group	Interviews with groups of people (anywhere from 4 to 12) selected because they share certain characteristics relevant to the questions of study. Interviewer encourages discussion and expression of differing opinions and viewpoints	• Studies participants in natural, real-life atmosphere • Allows for exploration of unanticipated issues as they are discussed • Can increase sample size in qualitative evaluation • Can save time and money • Can stimulate new ideas among participants • Can gain additional information from observation of group process • Can promote greater spontaneity and candor	• Interviewer has less control than in a one-to-one interview • Data are sometimes difficult to analyze • Must consider context of comments • Requires highly trained observer-moderators • Cannot isolate one individual's train of thought throughout

Method	Description	Advantages	Disadvantages
Phone Interview	One-to-one conversation over the phone	• Potentially lower cost • Anonymity may promote greater candor	• Not everyone has a phone • Unlisted numbers may present sampling bias • No opportunity to observe nonverbal gestures
Participant Observation (General)	Measures behaviors, interactions, processes by directly watching participants	• Spontaneous quality of data that can be gathered • Can code behaviors in a natural setting such as a lunch room or a hallway • Can provide a check against distorted perceptions of participants • Works well with a homogeneous group • Good technique in combination with other methods • Well suited for study of body language (kinesics) and study of people's use of personal space and its relationship to culture (proxemics)	• Quantification and summary of data are difficult • Recording of behaviors and events may have to be made for memory • Difficult to maintain objectives • Very time consuming and expensive • Requires a highly trained observer
Participant Observation (Participant as Observer)	The evaluator's role as observer is known to the group being studied and is secondary to his or her role as participant	• Evaluator retains benefits of participant without ethical issues at stake	• Difficult to maintain two distinct roles • Other participants may resent observer role • Observer's presence can change nature of interactions being observed

continued

Table H.3: [Continued]

Data Collection Method	Description	Advantages	Disadvantages
Participant Observation [Observer as Participant]	Evaluator's observer role is known and his or her primary role is to assess the program	• Evaluator can be more focused on observation role while still maintaining connection to other participants	• Evaluator is clearly an outsider • Observer's presence can change nature of the interactions being observed
Participant Observation [Complete Observer]	The evaluator has no formal role as participant; is a silent observer; may also be hidden from the group or in a completely public setting where his or her presence is unnoticed and unobtrusive	• More objective observations possible • Evaluator is not distracted by participant role • Evaluator's observations do not interfere in any way with the group's process if his or her presence is hidden	• If evaluator's presence is known, it can inhibit or change interactions of participants • If evaluator's presence is hidden, it raises ethical questions
Document Analysis	Unobtrusive measure using analysis of diaries, logs, letters, and formal policy statements to learn about the values and beliefs of participants in a setting or group. Can also include class reviews, letters to teachers, letters from parents, and letters from former students to learn about the processes involved in a program and what may be having an impact	• Diaries reduce problems of memory relating to when, where, with whom • Provides access to thoughts and feelings that may not otherwise be accessible • Can be less threatening to participants • Evaluator can collect and analyze data on own schedule • Relatively inexpensive	• Quality of data varies between subjects • Diaries may cause change in subjects' behaviors • Not well suited for low-literacy groups • Can be very selective data • No opportunities for clarification of data

	Description	Advantages	Disadvantages
Archival Data	Analysis of archival data from a society, community, or organization. Can include birth rates, census data, contraceptive purchase data, and number of visits to hospitals for sexually transmitted diseases	• More accurate than self-report	• Not all data are available or fully reported • Difficult to match data geographically or individually
Historical Data	Method of discovering, from records and personal accounts, what happened in the past. Especially useful for establishing a baseline or background of a program or of participants prior to measuring outcomes	• Baseline data can help with interpretation of outcome findings • Can help answer questions about why a program is or is not successful in meeting its goals • Provides a picture of the broader context within which a program is operating	• Can be difficult to obtain data • Relies on data that may be incomplete, missing, or inaccurate • May rely on participant's selective memory of events and behaviors • Difficult to verify accuracy
Secondary Analysis	Analysis of data that already exist (i.e., not the collection of new or original data)	• Considerably cheaper and faster than doing original studies • Evaluator can benefit from the research from some of the top scholars in the field, which for the most part ensures quality data • Other surveys may draw samples from the larger population	• May be difficult to find relevant data if dealing with a well-defined minority subgroup (since many surveys deal with national populations) • Can be used in irresponsible ways. If variables aren't exactly those you want, data can be manipulated and transformed in a way that might lessen the validity of the original research

continued

Data Collection Method	Description	Advantages	Disadvantages
		• Amount of previously collected data used is flexible (e.g., you might only extract a few figures from a table, use the data in a subsidiary role, or use them in a central role in your research) • Network of data archives in which survey data files are collected and distributed is readily available, making research for secondary analysis easily accessible	• Can involve large data files and difficult statistical packages (particularly in research of large samples)
Online Surveys	Usually questionnaires that are administered online through one of the many available online resources (e.g., SurveyMonkey.com)	• Less expensive (no postage or interviewer time) • Easier to make changes to questionnaire and to copy and sort data • Can be delivered to recipients in seconds, rather than in days as with traditional mail • Researcher can send invitations and receive responses in a very short time and thus receive participation-level estimates • Response rates on private networks are higher than with paper surveys or interviews • Respondents may answer more honestly • Participants can answer in minutes or hours, and coverage can be global	• Population and sample limited to those with access to computer and online network • Difficult to guarantee anonymity and confidentiality • Construction can be more difficult the first few times, due to a researcher's lack of experience • More instruction and orientation to the computer online systems may be necessary for respondents to complete the questionnaire • Computers have a much greater likelihood of "glitches" than oral or written forms of communication • Response rates are higher only during the first few days

is in recovering old documents or artifacts that may not be easily accessible.

It may be, for example, that program start-up events were recorded but they are in the possession of a former employee, or that client records are sealed by court orders. It may also be that there are no existing data because none were ever recorded. Existing data can be found in:

- Documents and reports
- Data sets

Documents and Reports

Reviewing existing documents is a process whereby we examine data that have been previously analyzed and summarized. In other words, other people have already studied the raw, or original, data and presented their interpretations or conclusions. Examples of such materials include published research studies, government documents, news releases, social service agency directories, agency annual reports, client reports, and worker performance reviews.

The data available in existing documents and reports are typically presented in either narrative or statistical form. Existing narrative data are presented as words or symbols that offer insight into the topic being addressed. Reading the last 10 annual reports for a program, for example, can shed light on the program's evolution. Examining training materials for workers can reveal strengths and weaknesses of program services. Reviewing client files can provide strong clues about underlying practice principles that drive client service delivery.

Existing statistical data involve numbers and figures that have been calculated from original raw data. These data provide us with information about specific client or program features in a summarized form. The most recent program annual report, for example, may state that client racial makeup is 35% African American, 40% Caucasian, 15% Hispanic or Latino, and 10% other. Or it may report that program clients, on average, received 10 more service hours compared with clients from the previous year. These reports rarely include the raw data used to formulate such summary statements, but they are informative.

By looking at what others have already done, we can save valuable time and frustration—learning from mistakes made by others and avoiding unnecessarily reinventing the wheel. Data and information gleaned from existing published reports and articles provide us with a picture of how much attention our evaluation questions have previously received, if any.

Additionally, we can find out whether other similar evaluations or studies have taken place. If so, what did they find? What measurement instruments were used, either successfully or unsuccessfully? In short, existing reports provide a starting point from which to begin and refine current evaluation plans.

Data Sets

Data sets, also called databases, store existing raw or original data and organize them such that all data elements can be connected to the source that provided them. For example, a typical client database for a program stores demographic data (e.g., age, race, and gender) for each client. Because data in existing data sets were collected for purposes other than answering our evaluation questions, they are called secondary data.

Before we get ahead of ourselves, it's important to note that data sets or databases can be manual or automated. Most social service programs use manual data sets, which amount to no more than a collection of papers and forms filed in a folder and then stored in a filing cabinet. In contrast, automated data sets store data electronically in computers. The format or setup of an automated database can mirror its manual predecessors, but because of the power of computers, it's far more sophisticated and efficient.

Even though many social service programs are beginning to automate, old data sets will likely remain in manual form until the day comes when an ambitious evaluator determines that the old data are needed to inform current evaluation questions. Whether manual or automated, databases can accommodate secondary data in both narrative and statistical form. Two common data sets that evaluators can tap into are:

- Census data
- Client and/or program data sets

Census data. Census data are periodic summaries of selected demographic characteristics, or variables, that describe a population. Census takers obtain data about variables such as age, gender, marital status, and race. To obtain data in specific topic areas, census takers sometimes obtain data for such variables as income level, education level, employment status, and presence of disabilities.

Census data are extremely useful for evaluations in that they aim to compare a program sample with the larger population. For example, is the racial or gender makeup of a program's clientele similar to that of the community at large? Census data also are useful for providing a general picture of a specific population at a certain point in time. The more data obtained during a census taking, the more detailed the description of the population.

The disadvantage of census data is that they can become outdated quickly. Census surveys occur every 10 years and take considerable time to compile, analyze, and distribute. In addition, they give only a general picture of a population. The census, for example, provides data only on the average age of residents in a community or the percentage of childless couples living in a certain area. Although these data are useful for developing an average community profile, they do not provide us with a clear idea of individual differences or how the members of the community describe themselves.

Client and/or program data sets. More and more social service programs rely on client and program data to produce reports that describe the services they provide. They most likely use data taken from client and program records. Client data sets consist of data elements that are collected as part of normal paperwork protocols. Intake forms, assessments, progress reports, and critical incident reports all produce a wealth of client data that range from client demographics to rates of treatment progress.

Program data sets encompass various administrative forms that are part and parcel of program operations. They include such things as time sheets, employee resumes and performance evaluations, audit sheets, accreditation documents, training and supervision schedules, and minutes of meetings. Program data sets also yield rich data, including variables such as number of clients served, worker demographics and qualifications, type of service provided, amount of supervision and training, and client outcomes.

There are two problems associated with client and program data sets. First, the data are often incomplete or inconsistently recorded. Because data collection occurred previously, it's usually not possible to fill in missing data or correct errors. Second, the data apply to a specific point in time.

If program conditions are known to change rapidly, then past data may no longer be relevant to present evaluation questions. For example, social service programs that rely on workers to collect client and program data and that suffer from high staff turnover rates are faced with the problem that data collected by past workers may not be pertinent to present situations.

Obtaining New Data

Existing data provide us with general impressions and insights about a program, but rarely can they address all questions of a current evaluation. As such, the activities of an evaluation almost always involve the process of collecting new or original data that can be obtained from:

- Individual interviews
- Surveys
- Group interviews
- Observations

Individual Interviews

Individual interviews with data sources can produce new, or original, data about social needs, program processes, or program outcomes. Interviewing is a data collection method that requires us to identify, approach, and interview specific people who are considered knowledgeable about our questions. Interviewees are sometimes referred to as key informants and can include various people: professionals, public officials, agency directors, program clients, select citizens, and minorities, to name a few.

Interviews can be formal, and they can use a structured interview schedule such as the one presented for a needs assessment in Box 10.1. Overall, face-to-face interviews with individuals are generally used to ask questions that permit open-ended responses. To obtain more detailed data, we simply develop additional questions to provide more structure and help probe for answers with more depth.

Question 4 in Box 10.1, for example, could be expanded so that key informants are asked to consider past or present services, or gaps in services. Structured interview schedules are used when we have some prior knowledge of the topic being investigated and we want to guide data sources to provide us with particular kinds of information.

On the other hand, when very little is known about our problem area, we can use informal unstructured interviews to permit more of a free-flowing discussion. Informal interviews involve more dialogue, which produces not only rich and detailed data but also more questions.

Suppose, for example, we want to learn more from a group of community residents who avoid using our social service program (needs assessment). We might begin each interview by asking a general question: What keeps you from using our social service program?

Depending on the responses given, subsequent questions may focus on better understanding the needs of our interviewees or on changing existing services to become more accessible. Both structured and unstructured interviews rely on interviewer–interviewee interaction to produce meaningful data.

Surveys

The main goal of surveys is to gather opinions from numerous people to describe them as a group. Such data can be collected using in-person or telephone interviews, or via mailed surveys. Surveys differ from the structured and unstructured interview schedules used in face-to-face data collection. Specifically, survey questions are narrower and yield shorter responses. Additionally, they do not rely on interviewer skills to generate a response.

Creating survey questions that yield valid and reliable responses is a prickly problem because it's a task that appears simple but is not. Consider the likely reactions of students if a teacher were to include a vague or confusing question on a class test. Generally speaking, people do not like or do not respond to questions that do not make sense or are presented ambiguously.

Whether surveys are conducted in person, by telephone, or by mail depends on several factors. Whatever the method of collecting data, all types of surveys contain basic tasks in their implementation. There are various steps that must be followed when sending a survey, such as a mailed satisfaction with services questionnaire (Hatry & Lampkin, 2003):

- Identify the specific information needed.
- Develop the questionnaire, with help from an expert if possible. Each question included should provide information related to one or more of the outcome indicators.
- Decide when to administer the questionnaire. For example, if a program seeks to help clients sustain an improved condition, then each client might be surveyed 6 or 12 months after completing the service. In other programs, clients could provide outcome information at the time the services are completed. Institutionalized clients might be surveyed periodically, for example, at 1-year intervals.
- Determine how the questionnaire will be administered. Common options include the following:

  - *Mail,* if addresses are available and most clients are literate (a low-cost method)
  - *Telephone interview,* if clients have telephones (a more time-consuming and expensive method)
  - *In-person interviews,* which will likely be too costly unless the questionnaire can be administered at the program's offices
  - *A combination of the aforementioned methods.* Consider low-cost incentives (free meals, movie tickets, or a chance to win a TV or other items) to improve the response rate.

- Assign staff to track which clients should be surveyed and when and to oversee the survey administration and ensure completion, including arranging for second or third mailings or telephone calls to nonrespondents.
- Enter and tabulate survey information, preferably using a computer to prepare reports.
- Provide and disseminate easily understood reports to staff and interested outsiders at regular intervals. Usually it's not appropriate to report on the responses of individual clients (and some programs may provide clients with a guarantee of confidentiality).
- Encourage use of the survey information to identify program weaknesses and improvement needs.

Given that one of the major disadvantages of mail surveys is a low response rate, we present the following strategies for increasing the number of respondents:

- Include a cover letter stating the purpose of the evaluation with each mailed survey. The letter confirms that all responses are confidential and is most effective when signed by a high-ranking official (e.g., program executive director, minister, school principal, or politician).
- Use extremely clear and simple instructions.
- Include a stamped, self-addressed return envelope with the survey.
- Include free incentives to potential respondents (e.g., movie passes, fast-food coupons, or a pencil with the agency logo).
- Send a follow-up letter to all respondents as a prompt to complete the survey.
- Offer respondents the opportunity to request the results of the evaluation.

Group Interviews

Conducting group interviews is a data collection method that allows us to gather the perspectives of several individuals at one time. They are more complex than individual interviews because they involve interaction between and among data sources. Three strategies for group interviews—presented from the least to most structured are:

- Open forums
- Focus groups
- Nominal groups

Open forums. Open forums have the least structure of the three group interview strategies. They are generally used to address general evaluation questions. Holding an open forum involves inviting stakeholders to discuss matters of interest to our evaluation. Open forums include such things as town-hall meetings or phone-in radio talk shows. They simply provide a place and an opportunity for people to assemble and air their thoughts and opinions about a specific topic.

Open forums are generally most useful for gaining reactions or responses to a specific event or problem. An executive director, for example, might hold an open forum for all program stakeholders to announce plans to conduct a program evaluation. The forum would provide stakeholders the opportunity to respond to the idea as well as give input. The advantage of public forums is that they offer widespread involvement. Their main disadvantage is that they tend to draw a deliberate and select group of people who have strong opinions (one way or another) that are not necessarily shared by all.

The procedures for carrying out an open forum are summarized as follows (Hatry & Lampkin, 2003):

- Identify the event or problem to be addressed.
- Allow individuals to spontaneously share responses and reactions.
- Record responses as given, without editing or discussion.

Focus groups. Focus groups aim to gather data for the purposes of exploring or testing ideas. They consist of individuals who are reasonably familiar with the topic slated for discussion but not necessarily familiar with each other. Focus groups involve an interactive discussion that is designed to gather perceptions about a predetermined topic of interest from a group of select people in an accepting and nonthreatening setting.

Conducting focus groups requires the skills of a group facilitator, who sets the ground rules for the group and helps to guide discussion. The facilitator, as a group leader, provides guidelines for the group process and aids the dialogue for group members. Questions prepared in advance help to set the parameters for discussion. Indeed, the questions presented earlier in Box 10.1 could be used to guide a focus group for a needs assessment.

The main task of focus group facilitators is to balance group discussion such that group members stay centered on the questions being asked but also stimulate one another to produce more in-depth and comprehensive data. The results of a focus group may show similar and divergent perceptions of participants.

The procedures for carrying out a focus group are summarized as follows (Hatry & Lampkin, 2003):

- Develop open-ended questions.
- Provide an orientation or introduction to the topic of focus.
- Allow time for participants to read or review material if necessary (maximum 30 minutes).
- Determine how data are going to be recorded (e.g., audiotape, videotape, observation, or note-taking).
- Have the facilitator begin with open-ended questions and facilitate the discussion.
- The four major facilitation tasks are
  - Prevent one person or a small group from dominating the discussion.
  - Encourage the quiet ones to participate.
  - Obtain responses from the entire group to ensure the fullest possible coverage.
  - Maintain a balance between the roles of moderator (managing group dynamics) and interviewer.
- When the responses have been exhausted, move to the next question.
- Analyze data from the group.

Nominal groups. The nominal group technique is a useful data gathering tool for evaluations because it provides for an easy way to collect data from individuals in a group situation. The composition of a nominal group is similar to that of a focus group in that it includes individuals who can answer a particular question of interest but may or may not know each other. A nominal group, however, is far more structured than a focus group, and group interaction is limited. The nominal group process involves members working in the presence of others but with little interaction.

The most obvious advantage of a nominal group is collecting data from numerous sources in an efficient manner. The nominal group process typically takes two to four hours, depending on the size of the group and the number of questions asked. Because of the game-like nature of the technique, participants can find the experience fun. When a cross-section of group participants is recruited, the process can yield a comprehensive response to evaluation questions.

The procedures for carrying out the nominal group technique are summarized as follows (Hatry & Lampkin, 2003):

- Develop open-ended questions.
- Provide six to nine people with a comfortable seating arrangement, preferably a circle.
- Give an overview of the group task, give each member a sheet with questions on it (and room to record answers), instruct members *not* to talk to each other, and allow time for individuals to record responses privately.
- Use a round-robin approach to list all answers from previous step. No discussion.
- Discussion focuses on clarifying what responses mean to ensure that everyone has a common understanding of each response.
- Individually rank top five responses.
- Round-robin to list rankings.
- Brief discussion for clarification if necessary.

Observations

Observation as a data collection method is different from interviewing and surveying in that the data source watches a person, event, or object of interest and then records what he or she sees. A major tenet of observation as a data collection method is that it produces objective data based on observable facts. Two types of observations are:

- Structured observations
- Participant observations

Structured observations. Structured observations occur under controlled conditions and aim to collect precise, valid, and reliable data about complex interactions. An impartial observer is trained to fix his or her eyes on particular persons or events and to look for specifics. The observation can take place in natural or artificial settings, but the conditions and timing of the observation are always predetermined. The data recorded redirect the trained observers' perceptions of what they see, and the observers are not directly involved with the people or the event being observed.

For example, a program may want to set up observations of parent–adolescent dyads to better understand how families learn to problem-solve together. The dimensions of problem-solving are predefined such that the observer knows precisely what to look for. It may be that the observer watches for each time the parent or child verbally expresses frustration with the other as they work through a problem.

Another dimension of problem-solving to watch for may be the degree of confidence parents convey to their children at the beginning, middle, and end of the problem-solving exercise. To obtain objective data, the observer cannot be directly or indirectly involved with the case being observed. In other words, workers and their supervisors are not eligible to observe families who are in their caseload.

Another evaluation effort may seek to describe exemplary cross-cultural supervision practices. In this scenario, the observer follows a protocol to tease out supervisory behaviors that demonstrate cultural competence. Once again, the rules for observation and recording data are set out ahead of time, and the observer adheres to these fixed guidelines. In this case, the observer records only observations related to cultural competence and not general competence, for example.

Because structured observations rely on observer interpretation, it's useful to capture the observation episode on videotape to allow for multiple viewings and viewers. The more precise the protocols for structured observation, the more consistent the data. Also, training observers to a level of unmistakable clarity about what to watch for and what to document is essential. The basic tasks in implementing regular trained observer measurements are as follows (Hatry & Lampkin, 2003):

- Identify what specific data are wanted.
- Develop the trained observer rating guide. Test the guide with a number of raters to make sure the rated items and rating categories are clear.
- Decide when the ratings will be made and how frequently they will be reported during the year.
- Select and train the observers.
- Assign staff to oversee the process, including (a) making sure the ratings are done on schedule, (b) periodically checking the ratings to make sure that each trained observer is still providing accurate ratings, and (c) providing retraining when necessary and training for new observers.
- Arrange for the ratings to be entered and tabulated, preferably electronically and using a computer to tabulate that information and prepare reports. (In recent years, many organizations have begun using handheld computers to record the ratings. The use of such computers can greatly reduce data entry, tabulation, and reporting time.)
- Provide and disseminate regular reports on the findings to staff and interested outside organizations. The reports should be clear and understandable.
- Encourage use of the rating information to identify program weaknesses and improvement needs.

Participant observations. Participant observation differs from structured observation on two main features: The observer is not impartial, and the rules for observation are far more flexible. As a participant in the event under scrutiny, the observer has a vested interest in what is taking place. An executive director could be a participant observer in a sobriety support group offered by her program, for example, given that she has influence in how the group is run and has a stake in the group's success.

The challenge for participant observers is to balance their dual roles so that data are based on fact and not personal impressions. The benefit of participant observation is that members of the group are in a better position to pick up subtle or cultural nuances that may be obscure to an impartial viewer. Consider the scenario of the parent–adolescent dyad working toward improving their problem-solving skills.

Choosing to use a participant observer such as the assigned worker or another family member may well influence data collection. Specifically, an observer who is personally known to the parent and adolescent can better detect verbal expressions of frustration or parent behaviors displaying confidence than can a stranger.

Unlike structured observers, participant observers interact with the people they are watching. In other words, the participant observer is free to have a dialogue with his or her research participants to verify observations and to check out interpretations. Participant observer interviews are unique in their tone and how they are carried out.

DATA COLLECTION PLAN

With the knowledge you gained from this tool and others, you are now in a position to develop a data collection evaluation plan. Table H.4 provides an example of all the ingredients that need to be put into such a data collection plan.

a = This column should list specifically what indicator(s) you are going to use to measure with each one of your program's objectives. Each indicator must come from the "outcomes" column in your logic model. Theoretically, you can have multiple indicators to measure the same program objective.

Realistically, and at a much more practical level, however, a program objective can easily be measured with only one indicator. Remember, each program outcome is a program objective. Thus each outcome on your logic model (as presented in Chapters 7 and 8) must be listed in your data collection plan.

b = This column should list specifically how you are going to measure each indicator in column *a*. For example, the indicators for self-esteem and social support can be measured many different ways. In our example, we chose two standardized measuring instruments:

1. The Rosenberg Self-Esteem Scale to measure self-esteem.
2. The Perceived Social Support Scale to measure social support.

c = This column should list specifically the person who is going to provide the data, via the use of your selected measuring instrument (*b*). In a nutshell, this person, called a data source, is the one who is going to complete the measuring instrument. Once again, a measuring instrument can be completed by a variety of different data sources.

d = This column should list specifically how the measuring instrument is going to be administered. Not only can you use a variety of measuring instruments to measure an indicator (*b*), but you also have a variety of options on how to administer them. For example, you can read the items, or questions, on the measuring instrument to your clients, or you can have your clients fill out the instrument themselves. You can also have clients complete them individually with no one around or in group settings such as parks, waiting rooms, and coffee shops.

Table H.4: Data Collection Evaluation Plan.

	a	b	c	d	e	f	g
	Indicator (from logic model)	*How indicator is measured*	*Who provides the data*	*How data are gathered*	*When data are gathered*	*Where data are gathered*	*Who collects the data*
Example	Increase the self-esteem of pregnant adolescents after they have their babies	Rosenberg Self-Esteem Scale	Client	1. Self-administered 2. Self-administered 3. Self-administered	1. Intake 2. Exit interview 3. 3 months after intervention	1. Waiting room 2. Worker's office 3. Client's home	1. Receptionist 2. Social worker 3. Case aid
Example	Increase the social support systems of pregnant adolescents after they have their babies	Scale of Perceived Social Support	Client	1. Self-administered 2. Self-administered in a group setting 3. Self-administered in a group setting	1. Intake 2. Last day of intervention 3. 1 month after intervention	1. Waiting room 2. In last group session 3. Group interview in coffee shop	1. Receptionist 2. Group leader 3. Research assistant

e = This column should state specifically the exact time frame in which the measuring instrument is going to be completed. Once again, there are many options available. Clients can complete measuring instruments at home on Friday nights before bedtime, for example, or at the beginning of your interview.

f = This column is closely related to the previous column (*e*). It should list the specific location of where the measuring instrument will be completed. For example, you can have your clients complete the Rosenberg Self-Esteem Scale in your program's waiting room, at home, or in your office.

g = This column should list specifically who is going to collect the data via the measuring instrument when it's completed. After the data source (*c*) has completed the data-gathering instrument (*b*), who's going to collect the completed instrument for analysis? And, more important, who is going to collate all the data into a data bank for further analyses?

SUMMARY

This tool covered some of the basic phases of all evaluations: sampling and data collection. Evaluators can choose from numerous sampling and data collection methods. The pros and cons of each must be assessed in light of the unique context for each evaluative effort. Ultimately, programs should strive to collect data from firsthand sources. Additionally, data collection methods ought to be easy for workers to use, fit within the flow of a program, and be designed with user input.

TRAINING AND SUPERVISING DATA COLLECTORS

In order to collect high-quality data that meet the standards of utility, accuracy, and propriety, it's important that data collectors be trained and supervised. Training can be formal or informal depending on planned activities and the experience level of the data collectors, but all training should aim to ensure that:

- Standards and procedures will be applied consistently
- Data collectors and their supervisors understand how the data will be used in the evaluation, how planned activities will be carried out, their respective roles and responsibilities, and how to handle events that may arise.

Even if your evaluation plan calls for using existing data, or data that would be collected as part of the intervention or other program activity, it's good to review your plans together so that data collectors and supervisors share the same understanding of the purpose of data collection, the data collection procedures, the division of labor, and any special data collection circumstances.

IDENTIFYING WHO NEEDS TO BE TRAINED

You can use a table like Table I.1 to help you think systematically about who should receive training. Table I.1 was completed using an example that involves an asthma education training intervention. Notice that we not only list the people who may be directly collecting data for the evaluation but also those who supervise data collection or whose participation is necessary to gain "access" to the data—in this case those who would be referring participants to the intervention.

Thinking broadly at this step will help you avoid difficulties later. The training needs of each of these groups may not be the same. By systematically thinking through the roles and training needs of each group, you can tailor your training to meet their needs.

SELECTING YOUR TRAINING METHOD

Training can take many forms, from informal to formal and from simple to complex. Your choice of methods will depend on your audience(s), the training needs you have identified, your training resources, and your personal style. Some training methods you might consider include:

- *Written instructions.* In some cases simple instructions on a data collection form may be sufficient.
- *Verbal instructions.* For simple data collection activities, verbal instructions may be sufficient (e.g., "Place completed forms in the box at the door before you leave"); however, we suggest pairing these with written instructions whenever possible.
- *Meetings.* It may be necessary to hold meetings with partners, stakeholders, or decision-makers to ensure access to the data you need for the evaluation.

Table I.1: **Data Collector Involvement and Training Needs for an Asthma Education Training Intervention.**

Data Collector/ Stakeholder/Other	Data Collection Type	Role in Data Collection	Training Needs
Asthma Educators	Pre- and post-intervention survey of asthma education program participants and attendance logs	• Maintain attendance log of all asthma education participants • Administer data collection questionnaires • Collect questionnaires • Keep questionnaires secure until collected by Evaluation Lead	• Data collection procedures • Attendance log procedures • Data collection logistics • Informed consent • Data handling and confidentiality
Evaluation Lead	Pre- and post-intervention survey of asthma education program participants and attendance logs	• Monitor randomly selected education sessions to assess consistency and quality of delivery • Collect questionnaires and attendance logs from asthma educators	• Data monitoring procedures • Data handling and confidentiality
Clinic Staff	Pre- and post-intervention survey of asthma education program participants	• Provide referrals to asthma education sessions	• Understand recruitment procedures

- *Memoranda of Understanding or data-sharing agreements.* Depending on institutional needs, it may be necessary to set out formal agreements for how data can be accessed. In such agreements, it's important to work out who will have access to data, under what circumstances, and when it will be available. It's also important to agree on the formats in which data will be made available and to be aware of any restrictions on the use of data. The contents of any agreements should be incorporated into your training activities.
- *Train-the-trainer.* In some cases you may have data being collected by people who

are also conducting an intervention (e.g., teachers conducting training with youth). In this situation you may want to embed your evaluation data collection training into the larger training on the intervention itself.
- *Formal data collector training.* For more complex data collection activities specific to the evaluation, and/or in cases where multiple data collectors are involved, we recommend that you hold a formal data collector training. If your situation calls for a more formal data collector training, using a variety of adult learning strategies and techniques will help you convey the important concepts (see Table I.4).

We anticipate that formal training will not be needed for most program evaluations. However, it's useful to know about these types of techniques, which can include both instructional approaches (e.g., didactic approaches, case examples or narratives, brainstorming, etc.) to convey knowledge and hands-on approaches (e.g., modeling, role-playing, small group and peer support, practice sessions, "on-the-ground" training, etc.) to teach skills.

Regardless of the approach you select, try to engage participants in active and interactive learning by asking and answering questions, being enthusiastic, and providing immediate positive *and* constructive feedback (e.g., "I liked how you did *X*. Next time I'd like to see you do *Y* as well."). Feel free to combine different types of techniques.

Formal trainings can range from a few hours to several days in length, depending on the complexity of your evaluation data collection approach. Typically, hands-on approaches take more time than presenting the information in lecture format. Be aware of how much time you will need, and try not to rush through the material.

If your evaluation design involves conducting data collection at different points in time, you may need to conduct training before each data collection period. If you will use the same data collectors during each time period, your training can serve more as a review of concepts. If you experience staff turnover or need to recruit one or more new data collectors during the data collection period, think about how you will train them.

DEFINING YOUR TRAINING TOPICS

Although your training will be customized to meet the needs of your evaluation, most training sessions will include the following:

- Background material about the data being collected that clarifies the type of data being collected, from whom, and for what purpose
- Instructions for data collection and data management, including roles and responsibilities

- Other topics, as needed, such as staff safety, team building, and special considerations in working with the intended audience

Background Material

Providing information about the purpose of the evaluation and how the data will be used will make data collectors feel more confident; motivate them to obtain high-quality data; help them make better decisions regarding the data collection; help them trouble shoot, answer respondent questions, and respond to unusual situations; and contribute to a more professional attitude.

A broader understanding of the evaluation will help data collectors appreciate how the evaluation standards informed the evaluation design and their role in maintaining those standards during implementation. Background material should include basic information about what kind of data will be collected, from whom, and for what purpose. It should also include information about who is sponsoring the evaluation and who will use the data to generate evaluation findings.

An evaluation overview statement can be developed and used for this purpose. For more formal data collector trainings, you should consider compiling a data collection handbook that includes the protocols, measuring instruments, instructions, contact numbers, and other supplementary materials that were developed for your evaluation. Data collectors can then use this handbook as a great reference after the training is completed.

Data Collection Instructions

Data collection instructions should cover every aspect of data collection, from identifying or locating appropriate respondents or records to processing the collected data. The need for clear instructions holds whether you have hired data collectors or will be using volunteers, such as teachers or parents, to record information in logs. These instructions should be detailed written instructions that leave no room for misinterpretation. In addition, all data collectors need to know their own specific roles and responsibilities as well as to whom they report and whom they should call with questions.

In some cases, data collectors work in teams and may need instruction on how to divide the work efficiently. Supervisors also need to be clear about their roles and responsibilities. Table I.2 provides additional details on training topics related to data collection and management.

Table I.2: **Common Data Collection Training Topics.**

Topic	Description
Data collection logistics	Training of data collectors should cover the logistics of the data collection: what, when, where, how, and from whom. Be sure to stress the importance of adhering to scheduling requirements that impact the quality of the evaluation, such as the timing of pre- and posttest data collection.
Identifying appropriate respondents/records	For some types of evaluation it is important to obtain data from only those respondents or records that meet the evaluation requirements. If data collectors understand the importance of adhering to the data collection protocol, they will be less likely to substitute respondents or records inappropriately, thus preserving the quality of the data.
Recruiting participants	Data collectors should be given detailed and explicit information about how to recruit participants or gain access to data. For instance, for survey data collection, high response rates are important. Interviewers or those administering questionnaires should be taught how to encourage a respondent to participate while at the same time protecting respondents' rights to refuse to participate.
Gaining access to data	Field workers who are abstracting records will need to learn what to say in order to gain admittance and request records. Despite having obtained the necessary organizational agreements or required clearances, data collectors may have to deal with gatekeepers or new staff who may be unaware of these agreements or who may find it burdensome to retrieve records or share offices.
Introducing the study and obtaining consent/ access	Data collectors should know how to provide informed consent to participants and how to gather and maintain the data collected according to ethical considerations and professional evaluation standards. Whenever possible, evaluation materials should include written scripts for how an evaluation should be introduced to participants or stakeholders as well as procedures for obtaining consent to participate in the evaluation.
Collecting unbiased data	Data need to be collected in a consistent and unbiased fashion in order to allow meaningful comparison and interpretation. Ensuring this type of consistency and neutrality in data collection should be a key consideration in training. For complex data collection instruments, it is good practice to develop a "Question-by-Question" manual that provides information about the intent of each question or item (e.g., "when we ask about asthma medications we mean only prescription medication and not over-the-counter or herbal remedies").

Table I.2. **(Continued)**

Topic	Description
	If interviews are planned, interviewers should be trained to read the questions as written and in the specified order, use a neutral tone of voice, and avoid interjecting comments or opinions. Focus group moderators need to make sure they do not ask leading questions and that they adequately guide the discussion to keep one person from dominating. For records abstraction, training should focus on which records are to be reviewed and precisely what information from the records is to be obtained.
Recording responses	Accurate recording of data is critical. Data collectors should have opportunities to practice recording and reporting data as part of the training. Encourage data collectors to make notes about any ambiguous responses. This will help data analysts better interpret the data later. You may want to measure the degree to which different data collectors record or code the same data in the same way.
Knowing when to terminate an interview	Sometimes interviewers should terminate or reschedule the interview. For example, if the respondent cannot focus or is experiencing difficulty comprehending or communicating, perhaps due to being emotionally upset, tired, or some other reason, then it is better to terminate or reschedule.
Data handling and security	Data collection procedures and training should address what to do with data once they are collected, how to protect the confidentiality and security of the data, who is allowed access, and what to do if any breach in security or confidentiality does occur. Data collectors need to learn these procedures and why data confidentiality and security are important.
Data collection supervision and monitoring	Regardless of who is collecting the data, it is important that there be a plan for supervision and monitoring to help ensure that data are being collected appropriately and that any issues can be resolved as they arise. Depending on the complexity of the data collection activity, supervisory responsibilities might be limited to training and quality checks but might also include a range of additional roles such as hiring data collectors, validating samples, supervising data entry, monitoring data collection, and coordinating with data analysts.
Routine methods for gathering feedback from data collectors	Ensure that you have a method for routinely gathering feedback from data collectors about any problems they have encountered or field observations they have that may necessitate reviewing data collection procedures or instruments. Devise means to share lessons learned among all data collectors and their supervisors while data collection is in progress. Keeping communication channels open, identifying emerging issues as soon as they arise, sharing critical information among all data collectors, and working together with them to develop effective solutions are among the best ways to safeguard the accuracy, propriety, and utility of any data collected.

Topic	Description
Data collector safety and security considerations	Depending on the location and timing of field work, safety and security considerations may be an important component in the training of data collectors. Training of field workers (e.g., home interventions) should include information on being alert, dealing with potential hazards (e.g., dogs, threatening situations), and using their best judgment. Equipping field workers with cell phones and pairing them to work together in a "buddy" system may be advisable in some circumstances. Training should emphasize that field worker safety and security is paramount and that they should avoid any situation in which they do not feel safe and call a supervisor for further instructions.
Working as a team	If you have multiple data collectors or individuals working on the data collection in different roles, it can be valuable to bring these individuals together formally or informally to explicitly discuss how to work together and how their roles complement one another. For example, it is often helpful for data analysts to attend data collector training in order to understand what types of data they may be receiving, as well as providing their perspective on what data they need to conduct a high-quality analysis. Roles and responsibilities as well as handling of data should also be explicitly discussed (e.g., To whom can a data collector give or transmit data? What should happen if that person is not available?).
Special considerations in working with the target audience	Your evaluation may involve data collection strategies from one or more target audiences. Ensure that data collectors understand any special considerations necessary for dealing with various types of audiences. Such issues may affect the protocol itself or the types of permissions that are needed (e.g., needing parental consent for evaluation data collection with children). They may also affect who is appropriate to include as a data collector (e.g., is it beneficial to try to match data collectors to participants by gender, language, age)? In other cases, data collectors should be made aware of any special considerations that may affect their perceptions or reception by the target audience.

For example, are there any cultural or religious customs or beliefs of which data collectors should be aware? Do participants have any disabilities that need to be accommodated? Would particular times be more or less beneficial? For professional audiences, what are the norms for professional conduct? You may be able to anticipate some of these issues because of prior work with target audience members. In other cases, data collectors' feedback can be used to revise data collection instructions to reflect these considerations. |
| Conducting data collection in a language other than English | This is a special case of working with the target audience (see above). Hire data collectors who are native speakers with similar dialect and culture, or train native speakers on local idioms and culture. If you use a translator, be sure the translator understands his/her role (e.g., lead focus group but not participate). |
| Practice sessions | As a pilot test of your data collection method(s), conduct practice sessions that are as realistic as possible. In general, such a practice would not be conducted with actual respondents but rather with people who closely resemble respondents (e.g., individuals who participated in an intervention prior to the evaluation data collection start; individuals of similar age or other demographic characteristics to those you are trying to recruit) or using fake or mock records.

This type of approach allows the data collector to practice all aspects of the data collection protocol. Typically a debriefing session would be held with data collectors to review any problems with the protocol itself as well as any areas where they may need additional assistance. |

Topics that are not necessary for most data collection activities but that may be relevant to your situation are listed in Table I.3.

TIPS FOR SUCCESSFUL DATA COLLECTION TRAINING

We have provided a number of ideas for how to train data collectors and the types of training topics that should be covered. We have also mentioned the need to supervise data collection activities in order to help ensure that data are collected in a timely manner and according to protocol.

In this section we offer a few tips to keep in mind as you develop your data collection procedures and your training approach. Although we anticipate that formal training will not be needed for most program evaluations, we conclude with a list of formal training techniques (Table I.4) that are most appropriate for use in large-scale data collection efforts.

- *Always conduct some type of data collection training.* Data collection training (either formal or informal) is needed for all data collection activities in your evaluation. You cannot assume that procedures will be intuitive or obvious to those conducting the data collection. Even with simple data collection procedures, it's better to be explicit to avoid later misunderstandings that can result in data that are not useful.
- *Experienced data collectors also need training.* Each data collection effort is different, and even experienced data collectors will benefit from the opportunity to think through the specific procedures for this evaluation and having time to practice.
- *Use high-quality trainers.* In multiperson data collection teams, when resources are scarce, you should recruit the best supervisors and trainers possible, even if this means recruiting less experienced data collectors. Poor supervision and/or training can impede

performance of even good data collectors, whereas good supervision and training can improve performance of both poor and good data collectors.

- *Ensure respondent comfort.* It's important that respondents feel comfortable with data collectors. In some cases, this may mean that you need to select your data collectors to be of similar racial, ethnic, linguistic, or geographic background to respondents.
- *Build data collection training into your evaluation schedule.* Don't underestimate the time it will take to be ready for data collection.
- *Think broadly about training needs.* Even if you are using a secondary data source, think about the procedures you will need to access the data, abstract the elements you need, and use it for your purposes. Make sure these procedures are explicit and well documented.
- *Emphasize to data collectors the importance of reporting problems and observations as they arise.* Data collectors are the members of the evaluation team closest to the evaluation implementation. Their observations can be invaluable.
- *Ensure appropriate documentation.* The training topics we have introduced are important even if you (or your evaluator) is the only one collecting data. You may not need a formal training, but it's still important to think through all aspects of your data collection activities and have procedures in place to deal with anticipated as well as unanticipated issues.

Being thorough and preparing written instructions help to ensure that your data collection approach is well documented and that others can step in to take over should it become necessary. The documentation also becomes a historical record of how you conducted your evaluation in case others wish to review your methods and/or undertake something similar.

Table I.4: **Formal Training Techniques.**

Topic	Instructional Approaches
Didactic approaches	Didactic approaches ensure that important content is conveyed to trainees and that key concepts and content are presented in a structured way. Areas that lend themselves to a didactic approach include an overview of the evaluation, understanding of evaluation standards, and a review of data collection instruments.
Case examples or narratives	Stories are a natural way of conveying information. Using short case examples or narratives may help trainees to work through various possible scenarios that may occur during data collection. Participants typically read or listen to a case example and then answer questions about how the situation was handled, what could be done differently, or how they might react in the same situation. Potential uses for this type of learning include ethical dilemmas, dealing with data collection challenges, and safety and security issues.
Brainstorming	The trainer may solicit ideas from the trainees to help them think about new approaches as well as allowing them to contribute ideas to enhance the data collection process itself. For example, participants can be encouraged to think as a group about how to deal with different types of respondent personalities or creative ways to deal with data collection challenges. For this type of training, develop your own list of topics ahead of time with approaches you think would be useful. Use these as prompts if the topics do not emerge from the group discussion. It is a good idea to document the data collection instructions developed by the group so that everyone is on "the same page" in terms of the final group decisions.
Topic	**Hands-On Approaches**
Modeling	Modeling techniques involve having a trainer model how a data collection situation should be handled and then allowing the trainees to practice the approach. This type of technique can be used, for example, in teaching your data collectors how to fill out data collection forms or abstract a "test" record.
Role-playing	Role-playing techniques simulate the actual data collection situation. Data collectors practice new skills and receive feedback in a safe and constructive setting. Training topics that can benefit from role-playing include obtaining informed consent, introducing the evaluation, recruiting participants, and answering tough questions.
Small groups and peer support	If you have a large group of data collectors or anticipate that participants will work as teams of data collectors, it may be valuable to divide participants into pairs or small groups. They can use the time to work through data collection logistics and decide how they will work together as a team. Small groups can also be used for role-playing or other hands-on activities to ensure that all participants have the opportunity to practice their skills and gain feedback from other participants.

- *Monitor the data collection process.*
Ongoing monitoring will tell you whether
data collection is proceeding as planned
and will allow you to intervene or provide
additional training or guidance as needed.
Situations that may indicate a need for
additional training include changes in the
protocol, unplanned deviations from the
protocol, implementation problems, or
complaints about the performance of data
collectors.

While the content and format of data collector
trainings will vary depending on the type of data
collection conducted, some elements of these types
of trainings are standard. You can use the following
checklist to see if you have included appropriate elements in your data collector training.

Have you . . .

- Provided background information to data
collectors to ensure they understand the
broader program and evaluation and can
accurately answer questions about the
evaluation?
- Ensured that data collectors have contact
information if they or participants have
additional questions?

- Included clear *written* instructions (whenever
possible) on how to conduct data collection?
- Reviewed *each* item to be collected and
provided information on the intent behind
collecting that item?
- Been explicit about expectations for data
collectors regarding use of professional
evaluation standards?
- Made sure that data collectors understand
"chain of custody" for what to do with data
that are collected, who can have access,
and how to safeguard data and respondent
information?
- Included discussion of schedule and logistics
for data collection, including plans for
ongoing communication with data collectors
throughout the evaluation?
- Reviewed any special considerations in
interacting with the intended audience?
- Communicated explicitly about what data
collectors should do in case of data collection
challenges?
- Provided opportunities for "hands-on"
skill-building activities (e.g., role playing,
practice sessions) if appropriate?

EFFECTIVE COMMUNICATION AND REPORTING

Throughout the phases of an evaluation, evaluators have the critical responsibility of providing effective communication about the evaluation planning, progress, and results. Effective and timely communication promotes understanding about the program's activities, resources, and outcomes and can engender important support for the program. It also demonstrates accountability, reminds people of the value of a program, and documents the progress of the evaluation so that learning from the program's experiences can occur along the way.

This tool provides guidance on developing a communication plan, identifying audiences, prioritizing messages, timing communications appropriately, matching communication channels and formats to audience needs, and using communications to build evaluation capacity.

DEVELOPING YOUR COMMUNICATIONS PLAN

Thinking strategically about who needs what information prior to evaluation implementation can significantly increase its usefulness. The types of information you share might include the purpose and details of the evaluation plan, progress updates, interim findings, and final report of findings.

Throughout the process, remember that your audiences may not always be clear on what they hope to get out of an evaluation, so asking them to periodically reflect on what they will do with the information you give them will help everyone by increasing the utility of the information provided.

Short Communications

The format for the communication may be anything from short communications, such as email messages, memos, newsletters, bulletins, oral presentations, executive summaries, to comprehensive final reports. Short communications are important tools for maintaining ongoing contact with stakeholders. Brief written communications can be used during all phases of the evaluation to quickly share information in a timely manner about the activities and progress of an evaluation. Memos or emails are sometimes the most efficient way to elicit feedback and discussion about ongoing activities; they may also be the most efficient mode for disseminating preliminary findings and recommendations to stakeholders.

Interim Progress Reports

Interim progress reports are typically short reports that provide select preliminary results from an ongoing evaluation. They are usually produced in anticipation of a more comprehensive report that will follow. An interim report can look much like a final report in its layout and content outline; it should be simple and presented in a style that maximizes stakeholders' understanding.

Timely interim reports may be valuable in generating discussions that effect changes or improvements in the program in time for the next phase of its implementation. Depending on the audience needs, these reports may be combined with the periodic evaluation reports.

Final Reports

Final reports are traditionally the most common form of reporting findings from an evaluation.

There are times when formal, comprehensive reports are appropriate and expected. In addition to thoroughly describing the program—its context, purpose, methods—final reports serve accountability needs and are useful for program funders and policymakers.

IDENTIFYING YOUR AUDIENCES

Most evaluations will have several audiences, such as:

- Program participants
- Evaluation sponsors or funders
- People who will make decisions about the program based on evaluation results
- Staff who plan or implement the program
- Advocates for or critiques of the program
- Others who are likely to be affected by the evaluation results

Often the primary audiences are the program's staff, the program's managers, or the evaluation's sponsors. In addition to those listed you might also consider others who, while interested in the results of the evaluation, are often distant from the program, such as future program participants, the general public, or special interest groups. In general, strive to ensure that your audiences are demographically representative of the entire population with which you want to communicate.

As the evaluation progresses, you may discover additional groups who will be interested in or impacted by the evaluation findings. As you identify these new audiences, be sure to add them into your communication planning and implementation efforts.

When thinking about these different audiences, remember that they are likely to prefer different types of information and formats in which they receive the information. For this reason, you should carefully consider the messages and formats for each audience and describe these choices in your communication and reporting plan.

REPORTING FINDINGS: PRIORITIZING MESSAGES TO AUDIENCE NEEDS

Even simple program evaluations can generate far more information than most audiences are willing to endure, let alone find useful. You must sift through the results of the data analyses and tailor your communications to specific audiences. Limiting your communications to the findings that are most relevant will enable your audience to invest their energy and limited time in actually using the information.

Different stakeholders will prioritize findings differently, so to do this sifting and tailoring effectively, it's important to have a clear understanding of the information needs of your various audiences, as well as to know about their capacity to use evaluation findings. For example, a recommendation for new recruiting procedures might be best highlighted with staff and immediate supervisors, while a recommendation for policy change would be more appropriate for administrators.

Always consider the level of knowledge the audience has about what is being evaluated and the evaluation itself when tailoring the message. It's important to provide sufficient background and context before sharing findings, since audience members often know only the activity, policy, or intervention that is being evaluated from their perspective. Providing the background and context will help to facilitate understanding and acceptance of the findings across multiple audiences.

Generally, the evaluation questions form a good organizing tool from which you can begin to aggregate and organize the information you plan to share. As part of Step 1 in the evaluation process (see Chapter 3), you have already identified stakeholder interests; the interpretation process (Step 5) is often an opportunity to actively engage stakeholders in identifying and prioritizing messages for the various audiences with whom you will be communicating. You can ask:

- Which findings will the audiences find most meaningful and useful? Why?
- What conclusions are being drawn?

- Which findings lend themselves to the development of recommendations?

The answers to these questions can help you prioritize the "take-home" messages you are developing.

Keep in mind that stakeholders may be reluctant to present negative findings and may suggest highlighting only positive ones. While this is understandable, it's important to remind stakeholders that, while positive findings assure the audience that the program is on the right track, negative findings are instructive and should be viewed as opportunities to improve the program. In other words, view the results with an eye to "how can we do better?" If necessary, you can refer to the propriety standard and note that, ethically, you are required to share complete evaluation findings.

Communicating Positive and Negative Findings

Documenting the strengths of a program is a major function and value of evaluation. Communicating strengths helps in planning, sustaining, and growing a program and may also help address anxiety about the evaluation process.

An equally important use of an evaluation is identifying areas that need improvement. These areas often reflect problems or weaknesses in a program that, when shared, may inspire a defensive, negative reaction. Anticipating the possibility of negative findings early in the evaluation process and actively communicating with stakeholders throughout data collection can help to prevent surprises at the end of the evaluation. This practice may also enable you to adjust your strategies to be sure you have sufficient information on program strengths and options for positive change. To this end, whenever possible, aim to develop messages that:

- Identify what worked and other strengths that can be built upon in future efforts.
- Share negative findings, emphasizing what has been learned and how it will influence the next course of action.

- Provide specifics about problems and situations, as appropriate, without betraying confidentiality.
- Avoid personalizing or critiquing individual performance.
- Focus on things that can be changed.

When summarizing and prioritizing messages, set explicit goals for each message and audience. Think about the conclusions, how the evaluation findings can be used, and what recommendations should be made. Consider what action(s) the audience can take. For example, do the data suggest that it would benefit the audience to:

- Increase knowledge and understanding of the initiative?
- Provide or support an increase in resources for the initiative?
- Change a program, policy, or practice?
- Reorganize or revise the initiative to make it more responsive?
- Overcome resistance to the initiative?
- Develop or promote methods for making the initiative more effective or efficient?

Creating a communication goal will help you identify the information needs that should be included in the messages you are developing.

While there is no right or wrong number of key messages, conclusions, or recommendations that can come from any evaluation, adult learning theory tells us that most people can comfortably comprehend and absorb five to seven points or ideas at a time. In light of this, you may find it useful to group the evaluation messages into categories or themes so as not to overwhelm the audience. The evaluation questions may help to inform some thematic categories.

TIMING YOUR COMMUNICATIONS

For evaluation findings to be useful, they must be communicated in a timely manner. As mentioned earlier, sharing interim findings at strategic points keeps stakeholders abreast of the process and engaged in the evaluation process. Interim findings may bring to light an implementation problem, such as the need to recruit a certain population that is currently being overlooked, allowing time to perhaps modify the recruitment approach.

Other opportunities to use the findings might emerge unexpectedly. For example, in the event an unanticipated funding announcement is released, your interim evaluation findings could be used to support the application. Maintaining and routinely updating communication messages can be helpful in capitalizing on such events.

The key is to think strategically and lay out plans for effectively communicating with your various audiences at appropriate intervals. Surprises at the end of the evaluation are never a good thing! You might find that the optimal time to communicate key or interim findings is during routine functions, such as at quarterly staff meetings or an annual retreat for policymakers. Remember that the more engaged you keep your audiences, the more ownership they feel of the process and, consequently, the more likely they will use your findings.

Matching Communication Channels and Formats to Audience Needs

Just as findings and messages must be tailored to the needs of different audiences, the mechanisms to effectively communicate with audiences will also vary. When deciding the channels and formats for communicating evaluation information, you should consider a number of factors.

Identifying the appropriate messenger is as important as carefully considering the messages to convey. When considering who should deliver the message, you might look for an individual who is highly respected and trusted in the local context, who has been involved in the evaluation, and who would be willing to present the findings (e.g., a well-respected physician, a leader of an organization, an elder). For example, in certain cultural traditions, having an elder spokesperson report on the evaluation shows acceptance of the results from a trusted figure.

Similarly, having a top official in an organization serve as the evaluation spokesperson can show that the results are of import and are to be taken seriously. Engaging a respected individual to report on the findings helps ensure that the information is viewed as credible. It may also help build evaluation capacity within the community, as discussion about the findings filters among community members and motivates people to act on what they have learned and to pursue further learning.

In other instances, the neutral, objective voice of the evaluator will be optimal. If you present the findings in person, be mindful of how you present yourself—for example, dress professionally yet in a manner that is appropriate to the local context (e.g., don't wear a suit if the setting is in a factory facility). Irrespective of who delivers the message, be sure the information delivered is accurate and complete and that it includes an appropriate balance of information free of biases favoring a particular interest or position.

Delivering Meaningful Presentations

Good presentations give meaning and context to evaluation findings. You may need to remind yourself that your audience may know little about evaluation or about the process undertaken to produce the information being communicated—therefore, it's important to provide a clear description of the issues so the audience understands the context for the information they are receiving. View the presentation as an opportunity to build evaluation capacity and increase the savvy of the evaluation consumer.

Covering the following items when presenting evaluation findings will help to assure that sufficient information is provided to meet audience needs:

- Description of the program and aspects of it that are being evaluated
- Description of stakeholders
- Evaluation purpose and evaluation questions
- Methodology used
- Data sources
- Findings
- Strengths and limitations
- Conclusions
- Recommendations

The depth in which any of these topics are addressed should be tailored to the audience. For example, a presentation to the general public should include a brief, simple presentation of the methods whereas a presentation delivered to scientists or evaluation peers should include a more detailed discussion of the methodology used.

To meet the propriety standard, evaluators must share both the evaluation findings and the limitations of the evaluation with everyone who may be affected. This should be done while balancing the feasibility of this level of communication. It may be helpful to remind the audience that the vast majority of evaluations are bound by resource limitations and that evaluators aim for the optimal balance between the information needs and the available resources.

As previously mentioned, you should use a broad and tailored strategy for communicating evaluation messages to meet the diverse needs of the audiences. Scheduling an evening presentation and offering childcare may reduce logistical barriers and increase the reach to particular community members. In some situations, it may be necessary to translate communications or to tailor the messages so they are appropriate to the literacy level of the audience.

The following are recommendations regarding some of the formats commonly used for communicating findings in oral presentations:

- Keep text brief and to the point
- Arrange text into digestible bites
- Use short sentences or bullet points
- Use big text
- Use clear fonts that are readable at a distance and distinguish headings (sans-serif typeface is preferable)
- Use lowercase text for better readability
- Incorporate graphs or charts to visually convey a message

When feasible, schedule time with stakeholders to discuss the evaluation findings. This interaction will build interest in and increase shared ownership of the evaluation. You can use this time as an opportunity to further clarify, tailor, and refine the messages based on feedback from stakeholders. To assure that your messages are communicated effectively, always use simple, clear, jargon-free language. Conclude by making specific recommendations that you expect your audience can implement.

In any evaluation, the analyzed data comprise the main content of what is communicated. The findings of an evaluation should include information about the data and an explanation of how the data were analyzed. The analysis results must sufficiently support each conclusion and recommendation.

"Data dumps" generally have little meaning to most audiences and therefore have little merit in a presentation of evaluation findings. Creating messages that adequately convey the data and their meaning requires a great deal of thought and creativity. Quantitative data can often be visually summarized and simply conveyed through the use of charts, graphs, and tables.

Graphs and charts can present statistical and complex data concisely. Charts are most useful for depicting processes, elements, roles, or other parts of some larger entity. Graphs are particularly useful for presenting data and relationships. They can illustrate trends, distributions, and cycles.

Tables and figures can make information more understandable and are especially effective if you have limited space or time to present information. They allow audiences to quickly absorb a large quantity of data while still conveying the key points of the evaluation findings. Visual representations of data can be illustrated in diagrams or visual forms of representation that reveal patterns, trends, and relationships that are otherwise not apparent in the text.

Diagrams, maps, or illustrations are often effective for conveying ideas that are difficult to express in words. In general, graphics need to be clear, precise, and limited in number. The goal of the graphic is to present one, clear message. An interpretation or explanation of graphics should be included to ensure accurate understanding.

In cases where you have collected both quantitative and qualitative data, you can use the qualitative data to complement and illustrate critical points found in the quantitative data. Be careful not to present more qualitative data than is needed to support your conclusions, especially in the form of quotations.

If you present a diagram using symbols, include a key that identifies or defines them. Evaluations that involve both qualitative and quantitative data should report a mix of results from each type of data.

Putting the Results in Writing

- **Evaluation report.** Developing a useful, comprehensive evaluation report requires an investment of time and resources, which limits the degree to which a report can be tailored to specific audiences. Usually, an evaluation report has more than one target population, so it's useful to organize a report to help specific audiences easily find the information most useful to them. This can be as simple as including headings such as "Recommendations for School Nurses" and "Recommendations for School Superintendents," for example.
- **Executive summary.** An executive summary is a vital section of any written report, given that many audiences will have limited time to invest in reading and reviewing a full-length report. The chief advantage of summaries is that they can be reproduced separately and disseminated as needed, often to busy decision-makers.

  Executive summaries usually contain condensed versions of all the major sections of a full report, highlighting the essential messages accurately and concisely. As with the full-length written report and oral presentation, summaries should be tailored to address the needs of particular audiences, emphasizing different program elements and findings. You may choose to create multiple, tailored executive summaries to assure that messages are meaningful to each audience.
- **Newsletters, bulletins, or brochures.** When you need to relay evaluation findings to a broad group of individuals in a form other than a lengthy report or oral presentation, consider using newsletters, bulletins, or brochures. These less formal media can

promote communication between the evaluator and stakeholders and enable presentation of findings as they emerge and at the end of the evaluation.

You can use a dedicated newsletter to communicate key evaluation findings from an evaluation or include an article about evaluation activities as part of an existing internal or external newsletter. Bulletins are similar to newsletters but are typically briefer and are dedicated to reporting periodically on a particular evaluation or project.
- **Brochures.** Brochures are typically intended to generate interest in the evaluation findings. A brochure can be as simple as a printed sheet folded twice. If your evaluation findings are positive, a brochure might also take the shape of a more comprehensive "marketing" folder with a variety of collateral pieces. In either case, it might include a brief description of the evaluation, an overview of the evaluation design, and the key findings and recommendations. This form of communication can be used to invite feedback and discussion on the evaluation or simply to inform readers of the evaluation's conclusions.

  As with other forms of presenting information, determine the type of communication best suited for your purpose and audience by considering your audience's interest, the desired frequency of publication, budget, availability of desktop publishing software and associated skills and resources needed, and scope of the dissemination effort.
- **Posters.** Posters and other visual displays of evaluation information can be designed for events such as conferences or meetings. Posters can also be advantageous because they can be displayed in a waiting room or other location, making the evaluation findings accessible to a wide range of audiences over time. They can also be used to promote interest and engagement in evaluation.

- **Social media.** Social media tools such as Facebook, YouTube, and Twitter offer innovative ways to communicate evaluation information. These tools and other emerging communication technologies can increase the timely dissemination and potential impact of evaluation; leverage audience networks to facilitate information sharing; expand reach to include broader, more diverse audiences; and facilitate interactive communication, connection, and public engagement.

COMMUNICATIONS THAT BUILD EVALUATION CAPACITY

Transforming the lessons learned from your evaluation experiences into opportunities to build evaluation capacity within your organization is one of the most important and more challenging aspects of the evaluation process. As part of their professional development, evaluators typically reflect on the evaluation process and make mental notes on what worked or what they would do differently next time.

By bringing stakeholders into this process—actively engaging them in problem-solving while implementing the evaluation—we can deepen their understanding of evaluation practice. Activities such as mock data review sessions and workshops on evaluation purposes, designs, methods, and other topics, along with remembering to work with stakeholders throughout the evaluation process, are critical to helping ensure the use of evaluation findings through stakeholder buy-in.

Additionally, the evaluation plan itself can be a valuable tool for documenting the implementation of the evaluation. Many evaluators make notes within the plan to chronicle what was done, what was revised, and how decisions were made. The plan can be supplemented with appendices tracking the use of evaluation findings and actions taken in response to the recommendations. These records are invaluable when planning subsequent evaluations and for showing the practical value of evaluation. Success stories and lessons learned from evaluations can be written up and shared in journal publications, at conferences, or less formally through blogs and listservs.

When operating in a collaborative, supportive environment, evaluators can use their effective communication skills to play an important role within the larger context of organizational learning. By working with organizational leaders to develop and support evaluation capacity building activities, evaluators can encourage the institutionalization of evaluation in program operations.

Organizational supports—such as making time available for skill building, allocating resources for evaluation, incentivizing learning, and creating expectations for openly discussing evaluation findings and their implications—demonstrate a commitment to building an evaluation culture.

DEVELOPING AN ACTION PLAN

To gain the maximum benefit from evaluation, it's imperative that the results of your efforts be put to use, whether to support program improvements or to guide other decision-making. We know from experience that evaluation results are more likely to be put to use if you take the time to develop an action plan.

An action plan is an organized list of tasks that, based on your evaluation findings, should lead to program improvement. It differs from a to-do list in that all the tasks focus specifically on achievement of your program improvement objectives.

If you identify more than one program area ready for improvement based on a single evaluation, we recommend creating an action plan for each improvement objective. Your evaluation may also identify program components that should be eliminated or components that are working well and should be sustained. Action plans are appropriate to guide these follow-up activities as well.

Since some stakeholders will be charged with implementing changes based on your evaluation findings, you will need to work with the stakeholders involved in designing the evaluation to create the action plan. They are likely to have important insights about how to best respond to the findings. Their involvement can help ensure that planned activities are both desirable and feasible, and they are more likely to participate in implementing changes if they have been involved in identifying actions to be taken.

We provide an example of an action plan in Table K.1. This format directly connects program improvement objectives to evaluation findings by including a brief summary of relevant evaluation findings, data on which findings are based, and proposed changes to respond to these findings. The majority of the plan focuses on specific action(s) you and your stakeholders will take to achieve your objectives, as well as identifying a person responsible for each activity, resources they need to accomplish it, and a timeline for completion.

The action plan template also includes an area listing the information you will use to monitor implementation of your action plan. Finally, the plan identifies the data you will use to determine whether the improvement you were seeking actually occurred.

Regularly reviewing the results of your action plan with your stakeholders will help you better utilize evaluation findings. If you have evidence that your program has improved, this marks an occasion for joint celebration. If more work needs to be done, your stakeholders can help focus your energies and support necessary changes.

Table K.1: Evaluation Results Action Plan.

Evaluation Result		Describe the key evaluation result that necessitates action						
Supporting Evidence		Describe the evidence that supports action						
		Plan of Action to Achieve Change				Monitor Change		
Change needed		Activities to implement change	Person responsible	Resources required	Due by	Indicators that change is implemented	Data sources	Indicators to monitor success of change	Data sources
Describe key change(s) you want to achieve based on this finding.		List activities that need to be carried out to make the change happen in the program.	List the person(s) who will assure each activity occurs.	List resources required for the activity.	Assign a due date by which the activity will be completed (the final date should be when the change will be in full effect).	Describe how you will know that the change is implemented as planned.	Describe what data you will need to have to know if change was implemented.	Describe how you will know the change to the program is working or not.	Describe the data you will need to measure success.

MEASURING VARIABLES

This tool will help you brush up on how you can measure variables in your evaluations. You should be somewhat familiar with the contents of this tool because much of it was covered in your foundational research methods course. As you know from this course, a concept such as depression can be defined in words, and, if the words are sufficiently well chosen, the reader of your final evaluation report will have a clear idea of what depression is.

When we apply the definition to a particular client, however, words may be not enough to guide us. The client may seem depressed according to the definition, but many questions may still remain:

- Is the client more or less depressed than the average person? If more depressed, how much more? Is the depression growing or declining?
- For how long has the client been depressed?
- Is the depression continuous or episodic? If episodic, what length of time usually elapses between depressive episodes?
- Is this length of time increasing or diminishing?
- How many episodes occur in a week?
- To what degree is the client depressed?

Answers to questions such as these will enable you to obtain greater insight into your client's depression—an insight essential for planning and evaluating a treatment intervention.

WHY MEASURE?

The word *measurement* is often used in two different senses. In the first sense, a measurement is the result of a measuring process such as in the following cases:

- The number of times Bobby hits his brother in a day (a possible frequency indicator for a practice objective)
- The length of time for which Jenny cries (a possible duration indicator for a practice objective)
- The intensity of Ms. Smith's depression (a possible magnitude indicator for a practice objective)

Measurement also refers to the measuring process itself; that is, it encompasses the event or attributes being measured, the person who does the measuring, the method employed, the measuring instrument used, and often also the result. Throughout our book, measurement is taken to refer to the entire process, excluding only the results. The results of any measurement process is referred to as *data*. In other words, measurement is undertaken to obtain data—objective and precise data, that is.

In any profession, from the social services to plumbing, an instrument is a tool designed to help the user perform a task. A tool need not be a physical object; it can just as easily be a perception, an idea, a new synthesis of known facts, or a new analysis of a known whole.

As we now know, an outcome evaluation is an appraisal: an estimate of how effectively and efficiently program objectives are being met in a practitioner's individual practice or in a social service program. In other words, an outcome evaluation can compare the change that has actually taken place against the predicted, desired change.

Thus an outcome evaluation requires knowledge of both the initial condition and the present condition of the practice and program objectives undergoing the proposed change. Therefore, it's necessary to have at least two measurements, one at the beginning of the change process and one at the end.

In addition, it's always useful—if possible—to take measurements of the objectives during the change process as well. Measurement, then, is not only necessary in the quality improvement process—it's the conceptual foundation without which the evaluative structure cannot exist.

A definition, no matter how complete, is useful only if it means the same thing in the hands of different people. For example, we could define a distance in terms of the number of days a person takes to walk it, or the number of strides needed to cross it, or the number of felled oak trees that would span it end to end. But since people, strides, and oak trees vary, none of these definitions is very exact. To be useful to a modern traveler, a distance must be given in miles or some other precisely defined unit.

Similarly, shared understanding and precision are very important in the social services. A worker who is assessing a woman's level of functioning, for example, needs to know that the results of the assessment are not being affected by her feelings toward the woman, her knowledge of the woman's situation, or any other biasing factor; that is, any other worker who assessed the same woman under the same conditions would come up with the same result.

Furthermore, you will need to know that the results of the assessment will be understood by other professionals, that the results are rendered in words or symbols that are not open to misinterpretation. If the assessment is to provide the basis for decisions about the woman's future, via your chosen treatment intervention, objectivity and precision on your part are even more important.

Objectivity

Some social workers believe that they are entirely objective; that is, they will not judge clients by skin color, ethnic origin, religious persuasion, sexual orientation, social economic status, marital status, education, age, gender, verbal skill, or personal attractiveness. They may believe they are not influenced by other people's opinions about a client—statements that the client has severe emotional problems or a borderline personality will be disregarded until evidence is gathered. No judgments will be made on the basis of the worker's personal likes and dislikes, and stereotyping will be avoided at all costs.

Social workers who sincerely believe that their judgment will never be influenced by any of the aforementioned factors are deluding themselves. Everyone is prejudiced to some degree in some area or another; everyone has likes and dislikes, moral positions, and personal standards; everyone is capable of irrational feelings of aversion, sympathy, or outrage. Workers who deny this run the risk of showing bias without realizing it, and a worker's unconscious bias can have devastating effects on a client's life.

A client may unwittingly fuel the bias by sensing what the practitioner expects and answering questions in a way that supports the worker's preconceptions. In extreme cases, clients can even become what they are expected to become, fulfilling the biased prophecy.

The art of good judgment, then, lies in accepting the possibility of personal bias and trying to minimize its effects. What is needed is an unprejudiced method of assessment and an unbiased standard against which the client's knowledge, feelings, or behaviors can be gauged. In other words, we require a measurement method from which an impartial measure can be derived.

Precision

The second ingredient of good measurement is precision, whose opposite is vagueness. A vague statement is one that uses general or indefinite terms; in other words, it leaves so many details to be filled in that it means different things to different people. There are four major sources of vagueness.

The first source of vagueness is the use of terms such as *often, frequently, many, some, usually,* and *rarely,* which attempt to assign degrees to a client's feelings or behaviors without specifying a precise unit of measurement. A statement such as "John misses many appointments with his worker" is fuzzy; it tells us only that John's reliability may leave much to be desired. The statement "John missed 2 out of 10 appointments with his worker" is far more precise and does not impute evil tendencies to John.

The second source of vagueness is the use of statements that, although they are intended to say something about a particular client, might apply to anyone; for example, "John often feels insecure, having experienced some rejection by his peers." Who has not experienced peer rejection? Nevertheless, the statement will be interpreted as identifying a quality specific to John. Our profession abounds with statements like this, which are as damaging to the client as they are meaningless.

A third source of vagueness is professional jargon, the meaning of which will rarely be clear to a client. Often professionals themselves do not agree on the meaning of such phrases as "expectations-role definition," "reality pressures," "pregnant pauses," and "creative use of silence." In the worst case, they do not even know what they mean by their own jargon; they use it merely to sound impressive. Jargon is useful when it conveys precise statements to colleagues; when misused, it can confuse workers and alienate clients.

The last source of vagueness is tautology: a meaningless repetition disguised as a definition; for example, consider the following:

- "A delinquent is a person who engages in delinquent behaviors."
- "John is agoraphobic because he is afraid of open spaces."
- "Betty is ambivalent because she cannot make up her mind."
- "Marie hits her brother because she is aggressive."
- "John rocks back and forth because he is autistic."

Obviously, tautological statements tell us nothing and are to be avoided. In summary, we need to attain objectivity and precision and avoid bias and vagueness. Both objectivity and precision are vital in the evaluation process and are readily attainable through measurement.

The measurement of variables—especially program objectives—is the cornerstone of all social work evaluation studies. Shining and formidable measuring instruments may come to mind, measuring things to several decimal places. The less scientifically inclined might merely picture rulers but, in any case, measurement for most of us means reducing something to numbers. As we know, these "somethings" are called variables, and all variables can take on different measurement levels.

LEVELS OF MEASUREMENT

As you know from your research methods course, the characteristics that describe a variable are known as its *attributes*. The variable *gender*, for example, has only two attributes—*male* and *female*—since gender in humans is limited to male and female, and there are no other categories or ways of describing gender.

The variable *ethnicity* has a number of possible attributes: *African American, Native American, Asian, Latino,* and *Caucasian* are just five examples of the many attributes of the variable ethnicity. A point to note here is that the attributes of gender differ in kind from one another—male is different from female—and, in the same way, the attributes of ethnicity are also different from one another.

Now consider the variable *income*. Income can only be described in terms of amounts of money: $15,000 per year, $288.46 per week, and so forth. In whatever terms a person's income is actually described, it still comes down to a number. Since every number has its own category, as we mentioned before, the variable income can generate as many categories as there are numbers, up to the number covering the evaluation participant who earns the most.

These numbers are all attributes of income and they are all different, but they are not different in *kind*, as male and female are, or Native American and Latino; they are only different in *quantity*. In other words, the attributes of income differ in that they represent more or less of the same thing, whereas the attributes of gender differ in that they represent different kinds of things.

Income will, therefore, be measured in a different way from gender. When we want to measure income, for example, we will look for categories (attributes) that are *lower* or *higher* than each other; on the other hand, when we measure gender, we will look for categories (attributes) that *are different in kind* from each other.

Mathematically, there is not much we can do with categories that are different in kind. We cannot subtract Latinos from Caucasians, for example, whereas we can quite easily subtract one person's annual income from another and come up with a meaningful difference. As far as mathematical computations are concerned, we are obliged to work at a lower level of complexity when we measure variables like ethnicity than when we measure variables like income.

Depending on the nature of their attributes, all variables can be measured at one (or more) of four measurement levels.

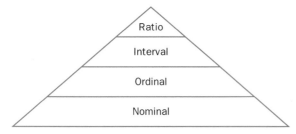

The lowest level of measurement is found at the bottom of the pyramid and the highest at the top.

Nominal Measurement

Nominal measurement is the lowest level of measurement and is used to measure variables whose attributes are different in kind. As we have seen, gender is one variable measured at a nominal level, and ethnicity is another. *Place of birth* is a third, since "born in California," for example, is different from "born in Chicago," and we cannot add "born in

California" to "born in Chicago," or subtract them or divide them, or do anything statistically interesting with them at all.

Ordinal Measurement

Ordinal measurement is a higher level of measurement than nominal and is used to measure those variables whose attributes can be rank ordered: for example, socioeconomic status, sexism, racism, client satisfaction, and the like. If we intend to measure *client satisfaction*, we must first develop a list of all the possible attributes of client satisfaction: that is, we must think of all the possible categories into which answers about client satisfaction might be placed.

Some clients will be *very satisfied*, one category, at the high end of the satisfaction continuum; some will be *not at all satisfied*, a separate category, at the low end of the continuum; and others will be *generally satisfied, moderately satisfied*, or *somewhat satisfied*, three more categories, at differing points on the continuum, as illustrated:

1. Not at all satisfied
2. Somewhat satisfied
3. Moderately satisfied
4. Generally satisfied
5. Very satisfied

The preceding is a 5-point scale with a brief description of the degree of satisfaction represented by the point (i.e., 1, 2, 3, 4, 5). Of course we may choose to express the anchors in different words, substituting *extremely satisfied* for *very satisfied*, or *fairly satisfied* for *generally satisfied*. We may select a 3-point scale instead, limiting the choices to *very satisfied, moderately satisfied*, and *not at all satisfied*; or we may even use a 10-point scale if we believe that our respondents will be able to rate their satisfaction with that degree of accuracy.

Whichever particular method is selected, some sort of scale is the only measurement option available because there is no other way to categorize client satisfaction except in terms of more satisfaction or less satisfaction. As we did with nominal measurement, we might assign numbers to each of the points on the scale. If we used the 5-point scale as illustrated earlier, we might assign a 5 to *very satisfied*, a 4 to *generally satisfied*, a 3 to *moderately satisfied*, a 2 to *somewhat satisfied*, and a 1 to *not at all satisfied*.

Here, the numbers do have some mathematical meaning. Five (*very satisfied*) is in fact better than 4 (*generally satisfied*), 4 is better than 3, 3 is better than 2, and 2 is better than 1. The numbers, however, say nothing about *how much better* any category is than any other. We cannot assume that the difference in satisfaction between *very* and *generally* is the same as the difference between *generally* and *moderately*.

In short, we cannot assume that the intervals between the anchored points on the scale are all the same length. Most definitely, we cannot assume that a client who rates a service at 4 (*generally satisfied*) is twice as satisfied as a client who rates the service at 2 (*somewhat satisfied*).

In fact, we cannot attempt any mathematical manipulation at all. We cannot add the numbers 1, 2, 3, 4, and 5, nor can we subtract, multiply, or divide them. As its name might suggest, all we can know from ordinal measurement is the order of the categories.

Interval Measurement

Some variables, such as client satisfaction, have attributes that can be rank-ordered—from *very satisfied* to *not at all satisfied*, as we have just discussed. As we saw, however, these attributes cannot be assumed to be the same distance apart if they are placed on a scale; and, in any case, the distance they are apart has no real meaning. No one can measure the distance between *very satisfied* and *moderately satisfied*; we only know that the one is better than the other.

Conversely, for some variables, the distance, or interval, separating their attributes *does* have meaning, and these variables can be measured at the interval level. An example in physical science is the Fahrenheit or Celsius temperature scale. The difference between 80 degrees and 90 degrees is the same as the difference between 40 and 50 degrees. Eighty degrees is not twice as hot as 40 degrees, nor does zero degrees mean no heat at all.

In social work, interval measures are most commonly used in connection with standardized measuring instruments, as presented in Tool M. When

we look at a standardized intelligence test, for example, we can say that the difference between IQ scores of 100 and 110 is the same as the difference between IQ scores of 95 and 105, based on the scores obtained by the many thousands of people who have taken the test over the years. As with the temperature scales mentioned previously, a person with an IQ score of 120 is not twice as intelligent as a person with a score of 60, nor does a score of zero mean no intelligence at all.

Ratio Measurement

The highest level of measurement, ratio measurement, is used to measure variables whose attributes are based on a true zero point. It may not be possible to have zero intelligence, but it's certainly possible to have zero children or zero money. Whenever a question about a particular variable might elicit the answer "none" or "never," that variable can be measured at the ratio level.

The question "How many times have you seen your social worker?" might be answered "Never." Other variables commonly measured at the ratio level include length of residence in a given place, age, number of times married, number of organizations belonged to, number of antisocial behaviors, number of case reviews, number of training sessions, number of supervisory meetings, and so forth. With a ratio level of measurement we can meaningfully interpret the comparison between two scores.

A person who is 40 years of age, for example, is twice as old as a person who is 20 and half as old as a person who is 80. Children aged 2 and 5, respectively, are the same distance apart as children aged 6 and 9. Data resulting from ratio measurement can be added, subtracted, multiplied, and divided. Averages can be calculated and other statistical analyses can be performed.

It's useful to note that, while some variables can be measured at a higher level, they may not need to be. The variable *income*, for example, can be measured at a ratio level because it's possible to have a zero income but, for the purposes of a particular study, we may not need to know the actual incomes of our evaluation participants, only the range within which their incomes fall.

A person who is asked how much he or she earns may be reluctant to give a figure ("mind your own business" is a perfectly legitimate response) but may not object to checking one of a number of income categories, choosing, for example, between the following:

1. Less than $5,000 per year
2. $5,001 to $15,000 per year
3. $15,001 to $25,000 per year
4. $25,001 to $35,000 per year
5. More than $35,000 per year

Categorizing income in this way reduces the measurement from the ratio level to the ordinal level. It will now be possible to know only that a person checking Category 1 earns less than a person checking Category 2, and so on. While we will not know *how much* less or more one person earns than another and we will not be able to perform statistical tasks such as calculating average incomes, we will be able to say, for example, that 50% of our sample falls into Category 1, 30% into Category 2, 15% into Category 3, and 5% into Category 4. If we are conducting a study to see how many people fall in each income range, this may be all we need to know.

In the same way, we might not want to know the actual ages of our sample, only the range in which they fall. For some studies, it might be enough to measure age at a nominal level—to inquire, for example, whether people were born during the Great Depression, or whether they were born before or after 1990. When studying variables that can be measured at any level, the measurement level chosen depends on what kind of data is needed, and this in turn is determined by why the data are needed, which in turn is determined by our evaluation question.

DESCRIBING VARIABLES

The purpose of measuring a variable is to describe it as completely and accurately as possible. Often the most complete and accurate possible description of a variable not only involves quantitative data (numbers) but also qualitative data (words). In an nutshell, the measurement of variables provides better:

- Correspondence
- Standardization

- Quantification
- Duplication

Correspondence

Correspondence means making a link between what we measure and/or observe and the theories we have developed to explain what we have measured and/or observed. For example, the concept of attachment theory can easily explain the different behaviors (variables) of small children when they are separated from—or reunited with—their mothers.

Measuring and recording children's behaviors in this context provide a link between the abstract and the concrete—between attachment (an unspecific and nonmeasurable concept) and its indicators, or variables, such as a child's behaviors (a more specific and more measurable variable).

Standardization

Variables can be complex, and the more complex they are, the more likely it is that people will interpret the exact same variable in different ways. Like concepts, a single variable can at times mean different things to different people even when using the same words.

Self-esteem, for example, can mean different things to different people. However, the perceptions linked to self-esteem (i.e., the empirical indicators of self-esteem) may be drawn together in the form of a measuring instrument, as they are in Hudson's *Index of Self-Esteem* (i.e., Figure L.1)

You may or may not agree that all of the 25 items, or questions, contained in Hudson's *Index of Self-Esteem* together reflect what you mean by self-esteem—but at least you know what Hudson meant, and so does everyone else who is using his measuring instrument. By constructing this instrument, Hudson (1982) has *standardized* a complex variable so that everyone using his instrument will measure self-esteem the same way.

Moreover, if two or more different researchers use his instrument with the same evaluation participants, they ought to get approximately the same results. The use of the word "approximately" here means that we must allow for a bit of error—something discussed at the end of this tool.

Name: _____ Today's Date: _____

This questionnaire is designed to measure how you see yourself. It is not a test, so there are no right or wrong answers. Please answer each item as carefully and as accurately as you can by placing a number beside each one as follows:

1 = None of the time
2 = Very rarely
3 = A little of the time
4 = Some of the time
5 = A good part of the time
6 = Most of the time
7 = All of the time

1. ___ I feel that people would not like me if they really knew me well.
2. ___ I feel that others get along much better than I do.
3. ___ I feel that I am a beautiful person.
4. ___ When I am with others I feel they are glad I am with them.
5. ___ I feel that people really like to talk with me.
6. ___ I feel that I am a very competent person.
7. ___ I think I make a good impression on others.
8. ___ I feel that I need more self-confidence.
9. ___ When I am with strangers I am very nervous.
10. ___ I think that I am a dull person.
11. ___ I feel ugly.
12. ___ I feel that others have more fun than I do.
13. ___ I feel that I bore people.
14. ___ I think my friends find me interesting.
15. ___ I think I have a good sense of humor.
16. ___ I feel very self-conscious when I am with strangers.
17. ___ I feel that if I could be more like other people I would have it made.
18. ___ I feel that people have a good time when they are with me.
19. ___ I feel like a wallflower when I go out.
20. ___ I feel I get pushed around more than others.
21. ___ I think I am a rather nice person.
22. ___ I feel that people really like me very much.
23. ___ I feel that I am a likeable person.
24. ___ I am afraid I will appear foolish to others.
25. ___ My friends think very highly of me.

3, 4, 5, 6, 7, 14, 15, 18, 21, 22, 23, 25

Figure L.1: **Hudson's *Index of Self-Esteem*.**

AUTHOR: Walter W. Hudson

PURPOSE: To measure problems with self-esteem.

DESCRIPTION: The *ISE* is a 25-item scale designed to measure the degree, severity, or magnitude of a problem the client has with self-esteem. Self-esteem is considered as the evaluative component of self-concept. The *ISE* is written in very simple language, is easily administered, and easily scored. Because problems with self-esteem are often central to social to social and psychological difficulties, this instrument has a wide range of utility for a number of clinical problems.

The *ISE* has a cutting score of 30 (+ or − 5), with scores above 30 indicating the respondent has a clinically significant problem and scores below 30 indicating the individual has no such problem.

Another advantage of the *ISE* is that it is one of nine scales of the *Clinical Measurement Package* (Hudson, 1982), all of which are administered and scored the same way.

NORMS: This scale was derived from tests of 1,745 respondents, including single and married individuals, clinical and nonclinical populations, college students and nonstudents. Respondents included Caucasians, Japanese, and Chinese Americans, and a smaller number of members of other ethnic groups. Not recommended for use with children under the age of 12.

SCORING: For a detailed description on how to score the *ISE*, see: Bloom, Fischer, and Orme (2009) or go to: www.walmyr.com.

RELIABILITY: The *ISE* has a mean alpha of .93, indicating excellent internal consistency, and an excellent (low) S.E.M. of 3.70. The *ISE* also has excellent stability with a two-hour test-retest correlation of .92.

VALIDITY: The *ISE* has good know-groups validity, significantly distinguishing between clients judged by clinicians to have problems in the area of self-esteem and those known not to. Further, the *ISE* has very good construct validity, correlating well with a range of other measures with which it should correlate highly, e.g., depression, happiness, sense of identity, and scores on the *Generalized Contentment Scale* (depression).

PRIMARY REFERENCE: Hudson, W.W. (1982). *The clinical measurement package: A field manual.* Chicago: Dorsey.

Figure L.1a: **Basic information about the *Index of Self-Esteem*..**

Quantification

Quantification means nothing more than defining the level of a variable in terms of a single number or score. The use of Hudson's *Index of Self-Esteem*, for example, results in a single number, or score, obtained by following the scoring instructions. Reducing a complex variable like self-esteem to a single number has disadvantages in that the richness of the variable can never be completely captured in this way.

However, it also has advantages in that numbers can be used in statistics to search for meaningful relationships between one variable and another. For example, you might hypothesize that there is a relationship between two variables: self-esteem and marital satisfaction.

Hudson has *quantified* self-esteem, allowing the self-esteem of any evaluation participant to be represented by a single number. He has also done this for the variable of marital satisfaction. Since both variables have been broken down to two numbers, you can use statistical methods to see whether the relationship you hypothesized actually does exist.

Duplication

In the physical sciences, experiments are routinely replicated. For example, if you put a test-tube containing 25 ounces of a solution into an oven to see what is left when the liquid evaporates, you may use five test-tubes containing 25 ounces each, not just one. Then you will have five identical samples of solution evaporated at the same time under the same conditions, and you will be much more certain of your results than if you had just evaporated one sample. The word *replication* means doing the same thing more than once at the same time.

In our profession, we can rarely replicate evaluation studies, but we can *duplicate* them. That is, a second researcher can attempt to confirm a first researcher's results by doing the same thing again later on, as much as is practically possible under the same conditions. Duplication increases certainty, and it's only possible if the variables being studied have been *standardized* and *quantified*.

For example, you could duplicate another researcher's work on attachment only if you measured attachment in the same way. If you used different child behaviors to indicate attachment and you assigned different values to mean, say, weak attachment or strong attachment, you may have done a useful study but it would not be a duplicate of the first.

CRITERIA FOR SELECTING A MEASURING INSTRUMENT

Now that you know why you need to measure program objectives, let us go on to look at *how* you measure them in the first place. To measure a variable, you need a measuring instrument to measure it with—much more about this topic in Tool M. Most of the measuring instruments used in social work are paper-and-pencil instruments like the one in Figure L.1.

Many other people besides Hudson have come up with ways of measuring self-esteem, and if you want to measure self-esteem in your study, you will have to choose between the various measuring instruments that are available that measure self-esteem. The same embarrassment of riches applies to most of the other variables you might want to measure. Remember that a variable is something that varies between evaluation participants. Participants will vary, for example, with respect to their levels of self-esteem.

You need some criteria to help you decide which instrument is best for measuring a particular variable in any given particular situation. There are five criteria that will help you to do this:

- Utility
- Sensitivity to small changes
- Nonreactivity
- Reliability
- Validity

Utility

To complete Hudson's *Index of Self-Esteem* (Figure L.1), for example, an evaluation participant must preferably be able to read. Even if you, as the evaluator, read the items to the participants, they must be able to relate a number between 1 and 7 (where 1 = *none of the time* and 7 = *all of the time*) to each of the 25 items, or questions.

Furthermore, they must know what a "wallflower" is before they can answer Item 19. If the participants in your study cannot do this for a variety of reasons, then no matter how wonderful Hudson's *Index of Self-Esteem* might be in other respects, it's not useful to you in your particular study.

Hudson's *Index of Self-Esteem* may take only a few minutes to complete, but other instruments can take far longer. The *Minnesota Multiphase Personality Inventory*, for example, can take three hours or more to complete, and some people may not have the attention span or the motivation to complete the task. In sum, a measuring instrument is not useful if your evaluation participants are unable or unwilling to complete it—for whatever reasons. If they do complete it, however, you then have to score it.

While the simple measuring instrument contained in Figure L.1 is relatively quick and simple to score, other instruments are far more complex and time consuming. Usually the simple instruments—quick to complete and easy to score—are less accurate than the more demanding instruments, and you will have to decide how prepared you are to sacrifice accuracy for utility.

The main consideration here is what you are going to do with the measurements once you have obtained them. If you are doing an assessment that might affect a client's life in terms of treatment intervention, referral, placement, and so on, accuracy is paramount and you will need the most accurate instrument (probably the longest and most complex) that the client can tolerate.

On the other hand, if you are doing an exploratory evaluation study where the result will be a tentative suggestion that some variable may be related to another, a little inaccuracy in measurement is not the end of the world and utility might be more important.

Sensitivity to Small Changes

Suppose that one of your practice objectives with your 8-year-old client, Johnny, is to help him stop wetting his bed during the night. One obvious indicator of the variable—bed-wetting—is a wet bed. Thus you hastily decide that you will measure Johnny's bed-wetting behavior by having his mother tell you if Johnny has—or has not—wet his bed during the week; that is: Did he or did he not wet his bed at least once during the week?

However, if Johnny has reduced the number of his bed-wetting incidents from five per week to only once per week, you will not know whether your intervention was working well because just the one bed-wetting incident per week was enough to officially count as "wetting the bed." In other words, the way you chose to measure Johnny's bed-wetting behavior was sensitive to the large difference between wetting and not wetting in a given week but insensitive to the smaller difference between wetting once and wetting more than once in a given week.

To be able to congratulate Johnny on small improvements, and of course to track his progress over time, you will have to devise a more sensitive measuring instrument; such as one that measures the number of times Johnny wets his bed per week. Often,

an instrument that is more sensitive will also be less convenient to use, and you will have to balance sensitivity against utility.

Nonreactivity

A *reactive* measuring instrument is nothing more than an instrument that changes the behavior or feeling of a person that it was supposed to measure. For instance, you might have decided, in the aforementioned example, to use a device that rings a loud bell every time Johnny has a bed-wetting accident.

His mother would then leap from sleep, make a checkmark on the form you had provided, and fall back into a tormented doze. This would be a sensitive measure—though intrusive and thus less useful—but it might also cause Johnny to reduce his bed-wetting behavior in accordance with behavior theory.

Clinically, this would be a good thing—unless he developed bell phobia—but it's important to make a clear distinction between an *instrument* that is designed to *measure* a behavior and an *intervention* that is designed to *change* the behavior. If the bell wakes up Johnny so he can go to the bathroom and thus finally eliminate his bed-wetting behavior, the bell is a wonderful *intervention*. It's not a good measuring instrument, however, because it has changed the very behavior it was supposed to measure. A change in behavior resulting from the use of a measuring instrument is known as a *reactive effect*.

The ideal, then, is a *nonreactive* measuring instrument that has no effect on the variable being measured. If you want to know, for example, whether a particular intervention is effective in raising self-esteem in girls who have been sexually abused, you will need to be sure that any measured increase in self-esteem is due to the intervention and *not* to the measuring instrument you happen to be using. If you fail to make a distinction between the measuring instrument and the intervention, you will end up with no clear idea at all about what is causing what.

Sometimes you might be tempted to use a measuring instrument as a clinical tool. If your client responded to Hudson's *Index of Self-Esteem* Item 13

(Figure L.1) that she felt she bored people all of the time, you might want to discuss with her the particular conversational gambits she feels are so boring in order to help her change them. This is perfectly legitimate so long as you realize that, by so doing, you have turned a measuring instrument into part of an intervention.

Reliability

A good measuring instrument is reliable in that it gives the same score over and over again provided that the measurement is made under the same conditions and nothing about the evaluation participant has changed. A reliable measuring instrument is obviously necessary since, if you are trying to track the increase in a client's self-esteem, for example, you need to be sure that the changes you see over time are due to changes in the client, not to inaccuracies in the measuring instrument.

Evaluators are responsible for ensuring that the measuring instruments they use are reliable. Hence, it's worth looking briefly at the four main methods used to establish the reliability of a measuring instrument:

- Test–retest method
- Alternate form method
- Split-half method
- Observer reliability method

Test–Retest Method

The test–retest method of establishing reliability involves administering the same measuring instrument to the same group of people on two separate occasions. The two sets of results are then compared to see how similar they are, that is, how well they *correlate*. A correlation can range from zero to 1, where zero means no correlation at all between the two sets of scores and 1 means a perfect correlation.

Generally, a correlation of 0.8 means that the instrument is reasonably reliable and 0.9 is very good. Note that there is a heading for "Reliability" in Figure L.1a, which means that Hudson's *Index of Self-Esteem* has "excellent stability with a 2-hour test–retest correlation of 0.92." The "2-hour" bit means, of course,

that the two administrations of the instrument took place two hours apart.

The problem with completing the same instrument twice is that the answers given on the first occasion may affect the answers given on the second. As we know from Tool E, this is known as a *testing effect*. For example, Ms. Smith might remember what she wrote the first time and write something different just to enliven the proceedings. She may be less anxious, or more bored or irritated the second time, just because there was a first time, and these states might affect her answers.

Obviously, the greater the testing effects, the less reliable the instrument. Moreover, the closer together the tests, the more likely testing effects become (e.g., Ms. Smith is more likely to remember the first occasion). Hence, if the instrument is reliable over an interval of two hours and you want to administer it to your study participants on occasions a day or a month apart, it should be even more reliable with respect to testing effects.

However, people may change their answers on a second occasion for reasons other than testing effects: They are having a good day or a bad day; or they have a cold; or there is a loud pneumatic drill just outside the window. However, a word of caution is in order. Sometimes clients complete the same measuring instrument every few weeks for a year or more as a way of monitoring their progress over time.

The more often an instrument is completed, the more likely it is that it will generate testing effects. Hence, social service programs that use instruments in this way need to be sure that the instruments they use are still reliable under the conditions in which they are to be used.

Alternate-Form Method

The second method of establishing the reliability of a measuring instrument is the alternate-form method. As the same suggests, an alternate form of an instrument is a second instrument that is as similar as possible to the original except that the wording of the items contained in the second instrument has changed. Administering the original form and then the alternate form reduces testing effects since the respondent is less likely to base the second set of answers on the first.

However, it's time consuming to develop different but equivalent instruments, and they must still be tested for reliability using the test–retest method, both together as a pair and separately as two distinct instruments.

Split-Half Method

The split-half method involves splitting one instrument in half so that it becomes two shorter instruments. Usually all the even-numbered items, or questions, are used to make one instrument, whereas the odd-numbered items make up the other. The point of doing this is to ensure that the original instrument is internally consistent; that is, it's homogeneous, or the same all the way through, with no longer or more difficult items appearing at the beginning or the end.

When the two halves are compared using the test–retest method, they should ideally yield the same score. If they did give the same score when one half was administered to a respondent on one occasion and the second half to the same respondent on a different occasion, they would have a perfect correlation of 1. Again, a correlation of 0.8 is thought to be good and a correlation of 0.9 very good. Figure L.1a under the "Reliability" section, shows that Hudson's *Index of Self-Esteem* has an internal consistency of 0.93.

Observer Reliability (Reliability of the Process)

Sometimes behaviors are measured by observing how often they occur, how long they last, or how severe they are. The results are then recorded on a straightforward, simple form. Nevertheless, this is not as easy as it sounds because the behavior, or variable, being measured must first be very carefully defined and people observing the same behavior may have different opinions as to how severe the behavior was, how long it lasted, or whether it occurred at all.

The level of agreement or correlation between trained observers therefore provides a way of establishing the reliability of the process used to measure the behavior. Once we have established the reliability

of the process, we can use the same method to assess the reliability of other observers as part of their training. The level of agreement between observers is known as *interrater reliability*.

Validity

A measuring instrument is valid if it measures what it's supposed to measure—and measures it accurately. If you want to measure the variable assertiveness, for example, you don't want to mistakenly measure aggression instead of assertiveness. There are several kinds of validity—in fact, we should really refer to the *validities* of an instrument. We now discuss a few that are most relevant to most of your evaluation needs:

- Content validity
- Criterion validity
- Face validity

Content Validity

Think for a moment about the variable self-esteem. To measure it accurately, you must first know what it is; that is, you must identify all the indicators (questions contained in the measuring instrument) that make up self-esteem, such as feeling that people like you, feeling that you are competent, and so on—and on and on and on . . . It's probably impossible to identify *all* the indicators that contribute to self-esteem.

It's even less likely that everyone (or even most people) will agree with all the indicators identified by someone else. Arguments may arise over whether "feeling worthless," for example, is really an indicator of low self-esteem or whether it has more to do with depression, which is a separate variable altogether.

Furthermore, even if agreement could be reached, a measuring instrument like Hudson's *Index of Self-Esteem* would have to include at least one item, or question, for *every* agreed-upon indicator. If just one was missed, for example, "sense of humor"—then the instrument would not be accurately measuring self-esteem.

In this case, because it did not include all the possible content, or indicators, related to self-esteem, it would not be *content valid*. Hudson's *Index of Self-Esteem*, then, is not perfectly content valid because it's not possible to cover every indicator related to self-esteem in just 25 items. Longer instruments have a better chance of being content valid (perhaps one could do it in 25 *pages* of items) but, in general, perfect content validity cannot be achieved in any measuring instrument of a practical length. Content validity is a matter of "more or less" rather than "yes or no," and it is, moreover, strictly a matter of opinion.

For example, experts differ about the degree to which various instruments are content valid. It's therefore necessary to find some way of *validating* an instrument to determine how well it is, in fact, accurately measuring what it's supposed to measure. One such way is through a determination of the instrument's *criterion validity*.

Criterion Validity

An instrument has criterion validity if it gives the same result as a second instrument that is designed to measure the same variable. A client might complete Hudson's *Index of Self-Esteem*, for example, and achieve a score indicating high self-esteem. If the same client then completes a second instrument also designed to measure self-esteem and again achieves a good score, it's very likely that both instruments are, in fact, measuring self-esteem. Not only do they have good criterion validity in that they compare well with each other, but probably each instrument also has good content validity.

If the same client does not achieve similar scores on the two instruments, however, then neither of them is criterion valid, probably one is not content valid, and both will have to be compared with a third instrument in order to resolve the difficulty. There are two categories of criterion validity:

- Concurrent validity
- Predictive validity

Concurrent validity. Concurrent validity deals with the present. For example, suppose you have an instrument (say, a reading test) designed to distinguish between children who need remedial reading services and children who do not. In order to validate the measuring instrument, you ask the classroom teacher which children she thinks need remedial reading services. If the teacher and your instrument both come up with the same list of children, your instrument has criterion validity. If not, you will need to find another comparison: a different reading test or the opinion of another teacher.

Predictive validity. Surprise, surprise—predictive validity deals with the future. Perhaps you have an instrument (say, a set of criteria) designed to predict which students will achieve high grades in their social work programs. If the students your instrument identified had indeed achieved high grades by the end of their MSW programs and the others had not, your instrument would have predictive validity. In sum, criterion validity, whether concurrent or predictive, is determined by comparing the instrument with another designed to measure the same variable.

Face Validity

Face validity, in fact, has nothing to do with what an instrument actually measures but only with what it *appears* to measure to the one who is completing it. Strictly speaking, it's not a form of validity. For example, suppose that you are taking a course on social work administration. You have a lazy instructor who has taken your final exam from a course he taught for business students last semester. The exam in fact quite adequately tests your knowledge of administration theory, but it does not seem relevant to you because the language it uses relates to the business world, not to social work situations.

You might not do very well on this exam because, although it has content validity (it adequately tests your knowledge), it does not have face validity (an appearance of relevance to the respondent). The moral here is that a measuring instrument should not only be content valid, to the greatest extent possible; it should *appear* content valid to the person who completes it.

Reliability and Validity Revisited

Before we leave reliability and validity, we should say something about the relationship between them. If

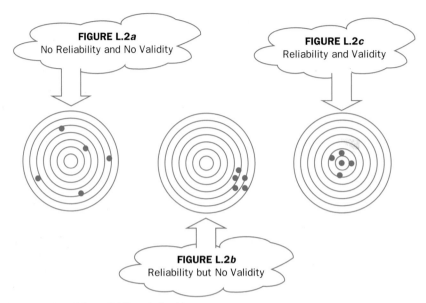

FIGURE L.2a
No Reliability and No Validity

FIGURE L.2c
Reliability and Validity

FIGURE L.2b
Reliability but No Validity

Figure L.2: **Targets illustrating the validity–reliability relationship.**

an instrument is not reliable, it cannot be valid. That is, if the same person completes it a number of times under the same conditions and it gives different results each time, it cannot be measuring anything accurately.

However, if an instrument *is* reliable, that does not necessarily mean it's valid. It could be reliably and consistently measuring something other than what it's supposed to measure, in the same way that people can be reliably late, or watches can be reliably slow. The relationship between validity and reliability can be illustrated with a simple analogy. Suppose that you are firing five rounds from a rifle at three different targets, as illustrated in Figure L.2 (Bostwick & Kyte, 1981).

- In Figure L.2a the bullet holes are scattered, representing a measuring instrument that is neither reliable nor valid.
- In Figure L.2b you have adjusted your sights, and now all the bullet holes are in the same place but not in the center as you intended. This represents a measuring instrument that is reliable but not valid.
- In Figure L.2c all the shots have hit the bull's eye: The instrument is both reliable and valid.

MEASUREMENT ERRORS

No matter how good the reliability and validity of a measuring instrument, no measurement is entirely without error. You can make two errors when you measure variables:

- Constant errors
- Random errors

Constant Errors

Constant errors, as the name suggests, are those errors that stay constant throughout the study. They stay constant because they come from an unvarying source. That source may be the measuring instruments used, the participants, or the evaluators themselves. Since we have already spent some time discussing the limitations of measuring instruments, we focus this discussion on errors caused by the evaluators and their evaluation participants.

Evaluation participants, with all the best intentions in the world, may still have personal styles that lead to errors in the study's results. If they are being interviewed, for example, they may exhibit *acquiescence* (a tendency to agree with everything the evaluators say, no matter what it is) or *social desirability* (a tendency to say anything that they think makes them look good) or *deviation* (a tendency to seek unusual responses).

If they are filling out a self-administered instrument, like Hudson's *Index of Self-Esteem*, they may show *error of central tendency*, always choosing the number in the middle and avoiding commitment to either of the ends. Moreover, they all have personal characteristics with respect to gender, age, ethnic background, and knowledge of the English language that remain constant throughout the study and may affect their answers.

Evaluators also have personal styles and characteristics. Interviewers can affect the answers they receive by the way they ask the questions; by the way they dress; by their accent, mannerisms, gender, age, ethnic background, even by their hairstyles. According to Gerald Bostwick and Nancy Kyte (1981), observers who are watching and rating evaluation participants' behaviors can commit various sins in a constant fashion, for example:

- *Contrast error*—to rate others as opposite to oneself with respect to a particular characteristic
- *Halo effect*—to think that a participant is altogether wonderful or terrible because of one good or bad trait, or to think that the trait being observed must be good or bad because the participant is altogether wonderful or terrible
- *Error of leniency*—to always give a good report
- *Error of severity*—to always give a bad report
- *Error of central tendency*—observers, like participants, can choose always to stay comfortably in the middle of a rating scale and avoid both ends

Since these errors are constant throughout the study, they are sometimes recognized and steps can be taken to deal with them. A different interviewer or observer might be found, for example, or allowances might be made for a particular participant's characteristics or style.

Random Errors

Random errors that are not constant are difficult to find and make allowances for. Random errors spring out of the dark, wreak temporary havoc, and go back into hiding. It has been suggested that eventually they cancel each other out, and, indeed, they might. They might not, as well, but there is little you can do about them except to be aware that they exist. According to Bostwick and Kyte (1981), there are three types of random error:

- *Transient qualities of the evaluation participant*—things such as fatigue or boredom, or any temporary personal state that will affect the participant's responses
- *Situational factors*—the weather, the pneumatic drill outside the window, or anything else in the environment that will affect the participant's responses
- *Administrative factors*—anything relating to the way the instrument is administered, the interview conducted, or the observation made. These include transient qualities of the evaluators (or whoever collects the data) as well as sporadic stupidity like reading out the wrong set of instructions.

IMPROVING VALIDITY AND RELIABILITY

When a measuring instrument does not achieve acceptable levels of validity and reliability—that is, when much error occurs—evaluators often attempt to redesign the instrument so that it's more valid and reliable. The following are a few techniques for improving a measuring instrument's reliability and validity (Monette, Sullivan, & DeJong, 2011):

- **Be clearer on what you are measuring.** Often, validity and reliability are compromised because the evaluator is not sufficiently clear and precise about the nature of the concepts being measured and their possible indicators.

Rethinking the concepts helps in revising the instrument to make it more valid.

- *Provide better training for those who will apply the measuring instruments.* This is especially useful when a measuring instrument is used to assess evaluation participants' feelings or attitudes. Previous studies show that people who apply an instrument can be intentionally and unintentionally biased and thus intentionally and/or unintentionally produce error.

- *Obtain the evaluation participants' personal reactions about the measuring instrument.* Those under study may have some insight regarding why the verbal reports, observations, or archival reports are not producing accurate measures of their behaviors, feelings, or knowledge levels. They may, for example, comment that the wording of questions is ambiguous or that members of their subculture interpret some words differently than the evaluator intended.

- *Obtain higher measurement levels of a variable.* This does not guarantee greater validity and reliability, but a higher level of measurement can produce a more reliable measuring instrument in some cases. So, when the evaluator has some options in terms of how to measure a variable, it's worth considering a higher level of measurement (e.g., nominal to ordinal, ordinal to interval).

- *Use more indicators of a variable.* This also does not guarantee enhanced reliability and validity, but a summated measuring instrument that has many questions, or items, can produce a more valid measure than one with fewer items. Thus the more items, the higher the reliability and validity.

- *Conduct an item-by-item assessment.* If the measuring instrument consists of a number of questions, or items, perhaps only one or two of them are the problem. Deleting them may improve the instrument's validity and reliability.

SUMMARY

Measurement serves as a bridge between theory and reality. Our program and practice objectives must be measurable. The measuring instrument we select to measure them will depend on why we need to make the measurement and under what circumstances it will be administered.

Measurement error refers to variations in an instrument's score that cannot be attributed to the variable being measured. Basically, all measurement errors can be categorized as constant errors or random errors. The next tool is a logical extension of this one: It presents the many different types of measuring instruments that are available for our use.

MEASURING INSTRUMENTS

This is the last tool in your evaluation toolkit. You can use it to review the various types of measuring instruments that are at your disposal for your evaluations. The type of measuring instrument you choose to measure your variables—usually program objectives—within your evaluation study depends on your situation: the question you are asking, the kind of data you need, the evaluation participants you have selected, and the time and amount of money you have available.

TYPES OF MEASURING INSTRUMENTS

In general, there are many different types of measuring instruments. We discuss only the five that are the most practical for your evaluation measurement needs:

- Journal and diaries
- Logs
- Inventories
- Checklists
- Summative instruments

Journals and Diaries

Journals or diaries are a useful means of data collection when you are undertaking an interpretive study that collects data in the form of words. They are usually not used as data collection devices within positivistic studies that collect data in the form of numbers. Perhaps in your interpretive evaluation you are asking the question, "What are women's experiences of home birth?" and you want your evaluation participants to keep a record of their experiences from early pregnancy to postdelivery.

With respect to the five criteria mentioned in Tool L, a journal is *valid* in this context to the extent that it completely and accurately describes the relevant experiences and omits the irrelevant experiences. This can only be achieved if the women keeping them have reasonable language skills, can stick pretty much to the point (e.g., will they include a three-page description of their cats or their geraniums?), and are willing to complete their journals on a regular basis.

A word is in order here about *retrospective data*, that is, data based on someone's memory of what occurred in the past. There is some truth to the idea that we invent our memories. At least, we might embellish or distort them, and a description is much more liable to be accurate if it's written immediately after the event it describes rather than days or weeks later.

The journal is *reliable* insofar as the same experience evokes the same written response. Over time, women may tire of describing, again, an experience almost identical to the one they had last week, and they may either omit it (affecting validity), change it a little to make it more interesting (again affecting validity), or try to write it in a different way (affecting reliability).

Utility very much depends on whether the woman likes to write and is prepared to continue with what may become an onerous task. Another aspect of utility relates to your own role as evaluator. Will you have the time required to go through each journal and perform a qualitative data analysis?

Sensitivity has to do with the amount of detail included in the journal. To some degree this reflects completeness and is a validity issue, but small changes in women's experiences as the pregnancy progresses cannot be tracked unless the experiences are each described in some detail.

Journals are usually very reactive. Indeed, they are often used as therapeutic tools simply because the act of writing encourages the writer to reflect on what has been written, thus achieving deeper insights, which may lead to behavior and/or affective changes. Reactivity is not desirable in a measuring instrument.

On the other hand, your qualitative evaluation study may seek to uncover not just the experiences themselves but the meaning attached to them by your evaluation participant, and meaning may emerge more clearly if she is encouraged to reflect.

Logs

You have probably used logs in your field placement, so we do not discuss their use in depth. When used in evaluation situations, they are nothing more than a structured kind of journal, where the evaluation participant is asked to record events related to particular experiences or behaviors in note form.

Each note usually includes headings: the event itself, when and where the event happened, and who was there. A log may be more valid than a journal in that the headings prompt the participant to include only relevant information with no discursive wanderings into cats or geraniums.

The log may be more reliable because it's more likely that a similar experience will be recorded in a similar way. It may be more useful because it takes less time for the participant to complete and less time for you to analyze. It's usually less sensitive to small changes because it includes less detail, and it may be somewhat less reactive depending on the extent to which it leads to reflection and change.

Inventories

An inventory is a list completed by the evaluation participants. For example, the following is an inventory designed to measure depression:

List below the things that make you feel depressed.

_____

_____

_____

This is valid to the degree that the list is complete and sensitive in that the addition or omission of items over time is indicative of change. It's useful if the participant is prepared to complete it carefully and truthfully; it's probably fairly reactive in that it provokes thought; and it's reliable in that the same experience should always result in the same entries on the list.

Checklists

A checklist is a list prepared by you. For example, a checklist designed to measure depression would include more items than shown but would follow this format:

Check below all the things that you have felt during the past week.

_____ A wish to be alone

_____ Sadness

_____ Powerlessness

_____ Anxiety

With respect to the five evaluative criteria presented in Tool L, the same considerations apply to a checklist as to an inventory except that validity may be compromised if you do not include all the possibilities that are relevant to your participants in the context of your study.

Summative Instruments

As you know from Tool L, rating scales obtain data from one question, or item, about the practice or program objective and summated scales present multiple questions, or items, to which the participant is asked to respond. Thus summated scales combine responses to all of the questions on an instrument to form a single, overall score for the objective being measured. The responses are then totaled to obtain a single composite score indicating the individual's position on the objective of interest.

Summated scales are widely used to assess individual or family problems, to perform needs assessments, and to assist other types of case- and program-level evaluation efforts. The scale poses a number of questions and asks clients to indicate the degree of their agreement or disagreement with each. As you know, response categories may include such statements as "strongly agree," "agree," "neutral," "disagree," and "strongly disagree."

It's our opinion that summated scales provide more objectivity and precision in the variable that they are measuring than the four types of measuring instruments mentioned earlier. Figure M.1 presents an excellent example of a standardized summative scale, and Figure M.1a shows how it can be scored. It measures one variable: client satisfaction with services. Notice that it only contains nine questions, or items, for the respondent to answer.

A longer version of Figure M.1 can be found in Figure M.2, which is another example of an excellent standardized measuring instrument. Notice once again that both Figures M.1 and M.2 measure the same variable: client satisfaction. They both can easily be used in a process evaluation—though not in an outcome evaluation since client satisfaction is never a program objective.

Figure M.3 is yet another great example of a standardized summative scale that measures client satisfaction with services; this one, however, has three related subscales, all combined in one measuring instrument.

A unidimensional summative measuring instrument (e.g., Figures. L.1, M.1, M.2) measures only one variable. On the other hand, a multidimensional one measures a number of highly related subvariables at the same time (e.g., Figure M.3). In short, a multidimensional instrument is nothing more than a number of unidimensional instruments stuck together. For example, Figure M.3 is a multidimensional summative measuring instrument that contains three unidimensional ones:

1. Relevance of received social services (Items 1–11)

2. The extent to which the services reduced the problem (Items 12–21)
3. The extent to which services enhanced the client's self-esteem and contributed to a sense of power and integrity (Items 22–34)

STANDARDIZED MEASURING INSTRUMENTS

Standardized measuring instruments are used widely in our profession because they have usually been extensively tested and they come complete with information on the results of that testing. Figures L.1, M.1, M.2, and M.3 are excellent examples of a summative standardized measuring instrument in that they all provide information about themselves in six areas:

- Purpose
- Description
- Norms
- Scoring
- Reliability
- Validity

Let's use Figures L.1 and L.1a from Tool L to illustrate the six bits of information they all contain.

Purpose is a simple statement of what the instrument is designed to measure. *Description* provides particular features of the instrument, including its length and often its *clinical cutting score*. The clinical cutting score is different for every instrument (if it has one, that is) and is the score that differentiates respondents with a clinically significant problem from respondents with no such problem.

In Hudson's *Index of Self-Esteem*, for example, people who score above 30 (plus or minus 5 for error) have a clinically significant problem with self-esteem and people who score less than 30 do not.

The section on norms tells you who the instrument was validated on. The *Index of Self-Esteem*, for example (see "Norms" in Figure. L.1a), was tested on 1,745 respondents, including single and married individuals, clinical and nonclinical populations, college students, and nonstudents, Caucasians, Japanese and

The questions below are designed to measure the way you feel about the services you have received. This is not a test, so there are no right or wrong answers. Answer each item as carefully and as accurately as you can by circling the appropriate number on the right.	None of the time	Very rarely	A little of the time	Some of the time	A good deal of the time	Most of the time	All of the time
1. People here really seem to care about me.	1	2	3	4	5	6	7
2. I would come back here if I need help again.	1	2	3	4	5	6	7
3. I would recommend this place to people I care about.	1	2	3	4	5	6	7
4. People here really know what they are doing.	1	2	3	4	5	6	7
5. I get the kind of help here that I really need.	1	2	3	4	5	6	7
6. People here accept me for who I am.	1	2	3	4	5	6	7
7. People here seem to understand how I feel.	1	2	3	4	5	6	7
8. I feel I can really talk to people here.	1	2	3	4	5	6	7
9. The help I get here is better than I expected.	1	2	3	4	5	6	7

Figure M.1: **Steve McMurtry's client satisfaction inventory (short form).**

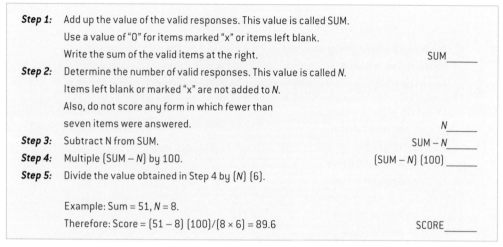

Step 1: Add up the value of the valid responses. This value is called SUM.
Use a value of "0" for items marked "x" or items left blank.
Write the sum of the valid items at the right.   SUM_____

Step 2: Determine the number of valid responses. This value is called *N*.
Items left blank or marked "x" are not added to *N*.
Also, do not score any form in which fewer than
seven items were answered.   *N*_____

Step 3: Subtract N from SUM.   SUM − *N*_____

Step 4: Multiple (SUM − *N*) by 100.   (SUM − *N*) (100)_____

Step 5: Divide the value obtained in Step 4 by (*N*) (6).

Example: Sum = 51, *N* = 8.
Therefore: Score = (51 − 8) (100)/(8 × 6) = 89.6   SCORE_____

Figure M.1a: **Scoring instructions for Steve McMurtry's client satisfaction inventory (short form).**

Chinese Americans, and a smaller number of other ethnic groups.

It's important to know this because people with different characteristics tend to respond differently to the sort of items contained in Hudson's *Index of Self-Esteem*. For instance, a woman from a culture that values modesty might be unwilling to answer that she feels she is a beautiful person all of the time (Item 3). She might not know what a wallflower is (Item 19), and she might be very eager to assert that she feels self-conscious with strangers (Item 16) because she thinks that women ought to feel that way.

It's therefore very important to use any measuring instrument *only* with people who have the same characteristics as the people who participated in testing the instrument. As another example, instruments used with children must have been developed using children.

Scoring gives instructions about how to score the instrument. We have discussed *reliability* and *validity* already. Summated standardized instruments are usually reliable, valid, sensitive, and nonreactive. It's therefore very tempting to believe that they must be useful, whatever the evaluation situation. More often than not, they *are* useful—provided that what the instrument measures and what the evaluator wants to measure are the same thing.

If you want to measure family coping, for example, and come across a wonderful standardized instrument designed to measure family cohesion, you must resist the temptation to convince yourself that family cohesion is what you really wanted to measure in the first place. Just remember that the variable being measured selects the instrument; the instrument doesn't select the variable.

Evaluating Instruments

There are several criteria that must be considered when it comes time to evaluate standardized measuring instruments that you think will accurately measure the variables in your evaluation study, particularly your outcome variable, or program objective (Jordan, Franklin, & Corcoran, 2014).

1. **The sample from which data were drawn**

   a. Are the samples representative of pertinent populations?
   b. Are the sample sizes sufficiently large?
   c. Are the samples homogeneous?
   d. Are the subsamples pertinent to respondents' demographics?
   e. Are the data obtained from the samples up to date?

CLIENT SATISFACTION INVENTORY (CSI)

This questionnaire is designed to measure the way you feel about the services you have received. It is not a test, so there are no right or wrong answers. Answer each item as carefully and as accurately as you can by placing a number beside each one as follows.

1 = None of the time
2 = Very rarely
3 = A little of the time
4 = Some of the time
5 = A good part of the time
6 = Most of the time
7 = All of the time
X = Does not apply

1. ___ The services I get here are a big help to me.
2. ___ People here really seem to care about me.
3. ___ I would come back here if I need help again.
4. ___ I feel that no one here really listens to me.
5. ___ People here treat me like a person, not like a number.
6. ___ I have learned a lot here about how to deal with my problems.
7. ___ People here want to do things their way, instead of helping me find my way.
8. ___ I would recommend this place to people I care about.
9. ___ People here really know what they are doing.
10. ___ I get the kind of help here that I really need.
11. ___ People here accept me for who I am.
12. ___ I feel much better now than when I first came here.
13. ___ I thought no one could help me until I came here.
14. ___ The help I get here is ready worth what it costs.
15. ___ People here put my needs ahead of their needs.
16. ___ People here put me down when I disagree with them.
17. ___ The biggest help I get here is learning how to help myself.
18. ___ People here are just trying to get rid of me.
19. ___ People who know me say this place has made a positive change in me.
20. ___ People here have shown me how to get help from other places.
21. ___ People here seem to understand how I feel.
22. ___ People here are only concerned about getting paid.
23. ___ I feel I can really talk to people here.
24. ___ The help I get here is better than I expected.
25. ___ I look forward to the sessions I have with people here.

Figure M.2: **Steve McMurtry's client satisfaction inventory (long form).**

SOCIAL SERVICE SATISFACTION SCALE

Using the scale from one to five described below, please indicate at the left of each item the number that comes closest to how you feel.

1 Strongly agree
2 Agree
3 Undecided
4 Disagree
5 Strongly disagree

1. ___ The social worker took my problems very seriously.
2. ___ If I had been the worker, I would have dealt with my problems in the same way.
3. ___ The worker I had could never understand anyone like me.
4. ___ Overall the agency has been very helpful to me.
5. ___ If friends of mine had similar problems I would tell them to go to the agency.
6. ___ The social worker asks a lot of embarrassing questions.
7. ___ I can always count on the worker to help if I'm in trouble.
8. ___ The agency will help me as much as it can.
9. ___ I don't think the agency has the power to really help me.
10. ___ The social worker tries hard but usually isn't too helpful.
11. ___ The problem the agency helped me with is one of the most important in my life.
12. ___ Things have gotten better since I've been going to the agency.
13. ___ Since I've been using the agency my life is more messed up than ever.
14. ___ The agency is always available when I need it.
15. ___ I got from the agency exactly what I wanted.
16. ___ The social worker loves to talk but won't really do anything for me.
17. ___ Sometimes I just tell the social worker what I think she wants to hear.
18. ___ The social worker is usually in a hurry when I see her.
19. ___ No one should have any trouble getting some help from this agency.
20. ___ The worker sometimes says things I don't understand.
21. ___ The social worker is always explaining things carefully.
22. ___ I never looked forward to my visits to the agency.
23. ___ I hope I'll never have to go back to the agency for help.
24. ___ Every time I talk to my worker I feel relieved.
25. ___ I can tell the social worker the truth without worrying.
26. ___ I usually feel nervous when I talk to my worker.
27. ___ The social worker is always looking for lies in what I tell her.
28. ___ It takes a lot of courage to go to the agency.
29. ___ When I enter the agency I feel very small and insignificant.
30. ___ The agency is very demanding.
31. ___ The social worker will sometimes lie to me.
32. ___ Generally the social worker is an honest person.
33. ___ I have the feeling that the worker talks to other people about me.
34. ___ I always feel well treated when I leave the agency.

Figure M.3: **Reid-Gundlach Social Service Satisfaction Scale.**

2. **The validity of the instrument**

   a. Is the content domain clearly and specifically defined?
   b. Was there a logical procedure for including the items?
   c. Is the criterion measure relevant to the instrument?
   d. Was the criterion measure reliable and valid?
   e. Is the theoretical construct clearly and correctly stated?
   f. Do the scores converge with other relevant measures?
   g. Do the scores discriminate from irrelevant variables?
   h. Are there cross-validation studies that conform to these concerns?

3. **The reliability of the instrument**

   a. Is there sufficient evidence of internal consistency?
   b. Is there equivalence between various forms?
   c. Is there stability over a relevant time interval?

4. **The practicality of application**

   a. Is the instrument an appropriate length?
   b. Is the content socially acceptable to respondents?
   c. Is the instrument feasible to complete?
   d. Is the instrument relatively direct?
   e. Does the instrument have utility?
   f. Is the instrument relatively nonreactive?
   g. Is the instrument sensitive to measuring change?
   h. Is the instrument feasible to score?

Advantages and Disadvantages

Like everything in life, there are advantages and disadvantages to standardized measuring instruments. Judy Krysik and Jerry Finn (2011) do a first-class job on summarizing them as follows:

Advantages

- Standardized instruments are readily available and easy to access.
- The development work has already been done.
- They have established reliability and validity estimates.
- Norms may be available for comparison.
- Most are easy to complete and score.
- In many instances, they are available free of charge.
- They may be available in different languages.
- They specify age range and reading level.
- Time required for administration has been determined.

Disadvantages

- The norms may not apply to the target population.
- The language may be difficult.
- The tone might not fit with the philosophy of the program, for example, deficit based versus strength based.
- The target population may not understand the translation.
- The scoring procedure may be overly complex.
- The instrument may not be affordable.
- Special qualifications or training might be required for use.
- The instrument may be too long or time consuming to administer.

Locating Instruments

Once you decide that you want to measure a variable through the use of a standardized instrument, your next job is to find it. The two general sources for locating such instruments are commercial or professional publishers and the professional literature.

Publishers

Numerous commercial and professional publishing companies specialize in the production and sale of standardized measuring instruments for use in the social services. They can be easily found on the Web. The cost of instruments purchased from a publisher varies considerably, depending on the instrument, the number of copies needed, and the publisher.

The instruments generally are well developed and their psychometric properties are supported by the results of several research studies. Often they are accompanied by manuals that include the normative data for the instrument. As well, publishers are expected to comply with professional standards such as those established by the American Psychological Association. These standards apply to claims made about the instrument's rationale, development, psychometric properties, administration, and interpretation of results.

Standards for the use of some instruments have been developed to protect the interests of clients. Consequently, purchasers of instruments may be required to have certain qualifications, such as possession of an advanced degree in a relevant field. A few publishers require membership in particular professional organizations.

Most publishers will, however, accept an order from a social work student if it's cosigned by a qualified person, such as an instructor, who will supervise the use of the instrument. Kevin Corcoran and Nikki Hozack (2010) along with Catheleen Jordan, Cynthia Franklin, and Kevin Corcoran (2014), have put together a nice list of selected commercial publishers that market standardized measuring instruments:

- Academic Therapy Publications, 20 Commercial Boulevard, Navato, CA 94947; www.academictherapy.com
- Achenbach, Thomas M., Department of Psychiatry, University of Vermont, 1 S. Prospect Street, Burlington, VI 05401–3444
- American Guidance Services, 420 Woodland Road, P.O. Box 99, Circle Pines, MN 55014; www.agsnet.com
- Associates for Research in Behavior Inc., The Science Center, 34th and Market Street, Philadelphia, PA 19104

- Biometrics Research, New York State Psychiatric Institute, 772 168th Street, Room 341, New York, NY 10032; www.wpic.pitt.edu/research/biometrics/index.htm
- California Test Bureau, 20 Ryan Ranch Road, Monterey, CA 93940; www.ctb.com
- Center for Epidemiologic Studies, Department of Health and Human Services, 5600 Fishers Lane, Rockville, MD 20857
- Consulting Psychologists Press, Inc., 577 College Ave, P.O. Box 11636, Palo Alto, CA 94306; www.cpp.com
- Educational and Industrial Testing Services, P.O. Box 7234, San Diego, CA 92107; www.edits.net
- Institute for Personality and Ability Testing, Inc., P.O. Box 188, 1062 Coronado Drive, Champaign, IL 61820; www.ipat.com
- Medical Outcomes Trust, 20 Park Plaza, Suite 1014, Boston, MA 02116–4313; www.outcomestrust.org
- Multi Health Systems Inc.,908 Niagara Falls Boulevard, North Tonawanda, NY 14120; www.mhs.com
- Pearson Assessments (formally NCS Assessments), 5605 Green Circle Drive, P.O. Box 1416, Minneapolis, MN 55440; www.pearsonassessment5.com
- Nursing Research Associates, 3752 Cummins Street, Eau Claire, WI 54701
- Person-0-Metrics, Inc., Evaluation and Development Services, 20504 Williamsburg Road, Dearborn Heights, MI 48127
- Pro Ed, 8700 Shoal Creek Boulevard, Austin, TX 78757; www.proedinc.com
- Psychological Assessment Resources Inc., P.O. Box 998, Odessa, FL 33556; www.parinc.com
- Psychological Corporation, 555 Academic Court, San Antonio, TX 78204; www harcourtassessment. com
- Psychological Publications Inc., 290 Conejo Ridge Road, Suite 100, Thousand Oaks, CA 91361; www.tjta.com

- Psychological Services, Inc., 3400 Wilshire Boulevard, Suite 1200, Los Angeles, CA 90010; www.psionline.com
- Research Press, P.O. Box 917760, Champaign, IL 61820; www.researchpress.com
- SRA/McGraw (formally Science Research Associates, Inc.), 155 North Wacker Drive, Chicago, IL 60606; www.sraonline.com
- Scott Foresman & Company Test Division, 1900 East Lake Avenue, Glenview, IL 60025
- Sigma Assessment Systems Inc., P.O. Box 610984, Port Huron, Ml 48061–0984; www.sigmaassessmentsystems.com
- SRA Product Group, London House, 9701 West Higgins Road, Rosemont, IL 60018
- US Department of Defense Testing Directorate Headquarters, Military Enlistment Processing Command, Attention MEPCT, Fort Sheridan, IL 60037
- US Department of Labor, Division of Testing Employment and Training Administration, Washington, DC 20213
- WALMYR Publishing Company, P.O. Box 12217, Tallahassee, FL 32317–2217; www.walmyr.com
- Western Psychological Services, 12031 Wilshire Boulevard, Los Angeles, CA 90025; www.wpspublish.com

- Wonderlic Personnel Test Inc.,1509 N Milwaukee Avenue, Libertyville, IL 60048–1380; www.wonderlic.com

Professional Books and Journals

Standardized measuring instruments are most commonly described in human service journals. The instruments usually are supported by evidence of their validity and reliability, although they often require cross-validation and normative data from more representative samples and subsamples.

Locating instruments in journals or books is not easy. Of the two most common methods, computer searches of data banks and manual searches of the literature, the former is faster, unbelievably more thorough, and easier to use. Unfortunately, financial support for the development of comprehensive data banks has been limited and intermittent.

Another disadvantage is that many articles on instruments are not referenced with the appropriate indicators for computer retrieval. These limitations are being overcome by the changing technology of computers and information retrieval systems.

Several services now allow for a complex breakdown of measurement need; data banks that include references from over 1,300 journals, updated monthly, are now available from a division of Psychological Abstracts Information Services and from Bibliographic Retrieval Services.

BOX M.1 MEASURING UNDERSERVED POPULATIONS

Instrument Bias

Researchers have debated measurement issues with racial/ethnic minorities for decades. Prominent among the debates has been the issue of testing the intelligence of ethnic minority children. Some researchers have argued that scores on standardized intelligence tests are underestimates of these children's actual abilities. The primary concern pertains to the standardization of the measuring instruments themselves.

It has been suggested that the samples utilized to standardize the instruments did not include enough ethnic minority children to provide the valid interpretation of the instruments' scores when they were used with ethnic minority children. Also, to do well on intelligence tests,

ethnic minority children must demonstrate proficiency with the European American culture.

On the other hand, there is no such requirement for European American children to demonstrate proficiency with ethnic minority cultures. By default, the European American culture is deemed "superior" to the ethnic minority culture.

Measurement Sensitivity

The lack of sensitivity of measuring instruments with ethnic minority populations has been well documented. However, these instruments continue to be used with populations for which they were not designed. The question of validity is apparent. As we know, validity addresses the extent to which a measuring instrument achieves what it claims to measure.

continued

BOX M.1 CONTINUED

In many cases we have no means to determine the validity of measuring instruments or procedures with ethnic minorities because ethnic minorities were not included in the development of instruments or procedures. Nevertheless, researchers have attempted to interpret results using culturally insensitive instruments. This undoubtedly has led to the misrepresentation and understanding of ethnic minorities.

Importance of Variables Measured

Of equal concern to the quality of measurement is whether or not the variables being measured are similarly important to all cultures and ethnic groups. The assumption that all groups value variables equally is another potential misuse of measurement and could assert the superiority of one group's values and beliefs over those of another. For example, when spirituality, a variable, is studied, it may be of greater importance for Native Americans than for other groups.

For a group that values spirituality, attainment of material possessions may be of lesser importance than spirituality. We know that there are often competing values in research. Thus we need to study those variables that are important to each group—not only important to the researcher—and attempt to further our understanding of the importance placed on their valued beliefs, attitudes, and lifestyles.

Language

Language also creates measurement issues. Some ethnic minorities lack facility with the English language, yet they are assessed with measuring instruments assuming that English is their primary language. There have been some efforts to translate measuring instruments into other languages, but few studies have been conducted regarding the equivalency of the translations from the original instruments to the newly translated ones. The results of translated versions may be different from those with the English versions.

Translators and interpreters have also been used to bridge the language barriers with ethnic minority populations. Some suggest that the presence of interpreters and translators influences participants' responses. The extent to which interpreters and translators influence the research participants' responses remains a contentious issue.

Observations

Qualitative studies using observational data collection methods are subject to misinterpretation as well. In observing nonverbal communication such as body language, for example, a researcher can easily misinterpret research participants' behaviors. In some Native American cultures, for example, direct eye contact of a subordinate with a person in authority would be deemed disrespectful. But in the European American culture, direct eye contact is indicative of respect. In this case, the unfamiliarity with the culture could easily lead a researcher to incorrectly interpret the eye-contact behavior.

In short, measuring instruments and procedures remain problematic with research studies that focus on ethnic minorities. The validity of studies using instruments insensitive to ethnic minorities has created erroneous and conflicting reports. Refinement of the instruments (and their protocols) is necessary to improve the understanding of ethnic minorities with respect to their own values, beliefs, and behaviors.

Nevertheless, most social workers will probably rely on manual searches of references such as *Psychological Abstracts*. Although the reference indices will be the same as those in the data banks accessible by computer, the literature search can be supplemented with appropriate seminal (original) reference volumes.

McKinney (2014), via Box M.1, presents a great discussion on the use of measuring instruments with underserved populations.

SUMMARY

In this tool we have briefly looked at measuring instruments—their types and where they can be found. This is the last tool in your toolkit. Hopefully these will be helpful to you when you need to "freshen up" on a particular topic.

Good luck in your professional career as a social worker, and most of all . . . happy evaluating.

Glossary

A PHASE In case-level evaluation designs, a phase (*A* Phase) in which the baseline measurement of the target problem is established before the intervention (*B* Phase) is implemented.

ABSTRACTING INDEXING SERVICES Providers of specialized reference tools that make it possible to find information quickly and easily, usually through subject headings and/or author approaches.

ABSTRACTS Reference materials consisting of citations and brief descriptive summaries from positivist and interpretive research studies.

ACCOUNTABILITY A system of responsibility in which program administrators account for all program activities by answering to the demands of a program's stakeholders and by justifying the program's expenditures to the satisfaction of its stakeholders.

ACCURACY A standard of evaluation practice that requires technical adequacy of the evaluation process; includes matters of validity, reliability, measurement instruments, samples, and comparisons.

ACTIVITIES The actual events or actions that take place as a part of the program.

AFFECTIVE PROGRAM OBJECTIVE An objective that focuses on changing an individual's emotional reaction to himself or herself or to another person or thing.

AGENCY A social service organization that exists to fulfill a broad social purpose; it functions as one entity, is governed by a single directing body, and has policies and procedures that are common to all of its parts.

AGENCY GOAL Broad unmeasurable outcomes the agency wishes to achieve; they are based on values and are guided by the agency's mission statement.

AGGREGATE-LEVEL DATA Derived from micro-level data, aggregate-level data are grouped so that the characteristics of individual units of analysis are no longer

identifiable; for example, the variable, "gross national income" is an aggregation of data about individual incomes.

AGGREGATED CASE-LEVEL EVALUATION DESIGNS The collection of a number of case-level evaluations to determine the degree to which a program objective has been met.

ALTERNATE-FORMS METHOD A method for establishing reliability of a measuring instrument by administering, in succession, equivalent forms of the same instrument to the same group of research participants.

ALTERNATIVE HYPOTHESIS *See* Rival hypothesis.

ANALYTIC GENERALIZATION The type of generalizability associated with case studies; the research findings of case studies are not assumed to fit another case no matter how apparently similar; rather, research findings are tested to see whether they do in fact fit; used as working hypotheses to test practice principles.

ANALYTICAL MEMOS Notes made by the researcher in reference to interpretive data that raise questions or make comments about meaning units and categories identified in a transcript.

ANNUAL REPORT A detailed account or statement describing a program's processes and results over a given year; usually produced at the end of a fiscal year.

ANTECEDENT VARIABLE A variable that precedes the introduction of one or more dependent variables.

ANTIQUARIANISM An interest in past events without reference to their importance or significance for the present; the reverse of presentism.

APPLIED RESEARCH APPROACH A search for practical and applied research results that can be utilized in actual social work practice situations; complementary to the pure research approach.

AREA PROBABILITY SAMPLING A form of cluster sampling that uses a three-stage process to provide the means to carry out a research study when no comprehensive list of the population can be compiled.

ASSESSMENT A professional activity that occurs prior to the intervention phase of practice in which a client's present level of functioning in relevant areas is assessed so that an appropriate intervention plan can be established.

ASSESSMENT-RELATED CASE STUDY A type of case study that generates knowledge about specific clients and their situations; focuses on the perspectives of the study's participants.

AUDIENCE The individuals (such as your stakeholders and other evaluation users) with whom you want to communicate the results of an evaluation.

AUDIT SHEET A checklist of all data to be recorded for a particular client and the dates by which these data are due; usually located on the cover of each client file.

AUDIT TRAIL The documentation of critical steps in an interpretive research study that allows for an independent reviewer to examine and verify the steps in the research process and the conclusions of the research study.

AUTHORITY The reliance on authority figures to tell us what is true; one of the ways of knowing.

AVAILABILITY SAMPLING *See* Convenience sampling.

AXES Straight horizontal and vertical lines in a graph upon which values of a measurement, or the corresponding frequencies, are plotted.

***B* PHASE** In case-level evaluation designs, the intervention phase, which may or may not include simultaneous measurements.

BACK-TRANSLATION The process of translating an original document into a second language, then having an independent translator conduct a subsequent translation of the first translation back into the language of origin; the second translation is then compared with the original document for equivalency.

BASELINE A period of time, usually three or four data collection periods, in which the level of the client's target problem is measured while no intervention is carried out; designated as the *A* Phase in single-system designs (case-level designs).

BASELINE DATA Initial information on a program or program components collected prior to receipt of services or participation in activities. Baseline data are often gathered through intake interviews and observations and are used later for comparing measures that determine changes in a program.

BASELINE MEASURE A numerical label assigned to a client's level of performance, knowledge, or affect prior to any intervention; the first measure to be made in any series of repeated measurements; designated as the *A* phase in formal case level designs.

BEHAVIORAL PROGRAM OBJECTIVE An objective that aims to change the conduct or actions of clients.

BENCHMARKS Measures of progress toward a goal, taken at intervals prior to the program's completion or the anticipated attainment of the final goal.

BETWEEN RESEARCH METHODS APPROACH Triangulation by using different research methods available in both the interpretive and the positivist research approaches in a single research study.

BIAS Not neutral; an inclination to some form of prejudice or preconceived position.

BIASED SAMPLE A sample unintentionally selected in such a way that some members of the population are more likely than others to be picked for sample membership.

BINOMIAL EFFECT SIZE DISPLAY (BESD) A technique for interpreting the *r* value in a meta-analysis by converting it into a 2×2 table displaying magnitude of effect.

BIOGRAPHY Tells the story of one individual's life, often suggesting what the person's influence was on social, political, or intellectual developments of the times.

CASE CONFERENCES An informal, or nonempirical, method of case evaluation that requires professionals to meet and exchange descriptive client information for the purposes of making a case decision.

CASE The basic unit of social work practice, whether it be an individual, a couple, a family, an agency, a community, a county, a state, or a country.

CASE STUDY Using research approaches to investigate a research question or hypothesis relating to a specific case; used to develop theory and test hypotheses; an in-depth form of research in which data are gathered and analyzed about an individual unit of analysis, person, city, event, society, etc.; it allows more intensive analysis of specific details; the disadvantage is that it is hard to use the results to generalize to other cases.

CASE-LEVEL EVALUATION DESIGNS Designs in which data are collected about a single client system—an individual, group, or community—in order to evaluate the outcome of an intervention for the client system; a form of appraisal that monitors change for individual clients; designs in which data are collected about a single client system—an individual, group, or community—in order to evaluate the outcome of an intervention for the client system; also called single-system research designs.

CATEGORIES Groupings of related meaning units that are given one name; used to organize, summarize, and interpret qualitative data; categories in an interpretive study can change throughout the data analysis process, and the number of categories in a given study depends upon the breadth and depth the researcher aims for in the analysis.

CATEGORY SATURATION The point in a qualitative data analysis when all identified meaning units fit easily into the existing categorization scheme and no new categories emerge; the point at which first-level coding ends.

CAUSAL RELATIONSHIP A relationship between two variables for which we can state that the presence of, or absence of, one variable determines the presence of, or absence of, the other variable.

CAUSALITY In outcome evaluation, when a program is deemed the agent that brings about change for clients as measured by its objectives using explanatory evaluation designs.

CD-ROM SOURCES Computerized retrieval systems that allow searching for indexes and abstracts stored on compact computer discs (CDs).

CENSUS DATA Data from the survey of an entire population in contrast to a survey of a sample.

CITATION A brief identification of a reference that includes name of author(s), title, source, page numbers, and year of publication.

CLASSICAL EXPERIMENTAL DESIGN An explanatory research design with randomly assigned experimental and control groups in which the dependent variable is measured before and after the treatment (the independent variable) for both groups, but only the experimental group receives the treatment (the dependent variable).

CLIENT DATA In evaluation, measurements systematically collected from clients of social service programs; ideally, data are collected in strict compliance with the evaluation design and procedures.

CLIENT LOG A form whereby clients maintain annotated records of events related to their practice objectives; structured journals in which clients record events, feelings, and reactions relevant to their problem.

CLIENT SATISFACTION A program variable that measures the degree to which clients are content with various aspects of the program services that they received.

CLIENT SYSTEM An individual client, a couple, a family, a group, an organization, or a community that can be studied with case- and program-level evaluation designs and with positivist and interpretive research approaches.

CLOSED-ENDED QUESTIONS Items in a measuring instrument that require respondents to select one of several response categories provided; also known as fixed-alternative questions.

CLUSTER DIAGRAM An illustration of a conceptual classification scheme in which the researcher draws and labels circles for each theme that emerges from the data; the circles are organized in a way to depict the relationships between themes.

CLUSTER SAMPLING A multistage probability sampling procedure in which the population is divided into groups (or clusters) and the groups, rather than the individuals, are selected for inclusion in the sample.

CODE The label assigned to a category or theme in a qualitative data analysis; shortened versions of the actual category or theme label; used as markers in a qualitative data analysis; usually no longer than eight characters in length and can use a combination of letters, symbols, and numbers.

CODEBOOK A device used to organize qualitative data by applying labels and descriptions that draw distinctions between different parts of the data that have been collected.

CODING (1) In data analysis, translating data from respondents onto a form that can be read by a computer; (2) In interpretive research, marking the text with codes for content categories.

CODING FRAME A specific framework that delineates what data are to be coded and how they are to be coded in order to prepare them for analyses.

CODING SHEETS In a literature review, a sheet used to record for each research study the complete reference, research design, measuring instrument(s), population and sample, outcomes, and other significant features of the study.

COHORT STUDY A longitudinal survey design that uses successive random samples to monitor how the characteristics of a specific group of people, who share certain characteristics or experiences (cohorts), change over time.

COLLATERALS Professionals or staff members who serve as indigenous observers in the data collection process.

COLLECTIVE BIOGRAPHIES Studies of the characteristics of groups of people who lived during a past period and had some major factor in common.

COLLECTIVIST CULTURE Societies that stress interdependence and seek the welfare and survival of the group above that of the individual; collectivist cultures are characterized by a readiness to be influenced by others, preference for conformity, and cooperation in relationships.

COMMUNICATIONS PLAN A document that describes: the communication needs and expectations for the project; how and in what format information will be communicated; when and where each communication will be made; and who is responsible for providing each type of communication.

COMPARATIVE RATING SCALE A rating scale in which respondents are asked to compare an individual person, concept, or situation, to others.

COMPARATIVE RESEARCH DESIGN The study of more than one event, group, or society to isolate explanatory factors; there are two basic strategies in comparative research: (1) the study of elements that differ in many ways but that have some major factor in common, and (2) the study of elements that are highly similar but different in some important aspect, such as modern industrialized nations that have different health insurance systems.

COMPARISON GROUP A nonexperimental group to which research participants have not been randomly assigned for purposes of comparison with the experimental group. Not to be confused with control group.

COMPARISON GROUP POSTTEST ONLY DESIGN A descriptive research design with two groups, experimental and comparison, in which the program's objective (dependent variable) is measured once for both groups, and only the experimental group receives the intervention (the independent variable).

COMPARISON GROUP PRETEST POSTTEST DESIGN A descriptive research design with two groups, experimental and comparison, in which the program's objective (the dependent variable) is measured before and after the intervention (the independent variable) for both groups, but only the experimental group receives the intervention.

COMPARISON GROUP A group not exposed to a program or treatment. Never randomly assigned. If randomly assigned then it is considered a control group.

COMPENSATION Attempts by evaluators or staff members to counterbalance the lack of treatment for control-group clients by administering some or all of the intervention (the independent variable); a threat to internal validity.

COMPENSATORY RIVALRY Motivation of control group members to compete with experimental group members; a threat to internal validity.

COMPLETE OBSERVER One of four possible research roles on a continuum of participant observation research; the complete observer acts simply as an observer and does not participate in the events at hand.

COMPLETE PARTICIPANT The complete participant is at the far end of the continuum from the complete observer in participant observation research; this research role is characterized by total involvement.

COMPLETENESS One of the four criteria for evaluating research hypotheses.

COMPREHENSIVE QUALITATIVE REVIEW A nonstatistical synthesis of representative research studies relevant to a research problem, question, or hypothesis.

COMPUTERIZED DATA SYSTEMS An automated method of organizing single units of data to generate summarized or aggregate forms of data.

COMPUTERIZED RETRIEVAL SYSTEMS Systems in which abstracts, indexes, and subject bibliographies are incorporated in computerized databases to facilitate information retrieval.

CONCEPT An understanding, an idea, or a mental image; a way of viewing and categorizing objects, processes, relations, and events.

CONCEPTUAL CLASSIFICATION SYSTEM The strategy for conceiving how units of qualitative data relate to each other; the method used to depict patterns that emerge from the various coding levels in qualitative data.

CONCEPTUAL FRAMEWORK A frame of reference that serves to guide a research study and is developed from theories, findings from a variety of other research studies, and the author's personal experiences and values.

CONCEPTUAL VALIDITY See Construct validity.

CONCEPTUALIZATION The process of selecting the specific concepts to include in positivist and interpretive research studies.

CONCURRENT VALIDITY A form of criterion validity that is concerned with the ability of a measuring instrument to predict accurately an individual's status by comparing concurrent ratings (or scores) on one or more measuring instruments.

CONFIDENTIALITY An ethical consideration in research whereby anonymity of research participants is safeguarded by ensuring that raw data are not seen by anyone other than the research team and that data presented have no identifying marks.

CONFOUNDING VARIABLE A variable operating in a specific situation in such a way that its effects cannot be separated; the effects of an extraneous variable thus confound the interpretation of a research study's findings.

CONSISTENCY Holding steadfast to the same principles and procedures in the qualitative data analysis process.

CONSTANT A concept that does not vary and does not change; a characteristic that has the same value for all research participants or events in a research study.

CONSTANT COMPARISON A technique used to categorize qualitative data; it begins after the complete set of data has been examined and meaning units identified; each unit is classified as similar or different from the others; similar meaning units are lumped into the same category and classified by the same code.

CONSTANT ERROR Systematic error in measurement; error due to factors that consistently or systematically affect the variable being measured and that are concerned with the relatively stable qualities of respondents to a measuring instrument.

CONSTRUCT See Concept.

CONSTRUCT VALIDITY The degree to which a measuring instrument successfully measures a theoretical construct; the degree to which explanatory concepts account for variance in the scores of an instrument; also referred to as conceptual validity in meta-analyses.

CONTENT ANALYSIS A data collection method in which communications are analyzed in a systematic, objective, and quantitative manner to produce new data.

CONTENT VALIDITY The extent to which the content of a measuring instrument reflects the concept that is being measured and in fact measures that concept and not another.

CONTEXTUAL DATA Empirical or subjective data that reflect the circumstances of the problem and help to explain the outcome or score.

CONTEXTUAL DETAIL The particulars of the environment in which the case (or unit of analysis) is embedded; provides a basis for understanding and interpreting case study data and results.

CONTRADICTORY EVIDENCE Identifying themes and categories that raise questions about the conclusions reached at the end of qualitative data analysis; outliers or extreme cases that are inconsistent or contradict the conclusions drawn from qualitative data; also called negative evidence.

CONTRIBUTING PARTNER A social work role in which the social worker joins forces with others who perform different roles in positivist and interpretive research studies.

CONTROL GROUP A group whose characteristics are similar to those of a program's participants but who do not receive the program services, products, or activities being evaluated. Participants are randomly assigned to either the experimental group (those receiving program services) or the control group. A control group is used to assess the effect of program activities on participants who are receiving the services, products, or activities being evaluated. The same data are collected for people in the control group and those in the experimental group.

CONTROL VARIABLE A variable, other than the independent variable(s) of primary interest, whose effects we can determine; an intervening variable that has been controlled for in the study's research design.

CONVENIENCE SAMPLING A nonprobability sampling procedure that relies on the closest and most available research/evaluation participants to constitute a sample.

CONVERGENT VALIDITY The degree to which different measures of a construct yield similar results, or converge.

CORRELATED VARIABLES Variables whose values are associated; values of one variable tend to be associated in a systematic way with values in the others.

COST-BENEFIT ANALYSIS An analytical procedure that not only determines the costs of the program itself but also considers the monetary benefits of the program's effects.

COST-EFFECTIVE When a social service program is able to achieve its program objectives in relation to its costs.

COST-EFFECTIVENESS ANALYSIS An analytical procedure that assesses the costs of the program itself; the monetary benefits of the program's effects are not assessed.

COST-EFFICIENT When a social service program is able to achieve its program objectives at less cost, compared to another program striving for the same objectives.

COVER LETTER A letter to respondents or research participants that is written under the official letterhead of the sponsoring organization and describes the research study and its purpose.

CREDIBILITY The trustworthiness of both the steps taken in qualitative data analysis and the conclusions reached.

CRITERION VALIDITY The degree to which the scores obtained on a measuring instrument are comparable to scores from an external criterion believed to measure the same concept.

CRITERION VARIABLE The variable whose values are predicted from measurements of the predictor variable.

CROSS SECTIONAL ANALYSIS When data are collected from a different group of clients at specified data collection points (e.g., program intake and exit) in an evaluation.

CROSS-CULTURAL COMPARISONS Research studies that include culture as a major variable; studies that compare two or more diverse cultural groups.

CROSS-EVALUATION STRATEGY As used in this book, this term refers to a strategy for assessing the mix, sequence, timing, and efficiencies across all priority evaluations.

CROSS-SECTIONAL RESEARCH DESIGN A survey research design in which data are collected to indicate characteristics of a sample or population at a particular moment in time.

CROSS-TABULATION TABLE A simple table showing the joint frequency distribution of two or more nominal level variables.

CULTURAL ENCAPSULATION The assumption that differences between groups represent some deficit or pathology.

CULTURAL RELATIVITY The belief that human thought and action can be judged only from the perspective of the culture out of which they have grown.

CULTURALLY EQUIVALENT Similarity in the meaning of a construct between two cultures.

CUT-AND-PASTE METHOD A method of analyzing qualitative data whereby the researcher cuts segments of the typed transcript and sorts these cuttings into relevant groupings; it can be done manually or with computer assistance.

D INDEX A measure of effect size in a meta-analysis.

DIRECTIONAL HYPOTHESIS *See* One-tailed hypotheses.

DIRECTIONAL TEST *See* One-tailed hypotheses.

DATA Isolated facts, presented in numerical or descriptive form, on which client or program decisions are based; not to be confused with information.

DATA ANALYSES The process of turning data into information; the process of reviewing, summarizing, and organizing isolated facts (data) such that they formulate a meaningful response to a research question.

DATA ARCHIVE A place where many data sets are stored and from which data can be accessed.

DATA CODING Translating data from one language or format into another, usually to make it readable for a computer.

DATA COLLECTION METHOD The way facts about a program and its outcomes are amassed. Data collection methods often used in program evaluations include literature search, file review, natural observations, surveys, expert opinion, and case studies.

DATA DISPLAY The manner in which collected data are set out on a page.

DATA SET A collection of related data items, such as the answers given by respondents to all the questions in a survey.

DATA SOURCES People or records that are the suppliers of data.

DATUM Singular of data.

DECISION DATA CHART A chart that lists, in chronological order, decisions to be made, the data needed to make each decision, and the data actually collected; used to ensure that adequate links exist between the data collected and the decisions made.

DECISION-MAKING RULE A statement that we use (in testing a hypothesis) to choose between the null hypothesis; indicates the range(s) of values of the observed statistic that leads to the rejection of the null hypothesis.

DEDUCTION A conclusion about a specific case(s) based on the assumption that it shares a characteristic with an entire class of similar cases.

DEDUCTIVE REASONING Forming a theory, making a deduction from the theory, and testing this deduction, or hypothesis, against reality; in research, applied to theory in order to arrive at a hypothesis that can be tested; a method of reasoning whereby a conclusion about specific cases is reached based on the assumption that they share characteristics with an entire class of similar cases.

DEMAND NEEDS When needs are defined by only those individuals who indicate that they feel or perceive the need themselves.

DEMANDS In needs assessment, something that is so desired by people that they are willing to "march" for it; to be differentiated from needs and wants.

DEMOGRAPHIC DATA Vital and social facts that describe a sample or a population.

DEMORALIZATION Feelings of deprivation among control group members that may cause them to drop out of a research study; a threat to internal validity.

DEMORALIZATION Feelings of deprivation among control group clients that may cause them to drop out of the evaluation study; a form of mortality that is a threat to internal validity.

DEPENDABILITY The soundness of both the steps taken in a qualitative data analysis and the conclusions reached.

DEPENDENT EVENTS Events that influence the probability of occurrence of each other.

DEPENDENT VARIABLE A variable that is dependent on, or caused by, another variable; an outcome variable, which is not manipulated directly but is measured to determine whether the independent variable has had an effect.

DERIVED SCORES Raw scores of research participants, or groups, converted in such a way that meaningful comparisons with other individuals, or groups, are possible.

DESCRIPTIVE DESIGN A design that approximates a true experiment, but in which the worker does not have the same degree of control over manipulation of the intervention process; also known as quasi experimental designs.

DESCRIPTIVE RESEARCH Research studies undertaken to increase precision in the definition of knowledge in a problem area where less is known than at the explanatory level; situated in the middle of the knowledge continuum.

DESCRIPTIVE STATISTICS Methods used for summarizing and describing data in a clear and precise manner.

DESIGN BIAS Any effect that systematically distorts the outcome of a research study so that the study's results are not representative of the phenomenon under investigation.

DETERMINISM A contention in positivist research studies that only an event that is true over time and place and that will occur independent of beliefs about it (a predetermined event) permits the generalization of a study's findings; one of the four main limitations of the positivist research approach.

DETERMINISTIC CAUSATION When a particular effect appears, the associated cause is always present; no other variables influence the relationship between cause and effect; the link between an independent variable that brings about the occurrence of the dependent variable every time.

DICHOTOMOUS VARIABLE A variable that can take on only one of two values.

DIFFERENTIAL SCALE A questionnaire-type scale in which respondents are asked to consider questions representing different positions along a continuum and to select those with which they agree.

DIFFERENTIAL SELECTION A potential lack of equivalency among preformed groups of research participants; a threat to internal validity.

DIFFUSION OF TREATMENTS Problems that may occur when experimental and control group members talk to each other about a research study; a threat to internal validity.

DIRECT OBSERVATION An obtrusive data collection method in which the focus is entirely on the behaviors of a group, or persons, being observed.

DIRECT OBSERVATION NOTES These are the first level of field notes, usually chronologically organized, and they contain a detailed description of what was seen and heard; they may also include summary notes made after an interview.

DIRECT RELATIONSHIP A relationship between two variables such that high values of one variable are found with high values of the second variable, and vice versa.

DISCRIMINANT VALIDITY The degree to which a construct can be empirically differentiated, or discriminated, from other constructs.

DIVERGENT VALIDITY The extent to which a measuring instrument differs from other instruments that measure unrelated constructs.

DOUBLE-BARRELED QUESTION A question in a measuring instrument that contains two questions in one, usually joined by an "and" or an "or."

DURATION RECORDING A method of data collection that includes direct observation of the target problem and recording of the length of time each occurrence lasts within a specified observation period.

ECOLOGICAL FALLACY An error of reasoning committed by coming to conclusions about individuals based only on data about groups.

EDGE CODING Adding a series of blank lines on the right side of the response category in a measuring instrument to aid in processing the data.

EFFECT SIZE In meta-analysis, the most widely used measure of the dependent variable; the effect size statistic provides a measure of the magnitude of the relationship found between the variables of interest and allows for the computation of summary statistics that apply to the analysis of all the studies considered as a whole.

EFFICIENCY ASSESSMENT An evaluation to determine the ratio of effectiveness or outcome to cost; does not contain data that may explain why the program is or is not efficient.

EMPIRICAL DATA Isolated facts presented in numerical or descriptive form that have been derived from observation or testing, as opposed to data derived from inference or theory.

EMPIRICAL Knowledge derived from one of the ways of knowing.

EMPIRICAL EVALUATION A method of appraisal based on the analysis of data collected by measuring instruments.

ERROR OF CENTRAL TENDENCY A measurement error due to the tendency of observers to rate respondents in the middle of a variable's value range, rather than consistently too high or too low.

ERROR OF MEASUREMENT *See* Measurement error.

ETHICAL EVALUATION PROJECT The systematic inquiry into a problem area in an effort to discover new knowledge or test existing ideas; the research study is conducted in accordance with professional standards.

ETHICS The moral practice of evaluation or the "code of right and wrong" for deciding how to handle data, how to interact with clients, and how to proceed in politically charged situations.

ETHICS IN RESEARCH Positivist and interpretive data that are collected and analyzed with careful attention to their accuracy, fidelity to logic, and respect for the feelings and rights of research participants; one of the four criteria for evaluating research problem areas and formulating research questions out of the problem areas.

ETHNICITY Implying a common ancestry and cultural heritage and encompassing customs, values, beliefs, and behaviors.

ETHNOCENTRICITY Assumptions about normal behavior that are based on one's own cultural framework without taking cultural relativity into account; the failure to acknowledge alternative worldviews.

ETHNOGRAPH A computer software program that is designed for qualitative data analyses.

ETHNOGRAPHIC A form of content analysis used to document and explain the communication of meaning, as well as to verify theoretical relationships; any of several methods of describing social or cultural life based on direct, systematic observation, such as becoming a participant in a social system.

ETHNOGRAPHY The systematic study of human cultures and the similarities and dissimilarities between them.

ETHNOMETHODOLOGY Pioneered by Harold Garfinkel, this method of research focuses on the commonsense understanding of social life held by ordinary people (the ethos), usually as discovered through participant observation; often the observer's own methods of making sense of the situation become the object of investigation.

EVALUABILITY ASSESSMENT An appraisal of a program's components and operations intended to determine whether a program can, in fact, be evaluated for outcome, efficiency, or process; mainly used to construct meaningful and measurable program objectives that are derived from the program's goal.

EVALUATION A form of appraisal using valid and reliable research methods; there are numerous types of evaluations geared to produce data that in turn produce information that helps in the decision-making process; data from evaluations are used to develop quality programs and services.

EVALUATION CANDIDATE As used in this book, this term refers to any program activity, initiative, or product that could be evaluated. A priority evaluation candidate is a program activity, initiative, or product that has been ranked (through a systematic process) as high priority for evaluation.

EVALUATION DESIGN The general conceptual framework used to develop the evaluation plan and guide the data collection to arrive at conclusions about the implementation of the program and the achievement of intended outcomes, including the logic model, the evaluation focus, and the protocol for collecting and analyzing data.

EVALUATION PLAN A written document describing the overall approach that will be used to guide an evaluation, including why the evaluation is being conducted, how the findings will likely be used, and the design and data collection sources and methods. The plan specifies what will be done, how it will be done, who will do it, and when it will be done.

EVALUATION PLANNING TEAM As used in this book, this term refers to a small group of evaluation stakeholders convened by your program to develop and regularly update your evaluation plan.

EVALUATION QUESTION A question related to a program's outcomes, outputs, indicators, or other definition of success. The goal of an evaluation's effort is to answer one or more evaluation question(s).

EVALUATION STANDARDS Developed by the Joint Committee on Standards for Educational Evaluation, evaluation standards are criteria upon which the quality of program evaluations can be judged. *See* Accuracy, Feasibility, Propriety, Utility.

EVALUATIVE RESEARCH DESIGNS Case- and program-level research designs that apply various research designs and data collection methods to find out whether an intervention (or treatment) worked at the case level and whether the social work program worked at the program level.

EXISTING DOCUMENTS Physical records left over from the past.

EXISTING STATISTICS Previously calculated numerical summaries of data that exist in the public domain.

EXPERIENCE AND INTUITION Learning what is true through personal past experiences and intuition; two of the ways of knowing.

EXPERIMENT A research study in which we have control over the levels of the independent variable and over the assignment of research participants, or objects, to different experimental conditions.

EXPERIMENTAL DESIGNS (1) Explanatory research designs or "ideal experiments"; (2) Case-level research designs that examine the question, "Did the client system improve because of social work intervention?"

EXPERIMENTAL GROUP In an experimental research design, the group of research participants exposed to the manipulation of the independent variable; also referred to as a treatment group.

EXPLANATORY DESIGN An attempt to demonstrate with certainty that specific activities caused specific reported changes in practice objectives. The professional manipulates certain factors in the intervention to gain a greater degree of control over the proceedings; also known as experimental designs.

EXPLANATORY RESEARCH "Ideal" research studies undertaken to infer cause–effect and directional relationships in areas where a number of substantial research findings are already in place; situated at the top end of the knowledge continuum.

EXPLORATORY DESIGN A process in which a professional assesses the effects of an intervention process for the purpose of building a foundation of general ideas and tentative theories that can later be examined by more rigorous evaluative methods.

EXPLORATORY RESEARCH Research studies undertaken to gather data in areas of inquiry where very little is already known; situated at the lowest end of the knowledge continuum. *See* Nonexperimental designs.

EXPRESSED NEEDS In needs assessment, the opinions and views of people who are directly experiencing a problem; also known as felt needs.

EXTERNAL EVALUATION An evaluation that is conducted by someone who does not have any connection with the program; usually an evaluation that is requested by the agency's funding sources; this type of evaluation complements an in-house evaluation.

EXTERNAL EVALUATION An evaluation that is conducted by someone who does not have any connection with the program; usually an evaluation that is requested by the agency's funding sources. This type of evaluation complements an internal evaluation.

EXTERNAL EVALUATOR An evaluator not affiliated with the agency prior to the program evaluation. Also known as third-party evaluator or outside evaluator.

EXTERNAL VALIDITY The extent to which the findings of a research study can be generalized outside the specific evaluation situation.

EXTRANEOUS VARIABLES *See* Rival hypothesis.

EXTRANEOUS VARIABLES Outside factors that occur at the same time as the intervention and thus may account for some of the measured change in practice objectives.

FACE VALIDITY The degree to which a measurement has self-evident meaning and measures what it appears to measure.

FACILITATIVE PRACTICE OBJECTIVE An objective that relates to the overall practice objective (it can be termed a practice subobjective); it also specifies an intended result and makes the achievement of the practice objective easier; constructed for the client's benefit.

FAIRNESS A standard of evaluation practice that requires evaluations to be conducted in a fair and ethical manner; includes the dissemination of evaluation results.

FEASIBILITY A standard of evaluation practice that requires evaluations to be conducted only under conditions that are practical and economically viable.

FEASIBILITY One of the program evaluation standards developed by the Joint Committee on Standards for Educational Evaluation. The feasibility standards are intended to ensure that an evaluation will be realistic, prudent, diplomatic, and frugal. *See* also Accuracy, Propriety, Utility.

FEEDBACK When data and information are returned to the persons who originally provided or collected them; used for informed decision-making at the case and program levels; a basic principle underlying the design of evaluations.

FIELD ERROR A type of nonsampling error in which field staff show bias in their selection of a sample.

FIELD NOTES A record, usually written, of events observed by a researcher; the notes are taken as the study proceeds, and later they are used for analyses.

FIELD RESEARCH Research conducted in a real-life setting, not in a laboratory; the researcher neither creates nor manipulates anything within the study but observes it.

FIELD-TESTED The pilot of an instrument or research method in conditions equivalent to those that will be encountered in the research study.

FILE DRAWER PROBLEM (1) In literature searches or reviews, the difficulty in locating studies that have not been published or are not easily retrievable; (2) In meta-analyses, errors in effect size due to reliance on published articles showing statistical significance.

FIRST-LEVEL CODING A process of identifying meaning units in a transcript, organizing the meaning units into categories, and assigning names to the categories.

FIRSTHAND DATA Data obtained from people who directly experience the problem being studied.

FLEXIBILITY The degree to which the design and procedures of a research study can be changed to adapt to contextual demands of the research setting.

FLOW CHART A diagram of client service delivery in which symbols are used to depict client movement throughout the service delivery system.

FOCUS GROUPS A group of people brought together to talk about their lives and experiences in a free-flowing, open-ended discussion which typically focuses on a single topic; a semistructured group interview.

FOLLOW-UP DATA Collecting client data (as measured by a program's objectives) at specific points after clients have exited the program (e.g., three months, six months, one year).

FORMAL CASE-LEVEL EVALUATION An empirical method of appraisal in which a single client is monitored via repeated measurements over time in order to examine change in a practice objective.

FORMATIVE EVALUATION A type of evaluation that focuses on obtaining data that are helpful in planning the program and in improving its implementation and performance.

FREQUENCY RECORDING A method of data collection by direct observations in which each occurrence of the target problem is recorded during a specified observation period.

FUGITIVE DATA Informal information found outside regular publishing channels.

GAINING ACCESS A term used in interpretive research to describe the process of engagement and relationship development between the researcher and the research participants.

GENERALIZABILITY Extending or applying the findings of an evaluation study to clients or situations that were not directly evaluated.

GENERALIZABLE EXPLANATION EVALUATION MODEL An evaluation model whose proponents believe that many solutions are possible for any one social problem and that the effects of programs will differ under different conditions.

GENERALIZING RESULTS Extending or applying the findings of a research study to individuals or situations not directly involved in the original research study; the ability to extend or apply the findings of a research study to subjects or situations that were not directly investigated.

GOAL A desired state of affairs that outlines the ultimate purpose of a program. This is the end toward which all program efforts are directed.

GOAL ATTAINMENT SCALE (GAS) A modified measurement scale used to evaluate case- or program-level outcomes.

GOVERNMENT DOCUMENTS Printed documents issued by local, state, and federal governments; such documents include reports of legislative committee hearings and investigations, studies commissioned by legislative commissions and executive agencies, statistical compilations such as the census, the regular and special reports of executive agencies, and much more.

GRAND TOUR QUESTIONS Queries in which research participants are asked to provide wide-ranging background information; mainly used in interpretive research studies.

GRAPHIC RATING SCALE A rating scale that describes an attribute on a continuum from one extreme to the other, with points of the continuum ordered in equal intervals and then assigned values.

GROUNDED THEORY A final outcome of the interpretive research process that is reached when the insights are grounded on observations and the conclusions seem to be firm.

GROUP EVALUATION DESIGNS Evaluation designs that are conducted with groups of cases for the purpose of assessing to what degree program objectives have been achieved.

GROUP RESEARCH DESIGNS Research designs conducted with two or more groups of cases, or research participants, for the purpose of answering research questions or testing hypotheses.

HALO EFFECT A measurement error due to the tendency of an observer to be influenced by a favorable trait(s) of a research participant(s).

HAWTHORNE EFFECT Effects on research participants' behaviors or attitudes attributable to their knowledge that they are taking part in a research study; a reactive effect; a threat to external validity.

HETEROGENEITY OF RESPONDENTS The extent to which a research participant differs from other research participants.

HEURISTIC A theory used to stimulate creative thought and scientific activity.

HISTORICAL RESEARCH The process by which we study the past; a method of inquiry that attempts to explain past events based on surviving artifacts.

HISTORY IN EVALUATION DESIGN The possibility that events not accounted for in a research design may alter the second and subsequent measurements of the dependent variable; a threat to internal validity.

HOMOGENEITY OF RESPONDENTS The extent to which a research participant is similar to other research participants.

HYPOTHESIS A theory based prediction of the expected results in an evaluation study; a tentative explanation of a relationship or supposition that a relationship may exist.

HYPOTHETICO-DEDUCTIVE METHOD A hypothesis-testing approach that a hypothesis is derived on the deductions based from a theory.

IDEOGRAPHIC RESEARCH Research studies that focus on unique individuals or situations.

IMPLEMENTATION OF A PROGRAM The action of carrying out a program in the way that it was designed.

INDEPENDENT VARIABLE A variable that is not dependent on another variable but is believed to cause or determine changes in the dependent variable; an antecedent variable that is directly manipulated in order to assess its effect on the dependent variable.

IMPACT The effect that interventions or programs have on people, organizations, or systems to influence health. While often used to refer to effects of a program that occur in the medium or long term, the expected impact can occur anywhere in the chain of outcomes, depending on the program.

IN-HOUSE EVALUATION An evaluation that is conducted by someone who works within a program; usually an evaluation for the purpose of promoting better client services; also known as an internal evaluation; this type of evaluation complements an external evaluation.

INDEPENDENT VARIABLE A variable that is not dependent on another variable but is said to cause or determine changes in the dependent variable; an antecedent variable that is directly manipulated in order to assess its effect on the dependent variable. Interventions are independent variables.

INDEX A group of individual measures that, when combined, are meant to indicate some more general characteristic.

INDICATOR A specific, observable, and measurable characteristic or change that shows the progress a program is making toward achieving a specified outcome.

INDIGENOUS OBSERVERS People who are naturally a part of the research participants' environment and who perform the data collection function; includes relevant others (e.g., family members, peers) and collaterals (e.g., social workers, staff members).

INDIRECT MEASURES A substitute variable, or a collection of representative variables, used when there is no direct measurement of the variable of interest; also called a proxy variable.

INDIVIDUAL SYNTHESIS Analysis of published studies related to the subject under study.

INDIVIDUALISM A way of living that stresses independence, personal rather than group objectives, competition, and power in relationships; achievement measured through success of the individual as opposed to the group.

INDUCTIVE REASONING Building on specific observations of events, things, or processes to make inferences or more general statements; in research studies, applied to data collection and research results to make generalizations to see if they fit a theory; a method of reasoning whereby a conclusion is reached by building on specific observations of events, things, or processes to make inferences or more general statements.

INFERENTIAL STATISTICS Statistical methods that make it possible to draw tentative conclusions about the population based on observations of a sample selected from that population and, furthermore, to make a probability statement about those conclusions to aid in their evaluation.

INFORMATION The interpretation given to data that have been collected, collated, and analyzed; Information is used to help in the decision-making process; not to be confused with data.

INFORMATION ANXIETY A feeling attributable to a lack of understanding of information, being overwhelmed by the amount of information to be accessed and understood, or not knowing whether certain information exists.

INFORMED CONSENT Procedures in which clients, or evaluation subjects, are told in advance about the major tasks and activities they will perform during an evaluation study; clients then participate in the evaluation study only if they are willing to engage in these activities.

INPUTS Resources that go into a program in order to mount the activities successfully.

INSTITUTIONAL REVIEW BOARDS (IRB'S) Boards set up by institutions in order to protect research participants and to ensure that ethical issues are recognized and responded to in the study's research design.

INSTRUMENTAL PRACTICE OBJECTIVE An objective that bears no apparent relation to the practice objective, but when accomplished will remove practical impediments to the attainment of the practice objective; constructed for the client's benefit.

INSTRUMENTATION ERROR Weaknesses of a measuring instrument, such as invalidity, unreliability, improper administrations, or mechanical breakdowns; a threat to internal validity.

INTAKE FORM A data collection instrument that is administered to clients at or near the point of entry into a social service program. The form typically asks questions about client demographics, service history, and reasons for referral to the program.

INTEGRATION Combining evaluation and day-to-day practice activities to develop a complete approach to client service delivery; a basic principle underlying the design of evaluations.

INTERACTION EFFECT Effects on the program's objective (the dependent variable) that are produced by the combination of two or more threats to internal validity.

INTERNAL CONSISTENCY The extent to which the scores on two comparable halves of the same measuring instrument are similar; inter-item consistency.

INTERNAL EVALUATION An evaluation that is conducted by someone who works within a program; usually an evaluation for the purpose of promoting better client services. This type of evaluation complements an external evaluation.

INTERNAL EVALUATOR An evaluator who is a staff member or unit from within the organization being studied.

INTERNAL VALIDITY The extent to which it can be demonstrated that the intervention (the independent variable) in an evaluation is the only cause of change in the program's objective (the dependent variable); soundness of the experimental procedures and measuring instruments.

INTEROBSERVER RELIABILITY The stability or consistency of observations made by two or more observers at one point in time.

INTERPRETIVE NOTES Notes on the researcher's interpretations of events that are kept separate from the record of the facts noted as direct observations.

INTERPRETIVE RESEARCH APPROACH Research studies that focus on the facts of nature as they occur under natural conditions and emphasize qualitative description and generalization; a process of discovery sensitive to holistic and ecological issues; a research approach that is complementary to the positivist research approach.

INTERQUARTILE RANGE A number that measures the variability of a data set; the distance between the 75th and 25th percentiles.

INTERRATER RELIABILITY The degree to which two or more independent observers, coders, or judges produce consistent results.

INTERRUPTED TIME SERIES DESIGN A descriptive evaluation design in which there is only one group and the program objective (the dependent variable) is measured repeatedly before and after the intervention (the independent variable).

INTERVAL LEVEL OF MEASUREMENT The level of measurement with an arbitrarily chosen zero point that classifies its values on an equally spaced continuum.

INTERVAL RECORDING A method of data collection that involves continuous, direct observation and documentation of an individual's behavior during specified observation periods divided into equal time intervals.

INTERVENING VARIABLE *See* Rival hypothesis.

INTERVIEW DATA Isolated facts that are gathered when research participants respond to carefully constructed research questions; data, which are in the form of words, are recorded by transcription.

INTERVIEW SCHEDULE A measuring instrument used to collect data in face-to-face and telephone interviews.

INTERVIEWING A conversation with a purpose.

INTRAOBSERVER RELIABILITY The stability of observations made by a single observer at several points in time.

INTRUSION INTO LIVES OF RESEARCH PARTICIPANTS The understanding that specific data collection methods can have negative consequences for research participants; a criterion for selecting a data collection method.

ITEMIZED RATING SCALES A measuring instrument that presents a series of statements that respondents or observers rank in different positions on a specific attribute.

JOURNAL A written record of the process of an interpretive research study. Journal entries are made on an ongoing basis throughout the study and include study procedures as well as the researcher's reactions to emerging issues and concerns during the data analysis process.

KEY INFORMANTS A subpopulation of research participants who seem to know much more about "the situation" than other research participants.

KEY INFORMANTS Individuals who are considered knowledgeable about the social problem that is being investigated and who provide new or original data through interviews. Examples are professionals, public officials, agency directors, social service clients, and select citizens.

KNOWLEDGE BASE A body of knowledge and skills specific to a certain discipline.

KNOWLEDGE CREATOR AND DISSEMINATOR A social work role in which the social worker actually carries out and disseminates the results of a positivist and/or interpretive research study to generate knowledge for our profession.

KNOWLEDGE PROGRAM OBJECTIVE An objective that aims to change a client's level of information and understanding about a specific social area.

KNOWLEDGE-LEVEL CONTINUUM The range of knowledge levels, from exploratory to descriptive to explanatory, at which research studies can be conducted.

LATENT CONTENT In a content analysis, the true meaning, depth, or intensity of a variable, or concept, under study.

LEVELS OF MEASUREMENT The degree to which characteristics of a data set can be modeled mathematically; the higher the level of measurement, the more statistical methods that are applicable.

LIMITED REVIEW An existing literature synthesis that summarizes in narrative form the findings and implications of a few research studies.

LITERATURE REVIEW *See* Literature search, Review of the literature.

LITERATURE SEARCH In a meta-analysis, scanning books and journals for basic, up-to-date research articles on studies relevant to a research question or hypothesis; sufficiently thorough to maximize the chance of including all relevant sources. *See* Review of the literature.

LOGIC MODEL A systematic and visual way to present the perceived relationships among the resources you have to operate the program, the activities you plan to do, and the changes or results you hope to achieve.

LOGICAL CONSISTENCY The requirement that all the steps within a positivist research study must be logically related to one another.

LOGICAL POSITIVISM A philosophy of science holding that the scientific method of inquiry is the only source of certain knowledge; in research, focuses on testing hypotheses deduced from theory.

LOGISTICS In evaluation, refers to getting research participants to do what they are supposed to do, getting research instruments distributed and returned; in general, the activities that ensure that procedural tasks of a research or evaluation study are carried out.

LONGEVITY In outcome evaluation, when client gains (as measured by a program's objectives) are maintained for a period of time after clients have exited the program (e.g., three months, six months, one year follow-up).

LONGITUDINAL CASE STUDY An exploratory research design in which there is only one group of research participants and the dependent variable is measured more than once.

LONGITUDINAL CASE-STUDY DESIGN An exploratory research design in which there is only one group and the program's objective (the dependent variable) is measured more than once; also referred to as a panel design, a cohort design, a developmental design, or a dynamic case study design.

LONGITUDINAL DESIGN A survey research design in which a measuring instrument(s) is administered to a sample of research participants repeatedly over time; used to detect dynamic processes such as opinion change.

MAGNITUDE RECORDING A method of data collection that involves direct observation and documentation of the amount, level, or degree of the practice objective during each occurrence.

MAINTENANCE PROGRAM OBJECTIVE An objective formulated in an effort to keep a program financially viable; constructed for the program's benefit.

MANAGEMENT INFORMATION SYSTEM (MIS) System in which computer technology is used to process, store, retrieve, and analyze data collected routinely in such processes as social service delivery.

MANIFEST CONTENT Content of a communication that is obvious and clearly evident.

MANIPULABLE SOLUTION EVALUATION MODEL An evaluation model whose proponents believe that the greatest priority is to serve the public interest, not the interests of stakeholders, who have vested interests in the program being evaluated; closely resembles an outcome evaluation.

MANUAL DATA MANAGEMENT Noncomputerized method of organizing single units of data to generate summarized or aggregate forms of the data.

MATCHED PAIRS METHOD A technique of assigning clients to groups so that the experimental and control groups are approximately equivalent in pretest scores or other characteristics, or so that all differences except the experimental condition are eliminated.

MATURATION Any unplanned change in clients due to mental, physical, or other processes that take place over the course of the evaluation project and which affect the program's objective; a threat to internal validity.

MEANING UNITS In a qualitative data analysis, a discrete segment of a transcript that can stand alone as a single idea; can consist of a single word, a partial or complete sentence, a paragraph, or more; used as the basic building blocks for developing categories.

MEASURE A label, usually numerical, assigned to an observation that has been subjected to measurement.

MEASUREMENT ERROR Any variation in measurement that cannot be attributed to the variable being measured; variability in responses produced by individual differences and other extraneous variables.

MEASUREMENT The process of systematically assigning labels to observations; in statistics, measurement systems are classified according to level of measurement and usually produce data that can be represented in numerical form; the assignment of numerals to objects or events according to specific rules.

MEASURING INSTRUMENT Any instrument used to measure a variable(s).

MEDIA MYTHS The content of television shows, movies, and newspaper and magazine articles; one of the ways of knowing.

MEMBER CHECKING A process of obtaining feedback and comments from research participants on interpretations and conclusions made from the qualitative data they provided; asking research participants to confirm or refute the conclusions made.

META-ANALYSIS A research method in which mathematical procedures are applied to the positivist findings of studies located in a literature search to produce new summary statistics and to describe the findings for a meta-analysis.

METHODOLOGY The procedures and rules that detail how a single research study is conducted.

MICRO-LEVEL DATA Data derived from individual units of analysis, whether these data sources are individuals, families, corporations, etc.; for example, age and years of formal schooling are two variables requiring micro-level data.

MISSING DATA Data not available for a research participant about whom other data are available, such as when a respondent fails to answer one of the questions in a survey.

MISSING LINKS When two categories or themes seem to be related, but not directly so, it may be that a third variable connects the two.

MISSION STATEMENT A unique written philosophical perspective of what an agency is all about; states a common vision for the organization by providing a point of reference for all major planning decisions.

MIXED RESEARCH MODEL A model combining aspects of interpretive and positivist research approaches within all (or many) of the methodological steps contained within a single research study.

MONITORING (program monitoring): The systematic collection and analysis of information as a project or program progresses to inform program management on the implementation, efficiency, and effectiveness of a program.

MONITORING APPROACH TO QUALITY IMPROVEMENT An evaluation that aims to provide ongoing feedback so that a program (or project) can be improved while it is still underway; contributes to the continuous development and improvement of a human service program. This approach complements the project approach.

MONITORING SYSTEM The evaluation design, protocols, and procedures that ensure systematic, complete, and accurate data collection; also includes a schedule for reporting and disseminating evaluation findings.

MORTALITY The tendency for clients to drop out of an evaluation study before it is completed; a threat to internal validity.

MULTICULTURAL RESEARCH Representation of diverse cultural factors in the subjects of study; such diversity variables may include religion, race, ethnicity, language preference, gender, etc.

MULTIGROUP POSTTEST ONLY DESIGN An exploratory research design in which there is more than one group and the program's objective (the dependent variable) is measured only once for each group.

MULTIPLE TREATMENT INTERFERENCE When a client is given two or more interventions in succession and the results of the first intervention may affect the results of the second or subsequent interventions; a threat to external validity.

MULTIPLE-BASELINE DESIGN A case-level evaluation design with more than one baseline period and intervention phase, which allows the causal inferences regarding the relationship between a treatment intervention and its effect on clients' target problems and which helps control for extraneous variables. *See* Interrupted time-series design.

MULTIPLE-GROUP DESIGN An experimental research design with one control group and several experimental groups.

MULTIPLE-TREATMENT INTERFERENCE Effects of the results of a first treatment on the results of second and subsequent treatments; a threat to external validity.

MULTISTAGE PROBABILITY SAMPLING Probability sampling procedures used when a comprehensive list of a population does not exist and it is not possible to construct one.

MULTIVARIATE (1) A relationship involving two or more variables; (2) A hypothesis stating an assertion about two or more variables and how they relate to one another.

MULTIVARIATE ANALYSIS A statistical analysis of the relationship among three or more variables.

NARROWBAND MEASURING INSTRUMENT Measuring instruments that focus on a single, or a few, variables.

NATIONALITY A term that refers to country of origin.

NATURALIST A person who studies the facts of nature as they occur under natural conditions.

NEEDS In needs assessment, something that is considered a basic requirement necessary to sustain the human condition; to be differentiated from demands and wants.

NEEDS ASSESSMENT Program-level evaluation activities that aim to assess the feasibility for establishing or continuing a particular social service program; an evaluation that aims to assess the need for a human service by verifying that a social problem exists within a specific client population to an extent that warrants services.

NEGATIVE CASE SAMPLING Purposefully selecting research participants based on the fact that they have different characteristics than previous cases.

NOMINAL GROUPS TECHNIQUE A group of people brought together to share their knowledge about a specific social problem. The process is structured using a round-robin approach and permits individuals to share their ideas within a group but with little interaction between group members; a structured group interview.

NOMINAL LEVEL OF MEASUREMENT The level of measurement that classifies variables by assigning names or categories that are mutually exclusive and exhaustive.

NONEXPERIMENTAL DESIGN An evaluation design in which participant data are gathered either before and after the program intervention or only afterwards. A control group is not used. Therefore, this design does not allow you to determine whether the program or other factors are responsible for producing a given change.

NONDIRECTIONAL TEST *See* Two-tailed hypotheses.

NONEMPIRICAL EVALUATION An informal method of appraisal that is not based on empirical data. It depends on theories and descriptions that a professional considers to be relevant to the case.

NONEXPERIMENTAL DESIGN A research design at the exploratory, or lowest, level of the knowledge continuum; also called preexperimental.

NONOCCURRENCE DATA In the structured-observation method of data collection, a recording of only those time intervals in which the target problem did not occur.

NONPARAMETRIC TESTS Refers to statistical tests of hypotheses about population probability distributions, but not about specific parameters of the distributions.

NONPROBABILITY SAMPLING Sampling procedures in which all of the persons, events, or objects in the sampling frame have an unknown, and usually unequal, chance of being included in a sample.

NONREACTIVE Methods of research that do not allow the research participants to know that they are being studied; thus, they do not alter their responses for the benefit of the researcher.

NONREACTIVITY An unobtrusive characteristic of a measuring instrument. Nonreactive measuring instruments do not affect the behavior being measured.

NONRESPONSE The rate of nonresponse in survey research is calculated by dividing the total number of respondents by the total number in the sample, minus any units verified as ineligible.

NONSAMPLING ERRORS Errors in an evaluation study's results that are not due to the sampling procedures.

NONSAMPLING ERRORS Errors in study results that are not due to sampling procedures.

NORM In measurement, an average or set group standard of achievement that can be used to interpret individual scores; normative data describing statistical properties of a measuring instrument, such as means and standard deviations.

NORMALIZATION GROUP The population sample to which a measuring instrument under development is administered in order to establish norms; also called the norm group.

NORMATIVE NEEDS When needs are defined by comparing the objective living conditions of a target population with what society—or, at least, that segment of society concerned with helping the target population—deems acceptable or desirable from a humanitarian standpoint.

NULL HYPOTHESIS A statement concerning one or more parameters that is subjected to a statistical test; a statement that there is no relationship between the two variables of interest.

NUMBERS The basic data unit of analysis used in positivist research studies.

OBJECTIVITY A research stance in which a study is carried out and its data are examined and interpreted without distortion by personal feelings or biases.

OBSERVER One of four roles on a continuum of participation in participant observation research; the level of involvement of the observer participant is lower than of the complete participant and higher than of the participant observer.

OBTRUSIVE DATA COLLECTION METHODS Direct data collection methods that can influence the variables under study or the responses of research participants; data collection methods that produce reactive effects.

OCCURRENCE DATA In the structured-observation method of data collection, a recording of the first occurrence of the target problem during each time interval.

ONE-STAGE PROBABILITY SAMPLING Probability sampling procedures in which the selection of a sample from a population is completed in one single process.

ONE-GROUP POSTTEST-ONLY DESIGN An exploratory research design in which the dependent variable is measured only once.

ONE-GROUP PRETEST–POSTTEST DESIGN A descriptive research design in which the dependent variable is measured twice—before and after treatment.

ONE-STAGE PROBABILITY SAMPLING Probability sampling procedures in which the selection of a sample that is drawn from a specific population is completed in a single process.

ONE-TAILED HYPOTHESES Statements that predict specific relationships between independent and dependent variables.

ONLINE SOURCES Computerized literary retrieval systems that provide printouts of indexes and abstracts.

OPEN-ENDED QUESTIONS Unstructured questions in which the response categories are not specified or detailed.

OPERATIONAL DEFINITION Explicit specification of a variable in such a way that its measurement is possible.

OPERATIONALIZATION The explicit specification of a program's objectives in such a way that the measurement of each objective is possible.

ORDINAL LEVEL OF MEASUREMENT The level of measurement that classifies variables by rank-ordering them from high to low or from most to least.

OUTCOME The results of program operations or activities; the effects triggered by the program (e.g., increased knowledge levels, skills, attitudes, affects, behaviors)

OUTCOME ASSESSMENT *See* Outcome evaluation.

OUTCOME EVALUATION The systematic collection of data to assess the impact of a program, present conclusions about the merit or worth of a program, and make recommendations about future program direction or improvement.

OUTCOME MEASURE The criterion or basis for measuring effects of the independent variable or change in the dependent variable.

OUTCOME-ORIENTED CASE STUDY A type of case study that investigates whether client outcomes were in fact achieved.

OUTPUTS The direct products of program's activities; immediate measures of what the program did, or produced.

OUTSIDE OBSERVERS Trained observers who are not a part of the research participants' environment and who are brought in to record data.

PAIRED OBSERVATIONS An observation on two variables, where the intent is to examine the relationship between them.

PANEL RESEARCH STUDY A longitudinal survey design in which the same group of research participants (the panel) is followed over time by surveying them on successive occasions.

PARAMETRIC TESTS Statistical methods for estimating parameters or testing hypotheses about population parameters.

PARTICIPANT OBSERVATION An obtrusive data collection method in which the researcher, or the observer, participates in the life of those being observed; both an obtrusive data collection method and a research approach, this method is characterized by the one doing the study undertaking roles that involve establishing and maintaining ongoing relationships with research participants who are often in the field settings, and observing and participating with the research participants over time.

PARTICIPANT OBSERVER The participant observer is one of four roles on a continuum of participation in participant observation research; the level of involvement of the participant observer is higher than that of the complete observer and lower than that of the observer participant.

PERCEIVED NEED: In needs assessment, the opinions and views of people who are not directly experiencing a problem themselves.

PERFORMANCE APPRAISAL The process of evaluating the efficiency and effectiveness of a staff person's work; a possible misuse of evaluation practice.

PERFORMANCE CRITERIA The observable aspects of a performance or product that are observed and judged in a performance assessment.

PERFORMANCE MEASUREMENT The ongoing monitoring and reporting of a program's accomplishments, particularly progress toward preestablished goals. It's typically conducted by program or agency management. Performance measures may address the type or level of program activities conducted (process), the direct products and services delivered by a program (outputs), or the results of those products and services (outcomes).

PERFORMANCE STANDARDS A generally accepted, objective form of measurement that serves as a rule or guideline against which an organization's level of performance can be compared. Frequently referred to as benchmarks.

PERMANENT PRODUCT RECORDING A method of data collection in which the occurrence of the target problem is determined by observing the permanent product or record of the target problem.

PILOT STUDY *See* Pretest (2).

PILOT TEST Administration of a measuring instrument to a group who will not be included in the evaluation study to determine any difficulties respondents may have in answering questions and the general impression given by the instrument.

POLITICS Individual actions and policies that govern human behavior, which, in turn, influence program decisions. Politically charged situations usually have an element of self-interest.

POPULATION An entire set, or universe, of people, objects, or events of concern to a research study, from which a sample is drawn.

POSITIVISM *See* Positivist research approach.

POSITIVIST RESEARCH APPROACH A research approach to discover relationships and facts that are generalizable; research that is "independent" of subjective beliefs, feelings, wishes, and values; a research approach that is complementary to the interpretive research approach.

POSTTEST Measurement of the dependent variable after the introduction of the independent variable.

POSTTEST ONLY DESIGN A nonexperimental design in which measures (data collection) are taken from the target population(s) after the activity/intervention. Since this is a nonexperimental design, it does not involve comparison groups/control groups.

POTENTIAL FOR TESTING One of the four criteria for evaluating research hypotheses.

PRACTICE OBJECTIVE A statement of expected change identifying an intended therapeutic result tailored to the unique circumstances and needs of each client; logically linked to a program objective. Practice objectives, like program objectives, can be grouped into affects, knowledge, and behaviors.

PRACTITIONER/RESEARCHER A social worker who guides practice through the use of research findings; collects data throughout an intervention using research methods, skills, and tools; and disseminates practice findings.

PRAGMATISTS Researchers who believe that both interpretive and positivist research approaches can be integrated in a single research study.

PRE-POSTTEST DESIGN This elementary quasi-experimental design involves the measurement of "outcome indicators prior to implementation of the treatment, and subsequent remeasurement after implementation. Any change in the measure is attributed to the treatment. Also known as a Before-After Design.

PREDICTIVE VALIDITY A form of criterion validity that is concerned with the ability of a measuring instrument to predict future performance or status on the basis of present performance or status.

PREDICTOR VARIABLE The variable that, it is believed, allows us to improve our ability to predict values of the criterion variable.

PREEXPOSURE Tasks to be carried out in advance of a research study to sensitize the researcher to the culture of interest; these tasks may include participation in cultural experiences, intercultural sharing, case studies, ethnic literature reviews, value statement exercises, etc.

PRELIMINARY PLAN FOR DATA ANALYSIS A strategy for analyzing qualitative data that is outlined in the beginning stages of an interpretive research study; the plan has two general steps: (1) previewing the data, and (2) outlining what to record in the researcher's journal.

PRESENTISM Applying current thinking and concepts to interpretations of past events or intentions.

PRETEST (1) Measurement of the dependent variable prior to the introduction of the independent variable; (2) Administration of a measuring instrument to a group of people who will not be included in the study to determine difficulties the research participants may have in answering questions and the general impression given by the instrument; also called a pilot study.

PRETEST TREATMENT INTERACTION Effects of the pretest on the responses of clients to the introduction of the intervention (the independent variable); a threat to external validity.

PREVIOUS RESEARCH Research studies that have already been completed and published; they provide information about data collection methods used to investigate research questions that are similar to our own; a criterion for selecting a data collection method.

PRIMARY DATA Data in its original form, as collected from the research participants; a primary data source is one that puts as few intermediaries as possible between the production and the study of the data.

PRIMARY LANGUAGE The preferred language of the research participants.

PRIMARY REFERENCE SOURCE A report of a research study by the person who conducted the study; usually an article in a professional journal.

PRINCIPLE OF PARSIMONY A principle stating that the simplest and most economical route to evaluating the achievement of the program's objective (the dependent variable) is the best.

PRIVATE CONSULTATIONS An informal method of case evaluation in which a social worker exchanges descriptive information about a client with another worker(s) to obtain solid advice.

PROBABILITY SAMPLING Sampling procedures in which every member of a designated population has a known chance of being selected for a sample.

PROBLEM AREA In social work research, a general expressed difficulty about which something researchable is unknown; not to be confused with research question.

PROBLEM-SOLVING PROCESS A generic method with specified phases for solving problems; also described as the scientific method.

PROCESS ANALYSIS *See* Process evaluation.

PROCESS EVALUATION A type of evaluation that aims to monitor a social service program to describe and assess (1) the services provided to clients and (2) how satisfied key stakeholders are with the services provided. Data are used to provide ongoing feedback in order to refine and improve program service delivery; also known as formative evaluation.

PROCESS-ORIENTED CASE STUDY A type of case study that illuminates the microsteps of intervention that lead to client outcomes; describes how programs and interventions work and gives insight into the "black box" of intervention.

PROFESSIONAL STANDARDS Rules for making judgments about evaluation activity that are established by a group of persons who have advanced education and usually have the same occupation.

PROGRAM An organized set of political, administrative, and clinical activities that function to fulfill some social purpose.

PROGRAM DATA In evaluation, measurements systematically collected about a program's operations. Ideally, the data are collected in strict compliance with the evaluation design and procedures.

PROGRAM DEVELOPMENT The constant effort to improve program services to better achieve outcomes; a basic principle underlying the design of evaluations.

PROGRAM EFFICIENCY Assessment of a program's outcome in relation to the costs of obtaining the outcome.

PROGRAM EVALUATION The systematic collection of information about the activities characteristics, and outcomes of programs to make judgments about the program, improve program effectiveness, and/or inform decisions about future program development.

PROGRAM GOAL A statement defining the intent of a program that cannot be directly evaluated. It can, however, be evaluated indirectly by the program's objectives, which are derived from the goal. Not to be confused with program objectives.

PROGRAM IMPACT MODEL A visual representation of a program impact theory, which is the conceptual theory for how a program is presumed to solve a problem or problems of interest.

PROGRAM IMPROVEMENT Increases in quality and efficiency of program efforts, especially increases in achievement of the program's intended outcomes and impacts. "Continuous program improvement" means a systematic approach throughout the life of the program to monitor, analyze, and take action based on evaluation and performance measurement findings.

PROGRAM MONITORING A program activity comprised of the ongoing collection, analysis, reporting, and use of collected program data.

PROGRAM OBJECTIVE A statement that clearly and exactly specifies the expected change, or intended result, for individuals receiving program services. Qualities of well-chosen objectives are meaningfulness, specificity, measurability, and directionality. Program objectives, like practice objectives, can be grouped into affects, knowledge, and behaviors. Not to be confused with program goal.

PROGRAM PARTICIPATION The philosophy and structure of a program that will support or supplant the successful implementation of a research study within an existing social service program; a criterion for selecting a data collection method.

PROGRAM PATHWAYS Program pathways are the means for accomplishing program outcomes. They comprise two parts. The *impact pathway* describes how the program is expected to cause change. The *process pathway* describes how the program is implemented.

PROGRAM PROCESS The coordination of administrative and clinical activities that are designed to achieve a program's goal.

PROGRAM RESULTS A report on how effective a program is at meeting its stated objectives.

PROGRAM STRUCTURE Fixed elements of a program that are designed to support social service workers in carrying out client service delivery. Examples include: staff–worker ratio, supervision protocols, support staff, training, and salaries.

PROGRAM-LEVEL EVALUATION A form of appraisal that monitors change for groups of clients and organizational performance.

PROGRAM Any set of related activities undertaken to achieve an intended outcome. For purposes of these guidelines and recommendations, "program" is defined broadly to include policies; interventions; environmental, systems, and media initiatives; and other efforts. It also encompasses preparedness efforts as well as research, capacity, and infrastructure efforts.

PROJECT APPROACH TO EVALUATION Evaluation that aims to assess a completed or finished program; this approach complements the monitoring approach.

PROPRIETY One of the program evaluation standards developed by the Joint Committee on Standards for Educational Evaluation. The extent to which the evaluation has been conducted in a manner that evidences uncompromising adherence to the highest principles and ideals (including professional ethics, civil law, moral code, and contractual agreements). *See* also Accuracy, Feasibility, Utility.

PROXY An indirect measure of a variable that a researcher wants to study; it is often used when the variable of inquiry is difficult to measure or observe directly.

PUBLIC FORUM A group of people invited to a public meeting to voice their views about a specific social problem; an unstructured group interview.

PURE RESEARCH APPROACH A search for theoretical results that can be utilized to develop theory and expand our profession's knowledge bases; complementary to the applied research approach.

PURISTS Researchers who believe that interpretive and positivist research approaches should never be mixed.

PURPOSE STATEMENT A declaration of words that clearly describes a research study's intent.

PURPOSIVE SAMPLING A nonprobability sampling procedure in which individuals with particular characteristics are purposely selected for inclusion in the sample; also known as judgmental or theoretical sampling.

QUALITATIVE DATA Data that measure a quality or kind; when referring to variables, qualitative is another term for categorical or nominal variable values; when speaking of kinds of research, qualitative refers to studies of subjects that are hard to quantify; interpretive research produces descriptive data based on spoken or written words and observable behaviors.

QUALITATIVE DATA Data that measure quality or kind.

QUALITY IMPROVEMENT PROCESS An ethical commitment to continually look for and seek ways to make services more responsive, efficient, and effective; a process that uses the data from all types of evaluations to improve the quality of human services.

QUANTIFICATION In measurement, the reduction of data to numerical form in order to analyze them by way of mathematical or statistical techniques.

QUANTITATIVE DATA Data that measure a quantity or amount; observations that are numerical.

QUASI-EXPERIMENT A research design at the descriptive level of the knowledge continuum that resembles an "ideal" experiment but does not allow for random selection or assignment of research participants to groups and often does not control for rival hypotheses.

QUESTIONNAIRE-TYPE SCALE A type of measuring instrument in which multiple responses are usually combined to form a single overall score for a respondent.

QUOTA SAMPLING A nonprobability sampling procedure in which the relevant characteristics of a sample are identified, the proportion of these characteristics in the population is determined, and participants are selected from each category until the predetermined proportion (quota) has been achieved.

RACE A variable based on physical attributes that can be subdivided into the Caucasoid, Negroid, and Mongoloid races.

RANDOM ASSIGNMENT The process of allocating clients to experimental and control groups so that the groups are equivalent; also referred to as randomization.

RANDOM ERROR Variable error in measurement; error due to unknown or uncontrolled factors that affect the variable being measured and the process of measurement in an inconsistent fashion.

RANDOM NUMBERS TABLE A computer-generated or published table of numbers in which each number has an equal chance of appearing in each position in the table.

RANDOM SAMPLING An unbiased selection process conducted so that all members of a population have an equal chance of being selected to participate in the evaluation study.

RANDOMIZED CROSS SECTIONAL SURVEY DESIGN A descriptive research design in which there is only one group, the program's objective (the dependent variable) is measured only once, the clients are randomly selected from the population, and there is no intervention (the independent variable).

RANDOMIZED LONGITUDINAL SURVEY DESIGN A descriptive research design in which there is only one group, the dependent variable is measured more than once, and research participants are randomly selected from the population before each treatment.

RANDOMIZED LONGITUDINAL SURVEY DESIGN A descriptive research design in which there is only one group, the program's objective (the dependent variable) is measured more than once, and clients are randomly selected from the population before the intervention (the independent variable).

RANDOMIZED ONE-GROUP POSTTEST-ONLY DESIGN A descriptive research design in which there is only one group, the program's objective (the dependent variable) is measured only once, and all members of a population have equal opportunity for participation in the evaluation.

RANDOMIZED POSTTEST-ONLY CONTROL GROUP DESIGN An explanatory research design in which there are two or more randomly selected and randomly assigned groups; the control group does not receive the intervention (the independent variable), and the experimental groups receive different interventions.

RANK-ORDER SCALE A comparative rating scale in which the rater is asked to rank specific individuals in relation to one another on some characteristic.

RATING SCALES A type of measuring instrument in which responses are rated on a continuum or in an ordered set of categories, with numerical values assigned to each point or category.

RATIO LEVEL OF MEASUREMENT The level of measurement that has a nonarbitrary, fixed zero point and classifies the values of a variable on an equally spaced continuum.

RAW SCORES Scores derived from administration of a measuring instrument to research participants or groups.

REACTIVE EFFECT (1) An effect on outcome measures due to the research participants' awareness that they are being observed or interviewed; a threat to external and internal validity; (2) Alteration of the variables being measured or the respondents' performance on the measuring instrument due to administration of the instrument.

REACTIVITY The belief that things being observed or measured are affected by the fact that they are being observed or measured; one of the four main limitations of the positivist research approach.

REASSESSMENT A step in a qualitative data analysis in which the researcher interrupts the data analysis process to reaffirm the rules used to decide which meaning units are placed within different categories.

RECODING Developing and applying new variable value labels to a variable that has previously been coded; usually, recoding is done to make variables from one or more data sets comparable.

REDUCTIONISM In the positivist research approach, the operationalization of concepts by reducing them to common measurable variables; one of the four main limitations of the positivist research approach.

RELEVANCY One of the four criteria for evaluating research problem areas and formulating research questions out of the problem areas.

RELIABILITY (1) The degree of accuracy, precision, or consistency of results of a measuring instrument, including the ability to reproduce results when a variable is measured more than once or a test is repeatedly filled out by the same individual, and (2) The degree to which individual differences on scores or in data are due either to true differences or to errors in measurement.

REPEATED MEASUREMENTS The administration of one measuring instrument (or set of instruments) a number of times to the same client, under the same conditions, over a period of time.

REPLICATION Repetition of the same research procedures by a second researcher for the purpose of determining whether earlier results can be confirmed.

RESEARCH ATTITUDE A way that we view the world. It is an attitude that highly values craftsmanship, with pride in creativity, high-quality standards, and hard work.

RESEARCH CONSUMER A social work role reflecting the ethical obligation to base interventions on the most up-to-date research knowledge available.

RESEARCH DESIGN The entire plan of a positivist and/or interpretive research study from problem conceptualization to the dissemination of findings.

RESEARCH HYPOTHESIS A statement about a study's research question that predicts the existence of a particular relationship between the independent and dependent variables; can be used in both the positivist and interpretive approaches to research.

RESEARCH METHOD The use of positivist and interpretive research approaches to find out what is true; one of the ways of knowing.

RESEARCH PARTICIPANTS People utilized in research studies; also called subjects or cases.

RESEARCH QUESTION A specific research question that is formulated directly out of the general research problem area; answered by the interpretive and/or positivist research approach; not to be confused with problem area.

RESEARCHABILITY The extent to which a research problem is in fact researchable and the problem can be resolved through the consideration of data derived from a research study; one of the four criteria for evaluating research problem areas and formulating research questions out of the problem areas.

RESEARCHER BIAS The tendency of evaluators to find results that they expect to find; a threat to external validity.

RESOURCES The costs associated with collecting data in any given research study; includes materials and supplies, equipment rental, transportation, training staff, and staff time; a criterion for selecting a data collection method.

RESPONSE BIAS The tendency for individuals to score items on a measuring instrument in such a manner that one score is reported for the majority of all items.

RESPONSE CATEGORIES Possible responses assigned to each question in a standardized measuring instrument, with a lower value generally indicating a low level of the variable being measured and a larger value indicating a higher level.

RESPONSE ERROR A type of nonsampling error in which the participants of an evaluation present themselves differently than they actually are, perhaps in a manner that is socially desirable.

RESPONSE RATE The total number of responses obtained from potential research participants to a measuring instrument divided by the total number of responses requested, usually expressed in the form of a percentage.

RESPONSE SET Personal style; the tendency of research participants to respond to a measuring instrument in a particular way, regardless of the questions asked, or the tendency of observers or interviewers to react in certain ways; a source of constant error.

REVIEW OF THE LITERATURE (1) A search of the professional literature to provide background knowledge of what has already been examined or tested in a specific problem area; (2) Use of any information source, such as a computerized database, to locate existing data or information on a research problem, question, or hypothesis.

RIVAL HYPOTHESIS A hypothesis that is a plausible alternative to the research hypothesis and might explain the results as well or better; a hypothesis involving extraneous or intervening variables other than the independent variable in the research hypothesis; also referred to as an alternative hypothesis.

RULES OF CORRESPONDENCE A characteristic of measurement stipulating that numerals or symbols are assigned to properties of individuals, objects, or events according to specified rules.

SAMPLE A subset of a population of individuals, objects, or events chosen to participate in or to be considered in a study; a group chosen by unbiased sample selection from which inferences about the entire population of people, objects, or events can be drawn.

SAMPLING ERROR (1) The degree of difference that can be expected between the sample and the population from which it was drawn; (2) A mistake in a research study's results that is due to sampling procedures.

SAMPLING FRAME A listing of units (people, objects, or events) in a population from which a sample is drawn.

SAMPLING PLAN A method of selecting members of a population for inclusion in a research study, using procedures that make it possible to draw inferences about the population from the sample statistics.

SAMPLING THEORY The logic of using methods to ensure that a sample and a population are similar in all relevant characteristics.

SCALE A measuring instrument composed of several items that are logically or empirically structured to measure a construct.

SCATTERGRAM A graphic representation of the relationship between two interval- or ratio-level variables.

SCIENCE Knowledge that has been obtained and tested through use of positivist and interpretive research studies.

SCIENTIFIC COMMUNITY A group that shares the same general norms for both research activity and acceptance of scientific findings and explanations.

SCIENTIFIC DETERMINISM *See* Determinism.

SCIENTIFIC METHOD A generic method with specified steps for solving problems; the principles and procedures used in the systematic pursuit of knowledge.

SCOPE OF A STUDY The extent to which a problem area is covered in a single research study; a criterion for selecting a data collection method.

SCORE A numerical value assigned to an observation; also called data.

SEARCH STATEMENT A preliminary search statement developed by the researcher prior to a literature search and which contains terms that can be combined to elicit specific data.

SECONDARY ANALYSIS An unobtrusive data collection method in which available data that predate the formulation of a research study are used to answer the research question or test the hypothesis.

SECONDARY DATA ANALYSIS A data utilization method in which available data that predate the formulation of an evaluation study are used to answer the evaluation question or test the hypothesis.

SECONDARY DATA Data that predate the formulation of the research study and which are used to answer the research question or test the hypothesis.

SECONDARY DATA SOURCES A data source that provides nonoriginal, secondhand data.

SECONDARY REFERENCE SOURCE A source related to a primary source or sources, such as a critique of a particular source item or a literature review, bibliography, or commentary on several items.

SECONDHAND DATA Data obtained from people who are indirectly connected to the problem being studied.

SELECTION–TREATMENT INTERACTION The relationship between the manner of selecting research participants and their response to the independent variable; a threat to external validity.

SELF ANCHORED RATING SCALE A type of measuring instrument in which respondents rate themselves on a continuum of values, according to their own referents for each point.

SELF-DISCLOSURE Shared communication about oneself, including one's behaviors, beliefs, and attitudes.

SELF-REPORT MEASURING INSTRUMENTS Measuring instruments such as questionnaires or rating scales in which clients answer questions about their individual experiences and perspectives.

SEMANTIC DIFFERENTIAL SCALE A modified measurement scale in which research participants rate their perceptions of the variable under study along three dimensions—evaluation, potency, and activity.

SEQUENTIAL TRIANGULATION When two distinct and separate phases of a research study are conducted and the results of the first phase are considered essential for planning the second phase; research questions in Phase 1 are answered before research questions in Phase 2 are formulated.

SERVICE RECIPIENTS People who use human services—individuals, couples, families, groups, organizations, and communities; also known as clients or consumers; a stakeholder group in evaluation.

SIMPLE RANDOM SAMPLING A one-stage probability sampling procedure in which members of a population are selected one at a time, without a chance of being selected again, until the desired sample size is obtained.

SIMPLE RANDOM SAMPLING A one-stage probability sampling procedure in which members of a population are selected one at a time, without chance of being selected again, until the desired sample size is obtained.

SIMULTANEOUS TRIANGULATION When the results of a positivist and interpretive research question are answered at the same time; results to the interpretive research questions, for example, are reported separately and do not necessarily relate to, or confirm, the results from the positivist phase.

SITUATION-SPECIFIC VARIABLE A variable that may be observable only in certain environments and under certain circumstances, or with particular people.

SITUATIONALISTS Researchers who assert that certain research approaches (interpretive or positivist) are appropriate for specific situations.

SIZE OF A STUDY The number of people, places, or systems that are included in a single research study; a criterion for selecting a data collection method.

SNOWBALL SAMPLING A nonprobability sampling procedure in which individuals selected for inclusion in a sample are asked to identify additional individuals who might be included from the population; can be used to locate people with similar points of view (or experiences).

SOCIAL DESIRABILITY (1) A response set in which research participants tend to answer questions in a way that they perceive as giving favorable impressions of themselves; (2) The inclination of data providers to report data that present a socially desirable impression of themselves or their reference groups. Also referred to as impression management.

SOCIAL WORK RESEARCH Scientific inquiry in which interpretive and positivist research approaches are used to answer research questions and create new, generally applicable knowledge in the field of social work.

SOCIALLY ACCEPTABLE RESPONSE Bias in an answer that comes from research participants trying to answer questions as they think a "good" person should, rather than in a way that reveals what they actually believe or feel.

SOCIOECONOMIC VARIABLES Any one of several measures of social rank, usually including income, education, and occupational prestige; abbreviated SES.

SOLOMON FOUR GROUP DESIGN An explanatory evaluation design with four randomly assigned groups, two experimental and two control. The program's objective (the dependent variable) is measured before and after the intervention (the independent variable) for one experimental and one control group, but only after the intervention for the other two groups, and only the experimental groups receive the intervention.

SPECIFICITY One of the four criteria for evaluating research hypotheses.

SPECIFICITY OF VARIABLES An evaluation project conducted with a specific group of clients at a specific time and in a specific setting which may not always be generalizable to other clients at a different time and in a different setting; a threat to external validity.

SPLIT-HALF METHOD A method for establishing the reliability of a measuring instrument by dividing it into comparable halves and comparing the scores between the two halves.

SPOT-CHECK RECORDING A method of data collection that involves direct observation of the target problem at specified intervals rather than on a continuous basis.

STAKEHOLDER A person or group of people having a direct or indirect interest in the results of an evaluation.

STAKEHOLDER SERVICE EVALUATION MODEL Proponents of this evaluation model believe that program evaluations will be more likely to be utilized, and thus have a greater impact on social problems, when they are tailored to the needs of stakeholders; in this model, the purpose of program evaluation is not to generalize findings to other sites, but rather to restrict the evaluation effort to a particular program.

STAKEHOLDERS People or organizations that are invested in the program or that are interested in the results of the evaluation or what will be done with results of the evaluation.

STANDARDIZED MEASURING INSTRUMENT A professionally developed measuring instrument that provides for uniform administration and scoring and generates normative data against which later results can be evaluated.

STATISTICAL REGRESSION The tendency for extreme high or low scores to regress, or shift, toward the average (mean) score on subsequent measurements; a threat to internal validity.

STATISTICS The branch of mathematics concerned with the collection and analysis of data using statistical techniques.

STRATIFIED RANDOM SAMPLING A one-stage probability sampling procedure in which the population is divided into two or more strata to be sampled separately, using random or systematic random sampling techniques.

STRUCTURED INTERVIEW SCHEDULE A complete list of questions to be asked and spaces for recording the answers; the interview schedule is used by interviewers when questioning respondents.

STRUCTURED OBSERVATION A data collection method in which people are observed in their natural environments using specified methods and measurement procedures. *See* Direct observation.

SUBJECTIVE DATA Isolated facts, presented in descriptive terms, that are based on impressions, experience, values, and intuition.

SUBSCALE A component of a scale that measures some part or aspect of a major construct; also composed of several items that are logically or empirically structured.

SUMMATED SCALE A multi-item measuring instrument in which respondents provide a rating for each item. The summation of items provides an overall score.

SUMMATIVE EVALUATION A type of outcome evaluation that assesses the results or outcomes of a program. This type of evaluation is concerned with a program's overall effectiveness.

SURVEY RESEARCH A data collection method that uses survey-type data collection measuring instruments to obtain opinions or answers from a population or sample of research participants in order to describe or study them as a group.

SURVEY A method of collecting evaluation data in which individuals are asked to respond to questions that are designed to describe or study them as a group; can be conducted by mail or telephone.

SYNTHESIS Undertaking the search for meaning in our sources of information at every step of the research process; combining parts such as data, concepts, and theories to arrive at a higher level of understanding.

SYSTEMATIC ERROR Measurement error that is consistent, not random.

SYSTEMATIC RANDOM SAMPLING A one-stage probability sampling procedure in which every person at a designated interval in the population list is selected to be included in the study sample.

SYSTEMATIC To arrange the steps of a research study in a methodical way.

TARGET POPULATION The group about which a researcher wants to draw conclusions; another term for a population about which one aims to make inferences.

TARGET PROBLEM (1) In case-level evaluation designs, the problems social workers seek to solve for their clients; (2) A measurable behavior, feeling, or cognition that is either a problem in itself or symptomatic of some other problem.

TARGETS FOR INTERVENTION A unit of analysis (e.g., individuals, groups, organizations, and communities) that is the focus for change in an evaluation. Criteria used to define targets include demographics, membership in predefined groups, and social conditions.

TEMPORAL RESEARCH DESIGN A research study that includes time as a major variable; the purpose of this design is to investigate change in the distribution of a variable or in relationships among variables over time; there are three types of temporal research designs: cohort, panel, and trend.

TEMPORAL STABILITY Consistency of responses to a measuring instrument over time; reliability of an instrument across forms and across administrations.

TEST–RETEST RELIABILITY Reliability of a measuring instrument established through repeated administration to the same group of individuals.

TESTING EFFECT The effect that taking a pretest might have on posttest scores; a threat to internal validity.

THEMATIC NOTES In observational research, thematic notes are a record of emerging ideas, hypotheses, theories, and conjectures; thematic notes provide a place for the researcher to speculate and identify themes, make linkages between ideas and events, and articulate thoughts as they emerge in the field setting.

THEME In a qualitative data analysis, a concept or idea that describes a single category or a grouping of categories; an abstract interpretation of qualitative data.

THEORETICAL FRAMEWORK A frame of reference that serves to guide a research study and is developed from theories, findings from a variety of other studies, and the researcher's personal experiences.

THEORETICAL SAMPLING *See* Purposive sampling.

THEORY A reasoned set of propositions, derived from and supported by established data, which serves to explain a group of phenomena; a conjectural explanation that may, or may not, be supported by data generated from interpretive and positivist research studies.

TIME ORIENTATION An important cultural factor that considers whether one is future, present, or past oriented; for instance, present-oriented individuals would not be as preoccupied with advance planning as those who are future-oriented.

TIME-SERIES DESIGN Research designs that collect data over long time intervals—before, during, and after program implementation. This allows for the analysis of change in key factors over time.

TRADITION Traditional cultural beliefs that we accept "without question" as true; one of the ways of knowing.

TRANSCRIPT A written, printed, or typed copy of interview data or any other written material that has been gathered for an interpretive research study.

TRANSITION STATEMENTS Sentences used to indicate a change in direction or focus of questions in a measuring instrument.

TREATMENT GROUP *See* Experimental group.

TREND STUDY A longitudinal study design in which data from surveys carried out at periodic intervals on samples drawn from a particular population are used to reveal trends over time.

TRIANGULATION OF ANALYSTS Using multiple data analyzers to code a single segment of transcript and comparing the amount of agreement between analyzers; a method used to verify coding of qualitative data.

TRIANGULATION The idea of combining different research methods in all steps associated with a single research study; assumes that any bias inherent in one particular method will be neutralized when used in conjunction with other research methods; seeks convergence of a study's results; using more than one research method and source of data to study the same phenomena and to enhance validity; there are several types of triangulation, but the essence of the term is that multiple perspectives are compared; it can involve multiple data sources or multiple data analyzers; the hope is that the different perspectives will confirm each other, adding weight to the credibility and dependability of qualitative data analysis.

TWO-PHASE RESEARCH MODEL A model combining interpretive and positivist research approaches in a single study where each approach is conducted as a separate and distinct phase of the study.

TWO-TAILED HYPOTHESES Statements that do not predict specific relationships between independent and dependent variables.

UNIT OF ANALYSIS A specific research participant (person, object, or event) or the sample or population relevant to the research question; the persons or things being studied; units of analysis in research are often persons, but they may be groups, political parties, newspaper editorials, unions, hospitals, schools, etc.; a particular unit of analysis from which data are gathered is called a case.

UNIVARIATE A hypothesis or research design involving a single variable.

UNIVERSE *See* Population.

UNOBTRUSIVE METHODS Data collection methods that do not influence the variable under study or the responses of research participants; methods that avoid reactive effects.

UNSTRUCTURED INTERVIEWS A series of questions that allow flexibility for both the research participant and the interviewer to make changes during the process.

USER INPUT In evaluation, when the persons responsible for completing a measuring instrument are involved in its creation; for example, when program workers have a say as to how the program intake form is developed.

UTILITY (1) A characteristic of a measuring instrument that indicates its degree of usefulness (e.g., how practical is the measuring instrument in a particular situation?), and (2) A standard of evaluation practice that requires evaluations to be carried out only if they are considered potentially useful to one or more stakeholders. *See* also Accuracy, Feasibility, Propriety.

VALIDITY (1) The extent to which a measuring instrument measures the variable it is supposed to measure and measures it accurately; (2) The degree to which an instrument is able to do what it is intended to do, in terms of both experimental procedures and measuring instruments (internal validity) and generalizability of results (external validity); (3) The degree to which scores on a measuring instrument correlate with measures of performance on some other criterion.

VALUATION Interpretation given to data produced by evaluations; the degree to which results are considered a success or failure.

VARIABLE A characteristic that can take on different values for different individuals; any attribute whose value, or level, can change; any characteristic (of a person, object, or situation) that can change value or kind from observation to observation.

VERBATIM RECORDING Recording interview data word-for-word and including significant gestures, pauses, and expressions of persons in the interview.

WANTS In needs assessment, something that is so desired by people that they are willing to "pay" for it; to be differentiated from demands and needs.

WIDEBAND MEASURING INSTRUMENT An instrument that measures more than one variable.

WITHIN-METHODS RESEARCH APPROACH Triangulation by using different research methods available in either the interpretive or the positivist research approaches in a single research study.

WORDS The basic data unit of analysis used in interpretive research studies.

WORKER COOPERATION The actions and attitudes of program personnel when carrying out a research study within an existing program; a criterion for selecting a data collection method.

WORKING HYPOTHESIS An assertion about a relationship between two or more variables that may not be true but is plausible and worth examining.

References

American Evaluation Association. (2004). *Guiding principles for evaluators.* Retrieved February 23, 2011, from http://www.eval.org/Publications/GuidingPrinciples Printable.asp

Black, T. R. (1999). *Doing quantitative research in the social sciences: An integrated approach to research design, measurement, and statistics.* Thousand Oaks, CA: SAGE.

Bostwick, G. J., Jr., & Kyte, N. S. (1981). Measurement. In R. M. Grinnell, Jr. (Ed.), *Social work research and evaluation* (pp. 181–195). Itasca, IL: F.E. Peacock

Centers for Disease Control and Prevention. (1999a). *Framework for program evaluation in public health.* Atlanta, GA: Author.

Centers for Disease Control and Prevention. (1999b). *Overview of the framework for program evaluation* (Revised November 2, 1999). Atlanta, GA: Author.

Centers for Disease Control and Prevention. (1999c). *Summary of the framework for program evaluation* (Revised August 14, 1999). Atlanta, GA: Author.

Centers for Disease Control and Prevention. (2001). *Introduction to program evaluation for comprehensive tobacco control programs.* Atlanta, GA: Author.

Centers for Disease Control and Prevention. (2005). *Introduction to program evaluation for public health programs: A self-study guide.* Atlanta, GA: Author.

Centers for Disease Control and Prevention. (2006). *Get smart: Know when antibiotics work. Evaluation manual: Step 2 — Describe the program.* Atlanta, GA: Author.

Centers for Disease Control and Prevention. (2010). *Learning and growing through evaluation: State asthma program evaluation guide.* Atlanta, GA: Author.

Centers for Disease Control and Prevention. (2011). *Introduction to program evaluation for public health programs: A self-study guide.* Atlanta, GA: Author.

Centers for Disease Control and Prevention. (2013). *Developing an effective evaluation report: Setting the course for effective program evaluation.* Atlanta, GA: Author.

Corcoran, K., & Hozack, N. (2010). Locating assessment instruments. In B. Thyer (Ed.), *The handbook of social work research methods* (2nd. ed., pp. 97–117). Thousand Oaks, CA: SAGE.

Council on Social Work Education. (2015). *Baccalaureate and masters curriculum policy statements.* Alexandria, VA. Author.

Dodd, C. (1998). *Dynamics of intercultural communication* (5th ed.). New York: McGraw-Hill.

Gabor, P. A., & Ing, C. (2001). Sampling. In R. M. Grinnell, Jr. & Y. A. Unrau (Eds.), *Social work research and evaluation* (7th ed., pp. 207–223). Isasca, IL: F.E. Peacock.

Gabor, P. A., & Sieppert, J. (1999). Developing a computer supported evaluation system in a human service organization. *New Technology In the Human Services, 12,* 107–119.

Ginsberg, L. H. (2001). *Social work evaluation: Principles and methods.* Boston: Allyn & Bacon.

Grinnell, R. M., Jr., & Unrau, Y. A. (Eds.). (2014). *Social work research and evaluation: Foundations of evidence-based practice* (10th ed.). New York: Oxford University Press.

Grinnell, R. M., Jr., & Unrau, Y. A., Williams, M. (2014). Introduction. In R. M. Grinnell, Jr. & Y. Unrau (Eds.), *Social work research and evaluation: Foundations of evidence-based practice* (10th ed., pp. 2–29). New York: Oxford University Press.

Haffner, D. W., & Goldfarb, E. S. (1977). But does it work? Improving evaluations of sexuality education, *SIECUS Report, 25,* 8–11.

Hall, E. T. (1983). *The dance of life: Other dimensions of time.* New York: Doubleday.

Harris, P. R., & Moran, T. (1996). *Managing cultural differences: Leadership strategies for a new world business* (4th ed.). London: Gulf.

Hatry, H. P., & Lampkin, L. M.. (2003). *Key steps in outcome management*. Washington, DC: Urban Institute.

Hoefstede, G. (1997). *Cultures and organizations: Software of the mind*. New York: McGraw-Hill.

Hornick, J. P., & Burrows, B. (1998). Program evaluation. In R. M. Grinnell, Jr. (Ed.), *Social work research and evaluation* (3rd ed., pp. 400–420). Itasca, IL: F. E. Peacock.

Hudson, W. W. (1982). *The clinical measurement package: A field manual*. Chicago: Dorsey.

Jordan, C., Franklin, C., & Corcoran, K. (2014). Standardized measuring instruments. In R. M. Grinnell, Jr. & Y. Unrau (Eds.), *Social work research and evaluation: Foundations of evidence-based practice* (10th ed., pp. 250–270). New York: Oxford University Press.

Kettner, P. K., Moroney, R. K., & Martin, L. L. (2012). *Designing and managing programs: An effectiveness-based approach* (4th ed.). Thousand Oaks, CA: SAGE.

King, J. A., & Stevahn, L. (2002). Three frameworks for considering the evaluator role. In K. E. Ryan, & T. A. Schwandt (Eds.), *Exploring evaluator role and identity* (pp. 45–65). Charlotte, NC: Information Age.

Krysik, J. L., & Finn, J. (2013). *Research for effective social work practice* (3rd ed.). New York: Routledge.

Lewis, R. D. (1997). *When cultures collide: Managing successfully across cultures*. London: Nicholas.

Maslow, A. H. (1999). *Toward the psychology of being* (3rd ed.). New York: Wiley.

McKinney, R. (2014). Research with minority and disadvantaged groups. In R. M. Grinnell, Jr. & Y. A. Unrau (Eds.), *Social work research and evaluation: Foundations of evidence-based practice* (10th. ed., pp. 141–164). New York: Oxford University Press.

Milstein, B., Wetterhall, S., & CDC Evaluation Working Group. (2000). A framework featuring steps and standards for program evaluation. *Health Promotion Practice, 1*, 221–228.

Monette, D. R., Sullivan, T. J., & DeJong, C. R. (2011). *Applied social research: A tool for the human services.* (8th ed.). Belmont, CA: Brooks/Cole.

Morrison, B. T., Conway, W. A., & Borden, G. A. (1994). *Kiss, bow, or shake hands: How to do business in six countries*. Holbrook, MA: Adams Media.

Mulroy, E. A. (2004). Theoretical perspectives on the social environment to guide management and community practice: An organization-in-environment approach. *Administration in Social Work, 28*, 77–96.

National Association of Social Workers. (1996). *Code of ethics*. Silver Spring, MD: Author.

National Educational Research Laboratory. Retrieved August 12, 2011, from http://educationnorthwest.org/webfm_send/311

Neuliep, J. W. (2000). *Communication: A contextual approach*. New York: Houghton-Mifflin.

Pecora, P. J., Kessler, R. C., Williams, J., O'Brien, K., Downs, A. C., English, D., . . . Holmes, K. E. (2005). *Improving family foster care: Findings from the Northwest Foster Care Alumni Study*. Retrieved June 28, 2014, from http://www.casey.org/resources/publications/pdf/improvingfamilyfostercare_es.pdf

Porter, R. E., & Samovar, L. A. (1997). An introduction to intercultural communication. In L. A. Samovar & R. E. Porter (Eds.), *Intercultural communication: A reader* (8th ed., pp. 5–26). Belmont, CA: Wadsworth.

Reviere, R., Berkowitz, S., Carter, C. C., & Ferguson, C. G. (1996). *Needs assessment: A creative and practical guide for social scientists*. Washington, DC: Taylor & Francis.

Rossi, P. H., Lipsey, M., & Freeman, H. E. (2003). *Evaluation: A systematic approach* (7th ed.). Thousand Oaks, CA: SAGE.

Russ-Eft, D. R., & Preskill, H. (2009). *Evaluation in organizations: A systematic approach to enhancing learning, performance, and change*. Philadelphia, PA: Basic Books.

Samovar, L. A., Porter, R. E., & Stefani, L. A. (1998). *Communication between cultures*. Belmont, CA: Wadsworth.

Sayre, K. (2002). *Guidelines and best practices for culturally competent evaluations*. Denver, CO: Colorado Trust.

Weinbach, R., & Grinnell, R. M., Jr. (2015). *Statistics for social workers* (9th ed.). Boston: Allyn and Bacon.

W. K. Kellogg Foundation. (1998). *Evaluation handbook*. Battle Creek, MI: Author.

W. K. Kellogg Foundation. (2004). *Logic model development guide*. Battle Creek, MI: Author.

Yarbrough, D. B., Shulha, L. M., Hopson, R. K., & Caruthers, F. A. (2011). *The program evaluation standards: A guide for evaluators and evaluation users* (3rd ed.). Thousand Oaks, CA: SAGE.

Credits

Box 2.1: Adapted and modified from: National Educational Research Laboratory. Retrieved August 12, 2011, from www.educationnorthwest.org/webfrm_send/311

Box 6.1: From: Sayre, K. (2002). *Guidelines and best practices for culturally competent evaluations*. Denver, CO: Colorado Trust.

Boxes 6.2 and M.1: From: McKinney, R. (2014). Research with minority and disadvantaged groups. In R. M. Grinnell, Jr. & Y. A. Unrau (Eds.), *Social work research and evaluation: Foundations of evidence-based practice* (10th. ed., pp. 141–164). New York: Oxford University Press.

Boxes 8.1–8.3: Adapted and modified from: Wilder Research. (2009). *Program theory and logic models*. St. Paul, MN: Author. Used with permission.

Box 12.1: Adapted and modified from: Hatry, H. P., Cowan, J., Weiner, K., & Lampkin, L. M. (2003). *Developing community-wide outcome indicators for specific services*. Washington, DC: Urban Institute. Reprinted with permission.

Box 13.2: Adapted and modified from: National Institute of Drug Abuse. Retrieved on November 5, 2014, from http://www.nida.nih.gov/impcost/impcost2.html.

Chapter 3; Table 1.1; Figures 3.1; 3.6a–3b; Boxes G.1–G.3; Tools A–D, F, G, I–K; and In-a-Nuthells: By Centers for Disease Control and Prevention. Adapted and modified from: Centers for Disease Control and Prevention (1999). *Framework for program evaluation in public health*. Atlanta, GA: Author; Centers for Disease Control and Prevention. (1999). *Overview of the framework for program evaluation* (Revised November 2, 1999). Atlanta, GA: Author; Centers for Disease Control and Prevention. (1999). *Summary of the framework for program evaluation* (Revised August 14, 1999). Atlanta, GA:

Author; Centers for Disease Control and Prevention. (2001). *Introduction to program evaluation for comprehensive tobacco control programs*. Atlanta, GA: Author; Centers for Disease Control and Prevention. (2005). *Introduction to program evaluation for public health programs: A self-study guide*. Atlanta, GA: Author; Centers for Disease Control and Prevention. (2006). *Get smart: Know when antibiotics work. Evaluation manual: Step 2—Describe the program*. Atlanta, GA: Author; Centers for Disease Control and Prevention. (2010). *Learning and growing through evaluation: State asthma program evaluation guide*. Atlanta, GA: Author; Centers for Disease Control and Prevention. (2011). *Introduction to program evaluation for public health programs: A self-study guide*. Atlanta, GA: Author; Centers for Disease Control and Prevention. (2013). *Developing an effective evaluation report: Setting the course for effective program evaluation*. Atlanta, GA: Author; and Milstein, B., Wetterhall, S., & CDC Evaluation Working Group. (2000). A framework featuring steps and standards for program evaluation, *Health Promotion Practice*, *1*, 221–228. Reprinted with permission.

Chapter 4: The section titled "The Four Standards" has been adapted and modified from: Yarbrough, D. B., Shulha, L. M., Hopson, R. K., & Caruthers, F. A. (2011). *The program evaluation standards: A guide for evaluators and evaluation users* (3rd ed.). Thousand Oaks, CA: SAGE. Used with permission.

Chapter 5: By Andre Ivanoff and Betty Blythe. Adapted and modified from: Ivanoff, A., Blythe, B., & Walters, B. (2008). The ethical conduct of research. In R. M. Grinnell, Jr. & Y. A. Unrau (Eds.). *Social work research and evaluation: Foundations of evidence-based practice* (8th. ed., pp. 29–59). New York: Oxford University Press.

Chapter 6: By Carol Ing, adjunct faculty member within the Child and Youth Care Program at Lethbridge College, 3000 College Drive South, Lethbridge, Alberta, Canada T1K 1L6.

Chapter 8: Adapted and modified from: Wyatt Knowlton, L., & Phillips, C. C. (2012). *The logic model guidebook: Better strategies for great results* (2nd ed.). Thousand Oaks, CA: SAGE. Used with permission.

Chapter 9 and all referenced Tools: By Centers for Disease Control and Prevention. Adapted and modified from: Centers for Disease Control and Prevention, National Center for Environmental Health, Division of Environmental Hazards and Health Effects, Air Pollution and Respiratory Health Branch Centers for Disease Control and Prevention. (2010). *Learning and growing through evaluation: State asthma program evaluation guide*. Atlanta, GA: Author. Used with permission.

Table 2.1: Koger, D. C., Early Childhood Consultant, Oakland Schools, 2111 Pontiac Lake Road, Waterford, MI 48328. Used with permission.

Table H.1: Adapted and modified from: Lampkin, L. M., & Hatry, H. P. (2003). *Key steps in outcome management*. Washington, DC: Urban Institute. Reprinted with permission.

Figures 1.2 and 1.3: From Mulroy, E. A. (2004). Theoretical perspectives on the social environment to guide management and community practice: An organization-in-environment approach. *Administration in Social Work, 28*, 77–96. Used with permission.

Figures 3.2 and 3.3: From W. K. Kellogg Foundation. (2004). *Logic model development guide*. Battle Creek, MI: Author. Used with permission.

Figures L1.1 and L1.1a: Walter W. Hudson. Copyright © 1993 by WALMYR Publishing Company and Steven L. McMurtry.

Scale can be obtained from WALMYR Publishing Co., P.O. Box 12317, Tallahassee, FL 12317–2217. Reprinted with permission.

Figures M.1 and M.1a: From: Steven L. McMurtry. Copyright © 1994 by WALMYR Publishing Company and Steven L. McMurtry. Scale can be obtained from WALMYR Publishing Co., P.O. Box 12317, Tallahassee, FL 12317–2217. Reprinted with permission.

Figure M.2: Adapted from: P. N. Reid & J. H. Gundlach, A scale for the measurement of consumer satisfaction with social services. *Journal of Social Service Research, 7*, 37–54. Copyright © 1983 by P. N. Reid and J. H. Gundlach. Reprinted with permission.

Tools E, H, L, and M: Adapted and modified from: Grinnell, R. M., Jr., & Williams, M. (1990). *Research in social work: A primer*. Itasca, IL: F. E. Peacock; Williams, M., Tutty, L. M., & Grinnell, R. M., Jr. (1995). *Research in social work: An introduction* (2nd ed.). Itasca, IL: F. E. Peacock; Williams, M., Unrau, Y. A., & Grinnell, R. M., Jr. (1998). *Introduction to social work research* (3rd ed.). Itasca, IL: F.E. Peacock; Williams, M., Unrau, Y. A., & Grinnell, R. M., Jr. (2003). *Research methods for social workers* (4th ed.). Peosta, IA: Eddie Bowers; Williams, M., Unrau, Y. A., & Grinnell, R. M., Jr. (2005). *Research methods for social workers* (5th ed.). Peosta, IA: Eddie Bowers; Grinnell, R. M., Jr., Williams, M., & Unrau, Y. A. (2008). *Research methods for social workers: A generalist approach for BSW students* (6th ed.). Peosta, IA: Eddie Bowers; Grinnell, R. M., Jr., Williams, M., & Unrau, Y. A. (2009). *Research methods for BSW students* (7th ed.). Kalamazoo, MI: Pair Bond; Grinnell, R. M., Jr., Williams, M., & Unrau, Y. A. (2012). *Research methods for social workers* (9th ed.). Kalamazoo, MI: Pair Bond; and Grinnell, R. M., Jr., Williams, M., & Unrau, Y. A. (2014). *Research methods for social workers* (10th ed.). Kalamazoo, MI: Pair Bond.

Index

Page numbers followed by *f* and *t* indicate figures and tables, respectively. Numbers followed by *b* indicate boxes.